Rhonda Lampton
740 624-8887

W9-CCI-946

God's War on Terror

ISLAM, PROPHECY
AND THE BIBLE

A fresh understanding of Biblical prophecy
from an Eastern perspective
as viewed by an ex-Muslim terrorist

By Walid Shoebat

✦⸝⸺ ✳ ⸺⸝✦

Cover Design: Graphics by Sher

For information, please e-mail the author at
walid@shoebat.com

ISBN: 978-0-9771021-8-1

1st Edition

Printed in the United States

PREFACE

From every area of the free world, strong evidence is reaching us of crimes and atrocities committed by Islamic fundamentalists in the name of Allah. A great many Muslims, "educated" people, and our elected leaders know about these crimes; those that do not know, do not know because they do not want to know. They do not ask questions because they are afraid of the answers. They fear the knowledge of what they are tolerating; but the ones among us who are open to seeking truth and justice, know how to differentiate between criminals and their victims. The people of the civilized world now have to prove by deed where they stand; mere words will not be believed by a world that witnesses the crimes against God's people and my Christian brethren.

In the past I have sinned greatly against God's people, but because of the grace I received through Christ, I am working to rescue them from injustice.

Walid Shoebat

ACKNOWLEDGEMENTS

This book has been my 15-year journey out of a lifetime experience of searching for answers regarding Bible Prophecy. As in the story of Moses, the introvert who faced the world's most powerful leader, I stand before of the prophets of Ba'al risking it all. If Moses was slow of speech, I too had my trouble with English being my second language. But thanks be to God for providing Aarons in my path. Such was Keith Davies my partner and manager who worked full-time assuring the completion of this book on time, and such was his wife Deborah for patiently assisting him to accomplish this mission; Such was Cheryl Taylor who helped with the editing, and prepared the book for desktop layout. Thanks also to Joel Richardson who partnered with me in writing this book, and to J. H. Hadley who came in at the end of this project to help edit. Each one contributed to reach our deadline for print.

Like Moses, this mission has had its blessings and its curses. The blessings provided by the Lord were a wealth of Biblical understanding; the opportunity to develop a deeper knowledge of long suffering and righteous anger. Yet, if Moses endured Pharaoh's curses so that God's people could be set free, I will accept the weight of this knowledge because it is essential in restoring America and the Church.

A special thanks goes to the two women God has placed in my path—to my wife who was the catalyst that enabled me to find the truth, and has borne the burden of many days when I am away from her and our two sons—to my mother who endured 35 years of suffering, living in exile against her will in a Muslim society, silently praying for my salvation.

Finally, thanks to you, my readers and supporters, who with your letters of encouragement and strong attendance wherever I go, means that we can continue the fight for truth and justice.

Walid

Section I

Winners vs. Losers

1

Your Glory or His? Choose Wisely!

✦┼══╼·✳·╾══┼✦

A few years from now, you will pull this diary off your bookshelf and blow the dust off the cover being unable to resist re-reading it, only to find out how prevalent it is to the times you live in. And when you do begin to read, you find yourself unable to stop partaking in the only wholesome addiction, praying to the Almighty that you never recover from it, for it uses a roadmap orchestrated for us by Him thousands of years ago. The efforts I put into it was like a quest to find a hidden treasure, with only one difference—I want to share all this wealth I found—with you. This new treasure I found, reminds me of a favorite movie in our family, *Indiana Jones and the Last Crusade*. In this film, the key regarding the quest for the Grail becomes Dr. Henry Jones's diary, for without it, no one can lay hands on the chalice that contained the power for eternal life, and so the fictional story goes. Henry is obsessed with the Grail and has spent his lifetime researching and documenting details in his diary to help locate the prized treasure. But he isn't the only one enchanted by its powers. The Nazis are in the hunt for it as well, yet for the wrong motive. They falsely believe that the Grail will bring them an eternal Nazi kingdom.

Both Henry and his son Indiana have fallen captive to the evil Nazis and lost the diary to them. Henry, after escaping with Indiana from Berlin insists on going back for the diary. Without it, no one can escape the lethal pitfalls and booby traps set up at the pathway to the temple housing the Grail. In an argument between Henry and his son, who did not want to go back into the lion's den, Indiana blasphemes the name of Christ. Henry slaps him looking straight into his eyes. "This is for blasphemy," he chastises. "The quest for the Grail is not archeology; it's a race against evil. If it is captured by the Nazis, the armies of darkness will march all over the face of the earth. Do you understand me?" Indiana replies "This is an obsession, Dad. I've never understood it. Never..." It seems that Indiana doesn't understand the deeper side of his father—which isn't merely obsession with the quest to find the Grail, but a desire to win the war against Nazism. Henry has faith in God, but Indiana is a doubting Thomas.

After all the commotion of going back to Berlin and rescuing the diary from the Nazis, the scene finally culminates with all of the movie's characters trying to reach the sacred spot: the Joneses, Salah, and Brody all reach the Canyon of the Crescent Moon, in Hatay near Äskenderun, the site of the temple housing the Grail. The Nazis capture them in the temple and a showdown between good and evil ensues. The Joneses are overcome by guns from the antagonist, Donovan, and his men. Donovan, in order to test the path to the Grail for booby traps, sends in a Turkish soldier to clear the way of cunning devices. Attempting to enter, he walks slowly, eyes darting, muttering a prayer under his breath. He approaches the spot where another decapitated Turkish soldier lies dead. He takes one more step—a fatal step, it turns out. We hear a roar, a woosh of air, and see the Turk's head fly off and bounce across the ground.

Realizing the futility of this, Donovan decides to send in an expert, so he appoints Indiana by pointing his gun at him "What do you say, Jones, ready to go down in history?" Indiana responds "As what, A Nazi stooge like you?" Donovan counters "Nazis?!—Is that the limit of your vision? The Nazis want to write themselves into the Grail legend and take on the world. Well, they're welcome. But I want the Grail itself, the cup that gives everlasting life. Hitler can have the world, but he can't take it with him. I'm going to be drinking to my own health when he's gone the way of the Dodo."

It seems that Donovan views Christ's mission on earth as nothing more than his own private key to personal health and wealth. Donovan believes in the power of the cup to bring eternal life. Indiana thought of it as a fairy tale. Of the two, I prefer Indiana. I'd rather have a doubting Thomas than a person who believes for the wrong motives, that Christ's mission is to bring them abundant material wealth and physical health. I see this every day on a massive scale throughout churches across America. Like Donovan, millions of Christians focus on their own personal gain without realizing that such pursuit is a curse, "an adulterous and wicked generation that seeks signs and wonders." (Matthew 12:39)

The different views on the Grail resemble what has been going on for centuries; divisions over the aim and purpose of Christ. With so many views, how do we follow *Christ's* diary? What is man's destiny and how will God's prophetic plan unfold? What is needed is an understanding of God's plan to help the billions of doubting Thomases and for everyone who desires eternal life. Such is the quest for understanding God's love letter— The Bible.

It parallels a statement in the movie; Kasim, the Christian Turk, and one of the knights of the cruciform sword and protector of the Grail, asks Indiana a question after finding Sir Richard's tomb:

"Whom does the Grail serve?" Kasim asks Indiana.

"Ask yourself, why do you seek the cup of Christ? Is it for His glory, or for yours?"

Christ is to be glorified in all we do, not just in our health and wealth, as some claim.

Donovan, who thought of himself as a believer, is actually seeking his own glory. He draws his pistol:

"The Grail is mine, and you're going to get it for me," he says to Indiana.

Donovan then shoots Henry, Indiana's father, forcing Indiana to enter the path of death. He proceeds forward. His hands open the Grail Diary and he reads from it:

"The Breath of God...Only the penitent man will pass. Only the penitent man will pass," he mutters to himself.

Indiana takes a few steps forward: "The penitent man will pass. The penitent man...The penitent man is humble before God."

He kneels before God. A razor sharp pendulum has been guarding a small corridor—the mechanism misses his head since he was bowing, confirming his need to follow the diary's instructions carefully, step by step. Holding the Grail Diary, his fedora now covered in cobwebs, Indiana reads to himself:

"The second challenge is the Word of God. Only in the footsteps of God will he proceed... The Word of God...The Word of..."

Indiana pulls away some cobwebs to reveal a cobblestone path. Each cobble is engraved with a letter he reads from the Diary:

"Proceed in the footsteps of the Word. The Word of God..."

The scene then goes back to his father Henry who lies on the ground speaking ahead of Indiana the words:

"The Name of God..."

The scene returns to Indiana, who mutters to himself:

"The Name of God...Jehovah."

Guided by the Diary, Indiana circumvents all the deadly booby traps, reaching a room where he finds a knight of the First Crusade, kept alive by the power of the Grail. Donovan and Elsa tentatively enter the room. The two of them slowly approach the collection of grails, and Donovan looks at them for a moment. Donovan turns to the knight asking:

"Which one is it?"

The knight advises Donovan and Elsa:

"You must choose. But choose wisely, for as the true Grail will bring you life, the false grail will take it from you."

Elsa looks at Donovan, smiles, and selects a beautiful chalice made of gold. Grinning, she hands it to Donovan and he holds it up to the light exclaiming,

"Oh, yes. It's more beautiful than I'd ever imagined!"

Donovan approaches a large vessel filled with water:

"This certainly is the cup of the King of Kings."

He gently fills the cup with water, proclaiming: "eternal life."

Donovan drinks from the cup. Looking at his reflection in the water, he can see that he has begun to age rapidly. He gasps:

"What is happening to me?"

Now nothing more than skeleton, Donovan crashes against the wall.

The wind blows away his remains, now turned to dust. Only his Nazi lapel pin remains.

The Grail Knight utters a telling phrase, "He chose...poorly."

At this point Indy spots an unassuming wooden cup with a gold interior worthy of a carpenter and almost unnoticed among the shinny, beautiful cups. Indy takes the small, wooden chalice, walks up to the vessel, dips the cup in it, and, after taking a deep breath, drinks from it. He turns to the knight. Grail Knight utters:

"You have chosen wisely."[1]

Though the movie is fiction, it reminds me of the real quest I made. I began to pray for a clear understanding after reading the Bible and the symbolic language and mystery in the Book of Revelation which contains prophetic declarations written by ancient prophets who wrote of great judgments against various nations. After my prayer, I began my quest. I read and re-read things I had never understood before. Searching the Scriptures from beginning to end, over and over again, I was on a journey to piece this great puzzle together. The knowledge I gained came gushing down upon me like a river, with spiritual water that quenched my every thirst. It was like a treasure hunt, uncovering one nugget at a time. After quite some time I had accumulated a treasure chest that I will be sharing with you in this book. That you truly want to own all this wealth and evidence, I am not sure. Let me warn you that this quest carries a heavy burden with many trials and tribulations. It could change your life—forever. For "The kingdom of heaven is like a treasure hidden in the field, which a man found and hid; and from joy over it he goes and sells all that he has and buys that field." (Matthew 13:44)

Putting a puzzle together is delicate work. You cannot switch pieces or the finished result will be distorted. Let me give you an example. Let's say that part of a puzzle game called "the Quest for the Grail" is to find "Eternal Life." You are given letter blocks and you are to put them together to create the correct word. The letters you are given are "**VALACRY**," and the hint given to solve this puzzle is "Salvation." The correct word is "Calvary," but one could take these same letters and come up with the word "Cavalry," insisting that a "Cavalry" could actually provide a sense of salvation. This argument would be absurd; Cavalry of course is not the correct answer to the puzzle.

I know that this is a simple example. Yet, there is much similarity between that example and the prophetic puzzle regarding the Messiah and what has been predicted of Him. The message is simple; the whole purpose of the first advent of the coming Messiah was Calvary. But our focus here will be to solve the puzzle regarding the Messiah's second coming. For such a mission, one cannot have missing or switched pieces. Everything must fit—like a glove.

At the end of the journey, after we have put the entire puzzle together, you will find yourself at a fork in this road of destiny. When you get there, you will need to choose. But make sure you choose wisely. You will have the same two choices that I had. But don't worry; to complete this puzzle, all we need to do is follow a simple manual with the easiest of instructions.

This writing will resemble the diary written by Henry, Indiana's father. It will simplify what others have made complex and will show how easy it is to find this eternal treasure. Each chapter will warn you of the lethal cunning devices, placed not by the guardians of our treasure as in the fictional movie, but by the evil forces that are about to be unleashed against us in the near future.

I will give you instructions on how to avoid pitfalls and how to pinpoint the booby traps to which so many fall prey, ultimately plunging them headlong into eternal damnation. You will learn how the "wicked one" functions; you will learn his schemes and his lies. The dialogue you and I will share will give you the most basic instructions first, for I am afraid your mind may not see everything clearly if I proceed too quickly. I know you might doubt, that's okay—everyone has some doubts.

So then, Mr. Doubting Thomas, I promise that by the time you finish reading this, you will never be the same. But beware, by the time you reach that fateful fork in the road, you will have to choose—choose wisely!

Are You a Fool or a Bigot? Choose Wisely!

THE FOOLS

L et me start from the beginning, not of my life as a terrorist, but from the point in time when I decided to become a Christian. As I began to express my views on university campuses all over America, many labeled me as someone who traded one extreme belief (terrorism) for another (Christian fundamentalism). In the West, many see American evangelicals as extreme, particularly outspoken people, who preach a radical message. Critics often link the fundamentalist Christians as essentially the same as the radical Muslims. But are these two groups the same? Christians may give leftists a headache, but Muslims would cut off their heads! To make a comparison between these two groups is mindless moral equivalency at its best. It could easily be said that such critics have tunnel vision. It would be easier for a camel to go through the eye of a needle than for a grain of wisdom to enter such hearts.

I have reviewed many books that are Anti-God and Anti-Christian, and I'm not bothered by them at all. That the *heart of man does not seek God and is at war with Him* simply proves the truth of the Bible. The spiritual war is on—everywhere. I see it when I walk into bookstores at airports as I travel to fight the "War on Terror." One can find many critical books laced with untruths about Christianity and the Bible. Some of these books are, The Da Vinci Code, The God Delusion, American Theocracy, The Baptizing of America, The End of Faith, Atheist Universe 'The Thinking Person's Answer to Christian Fundamentalism,' Thy Kingdom Come 'How the Religious Right Distorts the Faith and Threatens America,' Religion Gone Bad 'The Hidden Dangers of the Christian Right,' and God is Not Great.

Christopher Hitchens, the author of *God is Not Great,* must have a problem using his first name, which means 'Christ-bearer.' Even in the religious section, we find many anti-Christian books displayed on the shelves of bookstores.

Richard Dawkins, the author of The God Delusion, is a staunch believer in the Darwinian Theory of Evolution. He continually complains that teaching children about hell is a form of child abuse worse than sexual molestation.

"*Really?!*"

If Dawkins' children were kidnapped at gunpoint and he was given a choice between having his children listen to a sermon entitled "Hell" by John Hagee or having his children molested, would Dawkins *really* choose the latter? Highly doubtful! So then, is his primary concern for the children, or is it to use children in his argument to attempt to destroy faith in God? Dawkins further shows his concern for children (or lack thereof) in his position on abortion. Dawkins says that if no pain is involved, it should be completely acceptable to kill a baby, as long as it is still in the womb.

Is *pain* truly the main issue here? What about the issue of killing innocent babies?

If Dawkins really cares about protecting children, why does he promote killing them in the womb? Suppose Dawkins could decide the conditions acceptable to terminate a life, could others then decide to terminate Dawkins, as long as he was anesthetized with a sufficient quantity of painkillers?

Dawkins and his ilk would argue that the issue of abortion has nothing to do with God, for He does not even exist, and the faster we get this through our heads, the faster we will finally have peace. This is the thrust of the "Dawkins Gospel."

However, if God does not exist, why does Dawkins designate *himself* to play god by promoting the destruction of the unborn? Why create another creed to replace Christianity? Instead of his book title being The God Delusion, possibly it should be The Dawkins-is-God Delusion. Does Dawkins think it's okay to evolve himself into a god and decide the fate of an unborn child's life just because he believes in Evolution? Is Evolution a matter of science as they claim, or a philosophical religious message? Is it even Evolution, or is it Evilution?

If morality comes from man, who according to Dawkins is simply just another animal, why don't we see Dawkins walking naked in public, as all other animals do? The concept of clothes was one of the first moral instructions that *God* gave to man after man sinned. The Bible tells us that God made garments out of skins to cover Adam and Eve's nakedness (Genesis 3:21). No one has an excuse not to know we need to be covered. It is part of our *created* instinct! You don't have to be in the Garden of Eden and witness the fall of man to verify this truth. This is the Gospel—that Christ died to be our covering. When I was growing up as Muslim, I heard the argument that for one man to die in order that another may live is unfair and stupid. Yet this is the message of Salvation, and it can be seen everywhere, including in our daily food; we cannot live unless the innocent die for us. We survive by killing the living; either animals or plants—life must die for life to continue.

Truth is obvious, but a lie is a process of always casting doubt and suspicion. Mohammed's false "Gospel of doubt," that Christ was never crucified, and the leftists "Darwinian Gospel," that continues to reject what is clearly obvious all around us, are no match to the Christian Gospel. Where is the "Good News" within these false doctrines? I have seen it over and over again—Christ was right—when the world accuses, they accuse you of the things of which they themselves are guilty. They point the finger at you, then accuse you of being a finger-pointer. Dawkins should have plucked the delusion log from his own eye with his believing he's concerned about protecting children, before pointing to the spec in the eyes of Christians who simply want to save lives—both for the now and the hereafter. Dawkins can't disprove God's existence, yet I can prove He does exist. The lie that we cannot prove God's existence ends here. Everything God proclaimed so long ago in the Bible regarding past and the current events, He has fulfilled.

THE BIGOTS

W*hen I finally accepted living with the titles forced on me by Anti-Christians—being called a "Christian Fundamentalist," "American Islamophobic racist Kaffer," "divisive and xeno-phobic bigot," I gladly received my badge of honor, and decided to speak in churches and find other like-minded "bigots."*

One Sunday I sat in a pew and listened to the choir sing, "Behold He Comes." The lyrics "There's no God like Jehovah," reminded me of the Islamic creed uttered by every Muslim in the world who, throughout history, has marched forward wielding the force of the sword, singing "There is no god but Allah." Yet the song in church was not saying that no one else in the world has the right to worship their own gods, simply that there is *no God like Jehovah*—all the others are unqualified claimers and unworthy imposters.

The song reminded me of my journey in 1993, a quest to find the truth, and then choose between Allah and Jehovah. I will share my diary and findings here to demonstrate why I believe that God is Jehovah and why Allah is not God.

I can already hear some of you grumbling with all sorts of complaints that what I just said sounds bigoted. Perhaps you are one who thinks that I need to prequalify everything. Why should I? Unlike you, bigots do not have to prequalify anything. This is what I don't understand—if I was a terrorist, and the Bible helped tame me, why do the leftists still complain? Why argue with what works? But I've found that it usually takes a bigot to point out another bigot. It is rare to find those who are innocent pointing out bigots. Yet, in the

West when I express that "Allah is not Jehovah," I always get the standard response: "we all worship the same god." I hear this nonsensical politically-correct rhetoric every time I get into a discussion about theology. I am, at times, even tempted to abstain from carrying out any further discussion, after all, how does one object to such a "unifying creed?"

But I learned, now that I am an American 'bigot' who has lived in the U.S. for so many years, that we can thumb our noses at anything that doesn't suit our fancy, even to the point of believing there is no God at all. Such freedom, to think and critique anything we want, was exactly what so many Christians in America spilled their blood and died for, only to have to endure sneers by the haters of Christianity—all in the name of freedom.

Instead of attacking Islamic books that declare Jihad by the sword, and blame all world evils on Israel, and call for the killing of all Westerners; most of today's sophisticated politically-correct commentators simply aim their biggest guns at evangelicals such as Pastor John Hagee of Cornerstone Church or Pat Robertson of the 700 Club. According to the elitists of the American left, it is "the Christians" who are the source of all the evil.

Are we?

We have more courage than you leftists could ever muster. I dare your Christopher Hitchens, author of *God is Not Great,* to write a book titled "Allah is Not Great." It would be interesting to see how long a book like that would stay in print. Indeed, if these people are honest about what they say, why are they simply giving "lip service" to Jihadists, and at the same time keeping the real thrust of their war aimed at fighting one book—the Bible. Yet somehow they want us to sing in unison that we all worship the same God—only they demand that it be their god!

Do we all really worship the same god? Of course not! So why do they expect Christians to worship their god? It is apparent that evolution has skipped through the realm of science and become a religion—and beyond that, it has become the educational standard which is taught in our secular schools. Allah has skipped the realm of personal devotion, and has become a mandated constitution. So, if the new creed is true, that we all worship the same god, should we also hold hands with the Wiccans (those who practice a form of witchcraft)? Should we all declare 'Heil Satan?' After all, Satanists worship Satan as their God. And if we all worship the same god, does that mean they too worship the same God as everyone else, or are they the only exception? If so, just how many exceptions are there? Where do we draw the line? Or, perhaps they are all correct—they all worship the same god—and this god is Satan disguising himself as the true God.

We the Christians choose to stand alone and be resolved to never bow to your Baal. You're being hypocrites attempting to force us to say that "we all worship the same god." It would probably be an offense to everyone if we agreed to such a statement.

Do you see my point? I am damned if I agree and damned if I do not, for Jehovah is different from all other gods and idols you have erected.

NO, there is no God like Jehovah. He describes Himself as our Father and He is the Holy Spirit. Allah in the Qur'an is neither a father nor the Holy Spirit. In fact, Allah rejects such titles. I should know since I was a Muslim myself. So to insist that we are all worshipping the same god, by the liberals' own logic, would be to force 1.3 billion Muslims to believe that Jehovah and Allah are the same deity. That would be pushing Muslims into accepting the Christian concept of the Biblical God. Would they do that? Not a chance!

Right now you might want to accuse me of being divisive. Perhaps you think I should sing your song, and then all worship the "same god." But just because you believe in this creed and song that so many politicians are now singing, doesn't make it right for you to push your faith on 1.3 billion Muslims. And if not on them, why push it on me?

You might think that I am being a Christian fundamentalist bigot. Well, maybe I am. My diary will make my case as to why I chose this path; I believe in the America founded by Christians who spilled their blood in order that others might live. There is no country that I know of on earth that believes in this freedom and liberty more than America. This is truly a land where people "live and let live." What is ironic is that the left wants to protect the rights of the world's most notorious killers in Guantanamo while at the same time they promote the wholesale slaughter of the most innocent little lambs that God has to offer in the womb.

Many claim that the 'beautiful and peaceful' religion of Islam was "hijacked" forgetting that it was American airplanes carrying the living that were hijacked. Now some of those leaders, and their compatriots sit in Guantanamo enjoying Halal lamb chops—men whose creed is to "kill and let kill." Someone stole our Constitution and flipped it upside down!

It's a known fact that Christians spend and donate more than any other group to help feed the world's hungry. We are the ones who fight slavery. We are the ones who defend women's rights while leftists sit silently on their backsides. As I write this, there is a story running in the news about two young girls killed by their Muslim father for not wearing Hijab in Texas! Yet I hear no outrage from the left wing—for this story does not fit the template that liberals follow in their own war on Christianity. Indeed a devil must exist—how else can one explain the unity of beliefs between the leftists and Muslims? Leftists, like the Islamists, will never understand the fury they cause within me. They want to self-destruct at my expense and the expense of our national security. Leftists create a frustration that would cross a rabbi's eyes 'yada dada da.'

So, leftists, do me a favor, get out of my way, I have a country to save. Instead of labeling me as a conservative extremist, you need to label yourselves with such a title; while I am busy saving lives, you love to conserve energy, and collect plastic bottles and cans for recycling. Even though I agree with you on such issues, I, the bigoted Christian, have higher goals. I am not against people who want to use windmills and conserve fuel and natural resources, but don't ever become so extreme as to think that's all there is to life and eternity. Can't you see the hypocrisy and lies you promote?

Why do so many of the leading advocates of the global-warming-worry-warts drive cars the size of a tank, and then they have the 'chutzpa' to preach to you about conserving fuel! Why are you always so gullible as to believe them?

It is I, the one you call a "Jesus Freak" with the ministry of rebuke, telling other Americans who drive SUVs that they are addicted to Arab oil. This is what is aiding and abetting terrorism and funding the Wahhabist Saudi Arabia. While we try to find a better solution, leftists have prevented America from getting a temporary fix to our common addiction by simply digging for oil in Alaska. If global-warming is the issue, why not care about the entire globe. Why don't you focus on the Saudi Arabian environment instead of only that of Alaska?

Westerners confuse the terminology by calling leftists, liberals, when in fact we are the liberals. In this diary I will show how Americans read Eastern expressions and terms within the Bible yet interpret them through a Western lens. I will show how the West has misunderstood many Eastern allegories and riddles. The Christian Right doesn't seem to get it either. This critical analysis of Islam is dangerous; the subject that the anti-Christian books so carefully avoid.

Perhaps I should begin by being moderate and politically correct and state that I still agree with Muslims, Mohammed is indeed the prophet of Allah.

Does that ease things a little?

Okay, Mohammed is a prophet of Allah—but not of Jehovah. How is that for a start? Are you grinding your teeth now? I guess you are going to say that I should seek peace and not "divisiveness," another issue I have to deal with. Well, in this case I must choose divisiveness; Muslims are not my spiritual brethren. But generally it is the other way around— I am for peace, and you are divisive. I like peace, and it would be easy for you to create peace for me—just live and let me live.

Everywhere I go to speak I always get heckled by tree huggers and leftists. But I wonder... Was Russia better off with its type of god? Was the Middle East better off with Allah? Were the Japanese better off worshipping the emperor? Where Hindus better off believing in reincarnation? Are we better off worshipping the environment instead of having this earth serve some of our needs? Why not call all these divisive, and take that title away from me?

THE FOOLS PEACE PROPOSAL

Okay let us have peace your way; let us not offend the Muslims. You might ask, "How do we do this?" Well, I believe I know how. Are you ready? The whole concept of peace with Islam can be achieved in one day when all Americans, perhaps on the "4th of July" gather in football stadiums for an international peace rally. After singing the National Anthem, they must acknowledge the peace declaration the Muslims have been seeking for hundreds of years. You might ask, "What declaration?" All that Americans need to do is utter the Muslim creed for peace. Sounds simple. You might ask, "why not?" Okay, here it is, just say, "There is no God but Allah, and Mohammed is His messenger" (the Shahadatan). Then everyone will place an emblem or a badge on his or her forehead, as Muslims do at every demonstration or gathering you see around the world. The emblem can be seen here:

If you do that, you will have instant peace, and I mean instant. Here are some photos of Muslims carrying the Shahadatan banners to give you a glimpse of what else is ahead for you. Maybe you could open a factory to produce such banners so you'll be ready for the next 4th of July.

Osama Bin Laden made this point quite clear. So did Ahmadinejad and thousands of Muslim leaders. I can provide you with thousands of peace requests from Muslims. They all say the same thing: "we invite you to accept Islam." This is really the crux of the whole issue. One statement, that's all: "There is no God but Allah, and Mohammed is His messenger."

If America collectively would recite this, you would see hundreds of millions of Muslims demonstrating peacefully for a change. So why are these anti-Christian leftists not declaring this peace-creed in their books? Actually, they are already half-way there when they agree with the Muslims who blame Israel and America for all of this world's evils. "Is it really possible historic wars with Islam raged over one bloody sentence?" you might ask. Yes!

This offer, in fact, was the norm throughout Islamic history. The historian Edward Gibbon writes, "While the Persian monarch [Chosroes] contemplated the wonders of his art and power, he received an epistle from an obscure citizen of Mecca [Mohammed], inviting him to acknowledge Mohammed as the apostle of God. He rejected the invitation, and tore the epistle." Mohammed also sent a letter to Hercules the king of the Romans saying "Bismillah (in the name of Allah) from Mohammed the son of Abdullah, the Messenger of Allah, to the Hercules of the Romans. Peace upon the one who follows the guidance, I call you to Islam, 'aslim taslam' (embrace Islam and you will be saved), or have a treaty (covenant of security) with the Muslims, you will be saved." The year 629 was marked by the conquest of Arabia and the first war of the Muslims against the Roman Empire. Both the Persians and the Romans rejected Mohammed's peace offer. Eventually both fell to Islam. The Muslims persisted until they defeated them. Ahmadienejad and Bin Laden are very serious. The West has a choice to make peace or make war. To the Muslims, there are only two choices. Do you want peace? Then declare the Islamic creed and live in peace. Is this tempting or what? So then, why are you not saying it? Why are you being so 'bigoted' and against peace? Just declare it and you'll be spared the wrath. Choose this glittery golden chalice; Islam could be the truth after all. According to the Muslims, Islam is peace, peace, peace, and eternal life. There is one way to find out, just "dip and drink."

MY BIGOTED INTERVENTION

STOP! Do not become another Donovan. I was only playing the devil's advocate with you. If you drink this cup, you will have chosen poorly! You might be someone who knows nothing about life, maybe you are a student activist who simply objects to everything you can complain about: the environment, cultural diversity, interfaith dialogue, or maybe you want to fight Christians who believe in spanking and not sparing the rod. Perhaps you need to know that in Islam they do not believe in sparing you the sword. Maybe you are still in denial. If you are, may I suggest that for your next vacation you go to Mecca and carry a poster that says "We all worship the same god—Muslims, Christians, Jews, and Buddhists are all one—and Allah, Jehovah, God, and Buddha, are but the same God." You will learn that when it comes to God, Muslims will not simply draw a line in the sand, but on your neck. They will not spare you either the rod or the sword. You don't believe me? If you decide to accept my challenge, when you arrive at Mecca, you will see a sign with four arrows pointing to the city. There is a wide lane with a sign that reads: "Lil-Muslimeen

Fakat" which means "Muslims only." The right lane, which is narrow, has a sign that reads: "Ghayr Al-Muslimeen" which means "Non Muslims."

Make sure you choose "right lane" towards the narrow-gate, while you still have a chance to obtain eternal life. If you take the wide lane at the fork, you could die. And I mean *eternally*. Jesus said the way to eternal life is through the narrow gate. It is so easy to lose your life not only on earth, but eternally as well. I am trying to save lives. Muslims might kill you for making the wrong turn. So who is really a racist? Is it me or is it them? Ask yourself "how come you can't visit Mecca?" They will tell you it is because you are not Muslim. Actually, that is only half the truth. The full truth is that you are an unclean Kaffer. Do you ever wonder why no one in the world but Muslims want to visit Mecca—and only out of duty, never for a vacation?

Yet, when I hear of pilgrims traveling to Jerusalem, every cell in my body and soul cries out. Even Muslims long to go there these days. If Allah loves Mecca so much, then where is its spiritual electricity? If you removed the black stone, no one in the world would ever visit this arid desert city. Again, why is Jerusalem so attractive to the soul? The Jewish Temple has been destroyed twice, and still it is alive with electricity that comes from God! Jehovah God who said that He will even "make Jerusalem a trembling cup to all the surrounding peoples" (Zechariah 12:2). The fight is over beautiful Jerusalem not the arid Mecca. Allah cannot bring an electric charge that would cause non-Muslims to love such a place as Mecca. I see all sorts of signs "I love New York," "I left my heart in San Francisco," "Next Year in Jerusalem," but Mecca??? When we use the term "Holy Land," the whole world understands that is Israel, not Mecca. Even the Muslims who live in the Holy Land will go to Mecca once, yet deep in their hearts, they prefer Jerusalem, and visit it often.

In the 70s, I once asked my father about his pilgrimage experience to Mecca. His answer was a shock to my ears "Terrible, there were not enough rest rooms to accommodate the multitudes at mount Arafat and one would have to skip stepping on the human excrements, I felt nothing and saw nothing but a stampede of hundreds of thousands of people chanting and roaming round-about the Black Stone. By the time I was ready to kiss the holy object, a guard was whipping the frenzied mobs that were climbing on top of each other to reach the silver opening to the window in the Black Stone." Yet when I asked him about Jerusalem... when I was a boy, he would take me to a special place called the "Dome of the Spirit" on the Temple Mount, he said that he could not feel the presence of God in any place on earth as he did there. Every Friday he would go and cling to that spot. I used to joke with him that maybe he was a Jew whose ancestors converted to Islam long ago. In fact, there is some truth to that. We have F.M.F (Familial Mediterranean Fever), a genetic problem that originated in Israel thousands of years ago, and is also found among Armenians, Arabs and Turks, but it is most common amongst the Sephardim (Eastern Jews). I suspected something in my father's genes caused him to love that land and that spot. After all, the Shoebat clan stems from Shmuel bin Ādiyā, a Jew known for his exemplary courage. So why deny our Jewish connection. Many so-called Palestinians were originally Jews. In the village of Yatta near Hebron, for example, all were converted to Islam by force—originally they were all Jews. During demonstrations against Israel, Yattans would throw rocks harder than their Arab neighbors in Hebron, in an attempt to rid themselves of the stigma of having once been Jews. They chose to bow to Allah instead of Jehovah. This is why I do not agree with Rabbi Maimonides who said: "if Jews were given the choice of Allah or death, they should utter the creed of Islam and live." Did the Rabbi really believe this would save Jewish lives? Those who converted eventually saw their children absorb Islam, and the rest is history—their grandchildren and great-grandchildren stoned or killed other Jews. How is that saving Jewish life? Do you know how the Muslims were able to create the Janissaries, an elite fighting group who stormed the ancient world and forced nations to submit to Islam? This Turkish military group was comprised primarily of Christian children, who were kidnapped from their parents, then forcibly converted to Islam and made to fight Islam's battles against the Christians. It was simply easier for the liberal Christians to submit—fundamentalists usually chose the blade.

NEVER BOW. Listen to me, don't go to Mecca, and don't accept my challenge. If they searched your car and found the sign that reads "We all worship the same god–Allah—Jehovah—Buddha" you would be given a choice: either bow to Allah, adopt Islam and seek forgiveness, or instantly receive a razor-sharp, hand-held, crescent-shape pendulum that will send your head bouncing into "chop-chop square." This is a real place in Saudi Arabia and this is its real name. This may be too graphic, but I've heard that people still have a few seconds to hear and see even after they have been decapitated. Maybe the last thing you would hear is the sound of a multitude shouting, "Allahu-Akbar." In that case, if your mind is still functioning, make sure to quickly invite Jesus into your heart and don't worry—in the end He will reunite your body parts for a glorified resurrection.

So are you willing to bow to Allah? I think I already know your answer—"We are Americans. No one tells us what to do or what to believe." Maybe you are feeling some spark of patriotism. If so, possibly the issue for you is freedom—the very thing that your grandfathers bled and died for? Now you're beginning to remind me of William Wallace in Braveheart. Just before king Longshanks ordered Wallace's head cut off, he cried out one word **"freeeeeeedom."** I can sense that patriotism is all around now. You might even sing "God bless America." Have you ever asked yourself what these songs mean? Now you are in danger of becoming like me, an American 'bigot.' We are Americans, or at least I began to believe that, once I dumped my old bigoted beliefs, that Mohammed is a messenger of God. Is it bigotry to believe that Mohammed was commissioned from Allah, not Jehovah? If it is, then we are both bigots—may I suggest that you do what I did and go into a church with the rest of us sheep? You should find out what your destiny is before you end up in a box six feet under.

What you need to learn before you die is how evil works, lest you get eaten by wolves in sheep clothing. Christ said that He sends us out as sheep amongst wolves, so if you have no wolves in your life, it is because you are not one of His sheep. This diary will help you get out of your sheep costume and teach you how to have the Lamb of God in your innermost being. It will also teach you how wolves think and act. You might wonder, "Why become a sheep at all? It's better to be the wolf, a predator on top of the food chain." If so, then don't complain about us sheep whose only shield and sword is the Bible.

BIGOTS KNOW SACRIFICE, FOOLS DON'T

I am not a push-over. I know I am supposed to be afraid of releasing what I am writing here. After all, some fanatic Muslim might kill me. Well, as my fifteen year old son Theodore said "we are all dying, we can either die *for* something, or we can die *of* something." Leftists are chickens; at least this 'bigot' chooses to risk it all. Show me one leftist who confronts Islamic fanatics and I can show you a thousand Christians in the heartland of Islam risking their lives to save your hide—and the hide of millions of Muslims as well. Yes, and we even love Muslims more than you falsely claim to love them. However, true love doesn't coddle—it tells the truth. So what are you dying for? Or dying of? Everyone dies—sooner or later. So, come on in, and at least read all about my song, then decide freely if you want to sing along with the rest of us "bigots." Just don't forget, to leftists and Muslim apologists, you are already a bigot. Stop singing the lie that we all worship the same god and try my song for a change:

These are the days of Elijah
Declaring the Word of the Lord
And these are the days of your servant Moses
Righteousness being restored
And though these are days of great trials
Of famine and darkness and sword
Still we are the voice in the desert crying
Prepare ye the way of the Lord!
Behold He comes! Riding on the clouds!
Shining like the sun! At the trumpet call
Lift your voice! It's the year of Jubilee!
And out of Zion's hill salvation comes!
And these are the days of Ezekiel
The dry bones becoming as flesh
And these are the days of your servant David
Rebuilding a temple of praise
And these are the days of the harvest
The fields are as white in the world
And we are the laborers in your vineyard
Declaring the word of the Lord!
Behold He comes! Riding on the clouds!
Shining like the sun! At the trumpet call
Lift your voice! It's the year of Jubilee!
And out of Zion's hill salvation comes!
There's no God like Jehovah!
There's no God like Jehovah!
There's no God like Jehovah!   *Words and Music by Robin Mark*

CHRISTIANS—WAKE UP

On the night of His capture and then trial, Jesus went to pray, and came back to find His disciples sleeping. Today, again, the church is asleep! Even their childish dreams can be easily guessed by listening to the prayer requests in a typical Sunday school. I call most of these prayers, "Hemorrhoidal prayer requests." They are the typical petitions for healing from ailments and freedom from all pain or trials, as if Jesus' sole purpose is to heal the lame and the blind without us carrying our crosses.

I can see I'm pre-qualifying my statements here, because if I don't, I'm afraid you'll be offended and close this diary. I want to keep your attention in this fast-food world. Let me go on: I'm not saying that prayer for healing is wrong. What I am saying is that we have so many prayers without taking an iota of action. We pray about things we can easily take care of, so maybe we pray because we are lazy or afraid to deal with real situations. Every time I enter the lion's den, I hear people tell me they will pray for me, but no one helps me fight the lions.

I remember when I arranged to bring the terror-bombed Bus #19 from Israel and have it shipped to my church, the North Creek Church in Walnut Creek, California, to be "publicly displayed" as a wake-up call concerning terrorism. My pastor, John McNeff, had it moved to the back of the church where it could hardly be seen. "Why hide it?" you might ask. Well, he was afraid of reprisals. The church officials preferred to gather in the back of the church, make a speech, and pray. Even using the Xerox-machine to make copies about abortion was a problem at my first church. The pamphlet I *wanted* to copy, called for political action, and the elders were afraid of losing their 501(c)(3) tax exemption status. They chose to rather "just pray about it." On another occcasion, at Fair Oaks Baptist Church, I was commissioned to plan a day to honor Christian Martyrs. Instead of my elaborate event to honor these martyrs, my pastor Dennis Beaty objected—he wanted a simple evening event with a prayer vigil for the families of the dead martyrs. Frustrated with these things, I locked heads with my pastor, who told me that he is German and no one can "out-stubborn him." I told him that I was an ex-terrorist who had once been willing to die for Satan, and is now willing to *live or die* for Jehovah. I told him that I would fast from all food and drink until I died unless he changed his mind.

On the third day, the elders learned that they would have a dead-man on their hands and so they decided to stand by my plan instead of the pastor's desire. I organized an event and brought a speaker from the *Voice of the Martyrs*. Everyone from the church came and learned about the suffering Christians overseas. The next year, my 'German' pastor chose someone else to do the event—almost no one showed up. I'm convinced God is looking for 'crazies' who trust in Him. For Moses to take a million Jews and march them through the Red Sea was crazy. Yet Moses trusted in God. For Elijah to challenge the prophets of Baal was crazy. Yet Elijah trusted in God. For David to challenge Goliath was crazy. Yet David trusted in God. For Israel to enter the Promised Land and fight the giants was crazy. Yet they trusted in God. For Christ to carry His cross was crazy. Yet He trusted His Father. However, when I became Christian and chose to walk into a church, I realized fairly quickly, that most Christians are content to pray, praise, and sing—and do nothing more. This is fine, but do they even know what they are singing about? Moses was commanded to go for a prayer and worship service in the wilderness, but was stopped by Pharaoh. Like my German pastor, Pharaoh was stubborn, yet Moses, trusting in God, would out-stubborn anyone, including Pharaoh. How stubborn and crazy for God are *you*?

KNOWING WHAT YOU SING

Throughout my years of speaking to millions across this great nation, I've sung many songs with Christians in the West. Each time we've sung "Behold He Comes, Riding on the Clouds," I've asked the question, "where is He was going?" I haven't heard a correct answer to this question yet. How are these the days of Elijah, and why are the dry bones becoming flesh? Elijah fought the prophets of Baal, yet how do Christians resemble Elijah today, especially when odds are against Christians to bow down to Baal? Is there Baal worship today? I would argue that there is, but rather than taking action and fight these modern day worshippers of Baal, most would simply rather pray about it.

3

Putting Things Together

RUNNING INTO AN ANVIL

Speaking to the people in the West, I began to see how the U.S. is oblivious to what is about to come upon her. They sing songs and worship often without understanding what they are even saying. The songs become traditions. So far, only a handful of individuals have been able to answer the questions that I always ask: for what reason will Christ come to judge the nations? and what does the Lord do when He comes riding on the clouds?

As a Muslim, I spent a whole year trying to refute the Bible as a book that had been corrupted by the Jews and Christians. I believed the corruption was making God a Father, Son, and Holy Spirit. Yet, during my long search for the truth, instead of finding the alleged corruptions, further reading of the Bible made my head spin. It was like hammering an anvil. Though I thought I would only encounter lies, I was able to find the truth. And within the pages of the Qur'an, which I had thought was truth, I found as many lies as the grains in a pool of sinking sand. Was I able to find all the truth? Of course not, but enough truth to make me think, and re-think. There are so many things I can never prove or disprove. I was not able to dissect God in order to find out if He was three in one. But I came to realize that rather than the Christians, it was in fact, us, the Muslim world, who were spinning our heads trying to discover the unknown. But we had failed to consider the obvious realities that were right before us.

FUTUROLOGY 101

My turning point from being a Muslim terrorist began the day I spent the best ten dollars of my life to purchase a Bible. Perhaps the most crucial discovery I made was that the Bible is not simply a book filled with wise sayings and deep thoughts for personal meditation as is commonly thought. The Bible is many things, including a roadmap of destiny with many details concerning the future of humanity. For me, it was exciting to also realize that much of its focus is on the Middle East, where I was born and grew up. On a personal level, the Bible was also a mirror that showed me everything that was wrong in my own soul. You can only imagine what it did to this pride-filled Muslim when I studied detailed scenarios of the future rise and fall of Islamic nations and coalitions. I have taken courses during my college days in Psychology 101, English 101, and Sociology 101, but I never imagined taking a course, Futurology 101. Here I am not only talking about the predictive elements of the Bible. Pride is a disease worse than anything else that we could ever deal with. The effects that Hitler and Nazism had on the German people were far worse than the effects that the drug epidemic is having on modern day America. Today we see the rise of a similar pride epidemic that is growing on an international level in 55 Muslim states across the globe. As a result, we could very shortly be dealing with several Islamo-Nazi wars on numerous fronts around the world. Does the Bible predict such a cataclysmic event with so many Muslim nations? The answer is absolutely yes!

MY CREDENTIALS

In this diary, you will find an extensive course on the subject of Islam as predicted in the Bible. I will provide you with a fresh understanding of Biblical prophecy from an Eastern perspective and insight into the Bible as viewed by an ex-Muslim terrorist. I realize that these are not the greatest qualifications, particularly because I am not even a seminary graduate—but neither were many of Jesus' disciples. He chose Paul, a terrorist against Christians, and He transformed him into one of the greatest Christian ambassadors that has ever lived. Like Paul, I persecuted God's people, and like Christ, I was born in the same village as the King of Kings. I was born in the lowly area called the Shepherds Field, and like Jesus I was born on the first day that my parents arrived there from the United States. Don't worry, I am not here to declare that I am the One, I am but a "voice that cries in the wilderness," warning of things the Bible says are to come. I have walked where He walked and have breathed the air of the Middle East throughout my youth. My paternal Grand-father was the Muhktar, or chieftain, of the village. He was a friend and associate of Haj-Ameen Al-Husseni, the Grand Mufti of Jerusalem, and a notorious friend of Adolph Hitler. My Maternal Great Grandfather, F. W. Georgeson on the other hand, was the Mayor of Eureka, California, and a close friend of Winston Churchill, who wanted nothing more than the destruction of Hitler and Nazism. I was born from parents who were from opposite ends of the spectrum—both geographically and ideologically.

MY OFFER

All I can provide is my diary and my findings. In these, my course can only offer one guarantee: You will never read anything like this. You will read it again, and again, but never be bored of the subject. Throughout this course, you will also learn how to analyze the world around you and gain radar-like ability to recognize the rising evil that has lain dormant for a few decades: an evil that will dwarf Nazism. However, it is an evil that bears many parallels to Nazism—it even caused me to become bent on destroying Israel and attempting to kill Jews. It is not surprising then that I used to love Hitler. My heritage had a connection with Hitler's henchmen. They conspired with him on the Eve of the Final Solution to kill the Jews everywhere on the face of the globe. In the end they failed and, as a result, Israel was born. It was the world of hatred that caused the creation of the State of Israel. Now the world of hatred wants to destroy what they have created. In this detailed diary, you will discover how Islam is the missing link to the prophetic puzzle. Through the Bible, I came to understand that the world of hatred is its own enemy, and eventually this world of hatred became my enemy. What we need in such a world is to have our spiritual radar installed—fairly quickly. Or simply take out the old outmoded one and upgrade it. Consider this diary as an installation manual. It will never show you how to achieve health or wealth, but it will help you get your radar squeaky clean so you will never again fall for charlatans and snake-oil salesmen.

By the time you finish this course, you will thank God you took it for the rest of your life. And, I want to walk you through this journey with this book. In many ways, it was through understanding how real this prophetic knowledge that I discovered is, that I personally came to make the most important of all decisions—I, a Palestinian Muslim, determined from childhood to fight against Israel and the West with all of my being, chose instead to repent of my sins, and to become a follower of Jesus, the Messiah.

HOW I DID IT

I believe that as you journey into these findings with an open mind, you will find that the facts presented here make more sense than many of the wild and sensational ideas about prophecy that now dominate Western thought. When I began my research, I prayed continually for God's guidance, and then followed hermeneutical guidelines:

1. Gather much of the literal prophetic references to build the mold for End-Times events.
2. Apply the literal-mold over allegory and symbolism. This will give us an accurate picture of prophecy.

3. Follow a strict guideline by obtaining the meaning for all the symbolism in the Bible, from the Bible itself.

What I discovered was shocking. When I compared Islam, its purpose and eschatology, with all the prophecies in the Bible, not only did I discover that Islam was the antithesis of the Biblical faith, but that Islam also fits both the literal and the allegoric mold. Only after such extensive research is done, do we begin to find the perfect match to this Antichrist spirit. I will first present the spirit of Antichrist and compare Islamic prophecies with Biblical End-Times prophecy. Then I will take you on an extensive journey into the literal world of the Bible. Finally, I will apply these to the allegoric Books of Daniel and Revelation. The evidence you are about to examine is powerful.

SIMPLE OBSERVATIONS PROVE IT

Understanding the gravity of my conclusions, it is with absolute sobriety that I declare that this book will establish the fact that Islam is the religion of the Antichrist. I'm sure that will be a difficult pill for many people to swallow. But a simple observation regarding you doubters will prove my point.

How often do you find people who want to mess with Islam? Doesn't it seem to be an easier position to point to the finger at the Roman Empire, which has persecuted Christians in the past but which doesn't even exist any longer? How often do you hear that the European Union is the beast of the Book of Revelation? To such, I have but one challenge: Truth always stands against the tide of evil. To speak it and to fight for it is never comfortable. Standing against the Antichrist spirit is always risky. When you expose it, you risk death. Ask yourself, what would be the most uncomfortable thing to expose today, the European Union and the Catholic Church as the Antichrist and the Great Whore, or Islam? One can expose the Catholic Church and the European Union until they are blue in the face, and no one will berate them. Islam on the other hand, is a very different matter. Whenever we speak about Islam, there is massive pressure to pre-qualify our every statement. Objecting to Islam always brings controversy and outcries—even from non-Muslims who have never even really experienced Islam. We hear claims that Islam means "peace" and whoever criticizes it is characterized as a racist bigoted Islamophobe. Millions demonstrate when the Pope makes a simple comment. This is the very Pope that many Evangelicals mistakenly point to as leader of the Harlot of Babylon. Yet he often has shown more courage than many Evangelicals when shining the light of truth on Islam.

Muslims are responsible for the most powerful leader in the world, the president of the United States of America, George W. Bush, to give homage to Allah by proclaiming that

Allah is the same God that Christians worship. Muslims think this statement brings their dreams of the Islamization of the West even closer than ever—especially when George Bush says that Islam is "the religion of peace." This, from a Christian president who should know very well that the Antichrist spirit is the one who "by peace will deceive many." Even many conservative radio and television talk show hosts object to calling Islam a violent religion, yet feel free to equate the Bible with violence. The Western commentators say that the Islamic world simply needs to return to its own great and peaceful religious heritage. They say that all Muslims must jump on the bandwagon to fight that tiny minority who hijacked this loving religion. Imagine how I feel as a former Muslim to hear some ignorant Western commentator tell me that Islam means "peace." Yeah! and someday a unicorn riding on a cotton candy rainbow will come and take us all to Michael Jackson's Neverland where we will all live together in unity. Islam is peace? It brings an instant Fatwa against its critics, it threatens the stability of the entire globe, it infiltrates the West using oil wealth, and attempts to change our laws and constitution. Yet all of this was predicted in the Bible. Islam is the "peaceful religion" that ruthlessly persecutes the Church and the Jews, and even rules all of the landmass of every previous Biblical empire—the Egyptian, Babylonian, Persian, Grecian, and much of the Roman. Islam as a world power was wounded and appeared to be nearly dead. Yet it is now rising from the dead and is doing so with great speed. Islamic terror does not simply emanate from rag-tag organizations, but also from Islamic nations and mini-states within states. Today we have Islamist rule and influence in Iran, Afghanistan, Saudi Arabia, Lebanon, Sudan, Somalia, and that phony state of psychosis which is called Palestine. Islam is moving quickly to topple Pakistan in order to gain nuclear missiles. It is attempting to topple Egypt, Algeria, Jordan, and to gain political inroads in Turkey, where an Islamist government is already in place.

It is my prayer that this research will open your eyes to see and understand what convinced me that the Bible, unlike any other sacred text known to man, is indeed the very Word of God. And if you are a Muslim who is reading this, by the time you finish this course, you will either hate me or thank God that you read this book. But I hope you realize that I am not the source of this manual—I simply borrowed much of this wisdom from the oldest book ever written, the Bible. From the Bible, I was able to recognize that "faith is the substance of things hoped for, the evidence of things not seen" (Hebrews 11:1). Faith is an expected certainty of things we cannot prove, but has enough evidence for the future that we do not yet see. This evidence will give us complete assurance that we have wisely chosen the narrow path.

KNOCK KNOCK

Just come in. Have a seat. Care for a slice of apple pie? It's my favorite—it reminds me of America. My American mother used to make it when she was held against her will for 35 years in the Jordanian and then the Palestinian (not Israeli) occupied territory, which was the Biblical Judea. She always made a point to remind us of her country of origin. She risked her life many times attempting to escape back to her home. We were the only kids that ate American apple pie in our village. I still love it. It will always remind me of my mother's desire and prayer for freedom.

Buckle up. Let's take this journey together. Let me tell you what I discovered and why I changed my mind. Let me tell you why what sounds solid to many at times is, in reality, sinking sand.

I read the Bible alone, and prayed asking God for guidance, and then I believed. When I decided to find a church, I began to see that when it comes to many issues, there is a difference between traditional Christianity and the Bible. There is a world of Christians awaiting the coming of their Messiah, yet with only a glimpse of what He will do when He comes, or what we ought to do while He tarries. "For the revelation awaits an appointed time, it speaks of the end and will not prove false. Though it linger, wait for it; it will certainly come and will not delay." (Habakkuk 2:3)

My friend, Islam has risen again after decades of being dormant, and boldly challenges Christianity with its creed "There is no God but Allah, and Mohammed is his messenger." People demonstrate by the millions when the Pope makes a statement that "Islam must never be propagated through violence." They object that Islam is peace, yet they express this objection through violence. Having been born in Bethlehem of Biblical Judea, I must admit I never knew Christ and was raised to persecute Him and His people. All that time, I claimed, as a Muslim, to believe in Him. After all, to us He was a prophet of Allah.

Reading the Bible in 1993, I began to see not only the trouble within my soul, but with the West. I saw how we Muslims were again able to gain a foothold by crossing through your fortification with a Trojan Horse we called "peace" in an attempt to change your very foundations and constitution. I can see that Christians in the West lack the belief in their Bible and, unlike Elijah the prophet, whom every believer should emulate, they are afraid to challenge the prophets of Baal. Rather they fear name-calling and will not stand up and make their case from the Bible. While many attempt to defeat Islam through secularizing and moderating them, few will try the wisdom of old—the unchanging Word of God. Why not use what works? Today, millions of Muslims are finding transformation through the oldest tried method—conversion to Christianity. I myself was one of those who were convicted by my enemy's book—the Bible. I have become one of the remnant out of 1.3 billion Muslims and 2 billion claiming Christians, and like Elijah the prophet, I refuse to bow down to Baal. Just as John the Baptist "cried in the wilderness—prepare ye, for The Day of the Lord is at hand. Make straight the path..." (Isaiah 40:3)

So I invite you now on a journey into shocking contents that will change your life forever. Here you will find the results of my search for the truth. Here you will find an amazing amount of extensive research done regarding the subject of the Bible, how to interpret it, it's warning about evil, and what lies ahead regarding the rise of the harlot religion. *Yes this is Futurology 101.* Here we will study not only Bible prophecy, but also the Islamic beliefs regarding their own version of the End-Times, so that you may see these things as I saw them—through the Eastern eyes of a Muslim convert. I promise that you will see the ancient prophecies of the Bible in a new way that you had never considered before. After years of deep study of the Bible, I have assembled ample evidence for what I am about to say. I have prepared this detailed work, if I may say the best of my life, to show how, in the end, the truth will prevail and defeat the claim made by modern prophets of Baal that "there is no god but Allah." The trouble with Islam is not that Muslims are going back to fundamentalism and rising with violence, pride, and aggression, nor is it a problem of God forgetting to forewarn Christians. Rather, the problem is that the Church has fallen away and has ignored what the Bible says regarding its End-Times purpose and the rise and fall of Islam. You heard it right—the Bible has much to say regarding this pandemic the West calls radical Islam. I simply call it what it is—Islam.

This diary has been written to infuse you with the facts of what is to come—the rise of fundamental Islam and its fall and utter destruction. But before that day comes, we need to respond to Islam and urge a remnant of Muslims who are pre-ordained for salvation to come out of it.

≈4≈
Challenging Prophecy Analysts

Speaking to an audience of several of the most prominent prophecy authors in Dallas, Texas, I asked a question, "Besides the argument of whether Magog is Russia or not, can you name any literal references in the Bible to a nation that God destroys in the end-times that is not Muslim?"

I paused, waiting for someone to rise to answer the question. "No one is raising their hands. Is it because you can't find any?" Giving them all one last chance to answer this question. Yet, all of them failed to name a single nation that Jehovah-God will destroy that is not a Muslim nation. I know you might think of some that you picked up from current or old tradition,but please hold on, we will examine all of these in great detail.

As I speak at numerous churches, I always ask the same question, yet no one has been able to produce a valid response. Thus far, everyone I know who has tried was eventually convinced they did not have an answer. I hope I have gotten your attention! So why has the West missed this all along? Is it a lack of Scripture verses? This is hardly the case here. Is this interpretation solely mine? Again, I don't believe so. Many very prominent Christian leaders and scholars down through the years have written about the prominent role of Islam in the last-days. Their names are included in Chapter 70. So why should you be excited about this? Well, read on.

THE BEAUTY OF KNOWING THE FUTURE

Can you imagine living at the time just prior to Jesus' first coming? Being there and knowing well the correct interpretation of ancient prophecies? Or can you imagine being told by Daniel the prophet that a particular star would point you to the coming King of Kings? You would know what to prepare and how to be ready for the coming Messiah. Perhaps you could be one out of a handful of people to go down to Bethlehem and see the king lying in the manger. You might say that these events have come and gone. Well? What about His second coming? Would you like to know how to properly interpret the signs of His second coming? Maybe you don't even believe in a second coming. What you will find in this diary is overwhelming evidence. In the end, you will have one of the following choices to make: 1.) either the prophets of old had been very lucky and perfectly guessed the future, 2.) or there is a God and the prophets recorded man's future destiny. It is this challenge I present to my enemies which demands a verdict. It is for this reason that I follow the God of the Bible alone, and no other god. Go ahead; try to refute my points here—if you can.

CHRIST FIGHTS MUSLIM NATIONS

Even among so many Christians who claim to be experts on the subject of prophecy, I find as I question them on so many parts of the Bible, they actually lack understanding of many of the most important portions of Biblical prophecy. The most amazing prophecies in the Bible are hardly ever discussed today. *In every portrayal of Christ's return to the earth, He is fighting a nation that today is Muslim.* Try to imagine how I felt when I read Habakkuk 3, which says that in the last-days, God, the Holy One, would actually come to the earth on a mission to execute vengeance on Teman (Arabia) and Cushan (Sudan). "I saw the tents of Cushan in distress, the dwellings of Midian in anguish" (Habakkuk 3:7). Here Christ fights in battles against Arabia, Sudan and Somalia—all Muslim nations. I had to ask myself, if Allah and the God of the Bible are one and the same, why then does the Bible consistently portray God as being on the side of Israel and against the Muslims? As to the question that I asked earlier, "what does the Lord do when "He comes riding on the cloud?" the answer is found in the Book of Isaiah, chapter 19: He will come to *Egypt* to execute *vengeance*; "See Jehovah rides on a swift cloud and is coming to Egypt. The idols of Egypt tremble before him, and the hearts of the Egyptians melt within them." I appeal to the West; why are no prophecy teachers teaching this? Allah, the idol of Egypt and all the crescents on the tops of the mosques will shake and tremble. Indeed at this point, the world will proclaim as the song says, "there's no God like Jehovah." You might think, oh well, so what? What is so important about the fact that Jesus will deal with Egypt? He will judge many nations, even the whole world. Just hit the pause button on your Western presuppositions for a while. Again, in Isaiah I read that "the Lord, Jehovah Almighty would lop off the boughs of the 'great cedar' [Antichrist] with great power and 'Lebanon will fall before the Mighty One.'" (Isaiah 10:34) When I read this (in 1993), then I knew that Hezbollah (the Party of Allah) would gain a foothold in Lebanon. Today they have infested the whole nation. From a Muslim perspective, members of Hezbollah are faithful and holy warriors who are bent on destroying what they believe to be the evil nation of Israel. Yet the Bible teaches that in the Last-Days, Jesus Himself will fight against, and destroy, these anti-Israel forces from Lebanon. Again, I asked myself how could the Bible have nailed it so accurately so long ago? After listening to so many Westerners' view of Biblical prophecy, I realized they have it all wrong when they say that Christ will fight a coalition of European nations. Please don't assume by this that I am judging Western analysts. I had a much bigger log in my own eye because as a Muslim I was always taught that God Almighty would remain in heaven forever. In no way would He ever come down to the earth. It is far too beneath our pride-filled Allah and his dignity to do so. At least Western Christians understood that God would visit the earth. In Psalm 144:5-6, I read the following: "Bow thy heavens, O Jehovah, and come down: touch the mountains and they shall smoke." God will come down to the earth and touch the mountains? How does He touch mountains? He comes for war "Cast forth lightning, and scatter them: shoot out your arrows, and destroy them." Jesus will return to fight for the Jewish people and the Temple Mount in Jerusalem: "So shall the LORD of hosts come down to fight for mount Zion, and for the hill thereof." (Isaiah 31:4) Allah never said that he would come down to the earth. Only Christ who claimed to be God promised to physically return. Yet, in 1993 this thinking was blasphemy to me. Not only was I taught that Allah would never stoop so low as to come down to the earth, but I was also taught that Allah hates the Jews. But as I continued reading the Bible, I discovered that the Lord will judge the nations *specifically* based on their treatment of the Jewish people: "I will enter into judgment against them concerning my inheritance, my people Israel. For they scattered my people among the nations and divided up my land." (Joel 3:2) This is the answer to the second question I asked Christians: What is the reason for Jesus to judge these nations? The answer was right there in my face—He judges them based on their treatment, just or unjust, of the Jewish people and for a specific event "because they divided up my land." Indeed they have created a religious Islamic state of psychoses they have called Palestine. The language was inescapable and it was also obvious to me that passages such as these were speaking about the Israel of today. Israel has been sliced into two states and even now "Palestine" is divided between the West Bank run by the P.A. (Palestinian Authority) and Gaza which I call "Hamasistan."

It is issues like these, and verses that lay dormant, or not properly explained in Biblical commentaries, that I deal with extensively in this book. There are hundreds of verses and issues that have never been properly addressed by the Christian Church. I asked myself, why would Jehovah stand with Israel while Islamic tradition claims that in the Last-Days, Allah will appoint the very trees and rocks to cry out that "There is a Jew hiding behind me, come O faithful Muslim, come O servant of Allah, come and kill him"? Not a single male Jew will be left alive. However, I could not deny the fact that the Bible portrays Jesus the Messiah as returning to fight nations that come against Israel. In numerous passages, he actually confronts them by name. Even in Joel 3, where we find the judgment of the nations for dividing Israel, we read: "Now what have you against me, O Tyre and Sidon [Lebanon] and all you regions of Philistia [Gaza]; Are you repaying me for something I have done? If you are paying me back, I will swiftly and speedily return on your own heads what you have done." (Joel 3:4) It couldn't be more clear! It was as if Jesus himself was speaking directly to Hezbollah (Tyre and Sidon) and Hamas (Philistia) and challenging them regarding their blood-lust against the Jewish people. Their fight against Israel is in reality a declaration of war on the King Himself.

I had been an ally of the Philistia crowd. I hated Israel and attempted to kill Jews every chance I had. I had planted a bomb that exploded, and was part of the terrorist network in Israel, and in the United States. But in reality, I was fighting against God. Now I began to learn something new—that the Lord God Almighty will come down from His throne. This reality is evident throughout the Old Testament: "Arise O God, judge the earth, for all the nations are your inheritance." (Psalm 82:8) God Himself arises from His throne?! But which nations does He rouse Himself to fight? The nations that He wars against are well defined in Psalm 83 as a confederacy of Muslim nations allied against Israel: "They form an alliance against you—the tents of Edom and the Ishmaelites, of Moab and the Hagrites, Gebal, Ammon and Amalek, Philistia, with the people of Tyre. Even Assyria has joined them to lend strength to the descendants of Lot." (Psalm 83:5-8) When I looked at the several battles that Israel had fought against the Muslim countries from 1948 until today—some of which I personally witnessed first-hand, Israel always came out on top. If we Muslims were the good guys and Allah was on our side, why did we consistently lose against the "evil" Jews? As a radical Muslim and PLO terrorist, I knew that this is precisely what we were dreaming of doing—killing all Jews. I know I'm supposed to couch this in a more politically correct, moderate tone. Let me just say it again, without pre-qualifying my statement, all we wanted to do was, kill Jews. However, I'm afraid that the West will only learn this through more painful experiences with Islam. In the meantime, the West will continue asking the same old tired questions and will continue to apologize for its own existence, while it desperately believes against all hope that Islam is peaceful. I refuse to keep drinking that politically correct Cool-Aid—that everything will be just fine, that the Neverland Ranch awaits us all.

≈5≈
A World Gone Stupid

It is said that there are no stupid questions; that the only stupid question is the question that is not asked. That's true, but it depends on two conditions: 1.) if the question is basic, such as what is 1+1? 2.) the one asking the question is still a child. Yet the most common question I get does not fit either category, it comes from so-called intellectuals, show hosts, professors, and students, all of the same feather. That question is: "If you were a PLO terrorist why are you not in prison and why is the FBI not arresting you?" These allegedly well-educated students don't seem to understand the very nature of their enemy. It is an enemy that is bound and determined to defeat the United States and rid the world of both the Christians and the Jews. The very enemy that has planted 150 pro-terror Muslim Student Associations in the top 150 universities and colleges across this nation, that are paid to carry out their activities by funds from student tuitions. Yet the leaders of the Muslim Student Associations are never asked the kind of inquisition-like questions with which I am constantly being barraged. And, the Muslim Student Associations are never questioned, even though the evidence for terror supported by them is demonstrable and extensive. They want me in jail, and they want to release all of the terrorists who are enjoying gourmet meals, soccer games, snorkeling and outings in Guantanamo. George Orwell, eat your heart out! Well, let me answer the question that was just raised for some of you sitting-ducks who still don't get it. The reason the FBI has not arrested me can be explained in the images below. I was from the terror group that says "approved," and the only difference is the badge on their foreheads.

THIS MESSAGE IS BROUGHT TO YOU BY THE WEST, USING YOUR TAX
DOLLARS TO SUPPORT ONLY THE FINEST JEW-HATING TERRORISTS

The terrorist on the left has a badge on his forehead that says "Hamas" the one on the right says "Fatah." Courtesy of Cox and Forkum

If you don't get the message in the image then you need help. But that's ok, we all must start somewhere. I am no better. I had really believed that dying as a terrorist would send me to paradise. I had a much bigger log in my eye, so who am I to pick on the speck in yours? Fatah is the PLO and the PLO (changed after Oslo to PA) is recognized by the world as no longer a terrorist group. Even though they do exactly the same things that Hamas does—exactly—bombings, killings, assassinations, and terror funding from everywhere on the globe. So, nothing has changed. But since the Oslo Accord, PLO terrorists have the seal of approval from the White House. They enjoy visits from the top of the terrorist chain and funding to the tune of hundreds of millions. They even receive training by the United States. "War on Terror?" you might ask. Well, all I can say is, "War on Terror, my foot." Only God will fight that battle. Mankind will bend and fall for false peace with terrorists and liars. But why is the U.S. in bed with them?

The most common U.S. tactic has been to choose one bully over another in the hope that the least-worst of the two bullies takes control and that country would become slightly more moderate. In Afghanistan, the Northern Alliance was the preferred bully to fight the Taliban. But if the Northern Alliance is indeed "moderate," why would they also call for the killing of Christian converts? When Russia was advancing into Afghanistan, the United States helped the Muslim fanatics against Russia, thinking that fanatical Muslims were better than Communist Russians. This simplistic approach of the United States to Middle East problems has been devastating. Ever since the day they began aiding Islamists against Russia, the error of their ways has become increasingly obvious. The defeat of the Russians only served to bolster the radical Muslim confidence, which in turn sparked the rise of Islamic fundamentalism. This level of cockiness was especially evident when President Carter did nothing to help the Shah of Iran and allowed the most Radical Shi'a to take over the nation. For now, the U.S. sees the PLO as moderates, yet anyone who has ever heard of Al-Aqsa Martyrs Brigade should know that it was created by the PLO and is still funded by them as part of the global Islamic Jihad movement. The PLO is no different than Hamas. Remember, if it quacks like a duck, it is indeed a duck. Those in Lebanon are no different either; Hezbollah's militia can be seen doing the "Step March" imitating the Nazis. The only difference between Hezbollah and the Nazis is their chant—instead of Heil Hitler in German you hear Heil Allah in Arabic.

Additionally, Israel has a revolving door due to pressure from America and Europe. They have released more terrorists than any other nation on earth, despite the fact that throughout history, Israel has suffered from terrorism more than any other nation on earth. I am not sure if this is sheer stupidity or just plain evil.

To illustrate this stupidity, let me give you an example. Imagine a hundred terrorists storming into the Vatican and holding everyone hostage in the Pope's headquarters including all clergy and priests, exchanging fire with the authorities, ransacking the place, destroying ancient relics and such. What do you think should be done to these terrorists after they are caught? Yet something far worse than this has already happened.

To Catholics, the Pope is the Vicar of Christ. Yet the Church of the Nativity is THE place where Christ Himself was born. But all of the PLO terrorists who desecrated the birthplace of The King of Kings have been released from jail. What is most ironic about this story is that the Vatican itself called for the release of the gang that defiled the second holiest place for Christians worldwide. This type of minimalist response when it comes to terrorism in Israel is quite a pathetic phenomenon. To me, it is simply shameful. When I lived in the Holy Land, my whole family was involved in the Palestinian mockery and blasphemy of Jehovah God. Now that I live in America and see how the U.S. aids terrorism, at times I wonder why they have "In God we trust" on their money. It seems that American foreign policy displays more trust in the PLO than it does in God.

Consider the case of terrorist Atef Abiyat; one of the most wanted Palestinian PLO terrorists and fugitives in the West Bank. He was from my village of Beit Sahur in Bethlehem. He was directly responsible for the deaths of five Israelis. Abiyat was known as the "Commander of the Al-Aqsa Martyrs Brigade" in the Bethlehem area. There he was not a fugitive however, for in reality, these terrorists gained the support of the extended neighborhood. At his funeral, the entire community showed up to show support for his life as a terrorist and his success in killing Israelis. The whole city was there. It's an unwritten rule that anyone who blows up Jews gets the full support of the community, regardless if he is Hamas or PLO. Abiyat and two associates were killed after a car in which they were riding exploded in my village when the Israeli snipers hit him with a missile, in response for his responsibility in the deaths of three Israeli soldiers. Yet the Palestinian sources claim that Abiyat's death was another example of an innocent Palestinian who was randomly killed by the evil Israelis. Atef was related to Hussein Abiyat, one of the first Palestinian gunmen to be killed in the Intifada. He and two women bystanders died after helicopter missiles hit his car. The two ladies were relatives of mine, and another man who was injured in the strike was my first cousin who was with me when I bombed Bank Leumi in Bethlehem—the bank which sits adjacent to the Church of the Nativity where Christ was born. Abiyat, along with many of his family members helped suicide bombers purchased chemical compounds or explosives, planned the suicide bombing at the International Convention Center in Jerusalem, occupied the Church of the Nativity, Christ's birth place, desecrating it, and holding all the priests hostage. They even lit fires in the Church. Does anyone else wonder how the Islamic world respond if Jewish terrorists kidnapped some Muslim clerics in Saudi Arabia and occupied Mohammed's Masjid Al-Nabawi Mosque? The world saw how they behaved over a simple cartoon.

Yet with all of this (and more), the Vatican and the U.S. pressured Israel to set the terrorists who violated the Church of the Nativity free. These terrorists now reside in Italy, Greece, Ireland, and Portugal. Meanwhile, the Danish cartoonist and his family are living in hiding, moving from place to place, to avoid being assassinated.

In May 1985, over a thousand terrorists were released in exchange for three Israeli soldiers as part of the "Jibril deal." The terrorists who were released became the ideological and operational foundation for many terrorist activities in the years that followed. These releases are occurring constantly as a part of our war on terrorism; all the while Al-Qaeda is being hunted, PLO terrorists are being released to roam the streets. But this shouldn't be much of a problem, since these terrorists are only killing Jews! Whoever said that the Holocaust is over is a liar.

Now Primere Minister Ehud Olmert is entertaining a request to allow all of the terrorists who hijacked the Church of the Nativity to return home. After all, these poor souls are really not hijackers; they are simply victims whose *religion* has been hijacked. My cousin, Mahmud Khalil Awad-Allah, was also one released from prison after being given a life sentence for bomb planting and terrorism. This story is repeated a thousand times. The Israeli prison doors have become revolving doors, and the terrorists know it. International pressure eventually becomes too much, and Israel buckles to it, putting the terrorists back on the street to kill more innocent Jews. "Are we are fighting a War on Terror?" you might ask. Well, all I can say is, "War on Terror, my other foot."

Israel,
A Thorn in the Flesh

We wanted to destroy Christianity, America and every Jew. But it was my enemy's book that finally began my journey into critical thinking and led me to dig into my inner soul. What saved me were not deals, land concessions for peace, tolerance, interfaith dialogues, better jobs, secularism, or education. What saved me was conversion to believe in the God of the Bible. I kept asking myself over and over, how did the Bible perfectly predict all of our plans to destroy Israel and Christianity thousands of years in advance? Why was Jehovah defending Israel in the Bible? Why was it that whatever Allah loved, Jehovah hated, and whatever Jehovah loved, Allah hated? Allah hated Jews, Jehovah loved them. My life at this point was turning upside down and my head was spinning. But what disturbed me the most was the fact that in the end, Israel always won. What America needs is a victory just as they had when they crushed the Taliban. Israel needs to apply the same methods to Hezbollah. The destruction of Hezbollah needs to be complete until the stones and trees cry out, "Nasrallah is hiding behind me, come and kill him."

Yet the West has a long way to go to move beyond the fear of being labeled Islamophobic and realizing that the real phobia has always infected Muslims who fear Allah's threats as they occur in every other verse in the Qur'an. Even the terrorists are terrorized by the Qur'an. Yet the accusations of phobia are only cast upon the Christian nations who allow Islam to build mosques and Islamic centers by the thousands across their lands.

But Christianity is not the only problem for Islam; in reality, Israel is a thorn-in-the-flesh to Muslims worldwide. Yet, to God, Israel is His response to all the modern prophets of Baal. As terrorists, Israel drove us crazy! Allah didn't provide us with the favor of proving himself. But he promised that the stones and trees would "cry out" and betray the Jew hiding behind them so that we could come and kill him. The Gharqad tree, also called the Jewish "snitch" tree, is believed by Muslims to expose the hiding places of the Jews so that we can go and decapitate the last Jewish man. (The women we would keep alive as sex slaves.) Yet no Gharqad tree ever shouted during the 1948 war, the 1967 Six Day War, or the 1973 Yom Kippur War. Instead it was the Arabs who were all shouting for mercy after the surrender. So what went wrong? Where was Allah?

Egyptian born Sheikh Qaradawi, perhaps the most prominent and influential Muslim cleric in the Sunni world, responded to this issue in Kansas City speaking at a conference for the I.A.P (Islamic Association of Palestine). In an open forum supporting Hamas the terror organization, Qaradawi declared a common Muslim fundamentalist slogan—La Tu'adu Filisteen Illa Bil-Islam "we can never re-take Palestine unless we revert to Islam [completely]."[2] Qaradawi basically said what every Islamist is preaching—that we need to kick it up a notch. In other words, our Islam is not pure enough, not good enough, and not fundamentalist enough. We need to turn up the heat. Qaradawi declared to the Muslim crowd in Kansas City that Arab secularism and nominal Islam were the reason that we have lost all of our battles against the Jews. Our way of dealing with this dilemma was to argue that we were not serious enough with our Islam—we need to become even more aggressive. This is how Muslims chose to deal with the situation and thus, this is what much of the Muslim world is doing today.

So, now we are seeing several radical Muslim nations preparing for yet another attempt to destroy the nation of Israel. Meanwhile, the West only emboldens the Muslims by giving in to their demands of more "land for peace." After doing this, the West then has the gall to demand that Israel refrain from fighting back when they are assaulted daily by radical groups like Hamas or Hezbollah.

Neither land for peace or peace treaties will work, because according to Islam, in order to prove their Allah to be true, Israel MUST be destroyed. Since this is written in the Islamic prophecies it must take place, otherwise Allah is not God.

∽ 7 ∾
I Am Not
Alone

──✳──

What I was discovering in the Bible was beginning to open my eyes—Allah was not an awesome god, but Jehovah is. I also learned that I was not alone in my discoveries. Many Muslim converts from all over the world, upon becoming followers of Christ, and upon studying the prophecies in the Bible, also see many of the things that I saw.

Robert Livingstone, a Christian missionary to the Muslim World, recounts the occasion of going to hear the story of an Arab woman who had recently converted from Islam to Christianity. She had purchased a Bible from a book fair and hurried home to read it. Because she was accustomed to reading Arabic—which is read from right to left—she assumed that one should begin reading at the back of the Bible first. Thus, this women's first encounter with the Bible began with the Book of Revelation. Livingstone recounts this woman's experience: "As she began to read the book of Revelation, she was quickly astonished, and was shaken to the very core of her being. Suddenly the scales fell off of her eyes as she began to understand that everything she had believed her whole life was radically wrong. The shock was overwhelming, but the message of Revelation was clear to her. Its truth and power was so penetrating, she could not avoid the obvious conclusion. She would have to deny Islam, and whatever the consequences, become a follower of Jesus Christ. Fatima became one of the growing thousands of Muslims who are finding new life in Jesus Christ."[3]

This was not only a revelation for Fatima, but for Livingstone as well. Listening to Fatima's conclusions, Livingstone realized that perhaps his Western lens had clouded his perception of the Book of Revelation and Biblical End-Time prophecy in general. Over the next several years, with his understanding of Islam, Livingstone attempted to study Biblical prophecy through a different lens—through Eastern eyes. Not surprisingly, Livingstone's conclusions and mine are very similar.

Do you think this is simply an anomaly? I've got news for you. Some of the best and the greatest thinkers in Christian history have also seen Islam as Antichrist. In this diary we will examine some of these who supported the concept that Islam was Antichrist. There was Hilaire Belloc, Bishop Fulton Sheen, Gregory Palamus of Thessalonica, Vernon Richards, Sir Robert Anderson, Cyril of Jerusalem, Sophronius the Patriarch of Jerusalem (560-638), Maximus The Confessor (580-662), John of Damascus (676-749), Eulogius of Cordova, Paul Alvarus, and the Martyrs of Cordova. Even John Calvin and Jonathan Edwards the great American Revivalist both saw Islam as playing the major roll in the End-Times. With all of this, do I have your attention now?

≈ 8 ≈
Be As Wise As Serpents

✦

Satan is quickly approaching his final check-mate. He must destroy Israel to stop the Messianic Kingdom, yet with all his attempts to create his own kingdom on earth, and muster his forces as pawns against Israel, he is only fulfilling the very prophecies in Scripture that he so much wants to prevent. While Allah, who is Satan in disguise, thinks that stealing bits and pieces of Biblical prophecy is clever, he is unaware that he plays right into the very prophecies that were written thousands of years ago regarding his ultimate defeat. So instead of completely destroying the Jews to prevent the establishment of this state, they end up fulfilling Ezekiel 37, the valley of the dry bones, which explains how Israel will arise out of the ashes, and instead of Islam winning eternal life and destroying Israel, they will stand on Lucifer's side by attacking Israel, and without intention, usher in the Kingdom of Christ, while he goes the way of the dodo bird.

As a Muslim who fought to build my previous utopia by crushing the Judeo-Christian world, I was always taught that the Bible had long ago been corrupted by Christians and Jews. If this is true, then how did the Bible accurately predict what we Muslims were so clearly planning? Why is Allah, if he is indeed God, so afraid of us touching this manuscript? If indeed we had the truth, why were we so afraid of the Bible?

The Bible never warns Christians to run in fear from the texts of other religions. In fact the Bible says quite the opposite—"be as wise as serpents" (Matthew 10:16). In other words, Christians must understand how evil works, they must be aware of the evil that exists in the world. For some, this means actually studying the Qur'an and other Islamic sacred manuscripts in order to give insight to the rest of the Church. What one finds when reviewing Islam's prophetic worldview, is that Satan's best response to the Bible is to steal God's prophetic declarations.

Satan takes a shred of truth and then twists it, ultimately influencing lost souls like Al Gore, nudging him to predict global warming. Yet Global Warming was already predicted in Scripture long ago. Satan simply added his little twist to force America to sacrifice its industrial strength. Global Warming has nothing to do with the 'Lala-Land' of Al Gore or

CO_2 emissions. Any real Global Warming is caused by the heating of the sun itself. The Bible says that the earth will heat up from the sun: "Moreover, the light of the Moon shall be as the light of the Sun; and the light of the Sun shall be sevenfold—as the light of seven days!" (Isaiah 30:26) Global Warming has nothing to do with fossil fuel emissions, but is the result of so many drinking Satan's chalice "And men were scorched with great heat, and they blasphemed the name of God who has power over these plagues; and they did not repent and give Him glory." (Revelation 16:9)

How could people still blaspheme God even after they experience this "plague of heat?" Most Westerners read this and assume that it is merely mankind's stubbornness and hatred of God. To a certain extent this is true. But the real answer is that these peoples will be clinging to the satanic Allah, thinking that he is God and begging him for mercy, when instead they should be begging Jehovah, the One True and only God. In their mindset, they are already pleading to God. In other words, begging and praising Allah is already the greatest blasphemy. This stubborn attitude is right in front of us. All of the Muslim nations continue to be defeated by the little nation of Israel. So, the Muslims cling even harder to Allah and Islam when they should be praying to Jehovah and asking for His forgiveness. It is Satan's tactic to take bits and pieces of the Bible's prophetic insight, then add his own story in order to flip the ending upside down. Instead of being the nations that are judged by Jesus for attacking Israel, the Muslim apocalyptic prophecies portray the Muslims as eventually gaining victory over Israel for Allah. Do you see how the devil has setup the Muslims? They are in so deep, that they will never figure it out until the end.

Islam is such a barrel of contradictions. On one hand many Muslims will openly deny the Holocaust in front of Westerners and even deny Islam's roll in it. Yet on the other hand, they will secretly plot to achieve Mohammed's Final Solution. Beware of anyone who denies history, for if someone denies the Holocaust, they are also likely to deny the Crucifixion. It is very important that you understand what I mean by "deny the Crucifixion" since so many Christians also deny the crucifixion.

Are you stunned at what I said, that many claiming to be Christians deny the Crucifixion? Don't be, there are many Donovans and smart fools. Many are no different from Muslims. Please get one thing straight: Muslims DO NOT deny that a crucifixion took place, they simply say that it was Judas or someone else who was crucified instead of Jesus. Satan has tricked the Muslims into believing that it was his disposable pawn, Judas Iscariot who hung from the tree as a scapegoat to save Jesus' hide. As insane as it sounds, that is what Muslims believe.

But here's my question: Who do you put on that cross? Hanan Ashrawi, Arafat's right hand advisor before Arafat died, chose a Palestinian revolutionary "Jesus" to have been on the cross instead of the King of the Jews. If you don't believe in the Crucified King of the Jews, then you don't have the real Messiah. You might as well crucify Judas Iscariot. It doesn't matters how much you adore or wear your crucified Iscariot around your neck; all your praises and worship are in vain.

But if you reject what I am telling you, you're not all alone. Hundreds of millions of Muslims are on your side, you could all worship together. But worship some place hot to get used to the heat, because in the end there will be no air-conditioning—in hell.

For Muslims the dilemma will remain: if Allah is the truth, then Islam must be victorious over the Jews. The frustration that is experienced by so many Muslims is that these Islamic predications have not come to pass. Several battles against Israel and all have resulted in losses for Islam. The prophetic evidence for the truthfulness of their Allah has been tried and found wanting.

≈ 9 ≈
So Who Corrupted
The Bible?

Ignorance of Satan's evil schemes encompasses Muslims who do not realize that their Jihad eschatology only fulfills *Biblical* prophecy—while claiming that the Bible is corrupt! Ignorance also infests Christendom, for not seeing Islam in the Bible, in fact throughout the whole manuscript, as you shall see. After I respond with much prophetic evidence to the accusation leveled by Muslims against Jews and Christians as corruptors of Scripture ask yourself this question: Who really corrupted the Bible? *Who* really has attempted to change God's words? With the monumental amount of evidence presented, the conclusion will be clear: It is the very ones who accuse the Bible of corruption who are the true corruptors. You will see that they took select portions of Scripture and after they twisted it and laced it with deadly cyanide, they concocted a whole new Bible that they call the Qur'an and claim it is the final *Word of God*. Like their god, the accuser, the corruptors accuse the virtuous of corruption, the murderers accuse the innocent of murder, the haters accuse the righteous of hate, the warmongers accuse the peaceful of war, the lovers of death accuse those who love life with cowardice, while cowards who promote instant death are given the title of the brave. Murderers are martyrs, their funerals are weddings, and their victims are criminals unworthy of even a funeral. Their heaven is debauchery and their earth is a hell devoid of even the most innocent music or wedding dance. *Everything is turned upside down.* They can't see any of this until they are permitted to think—deeply— and exchange their holy cloak, these phony religious cellophane wrappings, with the fruit of love and longsuffering, in order to offer life as a living—not a dead—sacrifice. Scripture already proclaimed this phenomenon: "Woe to those who call evil good and good evil; who put darkness for light, and light for darkness; who put bitter for sweet, and sweet for bitter!" (Isaiah 5:20).

10

Even Western Experts Don't Get It

Westerners love to bank on Muslims who do not agree with Osama. But what these Western experts fail to realize is that for many of these so called "moderate" Muslims, their only disagreement with Osama is his timing. Here is my challenge to the West, which I know that no one can refute: Westerners do not understand that when it comes to the Muslim world, even the most "moderate" of Muslims, if they are religious, all believe in the coming of the Mahdi and the establishment of the Caliphate to rule the entire Globe by changing world laws to adapt the Islamic Sharia. The coming of the Mahdi to religious Muslims is as holy of a belief as the coming of Messiah is to Christians and Jews.

To many Muslims, Osama has simply acted in haste and did not gain the proper permission from officially sanctioned Islamic jurisprudence. According to orthodox Islamic jurisprudence, only a sitting Caliph has the authority to declare a global Jihad. Thus to many Muslims, Osama jumped the gun, if you will, he acted in haste. But thinking that someone acted too soon is very different than thinking that what someone did was actually evil.

I can share many examples of what the problem is with Westerners who don't know how to deal with Islam and Muslims. Every time some Westerner has tried to argue with me about Islam, I have clearly demonstrated to them that every devout or even semi-devout Muslim believes in the coming of the Mahdi.

One example occurred in Long Island, New York, at a Jewish-Christian conference during the lunch break. A Messianic Jewish rabbi and I were taken by a pastor to a restaurant across the street from the church. "I have been visiting this restaurant for so many years, it's owned by Muslims and never once did I experience any bad treatment" commented the pastor. "Really" I asked? Then the waiter came and handed us our menus. "Assalamu Alaikum" (peace be upon you) I said to the waiter, "Wa-Alaykum Assalam Warahmatullahi Wabarakatuh," replied the waiter, in English this means "and peace be upon you, Allah's mercy and His blessings." Once I gave the official Islamic greeting in perfect classical Arabic a degree of trust developed and we began our private chat in Arabic while the other two who knew no Arabic were chatting alone. He thought I was Muslim and we had a few laughs. I asked him in Arabic, "Do you believe this; I am sitting here with a Christian pastor and a rabbi?" I then began to quote Mohammed's famous End-Times prophecy of the trees and stones that cry out for Muslims to kill the Jews. "So what do you think?" I asked him, "Is it valid then to kill Jews?" "No," he replied, "the time is not ripe." Then he added, "We need to wait for the Mahdi!" and this was his last remark. Then he left. "So what did he say?" asked the rabbi who knew no Arabic, I replied, "For a Jew, today is your lucky day, you're not on the menu—yet."

Just recently, at a speaking event in Detroit, I was speaking with James Woolsey, the former director of the C.I.A (Central Intelligence Agency). He expressed his admiration of Sheikh Hisham Kabbani, who he said was his favorite moderate Muslim—after all Kabbani openly fights terrorism. I explained to Woolsey that Kabbani is a devout believer in the coming of the Mahdi. He is awaiting the Mahdi to come and establish Sharia law not only in America, but throughout the world. In fact, we will cite many of his comments in this book. But Mr. Woolsey was unable to respond. I believe that he was too shocked. You will find several of Kabbani's quotes cited throughout this book; as I said, he is a devout Mahdist. The West is encouraged when they see Muslims like Kabbani fighting terrorism, but they do not understand *why* he is fighting terrorism. For Kabbani, and millions of other Muslims like him, it is just a matter of timing.

At a speaking engagement in Los Angeles to a Jewish audience on Hanukkah in 2006, a moderate Muslim, Dr. Zuhdi Jasser of the American Islamic Forum for Democracy spoke. After his speech, I took him aside and asked him the question "Did Mohammed massacre the Jews of Banu Qurayza?" In which he answered "Yes, but they had a fair trial." Westerners would be shocked, this, out of the mouth of a moderate? This in a day and age when even the Pope made amends with Israel, yet for a Muslim it would be difficult. Why? Because the slaughter of the Jews was committed by the founders of Islam themselves—Mohammed, Omar his disciple, Ali his nephew, and the rest of the Caliphs, whether Umayyads, Abbasids, or Ottomans. Muslims always follow the example of Mohammed. When one questions a supposed moderate, it's always important to ask the right questions: Did Mohammed massacre the Jews of Arabia? Yes or no?

The question is a double-edged sword; if a Muslim denies it, then he has denied Islamic history and much of the text written in Al-Seera Al-Nabawiyeh (the Hadith), where deeds and works of Mohammed are documented. This would be like a Christian rejecting the New Testament. Unless he is liberal, he is cornered with the reality that Mohammed slaughtered innocent Jews. If they deny it, they are likely more liberal in their faith. If they acknowledge that this slaughter occurred, then they are forced to either justify it or condemn it. I have never heard a single Muslim both admit that this happened yet condemn it.

Similarly, I had a dialogue with Dr. Khaleel Mohammed, a professor at San Diego University and a member of the board of the Center for Islamic Pluralism. Dr. Khaleel would not denounce the Khaibar massacre of Jews. He refused to apologize for Mohammed who killed or exiled virtually every Jew in Arabia. The Christian Reformation started when followers returned to the Bible and to the founders of their faith, who all very clearly prohibited genocide and murder. As we see in Luke 6:27-28: "But I tell you who hear me: Love your enemies, do good to those who hate you, bless those who curse you, pray for those who mistreat you. If one strikes you on one cheek, turn to him the other also." Yet Muslims cannot have a similar reformation. There is not a single verse in the Qur'an that says "love your enemies." Islam cannot have a proper reformation because the very founders themselves, Mohammed (the prophet of Islam); the Sahaba (his companions); and the Caliphs all participated in jihad by killing infidels and anyone who opposed the Islamic system.

Am I saying that Zuhdi Jaser, Khaleel Mohammed, and Hisham Kabbani are pro-terror? No. What I am saying is that even experts like Woolsey, the ex-director of the C.I.A., don't fully understand this issue. One day he will fully understand, but in the meanwhile, the U.S. will try to find more Northern Alliances which eventually will go south, if and when a Mahdi is declared and accepted by the Muslim world.

The best way to understand this case is to bring a case-in-point. Let's even take a different religion altogether—Judaism. Take the Neturei Karta for example. These are the Orthodox Jews who are staunchly opposed to Zionism and the establishment of Israel. Why do they oppose Israel? To the Neturei Karta, the Kingdom of Israel must not be established until Messiah comes. But never before! They will oppose the establishment of Israel regardless of how many Jews suffer from the Diaspora or the Holocaust.

The Neturei Karta are very similar to the the Kabbanis, the Jasers, and the Khaleel Mohammeds of the Muslim world. These all reject any form of violent Jihad—*for now*. But when the Islamic Caliphate is established by the coming Mahdi, then it will be an entirely different situation. Then the fifteen percent of violent radicals in the Muslim world will become ninety percent. And the remaining ten percent of liberals who reject the Caliphate will be the first to go.

Just as the Jewish Neturei Karta is useful to Iran and the Jihadists, our Muslim "Neturei Kartas" are useful to us. But can we really trust these "for-now" moderates? Are these truly of the same feather as us? Yes and No. They are on our side, but only until the Mahdi arrives or the Caliphate is established. Then look out. The Messiah of the Jewish Neturei Karta however is vastly different from Islam's Mahdi. While the Messiah of Judaism will establish a kingdom in which the lamb will lay peacefully with the lion, in the Mahdi's world, the Jewish lambs are all slaughtered, as are the Buddhists and Hindus and Christians and liberal Muslims. Need I go on?

Then you have Jihadists acting like Muslim "Neturei Kartas." Why are these not openly Jihadists? It's because diplomatic jihad is every bit a part of the greater jihad. If "moderate" Muslims can influence U.S. foreign policy, to not take action against Islam's interests, then why would they need to blow anything up? So long as the goal is being achieved, the means is irrelevant. Although one can find liberal Muslims, rarely do we find moderate movements that call for genuine reformation within Islam other than for show in the U.S. and other Western countries. Image control is also a big part of the greater jihad. But don't be fooled. According to Khaleel Mohammed, as he described in our dialogue on *Front Page Magazine*, a major obstacle that stops the reformation of Islam is: "The status forced on Muslims by non-Muslim powers, so that Muslims, instead of trying to genuinely reform their religion, are instead forced to defend [it] against horrendous lies." In other words, according to Khaleel, the reason that moderates don't have time to fight against terrorism is because they are too busy fighting us, the "Islamophobes"—silencing dissidents is another form of jihad.

Who is Ushering in the Apocalypse, Christians or Muslims?

One of the most common accusations that self-described anti-Christian experts like to launch against Christians is that they are awaiting a fantasy utopian kingdom that belongs in "Lala-Land." But are Christians the only ones who are longing for a utopia? Everyone fights for their own version of a utopia; Communism, Nazism, Islamism, and even the worship of the Emperor in Japan were all founded on a utopian dream that failed miserably. Meanwhile the supposedly backward and hyper-religious, (or alternately wicked) Christian America managed to turn out on top. Yes, America is sinful in many respects. But at least we confess our sins out in the open. And America will continue to survive so long as the other utopian ideologies don't destroy us from within. I guarantee you that one of the biggest criticisms of this book will be that it emanates from a Christian Zionist who believes in a coming Armageddon. The left always claims that any Christians who are both pro-Israel and pro-Kingdom of Christ are going to inadvertently create an Apocalypse and claim its prophecy. *Are we, the Evangelical Christians creating, a self-fulfilled prophecy*?

The question that I have posed to many of these accusers, which none have been able to respond to is this: In order to establish Israel, did we the Christians conspire to orchestrate the Holocaust? Did we create and fulfill this prophecy? Or was it some other greater evil that was behind the effort to destroy the Jews? Who was truly behind the Holocaust which led to the fulfillment of Bible prophecy via the establishment of the State of Israel? Was it not Hitler and the agents of the devil? Of course it was.

The skeptics argue that it was the Balfour Declaration that created the state of Israel. Well, who was behind this declaration? It was Chaim Weizmann, a Jew. Were the Jews self-fulfilling prophecy? Chaim Weizmann and the first Zionists were far from religious. Were they making efforts to fulfill Bible prophecy? No one can provide any evidence of this. God will use the non-religious, the Muslims, and even Satan himself to fulfill His plans. None can stop Him. Simply because Christians believe the Bible, it does not logically follow that they are self-fulfilling prophecy.

Yet every time I speak at a Jewish event, I will hear the claim that we Christians are trying to usher in Armageddon. If true collaboration between Christians and Jews is desired, then why are such accusations being leveled? If Christians do not stand with Israel, we will be accused of being anti-Semitic, but if we stand with Israel, we are accused of ushering in Armageddon? I'm not following the logic here.

Back to the skeptics, if religious Jews were secretly behind the establishment of Israel, then why was Israel settled without East Jerusalem, the heart of every Jew? They accepted the fact that Jordan annexed East Jerusalem and Judea. Yet despite the fact that the Jews settled without East Jerusalem, the Arabs still continued their threats to destroy Israel. This eventually led to war in 1967.

Who ushered in this war? Israel? Did Israel force the Arabs to call for the destruction of the Jews? Yet what was the result of this Arab aggression? Israel won the 1967 Six Day War and East Jerusalem was given to Israel. Did Israel gain its original homeland by force? Yes—a force *from Above*. God finally declared a war on terror. After two thousand years, East Jerusalem was back in the hands of the Jewish people, just like the Bible said it would be (Zechariah 12:6). The Bible also predicts Jerusalem's soon-coming division. If anything, this proved Jehovah to me. People search for evidence for God, yet such proof is everywhere; just seek with all your heart, soul and might. In other words, no matter how you examine it, the ones who curse the Jews and the Bible, are the ones who will usher in all the nasty parts of the prophetic predictions. The ones who curse the Jews get the curses, and the Jews get the blessings. It's a proven law with much historical evidence that no logical man can deny. Nothing could be less non-self-fulfilling. Example: Hitler cursed them—he was cursed.

What was promised to Abraham, "I will curse those who curse you and bless those who bless you" still stands. It has no expiration date. If you hate Israel, hate obeying the Bible, you have chosen the chalice of death and you will be the one to usher in the fulfillment of Bible prophecy. You have chosen poorly and unless you repent, your destiny will be the same as Hitler's. But as you live out your part, may I ask one favor of you? What you do— you must do quickly (John 13:27). So if you are a leftist, you will claim that I am a religious freak who is ushering in the Apocalypse while you defend the terrorists who truly want to ignite Armageddon, even with the trees and the stones crying out to find a Jew and kill him.

Are you these stones and these trees? You too cry out to go after the Jews in Israel, driving them from their homes in Gaza and Hebron. You might just be the very stones and trees in this evil Muslim parable. Or perhaps you are the tree that Jesus warned about that bears no good fruit (Matthew 7:19). Don't worry, I won't cut you down, but He will.

So who are really self-fulfilling their prophecies? Using jihad to expand Islam and control the world is part of Islamic prophecy. Muslims are self-fulfilling these prophecies with all of their might. Yet few are trying to understand Islamic prophecy. What is so ironic is that Muslims do not see the human-origin of their actions. If someone warns they'll do you harm, and then does it, is that self-fulfilled prophecy?

What about the sudden explosion of devotion to Islam's so-called Messiah figure, "the Mahdi" that we are now seeing throughout the Muslim world? Did Christians also conspire to create this phenomenon? Did we force Iranian President Mahmoud Ahmadinejad to come to New York City and pray about the soon emergence of the Mahdi before the United Nations General Assembly in September of 2005? Ahmadinejad actually prayed, "O mighty Lord, I pray to you to hasten the emergence of your last repository, the promised one, that perfect and pure human being, the one that will fill this world with justice and peace." The Mahdi, who is referred to as: "the perfect human being who is heir to all prophets and pious men." The Mahdi is heir to all prophets? According to Islam, Mohammed is the final prophet and the perfect man. What Ahmadinejad was saying is that the Mahdi of Islam is essentially the reincarnation of Mohammed. According to Islamic prophecy, the Mahdi is the first of the major signs heralding the "Last-Days." This is confirmed by Ibn Katheer, the renowned Muslim scholar from the eighth century who stated that, "After the lesser signs of the Hour appear and increase, mankind will have reached a stage of great suffering. Then the awaited Mahdi will appear; He is the first of the greater clear, signs of the Hour."[2]

In 1976, the Muslim World League (Rabitah al-'Alam Al-Islami) issued a fatwa which declared that belief in a coming Mahdi is universal for all Muslims: "The Memorizers and scholars of Hadith have verified that there are reliable and acceptable reports among the Hadiths on the Mahdi; the majority of them are narrated through numerous authorities. There is no doubt that their status is unbroken and sound reports. And the belief in the appearance of the Mahdi is obligatory...none denies it except those who are ignorant of the Sunnah and innovators in doctrine."[3]

While tradition varies between Sunni and Shi'a regarding Mahdi's appearance onto the world stage, the core belief in his coming is not a sectarian issue, but is accepted by the majority of Muslims worldwide. Even in the United States, prominent and so-called "moderate" Muslim leader Sheikh Muhammad Hisham Kabbani, chairman of the Islamic Supreme Council of America has stated that, "The coming of the Mahdi is an established doctrine for both Sunni and Shi'a Muslims, and indeed for all humanity."

The renowned Harun Yahya also concurs: "Belief in the Mahdi has always been of great importance in the Islamic world. That applies to both Sunni and Shi'a faiths. Although there are some differences in the beliefs of these two major sects, the essence of the belief in the Mahdi is the same."[4]

∽ 12 ∾
Mahdi

Y ou can't imagine how I felt when I read the Bible and found so much that describes the Mahdi who I had learned so much about growing up. The shock to me was that, while a character identical to my Mahdi was seen throughout the pages of the Bible, this character was not called "the Mahdi", but rather "the Antichrist." Were the prophets of the Bible Islamophobes? After all, the Mahdi to us Sunni Muslims was "The rightly-guided and awaited One."[1] Shi'a Muslims refer to him as Sahib Al-Zaman "The Lord of the Age." This is exactly what the Bible calls Satan: "The lord of the age" (II Corinthians 4:4).

You might think that this is simply a coincidence. Once I am done demonstrating the dozens of similarities between Islam's system and that of the Antichrist, you will not be able to claim mere coincidence. You may want to create a chart, and using the laws of probability try to figure out what the real odds are. My guess is the odds would be one in trillions. Would you bet fifty cents on such odds? If not, why then gamble with your own soul? But what should really frighten everyone is that this Antichrist story is not simply a nightmare story that one reads about in some ancient sacred texts, but it is rapidly becoming a reality right before our eyes.

KHILAFA

A ccording to Islamic tradition, the Mahdi doesn't merely emerge as some vague great religious leader, he will return to reinstate the office of the Caliphate. Islam directs its followers: "If you see him, go and give him your allegiance, even if you have to crawl over ice, because he is the Vice-regent (Khalifa) of Allah, the Mahdi."[5] "For he will pave the way for, and establish the government of, the family [or community] of Mohammed...Every believer will be obligated to support him."[6]

HADITH

Briefly, the Hadith, or Sunna are the records of both the words and the deeds of the "prophet" Mohammed. In other words, the Qur'an is "thus says Allah" and the hadiths are "thus says Mohammed." The hadiths are crucial to understand when one debates with Muslim apologists. Whenever a non-Muslim brings up the issue of Islamic terrorism, the standard Muslim apologist will almost inevitably say something like, "show me a single verse in the Qur'an that teaches violence?" This has been a common technique to throw off Westerners, because whatever verse is given, it will then be explained away as speaking of self-defense or as commandments that were only given on one particular occasion. In other words, all of the commandments in the Qur'an which call Muslims to jihad are obsolete and not applicable today.

But this is sheer trickery. Public-image-jihad, remember? The first response to such a question should always be this question: Do you consider Mohammed to be the best authority to interpret the Qur'an? In other words, are the Hadith authoritative to all Muslims? This results in a Jesus style "checkmate," because if a Muslim denies the authority of the Hadith, then he is denying Mohammed's authority as prophet. Most often, the wiggly Muslim will claim that he does not believe in many of the Hadith (particularly the ones that you cite in the course of the discussion). But this argument will always end when a powerful Qur'anic verse is given that states "O you who believe, obey God and obey His Messenger and those in authority among you. If you fall into dispute about a matter, refer it back to God and His Messenger if you believe in God and the Last Day..." (Qur'an 4:59) After this, in accordance to this commandment from Allah, any Muslim who denies the Hadith is not only denying Allah's commandment, but Allah himself. This is comparable to a Christian denying the New Testament. In reality most wiggly Muslims do not deny the Hadith at all—they simply deny it in front of you.

Few Westerners realize that Muslims are allowed to conceal the truth regarding this issue when speaking to non-Muslims. The Sunnah is as important to a Muslim as the New Testament is to a Christian, "The Sunnah is everything besides the Qur'an that came from God's Messenger. It explains and provides details for the laws found in the Qur'an."[7] There are no serious scholars today who would deny the 200 or so commandments found in the Hadith, which promote nothing short of jihad by the sword—including unprovoked invasions for the sole purpose of advancing the worship of Allah.

Always keep in mind, the difference between Islam and Christianity can be summed up in one statement—Christianity is Calvary, Islam is Cavalry. The goal of Mohammed, the Khalifa, the Mahdi, and all obedient Muslims, is to achieve one goal and one goal alone—

to advance only Allah's glory as the supreme god by jihad; invitation first, then war until there are none left who will not say "There is no God but Allah, and Mohammed is His messenger." Allah commands all of his followers to engage in jihad until there is literally *no one left on the earth who does not worship Allah*: "Allah's Apostle said, 'I have been ordered to fight the people till they say: None has the right to be worshipped but Allah.'"[8]

CALIPH

Historically the Caliph is the supreme political, military, and administrative leader of all Muslims worldwide. Try to understand it this way; the Caliph is essentially the Vicar of Mohammed as the Pope is the Vicar of Christ to Catholics worldwide. The office and government of the Caliph is known as the Caliphate (Khilafat). It is the only form of government that is fully sanctioned by Islamic jurisprudence.

But since 1924, after nearly fourteen centuries of "divine rule," the office of the Caliph was finally abolished. Today, the movement throughout the Muslim world to reinstate the Caliphate is exploding with a force that is volcanic. With the mandate to have both seats of the Mahdi and Caliph in one, Mohammed said "There would be a caliph in the last period of my Ummah...He would be Imam Mahdi."[9] In other words, this last Khalifa, when he is installed, would be the Mahdi of the End-Times.

THE MUSLIM JESUS

The second most important Muslim end-time character is Isa-Almaseeh, the Muslim Jesus. The Islamic narrative regarding Jesus is drastically different from the historical and Biblical Jesus. The Jesus of Islam is in no way a "savior" or redeemer. He is merely one more prophet out of a long line of prophets sent by Allah. The special title of Messiah, although retained in the Islamic tradition, actually is void of any truly Biblical Messianic qualities. According to Islam, Jesus will not restore the nation of Israel to the Jewish people. Nor will Jesus' purpose be to save and deliver his faithful followers from the ongoing persecution of the Antichrist. In Islam, Jesus comes back as a radical Muslim to lead the Muslim armies, to abolish Christianity and to slaughter the Jews. As ironic and as perverted as that may sound, that is exactly what fundamental Muslims throughout the world believe and are awaiting. Are apocalyptic Christians behind this doctrine as well?

Section II

The Madhi vs. Antichrist
Why Are They So Similar?

13

Both Deny
The Trinity and The Cross

Out of the hundreds of parallels that exist between the Biblical Antichrist and the Islamic Mahdi, I have compiled the 43 most important ones. Get ready for a wild ride.

Most Western Christians understand Antichrist to only be an imposter—one who claims to be Jesus Christ, though he is not. This view lacks the deeper nuance that the Bible ascribes to the Antichrist. On the one hand, the Antichrist attributes to himself titles that belong to Jesus alone, but on the other hand he also bears several titles that exhibit his clear opposition to Christ and all that He stands for.

The "Anti" in Antichrist refers to the fact that he will be both against Christ and all that Christ stands for, while at the same time, he will also attempt to be a replacement for Christ. Antichrist will be Anti-Trinity, Anti-Son, Anti-Crucifixion, and Anti-God-in-the-flesh. Islam's theology fulfills these denials perfectly; every Muslim in the world denies all of these doctrines. Better than any other world religion, Islam is a perfectly tailored polemical response which stands firmly against the most crucial aspects of the nature of God as described in the Bible.

While Satan is not only called by the various titles that we would expect, such as "the evil one" or "the prince of darkness," often he also ascribes to himself various titles that belong only to God. The same can be said for the Antichrist—Satan's "son of perdition" who like his father, also displays a classic split-personality that claims attributes belonging to the true Messiah in order to demand obedience and worship. The Qur'an clearly denies the Trinity: "They blaspheme who say that Allah is the third of three." (Qur'an 5:73)

Yet the Bible affirms the Trinity, even in the Old Testament: "Come near to Me, hear this; I have not spoken in secret, from the beginning; From the time that it was, I was there, And now the Lord God and His Spirit Have sent Me." (Isaiah 48:16) Amazingly, in one verse we see it: "From the time that it was (from the beginning was The Word), I was there, and now the Lord God (The Father) and His Spirit (The Holy Spirit) have sent Me (The

Son)." Yet the Qur'an calls this blasphemy. What is more amazing is that the context of Isaiah 48 is a confrontation between God and the Harlot of Babylon (Lady of Kingdoms). This Harlot is definitely anti-Trinity.

ISLAM EXALTS MOHAMMED

This self-exaltation of Satan and his son of perdition is evident whenever Muslims, in their most important and significant declaration of faith, The Shahadatan declare that "There is no god but Allah and Mohammed is his messenger.'"

Nowhere in the Bible do we see an attempt to so elevate a prophet by placing him side by side with God in creedal form. It is unimaginable to think of a creed that demands, let's say, "There is no god but Jehovah and Ezekiel is His messenger."

Why so much emphasis on one particular prophet? Why would the Muslim creed not insist that Mohammed is *one* of Allah's messengers? But, *the* messenger! That makes him more important than Jesus Christ Himself! Why would Mohammed allow himself to be so elevated—even above Jesus himself?

Biblically speaking, the Antichrist will never say that he was the one who died on the cross; and he will deny that Jesus ever went to the cross. Nor will the Antichrist say that he is the Son of God or a member of the Trinity—he will deny all of these ideas. Throughout the Bible, the attributes of the Antichrist are always described as being entirely opposite the characteristics of Christ. While Jesus is called The Truth, the Antichrist is called the Father of Lies (John 8:44). Christ is called The Holy One; the Antichrist is called the Lawless One (II Thessalonians 2:8). Christ is The Son of God, while the Antichrist is the Son of Perdition (II Thessalonians 2:3). Christ is called The Mystery of Godliness; the Antichrist is called the Mystery of Iniquity (Revelation 17:5). He will not have the same name as Christ, yet he will claim just enough messiah-like attributes to form an effective camouflage to deceive the nations of the earth.

As we examine the attributes of Allah and his messiah figure, "The Mahdi," we will see that they perfectly match what the Bible has warned us of. In the many comparisons made, take special note, not only of the quantity of the similarities, but also of their incredible specificity.

14

Both Deny The Father
And The Son

octrinally, Islam and the Antichrist spirit are in perfect agreement because both deny the Trinity and the Divine Sonship of Christ, as the Bible describes: "Who is the liar? It is the man who denies that Jesus is the Christ. Such a man is the antichrist, he denies the Father and the Son. No one who denies the Son has the Father; whoever acknowledges the Son has the Father also." (1 John 2:22-23)

Whoever denies the reality of the Trinity and the fact that Jesus is the Son of God embodies the spirit of the Antichrist, *period*!

Knowing this, Antichrist will never say I am the Son of God, instead He will mock such a notion. This is crucial. The religion of Islam has as one of its most core and foundational beliefs, a blatant denial of Jesus as God's Son. This denial is found several times throughout the Qur'an. According to the Qur'an, whoever believes that Jesus is the Son of God commits a terrible blasphemy and is cursed by Allah. But beyond the fact that the Qur'an clearly teaches Antichrist doctrines, Islam has also created a perverted Jesus that is an affront to the historical Jesus of the Christian faith.

Growing up, I was always taught that when Jesus returns, he will declare himself to be a Muslim, He will deny all the claims of being God, or the Son of God, and lead many Christians to convert to Islam. Regarding those who do not convert to Islam, the Qur'an states that Jesus will be a witness against them on the Day of Judgment: "There is not one of the People of the Scripture (Christians and Jews) but will believe in him before his death, and on the Day of Resurrection he will be a witness against them." (Qur'an 4:159)

Muslim scholars explain that the phrase "will believe in him before his death" means that Christians and Jews will "confirm that he is alive and has not died and he is not God or the Son of God but [merely] His [Allah's] slave and Messenger, and Isa (Jesus) will testify against those who had called him Son of God."[10]

The so-called moderate Sheikh Kabbani agrees: "Like all prophets, Prophet Jesus came with the divine message of surrender to God Almighty, which is Islam. This verse shows that when Jesus returns he will personally correct the misrepresentations and misinterpretations about himself. He will affirm the true message that he brought in his time as a prophet, and that he never claimed to be the Son of God. Furthermore, he will reaffirm in his second coming what he prophesied in his first coming bearing witness to the seal of the Messengers, Prophet Mohammed. In his second coming many non-Muslims will accept Jesus as a servant of Allah Almighty, as a Muslim and a member of the Community of Mohammed."[11]

Ayatullah Baqir al-Sadr and Ayatullah Murtada Mutahhari, authors of *The Awaited Savior*, concur "Jesus will descend from heaven and espouse the cause of the Mahdi. The Christians and the Jews will see him and recognize his true status. The Christians will abandon their faith in his godhead" (sic).[12]

Once again, the canonized doctrines of Islam perfectly fulfill what the apostle John defined as the Antichrist spirit. The Bible warned Christians long ago to "test the spirits to see whether or not they are from God, because many false prophets have gone out into the world. By this you know the Spirit of God: every spirit that confesses that Jesus Christ has come in the flesh is of God. And every spirit that does not confess that Jesus Christ has come in the flesh is not of God. And this is the spirit of the Antichrist, which you have heard was coming, and is now already in the world." (I John 4:3)

The litmus test to know whether or not a spirit is from God or from the devil is specifically whether or not it acknowledges that Jesus Christ the Son of God has become a man. Any spirit that does not acknowledge this is from Satan and is the "spirit of the Antichrist." This by itself proves that Islam is possessed with an Antichrist spirit.

≈ 15 ≈

Both Are Blasphemous

✦━━✳━━✦

The Apostle John also adds "This is how you can recognize the Spirit of God: Every spirit that acknowledges that Jesus Christ has come in the flesh is from God, but every spirit that does not acknowledge Jesus is not from God. This is the spirit of the Antichrist, which you have heard is coming and even now is already in the world." (I John 4:2-3) "Many deceivers, who do not acknowledge Jesus Christ as coming in the flesh, have

gone out into the world. Any such person is the deceiver and the Antichrist." (II John 1:7)

From these verses, we learn that the antichrist is a spirit that is identified as a "liar" and a "deceiver" which specifically denies:

1. That Jesus is the Savior of Israel and the World.
2. The Trinity, or that Jesus is The Son of God.
3. That Jesus is God who came in the flesh.

Both Mohammed and his Mahdi perfectly embody this Antichrist spirit. Mohammed denied both "the Father and the Son." The Mahdi will come in Mohammed's spirit and will do the same. What is most holy to Christians is considered blasphemous in Islam, and what is holy in Islam is blasphemous to Christians. An understanding of Islam's reversalist or contrarian ideology is crucial for everyone who wants to understand Satan's attempt to contradict and undermine the basic teachings of the Bible.

Islam makes it one of its highest priorities to deny all of the above points regarding Jesus and His relationship with the Father. Just ask any Muslim, "what are your main objections to Christians" and their immediate response will be "Jesus is not the Son of God. Neither is He God. Neither is God our Father. Neither did He die on the cross." Try it.

My Catholic mother-in-law asked me prior to marrying her daughter "Do you believe in Jesus?" Being a Muslim I responded "of course." "Then you can marry my daughter," she said. However, had she asked me, "Do you believe He is the Son of God?" I would have said "Absolutely not."

The trick that Muslims use however, is that Islam teaches that Jesus is indeed the Messiah, after all the Qur'an calls him "Al-Maseeh." While it is true that Islam does retain the title of Messiah for Jesus, when one asks a Muslim to define what the title actually means in Islam, the definitions given are always hollow and fall entirely short of containing any truly Messianic substance.

In Islam, Jesus is merely another prophet in a very long line of prophets. Biblically speaking however, the role of the Messiah among other things also entails being a Divine Priestly Savior, a Deliverer, and the King of the Jews.

As we shall see throughout this book, rather than being a Messiah who saves or delivers Israel and all of his faithful followers in any way, in the Islamic traditions, Jesus instead returns to lead Israel's enemies against her in battle and to kill or convert all Jews and Christians to Islam. This would be the equivalent of calling Adolph Hitler—rather than Jesus—Israel's deliverer.

For now, we see that the apostle John informs us that just before the final hour, a very specific "spirit" will dominate the earth. This spirit will deny many of the essential Biblical octrines regarding who Jesus is and what He came to do. Islam could not epitomize this spirit any more perfectly. This spirit was "already in the world" (I John 4:3) even in John's time.

Several cults existed in John's day and continued with such a spirit. Islam stemmed from these Christian heretical groups such as the Gnostics and the Nestorians. While John's warning in the first century was speaking primarily to the heretical Gnostic Christians, when Islam came along, it literally adopted nearly every early Christian heresy and absorbed them all into one new heretical potpourri that we call Islam. As such, John's warning against the spirit of the Antichrist was virtually consummated in the religion of Mohammed, the greatest heresiarch that the world has ever known.

TAWHID AND SHIRK

In Islam the most essential belief is called Tawhid which refers to the strictest form of Unitarian monotheism imaginable—the absolute oneness of God. In Islam, God is utterly alone. And because adherence to Tawhid is the highest and most important commandment in Islam, then the greatest sin is called Shirk which is opposite of Tawhid. Shirk is idolatry, or "associating partners with God." As one Muslim group in Toronto has stated in their publication *Invitation to Islam*:

"Murder, rape, child molesting, genocide...These are all some of the appalling crimes which occur in our world today. Many would think that these are the worst possible offences which could be committed. But there is something which outweighs all of these crimes put together: It is the crime of shirk. As the Qur'an said: 'Surely, they have disbelieved who say: 'Allah is the Messiah (Jesus), son of Mary' but the Messiah (Jesus) said: 'O Children of Israel! Worship Allah exclusively...' (Qur'an 5: 72) This verse is evidence that those who associate with Allah are Kuffar and commit shirk akbar (greater shirk). If a person dies (committing shirk akbar) and never repents of it, he will be a permanent resident in hell-fire.'"[14]

While the unpardonable sin in the Bible is to deny, or *blaspheme*, the Holy Spirit as God, in Islam believing that God is the Holy Spirit is an unpardonable sin (Matthew 12:31). The Holy Spirit according to Islam is the angel who spoke to Mohammed. Yet the being that spoke to Mohammed bears far more resemblance to Lucifer than to any heavenly angel. Imagine that believing in the divinity of Christ is considered by many Muslims to be a far worse sin than committing murder!

Meanwhile, in the backwards world of Islam, the Muslims of Sudan are even now carrying out a literal genocide against the Black Sudanese while the rest of the Muslim world turns its collective head and looks the other way. But believe that Jesus is the Son of God and you stir up a hornet's nest. Neither the demons nor the Muslims can tolerate the truth that *Jesus Christ is the Son of God, and the Lord of All!*

ISLAM DENIES THE SON

This denial is found several times throughout the Qur'an: "In blasphemy indeed are those that say that God is Christ the son of Mary." (Qur'an 5:17) "They said, 'The Most Gracious has begotten a son!' You have uttered a gross blasphemy. The heavens are about to shatter, the earth is about to tear asunder, and the mountains are about to crumble. Because they claim that the Most Gracious has begotten a son. It is not befitting the Most Gracious that He should beget a son." (Qur'an 19:88-92) "...the Christians call Christ the son of Allah. That is a saying from their mouth; (in this) they but imitate what the unbelievers of old used to say. Allah's curse be on them: how they are deluded away from the Truth!" (Qur'an 9:30)

The Qur'an literally pronounces a curse on those who believe that Jesus is God's Son—people who say such things utter "gross blasphemies" and are likened to unbelievers or

Kuffar infidels. In his Institutes of Religion, Protestant Reformer John Calvin rightly stated that "[The Muslims], although they proclaim at the top of their lungs that the Creator of Heaven and earth is God, still, while repudiating Christ, they substitute an idol in the place of the true God."[15]

While Islam attempts to create an acceptable form of monotheistic worship, it not only leaves out the most essential aspects of a saving relationship with God, but it also confronts these things head on and calls them the highest forms of blasphemy. "Far be it from God that he should have a son!" These words encircle the inside of the Dome of the Rock Mosque in Jerusalem. This is the very location where for centuries God's people; the Jews, worshipped in their Temple awaiting their Messiah. This is also where Jesus, the Son of God, the Jewish Messiah, will someday rule over the earth. Islam has literally built a monument of unreserved defiance to this future reality.

But what is the "grievous penalty" that shall befall those who believe such things? According to Islamic narrative, Jesus will return to kill these, "polytheist Trinitarian Christians." But it does not end here. The Qur'an does not stop at denying that Jesus is the Son of God or that God exists as a Trinity.

ISLAM DENIES THE CROSS

With tears in his eyes, the apostle Paul warned the Thessalonians that, "many live as enemies of the cross of Christ." (Philippians 3:18). The Church Father Polycarp of Smyrna, a disciple of the Apostle John, also linked a denial of the cross to the Antichrist spirit in no uncertain terms when he said that "Everyone who does not confess that Jesus Christ has come in the flesh is an antichrist and whoever does not confess the testimony of the cross is of the devil...such a one is the firstborn of Satan"[16] It should not come as a surprise then that Islam also denies the most central event of all of redemptive history— the crucifixion of Jesus: "That they said (in boast), 'We killed Christ Jesus the son of Mary, the Messenger of Allah;' but they killed him not, nor crucified him, but so it was made to appear to them, and those who differ therein are full of doubts, with no (certain) knowledge, but only conjecture to follow, for of a surety they killed him not: Nay, Allah raised him up unto Himself; and Allah is Exalted in Power, Wise." (Qur'an 4:157-8)

Ironically, among Islamic scholars, there are actually numerous conflicting theories regarding exactly what happened to Jesus. As such, it is actually the Muslims who have "only conjecture to follow." But despite their inability to arrive at any form of consensus regarding what happened to Jesus, Muslims are very much in agreement on at least one issue: He never died on the cross!

≈ 16 ≈
Both Are Called Deceiver

When anyone picks up the Bible, they are almost immediately confronted with the fact that Satan is the greatest deceiver in history. It was shortly after having eaten the forbidden fruit that Eve said, "The serpent (Satan) deceived me, and I ate." (Gen. 3:13). In the New Testament, John the Apostle reminded us all that anyone who denies that Jesus has come in the flesh "is the deceiver and the antichrist." (II John 1:7). Paul the Apostle elaborates on the deceptive role of the Antichrist when he also warned that "The coming of the lawless one will be in accordance with the work of Satan displayed in all kinds of counterfeit miracles, signs and wonders, and in every sort of evil that deceives those who are perishing." (II Thessalonians 2:9-10) And as the Bible concludes, it encourages us all with the fact that in the end, "the devil, who deceived them, [will be] thrown into the lake of burning sulfur..." (Revelation 20:10)

Amazingly, all such unsavory descriptions of Satan are easily found scattered throughout the Qur'an (more detail later), but I will start with the most damning reference—Allah's bragging by calling himself Khayrul-Makireen, which literally means The Greatest of all Deceivers. (Qur'an 3:54) He refers to Himself with such title in Qur'an: 8, 30; 27, 50; 13, 42; 10, 21; (14, 46); (43, 79); 86, 15 f; 7,100.

Above, the first verse says "And they conspired, Allah also conspired, for He is the greatest of all deceivers" (Qur'an 3:54)

But what are the circumstances in Qur'an 3:54 that are causing Allah to be deceptive? Interestingly, the deception is regarding the story of Jesus, as verse 55 states, "When Allah said to Jesus, I shall cause you to die, then will raise you up to myself..." Allah deceived the people by not allowing Jesus to die on the cross and resurrecting Him instead.

As Christ was going about to do His father's work, Satan was concocting schemes for his firstborn Mohammed.

All of the most revered interpreters of the Qur'an; Ibn Katheer, Al-Tabari, Al-Jalalyn, and Al-Qurtubi, interpret Qur'an 3:54 as referring to Allah deceiving people to believe that Jesus was crucified when He was not. Qurtubi observes that some scholars have considered the words "the best of schemers" to be one of God's beautiful names. Thus one would pray, "O Best of Schemers, scheme for me!" Qurtubi also reports that the Prophet used to pray, "O God, scheme for me, and do not scheme against me!"[17]

How is it that in the Bible it is the Devil and his vessel the Antichrist that are repeatedly referred to as the schemers, liars and the deceivers; but in the Qur'an, it is Allah who is the greatest of all deceivers? Satan knows full well who he is, and as he was inspiring the Qur'an, he couldn't help but brag a little.

The Arabic word 'makara' means to deceive, scheme, hatch up, cook up, or connive. The Arabic Bible in Genesis 3:1 uses the same word for Satan.

In Ahl-Alquran (International Qur'anic Center) Sharif Sadeq explains the meaning of makara as attributed in the Qur'an "conniving is a weapon, like any other weapon, could be used for good or evil like a knife or a gun." According to Sharif, there are two types of conniving; one which is forbidden, the other noble.

BOTH ATTEMPT TO DECEIVE CHRISTIANS AND JEWS

Not only do Satan and Allah share the characteristic of being deceivers par excellence, they also both love to specifically target one group above any others—Ahlul-Kitab or "The people of the Book [the Bible]" as the Qur'an calls them. The Bible warns that Jews and Christians are Satan's favorite target, yet in the Qur'an, and all throughout this "sacred text," they are targeted by Allah. Does not Jesus warn "For false Christ's and false prophets will appear and perform great signs and miracles to deceive even the elect—if that were possible"? (Matthew 24:24) See, I have told you ahead of time. "So if anyone tells you, 'There he is, out in the desert,' do not go out; or, 'Here he is, in the inner rooms,' do not believe it."

As a Muslim I understood that according to Islamic tradition, the Mahdi will find some supposedly "lost" portions of the Old and New Testaments and even the Ark of the Covenant, and through these finds, he will argue with Jews and Christians, and win some to Islam. Ka'b al-Ahbar, an early Muslim commentator says, "He will be called 'Mahdi' because he will guide (yahdi) to something hidden and will bring out the Torah and Gospel from a town called Antioch."[18]

Alsuyuti, another classic Muslim scholar said that, "the messenger of Allah, may Allah bless him and grant him peace, said, 'He is called the Mahdi because he will guide the people to a mountain in Syria from which he will bring out the volumes of the Torah to refute the Jews. At the hands of the Mahdi, the Ark of the Covenant will be brought forth from the Lake of Tiberius and taken and placed in Jerusalem.'"[19]

Ad-Dani said that "he is called the Mahdi because he will be guided to a mountain in Syria from which he will bring forth the volumes of the Torah with which to argue against the Jews and at his hands a group of them will become Muslim."[20]

It is no wonder why Muslims cling to the fabricated Gospel of Barnabas. They are always trying to produce some sort of lost Gospel, believing that through such a discovery they will bring the whole Christian Church down.

THEY ARE ALL FOUND WANTING

I had always asked myself why Muslims were so specifically focused on attacking the integrity of the Bible; and today, not only Muslims, but the whole world. Even at most of the bookstores I visit, so many of the popular books are those that attack the historical Jesus and the reliability of the Bible. But rarely does one find a book that attacks the historical Buddha, the Bhagavad-Gita, the Book of Mormon, the Yazidi Al-Jilwah Black Book, or the Qur'an.

Why should they? For these lack any history or substance that is worthy of attack. Only a few Christians, who will probably be called 'bigots,' expose these books and show the lack of real evidence that they have.

So who is standing alone?

Who truly believes in The One God?

And who is uniting behind so many other gods?

Can we derive real historic accounts from the Book of Mormon?

Is there a single shred of evidence to prove the reality of any account in it?

The Qur'an also lacks any detail to derive much of the history it supposedly documents. Instead it only borrows apocryphal verses, and old folk tales.

I also asked myself this question: If the Jews were not truly God's people, then why did so many satanic empires and groups throughout history repeatedly make attempts to destroy them?

Muslims all over the world spend so much time repeating and hammering the claim that Israel does not belong in the land, that the Bible's history is fabricated, or simply that the Jews are evil.

Why is there so much focus on attacking and destroying the Jews?

And why are Muslims and Satan on the same side in this regard?

Why is it that one of Mahdi's goals is to win converts from among the Christians and Jews, primarily by casting doubts on the reliability of the Bible? Why doesn't the Mahdi focus on the Hindus or the Buddhists?

I have but one challenge to the false gods of all non-Biblical faiths: "Declare to us the things to come." (Isaiah 41:22)

If I may give the full challenge:

"Present your case, says the Lord. Bring forth your strong reasons, says the King of Jacob. Let them bring forth and show us what will happen; Let them show the former things, what they were, that we may consider them, and know the later end of them; or declare to us things to come. Show the things that are to come hereafter, that we may know you are gods; yes, do good or do evil, That we may be dismayed and see it together. Indeed you are nothing, And your works are nothing; He who chooses you is an abomination." (Isaiah 41:21-24)

Then the Lord continues: "Behold, the former things have come to pass, And new things I declared; Before they spring forth I tell you of them." (Isaiah 42:9)

Can the Qur'an show the former things?

Can the Book of Mormon show the former things? Not a shred of evidence for the claims they make about the Americas can be established. Regarding the Book of Mormon, the Smithsonian Institute stated that it "has found no archaeological evidence to support [the book's] claims."

The National Geographic Society, in a letter to the Institute for Religious Research, stated "Archeologists and other scholars have long probed the hemisphere's past and the society does not know of anything found so far that has substantiated the Book of Mormon."[21]

If the Smithsonian had the courage to say so, would they make similar statements about the Qur'an? Is there any proof for the existence of the peoples of Ad and Thamud "Irama that-il-I'tad" (the giants) as spoken of in the Qur'an? On the contrary, when archeology and Islam come together, we find more evidence of a Moon-god connection and old myths than to any real history.

Archeologists in the Middle East contribute to a publication called *Biblical Archeological Review* that monthly, through its challenges of the Bible, also finds much evidence attesting to historic confirmation of Scripture.

I ask "where is the Qur'anic Archeological Review?"

What happened to the "Book of Mormon Archeological Review?"

Have there been any Nephites and Lamanites found?

I challenge anyone to come up with such an institute and it will be short lived.

Indeed it has. Take Thomas Ferguson, a Mormon Archeologist who had been trying to find evidence for the Book of Mormon; the evidence he had desired to find to support the Book of Mormon did not turn up. In response to a letter Hal Hougey wrote in 1972 which reminded him that he had predicted in 1961 that the 'Book of Mormon' cities would be found within 10 years, Mr. Ferguson sadly wrote: "Ten years have passed...I sincerely anticipated that Book-of-Mormon cities would be positively identified within 10 years—and time has proved me wrong in my anticipation." (Letter dated June 5, 1972)

The same goes for the Muslims. Why would the Muslim authorities put such a tight lid on the volumes of the oldest Qur'ans found in Al-Masjid Al-Kabeer in Yemen? If I wish to purchase a facsimile copy of the Codex Vaticanus, I may do so. Why are copies of the Topkapi Manuscript, considered one of the oldest Qur'anic manuscripts, still sitting unexamined in the Topkapi Museum in Turkey? What are they afraid of? Why can't the oldest Qur'anic manuscripts face the same kind of critical examination that the most ancient Biblical manuscripts have endured for centuries?

I will tell you the reason: Because numerous aberrations from the standard Qur'anic text are found in all of these older manuscripts. Such aberrations, though not surprising to textual historians, are troublingly at odds with the orthodox Muslim claims that the Qur'an has reached us today exactly as it "came down" to Mohammed without a jot or dot missing.[22] Why would the Yemen and Turkish authorities close the door on the research?

The Dead Sea Scrolls were found to validate the authenticity of the Bible. In Qur'anic-style, typical Muslim challenge, may I say "bring your proof if you are truthful!" (Qur'an 27:64)

What about the future of mankind? Can the Qur'an or the Book of Mormon provide 8,362 verses of a prophetic nature?

Yet a prophecy from the Bible is fulfilled and the world goes mad over it—how can anyone explain Israel's return? "Fear not, for I am with you, I will bring your descendants from the East, and gather you from the West; I will say to the North 'Give them up!' And to the south, 'Do not keep them back!' Bring My sons from afar, and My daughters from the ends of the earth." (Isaiah 43:5-6)

While the Arabs kept them away for so long, eventually they failed. Russia held them back, they finally gave up. While the Arabs tried to destroy them, they failed, and even Allah could not destroy Israel.

The Arabs alone gave up 850,000 Jews from their lands.

Did Christians orchestrate this event to fulfill Scripture?

Allah is no savior, Jehovah is: "I, even I, am the Lord, And besides Me there is no savior." (Isaiah 43:11) and Israel is Jehovah's testimony " 'Therefore you are My witnesses' says the Lord, 'that I am God.'" (Isaiah 43:10)

It is this God that I serve, the one who "says to Jerusalem, 'You shall be inhabited, to the cities of Judah You shall be built.'" (Isaiah 44:26) God promised to restore Jerusalem and Israel and He is doing it.

We live in a world that overlooks evils far beyond anything that Israel does. God forbid that Israel should set up road closures, check points, or destroy a bomb factory in order to protect themselves from killers, yet Israel is the cause of a collective worldwide false testimony. Bookstores are filled with unfair critical analyses of Israel and the Bible. But the only books that one can find that criticize the Qur'an come from "Islamophobes" like me.

BOTH PRACTICE DECEPTION
SO, WHO IS LYING? CHRISTIANS OR MUSLIMS

The Biblical picture of the Last-Days is one where deception is the absolute rule of the day. Virtually every passage where the End-Times are discussed in the New Testament, the author stresses that believers are to be very careful that they not be deceived; "As Jesus was sitting on the Mount of Olives, the disciples came to him privately. 'Tell us,' they said, 'when will this happen, and what will be the sign of your coming and of the end of the age?' Jesus answered: 'Watch out that no one deceives you.'" (Matthew 24:3-4)

Jesus goes on to warn of the power of this deception "At that time many will turn away from the faith and will betray and hate each other, and many false prophets will appear and deceive many people...for false Christs and false prophets will appear and perform great signs and miracles to deceive even the elect—if that were possible. See, I have told you ahead of time." (Matthew 24:10-11, 24-25)

Likewise the Apostle Paul warned, "Concerning the coming of our Lord Jesus Christ and our being gathered to him...Don't let anyone deceive you in any way..." (II Thessalonians 2:1-3) A few verses later, he continues his warning describing the deception that the Antichrist brings as "a powerful delusion." (II Thessalonians 2:9-12)

Most Westerners have a hard time relating to the fact that purposeful exaggerations; covering of the truth; and outright, deliberate lying are actually part and parcel of the religion of Islam. Now, of course, if you bring this matter up to a Muslim, he will be quick to quote the Qur'an, "And cover not truth with falsehood, nor conceal the truth when ye know what it is." (Qur'an 2:42)

But unfortunately, if we dig just a little deeper to examine the meaning of this "thou should not lie" command and turn to the ancient Qur'anic commentary (Tafsir) by Ibn Katheer, we find a very different explanation: "Allah forbade the Jews from intentionally distorting the truth with falsehood and from hiding the truth and spreading falsehood. 'And mix not truth with falsehood, nor conceal the truth while you know the truth.' So Allah forbade them [the Jews] from two things; He ordered them to make the truth known, as well as explaining it...Qatadah said that, 'And mix not truth with falsehood' means, 'Do not mix Judaism and Christianity with Islam' 'while you know the truth' that the religion of Allah is Islam, and that Judaism and Christianity are [corrupted] innovations that did not come from Allah."[23]

The very verse that Muslims point to in an attempt to claim that they are forbidden from lying means nothing of the sort, but is instead a command to Jews not to lie to Muslims!

But this is the tip of the iceberg that the Western Titanic is colliding with. What lays beneath the surface and is hidden from the scene is far more ominous. While evangelism in Christianity is "the great news that Jesus died for you," take it or leave it, Islamic evangelism is violence with a shout of "Islam is victorious" and "Allah is great." For whom is this good news?

But before you awake to find out that you must make a choice between Allah and the blade, you need to understand how the victims of Islam get set up. It begins with the famous saying of Mohammed: "War is deception."[24]

During my college days in the early eighties I worked as an interpreter and counselor for the Arab students being paid through an American program called CETA (Comprehensive Employment and Training Act). While the grants came from the United States Government, my instructions came from representatives of the P.L.O., which at the time was considered a terrorist organization. Today, they are no longer considered a terrorist organization—that designation was dropped after Arafat applied the teachings of Mohammed and in 1993 signed what is known to Westerners as the Oslo Peace Accord, or the Oslo Hudna Accord as it is referred to by Muslims in the Middle East. Hudna is an Islamic term that refers to temporary treaties with non-Muslims that are used by the Muslims, solely to gain concessions, military and political strength.

Well, part of my job at CETA was to work on advertisements for events. The goal of our events was always to win American sympathy for the Palestinian cause. Actually, "win sympathy" may be a rather misleading expression. It was more like attempting to trick the gullible into our cause.

In Arabic, the advertisements for such events would openly use Jihad and anti-Semitic slogans calling for, "rivers of blood...support our Jihad to send student recruits to Southern Lebanon to fight the dirty Zionists...death to Israel...death to America..." The English version of the posters was a simple, "Welcome to a Middle Eastern cultural party, come and join a festival of song and dance, we will be serving roasted lamb and baklava..." Americans flocked for the food laced with our propaganda. Sure we had songs, they were all revolutionary songs in Arabic with nothing but the words of death and kill.

During my terror days, when I lied to Westerners they believed me, now that I am telling the truth, I am called a liar.

The biggest pathological lie was the psychosis we called "The Palestinian Cause." Muslims observe a ritual during their holy Hajj (Pilgrimage) to Mecca. Millions gather to "stone" an obelisk they call Satan. Palestinians carry out a parallel ritual in "Palestine" (Jerusalem). Only, instead of throwing stones at an obelisk, they position themselves atop the Temple Mount, Israel's holiest site, and the rocks are thrown down at the "Jew-Devils" who can always be found standing and worshipping at the Wailing Wall below. The daily headlines of these observances are guaranteed to attract gullible Westerners who flock to Jerusalem to film the stoning frenzies.

The Western media's holy mandate doesn't stop there; they run around the vicinity, ready to film the "Jew-Devil" as he sets up road blockades to protect his community and at times he is even filmed bulldozing a few olive trees to make way for a separation wall between themselves and the Muslim "saints." Yet the world cries out "how dare the 'devil' stop the influx of these 'holy pilgrims'?"

As long as the Muslims think of the Jewish people as "Jew-Devils" it makes it easier to confront them: The headlines tell of Jews clearing some trees to build an apartment complex at Har Homa. Next they are found guilty of destroying the environment on that piece of land, which he is then accused of taking. No one talks about how these lands were bought by the Jewish National Fund for double the market value from the Muslim landowners. Of course, it's not a sin to take money for land—even if it's from the "devil." Besides, these lands will come back to the "saints" from the hands of the unclean. My own grandfather sold lands which are now back in my family's possession.

None of the "saints" are concerned about Jewish claims of ownership of land they paid for, nor are they interested in listening to the cries of his children being murdered by stoning or explosions—it is a sacrilege to hear the voices of "demons." At times their bodies are so mangled, they can't even be recognized. The bits and pieces of ground human flesh is hand-picked by rabbis out of respect for the human body in order to give them a proper burial—regardless if the flesh belonged to the "Sainted" Muslim or the "Devil"

Jew. Dare the devil shoot down one of these holy ones who are bent on destroying the evil Jew, the cameras will be there to catch the "Jew-Devil" in the act.

The Jews are not allowed to set up search posts, a right to be exercised by only non-Jews. No thanks to 9/11, Westerners have come to accept being searched and having to wait in long lines at airports. What the West considers to be security measures is portrayed by Palestinians as harassments, occupation, oppression, closures and racism. The Western world is oblivious to collective Palestinian exaggerations. If indeed that is what we should call it. It is more like psychopathic lying in which the liar in this case truly believes his own lie and is even willing to die for it. One documentary titled *Paliwood* shows a Palestinian martyr procession in which the body accidentally falls off the coffin, then the coffin is lowered down to the ground, and the body miraculously rises from the dead and gets into the coffin, all on its own accord. The ironic thing about this true story is that many in the crowd saw this happen, yet they continued the march.

Muslim masses can lie in unison. If you think terrorists are all insane, then the Chairman of the Arab Psychiatric Association, Adel Sadeq must also be insane. Why else would he state to the media, "When the martyr dies a martyr's death, he attains the height of bliss...As a psychiatrist, I say that the height of bliss comes with the end of the countdown: ten, nine, eight, seven, six, five, four, three, two, one, zero. And then, you press the button to blow yourself up. When the martyr reaches 'one,' and then 'boom,' he explodes, and senses himself flying because he knows for certain that he is not dead...It is a transition to another, more beautiful world, because he knows very well that within seconds he will see the light of the creator. He will be at the closest possible point to Allah..." (Hadith Al Madina, Egypt, April 23, 2002).

Israel is always accused of racism, but in so many cases, it's the racist who accuses others of racism. You find this type of thing even in America. Obama's mentor is a great example. Pastor Wright fights racism against blacks by preaching sermons of nothing but hatred of whites. A racist is a paranoid person who daily swallows anti-phobia pills which causes him to accuse everyone else, except himself of courses, of racism and xenophobia. The intake of this psychopathic drug is amazingly not taken orally, but by watching and reading the media.

Discussions of Western gullibility during my college days, we would confirm their feelings by using half statements, "sure we hated Hitler," we said in front of Americans. But when we were all alone, we would say "we hate Hitler, he never got the job done." Half statements can create the totally opposite meaning.

We always viewed Westerners, including Christians, as a giant pack of politically-correct lemmings. And sadly, I must admit, our perceptions were not entirely unjustified. But now

I have learned to never point my finger at another's gullibility. For what we accuse others of, we are most often guilty of ourselves. After all, I had bought into the false doctrine that promoted the shedding of innocent blood (Proverbs 1:11), and I believed that killing oneself was a way to acquire salvation. Just how gullible can the wolves get? I have never seen sheep kill sheep, but wolves? We have civil unrest in Pakistan, Iran, Afghanistan, Lebanon, Sudan, Somalia, Algeria, the Philippines, Indonesia, Egypt, Occupied Judea...everywhere. Where the creed of the wolf thrives, everyone dies. The sheep are not the only ones dying—the wolves eat the sheep, but they are also killing each other without mercy.

The West needs to wake up from its slumber—the creed of the wolf teaches them to dress up as sheep, then trap the sheep. And for the past few decades, they have done a great job. The two doctrines that encourage this insidious form of religiously sanctioned deception are called Kitman and Taqiyya. The first is a command to deliberately conceal one's beliefs. It is a particular form of lying practiced primarily by Shi'ites and to a lesser degree by Sunnis. Imam Ja'far Sadiq, the sixth Imam of Shi'a Islam articulates this doctrine; "One who exposes something from our religion is like one who intentionally kills us" and "You belong to a religion that whosoever conceals it, Allah will honor him and whosoever reveals it, Allah will disgrace him."

Shi'a Muslims are commanded to purposefully hide what they truly believe in order to mislead outsiders as to the true nature of their religion. Contrary to Kitman, Christ encouraged His sheep "You are the light of the world. A city on a hill cannot be hidden. Neither do people light a lamp and put it under a bowl. Instead they put it on its stand, and it gives light to everyone in the house. In the same way, let your light shine before men, that they may see your good deeds and praise your Father in heaven." (Matthew 5:14-16) To Westerners, Kitman is more probably suited to deceptive politics than to religion. Muslims do not separate the two.

Taqiyya is virtually the same. A Shi'ite Encyclopedia describes Taqiyya as "Concealing or disguising one's beliefs, convictions, ideas, feelings, opinions, and/or strategies at a time of eminent danger, whether now or later in time, to save oneself from physical and/or mental injury. A one-word translation would be 'Dissimulation.'"[25]

Sunni Muslims argue that Kitman and Taqiyya as strictly a Shi'a doctrine. Yet, Ibn Abbas, the most renowned and trusted narrator of Islamic tradition in the sight of the Sunnis upholds the practice by Sunnis: "Taqiyya is (merely) the uttering of the tongue, while the heart is comfortable with faith."[26] "Nine-tenths of (the Islamic) religion is Taqiyyah (dissimulation), hence one who does not dissimulate has no religion." (Al-Kafi vol. 9 p. 110)

Christians throughout history chose to endure horrific and cruel torture, even martyrdom instead of denying their faith. The Qur'an admonishes Muslims "Let not the believers take for friends or helpers unbelievers rather than believers: if any do that, in nothing will there be help from Allah: except by way of precaution (prevention), that ye may guard yourselves from them (prevent them from harming you.)" (Qur'an 3: 28) Ibn Katheer explains the meaning of the verse: "Allah prohibited His believing servants from becoming supporters of the disbelievers, or to take them as comrades with whom they develop friendships…Allah warned against such behavior when He said, 'O you who believe! Take not my enemies and your enemies as friends, showing affection towards them. And whosoever of you does that, and then indeed he has gone astray from the straight path.' And, 'O you who believe! Take not the Jews and the Christians as friends; they are but friends of each other. And whoever befriends them, and then surely, he is one of them.' Allah said next, 'Unless you indeed fear a danger from them,' meaning, except those (Muslims) who in some areas or times fear for their safety from the disbelievers. In this case, such believers are allowed to show friendship to the disbelievers outwardly, but never inwardly. For instance, Al-Bukhari recorded that Abu Ad-Darda' said, 'We smile in the face of some people although our hearts curse them.'[27] Ibn Katheer—the Sunni Muslim scholar—then goes on: "Taqiyya is allowed until the Day of Resurrection."

But what wrong could come from practicing a doctrine to prevent the harm of the believers? After all, even Maimonides, the great Jewish physician and thinker, in his Epistle concerning apostasy and persecution by Muslims, writes to his fellow Jews, "Now we are asked to render the active homage to heathenism but only to recite an empty formula which the Muslims themselves knew we utter insincerely in order to circumvent the bigot … indeed, any Jew who, after uttering the Muslim formula, wishes to observe the whole 613 precepts in the privacy of his home, may do so without hindrance. Nevertheless, if, even under circumstances, a Jew surrenders his life for the sanctification of the name of God before men, he has done nobly and his reward is great before the Lord. But if a man asked me, 'shall I be slain or utter the formula of Islam?' I answer, 'utter the formula and live.'"[28]

The problem however, is that Kitman and Taqiyya extend the meaning of these terms, so that the word "harm" also encompass harm to one's reputation as a representative of Islam. So Muslims are allowed to lie even to protect the reputation of Islam. The renowned Muslim Philosopher Ibn Taymiyah from his book titled *The Sword Against the Accuser of Mohammed*, explains "Believers when in a weakened stage in a non-Muslim country should forgive and be patient with people of the book (i.e., Jews and Christians) when they insult Allah and his prophet by any means. Believers should lie to people of the book to protect their lives and their religion."[29]

Many Muslims will even lie for monetary gain: "After the conquest of the city of Khaybar by the Muslims, the Prophet was approached by Hajjaj Ibn `Aalat and told: 'O Prophet of Allah: I have in Mecca some excess wealth and some relatives, and I would like to have them back; am I excused if I bad-mouth you to escape persecution?' The Prophet excused him and said: 'Say whatever you have to say.'"[30]

With Islam, especially when it comes to issues of non-Muslims, it's 'any end that justifies any means,' even conspiracy to murder. Mohammed, the so-called "perfect man," serves as an example of Taqiyya: "Allah's Apostle said, 'who is willing to kill Ka'b bin Al-Ashraf who has hurt Allah and His Apostle?' Thereupon Muhammad bin Maslama got up saying, 'O Allah's Apostle! Would you like that I kill him?' The Prophet said, 'Yes.' Muhammad bin Maslama said, 'Then allow me to say a (false) thing (i.e., to deceive Kab).' The Prophet said, 'You may say it'"[31] and on another account, the murder of Shaaban Ibn Khalid al-Hazly: "It was rumored that Shaaban was gathering an army to wage war on Mohammed. Mohammed retaliated by ordering Abdullah Ibn Anis to kill Shaaban. The would-be killer asked the prophet's permission to lie. Mohammed agreed and then ordered the killer to lie by stating that he was a member of the Khazaa clan. When Shaaban saw Abdullah coming, he asked him, 'From what tribe are you?' Abdullah answered, 'From Khazaa.' He then added, 'I have heard that you are gathering an army to fight Mohammed and I came to join you.' Abdullah started walking with Shaaban telling him how Mohammed came to them with the heretical teachings of Islam, and complained how Mohammed badmouthed the Arab patriarchs and ruined the Arab's hopes. They continued in conversation until they arrived at Shaaban's tent. Shaaban's companions departed and Shaaban invited Abdullah to come inside and rest. Abdullah sat there until the atmosphere was quiet and he sensed that everyone was asleep. Abdullah severed Shaaban's head and carried it to Mohammed as a trophy. When Mohammed sighted Abdullah, he jubilantly shouted, 'Your face has been triumphant (Aflaha al-wajho).' Abdullah returned the greeting by saying, 'It is your face, Apostle of Allah, who has been triumphant. (Aflaha wajhoka, ya rasoul Allah).'"[32]

Such is the religion of peace, like the Hitler-Jugend who would turn in their own parents, in school we were taught that for Mohammed's sake we can even forsake our mothers and fathers, if they so instruct us to go against Islam then its lawful for us to kill them. We would do anything for our dead Führer who shall rise again as Mahdi. One example of such loyalty was the battle of Badr—Abu Ubaida killed his father, Abu Bakr Al-Siddiq was about to kill his son, Umar ibn Khattab killed his uncle. One Muslim apologist laments "Abu Ubaida fought and killed his father because he was an obstacle in the face of Islam and looked to stop Islam from dominating the Arabs at that time. Today, how often do we think about the obstacles that are facing the Muslims and preventing Islam from dominating the world? And when we do ponder upon these obstacles, we feel ourselves subdued, believing that which stands in our way in terms of obstacles are insurmountable? How often do we remember Allah (swt) describing the Muslims as the best nation brought forward to mankind, as mentioned in the Qur'an? Surely we must sacrifice and speak the word of truth to make the Muslims and non-Muslims aware of the beauty and justice of Islam, and how it can help to solve the problems that the Muslim world is plagued with today as well as the world at large. We should show similar courage and sacrifice to that of Abu Ubaida who was prepared to kill his father for the sake of his belief in Islam."[33]

Imam Al-Ghazali, one of the most famous Muslim theologians of all time, encourages lying so long as any positive or beneficial goal may be achieved: "Speaking is a means to achieve objectives. If a praiseworthy aim is attainable through both telling the truth and lying, it is unlawful to accomplish it through lying because there is no need for it. When it is possible to achieve such an aim by lying but not by telling the truth, it is permissible to lie if attaining the goal is permissible."[34] Talk about situational ethics. Imagine one of the Ten Commandments stating "Thow shall not lie, and thow shall not tell the truth, but one should do whatever is best to achieve victory." Ghazali also instructs Muslims to lie in order to attain material prosperity: "Know this that lying is not sin by itself, but if it brings harm to you it could be ugly. However, you can lie if that will keep you from evil or if it will result in prosperity."[35]

Abdullah Al-Araby rightly comments regarding the danger that the practice of lying in Islam is for the West: "The principle of sanctioning lying for the cause of Islam bears grave implications in matters relating to the spread of the religion of Islam in the West. Muslim activists employ deceptive tactics in their attempts to polish Islam's image and make it more attractive to prospective converts."[36]

Even many so-called moderate Muslims in order to protect the image of Islam, the Religion of Peace, after 9-11, began to lead a double life. One side expressed aggression to the West in private meetings, and the other side expressed tolerance and peace in front of Western audiences. Siraj Wahaj, the first Muslim to deliver the daily prayers and speeches of love, brotherhood, and harmony before the U.S. House of Representatives, in speaking to a Muslim audience in New Jersey said that Muslims should "take over the United States and replace its constitutional government with a caliphate. If we were united and strong, we'd elect our own emir (leader) and give allegiance to him. Take my word, if 6 to 8 million Muslims unite in America, the country will come to us."[37]

This "split-personality" is the cause of confusion because Americans in general and unfortunately even many government leaders, are not digging into what these leaders say in Arabic. Desperately wanting to believe the best of people in order to comfort themselves in times of great uncertainty, most Westerners swallow much of the Islamic deception—hook, line and sinker. Those few who are bold enough to speak the truth regarding the true nature of Islam are viewed and labeled as intolerant, hateful, bigoted, Islamophobes. One would think that Americans would be wise enough to wake up to this tired pattern by now, but apparently, ignorance truly is bliss. Until the front of the ship actually smashes headlong into the iceberg, that is.

⤝ 17 ⤞
Both Claim to be Messiah

✦

The Mahdi is to Muslims as Christ is to Christians—He is their awaited savior: "A figure more legendary than that of the Mahdi, the Awaited Saviour, has not been seen in the history of mankind. For the ultimate salvation of mankind he is the *Pole Star* of hope on which the gaze of humanity is fixed"[38], writes Ayatullah Baqir al-Sadr—the deceased father-in-law of Iraq's infamous Muqtada al-Sadr, in his book, *The Awaited Savior*.

University of Virginia Professor Abdulaziz Abdulhussein Sachedina in his scholarly work, Islamic Messianism, agrees: "The term 'Messianism' in the Islamic context is frequently used to translate the important concept of an *eschatological figure, the Mahdi*, who as the foreordained leader "will rise" to launch a great social transformation in order to restore and adjust all things under divine guidance. The Islamic messiah, thus, embodies the aspirations of his followers in the restoration of the purity of the Faith which will bring true and uncorrupted guidance to all mankind, creating a just social order and a world free from oppression in which *the Islamic revelation will be the norm for all nations*."[39]

Even the touted moderate Sheikh Kabbani, the darling of conservative Americans, is awaiting this Mahdi as Islam's primary messiah figure: "Jews are waiting for the Messiah, Christians are waiting for Jesus, and Muslims are waiting for both the Mahdi and Jesus. All religions describe them as men coming to save the world."[40]

What Muslims do not realize is that they are awaiting Antichrist. Jesus warned, *"For false Christs and false prophets will appear and perform great signs and miracles to deceive even the elect—if that were possible. See, I have told you ahead of time."* (Matthew 24:24-25)

JEWISH CONCEPT OF ANTICHRIST

Most Christians do not know that when it comes to the definition of Antichrist, Judaism agrees with them: "Satan Armilus is whom the Gentiles [Christians] call Antichrist." The legend of *Armilus*, as he is called, is expressed in the *Midrash Otot ha-Mashi'ah Midreshei Ge'ullah*, and is also documented in the Targums. The revered medieval Jewish sage Saadia Gaon records that in the End-Times—just prior to the age of redemption—an Anti-Messiah (Antichrist) figure would emerge and engage in a battle against the Jewish Messiah. The Jewish Messiah would kill Armilus and thus usher in the Messianic age of redemption for the Jewish people and the world.

Even his satanic connection is recorded by Jewish interpreters: "This Armilus [Antichrist] will deceive the whole world into believing that he is God and will reign over the entire world. He will come with ten kings and together they will fight over Jerusalem."[41]

In light of this, and when it comes to the issue of Antichrist, Christians and Jews while struggling over major differences in theology, need to unite fighting Mahdism, which is determined to, "govern the people by the Sunnah of their Prophet and establish Islam on Earth."[42] They proclaim that "Islam will be victorious over all the religions"[43] and only Islam will be practiced.

As we can see, all descriptions of the Mahdi according to Islam match those of the Antichrist as seen in the Bible.

⚞ 18 ⚟
Both Kingdoms Suffer
A "Head Wound"

✦══ ❋ ══✦

Biblically, the Empire of the Antichrist will not be a new empire; rather it will be the revival of a previously great empire that will have suffered what the Bible calls a "fatal head wound." (Revelation 13:3) But the wound will be healed and the empire will be revived from the dead as it were: "And the beast [Antichrist Empire] which I saw was like a leopard, and his feet were like those of a bear, and his mouth like the mouth of a lion. And the dragon gave him his power and his throne and great authority. And I saw *one of his heads as if it had been slain,* and his fatal wound was healed. And the whole earth was amazed and followed after the beast." (Revelation 13:2-3)

We will discuss at length in later chapters all the evidence concerning this "wound" as relating to an empire, and not the Antichrist as commonly understood by Western prophecy analysts. This empire is the Islamic Ottoman Empire which replaced the Roman Empire after the fall of it's remaining Eastern section, and was one of the world's greatest empires. But it was also the head of history's most anti-Christian empire. Ultimately it was dismantled and broken up by the Christian West.

Today the Caliphate exists only in the desires of hundreds of millions of Muslims worldwide who want to revive this beast that was slain on March 3rd, 1924. The last Caliphate—the Ottoman Caliphate—was officially abolished by the first President of the Turkish Republic, Mustafa Kemal Atatürk. The abolition of the Caliphate is profoundly significant for our study. For it was on this day that the Islamic Empire, led by a sitting Caliph for over fourteen hundred years suffered a fatal head wound. The position of "head of state" of the Islamic Empire was severed.

The magnitude of the fall of the Caliphate is as if the office of the Pope was forcefully abolished by anti-Catholic forces and it remained unfilled for nearly a hundred years. This would cause a devastating effect on Catholics worldwide. Likewise, without a Caliph, many Muslims literally feel as though the universe itself has been completely out of order for the past eighty plus years. Today Caliphate apologists argue: Christendom has its leader—

their vicar of Christ—so why can't Muslims have their vicar of Mohammed? After all, the office of the Pope is primarily symbolic?

But this is utter deception—the Papacy cannot justify from Scripture anything even close to Islam's Sharia law.

Today, we already hear Muslims loudly grieving over the head wound of the Caliphate. In a recent promotional video for Hizb-ut-Tahrir—an Islamic group whose goal is to restore the Caliphate: "The 3rd of March, 1924, the world was plunged into darkness. The Khilafah, [whose] light, spread from East to West for over a thousand years, was brought to an end. The consequences were unimaginable: death, destruction, chaos, exploitation. After 80 years of the absence of the Khilafah, the Muslim world has awakened from its slumber, and the Ummah [the community of all the world's Muslims] is ready to resume its political destiny. From the darkness will emerge a new light."[44] *Did you catch that?* "After 80 years of the absence of the Khilafah, the Muslim world has awakened from its slumber..." Throughout the world today, just as the mythological phoenix rose from its ashes, Islam is arising from the ashes of its past in order to claim its place as the most dominant world power. Islamists the world over are now seeking to return to the triumphant days when Muslims ruled the Middle East and non-Muslims were subservient.

Islam was wounded and nearly killed. But now it is attempting to resurrect itself, is it any wonder that in so many Muslim demonstrations you can see the same message.

Al-Muhajirun, demonstrating in England, set their main speaker to shout that "the world will soon recognize that Islam is the truth, and the giant of Islam shall rise again."

Why "rise again?"

Why use that word "again?"

It was two thousand years ago, the Bible predicted the Empire of the Antichrist would suffer precisely what we see in the wounded (and rising) Empire of Islam: "And I saw one of his heads as if it had been slain, and his fatal wound was healed and the whole earth was amazed and followed after the beast." (Revelation 13:3)

The Muslim world will revel as their confidence, pride, and a sense of strength increases every time they gain Western concessions and victories. This confidence is depicted in Scripture, "Who is like the Beast, and who can wage war with him?" (Revelation 13:4)

⌇ 19 ⌇
Both Work
False Miracles

❖

The Bible states that the Antichrist will display supernatural signs and perform false miracles in order to persuade the world that he is indeed the awaited Messiah: "Then that lawless one will be revealed...the one whose coming is in accord with the activity of Satan, with all power and signs and false wonders." (II Thessalonians 2:8-9)

The similarities between the Mahdi and Antichrist here are clear. Islamic tradition even confirms this: "Allah will give him power over the wind and the rain, and the earth will bring forth its foliage. He will give away wealth profusely, flocks will be in abundance, and the Ummah [Empire of Islam] will be large and honored..."[45] Antichrist is said to produce all kinds of false miracles while the Mahdi is said to have supernatural control over nature. This is yet another clear parallel to add to the probability chart. But don't put your pencil away just yet—we've just begun.

∞ 20 ∞
Both Ride A
White Horse

✦

What might be shocking to Western Bible Prophecy analysts is that Islam even confirms what is written in Scripture regarding Antichrist, who is described in Revelation 19:11 as riding on a white horse being none other than Imam Mahdi. The early Muslim transcription of prophet Mohammed's Hadith, Ka'b al Ahbar confirms this: "I find the Mahdi recorded in the books of the Prophets...For instance, the Book of Revelation says: 'And I saw, and behold a *white horse*. He that sat on him...went forth conquering and to conquer.'"[46] Egyptian authors Muhammad Ibn 'Izzat and Muhammad 'Arif then go on to say, "It is clear that this man is the *Mahdi* who will ride the *white horse* and judge by the Qur'an (with justice) and with whom will be men with *marks* of prostration on their *foreheads*."[47]

Muslim scholars do not reject the roll of Islam being Antichrist—they fully accept it. Even taking pride in marking their foreheads is in Islam. This is the work of Antichrist who will come riding on a white horse: "I watched as the Lamb (Jesus) opened the first of the seven seals. Then I heard one of the four living creatures say in a voice like thunder, 'Come!' I looked, and there before me was a white horse! Its rider held a bow, and he was given a crown, and he rode out as a conqueror bent on conquest." (Revelation 6:1-2) The seals that follow this rider are—war, famine, plagues, death, persecution, martyrdom of God's people, a great earthquake, and even the wrath of God. After this, the rider appears bent on conquest and the world completely slides in chaos. The rider is given a white horse, which is an attempt to imitate Jesus when He returns (Revelation 19:11). This imposter— the Antichrist—is also carrying a bow without any arrows. He is the bearer of false peace.

Our Antichrist is their Messiah—Muslim scholars open the Bible, read about the Antichrist, and see their Savior. This must be seen as quite ironic, if not entirely prophetic. Now you are beginning to see what I was faced with when I began to study the Bible, the **True Word of the Almighty God.**

∽ 21 ∾
Both Attempt to Change The Law

✦

So, who are the imperialists: Christians or Muslims? Who attempts to rule the world and force everyone to submit or be killed, Islam or Christianity? Who wants to change all laws globally and replace them with Sharia, Islam or Christianity?

According to the Prophet Daniel, "He [Antichrist] will speak against the Most High and oppress the saints and try to change the set times and the laws." (Daniel 7:25)

In this passage, we find an important clue; for by his actions, we can assess his origin. Not knowing how to deal with this piece of the puzzle, many students of Bible prophecy have speculated that the Antichrist will try to change cosmic laws. But the text infers no such thing. It simply says that he will desire to change two things: times (the accepted world calendar) and laws.

If we simply take the text at its face value, we find a simple warning that the Antichrist will attempt to change the times (calendar), legal systems, and constitutions. He will attempt to invoke Islam's evil laws worldwide to replace every other law and constitution.

Only God can change cosmic laws. So why teach that the Antichrist will change cosmic laws? Always be careful never to give attributes that belong to God and apply them to Satan.

The Mahdi fits the bill, for he will attempt to change the law by instituting Islamic Sharia law as far as he is able to do so. Who else other than a Muslim would desire to change the "times and laws"? Every Islamic activist organization is crying it—"Islam to the world!" What does this mean? It means they want Islam to replace *everything*— worship, law, and even the calendar. This activism already exists in every nation of the world. Behind all of the masks, they all desire to replace non-Islamic legal systems with Islamic Sharia law and replace every constitution with the constitution of the caliphate.

Do you think I am exaggerating? Earlier I gave the example of Siraj Wahaj. Again, he was the first "moderate" Muslim to deliver the opening prayer before the U.S. House of Representatives. Yet, when he spoke to a Muslim audience in New Jersey, what did he declare? Muslims should "take over the United States and replace its constitutional government with a caliphate."

Believe me; this Islamo-imperialist push for a caliphate is far more widespread than most think. Now let's address the issue of times. Besides the Gregorian calendar used by the West, there is also a Jewish, a Hindu, and a Muslim calendar, among others. But has there ever been a time when Jews or Hindus have tried to impose their religious calendars or laws onto the rest of the world? Islam, however, does have both its own calendar and laws, both of which are the first thing Islam has imposed in every country they've ruled.

Keep in mind that the text says he *attempts* to change set times and laws, yet he only succeeds partially, but never on a global scale, because like Nimrod in the story of the Tower of Babel, God will never allow the Antichrist to rule the entire world. Unlike most Western students of prophecy who think that the Antichrist governs the entire globe, God will stop Antichrist's attempt to create a one-world government system. Jesus is the *only* King who will accomplish a one-world government, and it will be ruled from Jerusalem.

The Islamic calendar is based on the career of Mohammed. It begins at the migration (*Hijra*) of Mohammed from Mecca to Medina.

Why do Muslims not establish this calendar from the time that Islam was founded in Mecca?

The answer to this is crucial. The Islamic dating system began from the time of its *conquests* in Medina: "The Islamic calendar testifies to the paramountcy of the Hijra by setting year one from the date of its occurrence. The year of the Hijra, 622 AD, is considered more significant than the year of Mohammed's date of birth or death, or that of the first Qur'anic revelation, because Islam is first and foremost a *political-military* enterprise. It was only when Mohammed left Mecca with his paramilitary band did Islam achieved its proper political-military articulation. The years of the Islamic calendar (which employs lunar months) are designated in English 'AH' or 'After Hijra.'"[48]

The Muslim calendar is viewed as being mandatory for all to observe: "It is considered a divine command to use a (Hijra) calendar with 12 (purely) lunar months without intercalation, as evident from...the Holy Qur'an."[49]

Not only does Islam view as a divine imperative the use of their unique religious calendar, it also has its own week. Unlike the Western rhythm of a week; Monday through Friday being the body of the work-week followed by Saturday and Sunday as the weekend, Islam holds Friday (the sixth day) as its sacred day of prayer. This is the day that Muslims meet at the mosque to pray and listen to a sermon (khutbat). Wherever Islam rules, it uses not only the Hijra calendar, its week also revolves around every Friday as the holy day.

According to Islamic traditions, Isa, the Muslim Jesus' primary purpose would be to oversee the changing of these times and laws, for it is he who is said to oversee the institution and the enforcement of the Islamic Sharia law all over the world: "According to Shalabi, Jesus will rule the Muslims according to the Divine Law (Sharia)."[50] "Jesus, the son of Mary, will descend and will lead them, judging amongst them according to the holy Qur'an and the Sunnah (law) of the Prophet Mohammed."[51]

So according to the Bible, the Antichrist is said to attempt to "change times and laws." The religion of Islam fulfills this description to an "absolute T."

22

Both Deny
Women's Rights

The Antichrist will have no regard for women's rights. Women will have no voice in his empire: "Neither shall he regard the gods of his fathers nor the desire of women." (Daniel 11:37) We have already seen Muslim countries in which women struggle to gain their desired rights. In Saudi Arabia, women struggle to acquire rights to drive a car. In Afghanistan, women struggle to gain a desired education. In Turkey, women struggle with laws attempting to gradually re-institute the Hijab.

The Antichrist will not only change constitutional laws, but civil laws as well. Everywhere in the Muslim world, women struggle to gain rights to be equal to their male counterpart. Women's rights in Islam are literally a fraction of what their male counterparts possess. According to Islamic law, a woman only inherits half of what a male inherits. In court, it takes the testimony of two women to equal the testimony of one man because Mohammed declared that women have half the mental capacity of a man.

Many prophecy analysts have speculated that Daniel 11:37 is stating that the Antichrist will not have any regards for that which was the desire of all Jewish women in Daniel's day—to give birth to Messiah.

This would be a strange interpretation since Messiah has already come and today we have no women with such desires. This disregard for women in Daniel 11:37 stems from the story of the fall of man: "And I will put enmity between thee and the woman and between thy seed and her seed. He shall bruise thy head and thou shall bruise His heel" (Genesis 3:15). This prophecy was made right from the beginning of humanity. It states that Satan will hate the woman and her seed who will crush the head of the Antichrist, the seed of Satan, and like his father, he has a deep disdain and hatred for women.

This is a commonality found in many satanic cults from fundamentalist Islam to fundamentalist Mormonism. In Daniel 11:37, the verse says nothing regarding a desire of women to give birth to the Messiah. It simply says that the Antichrist will show no regard for women—He hates women. In other words, women's rights are nil in the Empire of the Antichrist. The verse should be interpreted naturally. This is exactly what we see in Islam today. The subjection of women in Muslim societies—especially in Arab nations—is a reality that is on display for the whole world to see.

Some Western prophecy analysts have twisted this text and alluded to the idea that the Antichrist will be a homosexual or will simply show no desire for women. The text never said that he does not *desire* women, but that he does not *honor* their desires. This is a big difference.

Muslim apologists often make the claim that Islam exalts the status of women. If so, where is a Muslim woman's right to marry a non-Muslim? You rarely ever hear of Muslim women marrying Jewish or Christian men. Why?

Islam proclaims death to Muslim women who marrie out of their Muslim faith. Yet it allows Muslim men to marry non-Muslim women. Christianity on the other hand, admonishes both women and men not to marry out of the faith, yet, no where do we see any Christian edicts demanding the killing of anyone who marries out of the faith. In fact, it urges them to show good character, in order that the unbelieving spouse would see the beauty of Christianity. For anyone who knows Islam, the idea that Islam offers equality to women is simply comical.

Let's consider a few more facts. The Qur'an allows, even commands, men to beat their wives into subservience. This is no joke. If a wife doesn't listen to her husband, the husband is told to admonish her. If this doesn't work, he is told to make her sleep in a separate bed and is prohibited to have sexual intercourse with her. Out of all the punishments Islam prescribes to women, perhaps to some, this might be the favorite.

But if the wife still doesn't respect her husband's authority, the husband is told to beat her: "Men are in charge of women because Allah hath made the one of them to excel [over] the other, and because they spend of their property for the support of women. So the good women are, therefore, obedient and guard in the husband's absence what Allah would have them guard. As to those women on whose part ye fear disloyalty and ill-conduct, admonish them first. Next, refuse to share their beds. And last beat them; but if they return to obedience, seek not against them means of annoyance: For Allah is Most High, great above you all" (Qur'an 4:34).

It was not until I came to the U.S. that I heard the concept that "He who hates his wife hates himself" and is a slave to evil. Some Muslim translators have tried to water down the Qur'anic injunction for men to beat their wives. Again, they only do this for the English-speaking world. When it comes to wife-beating, Yusuf Ali (Islamic scholar who translated the Qu'ran into English, 1938) added the word "lightly" to his translation. But the word "lightly" is not in the original Arabic "Idribuhonna" (beat them).

But let's just say for the sake of argument that it was. What would that leave us with? The Qur'an still commands Muslims to beat their disobedient wives. Compare this Islamic injunction to the Biblical command to men: "Husbands, love your wives, just as Christ loved the church and gave himself up for her" (Eph 5:25). Compare this with Mohammed, who said, "I was shown the Hell-fire and that the majority of its dwellers are women."[52] Are women more evil or more disobedient than men? If so, were they born this way? Or, did Allah create women with more evil than men? This tradition displays the negative sentiment toward women that has been resident in Islam from the very beginning.

Muslims are not embarrassed when outsiders find out that Mohammed actually married his youngest wife Aisha when he was aged fifty-one and she was only six years old (some accounts say she was seven). He consummated the marriage when she was nine and he was fifty-four. The fact that this occurred is thoroughly documented within Islamic tradition by virtually every reliable collection of Hadith—it would be impossible to deny. "Aisha narrated that the Prophet married her when she was six years old and he consummated his marriage when she was nine years old, and then she remained with him for nine years (i.e., till his death)."[53]

When Mohammed died, he was 63 and his wife Aisha was only 18. If he had lived longer, he would have married someone even younger. Once, Mohammed looked at a baby girl named Um-Habiba while she was still nursing and said: "If she grows up while I am still alive, I will marry her."[54] This is the man that Islam calls a "prophet of God," the supreme example for all mankind and the perfect human being? A pervert and a pedophile! Did Mohammed consider whether or not this little baby would have any desire to marry an old man? Of course not, the girl's feelings were irrelevant to the "prophet." The simple truth is that Mohammed, and Islam, does not have "regard for the desire of women."

23

Both Rule Over
Ten Entities

A fter the Antichrist comes to power, the Bible says he will rule over ten other kings who will turn their authority over to him: "The ten horns you saw are ten kings who have not yet received a kingdom, but who for one hour will receive authority as kings along with the beast. They have but one purpose—to give their power and authority to the beast" (Revelation 17:12-13). In 2002 a plan for the reestablishment of the Caliphate was written by Abu Qanit al-Sharif al-Hasani of the Guiding Helper Foundation entitled, "*The Plan for the Return of The Caliphate.*" According to this plan, the Caliph would be assisted in his rule by a ten-member council of "Assistant Caliphs." These assistants, or council members, are similar to Ministers in many of today's governments.

In 2007, al-Qaeda in Iraq was busy attempting to establish its own Caliphate. As in Hasani's plan for the Caliphate, so also does al-Qaeda set in place ten ministers that we are told will rule under the coming Caliph in Iraq. "A Sunni insurgent coalition in Iraq announced Monday the appointment of an education minister to the group's so-called 10-member 'Islamic Cabinet,' set up in April to challenge the Iraqi government.'"[55]

So, once again we are faced with another striking similarity between Biblical prophecy and Islamic tradition. While the Caliph of the Muslims is said to rule over a council, or a cabinet of ten, the Antichrist is explicitly said to rule over ten "kings" or rulers who give their authority to him. The parallels just continue to roll. Did you remember to add this to your "growing probability" chart?

∞ 24 ∞
Both are the Source
Of Death and War

✛═══❉═══✛

In Daniel 11:37-38, we find an almost perfect summary of Islam. There we read about the Antichrist Empire's attempt to establish it's law, honor a war-like god, dishonor women's rights and encourage the Islamic Zakat (obligatory alms for jihad with gold and silver), all in one concise passage. This amazing passage alone should be enough to convince the most hardened skeptic that the Bible prophesied the coming of Islam.

As one who gives his allegiance to this war-god, the Antichrist, like his father the Devil, is portrayed as one who causes death and destruction. In the Bible, Satan is described as the one that possesses "the power of death, that is the Devil" (Heb. 2:4).

And yet in the Qur'an we find one title for Allah is Al-Mumeet. It is a name that is counted among the 99 beautiful names of Allah. It literally means, "the one who possess the power of death, causer of death, the slayer, and the taker of life or the destroyer of life." This title of Allah is nearly identical to the title that is given to Satan in the Book of Revelation: "They (the demons) had as king over them the angel of the Abyss, whose name in Hebrew is Abaddon (the destroyer), and in Greek, Apollyon" (Revelation 9:11).

What else do Satan and Allah have in common? Nearly every time that the Bible speaks about the Antichrist, it perfectly fits the spirit of Islam. Keep reading, you'll see.

≈ 25 ≈
Both Use
Military Force

Even the most moderate and ecumenical Muslim thinkers believe in the coming Mahdi to rule the world by military force. Harun Yahya, an allegedly moderate and prolific Muslim author, responds to a question posted on his website: "The Mahdi will invade all the places between East and West." Elsewhere, Yahya refers to the Mahdi's irresistible qualities as one who subdues the whole world: "Nobody can stand in the way of the Mahdi and dominion he will have over the world."

This is also strikingly similar to the Biblical description of the Antichrist who is said to declare war, "Who is like the Beast, and who can make war with him" (Revelation 13:4). In the Bible we are told the Antichrist "will devour the whole earth, trampling it down and crushing it" (Daniel 7: 23). It will be a confederacy known for its ferocity.

The Mahdi is portrayed throughout Islamic traditions as being the military leader of an Islamic "world revolution" that will defeat all other religions and political systems. Muslim author, Sideeque Veliankode, in his book *Doomsday: Portents and Prophecies*, writes: "The Mahdi will establish right and justice in the world and eliminate evil and corruption. He will fight against the enemies of the Muslims who would be victorious."[56] Al-Sadr adds, "He will reappear on the appointed day, and then he will fight against the forces of evil, lead a world revolution and set up a new world order based on justice, righteousness and virtue, ultimately the righteous will take the world administration in their hands and Islam will be victorious over all the religions."[57]

The Mahdi's means and method of accomplishing this world revolution will include multiple jihad campaigns. Abdualrahman Kelani, author of *The Last Apocalypse*, describes the many battles of the Mahdi: "Al-Mahdi will receive a pledge of allegiance as a caliph for Muslims. He will lead Muslims in many battles of jihad. His reign will be a caliphate that follows the guidance of the Prophet. Many battles will ensue between Muslims and the disbelievers during the Mahdi's reign."[58]

Without question, Islam views the Mahdi as one who advances Allah's glory over all the earth. He will use his military might and his mighty Islamic Empire to do so. On this point, both the Antichrist and the Mahdi are once again, completely indistinguishable.

∼ 26 ∼
Both Honor Their God
With Gold and Silver

In the Bible, the Antichrist dedicates gold and silver to his war god: "Instead of them, he shall honor the god of forces [war]: and a god whom his fathers knew not shall he honor with gold, and silver, and with precious stones, and pleasant things" (Daniel 11:38).

One of the five main obligatory pillars of Islam is for every Muslim to pay 'zakat' by giving one-fifth of their income—their gold, and their silver to honor and advance the cause of Allah: "Zakat is for the poor and the needy, and to free the captives and the debtors, and for the cause of Allah, and [for] the wayfarers; a duty imposed by Allah. Allah is omniscient, most wise" (Qur'an 9:60).

This is not only for the poor, but it's a tax to expand the rule of Allah. In fact, the Qur'an admonishes Muslims regarding zakat: "And those who hoard up gold and silver and do not spend them in the cause of Allah promise them a painful punishment. One day that [treasure] will be heated up in the fire of hell and their foreheads, their sides, and their backs will be branded with it: This is the treasure that you hoarded up for yourselves. Now taste what you have hoarded" (Qur'an 9:34-35).

Gold and silver that comes out of ones own savings, or is acquired through the booty of war for the cause of Allah, should have an amount allotted to share for the advance of Allah's cause through Jihad War. If this is not done, the Muslim would be punished for eternity.

So, who is carrying the pitch-fork and the branding iron? Believe it or not, the terrorists themselves *are* victims of terror. If you are a terrorist reading this, you have a way out— call on Jesus. Do it, try it, believe it, live it, trust Him and have *everlasting life*.

Just as Daniel predicted, zakat is a portion of gold and silver that is dedicated to Allah, the war-god of jihad.

While Christians tithe in order to fund the going forth of the gospel and to assist the needy and the poor, zakat under Islamic laws is often spent on global jihad. Since 9-11, the United States Homeland Security Administration has frozen dozens upon dozens of prominent Muslim zakat "charities" after it was revealed that a large percentage of their funds were actually going to terrorist groups such as al-Qaeda or Hamas. In 1999, Yousef-al-Qaradawi, the most highly respected "moderate" Muslim scholar in the Muslim world wrote the following regarding zakat: "The most honorable form of jihad nowadays is fighting for the liberation of Muslim land from the domination of unbelievers, regardless of their religion or ideology and fighting for such purposes in those occupied territories is the way of Allah for which zakat must be spent."[82]

Can there be any doubt that Muslims honor Allah, their "god of war" with their "gold and silver?" Do you see how Islam is a perfect match to the Biblical description of the Antichrist? Do you see how the Bible has already warned you, do you still want to argue that the Bible says nothing about Islam?

Hello, Captain Kirk? I am Mister Spock; I know the aliens better than you. I know I am a little bit different, but I am on your side and I want to save your ship before it's blown out of space. May I use your manual to point out the warnings? The author of this manual is, after all, from my neck-of-the-woods.

≈27≈

Both Honor a God of War and Advance His Glory Through War

⊹⸺✳⸺⊹

Antichrist "acts against the strongest fortresses with a foreign god, which he shall acknowledge, and advance its glory" (Daniel 11:39).

If the Antichrist is the strongest entity on earth, why does the Bible predict that he "acts against the strongest fortresses [military might]"? This would mean that he is not the strongest military. Why do Western prophecy analysts insist that Antichrist hold the most powerful military in the world? Who are the strongest fortresses? Which nations hold the strongest military might? Is it not the West? Muslims mourn the deadly wound that Islam received from the West. And they vow to revive their glory days through Jihad.

Also, who is this "foreign god"? How does Islam advance Allah's glory?

These are crucial questions to ask.

When viewing Islam, you must always keep in mind their creed: "There is no god but Allah and Mohammed is his messenger." It's the core of their faith. If you ask any Muslim what Islam is, they will immediately recite to you this creed. It is the First Pillar of Islam. This creed to advance Allah as the only god is carried out through Jihad which begins by an invitation to Islam (political Jihad), if the offer to take the mark of Islam is rejected, then advancing Allah's glory comes by Jihad war, in which the enemy is decapitated.

Volumes could be written on how Islam advanced Allah's glory. The first thing we need to focus on is Jihad itself. After years of analysis into the web of Islamic terror, I concluded that Islamic Jihad is *religious conditioning, using allusions of misery and glory days of the past in order to convert masses into becoming rage and pride-filled, remorseless killers and seekers of salvation by their own death. The goal is to re-establish a utopian theocratic world order where Allah and Muslims reign supreme and non-Muslims become subservient.*

That's what fundamental Islam is, and you will find out that everything in this dangerous movement fits within this definition. It's crucial that you keep this definition in mind; it will undoubtedly help as you watch biased news media coverage.

Today Islam focuses on the past when it ruled the ancient world.

DIDN'T CHRISTIANS HONOR A GOD OF WAR?

I am tired of Muslims pointing to the Crusaders as evidence for Christian hostility. Christians openly point out the errors made by the Crusaders; in fact, Christians use their own Scriptures to show the errors made by their fellow Christians. Yet rarely is it ever mentioned that the Crusaders were largely a response caused by Islamic injustices. Here we shall see which religion is truly violent and war-mongering—Christianity or Islam.

THE MAHDI – ADVANCE ALLAH'S GLORY THROUGH JIHAD

As we have seen, zakat to advance the cause of Allah by supporting jihad is one of the five main pillars of Islam. It is an obligatory aspect of Islam.

If we review Daniel 11:38-39 by applying Islam as the subject of these verses, we can clearly see that the Antichrist would be a Muslim. In verse 37 it predicts the dishonor of women and the disregard for their rights exactly as we see in the spirit and laws of Islam. Then in verses 38-39, the prophet Daniel amazingly predicted the combination of *Zakat* and *Jihad* to advance Allah's glory. We also see that the Antichrist honors a foreign god which he advances his name through war. Daniel could not have nailed it more precisely.

ANTICHRIST BY WAR ADVANCES HIS GOD

Many Westerners believe that the Antichrist is an atheist. They base this misconception on a phrase in Daniel 11:37: "he shall not give heed to any other god, for he shall magnify himself above all."

The first mistake in this analysis is dropping the word "other" from the interpretation; the text says he will not give heed to any "other" god.

How could the Antichrist be an atheist if the next verse says, "he shall honor the God of fortresses?" (Daniel 11:38)

How does Antichrist honor a god of fortresses, or a god of war?

You might counter that this is not a god, but is symbolic of power and might. Yet, when we continue to the next verse it says that he "act[s] against the strongest fortresses with [the help from] a foreign god, which he shall acknowledge, and advance its glory" (Daniel 11:39).

This verse is so clear and so shocking that it should unlock a major part of the prophecy puzzle. Yet few even pay attention to this. The Antichrist will show no regard "for any other god" (v. 37) accept this foreign god whom his ancestors did not know, but which he will "advance his glory" by war. The text logically speaks for itself. There is no doubt that a war god is involved and is fought for, to advance him. What do Westerners think when they see the most important creed of Islam carried through their Jihad that says *there is no god but Allah?*

The Antichrist cannot be an atheist. This is also confirmed by the prophet Habakkuk. There the Antichrist breaks the peace treaty and proclaims war in the name of his god: "Then his mind changes and he transgresses; He commits offense, ascribing this power to his god" (Habakkuk 1:11). He claims strength from his false god who promotes violence. The vision is "for the End-Times" (Habakkuk 2:3). "He always changes his mind and cannot be trusted. The Antichrist is the *most proud*" (Habakkuk 2:4).

They want to put down all other gods and religions throughout the globe and advance their god through war. The text is clearly portraying what we see in Islam today; even when we read that he declares war "against the strongest fortresses." What could that mean except what it plainly says—to declare war against the most powerful nations on earth? Jihadists already declared war on Europe and the U.S. However, the West seems oblivious to this fact. Who else could be as maniacal as Muslim fundamentalists to declare war on the powerful West? And it is all for the purpose of advancing their god, Allah. This is exactly what we see. *How did the Bible predict all of this?* Either the prophets guessed it perfectly, or indeed, there is an omniscient God. There is no third choice.

Keep in mind, the Muslims declared war on the Roman Byzantine Empire and won. They also won against Russia in Afghanistan. This is a formidable enemy with centuries of battle experience and political deception under their belts.

Another issue that often confuses students of prophecy is the notion that the Antichrist will magnify himself above all gods. How then could he follow a god?

What needs to be considered is that the Antichrist is Satan in the flesh (a man) and from the seed of Satan. He magnifies himself above every god and demands worship in the end. Satan attempts to emulate God and the relationship between the Father and the Son. This seeming contradiction between him honoring himself and honoring a god of war is resolved once we understand this. One can find seemingly contradicting verses when we examine Messianic prophecies as well. Yet, when we understand that Jesus was both God and God the Son, all the seeming contradictions are resolved.

Antichrist, Satan's "son of perdition," like his father, also displays a classic split-personality. He robs attributes that belong to the true Messiah in order to demand obedience and worship. Satan's exaltation of himself and his *son of perdition* to a god-like status is evident from the text.

We also see that the Antichrist does not honor "the god of his fathers." Fathers, of course, need not refer to a literal father, nor even to a grandfather—instead, "fathers" here is simply being used in the sense of "ancestors." This is a commonly used phrase in the

Bible that usually refers to Jehovah: "Say to the Israelites, 'Jehovah, the God of your fathers—the God of Abraham, the God of Isaac and the God of Jacob—has sent me to you'" (Exodus 3:15). This would be the god of Moses' ancestors.

JEWISH ANTICHRIST OR A MUSLIM ANTICHRIST

Jews love peace. In fact when I speak at Jewish events I always quote Golda Meier: "We will have peace when the Arabs love their children more then they hate us." Their faces shine at such a phrase, they love Golda's wisdom. Yet it is naïve to think that this will happen through hollow peace treaties. I always tell them that "We will have peace when the Jews love their children more than they love false peace."

Because the Antichrist is said not to worship the god of his fathers, some have concluded that the Antichrist will be an apostate Jew. Even if we accept this argument that he is a Jew by heritage, this would force the interpretation to make him a convert to another religion that honors a war-like god; Judaism does not honor a war-like god.

Islam fits, Judaism does not. Mohammed rejected his ancestral gods and advanced a new fabrication of a god named Allah. He then went on to "advance its glory." I repeat, Allah commands all of his followers to engage in *Jihad* until there is literally no one left on the earth who does not worship Allah: "Allah's Apostle said, 'I have been ordered to fight the people till they say: 'None has the right to be worshipped but Allah.'"[59]

Indeed, any honest analysis of the Antichrist must acknowledge that he is religious and a believer in a god. How else does the Antichrist "act against the strongest fortresses with a foreign god, whom he shall acknowledge"?

Although Israel signs a peace pact with the Antichrist, there is no textual evidence that the Jews will even accept the false Messiah as *their* Messiah. In fact the opposite is true. Throughout Scripture the Antichrist is portrayed as persecuting Israel. Shamefully, for centuries the Christian world has pointed its finger at the Jews as the source of the coming Antichrist, but the basis for a Jewish Antichrist comes from a couple of very weak arguments. The first is that the Jews would never trust a non-Jew to sign a false peace treaty. However, Israel signed a treaty with Yasser Arafat. Was Arafat Jewish? (Of course not!) The next argument comes from the interpretation of Daniel 11:37, that Antichrist does not "honor the god of his fathers" (Daniel 11:37), and since Antichrist's ancestors worshipped a "god" (singular) and not "gods" (plural), then the Antichrist must be a Jew because only Jews were monotheists who worshipped One God, while all other groups were polytheists.

Well Arafat, and all Muslims for that matter, also honor a singular god. The Antichrist could just as easily be a Muslim who rejects the pagan god of his ancestors. Zoroastrians worshipped a single god called *Ahura Mazda*. This would be the case of every Iranian Muslim. Even within the Arab Nations, it was common for each tribe to have its own god.

In no way does the Bible say that the Antichrist is a Jew, especially because Jews do not honor a god of war. Neither can we have a Jewish Antichrist ruling in what the Bible calls "The time of the gentiles."

Daniel 9 also rules out a Jewish Antichrist: "the people of the prince" were from the Eastern provinces of the Roman Empire from which the Antichrist must come. All these were gentiles who persecuted Jews. This should put an end to a Jewish Antichrist argument.

Yet this whole argument could be based on a problem with translation, the King James translators have it as "God of his fathers" rather than "the gods of his fathers." Unfortunately, the indictment of a Jewish Antichrist has persisted for centuries from this translation. If this is true, the question remains, what god does the Antichrist reject? There are two possible answers to this question. One answer is to point out the fact that the words used in this verse for *god* could also be translated as gods (plural) as most translations have it—NLT, NIV, ESV, NASB, RSV, ASV, HNV, GWT, BBS, TANAKH, WEB, Arabic Bible— all of these Bible translations have it interpreted the word as "gods," *plural*.

Most modern Western interpreters of prophecy actually reject the idea of a Jewish Antichrist. Dr. Tim Lahaye, Thomas Ice, Zola Levitt, Hal Lindsey, Arnold Fruchtenbaum, and many others join the list.

Dr. Arnold Fruchtenbaum, for example, states that "The fact the plural form of the word 'god' is used makes this a reference to heathen deities and not to God of Israel. There is much external evidence to show that this is the correct rendering of the Hebrew Text."[60]

The Hebrew word used here for God is not *Elohim* (the God) but rather elohei (gods). However, the difference is crucial. *Elohei* means *gods* in the sense of *idols*, as used in Deuteronomy. The verse states that the Antichrist will not worship the idols his ancestors worshiped. This would fit Mohammed exactly, whose main arguments with the pagans of Arabia were his rejection of the 360 gods in the Ka'ba. Thus the verse is saying that the Antichrist will not worship the idols of his ancestors, which is also Mohammed's claim. The verse need not be stating that the Antichrist will reject the immediate god of his actual father or grandfather.

In the end, the idea of a gentile Antichrist is far more supportable than a Jewish Antichrist. Throughout the Bible, those who persecuted the Jews from Pharaoh to Nebuchadnezzar and Antiochus to Nero, all of the great persecutors of the Jewish peoples were gentile rulers. All of the precursors to the Antichrist have been gentiles. Why should that change with this final Antichrist?

After all, Jews have never denied that God is our Father, neither did they deny He is the Holy Spirit (*Ruach Ha-Kodesh*). They do deny that Jesus is the *Son of God* and deny *His Deity*. This is no small matter, yet when it comes to Islam they supersede anyone with such a denial of all three truths.

The Antichrist is the leader of a Gentile coalition that is made up specifically of Muslim nations that will attack Israel. Or perhaps you think that the Muslims of the earth will unite under the leadership of a Jew?

ADVANCING ALLAH'S GLORY—AN ISLAMIC MANDATE

No serious intellectual can argue that Islam's Allah is the greatest war god history has ever known whose glory was advanced through war. Every Muslim is proud of the glory days when Islam ruled the ancient world. The god of the Qur'an demands endless war and the bloodshed of unbelievers: "Believers! Wage war against such infidels, as are your neighbors, and let them find you rigorous" (Qur'an 9:124).

This Jihad holy-war is mostly directed against Christians and Jews: "Make war upon such of those to whom the scriptures have been given as believe not in God and have forbidden His Apostle, and profess not the professor of truth, until they pay tribute out of hand, and they be humbled" (Qur'an 9:29).

Scriptures have been given to Jews and Christians, and throughout the entire Qur'an they are called the "people of the Book," or *Ahl-Al-Kitab*. The Qur'an commands Muslims: "O Prophet! Strive hard against the disbelievers and the hypocrites, and be harsh against them" (Qur'an 9:73). "O you who believe! Fight those of the disbelievers who are close to you, and let them find harshness in you, and know that Allah is with those who are the Pious" (Qur'an 9:123). "Kill the disbelievers wherever you find them" (Qur'an 2:191). "Slay or crucify or cut off the hands and feet of the unbelievers, that they be expelled from the land with disgrace and that they shall have a great punishment in world hereafter" (Qur'an 5:34). "Strike off the heads of the disbelievers,' and after making a 'great slaughter among them,' carefully tie up the remaining captives" (Qur'an 47:4).

This hatred that is built into Islam stems from the deceptive Satanic instructions propagated in Islam. Yet in the West, Islamic movements hide this violence by propagating the notion that Islam means peace. The Bible warns that, "Whoever hides his hatred has lying lips" (Proverbs 10:18).

Despite all of the lies and propaganda that we hear from Western Muslims these days, the Qur'an is clear that Jihad is obligatory and mandatory for all Muslims "Unless we go forth, (for Jihad) He (Allah) will punish us with a grievous penalty, and put others in our place" (Qur'an 9:39). "And He orders us to fight them on until there is no more tumult and faith in Allah is practiced everywhere" (Qur'an 8:39). "God has bought from the faithful their persons and their belongings against the gift of paradise; they fight in the way of Allah; they kill and get killed; that is a promise binding on Allah" (Qur'an 9:110). "Relent-not in pursuit of the enemy" (Qur'an 4:104). "O Prophet! Make war on the infidels and hypocrites, and deal rigorously with them" (Qur'an 66:9).

The concept of spreading ones religion through war is completely foreign to the Biblical mindset. Understand that Islam is not merely a personal belief (faith), but also a system of government and expansion. It cannot be separated from the tenants of war that form its very foundation. Many Muslim apologists will try to convince ignorant Westerners that the above quoted verses do not apply to Muslims today but were actually fulfilled during some specific time in Muslim history. Since Kitman and Taqiyya demand this deception, Westerners need to search and see all that is taught in the religious academies throughout the Muslim world since the very advent of Islam.

JIHAD—PAST OR FOR ALL TIMES

Muslims and liberals are always quick to quote Biblical verses from Joshua's conquests as evidence of violence in the Bible in an attempt to neutralize their own violence within Islam. Are they the same? Are Qur'anic Jihad commandments only to be applied historically?

This would be the greatest of lies ever.

The popular Muslim author and teacher Muhammad Saeed al-Qahtani, states, "Jihad is an act of worship, it is one of the supreme forms of devotion to Allah. They say that Jihad is only for defense. This lie must be exposed."[61]

Ibn Khaldun, the famous 14th century Islamic historian and philosopher in his classic and most notable work, the Muqaddimah says of jihad: "In the Muslim community, the holy war is a religious duty, because of the universalism of the (Muslim) mission and (the obligation to) convert everybody to Islam either by persuasion or by force. Therefore, the caliphate (spiritual), the royal (government and military) authority is united in Islam, so that the person in charge can devote the available strength to both of them at the same time."[62]

In his book, *Jurisprudence in Mohammed's Biography,* the renowned Egyptian scholar from Al-Azhar University, Dr. Muhammad Sa'id Ramadan al-Buti writes that offensive, not defensive, war is the "noblest Holy War" within Islam. "The Holy War (Islamic Jihad), as it is known in Islamic Jurisprudence, is basically an offensive war. This is the duty of Muslims in every age when the needed military power becomes available to them. This is the phase in which the meaning of Holy war has taken its final form. Thus the apostle of Allah said: 'I was commanded to fight the people until they believe in Allah and his messages.' The concept of Holy War (Jihad) in Islam does not take into consideration whether defensive or an offensive war. Its goal is the exaltation of the word of Allah and the construction of Islamic society and the establishment of Allah's Kingdom on earth regardless of the means. The means would be offensive warfare. In this case, it is the apex, the noblest Holy War."[63]

Jidad is to advance Allah's glory—*exactly as Daniel predicted!*

According to the Encyclopedia of Islam, "the fight is obligatory even when the unbelievers have not started it."[64]

The concept of Jihad in Islam is to literally attack unbelievers for the purpose of converting them to Islam, "by persuasion or by force," "even when they have not started it." This is quite clear; Mohammed and then his successors, Caliph Abu Bakr, Caliph Umar, and Caliph Uthman, from the Umayyad to the Ottoman, all attacked the surrounding nations offensively for the purpose of spreading Islam. These were not defensive wars. They were offensive wars whose goal was to force the victims to submit to Allah or be "crushed," plain and simple. So what part of "Jihad," "fight," or "kill" do Westerners not understand?

True Muslim scholars universally agree with the Qur'an which states: "O ye who believe! Fight those of the disbelievers who are near to you, and let them find harshness in you, and know that Allah is with those who keep their duty unto Him" (Qur'an 9:123).

THE SPREAD OF ISLAM

Ibn Katheer, one of the most widely accepted commentators of Islam comments, "Allah commands the believers to fight the disbelievers, the closest in area to the Islamic state, then the farthest. This is why the Messenger of Allah started fighting the idolaters in the Arabian Peninsula. When he finished with them...He then started fighting the People of the Scriptures (Jews and Christians). After Mohammed's death, his executor, friend, and Caliph, Abu Bakr, became the leader. On behalf of the Prophet, Abu Bakr started preparing the Islamic armies to fight the Roman cross worshippers, and the Persian fire worshippers. By the blessing of his mission, Allah opened the lands for him and brought down

Caesar and Kisra and those who obeyed them among the servants. Abu Bakr spent their treasures in the cause of Allah, just as the Messenger of Allah had foretold would happen. This mission (of world domination) continued after Abu Bakr at the hands of he whom Abu Bakr chose to be his successor. Umar bin Al-Khattab. With Umar, Allah humiliated the disbelievers, suppressed the tyrants and hypocrites, and opened the Eastern and Western parts of the world. The treasures of various countries were brought to Umar from near and far provinces and he divided them according to the legitimate and accepted method. Umar then died. Then, the Companions among the Muslims agreed to choose after Umar, Uthman bin Affan. During Uthman's reign, Islam wore its widest garment and Allah's unequivocal proof was established in various parts of the world over the necks of the servants. Islam appeared in the Eastern and Western parts of the world and Allah's Word was elevated and His religion apparent. The pure religion reached its deepest aims against Allah's enemies, and whenever Muslims overcame a community, they moved to the next one, and then the next one, crushing the tyrannical evil doers. They did this in reverence to Allah's statement, O you who believe! Fight those of the disbelievers who are close to you."[65]

Growing up as a Palestinian, I was never once taught that Jihad was anything other than one of Islam's most foundational tenants. Jihad was always taught as a war against the entire non-Muslim world. Islam, Allah, and Jihad are inseparable. Is it any wonder then that the Antichrist is said to honor "a god of war"? Unlike the god of any other major world religion, Allah fulfills this description. Jihad never ended, it simply received a death blow in 1924 from the West. It is mandated by every Muslim to continue Jihad until judgment day.

ADVANCING ALLAH'S GLORY—MOTIVES

When it comes to Islam, always think **Cavalry**, not **Calvary**.

So how has Satan persuaded millions of Muslims to die for Allah? This is the crux of the whole issue most Westerners don't understand. *Why blow yourself up? Why death?*

This is the cunningness of Satan—to persuade Muslims that God never died for them at Calvary, yet they must die for *him* in raids and military conquests.

So what motivates Muslims to fight and risk death?

Simply, Jihadism is a message of salvation—for one to die in the cause of Allah is an assurance of salvation and entry to paradise. It's a corruption of Christian dogma. The difference is that it's the shaheed (Martyr) who now can atone for his own sins. Therefore, dying in Jihad is the ultimate way to transit one's soul instantly to paradise. Salvation as understood in the Christian perspective is only through the death of one perfect man, Jesus Christ. In Islam, the idea of Christ dying for all humanity is rejected. In fact, this rejection is one of the main reasons Islam was founded. Islam considers this doctrine to be a corruption of the original faith, and views itself as the restoration of that original faith. Yet, Islam does retain a measure of Christianity's idea of salvation—that atonement is accomplished by death. However, the big difference is that in Islam, it's not the death of Christ that entitles you to heaven, but your own. So important is this concept, that a sha-heed in Islam can be an intercessor for 70 members of his/her family. Without this jihad-style death, you had better obtain enough merit to outweigh your sins so that you will go to paradise. This is a dilemma that confounds all Muslims.

The similarity in understanding this salvation is interesting. A suicide martyr is called "Fida'e," from the source word Fidyah (sacrificial lamb) as used in the Christian creed, and the best way for one to assure this salvation is to die in Jihad.

From a Christian perspective this is blasphemy, because a Muslim becomes like God. To say that you can obtain salvation by your own death, you have proclaimed yourself to possess attributes of God. It is no wonder why the Antichrist says "I will be like God."

The salvation occurs upon death and with the first drop of blood spilled, "A martyr has six bounties: He will be forgiven with the first drop of his blood that is spilt; He will see his place in Paradise (at the time of death); He will be saved from the 'Great Horror' (on the Day of Judgment); A Crown of Dignity will be placed on his head, which contains many conundrums, each one being more precious than this life and all that it contains; and He will have seventy-two women [virgins] of Paradise. Also, he will be allowed to intercede for seventy of his family members (who would have otherwise gone to hell)."[66]

Allah in the Qur'an gives this assurance of salvation "And never think of those who have been killed in the cause of Allah as dead. Rather, they are alive with their Lord, receiving provision" (Qur'an, Al-'Imraan:169). And to alleviate the thoughts of any pain it states: "The pain that a martyr feels at the time of death will be reduced so greatly that he will only feel as if he was stung by a mosquito." Abu Hurayrah narrated that the Prophet (PBUH) said: "A martyr only feels from the effect of being killed that which one would when being stung by a mosquito."[67]

Sure they do! How can anyone come back from the dead to prove such nonsense?

Martyrdom is indeed the highest aspiration of even the dwellers in heaven: "Anas bin Maalik, narrated that the Prophet said: 'Nobody who enters Paradise would ever wish to return to this life again, even if he was to be given the whole world and everything in it— except for a martyr; for he would wish to return and get killed ten times due to the honor that he received [in Paradise].' And in another narration: 'For what he finds as virtues of martyrdom.'"[68]

The goal of Jihad is to gain salvation:

"A Bedouin came to the Prophet, accepted Islam, and said: 'I wish to migrate (to Madeenah)'. So the Prophet asked some of his companions to take care of him. Then after a battle, the Muslims had gained some booty so the Prophet divided it and gave the Bedouin's share to some of his companions to look after, as the Bedouin was still at the rearguard. When the Bedouin returned, they gave him his share, so he asked them: 'What is this?' they replied: 'It is your share from the booty which the Prophet gave us to hold on to for you.' So the Bedouin took the booty and went to the Prophet and asked: 'What is this?' The Prophet said: 'Your share of the booty.' The Bedouin said: 'This is not why I believe in you and follow you; rather, I follow you so that I can get shot by an arrow right here, (and then he pointed to his throat) then die and enter Paradise.' The Prophet said: 'If you are sincere then Allah will grant you your wish.' After a short while, fighting resumed and the Bedouin's body was brought to the Prophet with an arrow in his throat at exactly the spot where he had pointed to the Prophet. Thereupon the Prophet said: 'He was sincere so Allah granted him his wish.' Then using his own garment, the Prophet shrouded the Bedouin, prayed the funeral prayer over him and was heard by his companions to say during the prayer: 'O Allah! This is Your slave who migrated for Your sake and was killed as a martyr — and I testify to this'. Which testimony could ever be more honorable, sincere and truthful than this great one given by the Prophet?"

SALVATION THROUGH THE BLOOD OF JESUS

Yet Salvation in Christianity is much different: "Jesus said unto them, Verily, verily, I say unto you, except ye who eats the flesh of the Son of man, and drinks his blood, ye has no life in you. Whoso eats my flesh, and drinks my blood, hath eternal life; and I will raise him up at the last day. For my flesh is meat indeed, and my blood is drink indeed; he that eat my flesh and drink my blood, dwells in me, and I in him" (John 6:53-56). Islam rejects the blood of Christ. How, then, can Christians be saved through the blood of Jesus? How can that assure salvation for anyone?

SALVATION THROUGH MOHAMMED'S BLOOD

While our understanding of these verses is purely symbolic, ask Abu Saad Khodri who stated in a strong Hadith in Sharh Hayat al-Sahaba, regarding partaking in the blood of Mohammed:

"When, at the battle of Uhud, the helmet-rings had been taken out of the Prophet's cheek, blood flowed from the radiant face of that Lord of the pure, and my father Malik Ibn Sinan sucked the wounds with his mouth, swallowing the blood. When they said to my father, 'Malik, is blood to be drunk?' my father replied, 'Yes, the blood of the Prophet of God I drink like a beverage.' At that time his Excellency, the Prophet, said, 'Whoever wishes to see one who has mixed my blood with his own, let him look at Malik Ibn Sinan: any one whose blood touches mine, him the fire of hell shall not desire.'"

Bizarre narrations like this are too many to quote. They speak of drinking Mohammed's urine and eating his excrement. Would such abominations be chosen over the precious blood of the sinless Lamb of God? Mohammed wanted to be a savior. Never has there ever been such a perverse heresy as Islam.

ADVANCING ALLAH'S GLORY—SEXUAL REWARDS

What do Muslims complain about when accusing the West of being run by international Zionism, with its Hollywood and sexual licentiousness? All of the perversity that we have in the West also exists in abundance in the Muslim paradise where there are "angels and young boys (handsome) as pearls well guarded" (Qur'an 52:24), "rivers of wine" (Qur'an 47:15), served with "goblets filled at a gushing fountain white and delicious to those who drink it." "It will neither dull their senses nor befuddle them" (Qur'an 37:40-48). "Rivers of milk of which the taste never changes; a joy to those who drink; and rivers of honey pure and clear" (Qur'an 47:15). "Bosomed virgins for companions: a truly overflowing cup" (Qur'an 78:31). These virgins are bashful and undefiled by man or demon.

Sexual enticements play an integral element in recruiting Jihadists. The late author and journalist Muhammad Galal Al-Kushk wrote; "The men in Paradise have sexual relations not only with the women who come from this world and with 'the black-eyed,' but also with the serving boys." According to Kurum, Al-Kushk also stated, "In Paradise, a believer's penis is eternally erect."[69]

A Hamas youth leader in a Gaza refugee camp told Jack Kelley of USA Today that, "most boys can't stop thinking about the virgins."[70] Sheikh Abd Al Fattah Jam'an speaking to Muslims in Palestine stated "What is waiting for the suicide bomber in paradise is a harem of beautiful virgins who are delicate and pure, esthetic, passive, with no personality or self or ego, whose only role is to sexually satisfy the shahid and be ever ready to fulfill his desires."[71] Many people think critics of Islam are making this up, but, in fact, they really teach this as doctrine.

Some delights do not have to wait until Paradise:

> "Ibn Fahd asked Al-Hajjaj 'I have some slave girls who are better than my wives, but I do not desire that they should all become pregnant. Shall I do azl (withdrawal) with them?' Al-Hajjaj said 'They are your fields of cultivation. If you wish to irrigate them do so, if not keep them dry.'"[72]

There are many references in the Qur'an where certain sexual privileges are reserved only for Mohammed: "Forbidden to you also are married women, except those who are in your hand as slaves, this is the law of Allah for you" (Sura 4:24). And in Qur'an 33:50 we read: "O prophet; we allowed thee thy wives to whom thou hast paid their dowries, and the slaves whom thy right hand possess out of the booty which Allah hath granted thee, and the daughters of thy uncle, and of thy maternal aunt, who fled with thee to Medina, and any believing woman who hath given herself up to the prophet, if the prophet desired to wed her, a privilege to thee above the rest of the faithful."

We had no problem with Mohammed taking advantage of this privilege. He married many wives and took several slave girls from the booty he collected from his victorious battles. We never knew how many wives he had and that question was always an issue for us to debate. We could debate the numbers, yet never question the moral justifications. One of Mohammed's wives was taken from his own adopted son, Zaid, as Allah declared that she was given to the prophet. Others were Jewish captives forced into slavery after Mohammed beheaded their husbands and/or families.

The Qur'an and Mohammed confirm this: "Thus [shall it be], and We will wed them with Houris [dark-eyed, celestial virgins], pure, beautiful ones."[73] "They shall recline on couches lined with thick brocade, and within reach will hang the fruits of both gardens. Therein are bashful virgins whom neither man nor jinnee will have touched [opening themselves] before them. Virgins as fair as corals and rubies."[74] "In each there shall be virgins chaste and fair. Dark eyed virgins sheltered in their tents whom neither man nor jinnee would have touched before. They shall recline on green cushions and fine carpets" (Qur'an 55:70-77). "We created the Houris and made them virgins, loving companions for those of the right hand. That which is coming" (Qur'an, 56:36). "As for the righteous, they shall surely triumph. Theirs shall be gardens and vineyards, and high-bosomed virgins for companions, a truly overflowing cup" (Qur'an 78:31-33).

The very same Qur'an and Sunna that served as the rules of conduct in the seventh century remain the basis for Islamic law today. Although many Muslim countries have banned such laws as a result of Western pressure, today the cry of the Muslim fundamentalist is to reinstate them, including slavery: "A slave is the property of his/her master. He/She is subject to the master's power, insomuch that if a master should kill his slave he is not liable to retaliation. With female slaves a master has the 'mulk-i-moot'at', or right of enjoyment, and his children by them, when acknowledged, has the same rights and privileges as his children by his wives. A slave is incompetent to anything that implies the exercise of authority over others. Hence a slave cannot be a witness, a judge, or an executor or guardian to any but his master and his children. A slave cannot inherit from anyone, and a bequest to him is a bequest to his master."[75]

You might ask; how can people believe this? This is a stubborn reality that seems so bizarre, and eludes many in the modern, secular West. Mohammed is famously known to have declared, "I have been ordered to fight the people till they say: "none has the right to be worshipped but Allah.'"[76] All this is done to honor his god Allah—the god of war. Unquestionably, Mohammed encouraged the spread of his religion by force, rape and even carnal sexual enticement.

One may argue that Christianity also has a goal of spreading its message throughout the earth. While this is true, Christianity does not have a goal of fighting against those who are not Christians, but rather, with love, presenting the gospel message, or "good news" to everyone in order that they have the choice to either freely accept or likewise reject God's offer of forgiveness and acceptance. As someone once said, "evangelism" (preaching the Christian message to non-Christians) is merely one beggar telling the other beggars where the food is. While Jesus, in calling new believers with "*Come to Me, all you who are weary and burdened, and I will give you rest. Take My yoke upon you and learn from Me, for I am gentle and humble in heart, and you will find rest for your souls. For My yoke is easy and My burden is light*" (Matthew 11:28-30). Mohammed calls his believers to something admittedly far more burdensome. Sounding somewhat like a parent trying to cajole their kids to finish up their broccoli, Mohammed says that killing infidels is actually good for you: "Warfare is ordained for you, though you may hate it; but it may happen that ye hate a thing which is good for you. Allah knoweth, but ye know not" (Qur'an 2:216).

When Western Muslims claim that the various verses which speak about Jihad are only about "overcoming adversity of injustice," they are serving up afresh the kool-aid of Jim Jones fame. What is so sad, however, is to see so many Westerners gobble this poisonous nonsense down. As one Muslim commentator has said, "Don't believe those moderate Muslims in the Western media who tell you that jihad means overcoming adversity."[77]

≈28≈
Both Condone Rape

Osama Bin Laden, you "Holier than thou" who cloaked himself with the turban and robes of "righteousness," who is the one who is immoral?

Christians always express that they are sinners. Muslim fundamentalists always express that they are a people who keep a "holier" lifestyle than the corrupt West. So, which one of the two is better in the eyes of God? Is it the one who sins and confesses or the one who claims holiness and yet defends their obvious sins?

I personally believe that when it comes to sin, most people fall into one of two categories: The ones who are bad yet think that they are good, or the good who always think they are bad.

The first are the type of people that will always tell you they are good. After all, they pay their taxes and obey traffic laws and such. Or, they pray five times a day, cover their body, and go to Hajj. The next group is the type of people who struggle with all sorts of issues in their lives, they confess their problems whatever they are, and maybe if they have a problem with something like alcohol or such, they seek help; and are always trying to better themselves, knowing that they can never attain perfection.

The Bible taught me that the second type of person is better in the eyes of God.

ANTICHRIST—RAPE OF JERUSALEM

Is rape in Islam only in ancient history? Few Westerners pay attention to the fact that Zechariah predicted the Antichrist army's rape of the Jewish women in Jerusalem: "Behold, the day of the LORD cometh, and thy spoil shall be divided in the midst of thee. For I will gather all nations against Jerusalem to battle; and the city shall be taken, and the houses rifled, and the women ravished" (Zechariah 14:2). But keep in mind, the Lord's feet shall stand in that day upon the Mount of Olives to save Israel from total annihilation.

JIHAD AND RAPE

This is nothing new to Islam. Even Mohammed condoned it. Take the fate of the tribe of Al-Mustaliq as an example. After being captured by Muslims: "We were lusting after women and chastity had become too hard for us, but we wanted to get the ransom money for our prisoners. Therefore, we wanted to use the "Azl" (Coitus Interruptus). We asked the Prophet about it and he said "You are not under any obligation to stop yourselves from doing it like that." Later on the women [after they were raped] and children were given for ransom to their envoys. They all went away to their country and not one wanted to stay although they had the choice."[78]

Allah is an utter pervert; why is the issue on be Coitus Interruptus? And where is the nobility in asking these women if they wished to stay? "The Antichrist will not honor the desire of women, nor will he respect their dignity." *And neither does Islam offer legitimate dignity to women!*

This is just the tip of the iceberg out of the annals of Muslim history. Abu Sa'id al-Khudri said: "The Apostle of Allah sent a military expedition to Awtas at the battle of Hunain. They met their enemy and fought with them. They defeated them and took them captives. Some of the Companions of the Apostle of Allah were reluctant to have intercourse with the female captives in the presence of their husbands who were unbelievers.' Therefore, Allah, the Exalted, send down the Qur'anic verse 'And all married women (are forbidden) unto you save those (captives) whom your right hand possess[es].'"[79]

IS THIS ONLY IN HISTORY?

Hardly, these rules still apply. Apologists for Islam always say that these issues reflect history during days of archaic civilizations and traditions. Even in recent times, hundreds of Chinese Indonesian girls/women (aged 10-55) have been gang raped brutally by Muslim Jihadis. Some victims were even raped in front of their family members or in front of an inhumane cheering crowd. Some of them were even thrown into the fire and burnt to death after being raped.

Yet, not many actions seem to have been taken to investigate all this or to help the victims. Not very many people seem to know or care about what happened.[80] Where is the liberal outrage? Oh yeah, that is reserved for George Bush and John Hagee.

Their are accounts of such rapes taking place from Pakistan to Egypt, and even all over Europe and Australia, with enough stories and testimonies to fill up a library. This dishonor to women is predicted and typical of the Antichrist spirit. From condoned pleasure marriage and sex with infants in the Shi'a circles to gang rapes promoted by Sunni Muslim scholars, there is much to be said about Islam and rape, yet I will only give a few examples since it is an anathema to God and to Christians.

In Australia's New South Wales Supreme Court in December 2005, a visiting Pakistani rapist testified that his victims had no right to say no, because they were not wearing a headscarf. Australians were outraged when Lebanese Sheik Faiz Mohammed gave a lecture in Sydney where he informed his audience that rape victims had no one to blame but themselves. Women, he said, who wore skimpy clothing, invited men to rape them. A few months earlier, in Copenhagen, Islamic mufti and scholar, Shahid Mehdi, created uproar when, like his peer in Australia, he stated that women who did not wear a headscarf were asking to be raped. And just to show that this mentality is not unusual within Islam, in 2004, the *London Telegraph* reported that visiting Egyptian scholar, and one of the most respected Islamic scholars in the Middle East, Sheik Yusuf al-Qaradawi claimed female rape victims should be punished if they were dressed immodestly when they were raped. He added, "For her to be absolved from guilt, a raped woman must have shown good conduct." [81]

So once again, Islam fulfills yet another Antichrist characteristic as prophesied in the Bible. The Prophet Zechariah warned the inhabitants of Jerusalem regarding the brutal nature of its future invasion.

Perhaps you are saying that rape is a common part of most wars, why single out Islam here?

We need to remember that the Antichrist invasion is not just any invasion—it is a religious invasion. These invaders will be followers of the Antichrist religion. They will be followers of the Antichrist and his war-god. Is it really all that difficult to figure out what the Bible is speaking about here? Islam is the only religion on earth whose "prophet" and whose legal system sanctions, yes even encourages, the rape of women—specifically after conquering an enemy. Meanwhile, world renowned Muslim "scholars" like Yusuf Qaradawi open their mouths and reveal Islam's inherently misogynistic attitudes toward women. It is undeniable. Believe me folks, Islam is the perfect fit like nothing else can be.

∾29∾

Both Usher in a
Seven Year Peace Treaty

Even the seven year "peace" treaty spoken of by Daniel can be found in Islam. Is it coincidence? Hardly! After rising to power, and as a prelude to his invasion of Israel, the Antichrist is said to confirm a peace-treaty with the nation of Israel for seven years: "He will confirm a covenant with many for one 'seven'" (Daniel 9:27). In context, this verse shows us that the Antichrist will "confirm" and not "establish" a peace treaty, as is commonly thought. He could confirm a peace treaty such as Oslo or the Saudi plan and revive them. This is a pre-existing agreement that will be re-established with Israel for seven years. However, the Bible also reveals that after only three and a half years, the Antichrist will break this seven year covenant.

As we have already discussed, Satan—through the Islamic prophecies—has set up the Muslims of the world to receive the Antichrist as their Messiah-Mahdi.

One Islamic tradition places the ascendancy of the Mahdi at the time of a final peace agreement between the Arabs and the Romans ('Romans' should be interpreted here as referring to Christians, or more generally, the West). Although this peace agreement is made with the "Romans," it is said to be mediated specifically through a Jew from the priestly lineage of Aaron. The peace agreement will be made for a period of seven years: "Rasulullah [Muhammad] said: 'There will be four peace agreements between you and the Romans [Christians]. The fourth agreement will be mediated through a person who will be from the progeny of Hadrat Haroon [Honorable Aaron—Moses' brother] and will be upheld for seven years."[83] Another Hadith speaks of the "reign" of the Mahdi this way: "He will divide the property, and will govern the people by the Sunnah of their Prophet and establish Islam on Earth. He will remain seven years then die, and the Muslims will pray over him." [84] "The Mahdi will fill the earth with equity and justice as it was filled with oppression and tyranny, and he will rule for seven years."[85]

So the seven year rule of the Mahdi is preceded by the seven year peace treaty which is said to be made with a descendant of Moses' brother, Aaron the Priest. Such a descendant would be a Cohen, or priest. Only priests are allowed among Jews to conduct the priestly duties of the Temple. This is important because the treaty that the Antichrist will initiate with Israel will also likely include an agreement to allow the Jews to re-build their Temple.

The question Western Christians always ask is how will the Jews rebuild the Temple if Muslims occupy the Temple Mount? How will the Muslims overlook the idea of Jews building a structure on the Temple Mount? The answer is that Islamic prophecy prescribes this, but only when the Mahdi appears.

∞ 30 ∞
Both Deceive and Destroy by Peace

The Bible warns us regarding the Antichrist that, "By peace he will destroy many." (Daniel 8:25)

Does that ring a bell? Who are saying that "Islam is a peaceful religion?" Had Western believers diligently read the Scriptures, we would not be in such a mess. The East needs your help, we have millions of Muslims converting to Christianity—many are awakening to the evil that Islam truly is. These converts can offer you much knowledge, yet they need your help: Christians suffer by the millions; my village of Bethlehem is now virtually void of Christians. Lands have been confiscated, including my own. Sacred locations including the Messiah's birthplace have been desecrated. Egyptian Coptic Christians are daily persecuted; their women kidnapped and raped. This is an S.O.S. Mister Spock, roger and out.

Peace demonstrators petitioning Israel always carry leaflets that say things like, "Stop the Cycle of Violence," yet violence in the Middle East almost inevitably comes as a result of false peace treaties which are never kept. Instead, they are almost always a stepping stone to further escalated violence. "Hudna" is a term all Westerners must learn. After 9/11, Westerners learned the word Jihad. Well, not exactly, they are still divided on whether the term means "holy war against all things non-Islamic" or "an internal struggle for self-betterment." In fact, the standard party-line peace-offering that "Jihad simply means inner struggle" is unheard of outside of the West. This definition is no where to be found. Even the Islamophilic scholar Reuven Firestone has acknowledged the dubious nature of the oral tradition (i.e., Hadith) upon which this alleged interpretation of jihad rests: "Its source is not usually given, and it is in fact nowhere to be found in the canonical collections [of Hadith]."[86]

Although the word Jihad standing by itself means "struggle," what Westerners need to focus on when reading the Hadith regarding Mohammed's Jihad is similar to the focus needed when reading Mein Kampf (My Struggle) by Adolph Hitler. Ask yourselves, "Struggle with what?" In time those who are leaning toward believing that Jihad simply means "struggle within" will understand—it will just take more lessons until they will see.

But the word *Hudna* needs to be understood as well. In the Muslim mind, Hudna is an Arabic term for a truce meant to produce a period of calm with an enemy in order to gain concessions, regroup, rearm, and re-attack at the appropriate time. This has been its purpose throughout Muslim history. Based on Islam's understanding of Mohammed's use of it, a Hudna could last as long as ten years.

Case in point. A particularly famous early Hudna was the Treaty of Hudaybiyya between Mohammed and the Quraysh tribe. According to Umdat as-Salik, a medieval summary of Shafi'i jurisprudence, Hudnas with a non-Muslim enemy should be limited to 10 years: "If Muslims are weak, a truce may be made for ten years if necessary, for the Prophet made a truce with the Quraysh for that long, as is related by Abu Dawud"[87]

Take for example the Oslo Peace Accords. Arafat relied on the term when he spoke about his commitment in 1994 to the Oslo Peace Accords. At a mosque in Johannesburg just a month after the signing, Arafat declared (not realizing that he was being taped) that the Accords were merely a way to facilitate his Jihad against Israel. Later, when challenged about this, he wiggled out of it by declaring that he was using the term Jihad in its most positive sense: A struggle against inner negative forces. So, Arafat presented himself as a "Jihad fighter for peace."[88]

Even Faisal Husseini, one of the PLO's highest level spokespersons clarified the meaning of the Oslo Accords to the world in an interview with an Egyptian newspaper:[89] "had the U.S. and Israel realized, before Oslo, that all that was left of the Palestinian National movement and the Pan-Arab movement was a wooden [Trojan] horse called Arafat...they would never have opened their fortified gates and let it inside their walls...The Oslo agreement, or any other agreement, is just a temporary procedure, just a step towards something bigger...distinguish the strategic, long-term goals from the political phased goals, which we are compelled to temporarily accept due to international pressure...Our ultimate goal is the liberation of all of historic Palestine, from the [Jordan] River to the [Mediterranean] Sea." In other words, Palestine will be created across the entire existing State of Israel.[90] The story of the Trojan Horse is synonymous to Islam's Hudna. Hamas agreed to several ceasefires between 1993 and 2003, none of which were honored. The West must understand these offers as mere tactical maneuvers to allow militant groups time to live to fight another day. At root, the current ceasefire between Israel and Hezbollah will eventually fail because, like all Hudnas to date, they are always broken. It would be sacrilege to keep them for too long. The Hamas Charter states: "For renouncing any part of Palestine means renouncing part of the religion; the nationalism of the Islamic Resistance Movement is part of its faith, the movement educates its members to adhere to its principles and to raise the banner of Allah over their homeland as they fight their Jihad: 'Allah is the all-powerful, but most people are not aware.'"[91] So any land deals as part of a Hudna should be an absolute anathema. Yet the idiocy continues and the West keeps biting the bait—every time. Hamas' Mahmoud Zahar reiterated after the recent electoral victory: "We have no peace process. We are not going to mislead our people to tell them we are waiting, meeting, for a peace process that is nothing." Zahar was echoing the Hamas Charter's declaration "[Peace] initiatives, the so-called peaceful solutions, and the international conferences to resolve the Palestinian problem, are all contrary to the beliefs of the Islamic Resistance Movement."[92]

Even though it seems that Hamas might reject any peace plan, rest assured that in the near future, they would, yet again, sign a Hudna. But now, you my Western friend know the difference—it will be yet another Trojan horse. I have stated this on record, so when it happens, you will remember.

What the West does not understand about Islamism is that Jihad is very systematic. It has stages. If Muslims have the upper hand, then Jihad is waged by force. If Muslims do not have the upper hand, then Jihad is waged through financial and political means. Since Muslims do not have the upper hand in America or Europe, they talk about peace in front of you while supporting Hamas and Hezbollah in the back room. The whole idea of Islam being a peaceful religion emanates from that silent stage of Jihad. Sheikh Qaradawi has taught Muslims this form of trickery at conferences in the U.S., I have it on video. At one conference, Qaradawi used the example of Salahu-Deen Al-Ayubi (Saladin). Saladin was asked to concede to peace with the verse from the Qur'an 8:61, "And if they incline to peace, then incline to it and trust in Allah." However, from Qur'an 47:35, he replied, "And be not slack so as to cry for peace and you have the upper hand."[93]

In Islam, conceding to peace means that the Islamic Umma (nation) is weak. But as soon as Islam becomes the stronger force, it switches into war mode and high-gear.

HUDAIBIYAH

To understand why God warns of false peace treaties, I need to explain an essential bit of Islamic history known as the Treaty of Hudaibiyah. During the early years of Mohammed's small but growing movement, the Muslims were in conflict with the tribe of Quraysh who were the guardians of the so-called "holy" city of Mecca. Mohammed and the Muslims had been kicked out of Mecca and were now living roughly two hundred miles to the north in Medina. During those days, the various surrounding Arab tribes would make a yearly religious pilgrimage to the pagan shrine in Mecca known as the Ka'ba (the Cube). But because the Quraysh and the Muslims were enemies, and because the Quraysh were much more powerful than the Muslims, they would not allow them to make any pilgrimages.

Then one night, Mohammed claimed to have received a revelation whereby he said that Allah told him that he and the Muslims would make the pilgrimage to Mecca. But as the Muslims were attempting to sneak into the city at a place called the Spring of Hudaibiyah, they were intercepted by Qurayashi troops. It was there that the men of Quraysh disrespected and shamed Mohammed in front of his men. They also refused the Muslims entry into Mecca. However, they did offer the Muslims a very generous deal. This deal became known as the Treaty of Hudaibiyah. Both parties agreed not to attack each other for ten years. Because the Muslims were by far the weaker and smaller group, the peace-agreement was clearly a generous deal on Quraysh's part. But Mohammed was humiliated and his Muslims were covered with shame. They were terribly embarrassed that their so-called prophet had been treated so poorly and did nothing to respond other than to roll over and agree to the treaty. They were also completely disillusioned because Mohammed had obviously prophesied falsely regarding the pilgrimage.

But Mohammed's response to his followers was typical of a false prophet—he simply painted a new bulls-eye around his arrow. Mohammed argued that Allah had never said that the Muslims would make pilgrimage "this year" but that they would simply make it someday. Al-Bukhari records this hilarious event when Umar said, "I went to the Prophet and said, 'Aren't you truly the Apostle of Allah?' The Prophet said, 'Yes, indeed.' I said, 'isn't our cause just and the cause of the enemy unjust?' He said, 'Yes.' I said, 'Then why should we be humble in our religion?' He said, 'I am Allah's Apostle and I do not disobey Him, and He will make me victorious.' I said, 'Didn't you tell us that we would go to the Ka'ba?' He said, 'Yes, but did I tell you that we would visit the Ka'ba this year?'"[94] Umar should have walked away at that point.

Knowing that his men were grumbling and that immediate action needed to be taken, Mohammed arose the following morning claiming that Allah had "sent down" another revelation explaining that what had happened was in fact a "great victory" for the Muslims. Remember that any time a pirate is allowed to live freely another day, this is considered a great victory.

This pattern of behavior is typical among Muslims even today. After every terrible military failure, Muslims will still triumphantly declare their victory. The recent clash between Hezbollah and Israel is a perfect example. But beyond declaring his failure a victory, Mohammed also turned the event around by declaring to his men the gladdest tidings of his latest revelation: All of the treasures, the women, and the children from the Jewish community of Khaibar would soon belong to them all! Mohammed announced that the majority of the booty and captives from any future conquests would belong to the Muslim soldiers who took part in the invasion. The incentive for Jihad had now been established, and this is where the bloodshed really began.

The Muslims instantly became the pirates of the desert. Within only weeks of being humiliated, Mohammed began attacking and pillaging several very wealthy Jewish villages. The Muslims who participated in these attacks reveled in their new found wealth as well as the many women and children that they took as slaves. Mohammed was also allegedly told by Allah that it was okay to use the captured women as sex-slaves—and this law still stands to this day. When other non-Muslim Arabs saw all the Muslims enjoying their wealth and slaves, the new converts suddenly began to pour into this Nimrod's religion like a mighty river. In the immediate period after this, the growth and expansion of the young Muslim movement was staggering.

Early biographies of Mohammed attribute this expansion directly to the period of peace that the Muslims enjoyed as a result of the Treaty of Hudaibiyah. Alfred Guillame in *The Life of Mohammed* writes "He (Allah) has wrought a near victory, the peace of al-Hudaybiyya. No previous victory in Islam was greater than this...In those two years double as many or more than double as many entered Islam as ever before."[95]

When the Treaty was made, the Muslims were less than 1,500, but within a mere two years the Muslim men alone were 10,000 strong. Between the Quraysh and the Muslims, the Muslims suddenly were the larger and more powerful group. So despite the ten-year peace treaty that Mohammed had agreed to, it was time for the Quraysh to pay. Mohammed and the Muslims wasted no time in breaking their end of the treaty. They attacked Mecca and the power of the Quraysh tribe was shattered. The Muslims were now the undisputed rulers of both Mecca and Medina.

The point of course in recalling all of this history is to demonstrate the certain fact that Mohammed was a brazen opportunist and a Nimrodian revolutionist. But he is also the supreme example for all Muslims today. As such, to this very day, Muslims do not view peace treaties in the same way that most people understand a "peace-treaty." To the Muslim mind, treaties are not binding agreements, but rather opportunities to grow stronger or buy time or to appear peaceful while preparing for war. But make no mistake, making peace treaties with the infidels simply for the sake of peace is never the ultimate goal. The only goal of Islam is victory over the whole world. Concepts such as honor, ethics, or obligations are afforded only a secondary importance against the supreme importance that is given to establishing the supremacy and domination of Islam throughout the whole world.

Muslims today all clearly understand "Hudaibiya" to be a code-word, which in brief means, "kiss the hand of your enemy until you have the opportunity to cut it off," or as the common Arabic saying goes "kiss the dog's mouth until you get what you need from him." *Do not be deceived.*

HUDAIBIYAH AS A MODERN MUSLIM POLITICAL TOOL

If you don't believe that anyone could be this blatantly subversive, then consider this: In May of 1994, Yasser Arafat addressed a group of Muslims in Johannesburg, South Africa. What Arafat didn't know was that he was being secretly recorded. At that time, things were looking really good for the Middle East Peace Process. Many felt as though tensions were winding down. But Arafat revealed the truth when he spoke of the ongoing "Jihad to liberate Jerusalem." Those Israelis who had trusted Arafat's previous promises of peace and good-will were shocked. But even more damning were Arafat's references to the Treaty of Hudaibyah. Referring to the Peace Agreement that he had only recently made with Israel, Arafat said "I see this agreement as being no more than the agreement signed between our Prophet Mohammed and the Quraysh in Mecca...The prophet had been right to insist on the agreement, for it helped him defeat the Quraysh and take over their city of Mecca. In a similar spirit, we now accept the peace agreement, but [only in order] to continue on the road to Jerusalem."[96]

In actuality, Arafat frequently made reference to the Treaty of Hudaibiyah and clearly expressed that it was a model for his own so-called "diplomacy." Though this allusion to the Treaty of Hudaibiyah was obscure to non-Muslims, Muslims were very familiar with it. Mentioning the Treaty in Johannesburg and often afterwards was Arafat's method of sending a clandestine message about his intentions toward Israel to his co-religionists. This is a common practice by Muslim leaders, but never when they know that "the enemy is listening." Only recently, the Malaysian Prime minister Datuk Seri Dr Mahathir Mohamad was also caught discussing the Treaty of Hudaibiyah as his model for diplomacy. "At Hudaibiyah Mohammed was prepared to accept an unfair treaty, against the wishes of his companions and followers. During the peace that followed he consolidated his strength and eventually he was able to enter Mecca and claim it for Islam...For well over half a century we have fought over Palestine. What have we achieved? Nothing. We are worse off than before. If we had paused to think then we could have devised a plan, a strategy that can win us final victory...The Qur'an tells us that when the enemy sues for peace we must react positively. True the treaty offered is not favorable to us. But we can negotiate. The Prophet did, at Hudaibiyah. And in the end he triumphed...The enemy will probably welcome these proposals."[97]

The Lure – Islam is Peace

AMAZING CONTRADICTIONS

Westerners always inquire and struggle to find moderate Muslims. Do they exist? If so, where are their Arabic websites? How many are there? If they exist, why are they only in English? Why do they only partially quote Muslim jurisprudence?

If one studies Islam carefully one would find two sets of codes, some abrogated Qur'anic verses and commands for peace used whenever objections against violence in Islam arise. Then you have other commands, exclusively for Muslims.

Muslims are quick to dish out fantastic quotes from Islamic sources claiming that Jihad means self-defense: "Fight in the cause of Allah those who fight you, but do not transgress limits; for Allah loves not transgressors." (Qur'an 2:190) Or the favorite, "Ten Commandments of Jihad" used by moderate imposters who quote Caliph Abu Bakr upon commissioning Muslims for Jihad expansions: "Listen and obey the following ten commands and instructions: Do not betray any one (if you give a pledge). Do not ever steal from the war booties. Do not breach your pledge of allegiance. Do not mutilate the body of the killed enemy fighters or deceased. Do not kill a child or a minor. Do not kill an elderly man or woman. Do not kill a woman. Do not pull out a date palm tree (or any other trees) and do not burn it either. Do not cut or destroy a fruit tree. Do not slaughter a female sheep, a cow, or a camel except for your (required) food. You surely will pass by some people who isolate themselves and are secluded for worship of Allah as monks and else, thus leave them alone and do not disturb them ever. You will, surely, stop at some people on the road, who will bring forth for you all types of food dishes. Whenever you eat their food utter the name of Allah each time you eat. You will, surely, pass by a group of people who shaved the hair in the center of their heads, and left the surrounding hair long braids. Go ahead; kill these people as they are the fighters and worriers who carry their swords against you, of the enemies. Go ahead, with the name of Allah."[98]

Isn't there a contradiction between "Jihad expansion" and all this talk of loving captive peoples? Why invade them in the first place? What transgression did Jerusalem do to Arabia to deserve Omar's invasion? Were the Muslims truly defending themselves when they invaded Spain? Then you have the most amazing contradiction from Al-Ghazali: One must go on jihad (i.e., warlike razzias or raids) at least once a year...one may use a catapult against them when they are in a fortress, even if among them are women and children. One may set fire to them and/or drown them...If a person of the Ahl al-Kitab [People of The Book—Jews and Christians, typically] is enslaved, his marriage is [automatically] revoked...One may cut down their trees...One must destroy their useless books. Jihadists may take as booty whatever they decide...they may steal as much food as they need."[99]

Professor Khalil Muhammad in a dialogue with me gave such loving quotes using Al-Ghazali the famous theologian, philosopher, and paragon of mystical Sufism, who is regularly quoted by the so called moderates as a prime example of moderate Islam. Even Western scholars like the eminent W. M. Watt describes Al-Ghazali as "acclaimed in both the East and West as the greatest Muslim after Mohammed, and he is by no means unworthy of that dignity."

Had Westerners studied Al-Ghazali regarding Jihad and the treatment of the vanquished non-Muslim dhimmi peoples, perhaps they would have not been deceived by peace.

Contemporary scholar Bassam Tibi sums it up this way: "At its core, Islam is a religious mission to all humanity. Muslims are religiously obliged to disseminate the Islamic faith throughout the world.[100] 'We have sent you forth to all mankind' (Qur'an 34:28). If non-Muslims submit to conversion or subjugation, this call (da'wa) can be pursued peacefully. If they do not, Muslims are obliged to wage war against them."[101]

Sure, Islam means peace—but only after submission.

GUILTY NO MATTER WHAT

Muslims believe that expansion through war is not aggression but love since only through Islam can we attain peace. In other words, "We are invading you for your own ultimate good."

"Yeah Right."

The resort to force to disseminate Islam, at least in the view of Muslims, is not harb (war), but rather they are seen as an act of bringing non-Muslims into "the house of peace" through what Islam calls futuhat; acts of "opening" the world to the peace of Islam. Ironically, Islam calls itself "The house of Peace" (Dar al-Islam), even though, the word Islam literally means submission, and it calls the non-Muslim world (who truly wants peace with Islam) "The house of War" (Dar al-harb). In other words, Islam says to the non-Muslim world, "Because you are such terrible war-mongers, we must attack and utterly conquer you." According to the Qur'an and to the authoritative commentaries of Islamic jurists, unbelievers who stand in the way, creating obstacles for the Da'wa (Islamic evangelism), are blamed for this constant state of war, for the Da'wa can be pursued peacefully if the subjects for Da'wa will only willingly submit. In other words, those who do not roll over and allow Islamic domination are the ones that cause wars and are responsible for them.

Only when Muslim power is weak, is Hudna (temporary truce) allowed (Islamic jurists differ on the definition of "temporary").[102]

The Bible is right: "by peace he will destroy many." But, how can peace destroy? Especially since destruction is the opposite of peace! Islam is truly an alternate universe where peace is used to destroy—exactly what the Antichrist will do. Islam's reversalist mentality is described precisely by the prophet Isaiah: "Woe to those who call evil good, and good evil; who put darkness for light, and light for darkness; who put bitter for sweet, and sweet for bitter!" (Isaiah 5:20)

It's not only the perverse logic that plagues Muslim jurisprudence, but a double-standard by Sharia that differs little between the Sunni and its Shi'ite strain. The Tabandeh Tract for example, which became the core ideological work upon which the Iranian government based its non-Muslim policy today states that, "Thus if a Muslim commits adultery his punishment is 100 lashes, the shaving of his head, and one year of banishment. But if the man is not a Muslim and commits adultery with a Muslim woman his penalty is execution...similarly if a Muslim deliberately murders another Muslim he falls under the law of retaliation and must by law be put to death by the next of kin. But if a non-Muslim who dies at the hand of a Muslim, has by lifelong habit been a non-Muslim, the penalty of death is not valid. Instead the Muslim murderer must pay a fine and be punished with the lash."[103]

This type of double standard encompasses all aspects of Islamic legal code. Thousands of cases-in-point can be found in Islam's Sharia: "Because Islam regards non-Muslims as on a lower level of belief and conviction, if a Muslim kills a non-Muslim...then his punishment must not be the retaliatory death, since the faith and conviction he possesses is loftier than that of the man slain...Again, the penalties of a non-Muslim guilty of fornication with a Muslim woman are augmented because, in addition to the crime against morality, social duty and religion, he has committed sacrilege, in that he has disgraced a Muslim and thereby cast scorn upon the Muslims in general, and so must be executed."[104] "Islam and its peoples must be above the infidels, and never permit non-Muslims to acquire lordship over them. Since the marriage of a Muslim woman to an infidel husband (in accordance with the verse quoted: 'Men are guardians over women') means her subordination is to an infidel, that fact makes the marriage void, because it does not obey the conditions laid down to make a contract valid. As the Qur'an says: "Turn them not back to infidels: for they are not lawful unto infidels nor are infidels lawful unto them (i.e., in wedlock)." (Qur'an 60:10)[105]

≈ 31 ≈

Both Break Treaties

+———— ✳ ————+

A ccording to Islam, the Mahdi will usher in the last seven years before judgment which will be the *Seven Years of Peace* Islam promises to establish, yet in Islamic Eschatology, he also kills all the Jewish men everywhere in the world. How is this peace?

These seven years of peace must then be broken.

This is already forewarned in the Bible: "He (The Antichrist) will confirm a covenant with many for one 'seven' [years] In the middle of the 'seven' [years] he will put an end to sacrifice and offering. And on a wing of the temple he will set up an abomination that causes desolation, until the end that is decreed is poured out on him." (Daniel 9:27)

How could it be that Islam's unholy intent is already predicted in the Bible? Why was Islam the only cult to copy Bible prophecy and become the antithesis to Christianity? Had Islam died, then none of these things written in the Bible would have come true. Islam is unique, though, and prophecies about it must be in the Bible. In fact, no other religion or cult has as many documented prophecies about itself as does Islam.

Antichrist will confirm a covenant that was previously stalled or broken. In the middle of the seven years, the Antichrist will violate the terms of this treaty and set up what the Bible calls an "abomination that causes desolation" on the Temple Mount. Of that treaty Isaiah also prophesied: "In that day the remnant of Israel, the survivors of the house of Jacob, will no longer rely on him who struck them down but will truly rely on Jehovah, the Holy One of Israel. A remnant will return, a remnant of Jacob will return to the Mighty God." (Isaiah 10:20-21)

The message is clear, by making treaties with nations and peoples who are in reality committed to their destruction, the Jewish people deceive themselves with the fanciful notion that they will achieve "peace and security" and thus escape the murderous plans of the surrounding peoples. Reality is that Israel's policies of appeasement have repeatedly resulted in agreements founded on mere wishful thinking that produced the exact opposite of what they had hoped for. Whenever the enemy finds it in *their favor* to do so, they break their agreements. This pattern has proven to be true with the Assyrians, the Babylonians, the Syrians, the Romans, and more recently with the Muslims. One might argue that the PLO was a secular organization. This is only partially true. The PLO wore a cloak of secularism, but in fact was Muslim. There is not a single Muslim country void of Sharia law.

TREATIES ARE NEVER KEPT

The Bible says repeatedly that this embrace of hollow feel-good agreements will ultimately result in Israel's near destruction. The message that Isaiah the prophet trumpeted to his people was that there was only one person they could truly "rely on" and this was the Messiah. He alone could be trusted and He alone would deal justly with Zion's cause.

Every treaty that Israel has committed to, from ancient times to modern day Oslo, Sharm el-Sheikh, and Wye, has had disappointing or even terrible results. Some may argue that Camp-David was a success—a deal in which Israel gave the entire Sinai Peninsula back to Egypt after Israel's victory in the Six-Day War—despite the fact that Israel gained this land legitimately after having been attacked by Egypt whose only requirement in exchange for regaining all of her lost land was a simple piece of paper with a promise not to attack Israel. But what do we find today? What has Israel gained from this agreement? Tunnels are dug daily from Egypt into Israel to smuggle weapons into Gaza so that the Palestinians can continue to kill Jewish civilians. During Mohammed's day, the Jews of Medina made an agreement to offer Mohammed asylum. What was the result at that time? In just a few short years, Mohammed had slaughtered thousands of Jews and destroyed entire Jewish communities. Times have not changed, nor has the Muslim practice of breaking treaties.

Even far before Mohammed's day, when the Hebrews left Egypt and approached the Promised Land, God issued them a command never to make a treaty with the various peoples that lived in and around what would come to be the Land of Israel "Be careful not to make a treaty with those who live in the land where you are going, or they will be a snare among you...Do not worship any other god, for Jehovah, whose name is Jealous, is a jealous God. Be careful not to make a treaty with those who live in the land." (Exodus 34:12-17) Later, even after the Jews had defeated the various tribes that lived in the land, they were still not allowed to make treaties with them. Instead God said, "You must destroy them totally. Make no treaty with them, and show them no mercy." (Deuteronomy 7:2-4)

THE UNFAIR JEHOVAH

Modern ears have difficulty with this. The poison of moral relativity has made it difficult to understand why God would have been so intolerant of other peoples. However, the simple fact of the matter is that the peoples that settled there were bent on Israel's destruction, while God for a thousand years offered them repentance and return. I always get asked everywhere I go, "What about Joshua who massacred the Canaanites?"

Yet, this is exactly what the U.S. did in Japan and Germany to end wars. It's a choice between preservation and suicide. The peoples that surrounded the Israelites wanted to destroy them and stop the plan of Israel. The Jewish people had an important and unique purpose in God's unfolding plan of redemption for the entire world. The job of the Jewish people was to become a holy people that could provide a holy womb that would bring forth the Messiah into the world. Through the Messiah, not only the Jewish people, but also the entire world would come to know Jehovah—the One True Supreme God.

But the peoples who lived in the land worshipped gods who were in reality demons. These demon-gods demanded such things as the sacrifice of the first-born child to be literally burned alive. But the situation is not different from the Canaanites or the Mayans who sacrificed humans to Satan. Would Westerners prefer to see ancient Mayan culture reinstated? Talk about Satanic cults and human offerings to evil, yet on a mass scale. If anything, no descendants of the Mayans want to go back to these days. The Spanish Inquisitions, with all their errors and greed seem to have done some good.

Satanic sacrifices never ended. In Palestine today, many Muslim parents willingly sacrifice their children to become human bombs for the sake of killing Jews. The people who lived in the Promised Land were spiritually sick just as we see the Palestinians behave. Plain and simple, God did not want their wicked ways to spread to the Jewish people. It was with good reason then that God commanded the Jewish people to refrain from ever making covenants or treaties with the various peoples of the land who worshipped false gods and demons—and they still do to this very day.

Unfortunately the Jewish people rarely obeyed God's command regarding their relationships with other nations. This theme is addressed in the "covenant with death" prophecy by Isaiah for the Last-Days: "Therefore hear the word of Jehovah, you scoffers who rule this people in Jerusalem. You boast, 'We have entered into a covenant with death, with the grave we have made an agreement. When an overwhelming scourge sweeps by, it cannot touch us, for we have made a lie our refuge and falsehood our hiding place.' So this is what the Sovereign Jehovah says: 'See, I lay a stone in Zion, a tested stone, a precious cornerstone for a sure foundation; the one who trusts will never be dismayed.'" (Isaiah 28:14-16) This passage ends with a call not to trust in the covenant offered by Antichrist, but rather in the "tested and precious cornerstone"—Jesus the Messiah.

~ 32 ~
Both Love War
For Booty

One cannot enter the world of Islam without being accustomed to Nasheed; a rhythmic poetry that is sung without musical instruments, which are totally prohibited in Islam. You would never hear musical instruments played in a mosque. Mohammed proclaimed musicians to be of the people dwelling in hell. Nasheed is much different than anything the Judeo-Christian world is accustomed to. To give a taste, perhaps I can share one of the most popular Islamic Nasheed songs:

> *We are those who built our forts*
> *Out of the skulls*
> *Which we brought from the land of the tyrant*
> *By force and on top of the booty*
> *Our Messenger is the one who made us*
> *Noble builders of glory*
> *Our Messenger is the sun of truth*
> *Who lit the face of the world.*

Does that sound like anything that you have ever sung in Church? Much history is rarely discussed regarding Muslims literally building mounds (forts) out of human skulls. If in doubt, study the memoirs of Baburnama of the Mughal Empire in which tens of millions were killed during Islam's invasions of India and decapitated heads were piled as trophies.

When I read the Bible it taught me that this type of bloodthirstiness was the cause of my separation from God: "But your iniquities have separated you from your God; and your sins have hidden His face from you, so that He will not hear. For your hands are defiled with blood, and your fingers with iniquity; your lips have spoken lies; your tongue has muttered perversity. No one calls for justice, nor does any plead for truth. They trust in empty words and speak lies; they conceive evil and bring forth iniquity. They hatch vipers' eggs and weave the spider's web; he who eats of their eggs dies, and from that which is crushed a viper breaks out. Their webs will not become garments, nor will they cover themselves with their works; their works are works of iniquity, and the act of violence is in their hands. Their feet run to evil, and they make haste to shed innocent blood; their thoughts are thoughts of iniquity; wasting and destruction are in their paths. The way of peace they have not known, and there is no justice in their ways; they have made themselves crooked paths; whoever takes that way shall not know peace." (Isaiah 59:2-8)

Such verses matched my heart perfectly. I began to understand that "The fear of the Lord is the beginning of knowledge, but fools despise wisdom and instruction." (Proverbs 1:7) This fool needed so much wisdom and instruction, not the instruction of evil: "'Come with us, Let us lie in wait to shed blood; Let us lurk secretly for the innocent without cause...We shall find all kinds of precious possessions, We shall fill our houses with spoil...' My son, do not walk in the way with them, Keep your foot from their path; for their feet run to evil, And they make haste to shed blood." (Proverbs 1:11-16) Such was the advice of my new Lord when I accepted the truth of the real Scriptures.

MOHAMMED AND BOOTY

Muslims are fascinated with the stories of Mohammed's conquests for land and booty. So important was the quest for booty that all Muslims were required to give a fifth of their treasure to Allah the war-god and his Nimrod Mohammed.

But what do they do when they find themselves out of money? Easy, the Qur'an says that "whatever ye take as spoils of war, lo! A fifth thereof is for Allah and for the messenger..." (Qur'an 8:41)

So if the Muslims were running low on Zakat, that was no problem, there was always more treasure from infidels to plunder. That is how Mohammed always handled being broke. Allah and Mohammed may have demanded one fifth, but they always paid their mercenaries well. When one reads the many Muslim traditions about this subject, it is quite apparent that Muslims truly ascribe to the proverb: "stolen bread is sweeter." (Proverbs 9:17) As the story goes, "A horseman came [to Mohammed] and said: Apostle of Allah, I went before you and climbed a certain mountain where I saw the Hawazin tribe all together with their women, cattle, and sheep, having gathered at Hunayn... Mohammed smiled and said: That will be the booty of the Muslims tomorrow if Allah wills..."[106] The great pirate of the desert sea smiled and did all that he could do to contain himself from yelling out "Booty Ahoy!"

People often look down on career politicians for never having actually worked a real job their whole life, yet what was Mohammed's job? He was a false prophet and a pirate—the greatest cult leader of ancient times, even modern times— Mohammed rules more people while dead than he did while alive.

The Qur'an even contains an entire chapter entitled Al-Anfal, which translates as "the Booty" or "the Spoils of war." It was there actually during the famous Battle of Badr that Mohammed allegedly received a revelation that his soldiers were allowed to keep all war booty for themselves, giving only five percent to Mohammed and for the poor: "And know that out of all the booty that ye may acquire (in war), a fifth share is assigned to Allah, and to the Messenger, and to near relatives, orphans, the needy, and the wayfarer." (Qur'an 8:41)

From the book Al-Hidayah, arguably the most widely read book of Islamic jurisprudence in the Muslim world, and used as a primary text in Islamic schools and seminaries, we read about this revelation and its effect as a motivating factor in the call to jihad:

"After the Battle of Badr, the verse dealing with the booties was first revealed. The verse introduced the rule for the first time that the spoils of war would be the property of the soldiers who actually take part in the battle...That is one of the reasons why the soldiers of Islam fought tooth and nail. They would get Paradise in case of death in a Holy War, and booty in the case of conquest. Jihad is therefore the best source of all acquisitions."[107]

Mohammed attacked numerous tribes, villages and cities in order to steal their wealth to give to his new followers, so also will the Mahdi imitate Mohammed. The Mahdi, during the seven years of peace proclaimed in Islam, will use the seized property and wealth of the nations that he defeats to distribute among his followers. One of the most popular traditions regarding the Mahdi is that "He will give away wealth profusely."[108] "In those years (the time of the Mahdi) my community will enjoy a time of happiness such as they have never experienced before. Heaven will send rain upon them in torrents, the earth will not withhold any of its plants, and wealth will be available to all. A man will stand and say, 'Give to me Mahdi!' and he will say, 'Take.'"[109]

If money can't buy you love, in the Muslim mindset, Jihad provides a certain bonus and can buy all the love you want, after all, if one risks their life, don't they deserve some compensation?

WHO TAKES BRIBES?

Every time I speak in an audience with Muslims present, there is at least one who would heckle me with the words "what did the Zionists pay you?" As if no informed person would ever express support for the nation of Israel apart from being bribed with the "blood money of those evil Jews." It's the same old anti-Semitic conspiratorial worldview that has always existed among the wicked. These anti-Semitic morons only prove my case.

Why is it that apologists for booty and Jihad will always accuse the ones who aren't bought with money of being bribed? Perhaps the very things people falsely accuse you of, they support because they themselves are guilty. A thief lacks trust because he thinks that others are like him. It is said that if you point a finger, pay close attention since three of your fingers are pointed towards yourself. Booty and corruption are part of the Islamic Ten commandments. With my new faith, the Bible clearly instructs its followers with the command "you shall not steal." Neither can you "lust after your neighbor's wife." As one Muslim author described what the Mahdi does when the masses cry out "Give to me Mahdi" that "Allah will sow love of him in the hearts of all people."[110] Who is, and with whose money is he, buying the support and love of the peoples?

ANTICHRIST AND BOOTY

In Isaiah chapter 10, the same theme continues, "Woe to the Assyrian (the Antichrist), the rod of my anger, in whose hand is the club of my wrath! I send him against a godless nation; I dispatch him against a people who anger me, to seize loot and snatch plunder, and to trample them down like mud in the streets. But this is not what he intends, this is not what he has in mind; his purpose is to destroy, to put an end to many nations." (Isaiah 10:5-7)

What does the Antichrist do in this passage? He comes to "seize loot and snatch plunder." This is identical to several other descriptions of the Antichrist found in Ezekiel and Daniel. In Ezekiel 38 for instance, we read of the motives in the Antichrist's heart: "I will plunder and loot and turn my hand against the resettled ruins and the people gathered from the nations, rich in livestock and goods, living at the center of the land." (Ezekiel 38:12) In Daniel we read of the Antichrist's plans: "When the richest provinces feel secure, he will invade them...He will distribute plunder, loot, and wealth among his followers." (Daniel 11:24)

But the final clincher that the Antichrist will be a Muslim is seen in Ezekiel 38, where it describes the war against Israel as carried out by a horde of Muslim nations, and then it gives the reason—to take booty and the spoils of war: "Sheba, and Dedan, and the merchants of Tarshish, with all the young lions thereof, shall say unto thee, Art thou come to take a spoil? Hast thou gathered thy company to take a prey? To carry away silver and gold, to take away cattle and goods, to take a great spoil?" (Ezekiel 38:13)

Not only are Daniel, Isaiah, and Ezekiel speaking about the same individual, but they are all also clearly speaking about the modern nation of Israel where the people have been resettled after being re-gathered from among the nations.

Antichrist, will attempt to curry favor and gain recruits through booty and bribes. In the second century, speaking of the Antichrist, the Church Father Ireneaus said that the Antichrist "pretends that he vindicates the poor."[111]

The Palestinian Hamas supporters claim that the Palestinian Authority are corrupt for stealing all the money sent to them by Europe and the United States, while Hezbollah provides water and food to Muslims in Lebanon, and Hamas provides health care to the poor Palestinians. The spirit of the Antichrist /Mahdi is already at work.

And so once again you can see how the behavior of the Antichrist—in both his motives and his actions—is matched perfectly by both Mohammed and his Mahdi.

⨳ 33 ⨳
Both Desire
World Domination

SO WHO DESIRES TO DOMINATE THE WORLD: AMERICANS OR MUSLIMS?

The Bible teaches that the Antichrist will strive for complete world domination. The Apostle John informs us that in the Last-Days, "power will be given to him over all peoples, and tongues, and nations." (Revelation 13:7) This is confirmed by Jewish tradition as well: "He will deceive the whole world into believing that he is God and will reign over the entire world."[112] What the Bible warns us of is exactly what Islam is. The renowned Muslim scholar Mawlana Sayid Abul Ala Mawdudi from the Indian subcontinent stated: "Islam is not a normal religion like the other religions in the world, and Muslim nations are not like normal nations. Muslim nations are very special because they have a command from Allah to rule the entire world and to be over every nation in the world." "Islam is a revolutionary faith that comes to destroy any government made by man. Islam doesn't look for a nation to be in a better condition than another nation. Islam doesn't care about the land or who owns the land. The goal of Islam is to rule the entire world and submit all of mankind to the faith of Islam. Any nation or power that gets in the way of that goal, Islam will fight and destroy. In order to fulfill that goal, Islam can use every power available every way it can be used to bring worldwide revolution. This is Jihad."[113]

WHO IS THIS NIMROD?

According to Islamic tradition, the Mahdi will lead "a worldwide Revolution." It is for this reason that the Bible in Micah 5 calls the Antichrist "Nimrod"—he is the rebellious one who will "cause all, the small and the great, and the rich and the poor, and the free men and the slaves" to receive a mark on their persons. (Revelation 13:16) Some may be tempted to think that such militaristic statements do not represent the beliefs of most modern Muslims. But in fact, even many Western, so-called moderate Muslims regularly express such beliefs. Abdullah al-Araby in his book *The Islamization of America* cites a very frightening letter from one Catholic Archbishop to the Pope as he describes his speech during an interfaith dialogue. An excerpt from his letter recounts that during the meeting, an authoritative Muslim figure stood up and spoke very calmly and assuredly, "Thanks to your democratic laws, we will invade you, thanks to our religious laws, we will dominate you."[114]

ARE YOU FIGHTING ANTICHRIST?

Are you simply sitting at church services, going home and, then returning again to get serviced with "positive and uplifting messages?" Or are you a sheep who was sent amongst the wolves? There is a way that you can find out. The real evil is usually the element that makes one nervous while they are confronting or exposing it. At one conference, I was speaking on Yom-Kippur in the largest synagogue in Los Angeles. The Rabbi felt comfortable to say as part of his exchange that the New Testament was riddled with violence. When he finished speaking, I stood up and asked him "Rabbi, when was the last time, and in front of an audience, did you ever say that the Qur'an is riddled with violence?" He said "Never." He chocked when I asked him, "do you feel that the Qur'an is riddled with violence?" I asked him one last question, "Why then Rabbi did you feel comfortable to say that the New Testament is riddled with violence, yet you dared not to say the same about the Qur'an?" That Rabbi was definitely not fighting Nimrod.

Telling the truth is not easy, and false accusations can be made with great ease. In Nazi Germany, no Nazi was afraid to falsely accuse the Jews of everything under the sun, yet how many dared to stand against the lies of the Nazis? Even in America, the media was virtually silent when six million Jews were massacred. Today the same phenomenon exists. I have spoken at many Jewish events. The comments I get from them are the same old usual fears. Jews have spent hundreds of millions in building Holocaust memorials so that the world will never forget. One of the events they like to remind the world of is Crystal-Nacht—the night when the Nazis burned the synagogue in Berlin and stormed thousands of homes throughout Berlin. Yet, when the Synagogue at Joseph's Tomb was burned in Israel—a synagogue much more important to Jewish history than the Berlin Synagogue—little was said about it in the West, or even among the very ones who swear that they will never forget. It is easy to fight dead Nazis—that takes little courage. The living Islamo-Nazi movement is a much different story. Yet it is an almost identical issue—but with a more dangerous twist—Islamists do not carry out their orders from the Fuehrer, their orders come straight from Allah and his Nimrod.

Nothing in these Holocaust Museums even mentions Joseph's Tomb. Concentrating on Holocaust memorials is a good thing, but it is not enough. The best way to honor those who were lost in the Holocaust is to truly continue the fight today against the spiritual inheritors of Nazism. It is good to honor and remember the dead, but what about the living? We say "never again" while the "never again" happens right in front of our eyes—despite all the Holocaust memorials. Christians are no better—the same things that happened to Joseph's tomb happened to the Church of The Nativity, Christ's birthplace, and we looked the other way. Most Jews and Christians in the West react as they see others act around them. They seem to seek more to be accepted in order to get respect, instead of gaining respect by strength and honor. No one on earth would ever consider telling a Muslim that he has no right to Mecca. Yet when a Jew or a Christian tries to simply pray quietly on the Temple Mount, they are immediately removed. And then their fellow Jews and Christians point their fingers at them and accuse them of being troublemakers. When Ariel Sharon simply walked on the Temple Mount, a war nearly erupted, and the Muslim world went on a frenzy with the majority of the West actually blaming Sharon for the violence that ensued.

While a Jew is not even allowed to walk on the Temple mount without riots erupting, Muslims have the audacity to claim that they literally own the entire globe. If you go to the website of almost any Mosque in the United States, you will invariably see a link to the Council on American-Islamic Relations. CAIR is a Washington based Islamic group that likes to present itself as a moderate Islamic civil rights group. Yet, according to Omar Ahmed, Chairman of the Board of CAIR, "Islam isn't in America to be equal to any other faith, but to become dominant." The Qur'an should be the highest authority in America, and Islam the only accepted religion on earth."[115] This is the same Omar Ahmed who tore into the Reverend Franklin Graham for calling Islam, "an evil religion." Mr. Ahmed addressed Graham in an open statement: "Learn more about Islam and Muslims before you repeat your erroneous and divisive statements about one of the three great Abrahamic religions, Judaism, Christianity, and Islam. Such statements only sow animosity and mistrust among Americans. As a religious leader you should instead work to rebuild our national foundation instead of trying to tear it down."[116]

Accusing every one of divisiveness and racism is typical of most Muslim organizations. Yet when one looks closely at such promoters of "love," it is easy to find out that they are the very one's who promote those things they accuse others of. Such is the spirit of Islam that speaks out of both sides of its mouth; one side intended for Western consumption and the other for Muslims. I will repeat this like a broken record, *what Westerners need to know is not what these groups say in English, but what they say in Arabic, Persian, and Turkish, etc.*

Daniel Pipes a scholar of militant Islam and director of the Middle East Forum, points out the case of one prominent American Muslim's open aspirations to take over America. Pipes introduced one Ismail Al-Faruqi, a Palestinian immigrant who founded the International Institute of Islamic Thought and taught for many years at Temple University in Philadelphia. "Nothing could be greater," Al-Faruqi wrote in the early 1980's, "than this youthful, vigorous, and rich continent [of North America] turning away from its past evil and marching forward under the banner of Allahu Akbar (Allah is Great)."[117]

In England, and throughout Europe, Islam has progressed in pride-filled strength far beyond that of Islam in America. Therefore, in such a context, we see aggressive statements being made far more openly. As far back as 1989 Europeans were shocked to see thousands of Muslims openly protest in the streets of Britain, France, Germany, Belgium and the Netherlands carrying signs with the provocative slogan, "Islam—our religion today—your religion tomorrow."[118]

Dr. Siddiqi, the head of the Muslim Institute, (now the Muslim Parliament of Great Britain) states "Jihad is a basic requirement of Islam and living in Britain or having British nationality by birth or naturalization does not absolve the Muslim from his or her duty to participate in Jihad."[119] Siddiqui does not exclude Britain from the places where "armed struggle" is necessary. Jihad is obligatory everywhere. And as time has passed, the call to Jihad in Europe has progressed to the point of being proclaimed openly in the streets by radical Muslim leaders.

The call to jihad is rising in the streets of Europe...In a town north of London, during the time Tony Blair was Prime Minister, a small group of young Britons...said they would like to see Prime Minister Blair dead or deposed and an Islamic flag hanging outside No. 10 Downing Street. They swear allegiance to Osama bin Laden and his goal of toppling Western democracies to establish an Islamic super state under Sharia law, like Afghanistan under the Taliban. They call the Sept. 11 hijackers the "Magnificent 19" and regard the Madrid train bombings as a clever way to drive a wedge into Europe.

Muslims in the West regularly refer to Islam as the "religion of peace." Yet of the roughly 400 recognized terrorist groups in the world, over 90 percent are Islamist groups. Over 90 percent of the current world-fighting involves Islamist terror movements.[120] The endless goal of moderate Muslim apologists is to make the claim that the radical terrorist groups are not behaving in an Islamic way. While many nominal and liberal Muslims have a strong disdain for the murderous behavior of many of the most violent groups, the terrorists are actually carrying out a very legitimate aspect of Islam as defined by Islam's sacred texts, scholars, and representatives. They are indeed behaving in an Islamic way. They are behaving like Mohammed and his successors. While it is often said that the terrorists have high-jacked Islam, in reality it is the so-called moderate Muslims who are trying to change the true teachings of Islam. Many in the West today are calling for a "reformation" within Islam. The problem is that this reformation has already happened and the most radical forms of Islam that we are seeing today are the result—violent Islam is true Islam. Yet few have the courage to declare the obvious.

The Bible warns us that in the Last-Days, the Antichrist would be given power, "over all peoples, and tongues, and nations." (Revelation 13:7) Today throughout the world, Islam is pushing for precisely that. In the days to come, it appears as if, although for a very short time, the Muslim Antichrist will come very close to accomplishing this goal.

≋ 34 ≋
Both Lead a
Turkish-Iranian Invasion

╬══✳══╬

Who is ushering in the Apocalypse: Christians or Muslims? The Bible describes that in the Last-Days, Israel will fight against a coalition of nations that are led by Turkey and Iran. In Zechariah 9:13 the Lord declares, "I will rouse your sons, O Zion, against your sons, O Yavan." In this passage, Israel is seen fighting against Ionia or Yavan. In several Bibles, this word is translated as "Greece." But Ionia/Yavan was simply a province that was located on the west coast of modern Turkey. This is crucial, because the clear context of this battle is the return of Christ: "Then Jehovah will appear over them" and fight on their behalf. So in the End-Times, at the time when Jesus returns, the Jews (Zion) will be engaged in a war with Turkey (Yavan). In Ezekiel 38 we learn that besides Turkey, Iran will also be a key player in the Last-Days assault against Israel: "Persia...will be with them, all with shields and helmets..." Persia is simply the ancient name for modern day Iran. We already see Iran today threatening Israel. What is so amazing is that Islamic tradition also contains prophecies that picture precisely these enemies waging war against Israel in the Last-Days. The difference, as usual, is that in the Islamic account, the Turks and the Iranians are portrayed as the righteous and are being led by the Mahdi, while the Jewish people are, as usual, portrayed as the wicked.

An Islamic prophecy speaks about an army of Muslims carrying Black Banners, with the creed of Islam written across them: There is no god but Allah, Mohammed is Allah's messenger. The black banner has always been the banner of Jihad. In this tradition, the Muslims are marching from Iran and are heading toward Israel to take Jerusalem for their Mahdi. After the Muslims have conquered Jerusalem, the Mahdi is said to use the Temple Mount as his seat of authority from which he will rule over the whole earth.

When Mohammed returned after his eight year exile from his home city of Mecca, he had with him an army of 10,000 Muslims who were carrying the black banners of Jihad. Written across these banners was the word "punishment." Likewise, the Mahdi when he invades Israel, he will be accompanied by a vast army carrying the black banners of Jihad, which today are seen in all of the Islamic Jihad videos and waved at all of the Muslim rallies throughout the world.

But the pertinent aspect of the tradition of the black flags is that the two nations that are specified that will accompany the Mahdi are both Turkey and Iran. Abdul Rahman al-Wahabi in the *The Day of Wrath* states: "The final battle will be waged by Muslim faithfuls coming on the backs of horses...carrying black banners. They will stand on the East side of the Jordan River and will wage war that the earth has never seen before. The true Messiah who is the Islamic Mahdi will defeat Europe, will lead this army of Seljuks [Turks]. He will preside over the world from Jerusalem because Mecca would have been destroyed."[121] The Seljuk Empire were Turks that preceded the Ottoman Empire. It covered the region of Turkey, Northern Iran, Syria, Iraq, Southern Caucasus, and Azerbaijan. Many Islamic scholars believe that the Mahdi will lead an army of Turks and will rule over Israel.

Expounding on the tradition of the black banners, the so-called "moderate" Sheikh Kabbani, the darling of many conservative Americans, states that the armies will come from the region of Iran: "Hadith indicate that black flags coming from the area of Khorasan [Iran] will signify [that] the appearance of the Mahdi is nigh. Khorasan is in today's Iran, and some scholars have said that this Hadith means when the black flags appear from Central Asia, i.e., in the direction of Khorasan (Iran), then the appearance of the Mahdi is imminent."[122]

Do you see how the "coincidences" keep piling up? But with God, there are no coincidences, no accidents, and thankfully, no surprises! While the Bible prophesied thousands of years ago that the Antichrist would lead an army of Turks and Iranians, so also does Islamic tradition state that their Messianic Mahdi would lead an army of Turks and Iranians against Israel. The prophecy predicts the destruction of Mecca. This would give an insight into the mindset of Islam's author, the devil. Satan knows that Arabia will be destroyed, and specifically Mecca. I will discuss this future prophesied event in later chapters. But for now, we need to remember that Satan's Biblical knowledge is not to be underestimated. The Bible states that in the Last-Days, Satan will know that his time is short (Revelation 12:12). How does he know this? What source is he using to find out this information? Again, Satan knows and understands Biblical prophecy better than we do. Never underestimate your enemy, especially when he has been around for thousands of years.

❦ 35 ❧
Both Exiled as
God

HOW MAHDI PROCLAIMS TO BE GOD

So who exalts man above God: Christians or Muslims?

"Pride goes before destruction, and a haughty spirit before a fall." Proverbs 16:18.

Christians are always accused by Muslims of exalting a man (Jesus) above God. Muslims take pride in the fact that their religion is the only one that correctly gives God honor and does not associate Him with any mortal man as Christians do. But is this really true? Do Muslims exalt God above men and angels? Do Muslims honor Jesus as much as they claim? Do Muslims only treat God as perfect?

Let's start with the most proud individual that exists, the Devil himself. Satan desires to be like God, and will spare no effort to achieve this end: "I will be like the most High" (Isaiah 14:14). This declaration more than any other displays the level of arrogance and pride that defines the very essence of who Satan is.

Throughout this book, I will repeat this point—what is the most holy in Islam is the most unholy in the Bible, and what is the most holy in the Bible is the greatest blasphemy in Islam.

Muslims believe that the spirit that revealed the Qur'an to Mohammed was the angel Gabriel (*Jibril* in Arabic). The utter blasphemy of Islam can be seen in that Jibril is called by such titles as *Ameer Al-Wahi* (The princely spirit), *Khazen Al-Quds* (The keeper of holiness), *Al-Ruh Al-Ameen* (The trusted spirit) and *Al-Ruh Al-Qodos* (the Holy Spirit)—all these titles from a Biblical perspective should belong to God and God alone.

As a Muslim, I had always argued that the idea of Jesus being God was utter blasphemy since from a Muslim's viewpoint, Jesus was only a man. But, I couldn't see the hypocrisy of my own beliefs. Islam teaches that the "angel" that Mohammed encountered is the Holy Spirit! Could anything be more transparently blasphemous?

While Muslims accuse Christians of blasphemy for calling Christ God, Mohammed, whose name means "The Praised One," is often treated by Muslims with a level of respect that should only be reserved for God alone. Yet they cannot see it. Why else would he be given such a glorious title?

In Scripture, names of prophets always pertain to glorifying God, never a man. But Muslims *do* exalt Mohammed beyond any other being—either in heaven or on earth. When something as petty as a cartoon of Mohammed is published, Muslims throughout the world protest with an indignation that is unparalleled. Buildings were torched, dozens of Christians all over the world were murdered, and the cartoonist and his family now live in exile. While Muslims adamantly deny that they exalt Mohammed to the place of God, whenever you read Muslim literature in English, you will always see the acronym PBUH which stands for *Peace Be Upon Him* following Mohammed's name. But this translation is misleading and inaccurate. In Arabic the phrase translated as PBUH is: *Salla Allâhû `A'layhî wa sallam*, which means, "the prayers and salutation of Allah be upon him [Mohammed]." Sala Allahu means "Allah prayed." How could Allah pray upon Mohammed? Ibn Katheer, the classical Qur'anic commentator corroborates this: "In the Arabic language, the basic meaning of Sala is supplication. In religious terminology, Sala is used to refer to the acts of bowing and prostration."[123]

So why do Muslims leave out the fact that the word "prayer" is present in this phrase? Because the phrase that is repeated by millions of Muslims everyday, actually means that Allah himself bows before and prays to Mohammed. This same phrase is even found in the Qur'an: "Allah and His angels pray upon the prophet. O ye who believe pray upon him and salute him with a worthy salutation" (Qur'an 33:56). Mohammed is the center of praise both in heaven and on earth: "He (Allah) has subjected to you (Mohammed) whatever is in the heavens and whatever is in the earth" (Qur'an 45:12). Yet despite these entirely blasphemous claims, it is the Muslims who endlessly accuse Christians of blasphemy; in the exaltation of Mohammed to the place that only Christ or God could occupy, we see the hypocritical and Luciferian nature of Islam. While Lucifer desires to be "like God," so also has Islam exalted created beings—both demons and false prophets alike—to the place of God. But why must Mohammed exalt himself as God?

The answer is found in II Thessalonians 2: "for [that day shall not come], except there come a falling away first, and that man of sin be revealed, the son of perdition; Who oppose and exalts himself above all that is called God, or that is worshiped; so that he as God sits in the temple of God, showing himself that he is God" (II Thessalonians 2:4).

Islam has a catch 22. Satan must deny the deity of Jesus because he wants to replace Him. How can Satan take over that position as Messiah and be worshipped and at the same time accept Jesus' deity? The best argument he could create is that Jesus is a mere man. How could a man become God? He must destroy the deity of Christ and establish himself instead, yet, at the same time he wants to be worshipped as God. He could not claim that Mohammed was God if he is to deny Jesus' deity.

Satan must direct this worship to Himself. The Bible has warned us that Satan will attempt to exalt his man, the Antichrist, over Christ. Islam does exalt Mohammed above Christ and downgrades Christ; likewise, the Mahdi is believed to have the spirit of Mohammed, and so, he will have the same attributes, and will also occupy the Temple Mount. All this is written in the Islamic annals.

From the day of their birth until their death, Muslims will hear it proclaimed millions of times that Mohammed is the most perfect man that has ever existed. Not only did we believe that he is superior to Christ, but we also believed that he actually shares many attributes and names with God Himself. In a book titled *The Perfect Man*, speaking of Mohammed, we read: "This earth has seen great men in the thousands, who achieved greatness in one area or another. Some of them even left their marks on the pages of history...Some of these great men might have influenced some aspects of human life in different ways and in different manners, but none has affected it in its totality...Even the Messengers of Allah, such as Hazrat Ibrahim (Abraham), Hazrat Musa (Moses) and Hazrat Isa (Jesus) who changed the course of history and influenced the lives of men by their teachings and outstanding personal example, have not left behind much from which present or future generations can get inspiration..."[124] "Allah...describes the personality of Mohammed (PBUH) in these words: 'And you stand on an exalted standard of character' (Holy Qur'an 68: V.4). Thus in the words of Allah, the standard of his character and personality is far above that of any other creation. He possessed the best and noblest qualities of the perfect man and was like a jewel illuminating the dark environment with his radiant personality, ideal example, and glorious message."[125] Islam requires all Muslims to believe that Mohammed is literally the best of all God's creation. Thirteenth century Islamic scholar Al-Bajuri explains: "It is obligatory (wâjib) on every legally responsible person to believe that he [Mohammed] is the best of all, and one who denies it commits a sin, is guilty of innovation, and deserves to be taught a lesson."[126] In order to support this idea, Muslims often point out that throughout the Qur'an, Allah has actually shared many of his names with Mohammed. This is viewed as a clear proof that from among all of the created order, Mohammed holds a uniquely exalted status unparalleled by anything or anyone else. He is given the title Al-Maqam-Al-Mahmud (The Glorious). Muslim scholar, Dr. G. F. Haddad, in an article with a blasphemous title, *The Best of Creation* states "[There is no] other Prophet [other than Mohammed] or angel-brought-near with whom Allah Most High shared as many of His own Names in the Qur'an as He did with the Prophet. With respect to his foremost name—Mohammed—peace be upon him, consider the poetic verse of Hassan ibn Thabit (RA): 'And He drew out for him [a name] from His own Name so as to dignify him greatly: The Owner of the Throne is the Glorious [Mahmûd], and this is the Praiseworthy [Mohammed]!'" 127 In other words, the name Mohammed is not a mere name for a man, according to the Qur'an, Allah, whose name is *Mahmud*, or the Glorious or the Praised One, named Mohammed after Himself. This is quite the claim. This is a further exaltation than the name Yeshua, which in English means Jehovah is our Salvation. Mohammed literally means The Praised One—The Most Praised.

Mohammed wanted to be like Christ. The Bible teaches that only Jesus is positioned at the right hand of God where He is the only one that intercedes for mankind: "Christ Jesus is He who died, yes, rather who was raised, who is at the right hand of God, who also intercedes for us" (Romans 8:34). One will never find in the Scriptures Ezekiel, Daniel, Amos, Habakkuk, or Jeremiah called "The praised one." From a Biblical perspective, this is blasphemous.

But speaking of Mohammed, Dr. Haddad writes, "'It may be that thy Lord will raise thee to a praised estate' (Qur'an 17:79), a station which the Prophet said none but he would receive. And this is the *Station of Intercession at the right of the Glorious Throne.*"128

Do you see how Islamic theology usurps the unique position of Christ and applies it to Mohammed? Islam will do the same with the Mahdi, Mohammed's ultimate successor. Do you see how crafty Satan's plan is? Like Mohammed, the Mahdi will claim to be exalted above all of creation and will literally sit in the Temple of God in Jerusalem declaring the same titles that belong to God alone. Islam has replaced the sinless one with a prophet of Satan. Think about this fact: Islam, the fastest growing religion in the world, is and has been from its inception, the quintessence of the very antichrist spirit that John the apostle warned us of. And now its curse is upon us.

⮜ 36 ⮞
Both Ascend to Heaven

Translation:
Praise be to Allah Who enabled His slave, Mohammed,
to make the journey at night from Masjid al-Haram
in Makkah to Masjid al-Aqsa

Desiring to imitate Christ as He ascended to heaven, this fallen star was the same one which according to the Qur'an transported Mohammed from the Al-Haram mosque in Mecca to Al-Aqsa mosque (the furthest mosque) in Jerusalem. In the *Mishkatu 'l-Masabih*, Mohammed describes his ascent through the seven heavens into the icy presence of the many-veiled Allah. This journey has come to be known as *Al-Isra-Wal-Mirajj*, the ascension to heaven or "Mohammed's Night Journey."

According to this claim, "Allah ordered Jibraeel to go down with seventy thousand angels to Mohammed (pbuh), and stand by his door. Allah, Mohammed's lord ordered these angels to summon Mohammed 'Accompany him to My [Allah's] presence.' According to the tale, Mohammed was awakened in the night by the angel, who sat Mohammed on a strange creature called Al-Buraq, or 'the lightning bolt.' Every Buraq had a crown on its forehead inscribed with the words: 'There is no god only Allah, Mohammed is the Messenger of Allah.' Arise, my Master, and prepare yourself cried the Buraq! Ride on the back of the Buraq, the heavenly creature that will carry you on your journey to the Rabb (Lord) of power through the land of the angels!" He [Mohammed] went to the paradise of buraqs and there he found forty million buraqs."[129]

This story has many similarities to the story of Lucifer, master of one third of the angelic host, the bright fallen angel who is mentioned in the Bible: "For you have said in your heart: 'I will ascend into heaven, I will exalt my throne above the stars of God'...You were in Eden, the garden of God...I will ascend above the heights of the clouds; I will be like the most High" (Isaiah 14:13-14). This story is not only regarding Lucifer the angel as he is cast out of heaven, but Lucifer the Antichrist-man as he claims to have ascended to heaven, "For you have said in your heart..." In Isaiah 14:12, this Lucifer is called a man: "Is this the man who made the earth tremble?" (Isaiah 14:16) When was this Lucifer a man? And when did he claim to have ascended to heaven? This story is identical to Mohammed's alleged heavenly ascension. It will also be the claim of the Mahdi since Islam makes him the same man as Mohammed.

In *Dua'a Nudbah* (the Prayer of Weeping) the classic Muslim poem about Mohammed's night journey, we read "...and made your East and West come under his feet, and harnessed for him the Buraq, and did make him ascend towards your heavens..."[130]

In the ultimate expression of pride, like Nimrod at the Tower of Babel, Mohammed claims to have succeeded in ascending to heaven. Likewise, the Mahdi, who has the spirit of Mohammed and with Lucifer dwelling in him, will also make the same claims.

≈ 37 ≈
Both are Described as a Beautiful and Wise Bird

Within many ancient cults from the Egyptian to the Mayan, one can often find the worship of feathered birds. The Bible also describes devils and demons with such language: "Babylon the great is fallen, is fallen, and is become the habitation of devils, and the hold of every foul spirit, and a cage of every unclean and hateful bird" (Revelation 18:2).

Tawoos al-Malaeka (the peacock of the angels), as its described in the annals of Islam is the name that Islamic tradition gives to Mohammed's heavenly transport that supposedly carried Mohammed into the seventh heaven and then ordered him to rule over all of mankind and the multitudes of demons.

God in the Bible addresses Satan with: "You had the seal of perfection, full of wisdom and perfect in beauty" (Ezekiel 28:12). This description is identical to the angel Mohammed encountered and described in the Qur'anic chapter of *Al-Najm* "the Star" as, "One Mighty in Power, the One endued with wisdom" (Qur'an 56:5,6). Is this coincidence?

Even the precious stones mentioned with regard to this angelic heavenly transport Al-Buraq, seem to fit what is written in Scripture regarding Satan: "His color was that of a peacock whose plumage was set with red rubies and corals, on which sat a white head of musk on a neck of amber. His ears and shoulders were of pure white pearls attached with golden chains, each chain decorated with glittering jewels. His saddle was made of silk lined with silver and gold threads. His back was covered with green emerald and his halter was pure peridot."[131]

Now compare the description of Mohammed's strange spirit guide with the description of Satan in the Bible "every precious stone was your covering: the ruby, the topaz, and the diamond; the beryl, the onyx, and the jasper; the lapis lazuli, the turquoise, and the emerald; and the gold, the workmanship of your setting and sockets was in you" (Ezekiel 28:13).

Many of Satan's descriptions almost match perfectly the descriptions of the Buraq, Mohammed's stead, that he rode to ascend to heaven. But beyond the ascension into heaven, this being, the Buraq is also described specifically as an angel of light.

Eventually Satan will be judged for "the iniquities of your trading" (Ezekiel 28:18). What does Satan trade in? The answer to this is simple—false religions and cults. The Muslim *Sufis* identify the spirit that inspired the Qur'an as the angel Jibril and refer to him as an angelic peacock: "God created the Spirit in a form of a peacock."

∼ 38 ∼
Both are
Beings of Lights

✦

The root word of Buraq (Mohammed's spirit guide) is "Brq" which means "lightning bolt" or "glowing light." The Bible describes Lucifer as "burning like a torch (or lamp)" (Revelation 8:10). This is exactly what the Qur'an describes Allah as: "a lamp." Allah in the Qur'an dedicates chapter Al-Noor (The Light) as the most significant description of Allah:

> "Allah is the *light of the heavens and the earth*; a likeness of His light is as a niche in which is a lamp, the lamp is in a glass, (and) the glass is as it were a *brightly shining star*, lit from a blessed olive-tree, neither Eastern nor Western, whose oil is nigh luminous though fire scarce touched it. Light upon light! Allah does guide whom He will to His light: Allah sets forth parables for men: and knows all things" (Qur'an 24:35-36).

Light of the heavens, and *brightly shining star* or luminous, are satanic titles—"Lucifer" literally means the *luminous one*. Satan desires to be the bright shining star.

Even the Mahdi is identified by the prophet Mohammed as the "peacock of all angels and of the dwellers of the heavenly realm, he is dressed and adorned with the cloaks of light.[132]

"Thus says the great prophet (Allah's prayers and supplications be upon him) Mahdi is the peacock of all angels and of the dwellers of the heavenly realm, he is dressed and adorned with the cloaks of light."

قال الرسول الأعظم (ص) المهدي كطاووس لأهل الجنة زينة لعينه كالبيب النور

Above Arabic script:
"Thus says the great prophet (Allah's prayers and supplications be upon him) Mahdi is the peacock of all angels and of the dwellers of the heavenly realm, he is dressed and adorned with the cloaks of light."

This "lightning bolt" described by Mohammed is described by Jesus: "I saw Satan fall like lightning from heaven" (Luke 10:18). The word Lucifer means "bearer of light," "luminous," or "the morning star." The Bible warns us regarding the manner in which Satan disguises himself "as an angel of light" (II Corinthians 11:14). John as well describes him: "I saw a star fallen from heaven to the earth. To him was given the key to the bottomless pit" (Revelation 9:1). This "star" is referred to as a "him," a person and not an actual star. The Qur'an even calls Allah "The Lord of star of Sirius" (Qur'an, chapter of *The Star*, 53:49).

The same star is described in Revelation 8:10: "Then the third angel sounded: And a great star fell from heaven burning like a torch (or lamp), and it fell on the third of the rivers and on the springs of water." The "waters" is likely allegoric of "peoples, multitudes, nations, and different tongues" which Satan spiritually destroys. (Revelation 17:15)

~39~
Both are
Pride-Filled

✦—◈—✦

Out of all the sinful and evil behaviors the Bible condemns, pride tops them all. The Qur'an on the other hand considers *Al-Mutakabbir*, which literally means, *The Most Proud One*, or the *One filled with pride*, as one of the 99 beautiful names of Allah. Describing how important pride is to Allah, He even cloaks Himself with it: "Pride is My Wear, Supremacy is My Dress, I will break anyone who vies with me, and for them I do not care."[133] And, "Glory be to the One who rightfully deserves to be called the Most Proud, He is Allah."[134] However, such attire is an abomination to God "I will punish the king of Assyria [Antichrist] for the willful pride of his heart and the haughty look in his eyes" (Isaiah 10:12).

Just as Allah links Himself with Pride, God links pride as the main behavior of 'the imposter' and the 'greatest adversary,' Satan: "Son of man, say to the ruler of Tyre [Antichrist] 'This is what the Jehovah, the Sovereign says' 'In the pride of your heart you say, 'I am''" (Ezekiel 28:2).

Muslims exulting in Allah's pride are evident from their declaration "Allahu Akbar" (Allah is greater!). It is usually yelled out loud in unison by Jihadists as a gesture of triumph. They are also the first words recited by the Muezzin as he cries aloud from the tip of minarets. It is the spark of every rally when one ignites the crowd shouting the word "Takbîr" (glorify His pride), the crowd then must respond "Allâhu Akbar" (Allah is greater, Allah, the most Proud). Every Muslim glorifies Allah in this manner: "Majesty and glory belong to Allah alone. This is pride in a god in the purest sense of the word."[135]

Both are Lords of This World
And The Underworld

Another title of Allah, *Malek-rab-Al-A'lameen* means "The Lord of the worlds" that is, this world, and the underworld: "O Allah, the Lord of the seven heavens and what-ever it shadows. Lord of the two worlds and whatever it is carrying. Lord of the wind and wherever it goes. Lord of the devils and whoever is unguided. I ask you all the good bless-ings in this country and the best of its people and the best of whatever it has. I seek refuge from all the evils of this country, the worst of its people and the worst of what it has."[136] Allah seems to have already been described in the Bible as "The god of this world who has blinded the minds of unbelievers, so that they cannot see the light of the gospel" (II Corinthians 4:4). "Now is the judgment of this world: now shall the prince of this world be cast out" (John 12:31). Mohammed definitely connected to the Lord of the Air and the god of demons.

In Ibn Ishaq's classic biography of Mohammed, we find an account of Mohammed praying to his lord: "O Allah, Lord of the heavens and what they overshadow, and Lord of the Devils and what into error they throw, and Lord of the winds and what they winnow, we ask Thee for the booty of this town and its people. We take refuge in Thee." Like the Antichrist in the Bible who is addressed the same way as Satan, Mohammed carries the same attributes as Allah: "Mohammed is the exemplar to both worlds, the guide of the descendants of Adam. He is the sun of creation, the moon of the celestial spheres, the all-seeing eye; the torch of knowledge, the candle of prophecy, the lamp of the nation and the way of the people; the commander-in-chief on the parade-ground of the Law; the gen-eral of the army of mysteries and morals; The lord of the world and the glory of 'But for thee;' ruler of the earth and of the celestial spheres."[137] Always, Mohammed is not far from such attributes given to His Lord: "He, and only he, is without question the most excellent of mankind; he and only he, is the confidant of God. The seven heavens and the eight gardens of paradise were created for him. He is both the eye and the light in the light of our eyes. He was the key of guidance to the two worlds and the lamp that dispelled the darkness thereof."[138]

This Lord of the Worlds is well-defined in Al-Fatiha (the opening) first chapter, and the most recited from the Qur'an: "In the name of Allah, the Merciful, and Compassionate. Praise be to Allah, Lord of the two worlds; the Merciful the compassionate, King of the Day of Judgment, You we worship and You we call upon. Guide us along the straight path. The path of those to whom You have given grace, Not those deserving anger nor those who have gone astray" (Qur'an, Al Fatiha).

But even more amazing is the that Allah is even claimed to be the Lord of the demons (Jinn in Arabic): "This is a Message sent down from the Lord of men and jinn (demons)" (Qur'an 69:43); "I only created jinn (demons) and man to worship me" (Qur'an 51:56). According to the Qur'an, demons are even said to have heard the Qur'an recited and decided to follow Allah as their lord. In this passage, the demons are actually declaring the greatness of Islam: "since we (the demons) have listened to the guidance of the Qur'an, we have accepted Islam: and any who believes in his Lord [Allah] has no fear of loss, force, or oppression" (Qur'an 72:13). How could Muslims follow a religion followed by demons.

Then in Qur'an 72:1-8 the Jinn describe their view of the Qur'an: "Say (O Mohammed): It is revealed unto me that a company of the Jinn gave ear, and they said: Lo! It is a marvelous Qur'an which guides unto righteousness, so we believe in it and we ascribe unto our Lord no partner. And (we believe) that He, exalted, be the glory of our Lord! Hath taken neither wife nor son, and that the foolish one among us used to speak concerning Allah an atrocious lie. And lo! We had supposed that humankind and jinn would not speak a lie concerning Allah; and indeed (O Mohammed) individuals of humankind used to invoke the protection of individuals of the jinn so that they increased them in revolt (against Allah); And indeed they supposed, even as ye suppose, that Allah would not raise anyone (from the dead), and (the Jinn who had listened to the Qur'an said): We had sought the heaven but had found it filled with strong warders and meteors" (Qur'an, Al-Jinn).

≈ 41 ≈

Both Are Called The "Son of The Dawn"

In the Qur'an, Allah is described as the Lord of the Dawn and the "bringer of evil." "Say I seek refuge with [Allah], the Lord of the Dawn from the mischief of the evil that He [Allah] has created... from the mischievous evil of Darkness as it becomes intensely dark" (Qur'an 114:1-3).

Right: "I seek refuge with [Allah] the Lord of the Dawn from the mischief of the evil that He [Allah] has created... from the mischievous evil of Darkness as it becomes intensely dark" (Qur'an 114:1-3).

Seeking refuge in Allah the Lord of the Dawn (Morning Star) from the evil entities he created is similar to what the Shamans do to ward off evil. This same Son of the Dawn, who the Bible attributes to all evil, havoc, and destruction of the earth: "How you have fallen from heaven, O morning star, son of the dawn! You have been cast down to the earth, you who once laid low the nations!" (Isaiah 14:12)

≈ 42 ≈
Both Are Afflicters

‡══·✳·══‡

Some Muslims get queasy when the 91st name of Allah Al-Darr is mentioned and even go as far as rejecting such title. Al-Darr happens to be the same word used to address vermin and anything nasty. It literally means the causer of harm, the afflicter and creator of all suffering. In the Bible, Satan is portrayed as the one who afflicts people with calamity and at times even with sickness and disease. His son of perdition, the Antichrist, is portrayed as one who afflicts the saints, and "the desolator." He is described as "the abomination" and "one who makes desolate" anything that is holy. He sets himself on the Temple of God which sparks the wrath of God to be poured on him: "until the full determined end is poured out on the desolator" (Dan 9:27). The prophet Job in the Bible had to endure the wrath of Satan, the afflicter. The term "afflicted by Job" became synonymous to testing our patience with Satan's afflictions. Would Job deny God? Can Satan win?

Despite Muslim uneasiness and rejection of such title, would any Muslim subtract one of the ninety-nine names of the beautiful names of Allah, to end up with only ninety eight? This in itself would cause some harm to the validity of Islam. Imagine if one uses such a name in the common usage of the names of Allah as customary for Muslim naming. Muslims love to connect the word "slave of" with every name and title of Allah—Abdul-Rahman (Slave of the Merciful), Abdul-Malek (Slave of The King), Abdul-Rauof (Slave of the Kind One), Abdul-Jabbar (Slave of The Mighty One, as in Kareem Abdul-Jabbar, the famous basketball player). Yet when it comes to Al-Darr, one would never ever find a Muslim with the name Abdul-Darr, How could such a name be one of the most beautiful names of Allah? Muslims know deep inside their inner soul that something is definitely wrong. Allah in Islam is understood to be the producer of not only good, but also of evil.

43

Both Are
Cast Out of Heaven

✦━━✦✵✦━━✦

The casting of Lucifer, the rebellious 'angel of light' out of heaven, along with his fallen angels, has a similar account in the Qur'an, with a slight adjustment—this angel is given the title of deity 'the Holy Spirit' and is commissioned to dispatch the host of angels down to earth commencing the advent of Islam and the new revelations of the Qur'an: "Say, The Holy Spirit has brought it (the Qur'an) down from your Lord, truthfully, to assure those who believe, and to provide a beacon and good news for all who submit" (Qur'an 16:102). Not surprisingly the one to dispatch this "Holy Spirit" to earth is none other than the lord of this world: "This (Qur'an) is a revelation from the Lord of the worlds" (Qur'an 26:192).

Upon my detailed investigation of Lucifer in the Bible, it always ended up matching all the attributes given to Allah in the Qur'an—if Lucifer is described in the Bible as an angel, he seems to fit the angel Mohammed encountered—if Lucifer claims to be God, so does Mohammed's angel claim attributes that belong to deity, for he is as Islam describes, "indivisible from Allah" who is breathed through Allah into all the living, becoming the agent of creation. To top this all, even the Biblical account of Lucifer being cast out of heaven, seems to have an account in the Qur'an—considered the holiest event in Islam:

> "We have sent it down to thee in the Night of Destiny, what do you know of this 'Night of Destiny?' The Night of Destiny is better than a thousand months. In it, the angelic hosts descend along with the [Holy] Spirit by command of their Lord [Allah], Peace shall it be until the rising of the Dawn (Morning Star)" (Qur'an 97:1-5).

Such blasphemies litter Mohammed's revelations. Muslims rarely question as to who is this "spirit" angel, the leader of this "descending angelic host." How, and why does he "descend to earth," and what is this "rising of this Morning Star?" Why is Allah "their Lord," proclaimed as the "Lord of these angels"? How could this angelic spirit be given a name of deity "the Holy Spirit"?

Allah is Rabul-Falaq (Lord of the Dawn) and it is the same title given to Lucifer in the Bible. Allah in the Qur'an proclaimed that His Spirit, the angelic medium, descended to earth with His angelic host as the holiest day in Islam. A similar account is described in the Bible: "The great dragon was hurled down—that ancient serpent called the devil, or Satan, who leads the whole world astray. He was hurled to the earth and his angels with him" (Revelation 12:9). This dark event parallels Islam's Night of Destiny known in Islam to have dual fulfillments: not only did this event commission Mohammed to spread Islam after the angel nearly choked him to death, but is also a night destined when the sky splits asunder and the angelic hosts come down to earth to proclaim judgment and begin the advent of Mahdi. Yet this End-Times event is described in the Bible with Lucifer, son of the morning (Isaiah 14:12)—an angel who is finally cast out and then possesses a "man" (v. 16) the Bible calls Antichrist. In Revelation 12:4, Satan and his fallen angels are cast out; the dragon, "drew a third of the stars of heaven and threw them to the earth." These same stars are the fallen angels: "And it waxed great, even to the host of heaven; and it cast down some of the host and of the stars to the ground, and stamped upon them" (Daniel 8:10). The prophecy concerning Petra in the land of Edom, has the same account with a similar long term application: "Though thou exalt thyself as the eagle, and though thou set thy nest among the stars, thence will I bring thee down, Says the LORD" (Obadiah 1:4). The same being is in Isaiah 14: "I will exalt my throne above the stars of God" (Isaiah 14:13).

Muslims everywhere need to ask themselves "why would this supremely holy event in Islam, so perfectly parallel an event that the Bible describes as being so completely evil?"

MUSLIM HOLY SPIRIT—DEIFICATION OF AN ANGEL

Islam was created by the author of confusion and knows little regarding the true God, the Holy Spirit, or the nature of God since the religion was so deeply influenced by the Gnostic and Christian heretics of Mohammed's time. On the one hand, Islam claims that the "Holy Spirit" is not God, on the other hand, it accuses anyone of heresy, who claims that the Holy Spirit was created: "Whoever says it [the Holy Spirit] is created (makhluk) is a heretic..." (Ibn Hanbal).

A major dilemma in Islam is that if indeed this Holy Spirit is God, then Islam would have confessed a similarity to Christianity by admitting one of the Godhead of the Trinity. This would be an anathema since Islam is vehemently anti-Trinity.

John of Damascus appropriately challenges Islam: "if Christians are accused by Muslims to have Shirk (associating "partners" with God) then, according to the Qur'an, Muslims should be accused of mutilating God by separating Him from His Word and His Spirit." This challenge still stands today.

If the Holy Spirit in Islam is an angel, the Bible describes Lucifer as an angel of light proclaiming himself as god. This deification of an angel is not absent from Islam even though Muslims deny this—most are unaware of it—the function of this angelic "Holy Spirit" in Islam is not some small function—for Islam ascribes to him attributes and acts exclusive to deity. This angel in the Qur'an is even involved in all creation by breathing life into the mother's womb: "But he fashioned him in due proportion, and breathed into him something of his Spirit. And he gave you (the faculties of) hearing and sight and feeling (and understanding): little thanks do ye give" (Qur'an, 32:9). "When I have fashioned him [Adam] (in due proportion) and breathed into him of My Spirit, fall ye down in obeisance unto him" (Qur'an, 38:72). "And (remember) her [Mary] who guarded her chastity: We breathed into her of Our Spirit, and made her and her son [Jesus] a sign for all peoples" (Qur'an, 21:91).

If this spirit was not claimed by Muslims to be God, how could it be involved in the act of creating, and how can a created being create? It is no wonder why Islam is so vague in explaining this spirit angel that Allah kept his nature as a secret—a mystery Muslims need not to question. When Mohammed was asked to explain exactly this angel's true identity: "They will ask thee concerning the Spirit. Say: The Spirit is by command of my Lord, and of knowledge you have been shown but a little" (Qur'an 17:85).

≈44≈
Both Are The
"Lord of Demons"

✦┼═══╋═✳═╋═══┼✦

Muslims are to seek refuge in what the Qur'an names Rabul-Falaq "the Lord of the Dawn." But from what are they seeking refuge? Ironically, it is against "the mischief of the evil that He (Allah) created...the mischievous evil of Darkness as it becomes intensely dark" (Qur'an 114:1-3). Allah is the producer of the mischievous evil of darkness, the very entity the Bible warns us we wrestle against: "the rulers of the darkness of this world" (Ephesians 6:12). These are indeed the works of "the prince of demons" (Matthew 12:24).

Only through the God of the Bible, was I able to see that Mohammed was standing on sinking sand and sought "refuge in the Lord of men and Jinn (demons), the King of men and demons, the God of men and demons" (Qur'an 114:1). Jinn are demonic "fiery spirits." This was the ruthless God of Islam, so ruthless that He said: "I swear by those who violently tear out souls and drag them to destruction" (Qur'an 79:1). Why would Allah swear by angels that tear out and destroy souls? Mawaridi states that these are the angels of the air which penetrate back and forth from heaven to earth. They are those who allegedly manage the affairs of Allah both in the heavenly and earthly realms. Biblically speaking, these Jinn can be none other than the hosts of demons that serve under their prince—the prince of the power of the air—who is none other than Satan.

～45～
Both Are Possessed

✦

The Qur'an was not inspired—inspiration is conveying God's thoughts and words, not dictating them. Each individual author of the books of the Bible was entirely conscious and brought to the Scriptures his own individual human style and personality. God used the human agents as His vessels, but He did not literally override them. The Qur'an was dictated to Mohammed; however, this is not inspiration—rather it is known as possession. All Muslims claim that, "The Prophet was purely passive—indeed unconscious: the book was in no sense his, neither it's thought, nor language, nor style: all was of Allah, and the Prophet was merely a recording pen."[139]

It is no wonder why Karen Armstrong became an apologist for Islam. Armstrong, a former nun who had similar experiences like Mohammed, with seizure-like religious hallucinations gives an account of the manner of Mohammed's initial encounter with the angel in the cave of Hira:

"Mohammed was torn from his sleep in his mountain cave and felt himself overwhelmed by a devastating divine presence. Later he explained this ineffable experience by saying that an angel had enveloped him in a terrifying embrace so that it felt as though the breath was being forced from his body. The angel gave him the curt command: 'iqra!' 'Recite!' Mohammed protested that he could not recite; he was not a kahin, one of the ecstatic prophets of Arabia. But, he said, the angel simply embraced him again until, just as he thought he had reached the end of his endurance, he found the divinely inspired words of a new scripture pouring forth from his mouth."[140] Alfred Guillaume however, in *The Life of Mohammed*, mentions that it was not actually until the third time that the "angel" had strangled Mohammed, demanding that he recite, that he finally did so."[141]

True divine encounters in the Bible always begin with "Do not be afraid" (Genesis 15:1, 26:24, 46:3, Daniel 8:15-19, 10:12, 19, Matthew 28:5, 10, Luke 1:13; 26-31, 2:10, Revelation 1:17). Even Mohammed himself believed that he was demon possessed and became distraught, even suicidal: "So I [Mohammed] read it, and he [Jibril] departed from me. And I awoke from my sleep, and it was as though these words were written on my heart... I thought, 'Woe is me poet or possessed...I will go to the top of the mountain and throw myself down that I may kill myself and gain rest.' So I went forth to do so and then when I was midway on the mountain, I heard a voice from heaven saying, O Mohammed! Thou are the apostle of God and I am Gabriel.'"[142] The reference to "poet or possessed" comes from Mohammed's belief that poets created their poetry under the inspiration of demons. At-Tabari, Islam's renowned historian explains: "The pre-Islamic Arabs believed in the demon of poetry, and they thought that a great poet was directly inspired by demons..."[143]

After the terrible experience, Mohammed returned home to his wife Khadija. Terribly disturbed, he: "returned with the Inspiration, his neck muscles twitching with terror till he entered upon Khadija and said 'Cover me! Cover me!' They covered him till his fear was over and then he said, O Khadija, what is wrong with me?' Then he told her everything that had happened and said, 'I fear that something may happen to me.'"[144]

It was not only Mohammed who suspected a demonic source behind his revelations, many of Mohammed's contemporaries also believed that his revelatory experiences were demonically inspired. The Qur'an records the following accusations that were leveled against Mohammed: "Yet they turn away from him and say: 'Tutored by others, a man possessed!'" (Qur'an 44:14) "What! Shall we give up our gods for the sake of a Poet possessed?" (Qur'an 37:36) The accusations became so bad that Allah even had to come to Mohammed's defense: "It (the Qur'an) is no poet's speech: scant is your faith! It is no soothsayer's divination: how little you reflect! It is revelation from the Lord of the Universe (Qur'an 69:41, 42). "No, your compatriot (Mohammed) is not mad. He saw him (Jibril) on the clear horizon. He does not grudge the secrets of the unseen, nor is this the utterance of an accursed devil" (Qur'an 81:22-25).

Many scholars were convinced that Mohammed was either an epileptic or demon possessed—or both. South African missionary John Gilchrist comments: "It should be pointed out that men can be subjected to a different type of seizure which very closely resembles epilepsy. During the life of Jesus a young boy was brought to him who was an epileptic (Matthew 17:15) and who suffered extreme forms of epilepsy (he would suddenly fall down, convulse, and be unable to speak). There is no doubt, however, that this epilepsy was not natural but demonically induced as all three records of the incident (in Matthew 17, Mark 9, and Luke 9) state that Jesus exorcised the unclean spirit in the child and healed the boy. Gilchrist continues: "Throughout the world missionaries have related cases of precisely this nature. To this day such phenomena are not uncommon among oriental ecstatic and mystics and they are widely reported."[145] The apostle Peter describes the experience of the authors of Biblical Scripture by referring to men who "spoke from God as they were, moved by the Holy Spirit" (II Peter 1:21). None of them however, ever questioned the source of their revelations; they never once asked if it was God or a demon that was speaking to them.

For well over a year, Mohammed admits that he was even "bewitched", whereby he would slip into an ecstatic spell and imagined that he was actually engaging in sexual relations with his wives, when he was in fact doing no such thing. In a reliable Hadith, Mohammed's favorite wife Aiesha recalls: "Magic was worked on Allah's Apostle so that he used to think that he had sexual relations with his wives while he actually had not."[146]

≈46≈
Both Practice
Beheading

≈✦≈

Beheading is the very heritage of Islam, carried out in God's name, and is exactly what the Bible warned us of: "And I saw the souls of those who had been beheaded because of their testimony for Jesus and because of the Word of God" (Revelation 20:4), and in a time that: "when anyone who kills you will think he is offering a service to God. They will do such things because they have not known the Father or Me. I have told you this, so that when the time comes you will remember that I warned you" (John 16:1-4). If only the Church would heed Christ's warning "remember that I warned you." This is hardly an atheist system—the only religion that still practices these is Islam.

If Westerners think that the well-publicized beheading of Nicholas Berg in 2004 with images of masked Muslims standing behind bound hostages in Iraq, Saudi Arabia, and elsewhere is their acquaintance to Islamic Terrorism, they need to think again. Rarely do Westerners examine Islam's history of the beheadings of hundreds of thousands of Christian Armenians and Christians from Smyrna. The future will prove of millions of Christians yet to be beheaded "in the name of Jesus."

Imagine all these suffering like the Wall Street Journal reporter Daniel Pearl did in 2002. To most Westerners however, Pearl was an anomaly. But was it? In 2004, Muslim beheadings seemed to have developed into quite a trend. For months there was just about weekly, a new story of foreigners and Christians being beheaded by Islamic radicals. Since that time, the beheadings have not stopped. In fact, it is likely that within weeks of your reading this, there will be a new beheading that will be posted by some Muslim group on the internet for the whole world to see.

But beheading in Islam by any means is not a new phenomenon, neither is it new to the so-called "hijacked Islam," as President Bush puts it, "the wholesome and wonderful religion of peace." And neither was it as apologists for Islam claim, "not an officially sanctioned Islamic practice," especially when beheading was carried out by its founder and chief—Mohammed: "Abdullah cut off Abba Hakam's head and carried it to his master. 'The head of the enemy of Allah!' exclaimed Mohammed joyously;—'Allah! There is no other god but He!'–'Yeah! There is no other!' responded Abdullah, as he cast the severed head at the Prophet's feet. 'It is more acceptable to me;' cried Mohammed, hardly able to contain his joy, 'than the choicest camel in all Arabia.'"[147]

Sadly the blood lust of Mohammed did not stop here. In 627 A.D. while laying a siege around the Jewish village of Qurayzah, the village surrendered and witnessed Allah at work, whose name is recited by every Muslim as the compassionate, the most merciful— ordered Mohammed to dig the infamous trenches. Ibn Ishaq, Islam's earliest biographer of Mohammed recounts, "Then they (Qurayza) surrendered...then he sent for them and struck off their heads in those trenches as they were brought out to him in batches... They were 600 or 700 in all, though some put the figures as high as 800 or 900...This went on until the apostle made an end to them."[148] Those were not enough, soon after this incident, Mohammed had 400 more Jews beheaded, then, another campaign of beheading festivals took place as he re-entered the city of Mecca, "Do you see the soldiers from Quraysh (from Mecca)?" He asked. "Go and pluck their heads." Would any Muslim scholar say that Mohammed slipped? Was there a confession like that of King David after killing Uriah the Hittite? If only that been the case. Even the most 'moderate' of Muslims when asked of this ghastly deed, they must justify these actions, for condemning these would deny Mohammed's prophetic career. This exemplary prophet, the model for all humanity, and whose words and deeds considered authoritative and inspired by Allah Himself: "If you love Allah, then follow me [Mohammed]" (Sura 3:31). "Ye have indeed in the Apostle of Allah a beautiful pattern of conduct for anyone whose hope is in Allah and the Final Day" (Sura 33:21). So was beheading ordained and even commanded for all the faithful till Mahdi's kingdom come. Even the trees will obey him and snitch on the last Jew alive. As the prominent Muslim Sheikh Qaradawi stated Mohammed's will on that final Judgment- Day: "Ya Muslim (O Muslim), Ya Abd-Allah" (O slave of Allah) Hatha Yahudi" (Here is a Jew) "Ta'ala waqta' ra'sah" (come and chop off his head).

All of Mohammed's disciples beheaded, hundreds of examples can be sited—Hadith, Muslim poetry, both ancient and modern, Muslim history, current events, and even graf- fiti *"We knock on the gates of heaven with the skulls of Jews,"* written on walls throughout Sharia dominated cultures.

The favorite of Muslims; Khalid bin al-Walid who earned the title, *The unsheathed Sword of Allah* who fought under Mohammed's leadership and under the first Caliph Abu-Bakr, was dispatched to extended Islam's peace proposal to the people of Persia: "In the name of Allah, the Compassionate, the Merciful. From Khalid bin al-Walid to the governors of Persia. Embrace Islam so that you may be safe. If not, make a covenant with me and pay the Jizyah tax. Otherwise, I have brought you a people who love death just as you love drinking wine."[149] When the Christians and Persians from Ullays turned down this peace offer, Khalid engaged them with an unfettered assault. The battle was so fierce that Khalid made a vow to Allah during the battle that if he defeated these resistors, he would make the canal that surrounded their village literally run with their blood. When the outcome was in Khalid's favor, it actually took a day and a half to behead all of the captives. The obstacle for Khalid was that the ravine of blood coagulated and Khalid's troops were forced to eventually release water into the canal in order that it would run red with the blood of the slain lest Khalid's vow be left unfulfilled.[150]

Some of Khalid's men wanted to meticulously fulfill his wishes "Even if you were to kill all the population of the earth, their blood would still not run... Therefore send water over it, so that you may fulfill your oath." Khalid had blocked the water from the canal. Now Khalid brought the water back, so that it flowed with spilled blood. Owing to this it has been called Blood Canal to this day."[151]

Even the prophet's grandkids did not escape the blade. Amir Taheri, an Iranian born journalist, in an article from the New York Post, May 14, 2004 entitled *Chopping Heads*, outlines several other incidents throughout Islam's history of the practice of beheading: "In 680, the Prophet's favorite grandson, Hussein bin Ali, had his head chopped off in Karbala, central Iraq, by the soldiers of the Caliph Yazid. The severed head was put on a silver platter and sent to Damascus, Yazid's capital, before being sent further to Cairo for inspection by the Governor of Egypt. The Caliph's soldiers also cut off the heads of all of Hussein's 71 male companions, including the one-year-old baby boy Ali-Asghar."[152]

Thus the pattern had been established and the principle that Mohammed had modeled now came back and touched his own family. Eventually stories of beheading came to fill Islam's history. Andrew Bostom, editor of *The Legacy of Jihad* points out that in the late fifteen century: "Babur, the founder of the Mughal Empire, who is revered as a paragon of Muslim tolerance by modern revisionist historians," recorded the following account of his own defeat of his infidel enemies: "Those who were brought in alive [having surrendered] were ordered beheaded, after which a tower of skulls was erected in the camp." While Islam's adventures in India, are rarely ever discussed in today, the estimated number of the slain in India alone was eighty million.

Skipping forward to a slightly more modern era, Taheri continues: "In 1842 the Afghani Muslims overtook the British garrison in Kabul and beheaded over 2,000 men, women, and children. The heads were placed on sticks around the city as decorations."[153] The practice continued during the 1980's, in Afghanistan, where an estimated 3,000 Soviet troops were beheaded by the Afghani Mujahideen, also common throughout the Iranian revolution: "In 1992, the mullahs sent a 'specialist' to cut off the head of Shapour Bakhtiar, the Shah's last prime minister, in a suburb of Paris. When the news broke, Hashemi Rafsanjani, then president of the Islamic Republic, and the example given by many Westerners as 'a moderate Muslim,' publicly thanked Allah for having allowed 'the severing of the head of the snake.'"[154] Taheri even makes reference to one Algerian "specialist" nicknamed Momo le nain (Mohammed the midget) who was recruited by an Islamic group known as the GIA specifically for the purpose of chopping off heads: "In 1996 in Ben-Talha, a suburb of the capital Algiers, Momo cut off a record 86 heads in one night, including the heads of more than a dozen children. In recognition of his exemplary act of piety, the GIA sent him [on a free trip] to Mecca for pilgrimage. Last time we checked, Momo was still at large somewhere in Algeria."[155] Taheri likewise relates the situation in Pakistan where, "Rival Sunni and Shi'ite groups have made a habit of sending chopped off heads of each other's activists by special delivery. According to one estimate, over 400 heads have been chopped off and mailed since 1990."[156] And beyond all of these very incriminating examples there are also the government sanctioned beheadings that take place weekly in Saudi Arabia after Friday prayers just outside the mosques. Over the past two decades, the Saudis have decapitated at least 1,100 people for alleged crimes ranging from drug running to witchcraft and apostasy, and in 2003: "The Saudi government beheaded 52 men and one woman... A condemned convict is brought into the courtyard; hands tied, and forced to bow before an executioner, who swings a huge sword amid cries from onlookers of 'Allahu Akbar!' Arabic for 'God is greater.'"[157]

What takes place during one of these beheadings is simply one of the most macabre things that you can imagine. With a very deliberate sawing and hacking motion, the head is severed. The "infidel" is heard screaming and gurgling until the knife passes through the throat in the exact same manner as a ritual animal sacrifice. In Islam, animal sacrifice is usually referred to as "Udhiyah or Dhabh." On Eid al-Adha (Day of Sacrifice), a Muslim holiday held during the Hajj (pilgrimage), an animal is often sacrificed. Before the animal is slaughtered, the knife wielder says Bismallah (In the Name of Allah) while others chant Yah Allah! (Oh Allah)

Like the sacrificial goat or calf, the human sacrifice is often seen sitting bound before his captors, shivering with fear. It is not unlike any other such sacrificial ritual that may have occurred in various Middle Eastern pagan cults over four thousand years ago. Only Islam, among all of the world religions, has adherents that still practice overt human sacrifice. With regard to the recent spate of ritualized beheadings that have been broadcast by Islamic fundamentalist groups, the language, the manners, and the rituals are identical to Islamic traditional animal slaughter, and all that with cries of Allahu Akbar. So, who is this Allah and what is this Allahu Akbar (Allah is greater), greater than who? What is so great with screaming this phrase while beheading Nicholas Berg, the Jewish-American contractor, Daniel Pearl another Jew, and Kim-Sun-il, the Korean translator and evangelical Christian? All three of these men loved Muslims and even attempted to help them. To my friends in the West; this is Islam. To my friends in the East, a choice needs to be made— the love of Allah or the love of Jehovah? This is the question. I have made my choice— there is no God like Jehovah.

IN SATAN'S FOOTSTEPS

Ritual beheading is nothing new—the Mayan civilization practiced human sacrifice with rituals of plucking out hearts and chopping off heads. Yet Islam today is not altogether unlike any one of these ancient pagan civilizations with all of the beheading and heart plucking. The one stipulation however is this—today the whole world must call this satanic cult a "religion of peace."

My Son, Theodore Shoebat has written a book entitled *In Satan's Footsteps*. I learned more from my 15-year-old son's book than I learned from nutty professors during my college days. He connects all evil to one source—Satan: "I will never forget my first trip to the Pyramids in Chichen Itza Mexico, seeing the ritual altars and the gigantic water-hole where they would throw the bodies. Sure, the Mayans had acquired great scientific knowledge, yet their science was intertwined in evil that was so deep it's shocking. Yes it's true, nothing is new. Germany, which was hailed as a beacon of knowledge and science, allowed itself to be caught up in the spell of one of the worst perpetrators of evil in history—Adolph Hitler. The quest leads us to ask—is there a devil? Can we trace his footsteps? What are the common denominators between these cults?"[158]

"The story of Satan can be seen all throughout the cults from time immemorial. Take Quetzalcoatl for example, god of civilization was identified with the planet Venus and with the wind; he represented the forces of good and light pitted against those of evil and darkness, which were championed by Tezcatlipoca. According to one epic legend, Quetzalcoatl, deceived by Tezcatlipoca, was driven from the ancient city Tula, the Toltec capital, and wandered for many years until he reached his homeland, the East coast of Mexico—where he was consumed by divine fire, his ashes turning into birds and his heart becoming the morning star. Another version has him sailing off to a mythical land, leaving behind the promise of his return."[159]

Similar with the war of Satan in heaven, Satan has duped the world into thinking of him as the underdog; he identifies himself with Venus, the star in the north and Quetzalcoatl as Messiah who will reclaim his position. It is no wonder that when I spoke to

Mormon missionaries and asked them for evidence that Christ visited the Americas their reply was Quetzalcoatl, the feathered serpent.

THIS IS NOT ISLAM?

Why is it so common to see Muslims only fighting those who expose Islamic atrocities, but rarely if ever fighting the ones who carry them out? Instead of demanding to stop the atrocities and change Sharia, they would rather defend the behavior with the typical, "this is not Islam! Islam should not be judged by the behavior of a few." But if they did, then their fight wouldn't need to be focused on "Islamophobes" who are simply reporting the atrocities, but they could concentrate on the Sharia which needs changing.

Even when one finds minority groups who call for such modifications in the Muslim world, they don't get a large following. Why? One might argue that they do not have much freedom of expression in Muslim nations where they live in tyranny.

We live in a world that loves to find excuses, and doesn't want to take responsibility for our actions. Even in the West where Muslims enjoy freedom of expression, you do not see a majority of Muslims calling for the much needed Muslim reformation? If most Muslims are really as "moderate" as many claim, how significant are the outcries against the Islamic Sharia law of Qisas? Qisas is the law of reciprocity, an Islamic version of an "eye for an eye" which states that: "no Muslim should be killed in Qisas for the killing of a disbeliever."[160] The death penalty for a Muslim is only applicable if he kills another Muslim. This leaves non-Muslims as free game with penalties such as prison or a fine.

On October 30, 2005, in the allegedly moderate Muslim nation of Indonesia, a Javanese trader named Hasanuddin Ida and five other men attacked and beheaded three young Christian girls—Arni Sambue (age 15), Theresia Morangke (15), and Alfita Poliwo (19) who were walking to school. At the end of Ramadan, Muslims are mandated to carry out specific acts of charity. Court transcripts show that Hasanuddin Ida believed that the beheading of Christians qualified as just such an "act of charity." The murders were planned. The girls had been stalked going to school. The girls' severed heads were dumped in plastic bags in their home village along with a handwritten note that said: "Wanted: 100 more Christian heads, teenaged or adult, male or female."

Although the law in Indonesia for such a crime requires execution, on March 20, 2007, Hasanuddin, the mastermind of the murders received a mere twenty years in prison. Two other men who also participated in the beheadings received only fourteen year sentences. Now juxtapose these sentences to that of Shapelle Corby, a 28 year old Australian woman, who was sentenced to 20 years in an Indonesian Prison for attempting to smuggle marijuana. Many in Australia think that Shapelle is innocent. Regardless, the message is clear: in Indonesia Western pot smugglers are given harsher sentences than those who stalk and saw the heads off of innocent young Christian girls. This example of injustice is one that is repeated thousands of times over throughout the Muslim world. The *Voice of the Martyrs* and *The Barnabas Fund* have collected hundreds of stories, updated daily, of Christians who are mistreated or even murdered without any legal repercussions for the Muslim murderer. Yet Muslims still try to play the "victim" card whenever they can.

One can find hundreds of Muslim websites littered with the typical twisted logic, playing the victim card while giving injunctions to kill the innocents. On an Internet interfaith discussion group forums.gawaher.com, one comment reads: "The kafirs (unbelievers) have been attacking Muslim countries killing Muslim people from the beginning of time... when we have done nothing. Like the people of Israel attack the Muslims from Palestine because they do it for the land and because they hate Arabs/Muslims... we defend them for Allah. We try and spread Islam, The one and only true word of Allah. They rejected it; therefore we are allowed to kill them. It is not forbidden to kill a kafir. Of course we want to by the will of Allah, peacefully live with them and teach them about the beautiful religion."

Killing in the name of Allah while playing the roll of victim, is nothing new in Islam. From its inception and throughout its history to this very day, beheading has been part and parcel of its religion. The Bible even predicted it for the Last-Days as the primary method by which martyrs would be killed. No other world religion or empire practiced systematic beheading like Islam. The Roman Empire's primary method of execution of non-citizens was crucifixion, while the Catholic Church was drowning or burning. Only Islam has such a long-standing historical tradition of beheading, with even, specific commandments recorded in its "holy book" to "strike off their necks" (Qur'an 47:4). By this, the martyrs will face the fate predicted in the Bible "And I saw the souls of those who had been beheaded because of their testimony for Jesus and because of the Word of God" (Revelation 20:4).

∼ 47 ∼

Both Desire
Israel's Destruction

┼──✵──┼

Whether we are discussing the Antichrist, the Mahdi or Isa (the Muslim Jesus), we can see that they all specifically target Jews and Christians for their campaigns of terror. Yet Muslims are quick to respond when accused of anti-Semitism that they don't hate Jews, they simply hate Zionism. I love the quote by Martin Luther King Jr. "You declare, my friend, that you do not hate the Jews; you are merely 'anti-Zionist.' And I say, let the truth ring forth from the high mountain tops, let it echo through the valleys of God's green earth: When people criticize Zionism, they mean Jews—this is God's own truth." If only many of the so-called civil rights leaders of today would follow the King's wisdom on this point.

Islam predicts the fate of Christians and Jews: "The Mahdi will offer the religion of Islam to the Jews and Christians; if they accept it they will be spared, otherwise they will be killed."[161] Centuries before Islam, the Bible predicted that Satan—through the Antichrist—will primarily target Jews and Christians for death or conversion during his final reign of terror—that the Antichrist will "wage war against the saints and kill them" (Daniel 7:21). The Apostle John mirrors Daniel's vision: "It was also given to him [the Antichrist] to make war with the saints and to overcome them" (Revelation 13:7). John also recounts seeing the Antichrist coming "up out of the abyss to make war with the saints, to overcome them and kill them" (Revelation 11:7). Interestingly, the Muslim Messiah seems to match the Biblical Antichrist, who, according to Islam, will slaughter the Jews and women.[162] It isn't surprising that Islam has Jews and women together following the Antichrist. In Islam, one of the main reasons for Jesus' return is, "to refute the Jews over the controversial issue that they killed Jesus. However Jesus will kill them including their leader, the Antichrist"[163] He will also not "regard the desire of women" (Daniel 11:37). "His [Antichrist] followers the Jews, will number 70,000. [Then] Jesus kills the Dajjal at the Gate of Hudd, near an Israeli airport, in the valley of "Ifiq." The final war between the Jews will ensue, and the Muslims will be victorious."[164]

Does Satan so specifically, so repeatedly, and so persistently target the Jews over and above all others? Yes! God loves Israel, and whatever God loves, Satan hates. Also, Jesus promised that he would not return until the Jews were established in their land and until they cry out, *"Blessed is He that cometh in the name of the Lord"* (Mat 15:24). This return to Israel with *Jews living in it* is emphasized by Jesus and every prophet in the Bible. Many claiming to be Christians are critical of Israel and support the establishment of a Palestinian state; they point that nowhere in the text of the New Testament do we have a mandate for such a state called Israel. However, in Matthew 10:23, Jesus describes the land as Israel, and it will be as such just prior to His return. Satan believes that by eliminating Israel he can extend his existence to rule this world and postpone his eternal judgment by God. It is for such a reason the Bible warns of this during the Last-Days—Jews will be sought out for destruction. In analyzing and studying Islamic eschatology, we are confronted with yet one more final holocaust, far worse than the previous holocaust that occurred under the Nazis. Speaking of Jews, Allah "placed enmity and hatred" against them (Qur'an 5:64). They are described as those who always "kindle the fire of war and strive to do mischief on earth" (Ibid). Apologists argue that these verses are limited to specific historical incidents in Mohammed's career. If so, why are these commands prescribed "until the Day of Judgment" (Ibid)?

This is not some mere temporary command. According to Islamic tradition, Jews not only start wars, they cause general mischief on the earth. Allah was so disgusted by the Jews, that he cursed them and literally transformed many of them into "apes and swine" assigning them the lowest "rank" among humankind (Qur'an 2:65; 7:166; 5:60). Among the more anti-Semitic and vocal Muslims, these verses have become absolute favorites. I could recall so many stories from my childhood in Bethlehem where this venomous hatred of the Jews was hammered into our little heads. I remember one instance when my class traveled to the Jerusalem zoo. Spectators had been throwing cigarettes at this one lone gorilla which had learned to pick up the cigarettes and smoke. Our Muslim teacher told us that this gorilla must originally be a descendant of the Jews.

HITLER LOVED ISLAM

Today I look back at this and I think of what the Nazis taught. The same Nazi ideology of the "vermin Jew" is now being taught throughout the entire Middle East. Yet Muslims claim that Hitler was a Christian. Most Westerners today are not historically savvy enough to note that Hitler was probably possessed by Allah since he preferred Islam over Christianity for Germany. In his memoirs, Albert Speer reported how Hitler expounded his views on Christianity to a visiting delegation of Arabs. Discussing the implications of the battle of Tours when Charles Martell, a German, defeated the advancing Muslim army, Hitler held forth: "Had the Arabs won the battle, the world would be Mohammedan today. For theirs was a religion that believed in spreading the faith by the sword and subjugating all nations to that faith. The Germanic peoples would have become heirs to that religion. Such a creed was perfectly suited to the Germanic temperament."[165] Hitler said that the conquering Arabs, because of their racial inferiority, would in the long run have been unable to contend with the harsher climate and conditions of the country. They could not have kept down the more vigorous natives, so that ultimately not Arabs but Islamized Germans could have stood at the head of this Mohammedan Empire.[166] Hitler concluded this historical speculation with, "You see, it's been our misfortune to have the wrong religion. Why didn't we have the religion of the Japanese, who regard sacrifice for the Fatherland as the highest good? The Mohammedan religion too would have been much more compatible to us than Christianity. Why did it have to be Christianity with its meekness and flabbiness?"[167]

Hitler even learned genocide from Islam. Adolph Hitler used what is now called the Armenian holocaust as his model for an even greater holocaust. Ottoman Turks developed techniques that were later used by the Nazis, such as piling 90 people into a train car with a capacity of 36, and leaving them locked in it for days—terrified, starving, and often dead.

"Hitler was even more impressed with how the Turks got away with genocide. On Aug. 22, 1939, Hitler explained that his plans to invade Poland included the formation of death squads that would exterminate men, women, and children. He asked, 'who, after all, speaks today of the annihilation of the Armenians?'"[168] Heinrich Himmler, a high ranking Nazi stated: "I have nothing against Islam because it educates the men in this division for me and promises them heaven if they fight and are killed in action, a very practical and attractive religion for soldiers."[169]

WHEN ARE CONTRADICTIONS NOT CONTRADICTIONS?

Muslim apologists defend the reputation of the Qur'an by alluding to peaceful verses in an attempt to whitewash the anti-Semitic rhetoric that fills the pages of the Qur'an. It is this type of serpentine "forked-tongue" deception that the Bible warned us of with regard to the Antichrist spirit that: "by peace he will destroy many" (Daniel 8:25). So, how does Allah deceive the faithful and sear the inner conscience to ignore all this peace in the Qur'an? Allah has hidden an ace under his sleeve perhaps like an asp shedding its old skin; the Qur'an has Nasekh, a hermeneutical rule that overrides the tolerant and peaceful verses that Islam considers obsolete—Mansookh. Islam holds to the notion that revelation is progressive, whereby whenever one comes across verses that seem to contradict one another; those newer revelations negate or cancel out the older ones. Anyone who grew up with even a minimal Islamic education understands this. In Mohammed's early career as a false prophet, he tried appealing kindly to the Jews to win them over, but when the sugar failed, he resorted to very bitter vinegar that composed the majority of curses and condemnation against Jews.

Yet Muslim apologists would deny everything when they speak in English, including this rule. But if the law of abrogation does not exist, then why are Muslims not permitted to drink wine? Especially since the Qur'an permitted it? Yet every Muslim from his youth is taught that this as an abrogated verse. Mohammed had to find a technique to change his mind. How would he then cover all the contradictions? The answer is simple—they are not contradictions, they have been abrogated.

But anti-Semitism in Islam is not limited to the Qur'an; it finds an even fuller expression in the infamous Hadith about the final slaughter of the Jews. This sacred text is continually repeated in Mosques throughout the Middle East: "The last hour would not come unless the Muslims will fight against the Jews and the Muslims would kill them until the Jews would hide themselves behind a stone or a tree and a stone or a tree would say: 'Oh faithful Muslim, or the servant of Allah, there is a Jew behind me; come and kill him.'"[170]

The enmity of Islam toward the Jews has existed since Islam's inception, yet today this enmity is blamed on Jews for founding the Nation of Israel and causing "the Palestinian plight." A growing opinion today is that if Israel ceased to exist, then the Jews would finally be left alone. If this is so, then why were there so many massacres committed against Jews by Muslims prior to the establishment of the state of Israel? Islam fills Muslim hearts with a hatred that proceeds forth from the very pit of hell. Consider the words of Hassan Nasrallah, the head of Hezbollah: "If they [Jews] all gather in Israel, it will save us the trouble of going after them worldwide."[171]

WHEN THE BRAVE ARE COWARDS

So it does not matter if the Jews had never entered their land or established a state, Nasrallah continues, "if we searched the entire world for a person more cowardly, despicable, weak and feeble in psyche, mind, ideology, and religion, we would not find anyone like the Jew. Notice, I do not say the Israeli."[172] To call the Jews cowardly and weak is hardly the truth. I clearly remember one particularly violent demonstration in my village in Beit

Sahur-Bethlehem when I was a teenager. We were all wielding knives and sticks, after having listened to a revolutionary song from the *Voice of Palestine Radio* calling for demonstrations the night before. They had played songs proclaiming Jews as cowards because they ran from stones. Yet as we threw our stones at them, the Israeli soldiers laid down their machine guns, and came towards us with batons, I will never forget their bravery—a dozen Jews approached hundreds of men. I injured one of them nearly to death. And although he was badly injured with his head gashed in, he stood back up. I asked myself that day about the song that said that the Jew was a coward. I wondered why the stones we threw didn't make him run—he was a coward, wasn't he? Every time the Jews tried to demonstrate that they didn't want to use excessive force against us, though they certainly could have, we took them for granted and considered it cowardly. But I soon began to realize that it was we who stood behind children who were the true cowards.

We hated Jews, period. Not just Zionists as we claimed. The *Muslim Student Association of UCLA* in front of Americans say that they only hate Zionism, yet in Arabic they chant in front of the Israeli Consulate "Death to the Jews."[173]

AND THE COWARDS ARE BRAVE

Today Islam and the Muslim world is undeniably the single-most anti-Semitic force on earth. Palestinians in particular use the anti-Semitic apocalyptic template as a basis for much of their actions against Israel. Sheikh Ibrahim Madhi, the former officially appointed Imam of the Palestinian Authority could not have made it any more clear: "the decisive battle will be in Jerusalem and its environs: 'The resurrection of the dead will not occur until you make war on the Jews...'"[174] it does not say "defend yourselves against the Jews," but "make war on the Jews." Muslims believe that this final slaughter will be an offensive battle. *Don't forget that.* Consider the following from "sermon" from the same Sheikh Mahdi:

> "Oh Allah, accept our martyrs in the highest heavens...
> Oh Allah, show the Jews a black day...
> Oh Allah, annihilate the Jews and their supporters...
> Oh Allah, raise the flag of Jihad across the land..."[175]

As the world is eagerly awaiting and believing for the peaceful co-existence of the Jewish and the Palestinian people, the very religious leaders of the Palestinian people, with the full support and approval of the political leadership are ceaselessly beating the drums for another final solution. As Moroccan cleric al-Maghili (d. 1505) said "Love of the Prophet [Mohammed] requires hatred of the Jews."[176]

≈48≈
Both Occupy
The Temple Mount

✦━✦━✦

As we were warned by Christ two millennia ago, the Antichrist will make the Temple Mount the specific location of his rule. Why would both accounts whether we study the Mahdi or the Antichrist—both desire to establish their rule from the Temple Mount, regardless that Jerusalem is not mentioned in the Qur'an? Why not Mecca or Medina? Antichrist wants to rule over Jehovah's Temple. In the early years of Islam, in order to coddle the Jews to his cause, Islam did exalt Jerusalem. But when his attempt failed, Mohammed turned on the Jews and made a practice of praying towards Jerusalem one of the "Mansookh" (cancelled) verses and the command to pray towards Mecca the "Naskh" (abrogating verse). Satan must control Jerusalem because he desires to sit in the true Temple so that he will be like the true God. Antichrist has a dual purpose, he is Anti or "against," yet he is also an "in place of" Christ.

While the Bible sets forth Jesus as the Messiah and the defender of Israel, Islamic tradition portrays the Mahdi and Jesus as joining with an army of Muslim warriors carrying their black flags of war against the Jews. The Mahdi like Saladin will lead this army to Israel and re-conquer it for Islam. The Jews will be slaughtered until very few remain and Jerusalem will become the location of the Mahdi's rule over the Earth. Ayatollah Ibrahim Amini, in his book, *Imam al-Mahdi, the Just Leader of Humanity* quotes the following hadith: "Armies carrying black flags will come from Khurasan. No power will be able to stop them and they will finally reach Eela (Baitul Maqdas in Jerusalem) where they will erect their flags." Baitul Maqdas or "the holy house" is referring to the Temple Mount in Jerusalem. Could placing flags with the slogan, "There is no god but Allah and Mohammed is his Messenger" in the Temple be the Abomination of Desolation?[177] Or could it be that a Black Stone image be set on the Holy of Holies?—only time will tell. In a particularly venomous manner, Egyptian authors, Muhammad ibn Izzat and Muhammad 'Arif comment on the above tradition: "The Mahdi will be victorious and eradicate those pigs and dogs and the idols of this time so that there will once more be a caliphate based on prophethood as the Hadith states...Jerusalem will be the location of the rightly guided caliphate and the center of Islamic rule, which will be headed by Imam al-Mahdi...That will abolish the leadership of the Jews...and put an end to the domination of the Satans who spit evil into people and cause corruption in the earth, making them slaves of false idols, and ruling the world by laws other than the Sharia (Islamic Law) of the Lord of the worlds."[178] This is astonishing; this evil one is on a mission to change the laws to Islamic Sharia. This law according to Islam came from Allah, the Lord of the worlds, that is, this world and the under world. After this, "He will oppose and will exalt himself over everything that is called God or is worshiped, so that he sets himself up in God's temple, proclaiming himself to be God" (II Thessalonians 2:4). Today, the Temple Mount, or in Arabic Haram Ash-Sharif, is the location of two Mosques and is considered to be the third holiest site of Islam. The above verse written by the apostle Paul indicates that there will be a rebuilt Jewish Temple in Jerusalem in the future. The apostle Paul says that the Antichrist will "set himself up in God's Temple," or more literally, "he takes his seat in the temple of God." This event was also taught by the early Christian Church. The early Church Father Irenaeus writes: "But when this Antichrist shall have devastated all things in this world, he will reign for three years and six months and will sit in the temple at Jerusalem; and then the Lord will come from heaven in the clouds, in the glory of the Father, sending this man and those who follow him into the lake of fire."[179]

Isaiah 14, commonly viewed as a description of Lucifer the fallen angel, yet a closer scrutiny of the verses reveals it as a prophecy against Antichrist, the man possessed by Lucifer after he is cast out of heaven, "Is this the man who made the earth tremble" (v. 16). Even defiling God's Holy Temple in Jerusalem could possibly allude to a northern location of the Third Temple: "I will sit on the Mount of Assembly, far away in the north." (v. 13b, KJV) The N.I.V reads, "I will sit enthroned on the mount of assembly, on the utmost heights of the sacred mountain." The footnote reads, "Hebrew Zaphon, which means north, or on the north side."

Psalm 48:2 also describes the Temple Mount, "It [the City of our God and his Holy Mountain] is beautiful in elevation, the joy of the whole earth. Like the utmost heights of Zaphon is Mt. Zion." This can only be referring to the Temple that was likely situated on the north side of the platform. Asher Kaufman, an expert on the Temple Mount believes that the original Temple lies 150 feet north of the Dome of the Rock where a copula was erected with several inscriptions: Qubat Al-Arwah (The Dome of the Spirits) and Qubat Al-Alwa (Dome of the Heights). Al-Arwah, or the spirits could have been intended to say "Al-Ruach" (The Spirit, Shekina Glory) in which the Holy Spirit rested.

As we have seen above, not only does the Mahdi-Antichrist desire to occupy Jerusalem as the capital of his Caliphate, but specifically he desires to sit in Baitul Al-Maqdas "the Holy House," on the Temple Mount in Jerusalem.

∞ 49 ∞
Our Messiah is Their Antichrist
And Their Antichrist is Our Messiah

✦

So we've seen that Islam's Messiah is identical to the Biblical Antichrist and it gets even worse, as a Muslim, I was also taught that the man who Christians believe is the Messiah—the one that will return from heaven to defend the nation of Israel—is the Antichrist of Islam's eschatology. The Antichrist is known as *ad-Dajjal* who claims to be the divine Messiah and will fight on the side of the Jews. We have seen how Islam's definition of Antichrist includes his leading 70,000 Jews and Christians into a battle with Isa, the Muslim Jesus who will kill the Antichrist in Lud. Indeed, Satan did not leave any ground uncovered. For even as Christians are repeatedly warned not to fall for false prophets and false messiahs, so also have Muslims been warned not to fall for the "deceptive" powers of the Dajjal. He is said to be a great deceiver who will have miraculous powers and who will temporarily hold power over the whole earth: "The Prophet was warning us that in the Last-Days there would be someone who would deceive all of humanity. The Dajjal will possess power over this world. Thus, Muslims must be careful not to have the love of the world in their hearts so they won't leave their religion and follow Him. He will be able to heal the sick by wiping his hand on them, like Jesus did, but with this deceit the Dajjal will lead people down the path to hell. Thus the Dajjal is the false Messiah, or Anti-Christ (*Massih ad-Dajjal*). He will pretend to be the Messiah, and deceive people by showing them amazing powers."[180] "the Dajjal will say to a Bedouin Arab, 'what will you think if I bring your father and mother back to life for you? Will you bear witness that I am your lord?' The Bedouin will say, 'Yes.' So two devils will assume the appearance of his father and mother, and say, 'O my son, follow him for he is your lord.'"[181] The Dajjal's deceptive signs are for the purpose of leading people into believing that he is actually their "lord." Muslim apologist, Abu Ameenah Bilal Phillips said of the Dajjal that he "will claim to be divine."[182] Muslim scholars universally agree with Phillips. As result of the fact that the Dajjal is, according to Islamic tradition, the false Jewish Messiah who claims to be God, Muslims believe that the Dajjal will thus claim to be both Jesus Christ by name and God Almighty.

As a Muslim, I was always taught that the Dajjal would be Jewish. If you go to the Islamic bookstores, you will find dozens of books warning Muslims about the coming evil

Jewish Antichrist. Emergence of the Dajjal, *The Jewish King* by Matloob Ahmed Qasmi is a big seller. Imam Sheikh Ibrahim Madhi of the Palestinian Authority articulated the Islamic perspective regarding the expectation of the Jewish people quite well in one of his sermons: "The Jews await the false Jewish Messiah, while we await with Allah's help...the Mahdi and Jesus, peace be upon him. Jesus' pure hands will murder the false Jewish messiah. Where? In the city of Lod, in Palestine. Palestine will be, as it was in the past, a graveyard for the 'invaders.'"[183]

Even many proclaiming Palestinian Christians like Samuel Shahid says of the Dajjal that he will be "the embodiment of the Jewish hope and longing. The bulk of his army is recruited from the Jews."[184] The sad thing is that many Christians in the West believe that the Antichrist is a Jew. The real Jesus of the Bible however, will indeed come as a divine defender of Israel and her people as Israel's spiritual children, the Christians. We can see that Satan's strategy in blinding the minds of the Muslims in order that when the real Jesus returns, the Muslims will already have been prepared to reject him as the great deceiver and false Jewish Messiah.

At least six hundred years before Islam ever existed, the Jewish Prophets and the Jewish Apostles described the event of Jesus returning to Israel, defeating her enemies and finally gaining full acceptance among the Jewish people: "In that day I (The Lord) will set out to destroy all the nations that attack Jerusalem. And I will pour out on the house of David and the inhabitants of Jerusalem a spirit of grace and supplication. They will look on me, the one they have pierced, and they will mourn for him as one mourns for an only child, and grieve bitterly for him as one grieves for a firstborn son" (Zechariah 12:10). "And so all Israel will be saved, as it is written: 'The deliverer will come from Zion; he will turn godlessness away from Jacob'" (Romans 11:26).

When Jesus returns, "to destroy all the nations that attack Jerusalem," he will be physically present in Israel. At this time, it is said that those Jews who are alive in Israel will realize that He is "the one they have pierced, and they will mourn for him." Thus the acknowledgement of Jesus as the genuine Jewish Messiah and divine Savior will fill their hearts and, "so all Israel will be saved." But this will only serve to confirm the suspicions of the Muslims. This will be proof that he is the Dajjal!

Muslims are expecting Jews to acknowledge the Dajjal as the divine Jewish Messiah, thus in the Islamic mind, the Jesus of Biblical tradition will fulfill the three most primary Islamic expectations of the Dajjal. Clearly, these traditions will be used by Satan, not only to preempt the Muslims of the earth from receiving the real Jesus when He comes, but literally to empower them to attack Him.

≈50≈
Both Stop
The Rain

Why would Islam parallel the works of the two great witnesses in Revelation to the works of the Dajjal? Mohammed warned Muslims of the Dajjal that he will work all kinds of miracles, controlling the weather and bringing drought or rains:

"Then he (ad-Dajjal) will command the sky to rain, and the earth to bring forth vegetation, and their cattle will come back to them in the evening, with their humps very high, and their udders full of milk, and their flanks stretched."[185] "The false messiah (al-Maseeh al-dajjaal) is the liar who leads people astray, the messiah of misguidance who will tempt people by means of the signs that he is given, such as bringing down rain, reviving the earth to bring forth vegetation, and other 'miracles.'"[186]

Yet the Bible in nearly an identical fashion portrays the great works of the Two Witnesses as being able to "have power to shut heaven that it rain not in the days of their prophecy: and have power over waters to turn them to blood, and to smite the earth with all plagues, as often as they will" (Revelation 11:6). Islam is set up to kill the Two Witnesses that testify of the coming Christ. In the Book of Revelation, we find the description of these two eschatological characters. In brief, they are two Old Testament prophets who will appear in Jerusalem a couple of years prior to the return of Jesus, during the reign of Antichrist. They will be identified as great miracle workers:

"And I will give power unto my two witnesses, and they shall prophesy a thousand two hundred and threescore days, clothed in sackcloth. These are the two olive trees, and the two candlesticks standing before the God of the earth. And if any man will hurt them, fire proceeded out of their mouth, and devoured their enemies: and if any man will hurt them, he must in this manner be killed. These have power to shut heaven that it rain not in the days of their prophecy: and have power over waters to turn them to blood, and to smite the earth with all plagues, as often as they will" (Revelation 11:3-6).

The two witnesses will fulfill a forerunner role similar to the ministry of John the Baptist who prepared the people for the "first" coming of Jesus in the first century.

In light of the confluence of these traditions and Scriptures, consider now the following scenario: The city of Jerusalem is under either the complete or partial control of the Muslim Caliph. During this time, two Jewish individuals emerge on the scene and begin to declare that the Mahdi is a deceiver and the chief henchman of Satan. They declare that Jesus of Nazareth is indeed the Messiah, the Son of God and the only true way of salvation. They declare that Islam is a sham and the religion of the devil. In the midst of this, these individuals work great miracles and have great success in winning many people to their cause. Not only would these individuals be Messianic Jews who proclaim that Jesus (Yeshua) is the Messiah, but they would also literally claim to be Old Testament prophets of Jehovah. In all of this, these individuals would fulfill many of the Muslim apocalyptic traditions and expectations of the Dajjal—or deceivers to come. Clearly these individuals would be immediately branded by Muslims as being dajjals and their deaths would be sought with ferocity that we cannot imagine.

≈ 51 ≈
Both Enjoy
Desecrating Bodies

As we read the narrative about the Two Witnesses, we see that after these two prophets are killed by the Antichrist, their dead bodies are left on display in the streets of Jerusalem. This practice of displaying the dead bodies of enemies or criminals in public places is a distinctly Islamic practice and is still done to this day. In typical Palestinian fashion, the two witnesses are finally killed and their bodies are desecrated:

> "And when they shall have finished their testimony, the beast that ascended out of the bottomless pit shall make war against them, and shall overcome them, and kill them. And their dead bodies shall lie in the street of the great city, which spiritually is called Sodom and Egypt, where also our Lord was crucified. And they of the people and kindred and tongues and nations (Gentiles) shall see their dead bodies three days and an half, and shall not suffer their dead bodies to be put in graves. And they that dwell upon the earth shall rejoice over them, and make merry, and shall send gifts one to another; because these two prophets tormented them that dwelt on the earth. And after three days and a half the spirit of life from God entered into them, and they stood upon their feet; and great fear fell upon them which saw them. And they heard a great voice from heaven saying unto them, Come up hither. And they ascended up to heaven in a cloud; and their enemies beheld them" (Revelation 11:7-12).

Often times the bodies are even dragged through the streets for all to see. Of course, most of us still remember the stripped body of the U.S. soldier that was dragged through the streets of Mogadishu in 1993 or the charred bodies of Americans strung up in Iraq. The purpose of these acts is to shame the dead and to scare any others who might consider committing a similar "crime." It is also a sick celebration of victory. Only recently, this practice has been seen in Afghanistan. According to *Can West News Service*, on December 19, 2006: "26 local Afghan men were executed by the Taliban yesterday and their headless bodies put on public display around a local village, in a morbid attempt to dissuade other civilians here from assisting NATO and Afghan National Security Forces operating in the area...Their heads were removed and their bodies were hanged from trees in and around Bazar Talukan, a small agrarian village."[187] As recently as February of 2007, in Saudi Arabia, America's biggest Arab ally, four men who were charged with robbery were publicly beheaded and crucified: "The bodies of four Sri Lankans beheaded in Saudi Arabia have gone on public display, in what was said to be an effort to halt a rise in crime committed by foreigners. The gang was executed on Monday at a public square in a busy market district of the capital, Riyadh...*The al-Riyadh Newspaper* reported that the men had been 'crucified'—tied to wooden beams after beheading—as part of moves to deter other foreigners from crime...The desert kingdom, home to Islam's holiest shrines, says it applies strict Islamic law."[188]

CELEBRATE AND GIVE AWAY GIFTS

Beyond the fact that Islam has a long-standing pattern of publicly displaying dead bodies after killing them in accordance with Islamic law, we also see that after the Two Witnesses are killed, that the people will celebrate their deaths as if it were Christmas: "And they that dwell upon the earth shall rejoice over them, and make merry, and shall send gifts one to another" (Revelation 11:10). Almost no one will forget the TV images of Muslims from Kabul to Kuala Lumpur, from Amman to Tehran dancing in the streets and celebrating after 9-11. In Palestine, we saw candy being given away in the streets until Yasser Arafat threatened the lives of AP reporters to stop showing what was really taking place. This type of *schadenfreude*—the taking of pleasure and rejoicing in the misfortune and pain of non-Muslims is an ever-present reality throughout the Muslim world. It is not even uncommon to see or hear of the mothers of suicide bombers celebrating the fact that their child was able to kill some "enemies of Islam." How much more if the greatest thorns in the side of the Islamic world were both killed on the same day? The Muslim world would virtually explode with joy and songs of excitement. I can see the party streamers and confetti even now. And so, in both the public display of the dead as well as the giving of gifts to celebrate the deaths of "infidels," we see distinctly Islamic practices. It should now be clear to everyone that Islam has taken those things that the Bible calls evil and has made them good. Islam has taken the Biblical Antichrist and has made him its Messiah. Yet Islam has taken the Biblical Messiah and has made him the Antichrist. This is the backwards world of Islam. Islam is a *reversalist* religion. As John Calvin the protestant reformer rightly observed "That was the 'Gospel' of Mahomet (Mohammed)—to turn all things upside down and to bring all things into confusion..."[189]

While Islam denies the fact that Christians and Jews will ever find eternal life, it claims that murderous suicidal martyrdom operations carried out against Christians and Jews are the key to eternal life and paradise. Islam calls rape and stolen booty the rewards of righteousness. Islam refers to the aggressive imperialistic invasion of a sovereign nation as *Futuhat* (liberation), but when a nation is genuinely liberated from tyranny, it is called "aggression," and "occupation." Islam calls Jews monkeys and terrorists holy. It forbids even music, calls joy evil and the oppression of women righteousness.

Section III

Literal References to Christ's Wars With Muslim Nations

～52～

Messiah in Person Defeats Muslims Lead By The Mahdi

All in all, we have clearly seen that Islam is the Antichrist religion, but the evidence that Islam is *the* Antichrist religion? Well, more shocking facts are yet to come. Previously we have presented much circumstantial evidence, now in Part III we will examine hard-hitting *DNA*-conclusive arguments to support our theory.

When comparing Old Testament heroes with Messiah, it is common to focus on Joseph as the suffering Messiah and David as King Messiah. Joseph's rejection by his brothers signifies Israel's rejection of Christ. David is a type of King Messiah because Christ's kingdom will be established in Jerusalem. But the one character in the Bible, that is virtually never focused upon when searching for types of Christ is Gideon—the warrior Messiah. Gideon is crucial if we want to understand what the Messiah will do during His war expeditions after He sets foot on the Mount of Olives to fight for the Battle of Jerusalem. Though it is rarely discussed, Christ, like Gideon will fight against "Midian." The Bible refers to Midian as Ishmaelites (Judges 8:22). They are the descendants of Abraham's fourth son with his concubine Keturah.

Like Gideon, the Bible portrays Christ as fighting against the inhabitant's of Arabia: "God came from Teman, the Holy One from Mount Paran. His glory covered the heavens and his praise filled the earth. His splendor was like the sunrise; rays flashed from his hand, where his power was hidden" (Habakkuk 3:3-4). *Jesus in person* is returning from battle out of Teman in Arabia. How often is this discussed in churches? Jesus will physically return and will judge not only the inhabitants of Arabia, but also Cush, which includes the modern day Islamist nations of Sudan and Somalia: "I saw the tents of Cushan in distress, the dwellings of Midian in anguish" (Habakkuk 3:5-6).

Midian refers to the regions east of the Jordan River and southwards on into modern Saudi Arabia. This is the heart of Islamic territory. Portrayals of battles like this, with Christ fighting against Muslim nations, are actually found throughout the Old Testament. The enemies that come against Christ are described as this: "They come for violence; their faces are set like the east wind. They gather captives like sand. They scoff at kings, and princes are scorned by them" (Habakkuk 1:9-10). The enemies like the east wind are the locusts of Arabia and the kings of the East.

And in case someone thinks that this is simply one minor war expedition by Messiah against Muslims, but that the real showdown is with an European Antichrist, consider the context of Habakkuk. It is the final battle of Messiah against the Antichrist who is described as, "the most proud," (Habakkuk 2:4) who breaks the peace treaty and proclaims war in the name of his god. "Then his mind changes and he transgresses; He commits offense, ascribing this power to his god" (Habakkuk 1:11). He breaks the treaty claiming this is not an offense; for such has been sanctioned by his false god who promotes violence—exactly what Islam permits in its Hudna. The context of Habakkuk's vision is for the End-Times: "For the vision [is] yet for an appointed time, but at the end it shall speak, and not lie: though it tarry, wait for it; because it will surely come, it will not tarry" (Habakkuk 2:3). Antichrist always changes his mind and cannot be trusted. He also uses wine (oil) to pressure the nations (Habakkuk 2:5).

Though Antichrist is strong, his weapons will not help him, because God will allow his missiles to be used against him for his own destruction: "You thrust through with his own arrows the head of his villages. They came out like a whirlwind to scatter me; their rejoicing was like feasting on the poor in secret" (Habakkuk 3:14). Like Daniel, Habakkuk is asked to write this vision for an appointed time (Habakkuk 2:3), which is in the End-Times, at the coming of the Messiah.

But in case you are still not convinced that Christ wars with Muslims, or that this passage is only a minor passage out of so many others, the Book of Numbers, in one of the earliest, clearest and most direct Messianic prophecies in the Bible, also speaks about the coming of the Messiah to specifically destroy and conquer these same peoples. This prophecy was made by Balam and was given to Balak, the King of the Midianites: "A star will come out of Jacob; a scepter will rise out of Israel. He will crush the foreheads of Moab, the skulls of all the sons of Sheth. Edom will be conquered; Seir, his enemy, will be conquered, but Israel will grow strong. A ruler will come out of Jacob and destroy the survivors of the city" (Numbers 24:17-19). The Messiah is portrayed as descending from Jacob and possessing the "scepter"—a clear reference to his future rule over Israel. But what is it he will accomplish when he rules over Israel? He will utterly destroy his enemies which consequently are also the enemies of Israel. These three names Moab, Edom, and Seir are all referring to the same general people and the same general region. It is the peoples who lived to the east and southeast of Israel. Is Europe located immediately to the southeast of Israel? Or is this the location of Arabia?

Ezekiel 35 speaks of the judgment of Mount Seir (v. 1) and connects it with Edom: "As you rejoiced because the inheritance of the house of Israel was desolate, so I will do to you; you shall be desolate, O Mount Seir, as well as all of Edom—all of it! Then they shall know that I am the Lord" (v. 15). Greater Edom encompasses the land from Teman to Dedan which today is from Yemen to Saudi Arabia.

When Jesus returns to take hold of his scepter and destroy "his enemies," who are they? They are the Arab peoples to the east of Israel. In Isaiah, the theme is repeated: "[The Lord] will swallow up death forever. The Sovereign LORD will wipe away the tears from all faces; he will remove the disgrace of his people from all the earth. Jehovah has spoken" (Isaiah 25:8).

Has this happened yet or is this referring to the period after Christ has returned? Unless death has already been swallowed up and I have missed it, this is clearly about the return of Christ. "The hand of Jehovah will rest on this mountain (Zion); but Moab will be trampled under him as straw is trampled down in the manure" (Isaiah 25:10). God doesn't seem too worried about using polite or politically correct language here. Once again, the Messiah comes back to trample Moab. He is pictured as standing with His hand of blessings resting on Israel while his foot is pressing against the neck of Moab.

For those who hold to the European Antichrist paradigm, why does God specifically mention Moab and not any nations from Europe? If you take a *face-value* approach to interpretation, which is more reasonable to conclude; that this passage is pointing to the final End-Time defeat of the modern day physical and spiritual descendants of Moab, or that this passage is allegorically pointing us to Europe? Let's get real here. The Bible simply does not teach a European Antichrist paradigm.

ISAIAH 63—A MOST AMAZING PROPHECY

The Prophecy of Isaiah 63 concludes with the Messiah emerging out of Edom with his robes literally drenched with blood from the multitudes of those that he has slaughtered. That's right. Have you ever seen Messiah portrayed this way? He left as a lamb, but he returns as a mighty conquering lion: "Who is this coming from Edom, from Bozrah, with his garments stained crimson? Who is this, robed in splendor, striding forward in the greatness of his strength? 'It is I, speaking in righteousness, mighty to save.' Why are your garments red, like those of one treading the winepress? 'I have trodden the winepress alone; from the nations no one was with me. I trampled them in my anger and trod them down in my wrath; their blood spattered my garments, and I stained all my clothing. For the day of vengeance was in my heart, and the year of my redemption has come'" (Isaiah 63:1-4).

Ezekiel 25 also reveals exactly how God feels about Edom: "Thus Says the Lord God; "Because that Edom hath dealt against the house of Judah by taking vengeance, and hath greatly offended, and revenged himself upon them. Therefore thus says the Lord God; I will also stretch out mine hand upon Edom, and will cut off man and beast from it; and I will make it desolate from Teman; and they of Dedan shall fall by the sword" (v. 13).

Teman is in Yemen, while Dedan was an ancient city in central Saudi Arabia that is now known as Al-Ula. Because of the use of both Teman and Dedan, we are to understand that the entire landmass stretching southward along the Red Sea and well into central Saudi Arabia is being highlighted. The Jewish Tanakh translates this verse; "from Teman to Dedan." This is a massive area.

The Book of Obadiah also focuses on the destruction of Edom: "Shall I not in that day," Says Jehovah, "even destroy the wise men out of Edom, and understanding out of the mount of Esau?" (Obadiah 8) As in the previous passages, so also in Obadiah, this is clearly referring to the period preceding Christ's rule over the earth: "And saviors shall come up on mount Zion to judge the mount of Esau; and the kingdom shall be Jehovah's" (Obadiah 21).

This next passage will no doubt infuriate many Muslims. After Jesus destroys the Muslim nations, the prophet Zephaniah makes it clear that the remaining Israelites will possess the Muslim lands: "Jehovah Almighty, the God of Israel [declares], 'surely Moab will become like Sodom, the Ammonites like Gomorrah—a place of weeds and salt pits, a wasteland forever. The remnant of my people will plunder them; the survivors of my nation will inherit their land'" (Zephaniah 2:9).

MESSIAH IN PERSON DEFEATS EGYPT

Isaiah spoke much regarding the day when Messiah would return in glory in the clouds to execute judgment against His enemies: "See, the Lord, Jehovah Almighty, will lop off the boughs with great power. The lofty trees will be felled; the tall ones will be brought low" (Isaiah 10:33). Again, who are these enemies? Among the many listed, Isaiah specifically names both Egypt and Lebanon: "See, Jehovah rides on a swift cloud and is coming to Egypt. The idols of Egypt tremble before him, and the hearts of the Egyptians melt within them" (Isaiah 19:1). Who comes on the clouds? This is Messiah personally coming to defeat Egypt. Obviously Egypt is a Muslim nation.

The "Mighty One" in Isaiah 10:33-34 who destroys Lebanon is the Messiah who fights on the day of the Lord: "So the light of Israel be for a fire, And His Holy One for a flame; it will burn and devour his thrones and His briers in one day" (Isaiah 10:17). Egypt will be largely destroyed: "The Lord will utterly destroy the tongue of the Sea of Egypt; With His mighty wind He will shake His fist over the River, and strike it in the seven streams" (Isaiah 11:15). The Nile empties itself into the Mediterranean Sea by seven streams. The Bible predicts: "they shall fly down upon the shoulder of the Philistines toward the West; together they shall plunder the people of the East; they shall lay their hand on Edom and Moab; and the people of Ammon shall obey them" (Isaiah 11:14).

MESSIAH PERSONALLY JUDGES LEBANON

In Isaiah 10:34 an amazing declaration is made that, "Lebanon will fall by The Mighty One." This is the Messiah who will judge the anti-Israeli elements within Lebanon and all of Lebanon will bow before Him. I can see some argue that "The Mighty One" here is God the Father in heaven and not the Messiah on earth. Yet Isaiah 19:20 leaves no question: "He will send them a Savior and a Mighty One, and He will deliver them." Who is the Savior? How is He sent? In the Psalms Messiah is portrayed as a soldier and a fighter with the same reference: "Mighty One" "Gird Your sword upon Your thigh, O Mighty One, With Your glory and Your majesty" (Psalm 45:3). In Zephaniah 3 this "Mighty One" is in physically present in Israel's midst: "The LORD your God in your midst, The Mighty One, will save" (Zephaniah 3:17). It is clear that this is the Messiah. God the Father is utterly transcendent. He is not physically present in Israel.

This prophecy regarding Lebanon is also the judgment against the Antichrist: "O my people, who dwell in Zion, do not be afraid of the Assyrian. He shall strike you with a rod and lift up his staff against you, in the manner of Egypt" (Isaiah 10:24-25). Antichrist will be responsible for the destruction of Lebanon: "For the violence done to Lebanon will cover you, and the plunder of beasts which made them afraid, Because of men's blood and the violence of the land and the city, And of all who dwell in it" (Habakkuk 2:17). God will punish Islam for what they have done in Lebanon with rape and pillage of Christians in that nation.

In the Book of the prophet Joel, we read about the judgment of the nations when Christ returns: "I will gather all nations and bring them down to the Valley of Jehoshaphat. There I will enter into judgment against them concerning my inheritance, my people Israel, for they scattered my people among the nations and divided up my land." (Joel 3:2) Do you see why Christ judges the nations? It is because of their sins against Israel. But which nations are specified as being guilty of this crime? "Now what have you against me, O Tyre and Sidon (Lebanon), and all you regions of Philistia (Gaza) are you repaying me for something I have done? If you are paying me back, I will swiftly and speedily return on your own heads what you have done." (Joel 3:4) It is likely that even Hezbollah (Tyre) and Gaza's Hamas (Philistia) are confronting the Messiah of Israel. Of course, at this point they have been duped by Satan to think that He is the Dajjal when in fact it's the Muslims who are following the false Messiah.

This pattern is also found in the Book of Jeremiah who also very clearly describes Jesus pouring out his wrath against the enemies of Israel at the end of the age: "This is what Jehovah, the God of Israel, said to me: 'Take from my hand this cup filled with the wine of my wrath and make all the nations to whom I send you drink it.'" (Jeremiah 25:15) So who are the nations God says on whom He will pour out his wrath? The list follows. As you read the list, ask yourself if the emphasis is on the Middle East or Europe: "Pharaoh king of Egypt, his attendants, his officials and all his people, and all the foreign people there; all the kings of Uz; all the kings of the Philistines—those of Ashkelon, Gaza, Ekron, and the people left at Ashdod, Edom, Moab and Ammon; all the kings of Tyre and Sidon; the kings of the coastlands across the sea; Tema, Buz and all who are in distant places; all the kings of Arabia and all the kings of the foreign people who live in the desert; all the kings of Zimri, Elam and Media; and all the kings of the North, near and far, one after the other—all the kingdoms on the face of the earth. And after all of them, the king of She-shach will drink it too... for I am calling down a sword upon all who live on the earth, declares Jehovah Almighty" (v. 19-26, 29).

Again, the word used for earth is "eretz" and need not literally refer to every last nation on the whole earth. If it were, then what would be the point of providing all of these names? The nations that are named however are all Middle Eastern Muslim nations. Is this a coincidence? Of course not!

Whenever the sword of Messiah's wrath is mentioned, the Muslim nations are always mentioned as suffering God's judgment. For Isaiah also prophesied: "My sword has drunk its fill in the heavens; see, it descends in judgment on Edom, the people I have totally destroyed. The sword of Jehovah is bathed in blood, it is covered with fat—the blood of lambs and goats, fat from the kidneys of rams. For Jehovah has a sacrifice in Bozrah and a great slaughter in Edom...Their land will be drenched with blood, and the dust will be soaked with fat. For Jehovah has a day of vengeance, a year of retribution, to uphold Zion's [legal] cause. Edom's streams will be turned into pitch, her dust into burning sulfur; her land will become blazing pitch!" (Isaiah 34:3-9)

The sword of Jehovah's wrath is against whom? Once again, it is Edom—the Muslim enemies of Israel. Why is Jesus judging Edom? It is to "uphold Zion's legal cause." (Isaiah 34:8) Time and time again, prophet after prophet, God's judgment is specified as being leveled against Muslim nations. Jesus himself is waging battle against the Muslim armies.

WHY DID THE WEST MISS THIS?

It is common in the West when someone initiates a prophecy discussion that the discussion is immediately turned to The Book of Revelation. Even on most prophecy documentaries they begin and revolve around allegorical passages from the Book of Revelation—the last book of the Bible. Why not start from the beginning? Why not start with the many literal references in the Bible regarding prophecy?

Instead of jumping right into an examination of the various allegorical visions and dreams about beasts, horns, dragons, and so forth, why not start with what is clear and straightforward? This would be a much more reasonable approach, would it not? When attempting to form a solid Biblical basis for understanding the Antichrist system, one needs to rely on the full council of Scripture, not merely the last and most mysterious book in the Bible.

While the prophetic snap-shots found in Revelation or the Book of Daniel are very important, they are only a small part of the much larger pool of information that the Bible has given us. Too many interpreters begin with these few snap-shots and when their conclusions are not supported by the wealth of other prophetic passages, they usually either twist those passages to conform to their established presumptions or they just ignore them altogether.

But we cannot take such a "pick-and-choose" approach. Again, in order to form an accurate and truly Biblical perspective on the End-Times, we must rely on the complete and full counsel of Scripture. In order for any theory or position to be convincing and more universally received by the Church, it is necessary that all of the passages be sufficiently reconciled—they must all come together cohesively in order to paint one consistent picture. In the following chapters we will show how all the prophetic Scriptures regarding the end of days will fit the scenario that is described in this chapter.

⁓ 53 ⁓

The Battle for Jerusalem
What Will Christians Do
Before and After the Rapture?

THE PRO-ISRAEL CHRISTIAN FORCES

Just the mention of the Christian "Zionist Lobby" has built such a stigma that any Christian group that supports Israel gets this label as a warning for everyone to stay away. Yet the ones that are the most rejected and tossed away by the world are the very ones with a very important mission that Messiah collects on His Day. Instead of sending them as ambassadors, now they instantly enlist and obtain an immortal body to become His Great Army commissioned to do battle for Jerusalem. This concept is virtually undiscussed anywhere in the Church.

Consider now the case of the coming of the Messiah as found in Micah 5. Western Christians refer to this chapter simply as the Christmas story and a prophecy of the place of Jesus' birth. Yet a careful study of this chapter in conjunction with Joel 2 reveals that at the time of the second coming, there will also be several nations that will come to the aide of Israel as well as raptured believers who come down with Christ to aid Israel in defeating the Antichrist and his Muslim hordes. I know, you're shocked because I stated that this enemy is Muslim—just keep reading. I have included the full text of the chapters we will discuss so you can refer to them in detail. It is better not to accept any claim, mine included, unless you examine each word from the text like a good Berean. May I suggest you review the underlined verses first, then go and study the full chapter of Micah 5:

> "¹⁾Now gather yourself in troops O daughter of troops; he has laid siege against us; they will strike the judge of Israel with a rod on the cheek. ²⁾But you, Bethlehem Ephrathah, though you are little among the thousands of Judah, yet out of you shall come forth to me the one to be ruler in Israel, Whose goings forth are from of old, from everlasting. ³⁾Therefore he shall give them up, until the time that she who is in labor has given birth; then the <u>remnant</u> of <u>his brethren</u> shall return to the children of Israel. ⁴⁾And he shall stand and feed *his flock* in the strength of the LORD, in the majesty of the name of the LORD His God; and they shall abide, for now he shall be great

to the ends of the earth; 5)and this *one* shall be peace. When the Assyrian comes into our land, and when he treads in our palaces, then we will raise against him seven shepherds and eight princely men. 6)They shall waste with the sword the land of Assyria, and the land of Nimrod at its entrances; thus he shall deliver *us* from the Assyrian, when he comes into our land and when he treads within our borders. 7)Then the remnant of Jacob shall be in the midst of many peoples, like dew from the LORD, like showers on the grass that tarry for no man nor wait for the sons of men. 8)And the remnant of Jacob shall be among the Gentiles, in the midst of many peoples, like a lion among the beasts of the forest, like a young lion among flocks of sheep, who, if he passes through, both treads down and tears in pieces, and none can deliver. 9)Your hand shall be lifted against your adversaries, and all your enemies shall be cut off. 10)And it shall be in that day, says the LORD, that I will cut off your horses from your midst and destroy your chariots. 11)I will cut off the cities of your land and throw down all your strongholds. 12)I will cut off sorceries from your hand, and you all have no soothsayers. 13)Your carved images I will also cut off, and your sacred pillars from your midst; You shall no more worship the work of your hands; 14)I will pluck your wooden images from your midst; Thus I will destroy your cities. 15)I will execute vengeance in anger and fury on the nations that have not heard. Let's walk through it together, now gather thyself in troops, O daughter of troops: he hath laid siege against us: they shall smite the judge of Israel with a rod upon the cheek" (Micah 5)

In verse 1 of Micah 5 above, the Messiah is struck in accordance with Isaiah 53 where the Messiah is smitten and afflicted. This is also in alignment with Genesis 3:15 where God prophesied to Satan the serpent that he would one day strike the heel of the Messiah. Though Satan smites the "judge of Israel," God has a response: "But thou, Bethlehem Ephratah, though you be little among the thousands of Judah, yet out of you shall he come forth unto me that is to be ruler in Israel; whose goings forth have been from of old, from everlasting." (Micah 5:2)

The Gospels record that this passage was referenced by the chief priests. (Matthew 2:4-5) The Jews of Jesus day knew this passage well. They longed for its fulfillment because it says that: "Israel will be abandoned until the time when she who is in labor gives birth and the rest of his brethren return to join the Israelites" (v. 3).

How is Israel abandoned?

Who is "she who is in labor?"

Who are these that He calls "His Brethren?"

These terms are so crucial. Indeed, we need to explain this whole scenario carefully.

So let's start at the beginning. In order to explain Micah 5 we need to first connect it with all that is taught in Joel. With patience, slow and careful reading you will get it, and when you do, you will never be the same. Do you know why I say that you will never be the same? Because if you are a Christian who loves the God of Israel, you will come to understand how you will be involved in the unfolding of all of this. You will also see the necessity to stand with Israel. You will finally understand why so many ministries stand with Israel's right to the land and to stop this nonsense that Israel doesn't matter. You will finally understand what God has been talking about this whole time and how He reconciles between Himself, His adopted children, and brethren (Christians) and His physical brethren—Israel. Remember—read slowly. Take your time. It is crucial to start with the Book of Joel to see why and how Christ rescues Israel in accordance with Micah 5. Joel 2 also speaks of this rescue mission:

> 1)Blow the trumpet in Zion, and sound an alarm in My holy mountain! Let all the inhabitants of the land tremble; for the day of the LORD is coming, for it is at hand: 2)A day of darkness and gloominess, a day of clouds and thick darkness, like the morning clouds spread over the mountains. A people come, great and strong, the like of whom has never been; nor will there ever be any such after them, even for many successive generations. 3)A fire devours before them, and behind them a flame burns; the land is like the Garden of Eden before them, and behind them a desolate wilderness; surely nothing shall escape them. 4)Their appearance is like the appearance of horses; and like swift steeds, so they run. 5)With a noise like chariots over mountaintops they leap, like the noise of a flaming fire that devours the stubble, like a strong people set in battle array. 6)Before them the people writhe in pain; all faces are drained of color. 7)They run like mighty men, they climb the wall like men of war; every one marches in formation, and they do not break ranks. 8)They do not push one another; every one marches in his own column. Though they lunge between the weapons, they are not cut down. 9)They run to and fro in the city, they run on the wall; they climb into the houses, they enter at the windows like a thief. 10)The earth quakes before them, the heavens tremble; the sun and moon grow dark, and the stars diminish their brightness. 11)The LORD gives voice before His army, for His camp is very great; for strong is the One who executes His word. For the day of the LORD is great and very terrible; who can endure it? 12)"Now,

therefore," says the LORD, "Turn to Me with all your heart, With fasting, with weeping, and with mourning." 13)So rend your heart, and not your garments; return to the LORD your God, for He is gracious and merciful, slow to anger, and of great kindness; and He relents from doing harm. 14)Who knows if He will turn and relent, and leave a blessing behind Him—a grain offering and a drink offering For the LORD your God? 15)Blow the trumpet in Zion, consecrate a fast, call a sacred assembly; 16)Gather the people, sanctify the congregation, assemble the elders, gather the children and nursing babes; let the bridegroom go out from his chamber, and the bride from her dressing room. 17)Let the priests, who minister to the LORD, weep between the porch and the altar; let them say, "Spare your people, O LORD, and do not give your heritage to reproach, that the nations should rule over them. Why should they say among the peoples, 'Where is their God?'" 18)Then the LORD will be zealous for His land, and pity His people. 19)The LORD will answer and say to His people, "Behold, I will send you grain and new wine and oil, and you will be satisfied by them; I will no longer make you a reproach among the nations." 20)"But I will remove far from you the Northern army, and will drive him away into a barren and desolate land, with his face toward the Eastern sea, and his back toward the Western sea; His stench will come up, and his foul odor will rise, because he has done monstrous things." 21)Fear not, O land; be glad and rejoice, For the LORD has done marvelous things! 22)Do not be afraid, you beasts of the field; for the open pastures are springing up, and the tree bears its fruit; the fig tree and the vine yield their strength. 23)Be glad then, you children of Zion, and rejoice in the LORD your God; for He has given you the former rain faithfully, and He will cause the rain to come down for you—the former rain, and the latter rain in the first month 24)the threshing floors shall be full of wheat, and the vats shall overflow with new wine and oil. 25)"So I will restore to you the years that the warming locust has eaten, the crawling locust, the consuming locust, and the chewing locust, my great army which I sent among you 26)you shall eat in plenty and be satisfied, and praise the name of the LORD your God, who has dealt wondrously with you; and My people shall never be put to shame. 27)Then you shall know that I am in the midst of Israel: I am the LORD your God and there is no other. My people shall never be put to shame. 28)And it shall come to pass afterward that I will pour out My Spirit on all flesh; your sons and your daughters shall prophesy, your old men shall dream dreams, your young men shall see visions. 29)And also on My menservants and on My maidservants I will pour out My Spirit in those days. 30)And I will show wonders in the heavens and in the earth: Blood and fire and pillars of smoke. 31)The sun shall be turned into darkness, and the moon into blood, before the coming of the great and awesome day of the LORD. 32)And it shall come to pass that whoever calls on the name of the LORD shall be saved. For in Mount Zion and in Jerusalem there shall be deliverance, as the LORD has said, among the remnant whom the LORD calls." (Joel 2)

LOCUSTS ARE LOCUSTS AND PEOPLE ARE PEOPLE

One misconception must be cleared. In Joel 2 many think that it's primarily speaking of an army of literal locusts. How so? These are human beings: "A people come, great and strong, the like of whom has never been; nor will there ever be any such after them" (Joel 2:2). These are not locusts but human beings with glorified bodies that do not die and cannot be killed: "Though they lunge between the weapons, they are not cut down" (Joel 2:8). Locusts do not fight in formation as these do: "they shall not break their ranks" (v. 7).

The context of Joel 2 is not to be confused with Joel 1. The locusts in Joel 1 are literal locusts that swept throughout Israel and kept it desolate for two millennia. It is known that these swarms of locusts would invade the land from the Sahara, although these swarms ceased in 1959. Eilat had a minor hit in 2004, but the rest of Israel was spared. But this recent swarm was minor compared to the swarms of the past: "...in our times we have seen swarms of locusts cover the land of Judea, which upon the wind rising have been driven into the first and last seas; that is, into the Dead sea and Mediterranean sea; and when the shores of both seas have been filled with heaps of dead locusts, which the waters have thrown up, their rottenness and stench have been so very noxious as to corrupt the air, and produce a pestilence among men and beasts."[1] The swarms can reach great sizes: a swarm across the Red Sea in 1889 was estimated to cover two thousand square miles. A swarm is estimated to contain up to 120 million insects per mile.[2]

Everyone knew of the locusts that invaded the land. My family would tell me of one particular locust invasion that occurred before Israel was established in which they had to close the wooden doors and window shutters. They could hear the swarms as they came and left within minutes. After they opened their windows, everything green was gone. The locusts would reach the Mediterranean and find nothing green left to eat and the miles of dead heaps of locusts would cover the shores of Israel. These accounts of locust invasions continued until Israel was restored as a nation: "And I will restore to you the years that the locust hath eaten, the cankerworm, and the caterpillar, and the palmerworm, my great army which I sent among you." (Joel 2:25)

JOEL 2 – THE CHRISTIAN ARMY

ARMY OF JOEL 2—WHO ARE THEY?

Many regard the army of Joel 2 to be an evil army coming against Israel. They perceive this because this army greatly destroys by fire. But this is not sufficient evidence to conclude that the army of Joel 2 is an enemy of Israel. It's simply misplacing the correct pieces of this puzzle. Psalm 50, Isaiah 13, Daniel 7, Zechariah 14, Matthew 24:31 and Joel 2 are the correct pieces that speak of the same story with both war and the Rapture in all six passages. The context of all these passages is the war and the catching away (Rapture). Whether the Rapture is a Pre-Tribulation, Mid-, or Post-Tribulation event is irrelevant at this point. The text is unclear in these as to the timing of the Rapture and could be argued by some to support a Post, yet we know that the battle itself will occur at the end of the Tribulation as commonly agreed. Whether the Rapture takes the believers before the seven years, then prepares them to come down for this battle later; or in the Middle; or we are caught up at the tail end to instantly participate in this, the timing is of no concern to Easterners; I predict that Westerners will wrestle with this issue and with each other until "The Kingdom comes."

THE WAR—DESTRUCTION BY FIRE

Just because there is destruction in Joel 2, it doesn't mean a wrong has been committed. God destroys nations for attacking Israel. This is not to be confused with the Destroyer, whose actions are for evil.

"A fire shall devour before Him, and it shall be very tempestuous all around Him." (Psalm 50:3)

This is commonly agreed by most scholars to be speaking of Christ. He comes to destroy the enemies of Israel by fire. Which agrees and correlates perfectly with Joel 2: "A fire devours before them, and behind them a flame burns." (Joel 2:3) It also agrees with Daniel 7:10: "A fiery stream issued and came before Him. A thousand thousands ministered to Him." (Daniel 7:10) Scholars agree that both Daniel 7:10 and Psalm 50:3, are speaking about the Messiah's coming. So why would anyone not also conclude that Joel 2 is speaking about the coming of the Messiah? The argument is that in Psalm 50:3 and

Daniel 7, they are addressing a single person—Messiah, while Joel 2 is regarding a multitude of people.

But this is not entirely accurate, as in Daniel 7:10, Messiah has a *thousand thousands* with Him. Who are these thousand thousands? These are the multitudes of believers as commonly agreed. This is the Messiah and his followers.

Isaiah 13 also speaks of these followers. In Isaiah 12:6 it says: "Cry out and shout, O inhabitant of Zion, for great is the Holy One of Israel in your midst!" With Messiah being on earth in Israel's midst, the call is on the sanctified ones: "I have also called My mighty ones for My anger—those who rejoice in My exaltation." (Isaiah 13:3) Who are these "mighty ones?" Everyone would agree that these who exalt God are believers. They are His "mighty ones" and are called for "His anger" and to fight with Him in battle: "The Lord of hosts musters the army for battle." (Isaiah 13:4) Why is He calling them "mighty ones?" They must have glorified bodies. Then He calls them an "army." There can be no doubt that these are His followers. These are the same people in Joel 2:11: "The Lord gives voice before His army" (Joel 2:11). All of these passages fit together perfectly. Joel 2 covers both the Rapture and the War as well.

Yes, you read it right—War.

Western Christians cannot get a grip over this issue—they will be fighting a war against an Islamic invasion—the Battle for Jerusalem. It will be the last war that will finally bring peace. Yet Western Christians rarely talk about the literal war that we will be in after the Rapture. In the East, Christians already cry out, "how long O Lord?" Meanwhile Westerners argue about the timing of the Rapture. Every time the subject of the Rapture comes up, a sword fight almost ensues and casualties of war are counted on all sides as people walk out of churches to join others of their Rapture-timing persuasion. In the East, few are concerned with this Western argument; there is a land that is already in the Tribulation.

Please don't get me wrong, I am not saying that we are in the Great Tribulation period. I would hate it if you put words in my mouth. I have had people who accuse me of having a position. Well I do daily pray for a Pre-Tribulation Rapture, and always prepare for a Post. I am of neither position. You will find no Scripture that states we should squabble over the timing of the Rapture. The Scriptures say to be ready, so start packing. Now you might ask, "What do we need to pack?" The answer is, nothing; you will receive your instructions once you meet with the King in the air. Are you ready? My job is simply to cry out—prepare the way, make straight the crooked roads, choose the narrow gate, choose wisely, choose Jerusalem for Israel not for the Muslims.

Even my position on the Rapture which is having "no position" gets me in trouble in the West. Will we ever get beyond such arguments? When Muslim Fundamentalists take over a Christian society and begin to behead, they never ask what Rapture position any of their victims hold, neither do they ask their denomination. In the case of Islam we all need to unite.

Now I just might get accused of being one of these who promote the One World Church. Not hardly. A One World Church would be a disaster in my opinion. It is good to have some differences; the ministry of Rebuke is an absolute necessity. It needs however, to switch from non-essentials to absolute essentials. As Islamic persecution increases, we shall see a dwindling of these non-essential arguments. This is why at times I pray for persecution. Satan fooled himself thinking that by killing us he would win. The fact is that everything Satan does ends up being used by God for good—when the crowds cried "crucify Him" God cried out "It is finished." What a great victory. Okay, back to the subject.

RAPTURE

Both Isaiah 13:3-4 and Joel 2:11 are speaking about The Lord's army. How could this army be bad? This army of the Lord in Joel 2 is the army that has just been Raptured: "Let the bridegroom go out from His chamber. And the bride from her dressing room" (Joel 2:16). Anytime the bridegroom goes out to meet the bride, it is none other than the Rapture. The purpose of the Rapture is this battle, and is clearly the same as in Psalm 50:4: "Gather My saints together to Me, Those who have made a covenant with Me by sacrifice" (Psalm 50:4).

This is a powerful verse that makes a powerful argument. The "gathering together unto Him" (II Thessalonians 2:1) are His saints that have a covenant with Him by sacrifice. Only believers will qualify. Psalm 50:4 are indeed the saints, the ones who awaited Messiah and sacrificed animals prior to His first coming, and the ones who accepted Him after the cross—the dead in Christ rise first, then the ones who are alive will follow.

The language in Psalm 50:4 is the same as in Matthew 24:31: "And He will send His angels with a great sound of a trumpet, and they will gather together His elect from the four winds, from one end of heaven to the other." Gather together His elect for what? God is not the author of confusion. He has a purpose for doing things. The Rapture has many purposes, yet the Bible sets forth as one of the clear reasons a very practical one—the Raptured believers are coming with Christ to participate alongside Him in the great battle of Jerusalem as described in Zechariah 14:5: "Then you [Israel] shall flee through My mountain valley, For the mountain valley shall reach to Azal. Yes, you shall flee as you fled from the earthquake in the days of Uzziah king of Judah. Thus the LORD my God will come, and all the saints [believers] with You" (Zechariah 14:5). *God will come and all the saints are with*

Him? This reconciles Psalm 50, Isaiah 13, and Zechariah 14 with Joel 2. They all fit together perfectly.

In Zechariah 14:5 the context is clear—the saints are with Him in this battle. In Zechariah 14:3 it states: "The Lord will go forth and fight...His feet will stand in that day upon the Mount of Olives...and the Mount of Olives shall be split in two." The earthquake is the same earthquake that we read about in Joel 2: "the earth quakes before them." The Lord goes down to Jerusalem for a fight (Joel 2:10): "the Lord will go forth and fight." This is to spare Israel from destruction. The whole context of Zechariah 14 is the Battle over Jerusalem. This matches what is written in Joel 2: "Let them say, "Spare your people O Lord, and do not give your inheritance to reproach, that the nations should rule over them. Why should they say among the peoples, 'Where is their God?' Then the Lord will be zealous for His land, and pity His people." (Joel 2:17-19) They are the army of Joel 2 and the people to be spared are the remnant of Israel. If the "inheritance" is the church, then where is The Church's land? The verse is clear: "the Lord will be zealous for His land" which is always the greater Land of Israel.

For many Christians, the land of Israel is insignificant. But it is not insignificant to God. In fact, he clearly returns to judge those nations that divided His land. (Joel 3:2) The bride, His church, is involved in this battle with glorified bodies that do not die: "Though they lunge between the weapons, they are not cut down" (Joel 2:8).

They are not cut down? These people in Joel 2 can lunge between the weapons and do not die. When do these people become impervious to weapons? How do they become indestructible? It is only when they receive their glorified bodies.

Some argue with me on this issue, that these people simply lunge between the weapons and not into them, which is why they are not killed. If this argument is true, what is the purpose of the verse? Where is the miracle? The context is speaking of the miraculous— they run on the walls (v. 9). How can people run on walls? With glorified bodies, we can not only walk on walls, but walk through them. In verse 11, these are the Lord's army: "The Lord gives voice before His army" (Joel 2:11). This must be the Lord's army. This leaves no question that the army of Joel 2 are the good guys. In Zechariah 14:5 the army is defined: "all the saints with you." They are the saints—both the martyred and the living.

THE MARTYRS REVENGE

The ones that Islam kills will come back to haunt them. It is these who are the real martyrs and not these evil Muslim "Shahids"—the suicide bombers who blow up innocent men, women and children. Remember, the enemy robs everything that belongs to us, and then applies it to his people. He then takes everything that *they* are guilty of, and applies that to us. Here I will show who the true martyrs are.

There is a debate that the, "marriage supper of the lamb" and the "marriage supper of the Great God" are two separate events.

What we first need to consider is that there is a purpose for everything: God is a God of order and purpose. In Revelation 19:7 we read: "Let us be glad and rejoice, and give honor to him: for the marriage of the Lamb is come, and His wife hath made herself ready" as shown in the following: "Behold, I show you a mystery; We shall not all sleep, but we shall all be changed, In a moment, in the twinkling of an eye, at the last trump: for the trumpet shall sound, and the dead shall be raised incorruptible, and we shall be changed. For this corruptible must put on incorruption, and this mortal [must] put on immortality. So when this corruptible shall have put on incorruption, and this mortal shall have put on immortality, then shall be brought to pass the saying that is written, Death is swallowed up in victory. O death, where [is] thy sting? O grave, where is thy victory? But thanks be to God, which giveth us the victory through our Lord Jesus Christ" (1 Corinthians 15:51-55).

He (the bridegroom) and the bride (the believers in Messiah), prepare for war leading up to the Marriage Supper of The Lamb. That is, believers in Messiah will participate in the Battle for Jerusalem prior to the Marriage Supper of the Lamb. "Let the priests, the ministers of the LORD, weep between the porch and the altar, and let them say, Spare thy people, O LORD, and give not thine heritage to reproach, that the heathen should rule over them: wherefore should they say among the people, Where is their God? Then will the LORD be jealous for his land, and pity his people" (Joel 2:17-18). The Book of Joel describes a single event—the Day of the Lord and the Battle of Armageddon.

Both Joel 2 and I Corinthians 15 are passages speaking about the incorruptible body. But Joel 2 contextualizes this by placing the timing of this glorification of the believers' bodies at the Great War for Jerusalem. In Joel 2, this incorruptible body is fighting on the Day of The Lord: "Blow ye the trumpet in Zion, and sound an alarm in my holy mountain: let all the inhabitants of the land tremble: for the day of the LORD cometh, for it is nigh at hand" (Joel 2:1).

Again in both passages there is the trumpet. Joel describes this day as: "A day of darkness and of gloominess, a day of clouds and of thick darkness, as the morning spread upon the mountains: a great people and a strong; there hath not been ever the like, neither shall be any more after it, even to the years of many generations. Fire devours before them; and behind them a flame burns: the land is as the Garden of Eden before them, and behind them a desolate wilderness; yea, and nothing shall escape them" (Joel 2:2-4). "Neither shall one thrust another; they shall walk every one in his path: and when they fall upon the sword, they shall not be wounded" (Joel 2:8).

Here these fighters cannot be wounded because they have incorruptible bodies as described in I Corinthians 15. Muslims claim that those who die in their evil battles that they offer to Molech/Allah are martyrs and that their corpses do not corrupt. What utter rubbish and nonsense! They steal verses from Scripture and apply them to their dead criminals. This is the type of blasphemy that Islam offers. If this is true, they should keep the corpses for a few days and see how fast they swell and stink. Joel presents the believers as super-human and this event as a definite tribulation: "They shall run to and fro in the city; they shall run upon the wall, they shall climb up upon the houses; they shall enter in at the windows like a thief. The earth shall quake before them; the heavens shall tremble: the sun and the moon shall be dark, and the stars shall withdraw their shining. And the LORD shall utter His voice before His army: for His camp is very great: for He is strong that executes His word: for the day of the LORD is great and very terrible; and who can abide it?" (Joel 2:9-11)

The "sun and the moon" being dark are none other than The Day of The Lord. Yet on that day, He speaks to His army in preparation for this battle of the Day of the Lord. Messiah is here in person, leading the defense of Jerusalem. This confirms that believers will fight physically in Jerusalem. Our fight in this world may be against spiritual forces, against powers and principalities, but this struggle will confound us in the physical realm too; Scripture makes that explicit. This declaration of the Lord before His army is supported in Revelation 19:15: "And out of His mouth goes a sharp sword, that with it He should smite the nations: and He shall rule them with a rod of iron: and He treads the winepress of the fierceness and wrath of Almighty God."

This "sharp sword" coming out of His mouth is the proclamation of war as written about in Joel 2:11: "And the LORD shall utter his voice before his army." Some people claim that this "sword" is simply God destroying the enemies miraculously. Yet, the utterance from Messiah's mouth is a command: "I beheld till the thrones were cast down, and the Ancient of days did sit, whose garment was white as snow, and the hair of his head like the pure wool: his throne was like the fiery flame, and his wheels as burning fire. A fiery stream issued and came forth from before him: thousand thousands ministered unto him, and ten thousand times ten thousand stood before him: the judgment was set, and the books were opened" (Daniel 7:9-10).

It's a command, an order, and a proclamation. Revelation 19:14 speaks of the Lord's army: "And the armies which were in heaven followed him upon white horses, clothed in fine linen, white and clean." Joel 2:16 describes it this way: "Gather the people, sanctify the congregation, assemble the elders, gather the children, and those that suck the breasts: let the bridegroom go forth of his chamber, and the bride out of her closet."

Here is the Rapture in which the bridegroom (Messiah) meets the bride (Messiah's followers) to participate in The Marriage Supper of The Lamb. The text continues to tell us what is to come: "Let the priests, the ministers of the LORD, weep between the porch and the altar, and let them say, Spare thy people, O LORD, and give not thine heritage to reproach, that the heathen should rule over them: wherefore should they say among the people, Where is their God?" (Joel 2:17)

Immediately after this intercessory cry is let out, the saints are transferred into the army to actually help fulfill their own prayers. In Revelation 19:13: "And He was clothed with a garment sprinkled with blood; and his name is called The Word of God... And the armies that were in heaven followed him upon white horses, clothed in fine linen, white and clean. And out of his mouth goes a sharp sword, that with it he should smite the nations, and he shall rule them with a rod of iron; and he treads the winepress of the fierceness and wrath of Almighty God. And he hath on his vesture and on his thigh a name written, KING OF KINGS, AND LORD OF LORDS."

The armies followed Him to earth, in order to "smite the nations." Notice, the armies are "clothed in fine linen, white and clean."

According to Revelation 19:7-8, this is the attire of the bride of Christ. Many argue that His armies are angelic hosts, yet Scripture alludes to martyred-saints. Look out Islamo-Facist, here they come: "And when he had opened the fifth seal, I saw under the altar the souls of them that were slain for the word of God, and for the testimony which they held: And they cried with a loud voice, saying, How long, O Lord, holy and true, dost thou not judge and avenge our blood on them that dwell on the earth? And white robes were given unto every one of them; and it was said unto them, that they should rest yet for a little season, until their fellow servants also and their brethren, which should be killed as they were, should be fulfilled" (Revelation 6:9-11).

The believers, who are with the Lord, are given white robes, the same garments in which the armies are dressed. Messiah will come for battle with His army of believers: "Who is this that comes from Edom (Arabia) from Bozrah in garments stained crimson? Who is this so splendidly robed, marching in his great might? It is I, announcing vindication, mighty to save. Why are your robes red, and your garments like theirs who tread the wine press? I have trodden the wine press alone, and from the peoples no one was with me; I trod them in my anger and trampled them in my wrath; their juice spattered on my garments, and stained all my robes. For the day of vengeance was in my heart, and the year for my redeeming work had come. I looked, but there was no helper; I stared, but there was no one to sustain me; so my own arm brought me victory, and my wrath sustained me. I trampled down peoples in my anger, I crushed them in my wrath, and I poured out their lifeblood on the earth." (Isaiah 63:1-6)

"I (the Lord) will send a fire into Teman: and it shall devour the houses of Bozrah." (Amos 1:12)

These (Teman, Bozrah, etc.) are Muslim nations today. And the Lord is fighting them. This will be the day when Christians will finally participate in executing justice. Yet most Christians believe that a sword will come out of His mouth and poof! The enemy will be gone. Not so. The blade protruding from His mouth is symbolic, representing the Messiah's judgment upon the nations. In other words Messiah will let the Christians have at it. And indeed we will. *This will indeed be the day when Christians participate in executing justice.*

The false bravery of Muslim warriors, the wolf packs that rape and kill innocent Christian women in Armenia, Sudan, and Lebanon will see the day when these women come back at them and their cowardly faces are wrenched with pain: "Before them the people writhe in pain; all faces are drained of color" (Joel 2:6). That's right, you cowards that kill yourselves and others. Kim-Sun-il, the Korean translator that you killed is coming back. As the Messiah returns, so will he. This time it is you who will beg for your life while your teeth gnash with trembling and fear. What goes around will come around. *God is just!*

Zechariah 14:4 states that the Messiah will stand on the Mount of Olives with an earthquake, as he comes for the battle in Jerusalem. According to Christian doctrine, the nation of Israel was punished with 2000 years of Diaspora for not paying attention to "the time of thy visitation." (Luke 19:44) Is it possible that the same problem will occur on His Second Coming? The issue was ignorance: "my people are destroyed from lack of knowledge" (Hosea 4:6). This is the attitude of some people today, "We will find out when He comes" or "We'll know the truth when we die."

It could be argued that they did not recognize His First Coming because they didn't care how He was to come; they simply followed the mainstream interpretations of the most famous rabbis who said that the Messiah would defeat Rome. Noah preached for 120 years and not one person outside of his family listened to him: "And God spared not the old world, but saved Noah the eighth person, a preacher of righteousness, bringing in the flood upon the world of the ungodly" (II Peter 2:5).

Every word regarding Messiah's Second Coming is crucial. How else could we distinguish between the Antichrist, who performs signs and wonders, and the Messiah, who also performs signs and wonders? Most Christians' attitude towards Israel is, at best, lukewarm, and so they must meditate on the written word of God to recognize that the Messiah is coming back for Israel and He will fight for her, so we ought to decide which side we are on right now. Do we sit by while her enemies try to crush her and say, "God will take care of it?"

The Lord will "catch up" the believers literally in the clouds and in His timing, they will descend together on earth to fight for Israel in the battle of Armageddon: "For the Lord Himself shall descend from heaven with a shout, with the voice of the archangel, and with the trump of God: and the dead in Christ shall rise first" (I Thessalonians 4:16).

The Bible says that we ought to focus on His coming again and our meeting Him and being with Him. Messiah is simply coming for Israel to save his people, the Jewish nation, with his saints, and these saints are none other than the true Christians who rise up to meet him in the air and then descend down to fight the enemy on the ground: "So the angel that communed with me said unto me, Cry thou, saying, Thus Says the Lord of hosts; I am jealous for Jerusalem and for Zion with a great jealousy" (Zechariah 1:14).

The Lord is greatly concerned for Jerusalem his Holy City and his people of Israel, to the point where He is jealous for His people and will fight for them in the Last-Days: "And I am very sore displeased with the heathen that are at ease: for I was but a little displeased, and they helped forward the affliction" (Zechariah 1:15).

The Lord is very angry that the Muslim hordes round about have made the lives of Jewish people very hard and bitter, and other nations have stood by passively or even applied greater pressure on Israel. In light of this, we need to consider:

- The Muslim nations are bent on destroying Israel and driving her people into to the sea.
- Most Western nations sit there trying either to negotiate impossible peace deals or to force sanctions on Israel through the United Nations.
- Most Christians are lukewarm and don't really care.

CHRISTIANS FIGHT FOR ISRAEL

Again, in Joel 2 it is clear why this army is at work: "Let them say, 'Spare Your people O Lord, and do not give your inheritance to reproach, That the nations should rule over them. Why should they say among the peoples, 'Where is their God?' Then the Lord will be zealous for His land, and pity His people" (Joel 2:17-19). At the end of the age, true believers should have this intercessory cry on their hearts. They should be spiritual intercessors and even political activists. As the spirit of anti-Semitism spreads even in the Church, Israel needs friends who will stand by her to the very end. Thus it will be these who will enjoy Israel's new beginning. These are the saints that love Israel and who care about the land. Psalm 102 gives a litmus test: "For Your servants take pleasure in her stones, and show favor to her dust" (Psalm 102:14). This is the attitude of Christian pilgrims to Israel. They love to take home a sample of dust or dirt or olive wood from the land. This is the behavior that is consistent with those who love Israel. If Islam truly loved the land of Israel, then why was it a desolate wilderness until the Jews began to immigrate to it? At a pro-Palestine Christian event someone said that the real stones were the "living stones"—"the Palestinians." If so, why didn't God say so? He would have called them "Palestinians," yet He didn't. They are deceived by their own rebelliousness.

Keep in mind that as the story continues in Joel 3, it is the judgment of the enemies of Israel. If anyone hates Israel, they also must hate God and would not have a desire to participate in this battle against Israel in Armageddon. Just look at the conclusion of Joel: "I will also gather all nations, and bring them down to the Valley of Jehoshaphat; And I will enter into **judgment** with them there On account of My people, My heritage Israel" (Joel 3:2). Do you see that word in bold? How crucial is that word? The division of Israel and creating a Palestinian state will be the reason for this judgment: "for they scattered my people among the nations and divided up my land" (Joel 3:2). Christians cannot be pro-Palestine or advocates for a Palestinian state that calls for carving out Israel in order to weaken that nation. Dividing Israel is pro-Antichrist, who divides the land for gain. One cannot be pro-Christ and pro-Antichrist at the same time. Yet this spirit is increasingly infiltrating certain quarters of the Church today.

JOEL'S WAR IS WITH ISLAM

The war over the land is with Muslim nations. Just read verse 4: "Indeed. What have you to do with Me, O Tyre and Sidon, and all the coasts of Philistia? Will you retaliate against Me?" (Joel 3:4) Lebanon (Tyre) and Muslim Gaza (Philistia) confront the Messiah Himself and lose: "will you retaliate against Me?" Gaza (Hamas) and Lebanon (Hezbollah) today are filled with radical Islam. They already attack Israel. Hezbollah literally means "the Party of Allah." So it will be Allah's Party against Jehovah's Party.

CHRIST IS PRESENT

In this battle the Lord is in Israel in Joel 2: "They shall know that I am in the midst of Israel" (Joel 2:27). The context of Joel 2 is not simply one of some random army that comes against Israel, but rather an army that Messiah leads. He is "in the midst" of Israel along with all of His followers from through the ages. This reality is again expressed in Joel 3: "So you shall know that I am the Lord your God, Dwelling in Zion My holy mountain" (Joel 3:17) Again, Joel 3 is speaking about the Battle of Armageddon in "the Valley of Jehoshaphat" (Joel 3:2). And yet which nations are specified here as being judged? It is none other than Egypt and Arabia: "Egypt shall be a desolation, And Edom a desolate wilderness, Because of violence against the people of Judah, For they have shed innocent blood in their land" (Joel 3:19).

AMOS

Once one begins to understand these themes, they suddenly begin to appear throughout the bible. The Book of Amos also ties into these themes. In the prophecy of Amos, we have Lebanon, Gaza, Egypt, and Arabia, all being marked for destruction within the context of the Lord's return: "The Lord roars from Zion, And utters His voice from Jerusalem." (Amos 1:2) Here, the Lord Himself roars from Jerusalem. Again, whenever God Himself is described as being physically present on the earth, we are reading about the Messiah. Yet what is He doing in this passage? He destroys Syria, Arabia, Gaza, and Lebanon:

Thus says the LORD: "For three transgressions of **Damascus**, and for four, I will not turn away its punishment, because they have threshed Gilead with implements of iron.[4] But I will send a fire into the house of Hazael, Which shall devour the palaces of Ben-Hadad.[5] I will also break the gate bar of Damascus, and cut off the inhabitant from the Valley of Aven, and the one who holds the scepter from Beth Eden. The people of Syria shall go captive to Kir," Says the LORD.[6] Thus says the LORD: "For three transgressions of **Gaza**, and for four, I will not turn away its punishment, because they took captive the whole captivity to deliver them up to Edom.[7]. But I will send a fire upon the wall of Gaza, Which shall devour its palaces.[8] I will cut off the inhabitant from Ashdod, and the one who holds the scepter from Ashkelon; I will turn My hand against Ekron, And the remnant of the Philistines shall perish," Says the Lord GOD.[9] Thus says the LORD: "For three transgressions of **Tyre**, and for four, I will not turn away its punishment, because they delivered up the whole captivity to Edom, and did not remember the covenant of brotherhood.[10] But I will send a fire upon the wall of Tyre, Which shall devour its palaces."[11] Thus says the LORD: "For three transgressions of **Edom**, and for four, I will not turn away its punishment, because he pursued his brother with the sword, and cast off all pity; His anger tore perpetually, and he kept his wrath forever.[12] But I will send a fire upon Teman, Which shall devour the palaces of Bozrah."[13] Thus says the LORD: "For three transgressions of the people of **Ammon**, and for four, I will not turn away its punishment, because they ripped open the women with child in Gilead, that they might enlarge their territory.[14] But I will kindle a fire in the wall of Rabbah, and it shall devour its palaces, amid shouting in the day of battle, and a tempest in the day of the whirlwind.[15] Their king shall go into captivity, He and his princes together," Says the LORD. (Amos 1)

While the defeat of these armies will primarily come from the Lord, part of their defeat is due to the fact that they turn on one another: "It shall come to pass in that day that a great panic from the Lord will be among them. Everyone will seize the hand of his neighbor" (Zechariah 13:13). These are the nations that surround Israel which God gathers for judgment. And in typical Islamic style, we see that they also kill each other: The usual Sunni killing Shi'a, Hamas killing the PLO, Iranians killing Iraqis, Iraqis killing Kuwaitis, Egyptians killing Libyans, Arabs killing Turks...Pray that many more Muslims will awaken to see the futility of following Satan. This can only be revealed as they begin to read and understand the Bible—the Word of the True Living Jehovah. From the very inception of Islam, immediately after Mohammed died, the Muslims began to kill other Muslims. This killing continued until today and will be continued until Messiah settles it.

It should be easy for Muslims to see their fate; "I will gather all nations."

MATTHEW 25 vs. JOEL 3

It is crucial to understand why Matthew 25 and Joel 3 are referring to the same event—the judgment of the gentile nations for their mistreatment of Israel. In Matthew 25, it is regarding the judgment of the nations according to how they treated Jesus' "Brethren." In Joel 3 Jesus again judges the nations specifically according to their treatment of Israel. So who are Jesus' Brethren? Is it Israel or the Church? How many gathering of the nations are there? There is only one:

Zechariah 14:2 "all the nations will be gathered before Him"
Matthew 25:32 "I will also gather all nations"
Joel 3:2 "I will gather all nations"

All throughout the Bible there is only a single judgment of the nations. Remember, this is not the Bema judgment that comes after the Millennium. This is the judgment when the Lord gathers the nations for judgment regarding their injustices toward the nation of Israel.

"My Brethren"
Are They Israel Or The Church?

In that famous parable about the judgment of the Sheep and the Goats, the nations and peoples are divided up according to how they treated Jesus' "brethren." But who are Jesus' brethren? Some say that this is the Church, others say Israel. In all the passages that we have looked at which describe the battles that take place when Jesus returns, they are all concerning the nation of Israel. In fact, the centrality of Israel in all end-time prophecy is an essential part of the picture that many Westerners fail to acknowledge. The usage of brethren can be used in more than one way. It can mean literal brethren, as in the case when Moses predicted the coming of Christ: "a prophet from the midst of thee, of thy brethren" (Dueteronomy 18:15). There are also spiritual brethren who are those who do the will of The Father. (Matthew 12:49-50)

When trying to determine which way Jesus was using the term in the parable of the Sheep and the Goats, we must look at the proper context of the passage. Matthew 25 cannot be separated from the rest of Scripture.

Again, there is only one "gathering of the nations" against Israel: "I will gather all nations" (Zechariah 14:2). "All the nations will be gathered before Him" (Matthew 25:32). "I will also gather all nations" (Joel 3:2). Any honest reading of Joel 2 will have to conclude that the nations are judged according to their treatment of Israel. This passage is literal and is not meant to be read symbolically or allegorically in any way. So if Jesus will judge the nations according to their injustices against Israel, it also only stands to reason that this truth would also be declared in the Parable of the Sheep and the Goats that is found in Matthew 25. Again, a reasonable hermeneutic always uses the clear and literal passage to illuminate the allegorical or difficult passages. Joel 2 declares in no uncertain terms that the nations will be judged according to their treatment of Israel. Matthew 25 teaches the same thing. The "brethren" in Matthew 25 are the Israelites, who are Jesus' relatives, according to the flesh.

In Matthew 25, Jesus tells the story: "I was hungry and you gave Me food...thirsty and you gave Me drink...in prison and you visited Me...a stranger and you took Me in...naked and you clothed Me."

"In prison...Sick?" When was Jesus sick or in prison?

If you want to know when Jesus was in prison or hungry or naked, then simply watch some Holocaust footage. There, you will see Him.

"Yes, but what does that have to do with Salvation?" This is the typical question I get. Well, maybe I will respond by asking a Jesus-style question: Antichrist will divide Israel; he wants to also divide Jerusalem between Israel and Islam. In Joel 3, God is in the valley of Jehoshaphat (which means the Lord judges). There He will judge all who participated in dividing up His land. Read it carefully. Now, if Antichrist wants Jerusalem divided, and Christ condemns this division. Yet you are for this division, which side are you on? Christ's or Antichrist's? Can one be on the side of Christ *and* on the side of Antichrist as well? There are always tests and evidences for one to check to see if they are producing God's fruit. Without any real fruit, you were never saved.

Is this all too difficult for you to swallow? Well, everyone must swallow—either swallow God's Word, or swallow His wrath. The choice is yours. I urge you however to choose the narrow gate, the right side on the fork ahead. Choose wisely, for the right choice will give you eternal life, and the wrong one will take it from you.

Maybe I can share the wisdom of this in the parable of the *Two Christian Nazis During the Holocaust*, on a Sunday morning, a pastor walked by nicely dressed going to church. He swerves out of the way from the sidewalk where a thin Jewish woman with her two starving children were begging, "Please, I have had nothing to eat and we are practically naked, please a piece of bread, a blanket." she says.

Unconcerned the pastor removes her clinging hand, obviously getting his fine garments dirty. "Lady, I am on my way to church, I have washed, and can't you see that I am busy doing the Lord's work?" Then a man by the name of Oscar Schindler walks by. And though he belonged to the Nazi Party, he was defiant and hated Hitler. He stops, takes the woman and her children in his car, puts her to work in his factory and keeps her and her children alive. Which one of the two did the work of God? Was it the pastor or the repentant Nazi? You might argue that the pastor who claimed to be doing God's work. Yet when God's work was right in front of his eyes, he stepped aside. The days ahead will hold many tests for all of us. Choose wisely!

There will be so many who prayed the Salvation prayer with their lips, yet never intended it with their hearts. Many who will call Him "Lord, Lord, we healed in Your name, we cast out demons in Your name." Many who preach health and wealth in the name of

Jesus. But do they truly do the work of God? You see them continually asking for big funds, while driving nice cars, always talking about their ministry that is in need. They talk about how the Lord will *richly bless you* with *abundant material blessings*, all you have to do is send money to them first. Beloved, beware how you spend your money. Always choose wisely.

Now allow me to continue to expand on the suffering people of Matthew 25 and why it must be Israel.

HE SUFFERED LIKE ISRAEL

In Isaiah 63, concerning the judgment of Edom (The Arabs), the secret is given regarding Israel in verse 9: "in all their affliction He was afflicted." Amazing—in every detail of the many afflictions of Israel, the Lord Himself suffered? Yes. Do you think that I found the Bible amazing for mundane and simple reasons? Do you really think that I left Islam and all of its pride for just a weak argument? So, they were silent as they died—He was silent as the crowd mocked Him before and during the cross. One can watch the footage, they died in amazing silence. If they were strangers and in prisons (Ghettos in the West, and Mellahs in the Middle East), so was He in prison. If they were starving, so was He. Even in their death, literally naked, so was His death, He was naked.

Can anyone imagine such horrible death and shame the Jews suffered in Nazi Germany? No one can forget the scenes of Rabbis' beards being ripped out, or the flogging of Jews in the concentration camps. "I gave My back to those who struck Me, And My cheeks to those who plucked out the beard; I did not hide my face from shame and spitting" (Isaiah 50:6). Indeed, neither did they hide their faces it's all on film—watch it.

Even Messiah's face being slapped had to be fulfilled by the Jews. Jews living in Muslim lands for centuries had to be slapped on the face as a custom. A Jew living in Tunisia recounts how they were treated as "dhimmis" (subjected people) under Islam. "The Jew is prohibited in this country to wear the same cloths as a Muslim and may not wear a red tarbush. He can be seen to bow down with his whole body to a Muslim child and permit him the traditional privilege of striking him on the face, a gesture that can prove to be of the gravest consequences. Indeed, the present writer has received such blows. In such manners the offenders act with complete impunity, for this has been the custom from time immemorial."[3]

As Christ died, so did the nation of Israel. In the resurrection even as Christ rose on, "the third day" (1 Corinthians 15:4) so also did the Jewish people revive as a nation: "After two days He will revive us; On the third day He will raise us up" (Hosea 6:2.) A day with the Lord is as a thousand years, so also, did the Nation of Israel arise "after two days" and was born in one day—May 14th, 1948: "Shall a nation be born at once? For as soon as Zion was in labor she gave birth to her children" (Isaiah 66:8).

When Jesus was held captive, the Gentiles cast lots for His garments: "Parted His garments, casting lots upon them, what every man should take" (Mark 15:24). This is also symbolic of Israel being sold into slavery to the Gentiles: "They have cast lots for my people and have given a boy for a harlot, and sold a girl for wine, that they might drink" (Joel 3:3).

ZION IN LABOR

In Isaiah 66:8, how was Zion in labor? It was through the Holocaust and the persecution of the Jews in Europe and the Middle East, that 850,000 exiled Jews from the Middle East were forced to flee to Israel. This was the birth of a nation. After labor comes birth and joy. Can all of this be orchestrated? Self fulfilled prophecy?

Micah 5 ends all arguments. There the Messiah from my village of Bethlehem is rejected. Therefore He "gives them up until the time that she who is in labor has given birth" (v. 3). This is Israel. It is the same story that is told in, Isaiah 66:8 and in Micah 5:3. There it is clear who the "brethren" are: "Then the remnant of His brethren shall return to the children of Israel." Sadly, only "a remnant" of Jews—not all—will migrate to Israel. No one can question that these brethren are Israel.

It is not necessary for all Jews to be in Israel for Messiah to re-appear. In Psalm 22:22, we read: "I will declare Your name to my brethren" (v. 22), the next verse continues, "All you descendants of Jacob glorify Him" (v. 23). One cannot escape the fact that Israel is found in every nook and cranny of Scripture. The very destiny of mankind is intimately tied to the Nation of Israel. Even the very suffering, death and resurrection of Jesus are mirrored in the Nation of Israel. If one doubts this, then I challenge you to explain Psalm 129:3-5 that describes the hatred of Messiah: "The plowers plowed on my back; They made their furrows long." This is regarding the Messiah's suffering as He was whipped and the skin of His back peeled off. But in the next verse, the focus shifts: "Let all these who hate Zion Be put to shame and turned back." Do you see how Jesus identifies Himself with Zion? This is identical to the pattern that we see in Matthew 25 and the Parable of the Sheep and the Goats.

In the Book of Jeremiah, the Lord speaks of Babylon tormenting Israel. But pay attention to the language: "Let the violence done to me and my flesh be upon Babylon" (Jeremiah 51:35). The Lord relates to Israel as His physical body: "the inhabitant of Zion will say; 'and my blood be upon the inhabitants of Chaldea!'" (Jeremiah 51:35)

～55～
God Will Raise
Seven Allied Nations

In Micah 5, the coming Messiah was specifically to be a sign to the Israelites that an epoch had ended. No longer would they be abandoned by God. They would live securely under the leadership of the Messiah: "He will stand and shepherd his flock in the strength of Jehovah, in the majesty of the name of Jehovah his God. And they will live securely, for then his greatness will reach to the ends of the earth" (Micah 5:4). Israel would no longer have to fear its enemies. The greatness of this Messiah would reach to the ends of the earth. But it is the next verse that is so essential to consider. For here we are told that this Messiah would deliver Israel from the invading Antichrist, whom the passage links to Nimrod the founder of Babel, and refers to him as, "the Assyrian." "And this man [the Messiah] shall be the peace, when the Assyrian shall come into our land: and when he shall tread in our palaces, we will raise against him seven shepherds, even eight principled men. They will rule the land of Assyria with the sword, the land of Nimrod with drawn sword. He [Messiah] will deliver us from the Assyrian when he invades our land and marches into our borders" (Micah 5:2-6).

The Assyrian (Antichrist) will attack Israel. Messiah will be the one to defeat him and establish true peace. It also says that in the midst of this, "seven shepherds, even eight principled men" will be raised up by God to participate in the defeat of the Antichrist.

Remember what the verse says, "we will raise against him seven shepherds, even eight principled men. They will rule the land of Assyria with the sword, the land of Nimrod with drawn sword."

They, the seven shepherds will destroy Assyria and Nimrod.

This is crucial. God will raise seven allies to help Israel in fighting against the Antichrist. These seven shepherds are rarely if ever discussed. The Bible describes in many cases that He will raise nations from the ends of the earth, far from the Middle East, to destroy Antichrist. Is it possible that seven righteous nations will stand on the side of Christ and Israel in the end? Could America be on this list of righteous defenders?

I've had many people argue with me that the 'Seven Shepherds' are from amongst Israel. But in Biblical symbolism, *Shepherds* are leaders of nations. A passage from the Book of Jeremiah reveals this. Consider first the following passage: "Woe be unto the pastors that destroy and scatter the sheep of my pasture! says the LORD. Therefore thus says the LORD God of Israel against the pastors that feed my people; Ye have scattered my flock, and driven them away, and have not visited them: behold, I will visit upon you the evil of your doings, says the LORD. And I will gather the remnant of my flock out of all countries whither I have driven them, and will bring them again to their folds; and they shall be fruitful and increase. And I will set up shepherds over them which shall feed them: and they shall fear no more, nor be dismayed, neither shall they be lacking, says the LORD." The "pastors" in this passage are the leaders of the nations that did not care for the Jews during the many years of their having been scattered among the Gentile nations. In verse 3, God says that he is going to gather the remnant of his flock out of all countries where He has driven them. He will bring them again to the folds; and they shall be fruitful and increase. Verse 4 tells us that He is going to give them "new shepherds" that will feed them, take care of them and remove the cause of their fears.

During the Diaspora, God drove the Jewish people into all of the gentile nations of the world. During this time, He will hold all of these nations responsible for Israel's welfare and safe keeping. In this passage, he refers to the leaders and governments of these nations as "Pastors or Shepherds." He is warning the nations that have mistreated Israel that, "He would visit upon them the evil of their doings." In other words, He is going to punish them for the way they have treated His people Israel.

Then God promises to give Israel new shepherds who would take good care of them. How have the Jewish people been treated since coming to the United States? Throughout history, the Jews have been persecuted in nearly every nation of the world, but not so in America. America was the first country in the world to give the Jewish people equal citizenship. And we are blessed because of it. At the present time there are more Jews living in America than any nation in the world including the nation of Israel itself. We have six million living in America compared to 4.8 million there.

God has indeed given Israel new Shepherds and has delivered them from the fear of persecution in these countries. In America the Jewish people prosper more than they have ever prospered in their entire history. So much so that most Jewish people in America have no desire to return to Israel. God is blessing them here, but there are other countries that treat the Jews well also. We are the countries (shepherds) that God has provided in order to bless the Jewish people. During the tribulation, by the grace of God, the U.S. will continue to defend Israel against the Antichrist. In fact, if we are among the seven righteous nations, then we will actually participate in fighting against the Antichrist. This is why he will call for help from other nations. At the latter part of the Tribulation, Israel will be nearly wiped out. Yet according to Daniel 11, the Antichrist will send for nations to come and help him go down against Jerusalem for the Battle of Armageddon. Think about this for a moment. We all know that the Antichrist is going to invade Israel and go into the temple to declare himself as God. Since he has already taken Israel, why would he be in a position to have to re-take it at the end of the seven years? The answer to this question is that he will be forced to leave Israel sometime between the middle and the end of the seven years of tribulation. Israel's allies will be the reason that he will come down. He will be coming to make war with us and the other nations who are helping Israel.

Now let's return to Micah 5: "And this man shall be the peace, when the Assyrian shall come into our land: and when he shall tread in our palaces, then shall we raise against him seven shepherds, and eight principal men. And they shall waste the land of Assyria with the sword, and the land of Nimrod in the entrances thereof: thus shall he deliver us from the Assyrian, when he cometh into our land, and when he treads within our borders" (Micah 5:5-6).

The seven shepherds are the seven nations who take care of the Jews that live within her boundaries. They will also stand with Israel against the Antichrist. The eight principal men are the seven leaders of these nations with Jesus himself as the eighth. These Scriptures declare it to be so. In the 5th verse it says, "And this man shall be our peace, when the Assyrian shall come into our land."

What many fail to realize is the regional nature of the Antichrist Kingdom. The final Antichrist Empire will be centered in the Middle East. The Antichrist will not literally rule every last nation on the planet. While the Bible does lay out for us the general framework for what the final days will look like, it does not necessarily fill in every last detail. We do not know for sure, for instance, what will become of Greenland or New Zealand. We cannot confidently conclude what will happen to America, Germany, England, or Russia in the Last-Days. Many Americans believe that America will not exist and will be destroyed by Antichrist; they conclude this because America is not mentioned in the Bible. But one could ask why any number of prominent nations is not mentioned in Bible prophecy. Does their lack of having been discussed necessarily mean that they will all be destroyed, or is this primarily due to the fact that the Middle East is the primary emphasis of Bible prophecy? After all, some Western nations are mentioned in the Bible—Spain and Rome. Yet they are never specifically mentioned in connection with judgment. The only nations that are ever mentioned by name in connection with Christ's judgment are Muslim nations. As the Apostle Paul warned, "We must be careful not to go beyond what the Scriptures state." (I Corinthians 4:6)

❦ 56 ❦

When Lucifer Becomes A Man

ANTICHRIST IN THE BOOK OF ISAIAH

Lucifer will possess the Antichrist, but where is this possession mentioned in Scripture? Rarely when I ask this question do I get a response. The answer to this question can be found in Isaiah 14. The ultimate context of Isaiah 14 cannot be ancient Babylon, although ancient Babylon was a type. Isaiah 14:1 declares that this passage is speaking about the return of the Jews to Israel with Gentile believers joining them: "For the LORD will have mercy on Jacob, and will yet choose Israel, and set them in their own land: and the strangers shall be joined with them, and they shall cleave to the house of Jacob" (Isaiah 14:1).

Then in Isaiah verse 25, we have the *Assyrian* (The Antichrist) who is also called the *King of Babylon*. The passage refers to this King of Babylon/Assyrian as Lucifer: "O [Lucifer] Morning star, the son of the dawn, How you have fallen from heaven" (v. 12). The passage is clearly speaking about the fall of the angel Lucifer who we often call Satan or the Devil.

The passage begins with Lucifer's rebellion: "I will ascend into heaven. I will exalt my throne above the stars of God. I will also sit on the mount of the congregation on the farthest sides of the north I will ascend above the heights of the clouds I will be like the Most High" (v. 13-14).

But then, just a couple of verses later, in the midst of describing Lucifer's humiliation and destruction, it says: "Those who see you stare at you, they ponder your fate: 'Is this the man who shook the earth and made kingdoms tremble?'"

When was Lucifer a man? At what time in human history has Satan the cherub ever manifested himself as a man? Clearly, this passage is speaking about the Antichrist who is in essence Satan in the flesh: "Have you also become as weak as we? Have you become like us?" (v. 10)

The context makes it clear that Isaiah is not referring strictly to Nebuchadnezzar, the King of Babylon but rather to the Antichrist of whom Nebuchadnezzar was merely a shadow or a type. Nebuchadnezzar certainly has never fallen from heaven. Nor was Nebuchadnezzar or any Assyrian king ever defeated in Israel: "I will break the Assyrian in My land, and tread him underfoot" (v. 25).

So clearly the primary context of this passage is yet future. It is about the End-Times. The theme of this is yet-future defeat of the Antichrist by the Messiah in Israel runs throughout the prophecies of Isaiah and Micah.

This passage also contains the five 'I wills,' which are *five claims of pride* that are made. The mystery of these five 'I wills' are resolved by viewing them as coming from the mouth of the Antichrist who will be a man.

"*I will ascend into heaven*." Muhammad already claimed to have ascended to heaven in the Isra wa Al-Mi'rajj. It is likely that the Mahdi will also make the same claim.

"*I will exalt my throne above the stars of God*." Muhammad already claimed to possess a position that is far above all angels (stars).

"*I will also sit on the mount of the congregation on the farthest sides of the north*." The Mahdi or the Antichrist is said to rule from Pergamum (Revelation 2:12-13) which Christ proclaimed would be the future seat of Satan. This is on the sides of the northern lands (Asia Minor / Turkey) as we shall later study in detail.

"*I will ascend above the heights of the clouds*." This declaration is essentially a repeat of the first proud declaration: "*I will be like the Most High*." Both Muhammad and Mahdi have given themselves or have been ascribed titles that belong to Jehovah alone.

ISAIAH 14

1)For the LORD will have mercy on Jacob, and will still choose Israel, and settle them in their own land. The strangers will be joined with them, and they will cling to the house of Jacob. 2)Then people will take them and bring them to their place, and the house of Israel will possess them for servants and maids in the land of the LORD; they will take them captive whose captives they were, and rule over their oppressors. 3)It shall come to pass in the day the LORD gives you rest from your sorrow, and from your fear and the hard bondage in which you were made to serve, 4)that you will take up this proverb against the king of Babylon, and say: How the oppressor has ceased, the golden city ceased! 5)The LORD has broken the staff of the wicked, the scepter of the rulers; 6)He who struck the people in wrath with a continual stroke, He who ruled the nations in anger, is persecuted and no one hinders. 7) whole earth is at rest and quiet; they break forth into singing. 8)Indeed the cypress trees rejoice over you, and the cedars of Lebanon, Saying, Since you were cut down, No woodsman has come up against us. 9)Hell from beneath is excited about you, to meet you at your coming; It stirs up the dead for you, All the chief ones of the earth; It has raised up from their thrones All the kings of the nations. [10]They all shall speak and say to you: Have you also become as weak as we? Have you become like us? [11]Your pomp is brought down to Sheol, and the sound of your stringed instruments; the maggot is spread under you, and worms cover you. [12]How you are fallen from heaven, O Lucifer, son of the morning! How you are cut down to the ground, you who weakened the nations! [13]For you have said in your heart: I will ascend into heaven, I will exalt my throne above the stars of God; I will also sit on the mount of the congregation on the farthest sides of the north; [14] I will ascend above the heights of the clouds, I will be like the Most High. [15]Yet you shall be brought down to Sheol, To the lowest depths of the Pit. [16]Those who see you will gaze at you, And consider you, saying: Is this the man who made the earth tremble, Who shook kingdoms, [17]Who made the world as a wilderness And destroyed its cities, Who did not open the house of his prisoners? [18]All the kings of the nations, All of them, sleep in glory, Everyone in his own house; [19]But you are cast out of your grave Like an abominable branch, Like the garment of those who are slain, Thrust through with a sword, Who go down to the stones of the pit, Like a corpse trodden underfoot. [20]You will not be joined with them in burial, because you have destroyed your land and slain your people. The brood of evildoers shall never be named. [21]Prepare slaughter for his children Because of the iniquity of their fathers, lest they rise up and possess the land, and fill the face of the world with cities. [22] I will rise up against them, says the LORD of hosts, And cut off from Babylon the name and remnant, and offspring and posterity, says the LORD. [23]I will also make it a possession for the porcupine, and marshes of muddy water; I will sweep it with the broom of destruction, says the LORD of hosts. [24] LORD of hosts has sworn, saying, Surely, as I have thought, so it shall come to pass, And as I have purposed, so it shall stand: [25] I will break the Assyrian in My land, And on My mountains tread him underfoot. Then his yoke shall be removed from them, and his burden removed from their shoulders. [26]This is the purpose that is purposed against the whole earth, and this is the hand that is stretched out over all the nations. [27]For the LORD of hosts has purposed, And who will annul it? His hand is stretched out, and who will turn it back? [28]This is the burden which came in the year that King Ahaz died. [29]Do not rejoice, all you of

Philistia, Because the rod that struck you is broken; For out of the serpent's roots will come forth a viper, And its offspring will be a fiery flying serpent. 30)The firstborn of the poor will feed, and the needy will lie down in safety; I will kill your roots with famine, and it will slay your remnant. 31)Wail, O gate! Cry, O city! All you of Philistia are dissolved; for smoke will come from the north, and no one will be alone in his appointed times. 32)What will they answer the messengers of the nation? That the LORD has founded Zion, and the poor of His people shall take refuge in it.

ANTICHRIST'S TITLES—LINK TO MUSLIM NATIONS

There are more Biblical hints to show that this Antichrist is Muslim from the titles that the Bible ascribes to him. Consider the following titles: the Assyrian, the Prince of Tyre, the King of Babylon, and Pharaoh of Egypt. This may seem rather simple, but if the Bible calls the Antichrist the Assyrian, then isn't it irresponsible to conclude that the Antichrist will come from Rome or any other European nation? Doesn't it only make sense to conclude from this title that he will come from the region of the ancient Assyrian Empire?

Why is it that the most popular end-time paradigms completely ignore these titles when attempting to discern the Antichrist's nation of origin?

If the Antichrist is the King of Babylon, then isn't it only reasonable to conclude that he will rule over the region of ancient Babylon? Wouldn't it be awfully strange to conclude that "the King of Babylon" will rule over Luxemburg, Germany or Rome? Yet innumerable Bible teachers who claim to be literalists do exactly this.

So what regions will the Antichrist come from and what regions will he rule over? This is actually quite simple: As the Assyrian, the Antichrist will come from the regions of ancient Assyria which today encompasses the areas of several modern Muslim nations. As we move on, we will see this location substantiated over and over again.

As the King of Tyre, the Antichrist will also rule over Lebanon. Of course, as we have already seen, there is much in the prophetic verses regarding Lebanon. And of course, we see all the trouble that is stirring today in the land of Lebanon, the stronghold of Hezbollah. As the King of Babylon, the Antichrist will rule over Iraq, Iran, and the Arabian Peninsula. As Pharaoh, King of Egypt, the Antichrist will rule over Egypt.

The title King of Tyre (Lebanon) is not some allegory for a European Antichrist, nor is the Biblical declaration that "Lebanon shall fall by The Mighty One" (Isaiah 10:34) an allegorical description of the fall of Rome. It is just what it says it is—Christ Himself will deal with the anti-Israeli elements in Lebanon.

How can Antichrist fit all these titles? How can He be a king of Babylon, a Pharaoh of Egypt, and the Assyrian?

Well, in order to respond to this question, I will ask you, how could Jesus come from Egypt, Nazareth, and Bethlehem as the various Scriptures prophesied?

Yet, all of the above are true.

Antichrist also can be a ruler of Babylon, Assyria, Syria, Lebanon, Egypt, and Turkey.

This is why critics of the Bible keep finding what seem to be contradictions. God ordained it this way so that evil will never get it. They are always busy finding problems.

Books have been written to criticize the Bible. Yet when I attempted to hammer this anvil, it was the anvil that bent my pride. A soul that refuses to submit to daily tilling of its inner fields will end up with nothing but thorns and thistles. They asked Jesus why do you speak in parables. He explained that he did so in order that the spiritually blind would not get it. (Matthew 13:13-15) Only those who truly seek truth will find it.

Does that mean that God is not fair? Rather God knows the hearts of men, and He has chosen to reveal His secrets to the humble and the lowly. But the wicked will continue to serve evil. Hardcore Nazis chose to die for Hitler, even after they witnessed the truth. In the end, they still chose suicide. Even the ones who were sentenced after Nuremberg still chose to praise Hitler moments before their death.

This Islamo-Nazi system will be similar; many will reject the truth no matter what—even after Jesus returns and still calls on them to repent. Why else will Jesus fight them? Even when the great hail falls on them, they will still curse God. Why? It's because they have been setup with false prophecy. They will still think that their misery is a sacrifice for Allah, when in reality it's a sacrifice to Satan. This is why it's a mystery for Westerners to understand why the Muslim armies will continue to fight against Jesus even after it is obvious that He is the real deal. Why can't Muslims see that Israel has defeated them against all odds several times? It's because Islam predicts Israel's return as well, only to be destroyed by Islam. When Islam loses, they simply think that they need to kick the Islamo-heat up a notch. Yet no one is daring to tell them the truth, everyone is so afraid to insult Muslims. You need to show them the truth with love. How does one claim to love another by fearing them? I have chosen Elijah's method to challenge the prophets of Baal to their face. *The Lord is calling on believers in these Last-Days to be bold in their love and fearless in their proclamation.*

THE GOLDEN CITY

The context of Isaiah 14 is regarding Israel's return: "For the LORD will have mercy on Jacob, and will still choose Israel, and settle them in their own land" (v. 1). When the Lord appears and leads them, Israel will rejoice, for the city that caused all the trouble is destroyed. This in my opinion is Mecca, the city decked with gold, or possibly Medina, called in Arabic Al-Madina Al-Munawarah (the city of light). This is very similar to the city that God condemns in the Last-Days: "That you will take up this proverb against the king of Babylon, and say: How the oppressor has ceased, the golden city ceased!" (v. 4) This city cannot be ancient Babylon because the context of the prophecy is the End-Times. Ancient Babylon no longer exists as a great city, but rather as an ancient ruin. Isaiah 14 speaks of Satan's destruction along with his "holy" city. As such, the end time spiritual or "mystery" Babylon is a city that exists in the world today.

HOW ISAIAH 9 TIES IN WITH ISAIAH 14

Study the underlined portions of the following passage in Isaiah 9:

1)Nevertheless the gloom will not be upon her who is distressed, As when at first He lightly esteemed The land of Zebulun and the land of Naphtali, And afterward more heavily oppressed her, By the way of the sea, beyond the , In Galilee of the Gentiles. 2)The people who walked in darkness have seen a great light; those who dwelt in the land of the shadow of death, upon them a light has shined. 3)You have multiplied the nation and increased its joy; they rejoice before You According to the joy of harvest, as men rejoice when they divide the spoil. 4)For You have broken the yoke of his burden And the staff of his shoulder, The rod of his oppressor, As in the day of Midian. 5)For every warrior's sandal from the noisy battle, And garments rolled in blood, Will be used for burning and fuel of fire. 6)For unto us a Child is born, unto us a Son is given; and the government will be upon His shoulder. And His name will be called Wonderful, Counselor, Mighty God, Everlasting Father, Prince of Peace. 7)Of the increase of His government and peace there will be no end, upon the throne of David and over His kingdom, to order it and establish it with judgment and justice from that time forward, even forever. The zeal of the Lord of hosts will perform this. 8)The Lord sent a word against Jacob, and it has fallen on Israel. 9)All the people will know— Ephraim and the inhabitant of Samaria—who say in pride and arrogance of heart: 10)"The bricks have fallen down, but we will rebuild with hewn stones; the sycamores are cut down, but we will replace them with cedars." 11)Therefore the LORD shall set up the adversaries of Rezin against him, and spur his enemies on, 12)The Syrians before and the Philistines behind; and they shall devour Israel with an open mouth. For all this His anger is not turned away, but His hand is stretched out still. 13)For the people do not turn to Him who strikes them, nor do they seek the LORD of hosts. 14)Therefore the LORD will cut off head and tail from Israel, Palm branch and bulrush in one day. 15)The elder and honorable, he is the head; the prophet who teaches lies, he is the tail. 16)For the leaders of this people cause them to err, and those who are led by them are destroyed. 17)Therefore the Lord will have no joy in their young men, nor have mercy on their fatherless and widows; for everyone is a hypocrite and an evildoer, and every mouth speaks folly. For all this His anger is not turned away, but His hand is stretched out still. 18)For wickedness burns as the fire; it shall devour the briers and thorns, and kindle in the thickets of the forest; they shall mount up like rising smoke. 19)Through the wrath of the LORD of hosts the land is burned up, and the people shall be as fuel for the fire; man shall spare his brother. 20)And he shall snatch on the right hand and be hungry; He shall devour on the left hand and not be satisfied; every man shall eat the flesh of his own arm. 21)Manasseh shall devour Ephraim, and Ephraim Manasseh; together they shall be against Judah. For all this His anger is not turned away, but His hand is stretched out still.

SHORT TERM

The short-term historical context of Isaiah 9 relates to the looming threat for the Jews who were at that time divided between two kingdoms; the Northern Kingdom, often referred to as Israel or Ephraim, and the Southern Kingdom, often referred to as Judah. The looming threat of an Assyrian invasion was hanging over both of them.

Through Isaiah, God was repeatedly calling out to his people to place their full trust in Him rather than trusting in political alliances. God's answer to the threat was the promise of the Messiah—a child who would be born from the line of David. (Isaiah 9:6)

LONG TERM

The Messiah, this "child that was born unto us" would be the one to deliver Israel from the Assyrian invasion. Yet, this never occurred at any time in history. The Assyrian army invaded the Northern Kingdom (v. 8-21) and dragged much of the inhabitants away into exile. But as for the Messiah defeating the Assyrian, this never happened—it is yet to come.

The prophecies about the Assyrian are ultimately about the Antichrist. When the Assyrian invades the land of Israel, then it is Jesus the Messiah who will personally defeat him. This is the final showdown between Jesus and the Antichrist. Isaiah also reveals that after the Assyrian is defeated, the people of Israel will then rule over the land of Assyria. Has there ever been a time in history that the Jews ruled over the land of Assyria? This is definitely speaking of the future.

After Jesus returns, the Jews will rule over and posses the whole Middle East. It will be like the wars of 1948 and 1967 in which Israel was surrounded on all sides. Israel used King David's method and instead of facing the giant with a sword, he exercised a pre-emptive strike with precision bombing and brought down Islam's Goliaths on all sides. Instead of losing land, the Jewish nation was able to take land from all of their attackers.

Many are surprised to find out that the full contexts of some of the most famous Messianic prophecies in all of Scripture are in reality significant end-time prophecies describing the showdown between Messiah and the Muslim Antichrist. The Messiah's primary purpose in these many passages is always to fulfill his prophesied role as the one who would crush the Assyrian and deliver his people Israel. As God prophesied to Satan long ago, in the end it would be like David and Goliath. The Messiah will crush Satan's head (Genesis 3:15). The evidence that I personally witnessed as a child in 1967 proved to the world that Jehovah was indeed greater than Allah. The War of 1967 and 1973 are not the last major wars Israel will encounter. There is another war, in which the Gideon-like Messiah will crush the followers of Baal. At that time, Jehovah, the God of Israel and the adopted Christians who love Him will reign supreme over the earth.

The passage is about the time when "the child" born unto us becomes the King: "Unto us a child is born, to us a son is given, and the government will be on his shoulders. And he will be called Wonderful Counselor, Mighty God, Everlasting Father, and Prince of Peace. Of the increase of his government and peace there will be no end. He will reign on David's throne and over his kingdom, establishing and upholding it with justice and righteousness from that time on and forever. The zeal of Jehovah Almighty will accomplish this" (Isaiah 9:6-9).

Few ever take the time to read the fuller context of this passage. If they did, they would see that what the Messiah accomplishes is the crushing of the enemies of Israel, just as Gideon did to Midian: "For as in the day of Midian's defeat, you have shattered the yoke that burdens them, the bar across their shoulders, and the rod of their oppressor. Every warrior's boot used in battle and every garment rolled in blood will be destined for burning, will be fuel for the fire" (v. 1-5).

Thus Jesus, the King Messiah, the Mighty God, will deliver Israel from the Assyrian, in the same way that Gideon delivered Israel from the Midianite armies. After that time, Jesus will rule on King David's throne forever as the Prince of Peace.

Again, the problem is that this deliverance and physical rule never occurred in history. Instead, the Assyrians chipped away at ancient Israel and Judah with waves of invasions (v. 8-21). The Assyrians were soon followed by the Babylonians. The end result was the complete desolation of both kingdoms. The ultimate deliverance did not come; the "yoke" was not shattered. And thus this famous Messianic prophecy can only be a reference to the future Last-Days.

JESUS WILL CRUSH THE ANTICHRIST-MAHDI

This crushing of Islam and the Mahdi-Antichrist with his Muslim hordes will occur in the Valley of Jehoshaphat (Joel 3), which the Book of Revelation refers to as the "Wine-press of his wrath." God will finally squash the Muslim hordes like grapes: "I will crush the Assyrian in my land; on my mountains I will trample him down. His yoke will be taken from my people, and his burden removed from their shoulders. This is the plan deter-mined for the whole world; this is the hand stretched out over all nations. For Jehovah Almighty has purposed, and who can thwart him? His hand is stretched out, and who can turn it back?" (Isaiah 14:25-27)

In Isaiah 10, the Lord promises that after he has finished chastising his people, he will, "punish the king of Assyria for the willful pride of his heart and the haughty look in his eyes" (v. 12). Then, "The Light of Israel will become a fire, their Holy One a flame." (v. 17) Who is the Holy One of Israel that will become a fiery warrior? This is none other than Jesus the Warrior King. Yet when has Jesus ever fulfilled this prophecy? It has never hap-pened in history, but it will happen soon. Israel will also fight: "The light of Israel will become a fire." This passage is also very similar to Obadiah 1:18: "The house of Jacob shall be a fire, And the house of Joseph a flame; But the house of Esau [shall be] stubble."

Most think that Messiah fights Antichrist solo, sort of like Zorro who at the end of the movie, fights on the roof of the castle and kills the bad guy who falls down to his death, then "Finale" and it's all over. But Israel fights alongside its Messiah. Likewise, so do the other seven shepherds that God will raise up, so also will the raptured believers fight along-side their King. Together, all of these will utterly decimate the Antichrist's kingdom. I know that this is difficult for Westerners to swallow. But everything that God does is done with the partnership of his people. We will discuss this in much greater detail as we move on.

As the passage progresses, in verse 26, "Jehovah Almighty will lash them with a whip, as when he struck down Midian at the rock of Oreb." Once again, Jesus is referred to as Jehovah Almighty who will lash the Antichrist in like fashion to Gideon who destroyed the Midianites. In Isaiah 31:4, the Bible says that, "The Lord will come down to fight for Mount Zion...then Assyria will fall by a sword that is not of man; a sword, not of mortals, will devour them." Again, not to belabor this point, but it needs to be driven home. Jesus never fought any physical battles against Assyria during His First Coming; therefore, this must refer to *Christ's Second Advent.*

Literal References in Isaiah of Muslim Nations Set for Judgment

Y ou might object that I am always referring to the armies that fight Messiah as Muslim. Would you like me to call them Buddhists, or European post-modern pacifist metrosexual agnostics? Do you think that all these nations the Bible mentions by name that are Muslim, and have been from time immemorial, will suddenly convert to Buddhism?—or to some other universal One-World religion as some teach? You might object that no one knows what the religion of these people will be. You may suggest that we will have to wait and see.

Do you challenge other books that point to the Catholics, Rome and Europe with names of nations and faiths? Maybe they need to change their books? After all, no one knows what religion they will be until this whole scenario unfolds, correct?

Sorry! My argument stands, for I *have* literal names of *literal nations*, while the others make assumption upon assumption. There is no legitimate reason for switching Rome with Edom or Spain with Babylon. How does one get a "Nicolai Carpathia" out of Assyria, Edom, Moab or Midian?

Much of the Book of Isaiah is devoted to the final clash between the Messiah and the Antichrist. Yet when we actually look at the specific nations which so many of the "prophetic oracles" or "burdens" are directed against, they are all Muslim nations. Consider the nations that are emphasized: *Babylon*—Isaiah 13; *Assyria and the Philistines (Palestinians)*—Isaiah 14; *Moab*—Isaiah 15; *Damascus*—Isaiah 17; *Cush (Sudan and Somaliland)*—Isaiah 18; *Egypt*—Isaiah 19; *Egypt and Cush*—Isaiah 20; *Babylon (Iraq and Arabia) and Edom (Arabia)*—Isaiah 21; *Tyre (Lebanon)*—Isaiah 23 .

Does this sound like a ten-nation European confederation to you? Or does it sound like a coalition of Muslim nations from the Middle East? Remember, the context of these chapters is the destruction of the Assyrian (Antichrist), and just as the destruction of the Assyrian is in the future, so are the judgments against these nations also future. His destruction is described in Isaiah 14:25: "That I will break the Assyrian in My land, and on My Mountains tread him underfoot."

EGYPT—DESTROYED BY CHRIST (ISAIAH 19)

Christ Himself defeats a portion of Antichrist's armies in Egypt: "Behold, the Lord rides on a swift cloud, and will come into Egypt" (Isaiah 19:1). This is crucial and valuable verse as it puts the context of Isaiah 19 within Messiah's second coming, for the *Lord Himself comes down* "on a swift cloud entering Egypt" (Isaiah 19:1). Israel also will fight against Egypt: "And the land of Judah shall be a terror unto Egypt" (v. 17). Since this war has never happened historically, it must be in the future. Also, the fact that the text tells us that Messiah will carry out this mission clearly places it in the future. Egypt will also have a civil war: "And I will set Egyptians against Egyptians: and they shall fight every one against his brother, and every one against his neighbor; city against city, kingdom against kingdom" (Isaiah 19:2).

Christ comes to fight Egypt because the Antichrist will occupy Egypt. "And the Egyptians will I give over into the hand of a cruel lord; and a fierce king shall rule over them, Says the Lord, the LORD of Hosts" (Isaiah 19:4). This is also confirmed in Daniel 11:42: "He [Antichrist] shall stretch out his hand against the countries, and the land of Egypt shall not escape."

Christ will ultimately rescue a remnant of Egypt from Antichrist: "In that day shall five cities in the land of Egypt speak the language of Canaan, and swear to the LORD of Hosts; one shall be called, the city of destruction" (v. 2-3). Many of the Egyptians will become like the Messianic Jews and love to speak Hebrew.

The oppressed Coptic Egyptians will be rescued by Messiah: "And it will be for a sign and for a witness to the LORD of Hosts in the land of Egypt; for they will cry to the LORD because of the oppressors, and He will send them a Savior and a Mighty One, and He will deliver them." (Isaiah 19:20) The Egyptian Coptics are increasingly being oppressed by the Muslim majority, and even by the government. But if God sees their cause as being important enough to personally rescue them, then, why are we so silent about the suffering Coptic Christians of Egypt?

THE GREAT EARTHQUAKE (ISAIAH 24)

In chapter 24 of Isaiah a reason is given for the punishment of these nations: "they have transgressed the laws, changed the ordinances" (Isaiah 24:5). This is speaking about the Antichrist who attempts to change times and laws (Daniel 7:25).

The Qur'an also speaks of a great earthquake but unlike Isaiah, the Qur'an does not warn that this judgment is against Muslim nations. "O Mankind! Fear your Lord. Surely the earthquake of the Hour (of Doom) is a tremendous thing. On the day when you behold it, every nursing mother will forget her nursing and every pregnant one will be delivered of her burden, and you will see mankind as if they were drunk, yet they will not be drunk, but the Doom of Allah will be strong (upon them)" (Qur'an 22:1-2).

Do you see how thoroughly Satan has duped the Muslims? When they see the great earthquake, they will believe that Allah and their book, was right on track. But in fact, God will punish them.

In Isaiah, *Jehovah declares*: "The foundations of the earth are shaken" (Isaiah 24:18), "the windows from on high are open" (v. 18) "earth is split open" (v. 19) "the earth reels to and fro like a drunkard" (v. 20). In Isaiah, judgment is even proclaimed on the fallen angels and the kings of the earth: "And it shall come to pass in that day, [that] the LORD shall punish the host of the high ones [that are] on high, and the kings of the earth upon the earth. And they shall be gathered together, [as] prisoners are gathered in the pit, and shall be shut up in the prison, and after many days shall they be visited. Then the moon shall be confounded, and the sun ashamed, when the LORD of Hosts shall reign in mount Zion, and in Jerusalem, and before his ancients gloriously" (Isaiah 24:21-23).

The tossing of the nations into the "pit" is a common theme that we need to take note of: *"They (the nations) shall be gathered together, as prisoners are gathered in the pit, and shall be shut up in the prison."* This is also described in detail in Ezekiel 31 and 32 with Antichrist thrown into the pit and the names of every nation that is thrown in with him, all of which are Muslim nations today. Truly the Muslims have been duped. Pray that many more Muslims will continue to wake up and turn to Jehovah God and His Son Yeshua, the Messiah.

DESTRUCTION OF MOAB BY CHRIST (ISAIAH 25)

Moab, like Egypt, is destroyed by Messiah Himself; "And it shall be said in that day, Lo, this is our God; we have waited for Him, and He will save us: this is the LORD; we have waited for Him, we will be glad and rejoice in His salvation. For in this mountain shall the hand of the LORD rest, and Moab shall be trodden down under Him, even as straw is trodden down for the dunghill." (Isaiah 25:9-10)

Moab is trodden down under the foot of the Messiah. While the Messiah's hand of blessing is resting on the head of Zion, His foot is on the neck of Moab, as He pushes his head into the dung.

The comment that I frequently hear is that Islam will be destroyed several years prior to the coming of Christ. Most prophecy teachers argue that this will set the stage for the *European Antichrist* and the Battle of Armageddon.

My response is that, in every passage investigated thus far, Christ *personally* fights nations that are all Muslim. In the last passage (Isaiah 25:9-10) at the time of his return, we have Christ fighting Moab. Why do *you* think God is always placing emphasis on the Muslim nations? Where are all of these European nations that He will allegedly fight?

Isaiah 25 is the reconciliation between Israel and her Messiah. Yet within this setting Moab is destroyed. Instead of Moab destroying Israel, God will spare His people from the wrath to come. "Come, my people, enter thou into thy chambers, and shut thy doors about thee: hide thyself as it were for a little moment, until the indignation be overpast. For, behold, the LORD cometh out of His place to punish the inhabitants of the earth for their iniquity: the earth also shall disclose her blood, and shall no more cover her slain" (Isaiah 26:20-21).

ANTICHRIST JUDGED

"In that day the LORD with his sore and great and strong sword shall punish leviathan the piercing serpent, even leviathan that crooked serpent; and he shall slay the dragon that is in the sea" (Isaiah 27:1). This is judgment of Antichrist, the dragon, the snake, the leviathan—the Devil. But the destruction of the Antichrist is spoken of all within the context of the remnant of Muslim nations repenting: "And it shall come to pass in that day, that the great trumpet shall be blown, and they shall come which were ready to perish in the land of Assyria, and the outcasts in the land of Egypt, and shall worship the LORD in the Holy Mount at Jerusalem" (Isaiah 27:13).

The nations are finally freed from the grip of Islam and its Antichrist-Mahdi. The remnant of Islamic Assyria and Egypt will come to worship the Lord, not in Mecca, but in *Jerusalem*! They are no longer Muslim, but like myself, they are ex-Muslim believers in Christ—speaking much better Hebrew, of course.

THE COVENANT WITH DEATH (ISAIAH 28)

The covenant with death as described in Isaiah 28 is of a dual meaning. The first is the story of mankind entering a covenant with death in the garden. When Adam and Eve partook of the forbidden tree, humanity, in essence, signed a covenant with death. This covenant was initiated by Satan; but through sacrificial offering, God provided a way out.

Likewise, Antichrist, the devil will initiate a false covenant and divide Israel for gain: "Your covenant with death will be annulled, and your agreement with Sheol will not stand. When the overflowing scourge passes through, Then you will be trampled by it" (Isaiah 28:18).

Throughout the Prophecy of Isaiah, God *repeatedly* warns His people never to trust in political alliances, but to *trust in Him alone*. But like the situation in Isaiah's day, so also will be the Last-Days. Israel will rely on political alliances, peace treaties, and promises of "peace and security." The Bible says that Israel will willingly accept the peace-treaty made with the Antichrist who "will confirm a covenant with many for one 'seven'" (Daniel 9:27).

But then this Assyrian-Antichrist will renege on his agreements and will invade the land: "that has recovered from war, whose people were gathered from many nations to the mountains of Israel" (Ezekiel 38:8).

We can see Israel's prime minister and x-mayor of Jerusalem Ehud Olmert attempting to make peace deals. But the Bible warns: "You scoffers who rule this people in Jerusalem. You boast, 'We have entered into a covenant with death, with the grave we have made an agreement. When an overwhelming scourge sweeps by, it cannot touch us, for we have made a lie our refuge and falsehood our hiding place.'...Your covenant with death will be annulled; your agreement with the grave will not stand. When the overwhelming scourge sweeps by, you will be beaten down by it." (Isaiah 28:14-18)

The Assyrian will strike them down until finally the remnant of Israel will turn back to God and repent for trusting in false promises made with the surrounding nations.

This will ultimately happen when the remnant of Israel says "Blessed is he who comes in the name of the Lord" as Jesus prophesied in Matthew 23:39. In other words, the remnant of Israel will come to realize that indeed the child, the Wonderful Counselor, Prince of Peace—Jesus the Messiah—is their only hope.

CHRIST'S INTERVENTION (ISAIAH 29-30)

Here in Isaiah 29-30, we have the account of Messiah finally defeating Islam. This account parallels the war of King David with the Philistines: "For the Lord will rise up as at Mount Perazim, He will be angry as in the Valley of Gibeon—That He may do His work, His awesome work, and bring to pass His act, His unusual act." (Isaiah 28:21) Delusions, starvation, and thirst will hit all the enemies that encamp against Israel: "as when a hungry man dreams that he is eating, but he awakens, and his hunger remains; as when a thirsty man dreams that he is drinking, but he awakens faint, with his thirst unquenched. So will it be with the hordes of all the nations that fight against Mount Zion." (Isaiah 29:8) I have stated it for many years that food prices and food shortages will be a major problem in Muslim nations, and this phenomenon will only increase.

This defeat of the enemies will be a mercy. That which is bad will be turned into good for the Jewish people. As the Holocaust was evil, from that darkness, Israel was born. 9/11 was a wakeup call, at least for a short while. Pearl Harbor awoke America to Japan's threat. Sin and evil are like manure, it first smells, yet the sun shines over it, it dries, and in the end it helps the increase of fruit. Nothing Satan does will ever work—he urged the crowd to crucify the Lord, but the evil he intended, Christ's crucifixion, broke the veil, so that, what Satan began in the garden, failed. The only thing that remains now is for the Messiah to crush Satan.

At times, as Christians we need to see through God's lens. For what appears as peace is often a curse. Peace with Hitler was a curse; Chamberlain went to Hitler and then declared: "Peace in our times!" Yet there was no peace—only deceit. Churchill was right—war was the solution. Yet he was accused of being a warmonger. There is a time for peace, but there is also a time for war. The day will come when there will be a true war to end all wars. Without the final war of the Messiah against wicked nations, the entire Bible story would be a story of injustice. When the meek of the earth turn the other cheek, they are deferring justice and their cause to the Lord. Unless God Himself eventually comes down and literally vindicates and executes justice then all cheek-turning is meaningless and unjust. Justice requires that Jesus eventually wage war on behalf of His people. There is a time for war! Israel has had its share of peace treaties, yet not one has brought peace. But Israel continues to offer mercy to the nations that continually attack her. These peace treaties are all the same, as Chamberlain went to Hitler, Israel will go down to Egypt seeking peace from Pharaoh: "That walk to go down into Egypt, and have not asked at my mouth; to strengthen themselves in the strength of Pharaoh, and to trust in the shadow of Egypt! Therefore shall the strength of Pharaoh be your shame, and the trust in the shadow of Egypt your confusion" (Isaiah 30:1-2).

Israel's peace with Egypt is a farce. Israel gave up the Sinai for a peace that only brought them explosives smuggled via Egypt into Gaza. And there will be future false peace deals with Egypt as well. And their results will be equally fruitless.

In Isaiah, Jerusalem is mentioned in this list of nations that are judged as well. However, it is important to distinguish the difference between God's chastisement and God's judgment. God chastises those he loves, but punishes his enemies. The Muslim nations are all marked for a severe judgment, while Jerusalem is marked for God's equally severe correction. The final portion of Isaiah 10 tells us of the ultimate results and good news that come from God's chastisement of Israel: "The remnant of Israel, the survivors of the house of Jacob, will no longer rely on him who struck them down but will truly rely on Jehovah, the Holy One of Israel. A remnant will return, a remnant of Jacob will return to the Mighty God" (Isaiah 10:20-21).

Despite having trusted in the Antichrist's false promises, Israel will rely on their Messiah who will "reign on David's throne and over his kingdom, establishing and upholding it with justice and righteousness from that time on and forever. The zeal of Jehovah Almighty will accomplish this" (Isaiah 9:9).

≈58≈
Literal References for Satan And The Muslim Nations Thrown Into Hell

✦✦✦

FROM EZEKIEL 28-32

Westerners mostly track Antichrist in the Book of Revelation, but they rarely do an inductive analysis of the literal names of nations he leads with him in battle against Israel, and in the end he is judged and is thrown into hell (the pit). Ezekiel 28-32 are perhaps the best chapters of the most amazing of all literal references to these Muslim nations that suffer in this judgment along with the Mahdi-Antichrist. These Muslim nations are not destroyed prior to the Battle of Armageddon as Western teachers often claim. They do not usher in the rise of Antichrist. *They are with him.*

To anyone who loves Bible Prophecy, Ezekiel 28-32 includes the Antichrist with the names of his army of nations cast into hell (Revelation 19:20-21), his fall as an angel and his pride and declaration to be God: "Because thou hast set thine heart as the heart of God." (Ezekiel 28:6) exactly as Paul described Antichrist: "the son of perdition, Who opposes and exalted himself above all that is called God, or that is worshiped." (II Thessalonians 2:1)

God provides a mix of nicknames for Antichrist. In the prophecy of Isaiah, the Antichrist was called the Assyrian, but here in Ezekiel, he is called the King of Tyre (King of Lebanon). The first hint that the passage is speaking about Satan dwelling in the body of the Antichrist and thus proving that Ezekiel 28 is not strictly an historical reference to an historical figure, for how else is this "King of Tyre" in "Eden the garden of God" and is called "The guardian Cherub" (guardian angel).

"Son of man, take up a lamentation upon the king of Tyrus, and say unto him, Thus Says the Lord God; Thou sealest up the sum, full of wisdom, and perfect in beauty. Thou hast been in Eden the garden of God." (Ezekiel 28:12)

When was the King of Tyre ever in "Eden, the garden of God?" But Satan was certainly there. He was the angel of light:

"You were anointed as a guardian cherub (angel), for so I ordained you. You were on the Holy Mount of God; you walked among the fiery stones. You were blameless in your ways from the day you were created until wickedness was found in you" (Ezekiel 28:14, 15).

This passage is clearly speaking of someone other than a mere historical king. The anointed cherub who once walked on "the Holy Mountain of God" and among the "fiery stones" is the rebellious angel, none other than the Devil himself. "By the multitude of thy merchandise they have filled the midst of thee with violence, and thou hast sinned: So I drove you in disgrace from the Mount of God, and I expelled you, O guardian cherub, from among the fiery stones" (Ezekiel 28:16).

Who else was driven in disgrace out of the presence of God in Heaven other than Satan? And what merchandise is this rebellious angel selling? The father of lies is peddling a false religion that promotes violence—"they have filled the midst of thee with violence."

Yet as Ezekiel makes clear, despite the Antichrist's self-exaltation, he will be severely rebuked by the Lord: "Wilt thou yet say before Him that slays thee, I am God? But thou shall be a man, and no God, in the hand of Him that slay thee" (Ezekiel 28:9).

The context of Ezekiel 28 includes Israel in End-Times:

"Thus says the Lord GOD; When I shall have gathered the house of Israel from the people among whom they are scattered, and shall be sanctified in them in the sight of the heathen, then shall they dwell in their land that I have given to my servant Jacob. And they shall dwell safely therein, and shall build houses, and plant vineyards; yea, they shall dwell with confidence, when I have executed judgments upon all those that despise them round about them; and they shall know that I am Jehovah their God" (Ezekiel 28:25).

Obviously, Israel has been re-gathered as a nation. Even the production of fruit; Israel today produces an abundance of fruit from her vineyards to satisfy the needs of many countries: wheat, barley, grapes, figs, pomegranates, olives, dates, and of course, Jaffa oranges.

When we recognize the fact that Ezekiel 28 is about the Antichrist and his dealings with Israel after she has been re-gathered as a nation, we can easily see that this passage is yet another end-time prophecy.

Antichrist is finally cast "into the pit":

"Thus says the Lord GOD; in the day when he went down to the grave I caused mourning: I covered the deep for him, and I restrained the floods thereof, and the great waters were stayed: and I caused Lebanon to mourn for him, and all the trees of the field fainted for him. I made the nations to shake at the sound of his fall, when I cast him down to hell with them that descend into the pit: and all the trees of Eden, the choice and best of Lebanon, all that drink water, shall be comforted in the nether parts of the earth. They also went down into hell with him unto them that be slain with the sword; and they that were his arm, that dwelt under his shadow in the midst of the heathen. To whom art thou thus like in glory and in greatness among the trees of Eden? Yet shall thou be brought down with the trees of Eden unto the depths of the earth: thou shall lie in the midst of the uncircumcised with them that be slain by the sword. This is Pharaoh and all his multitude, says the Lord GOD" (Ezekiel 31:15–18).

This is a parallel to Satan in Isaiah 14:

"But you are brought down to the grave, to the depths of the pit. Those who see you stare at you, they ponder your fate: "Is this the man who shook the earth and made kingdoms tremble, the man who made the world a desert, who overthrew its cities and would not let his captives go home?" (Isaiah 14:15-17)

Satan, the man (Antichrist) is brought down "to the pit": "They shall bring thee down to the pit, and thou shall die the deaths of them that are slain in the midst of the seas" (Ezekiel 28:8). "In the midst of the seas" (a symbolic term used to refer to the nations), shall the Antichrist be killed and thrown to the pit.

THE MUSLIM NATIONS CAST INTO THE PIT OF HELL

The specific nations mentioned for judgment alongside the Antichrist are listed below in order. Because ancient boundaries have changed, there is some overlap and some nations are repeated.

LEBANON:

The context of Ezekiel 28 is definitely End-Time—no longer will Israel's neighbors be painful briers or thorns in her side. The rockets launched from Lebanon to prick Israel daily will finally cease forever.

"The word of Jehovah came to me: Son of man, set your face against Sidon (Lebanon); prophesy against her and say: 'This is what the Lord God says:' I am against you, O Sidon, and I will be glorified in the midst of thee. They will know that I am Jehovah, when they have executed judgments in the midst of her and show myself holy in her midst. I will send a plague upon her and make blood flow in her streets. The slain will fall within her, with the sword against her on every side. Then they will know that I am Jehovah. No longer will the people of Israel have malicious neighbors who are painful briers and sharp thorns. Then they will know that I am the Lord God" (Ezekiel 28:20-24).

EGYPT

Antichrist is also called "Pharaoh King of Egypt" (Ezekiel 29:3) and like Ezekiel 28 there can be no doubt that this is Satan, "great monster who lies in the midst of the rivers." (Ezekiel 29:2) It is possible that "my river is mine" (v. 3) is concerning blocking Israel from the Strait of Tiran. This is nothing new; I personally witnessed the war of 1967. On May 18, Egypt's president, Gamal Abdul Nasser, demanded the withdrawal of UN forces from Gaza and Sinai; Secretary General Thant promptly acceded and removed the UNEF. Four days later, Nasser announced a blockade of Israeli shipping at the Strait of Tiran, an action that Israel has stressed since the 1956 War would be tantamount to a declaration of war. Jordan and Iraq rapidly joined Syria in its military alliance with Egypt.[4]

Ezekiel 29 concludes the destruction of Egypt "Egypt will become a desolate wasteland. Then they will know that I am Jehovah" (Ezekiel 29:9). Ezekiel 30 gives even more detail: "For the day is near, the day of Jehovah is near—a day of clouds, a time of doom for the nations. A sword will come against Egypt, and anguish will come upon Cush. When the slain fall in Egypt, her wealth will be carried away and her foundations torn down" (Ezekiel 30:3-4) They will even become slaves for Israel: "The labor of Egypt and merchandise of Cush, And of the Sabeans, men of stature, shall come over to you, and they shall be yours" (Isaiah 45:14).

EGYPT, SUDAN, LIBYA, TURKEY AND ARABIA

But far from being a judgment against Egypt alone, this portion of the prophecy is also leveled against; Sudan, Libya, Algeria, Tunisia Morocco, Turkey and Arabia: "Cush and Put, Lydia and all Arabia, Libya and the people of the covenant land will fall by the sword along with Egypt" (Ezekiel 30:5). Put or Phut is a reference to North Africa and includes the regions west of Egypt. Lydia was a central western region of Turkey. They will all be destroyed along with the Antichrist. These nations are in "league" or in "covenant" and allied with the Antichrist.

SYRIA, IRAQ, IRAN, AND TURKEY

"Assyria is there and all her company: his graves are about him: all of them slain, fallen by the sword: Whose graves are set in the sides of the pit, and her company is round about her grave; all of them slain, fallen by the sword, which caused terror in the land of the living" (Ezekiel 32:22–23). Assyria and "all her company" could include several Middle Eastern nations including Syria, Iraq, Iran, and Turkey as well as Egypt, Lebanon, Jordan and Saudi Arabia. They will all be cast into the pit.

IRAN

"There is Elam and all her multitude round about her grave, all of them slain, fallen by the sword, which are gone down uncircumcised into the nether parts of the earth, which caused their terror in the land of the living; yet have they borne their shame with them that go down to the pit" (Ezekiel 32:24). Elam encompasses the region of modern day Iran and perhaps regions of Afghanistan. Again we see that they also will, "go down to the pit" along with the Antichrist.

BUT MUSLIMS ARE CIRCUMCISED

Now, some will argue that the people who are destroyed in this passage are uncircumcised and thus they cannot be Muslim, but this reasoning is not necessarily correct. Let's look at the use of the word circumcision. In Ezekiel 44:7, God is angry because foreigners who are "uncircumcised in the heart and uncircumcised in the flesh" are profaning His sanctuary. This and many other passages reveal that there are two aspects to circumcision; one is of the heart (arel leb) and circumcision of the flesh (arel basar). In the passage in Ezekiel 32, only the word arel is used, and so it is impossible to distinguish between the two. We know that circumcision is the mark of God's covenant with Abraham and Isaac. (Genesis 17:19) Because all male members of the household were circumcised (Genesis 17:12–13), Ishmael was therefore circumcised—even though the covenant was not made with him.

And it may also be noted that some rabbinic interpreters also do not see this verse as ruling out Muslims. Technically Orthodox Jews do not consider Muslim circumcision to be complete circumcisions as Muslims only remove the prepuce or outer foreskin, while the Jews also remove the pariah or the inner foreskin.

TURKEY AND THE TURKIC NATIONS SOUTH OF RUSSIA

The Turkic Nations include nations such as Azerbaijan, Kazakhstan, Kyrgyzstan, Tajikistan, Uzbekistan and Turkmenistan:

"There is Meshech, Tubal, and all her multitude: her graves are round about him: all of them uncircumcised, slain by the sword, though they caused their terror in the land of the living. And they shall not lie with the mighty that are fallen of the uncircumcised, which are gone down to hell with their weapons of war: and they have laid their swords under their heads, but their iniquities shall be upon their bones, though they were the terror of the mighty in the land of the living." (Ezekiel 32:26-27)

JORDAN, SAUDI ARABIA

"There is Edom, her kings, and all her princes, which with their might are laid by them that were slain by the sword: they shall lie with the uncircumcised, and with them that go down to the pit" (Ezekiel 32:29) In the strict sense, Edom is comprised of the southern parts of Jordan but here the text states "her kings" (plural). This encompasses Arabia. In many passages, Edom has come to represent the greater portion of the enemies of Israel that live to her south and east.

TURKEY, LEBANON

"There be the princes of the north, all of them, and all the Sidonians, which are gone down with the slain; with their terror they are ashamed of their might; and they lie uncircumcised with them that be slain by the sword, and bear their shame with them that go down to the pit" (Ezekiel 32:30). All the "princes of the North" refers to Turkey and her allies. And Sidon once again refers to Lebanon. They are both cast "down to the pit."

CONNECTING TO REVELATION

Now that we understand the context of Ezekiel 27-32—namely the judgment of the Antichrist and the Muslim nations that follow him—we can now better understand certain portions of the Book of Revelation. Most Western interpreters would never consider Ezekiel 27-32 as the interpretive basis for understanding Revelation 19. Yet it is these passages that we just reviewed that are one of the premiere Old Testament foundations for the following passage which concludes the Biblical revelation concerning the judgment of Antichrist and the Muslim nations that follow him: "And the beast was taken, and with him the false prophet that wrought miracles before him, with which he deceived them that had received the mark of the beast, and them that worshiped his image. These both were cast alive into a lake of fire burning with brimstone. The rest of them were killed with the sword that came out of the mouth of the rider on the horse, and all the birds gorged themselves on their flesh" (Revelation 19:20, 21).

Some might object, here the beast and the false prophets are cast alive, while the other references in Ezekiel Pharaoh is killed. How then could this Pharaoh of Egypt thus be the Antichrist?

The answer to this is simple—does God punish the dead while they are dead? Does God punish a dead carcass and forget to punish the soul? Everyone who is cast into hell is physically dead. But their soul lives. How else can they be punished? The trouble with many interpretations is when men try to over analyze God and how He manages certain affairs. This is why it's a fruitless discussion when one enters into a debate with Muslims over the Trinity. They love to debate what mankind cannot fathom. They speak of an unknown God, yet they expect us to almost bring the Almighty so low and examine Him in a laboratory in order to dissect Him into three parts to prove them wrong?

The problem with most people is that they get hung up more on the allegory and the unknown, yet they ignore the obvious. Even scientifically we observe the world around us, we do not see the electro-magnetic waves, yet we believe they exist because we hear the radio. As the Bible states: "Faith is the substance of things hoped for the evidence of things not seen" (Hebrews 11:1).

≈59≈
Literal References of Christ Fighting an Islamic Alliance in the Psalms

"Arise O God, judge the earth, for all the nations are your inheritance" (Psalm 82:8).

CHRIST ARISES FROM HIS THRONE

Even from the very beginning of the Psalms, the purpose of God is clearly declared: "Why do the nations rage and the people plot a vain thing? The kings of the earth set themselves, the rulers take counsel together, against the Lord and against His Anointed, saying, 'Let us break their bonds in pieces, and cast away their cords from us'" (Psalm 2:1-3).

The Lord responds to the protests of the Gentile nations: "Yet I have set My King on My holy hill of Zion. I will declare the decree: The Lord has said to me, 'You are my Son, today I have begotten you. Ask of Me, and I will give you the nations for your inheritance, and the ends of the earth for your possession" (Psalm 2:6-8).

The Lord is speaking about His Messiah "Today I have begotten You" (v. 7) addresses the nations forming through crafty counsel a plot against the Messiah and Israel. The attack on Israel is viewed by God as an attack on the King Himself. These nations rage against "the Lord and His Anointed One" (v. 2). They blaspheme the Father and the Son" (I John 2:22).

Here we see another clear articulation of the Antichrist theology that the kings of these nations confess. One can hear them collectively declaring, "There is no god but Allah, and Mohammed is his messenger. And God has no Son!" To which the Lord responds, "You actually dare to stand against the Lord and against His Anointed?" And then He laughs in scorn and offers them this final warning: "You kings, be wise; be warned, you rulers of the earth. Serve Jehovah with fear and rejoice with trembling. Kiss the Son, lest he be angry and you be destroyed in your way, for his wrath can flare up in a moment. Blessed are all who take refuge in him" (v. 10-12).

It is crucial to understand the theme of Psalm 79 to Psalm 83 is God Himself arising from his throne to judge the nations that attack Israel at the end of the age: "Arise O God, judge the earth, for all the nations are your inheritance" (Psalm 82:8).

Jesus, who is seated at the right hand of the father, comes down for the final clash between the Lord and his enemies. This is no small matter and is one of the most amazing descriptions of God fighting nations that are all Muslim:

"Do not keep silent O God, do not hold Your peace, and do not be still, O God! For behold Your enemies make a tumult. And those who hate you have lifted up their heads. They have taken crafty counsel against Your people, and consulted together against your sheltered ones. They have said 'Come, and let us cut them off from being a nation, that the name of Israel be remembered no more.' For they have consulted together with one consent; they form a confederacy against You: the tents of Edom and the Ishmaelites, Moab and the Hagrites; Gebal, Ammon and Amalek, Philistia with the inhabitants of Tyre. Assyria also has joined with them; They have helped the children of Lot" (Psalm 83:1-8).

This battle cannot be historic. There are several reasons within the text that show us that this is an End-time battle with Islam:

1. God is physically present on the earth "do not be still O God" (v. 1), "Arise O God" (82:8), "Return we beseech You O God of hosts" (80:14) is the same as Israel's prayer: "blessed is He who comes in the name of the Lord" (Matthew 23:39).

2. This event is caused by the defiling of the Temple of God: "O God, the nations have come into Your inheritance; Your holy temple they have defiled" (79:1).

3. The Bible calls these peoples God's enemies. This is seen in the fact that the Psalmist calls them, "Your enemies" who "form a confederacy against You." One cannot claim to be on the side of God and against Israel. God declares that the enemies of Israel are His enemies: "Pour out Your wrath on the nations that do not know You. And on the kingdoms that do not call on Your name" (79:6).

4. These enemies who hate God are religious and not atheists: "The haters of the Lord pretend submission to Him" (Psalm 81:15).

    The word "Islam" literally means submission. To be a Muslim is to submit to the will of Allah. That these peoples think in their minds that they are in submission to God when in reality they hate and blaspheme Him is yet another clear indication as to the identity and religion of these peoples. Blasphemy is to deny God's edicts. Here God declared that the land belongs to Israel. To deny that is blasphemy. This is how crucial Israel is when it comes to faith in God.

5. That Israel is sheltered and living in her land. This is not the persecution of Israel in the Diaspora.

6. There is simply no evidence of any attack against Israel by such a confederacy of Arabs with Lebanon, Gaza and Assyria attacking Israel in the past. Psalm 83 is a prophecy of the final showdown. Notice that this prophecy is a confederacy or coali-

tion of nations: "They form a confederacy against you" (83:5) In the first verse, Israel's enemies are God's enemies, for they conspire against the Jews: "those whom God cherishes," (83:3) then the collective objective of God's enemies is declared: "Come... let us destroy them as a nation, that the name of Israel be remembered no more" (v. 3). God being zealous for Israel's name is being zealous for His own name.

7. Amazingly, the Bible even predicted so accurately that Philistia (Gaza) would be joined with the inhabitants of Tyre (Lebanon): "Philistia with the people of Tyre" (v. 7) we have seen these two collectively bomb Israel and carry each other's banners and each group launching rockets against Israel in unison. As Hassan Nassrallah, the leader of Hezbollah launched his rockets from Lebanon; Hamas was backing him up by launching its own Qassam rockets over every town in Israel that they could reach.

8. This event occurs when Israel is a nation: "Revive us" (80:18) "Restore us" (80:19, 80:3) and Israel is saved: "and we shall be saved" (80:19).

9. Many Arabs will also be saved: "O my God, make them like the whirling dust. Like the chaff before the wind. As the fire burns the woods, And as a flame sets the mountains on fire, so pursue them with your tempest and frighten them with your storm. Fill their faces with shame that they may seek your name, O Lord [Jehovah]" (Psalm 83:13-16). God's purpose for judging these nations is not some petty revenge or hatred; it is rather an appeal to these nations to reconcile with God and recognize His authority: "that men may know that thou, whose name alone is Jehovah, art the Most High over all the earth" (Psalm 83:18).

THE NATIONS OF PSALM 83

On May 26, 1967, as a multi-national Arab coalition was poised to attack Israel, Egyptian President Nasser almost seemed to have been quoting directly from this Psalm when he declared, "Our basic goal is the destruction of Israel."[5] Azaam Pasha, Secretary General of the Arab League announced, "This will be a war of extermination and momentous massacre which will be spoken of like the Mongolian massacres and Crusades." And to this day, we hear the repeated declarations made by numerous Muslim leaders who call for the destruction of Israel. But what makes this Psalm so important is that after recording the shared plans of the Last-Days enemies of God, it actually lists exactly who these nations are. "With one mind they plot together; they form an alliance against you" (v. 5). The nations of this coalition or alliance are the following:

Edom—which extends from Jordan to Saudi Arabia (see Ezekiel 25) Edom is described as extending from Teman to Dedan (Arabia).

Moab, Ammon, children of Lot—Jordan

Gebal—According to the Unger's bible dictionary, this is in Lebanon, 25 miles north of Beirut

Tyre—Again in Lebanon, today center for Hezbollah

Philistia—Gaza, today the center for Hamas

Ishmaelites and Hagarites—Arabs in general

Assyria—these are Iraq, Syria, and Turkey. At it's height it included Egypt and Iran as well.

Amalek—Jordan, southwest of the Dead Sea (Genesis 14:7)

And so we have a coalition of Muslim nations consisting of at least Turkey, Iraq, Jordan, Egypt, Syria, Lebanon, Saudi Arabia, and Palestine all bent on destroying Israel. This is nearly a perfect prediction of the nations whose battle cry we have heard over the past fifty years, since the establishment of the Jewish state. Just recently, even the Iranian President's chants of "death to Israel" and statements to the effect that Iran would "wipe Israel off the map" almost mirror this verse perfectly. The similarity of this prophecy to what we are seeing in the modern day Middle East is undeniable.

And indeed in modern times, we have witnessed at least a partial fulfillment of this Scripture in both the 1948 Arab-Israeli War and the 1967 Six Day War. In both of these wars, against tremendous odds, Israel triumphed—a reflection indeed of Israel's first birth when Joshua triumphed on the seventh day of a six-day battle. When Menachem Begin visited the Western Wall for the first time following its liberation in 1967, this was his prayer: "God of our Fathers, Abraham, Isaac, and Jacob, Lord of Hosts, be Thou our help. Our enemies encompassed us about; yea they encompassed us about and arose to destroy us as a people. Yet has their counsel been destroyed and their schemes will not be accomplished."

But apart from prophesying thousands of years into the future regarding Israel's enemies, what other important information does this Psalm convey?

One must keep in mind, that God sees Israel's sufferings as His. Even in the very prophecies about the Messiah, they all parallel Israel's sufferings: "Many bulls have surrounded Me; Strong bulls of Bashan have encircled Me" (Psalm 22:12). This is definitely a prophecy about the Messiah, yet it also speaks of the strong enemies of Israel that surround her. Specifically, Bashan points to Syria. But despite all of their wicked plans, in the end, they will be destroyed by Israel: "The nations surrounded me but in the name of the Lord I will destroy them" (Psalm 117:10).

ARMAGEDDON AND LEBANON (PSALM 29)

In Psalm 29 we find a clear connection between the Battle of Armageddon and the nation of Lebanon: "The voice of the Lord breaks the cedars, Yes, the Lord splinters the cedars of Lebanon" (Psalms 29:5) Muslim Lebanon will be destroyed. But this passage is speaking about the Battle of Armageddon: "The voice of the Lord shakes the wilderness; The Lord shakes the wilderness of Kadesh." (Psalm 29:8) Kadesh is the valley of Megiddo "Har-Megiddo"—Armageddon: "And he gathered them together into a place called in the Hebrew tongue Armageddon" (Revelation 16:16). This is an End-Times event: "And in His temple everyone says, "Glory!" (v. 9) "And the Lord sits as King forever." (v. 10) Jesus is clearly pictured here as the Warrior Messiah: "Gird Your sword upon Your thigh. O Mighty One" (Psalm 45:3). This Mighty One is also the Immanuel, the God with us: "The Lord of hosts is with us" (Psalm 46:11).

MY OWN EXPERIENCE

When I was a young boy in Jericho, the American Consulate sent representatives from Jerusalem when they heard that a major war was about to erupt. They started evacuating all Americans in the area; and because my mother was an American, they came to rescue her. My father, however, refused the offer to leave because of his love for his religion and country and because he did not want his children growing up in America to become soldiers in the war with Vietnam.

The Six Day War began, and the Jews captured old Jerusalem and the rest of Judea. The Israeli victory was a great disappointment to Arabs and Muslims worldwide. I remember the thunder of the bombs and clatter of machine guns that continued for six days and nights. As the Arabs ran in fear from the Israelis and crossed the Jordan River, many of their fellow citizens and neighbors in Jericho began looting the stores and houses. The Israeli soldiers announced that everyone should post a white flag on their gate. Israel won the war in six days, and on the seventh day, Rabbi Goren blew the ram's horn on the Wailing Wall in Jerusalem, declaring victory.

Many see this war as a parallel to Joshua at Jericho, when Joshua and the Israelites marched around the walls of Jericho for six days. On the seventh day, they marched around the city seven times. On the seventh day, the priests blew the trumpets and the people shouted with one voice, the walls tumbled, and the Israelites took the city. The Arabs have lost every war they waged against Israel, exactly as the Bible prophesied. Yet after all these losses, we still hoped for that one victory, which we believed was all that was necessary to destroy Israel. Many Muslims in the land claim that Israel is God's punishment for allowing bad governments to rule the Islamic world. This belief is what fuels the attempts by majority Muslim populations to topple ruling governments.

Consider the words of former Syrian President Hafez Assad: "The Arabs are willing to lose several wars to come with Israel. All they need to do is defeat Israel once." Yet the God of Israel has promised, "They shall not be pulled up" (Amos 9:15). The Arab and Muslim worlds continue to try, but God has promised that they will fail. Arabs feel that the God of the Bible is biased toward the Jews, but the Lord desires that the Arab people all turn to Him (the One True God). We should not ignore the many verses that declare punishments against Israel. After the Jews refused to accept Christ's sacrifice, the final offering for sin, the Temple was destroyed and the great "Diaspora" began. The Jews were scattered into all the earth, separated from their homeland and far from Jerusalem. God allowed them to be killed and suffer more than any other people in the world. There are no other people in history who have tasted the agony of war and pain more than the Jews have; they are the true refugees of the earth.

A SIGN FROM GOD

In July of 2006 during the height of the Israeli-Hezbollah conflict a miracle was reported on news outlets across the world. An Irish construction worker operating a backhoe happened to notice something very unusual in the swampy peat that he was about to dig up. His find turned out to be an ancient 20-page portion of the Psalms dated to the years 800-1000 A.D. Experts say that the manuscript had been laying in the mud for the past 1,000 to 1,200 years. The National Museum of Ireland issued a statement saying, "In discovery terms, this Irish equivalent to the Dead Sea Scrolls is being hailed by the museum's experts as the greatest find ever from a European bog."[6]

The museum's director, Pat Wallace referred to the find as a "miracle find," telling the Associated Press, "it's unlikely that something this fragile could survive buried in a bog at all, and then for it to be unearthed and spotted before it was destroyed is incalculably more amazing."[7]

But what is even more miraculous than the nature and the manner in which the book was found, is the timing of the find and the nature of the manuscript that was found. For not only did the find occur at the height of the Israeli-Hezbollah conflict, but the Psalter itself was found opened to Psalm 83. A very fitting Psalm indeed to be found in the midst of a historical conflict between Israel and the Iranian and Syrian backed Hezbollah.

BOTH DESECRATE JEWISH HOLY PLACES

Antichrist will desecrate Jewish holy places. The spirit of Antichrist can be seen when Muslims desecrate all Jewish places of worship in Judea. This will continue until the Muslim Antichrist himself defiles the Temple. Psalm 74 refers to the Muslim people because they are the only ones that carry out such desecrations. It is difficult for students of the Bible at times to identify prophecies that pertain to current events because many subconsciously view the Bible as speaking only about historic events. While the prophets did speak about current events in their day, even these historic events contained shades of end time prophecies as well. Oftentimes, when a prophet was speaking of events that occurred in his day, he would also layer into the prophecies information about the End-Times as well.

Psalm 74 begins with: "O God, why hast thou cast us off for ever? Why doth thine anger smoke against the sheep of thy pasture?" Israel has been cast off for its sins and the Jews believe God has neglected them. In Psalm 74:2 we hear their plea, "Remember thy congregation, which thou hast purchased of old; the rod of thine inheritance, which thou hast redeemed; this mount Zion, wherein thou hast dwelt." Mount Zion is the Temple Mount. Psalm 74:3 says, "Lift up thy feet unto the perpetual desolations; even all that the enemy hath done wickedly in the sanctuary." Who has done and will do wickedly in God's sanctuary, but the present occupiers—the Islamic crowds who daily pollute the sanctuary with their abominations? One of the most egregious examples is the construction (or rather, destruction) project undertaken by the Waqf, the Muslim religious authority that controls the Temple Mount. The purpose of the project is to create a second entrance to the al-Marawani Mosque, which is located under the southeastern quadrant of the Mount—an area popularly, although mistakenly, known as Solomon's stables.

The huge underground mosque attracts thousands of worshippers, so there is no question that a second entryway is important for safety reasons. However, the Waqf's decision to haul material from the area and dump it in the dead of night in the nearby Kidron Valley has come under attack as irresponsible destruction of an important archaeological site. Israeli archaeologists called for a professional, controlled excavation to no avail. Now the only remaining option is for personnel from the Israel Antiquities Authority (IAA) to sift through the dump in the Kidron Valley in the hopes of gaining some raw data, but unfortunately, without context. They dig up precious Jewish artifacts and destroy them to prevent the Jews from claiming the site of their temple; they do this because they worship a God who is not the God of Israel, the one true God. Under the direction of the Muslim authorities, bulldozers cart away huge mounds of earth from underneath the Temple

Mount in Jerusalem, one of the most revered and sacred sites in the world. Israeli archaeologists are outraged, claiming that the Muslim authorities are damaging the inside of the Mount's eastern retaining wall and destroying priceless historical data in the process. The Muslims have also attacked synagogues in Israel and throughout the world, including Turkey and Tunisia.

Today Roman Catholics do not burn synagogues or attack Jewish shrines nor do Jews ever destroy churches or mosques. Yet Muslims have gone so far as to desecrate the tombs of Abraham, Sarah, Rachel, and Joseph. "Thine enemies roar in the midst of thy congregations; they set up their ensigns for signs" (v. 4).

Psalm 74:5 refers to the man or men who cut down trees that built God's holy sanctuary with "axes and hammers." "A man was famous according as he had lifted up axes upon the thick trees." And we are told in Psalm 74:6. "But now they break down the carved work thereof at once." This reference to breaking down the carved works (v. 6) is fulfilled not only by the destruction accomplished by the Waqf, but also by the destruction of Joseph's Tomb in Shechem in present-day Nablus. Palestinians relentlessly hammered at the tomb with pick axes and hammers to pry the stones apart. Muslim mobs burned and destroyed Joseph's tomb and then danced in celebration. Over sixteen synagogues were desecrated in Judea, literally all the synagogues in Judea. "They said in their hearts, Let us destroy them together: they have burned up all the synagogues of God in the land" (v. 8-9).

What else could fulfill these Scriptures more precisely than these acts of violence and desecration in these holy places? "They have cast fire into thy sanctuary, they have defiled by casting down the dwelling place of thy name to the ground." (v. 7) Muslims hate the Jews. As they commit violent acts against the Jews, they deny the God of Israel His place to be worshiped. With their voices and with ensigns, they proclaim that only Allah is god; they are against the one true God. "We see not our signs: there is no more any prophet: neither is there among us any that knoweth how long" (v. 9).

Today Jews in Israel are perplexed as never before as to how long this violence can continue. Synagogues are burned, just as prophesied in this Scripture. Yet Jews in America simply want to erect monuments and memorials for the Holocaust. While this is good to declare that one must "never forget", what about remembering the Jews that are still living? While Jews must never forget the shattering of all of that fine crystal during ChrystalNacht, why are they so silent on the splintering of their Patriarch Joseph's tomb?

They are silent because of passivity and fear. Such fear that only emboldens the Muslims even more. Throughout the Bible, fear is an element that Israel had to deal with. It continued until Moses, Joshua, Gideon, David and so many more examples rose up and gained victories for Israel through the power of Jehovah.

Israel will continue to live in this fear until Messiah comes and fights the world's Goliath, the Muslim beast. It will end when Messiah crushes the head of Leviathan just as David crushed the head of Goliath. Psalm 74 speaks of this glorious day. The violence against the Jews will continue until the end of the Tribulation: "You break the heads of leviathan in pieces, and gave him to be meat to the people inhabiting the wilderness." The seven-headed beast of Revelation is destroyed. "Remember this, that the enemy has reproached, O LORD, and that the foolish people have blasphemed thy name. O deliver not the soul of thy turtledove unto the multitude of the wicked: forget not the congregation of thy poor forever. Have respect unto the covenant: for the dark places of the earth are full of the habitations of cruelty. O let not the oppressed return ashamed: let the poor and needy praise thy name. Arise, O God, plead thine own cause: remember how the foolish man reproaches you daily. Forget not the voice of thine enemies: the tumult of those that rise up against thee increase continually" (Psalm 74: 14-23).

This passage agrees with both Joel 3 and Matthew 25. The core of this issue is the oppression of Israel. God will arise, as written in Hebrew: Kumma Elohim, "Arise O God", and "when God arose to judgment" (Psalm 75:9). "Return we beseech You, O God of hosts" (Psalm 80:14) "the mountains (nations) melt like wax at the presence of the Lord of the whole earth" (Psalm 97:5). All these references confirm that He will come down from heaven and respond to the cruelty of the Muslim multitude for killing the Jewish people and for destroying His holy places: "You will arise and have mercy on Zion" (Psalm 102:13).

This will be a time of spiritual revival in Israel: "Revive us" (Psalm 80:18), and "restore us" (Psalm 80:19). Both of which correspond to Hosea 6: After two days he will revive us; on the third day he will restore us, that we may live in his presence" (v. 2).

This revival comes in the midst of great persecution from Islam as He reminds His people: "I will make mention of Rahab and Babylon to those who know Me; Behold O Philistia and Tyre with Ethiopia" (Psalm 87:11).

They conspired, all of them—Arabia (Babylon), Gaza (Philistia), and Lebanon (Tyre) together with other Islamic nations to destroy the Jews. They plan first to destroy the Saturday people (the Jews) and then the Sunday people (the Christians).

Kumma Elohim is a desperate appeal to God to arise from His throne and come to the earth to fight the enemies of Israel as seen in Psalm 82:8, which is immediately followed by the judgment of Muslim nations in Psalm 83.

Of Israel the Lord states: "Woe is me, that I dwell Meshech, That I dwell amongst the tents of Kedar! My soul has dwelt too long with one who hates peace. I am for peace; but when I speak, they are for war" (Psalm 120:5-7). They desire peace, they have come out of captivity, while their enemies still desire war and speak falsely of Israel: "Or what shall be done to you, You false tongue" (v. 3) *Oh Lord—come quickly!*

≈60≈
Literal References for Ezekiel 38
The Controversy Over Rosh

"The word of the LORD came to me: 'Son of man, set your face against Gog, of the land of Magog, the chief prince (Rosh) of Meshech and Tubal'; prophesy against him and say: This is what the Sovereign LORD says: I am against you, O Gog, chief prince of Meshech and Tubal. I will turn you around, put hooks in your jaws and bring you out with your whole army...Persia, Cush and Put will be with them, all with shields and helmets, also Gomer with all its troops, and Beth Togarmah from the far north with all its troops—the many nations with you. "Get ready; be prepared, you and all the hordes gathered about you, and take command of them...In future years you will invade a land that has recovered from war, whose people were gathered from many nations to the mountains of Israel, which had long been desolate. They had been brought out from the nations, and now all of them live in safety. You and all your troops and the many nations with you will go up, advancing like a storm; you will be like a cloud covering the land." (Ezekiel 38:1-9)

One of the most popular prophecies of the Bible that has captured the attention of prophecy students is the "Battle of Gog and Magog" that is found in Ezekiel 38. The passage speaks of a coalition of nations that attack Israel, who are all led by the nation of "Magog." Many prophecy teachers claim that Magog is Russia which will be destroyed alongside with Islamic nations. This must occur in order to usher in the Battle of Armageddon and the coming of Christ. But these two arguments are unfounded and totally depend on pure conjecture.

So, is Russia the nation of the Antichrist? Or is the Battle of Gog and Magog a separate battle distinct from the Battle of Armageddon? Are Gog and the Antichrist one and the same? Does Gog come from Russia?

We will examine the main arguments:

DOESN'T RUSSIA ARM MUSLIM NATIONS?

The most common argument for this assumption is that Russia is supplying arms to Iran (Persia) and other Muslim nations. But selling weapons does not amount to primary evidence for anything Biblical. The United States supplied Saudi Arabia with weapons. They also gave weapons to Afghanistan during the Cold War in order to defeat Communism. In doing so, they aided the *Mujahideen* and indirectly created the Taliban. It was the United States that forced Israel to allow elections for the Arabs in Jerusalem— and now we have "Hamasistan" in Gaza. The United States twisted Israel's arm to pull out of Lebanon and now we have Hezbollah practically running that country. The United States, under Jimmy Carter, gave the cold shoulder to the Shah of Iran and did nothing when Khomeni and the *Mujahideen-Khalq-Iran* took over. But do these destructive acts of ignorance tie the U.S. into End-Times prophecy? Yet in Joel Rosenberg's runaway best-seller, *Epicenter*, it is this type of evidence that is used as the primary support for seeing Russia as the key player in the coming "Gog and Magog" battle against Israel. But circumstantial evidences cannot be used as substitutes for solid Scriptural evidences. Circumstances change, but God's Word does not.

So do the above mentioned acts of the United States make them the Biblical Gog or the land of the Antichrist? Well, it certainly seems at times that the U.S. is under an Antichrist spell. And Satan certainly wants nothing more than to weaken the somewhat righteous nations that stand with Israel and spread the Gospel throughout the earth. But Western naiveté and mediocre minds of American politicians would be no match for fourteen centuries of Islamic deception. The Bible warned Christians long ago to be wary of their enemy's pathological lies: "be as wise as serpents and as innocent as doves," (Matthew 10:16).

The only one who knows Russia's future for certain is God. When Russia stood with Nazi Germany, many concluded that Hitler was the European Antichrist. They were wrong. As soon as Stalin was betrayed by Hitler, Russia fought against Germany. If so many prophecy analysts were wrong then, is there a chance that they are also wrong again? During the Cold War, numerous prophecy analysts focused on Communist Russia as a major player in the End-Times. Of course she was. She was the enemy of America and everyone knows that God is an American, right? But then the superpower collapsed and its Muslim parts created their own Commonwealth of Independent States (C.I.S.). Few pay attention to the fact that they all are mentioned by their ancient names in the Bible.

ISN'T "ROSH" RUSSIA?

This controversy has been brewing for years. Much of the controversy revolves around the way that the word "Rosh" in Ezekiel 38:2 is translated. Some Bibles translate the word as a proper noun, "Rosh" and others as "the chief prince."

Those who argue that Rosh is a proper noun almost universally argue that it is referring to the modern nation of Russia.

Others object. Dr. Charles Ryrie, for example, takes issue with the translation of Rosh as a proper noun. He writes: "'The prince of Rosh' is better translated as 'the chief prince of Meshech and Tubal.'"[8]

While the NASB translates this verse as, "the prince of Rosh" in Ezekiel 38:2 and 39:1, a marginal note in 39:1 reads, "chief prince of Meshech." Yet Meshech and Tubal are not linked with a place called Rosh in any of its other occurrences in the Bible. (See Gen. 10:2; 1 Chron. 1:5; Isa. 66:19;[8] Ezekiel 27:13; 32:26)[9] So it is extremely unlikely that in these two cases, Rosh would suddenly take on an entirely different meaning from that used elsewhere in the Old Testament.

In his book, *Iran, The Coming Crisis*, Bible prophecy teacher Mark Hitchcock refers to Wilhelm Gesenius, one of the most respected Hebrew scholars of modern times to support the position that Rosh should be translated as a proper noun. Hitchcock also points out that the Septuagint—a first century B.C. Greek Translation of the Old Testament—also uses Rosh as a proper noun.

As impressive as a reference as Genesius is, it must be remembered that he was a lexicographer and grammarian, but not an authority on ancient history. Nor do other greatly respected lexicographers all agree with Genesius. Another equally respected Hebrew Lexicon is the Brown-Driver-Briggs (B-D-B) Lexicon. It is the work of three famous lexographers of the Hebrew language. The B-D-B Lexicon indicates that there is no identity known for the word "rosh" as a personal name.

The far more reasonable translation of the Hebrew word rosh in Ezekiel 38 is, "head of" or "chief". The word Rosh appears nearly 600 times in the Bible, and all but once, it is interpreted as meaning "head, chief, top, best" or something similar. Why, then, would we make an exception here and translate it as a proper noun? The word Rosh here is the Rosh that we find in the Rosh Hashana—The chief day of the year—the Jewish New Year.

According to Bible scholar Dr. Merrill F. Unger, "Linguistic evidence for the equation [of Rosh with Russia] is confessedly only presumptive."[10]

So who then is right? Is Rosh a proper noun? Or does Rosh mean "chief"?

Theologian and historian Edwin Yamauchi notes that even if one translated the Hebrew rosh as a proper name, it can have nothing to do with modern Russia. He writes, "This would be a gross anachronism, for the modern name [of Russia] is based upon the name Rus, which was brought into the reign of Kiev, north of the Black Sea, by the Vikings only in the Middle Ages."[11] That means that it would have been nearly two thousand years after the time of Ezekiel that the supposed "Rosh peoples" became the "Russians."

Prophecy teacher Mark Hitchcock argues that Yamauchi's argument stands in direct opposition to the arguments presented by the Hebrew scholars Gesenius, James Price, and Clyde Billington.[12] But do these scholars really substantiate Hitchcock's arguments? When one actually looks them up, they do not.

Hitchcock quotes Billington, "Those Rosh people who lived to the north of the Black Sea in ancient and medieval times were called the Rus / Ros / Rox / Aorsi from very early times...From this mixture with Slavs and with the Varangian Rus in the 9th century, the Rosh people of the area north of the Black Sea formed the people known today as the Russians."[13] Did you notice that? Billington admits that the "Rus" did not even become "Russians" until they migrated and intermarried with Slavic peoples from the north in the 9th century. That is over fifteen hundred years after Ezekiel penned this prophecy.

While Hitchcock conveniently selected quotes from Billington to support the idea that the ancient Rus peoples through intermarriage, and migration eventually became "the Russians," he failed to explain that Billington did not place "Rosh" geographically in Russia at the time of Ezekiel. Instead Billington argues that the Rus peoples lived to the north of the Black Sea: "From a variety of sources it is known that a people named the Ros or Rus lived in the same area near the Black Sea where the Tauroi people lived."[14] Geographically north of the Black Sea would be the Ukraine. Billington adds "early Byzantine Christian writers identified the Rosh people of Ezekiel 38-39 with an early group of people of southern Russia whom they called the 'Ros.'"[15]

While this may be true, the Byzantine era was thousands of years after Ezekiel. Why must those who support a Russian presence in Bible prophecy jump forward nearly two thousand years to twist Ezekiel's words? At best, Billington puts Rosh in the Ukraine, north of the Black Sea or possibly in southern Russia which would be the Muslim regions of Georgia and Chechnya.

And what about Bible scholar James D. Price, whom Hitchcock simply mentions as a refutation to anyone who objects? In an article in the *Grace Theological Journal*, Price identifies Rosh as "a well-known land in antiquity on the banks of the Tigris river, bordering on Elam and Ellipi," in the far western part of modern Iran.[16] So now Rosh is in Iran? Why does Hitchcock only cite Billington but not Price? One man's argument might sound good, until they are examined by another.

But ultimately here's the real problem with Hitchcock's approach: In all of the names mentioned in Ezekiel 38, Hitchcock locates where they existed in Ezekiel's day and then identifies the nations that now occupy those regions as key players in the Gog Magog invasion. So if during Ezekiel's day, Magog was located in Asia Minor, then Magog comes to represent modern day Turkey. This is the geographical method of identifying the names listed. Hitchcock uses this method to identify every one of the eight names—except Rosh. When we get to Rosh, then Hitchcock's methodology is suddenly switched up. With Rosh, Hitchcock's method is to use "the ancestral migration" method. So although the Rosh peoples of Ezekiel's day may have lived in the region that is modern day Ukraine, (others as we just saw, argue otherwise) Hitchcock does not identify them with the Ukraine. Instead he identifies them with the nation that their ancestors—after migrating and intermarrying with the Slavic people to the north—eventually founded, which is Russia. But why suddenly change methods? If we applied the ancestral migration method with every other name, we would have an absolute mess. Tracking the intermingling and migration of numerous ancient peoples is often an exercise in futility. The history of this world is the story of the intermingling and migration of every race tribe and people. As such, the regional method is by far preferred and should be stuck with.

So even if Rosh is interpreted as a proper noun, it could point to the Ukraine, Chechnya or Georgia and possibly even Iran. But to point to one small tribe that possibly lived north of the Black Sea as proof to point to the vast nation that is Russia is highly irresponsible.

Now let's examine the identity of the other nations that will be involved in the Great Battle.

MAGOG

Magog encompasses Asia Minor. But some prophecy teachers try to claim that Magog is also pointing to Russia. Tim Lahaye, author of the best-selling *Left Behind series*, points to Josephus' identification of Magog as "the land of the Scythians—the ancient northern nomadic tribes who inhabited the territory from Central Asia across the southern Steppes of modern Russia."[17]

Lahaye's assessment of the Scythians is accurate, yet it proves the point that if Magog is the Scythian territory, then this land mass is in the southern region of the former USSR, but not Russia proper.

The problem with using this method to see Russia in Ezekiel's prophecy, however, is that the southern Steppes of modern Russia include portions of the former USSR. Still, it is not part of modern Russia proper. These Muslim states split from Russia when Communism fell.

Ancient Scythia includes the regions of Asia Minor (Turkey) and the several Central Asian states (Turkmenistan, Kazakhstan, Tajikistan, Uzbekistan, etc.). These are all Muslim nations.

Analysis that supports the "Magog Russia theory" uses correct references, but draws faulty conclusions. The theory is based on the assumption that Russia proper would always control the southern Muslim states, but to everyone's surprise, Communism fell and the Soviet Union collapsed. The unexpected split seems not to have effected Western analysts' interpretation of end-time events.

Prophecy author Grant Jeffrey, who also interprets Magog as Russia by quoting Rawlinson, says, "The areas...that were ruled by the Scythians are located south of Russia and in the *southern republics of the Commonwealth of Independent states* (the former USSR)."[18] Although Jeffrey correctly quotes Rawlinson, he insists on seeing Russia in Ezekiel's prophecy since this theory had become a standard interpretation.

The Latin Church Father Jerome says that Magog denotes, "Scythian nations, fierce and innumerable, who live beyond the Caucasus and the Lake Maeotis, and near the Caspian Sea, and spread out even onward to India, which represents the Assyrian Mat Gugi, or 'country of Gugu,' 'the Gyges of the Greeks.'"

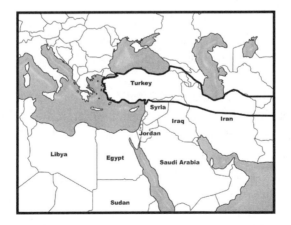

Magog: Turkey, Syria, Northern Iran and The Turkic Regions of Central Asia

The Matthew Henry Complete Commentary speaks of this diversity of opinion. "Some think they find them [Gog and Magog] afar off, in Scythia, Tartary, and southern Russia. Others think they find them nearer the land of Israel, in Syria, and Asia the Less Turkey. (Matthew Henry, Bible Commentary)

Josephus also points to the Scythians as Magog: "Magog founded the Magogians, thus named after him, but who by the Greeks are called Scythians."

But again, where was the "Scythian" territory of Magog? It was not Russia.

The Schaff-Herzog Encyclopedia of Religious Knowledge, citing ancient Assyrian writings, places the location of Magog in the landmass between ancient Armenia and Media[19]—in short, the Republics south of Russia and north of Israel, comprised of Uzbekistan, Kazakhstan, Turkmenistan, Azerbaijan, Turkestan, Chechnya, Turkey, etc.

I agree with all these quotes and I add; *these are all Muslim nations.*

Many who support the "Magog Russia theory" also use Hesiod as an example. Hesiod, the father of Greek didactic poetry, identified Magog with the Scythians in the 7th century B.C.[20] Philo as well, in the first century, identifies Magog with Turkey and the *southern steppes* of the former USSR—that entire northern region is described in Ezekiel 38 as the *"remote parts of the north."*[21]

Some argue that because the passage points to the "farthest north," it must be referring to Russia. But the word "farthest" is not to be found in the Hebrew.

Another interesting point is that in Ezekiel 39:18 the dead bodies of the fallen soldiers of Magog are called, "fatlings of Bashan." While most Bible encyclopedias identify Bashan with Syria, there is also an area called Bashan in the Caucasus or the Caucasian Region. But one cannot call Russians "fatlings of Bashan."[22]

If we examine some of the greatest Biblical references, like the *Macmillan Bible Atlas, Oxford Bible Atlas*, and The *Moody Atlas of Bible Lands*, they all locate Magog, Meshech, Tubal, Gomer and Beth Togarmah in Asia Minor, and not Russia.

Are they all wrong?

Another important point is that Meshech and Tubal must be tied to Magog, yet these are in Asia Minor and not Russia. Magog is specifically referred to as the region of "the land of Magog, chief prince (head or leader of) of Mesheck and Tubal." (Ezekiel 38:2) Because Meshech and Tubal are regions of Turkey—Magog must thus be related to Turkey. Otherwise the passage would make little sense. How could Russia be the head over regions of Turkey? It makes better sense to conclude that Gog is a leader from the land of Magog and the leader of Meshech and Tubal, all of which are in Turkey.

When it comes to the geographic location of Meshech and Tubal, you will never find a serious historian, Bible dictionary or Bible map that would agree with any of the proponents for a Russian location. What you will find written by supporters of the Magog Russia theory are words like "probably" "possibly" and "maybe" interspersed throughout their arguments.

One common denominator in the argument over the Gog and Magog story is that everyone at least agrees that *Gog is Prince of Meshech and Tubal.* No serious historian would argue that Meshech and Tubal are not in Turkey. If we go with the translation that Gog is "prince of Rosh, Meshech and Tubal" are we then to say that Gog rules both Russia and Turkey?

You might want to counter that Gog could indeed be the chief over this whole confederacy. But apart from the fact that these two nations have warred against each other from time immemorial, why didn't the Bible then give him the title of "prince of Rosh, Meshech, Tubal, Persia, Phut, and Cush"?

Gog is of the land of Magog, a very specific place, and he is the ruler of his domain; "Meshech and Tubal," which must be associated with Magog. All these are given for locators and are not intended to lead us into a wild goose chase or a genealogical and historical puzzle.

It is actually far simpler than some make it.

The error of the Russian theory arose from the *Scofield Study Bible*, which identifies *Mesheck and Tubal* with the modern Russian cities of *Moscow and Tobolsk*. The only basis for this interpretation is the somewhat similar sound of the two words. Thus: Meshech sounds like Moscow, and Tubal sounds like Tobolsk. However, one cannot simply take a word from an ancient Semitic language (in this case, Hebrew) and find a correlation to a modern name from a drastically different language (in this case an early form of Scandinavian) simply because the two words "sound the same." While this may be convincing to some for the sole reason of phonetics, it is very irresponsible hermeneutics.

Tim LaHaye for example explains the reason that we may know that Ezekiel 38 and 39 "can only mean modern-day Russia" is because of "etymology," that is, by studying the origin of words.

If phonetics is the yard stick to prove where Gog comes from, then Meshech fits best with the ancient Moschi/Mushki far better than it does with Moscow. Likewise Tubal fits far better with the ancient Tubalu peoples than it does with modern Tobolsk, especially because the two locations were well known regions of Asia Minor Ezekiel's day. There is no need to look any further.

Even Hitchcock admits that Meshech and Tubal are in modern Turkey, or possibly in parts of southern Russia and northern Iran.[25] Yet Hitchcock chose *Russia* for Rosh and *Turkey* for Meshech and Tubal. As I mentioned above, this forces a strange reading of the passage that combines Turkey and Russia under a single ruler as Gog is the prince of Rosh, Meshech and Tubal.

I presume that knowledge and refinement are increasing the closer we get to the actual events. What is missing is a humble stern gradual correction and refinement as we watch the Middle East. I am not saying that our Western Christian prophecy authors have tried to hide something or had any hidden agenda. That would be unfair to say, they are simply teaching what they have been taught by their teachers who taught the same false conclusions. Much of the other material on prophecy presented by Hal Lyndsey, Tim Lahaye, Grant Jeffrey and Mark Hitchcock are excellent and worthy of the edification of the Church. But on this point, the wild geese have migrated and they are wasting their time chasing them so far to the north. Turkey is far enough.

MESHECH

Meshech appears in Assyrian texts as Muski or Musku from 1200 B.C. onwards. The people of Musku were known to be aligned with Tubal. There is little doubt that the frequent Biblical association of Meshech and Tubal (Genesis 10:2; Ezekiel 27:13; 32:26; 38:2-3; 39:1; I Chronicles 1:5) reflects this ancient political alliance in central Asia Minor during Ezekiel's day.[24]

Like Magog, the support for Meshech and Tubal to be in Asia Minor gains the blessings of historians even in Ezekiel's day— Herodotus tells us that the name of the Cappadocians (Katpatouka) was applied to them by the Persians, while they were termed by the Greeks "Syrians" or "White Syrians" (Leucosyri). One of the Cappadocian tribes that Herodotus mentions are the Moschoi, associated by Flavius Josephus with the Biblical figure Meshech, son of Japheth, "and the Mosocheni were founded by Mosoch; now they are Cappadocians."[26]

Cappadocia of course, is in Turkey. Yet some still try to associate Mesheck with Moscow. Again, unless one can legitimately trace the roots of a particular word back to its Hebrew origin, then the argument is based on extremely weak evidence. This error is caused by relying on words similar in their sounding, a common thing within certain prophecy circles. Some have even gone so far as to claim that "Gomer" is referring to Germany. This position has some serious flaws. First, in order to make the root word for "Gomer" to work with "Germnay" one must reverse the "R" and the "M." Ezekiel wrote of GMR not GRM. Such a reversal is completely unwarranted. Furthermore, this similarity and inversion is based upon a comparison of Ezekiel's GMR with a modern English (from Latin) designation for *Deutschland*. Clearly, the similarity is only superficial and only serves to highlight the American-centric mentality of so many American prophecy teachers who forget that the Bible was not written for English speakers. These two errors rule out, absolutely, any possible identification of Gomer with Germany.[27]

Imagine how foolish the use of this methodology could become: One could even go so far as to make Biblical Javan be referring to Japan or Saksin be Anglo-Sakson—after all, they sound similar, do they not? Another could argue that Scythia is in Scotland, which is inhabited by "Scots" since "Scyths," and "Scots" can be mildly manipulated to sound similar. Yet some serious Bible teachers follow this flawed approach and equate Tubal with "Tblisi" in Georgia.[28]

But try to follow the logic: Even if it were true, that some particular modern nation adapted a name that related to its ancient ancestors, it does not override its original location. This would be like saying that because there is a Bethlehem in Pennsylvania, the Messiah must be from Pennsylvania. Scythia is in Eurasia and not in Scotland or Siberia. Even Spain or the Iberians are of Anatolian origin (Celtiberian) and descend from Gomer. So are the Celtic, the Gaels, the Irish, the Welsh, the Britons and the French who trace themselves to Gomer part of the Gog coalition also? And if not, then why are we including Russia simply because she may have descended from the Rosh? There is no difference between the two.

If phonetics and migration patterns are the yardstick that God has ordained for us to identify these nations, then we are in serious trouble because we will be forced to ultimately include virtually every nation in Europe. Then by adding Cush and Phut who are the children of Ham, we can also include all of Africa in Gog's coalition. We can even theorize that China came from Mongolia who is linked to the ancient Magogite/Scythians as well. In fact, if we continue with the lineage and migratory path then we might as well include the whole globe. The U.S. has peoples from every ancient people imaginable, so is the U.S. also part of the Gog coalition?

But if the ancestral, migration method is the method that we need to be using, why then would the Bible go through all of the effort of giving us the names of nations? Why not simply say that Gog is chief prince of the entire globe, and then forget about providing us with all of these ancient names? Why simply pick on the Russians? Why not the Scots, the Irish, the Eskimos...?

Had God intended a European nation to be included in the Gog coalition, He would have simply mentioned them. Iberia is mentioned in the Bible. So is Chittim, which was the ancient name for Rome—did God forget to mention it in this prophecy?

Now, if we take the Scyths equal Scots argument and make a Study Bible that declares this as if it is fact, when it becomes popular, would it thus become true?

Popularity and truth have always struggled with each other. Churchill was not popular when he pointed out the facts regarding Nazism. Lady Aster told him that she hated him, that his opinion is not popular, and that if she were his wife, she would poison his tea. Churchill obliged and responded with "Ma'am, if I was *your* husband, I'd gladly drink it."

The argument falls not from only historians who would refute the Meshech is Moscow argument, but from the Bible itself and even many who support the Russia theory since Meshech and Tubal are mentioned in Ezekiel 27:13 as trading partners with ancient Tyre. Tyre was in what is today Lebanon. No serious teachers are willing to say that Moscow traded with Lebanon thousands of years ago. Even Hitchcock agrees: "It is highly doubtful that ancient Tyre was trading with people as far north as Moscow and Tobolsk."[29]

Even though Hitchcock argues for Russia being Rosh, he admits that Meshech, Tubal, Gomer, and Beth Togarmah are all in Turkey.[30] He's ninety percent there.

Taking Hitchcock's argument that the word "Rosh" is Russia, then Gog of the land of Magog who is the prince of all "Russia" and 'Meshech/Tubal' (Turkey). Such a merge must occur between these nations that have always been in conflict with each other. Yet a merging with Turkey and other Turkic Muslim nations is quite plausible, especially that Turkey could be rejected from the E.U.

In fact, it is questionable whether or not Moscow and Tobolsk were even populated in Ezekiel's day. Hitchcock then identifies a more reasonable solution "A closer study of these names reveals that Meschech and Tubal are the ancient Moschi/Mushki and Tubalu/Tibareni peoples who dwelled in the area around, primarily south of, the Black and Caspian Seas in Ezekiel's day.

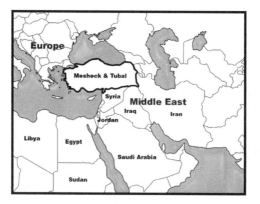

Region of Meshech and Tubal: Modern Turkey

These nations today are in the modern country of Turkey, possibly parts of southern Russia and northern Iran.[31]

Admittedly and correctly Hitchcock writes "Magog today probably represents the former underbelly of the Soviet Union: Kazakhstan, Kirghizia, Uzebekistan, Turkmenistan, and Tajikistan.[32] All these are Muslim.

Meshech was located near what was known as Phrygia, in central and western Asia Minor (Turkey), while Tubal was located in Eastern Asia Minor (Turkey). So with Meshech and Tubal, we are dealing with portions of modern Turkey. Today this region is all Muslim.

GOMER

Gomer is in Turkey not Russia or Germany. This is the land of ancient Kimmeria.[33] Gomer, it seems to be almost universally agreed upon among scholars "refers to the Celtic Cimmerians of Crim-Tartary."[34] Gomer is well known to the ancient world as Gimarrai of north central Asia Minor (Cappadocia). These people are also known as the Cimmerians. This seems to be the simplest, most obvious interpretation.[35]

So Gomer is Gimarra or Cimmeria in Cappadocia. Cappadocia is simply central Turkey, again, another Islamic region.

TOGARMAH

Beth Togarmah is also in Turkey. Togarmah or *Tilgarimmu* was a city state in Eastern Anatolia (Asia Minor, modern Turkey), more specifically, as Ryrie states, "the south-eastern part of Turkey near the Syrian border." This identification is generally acknowledged by all [36] Once more then we have another region that is in present day Turkey.

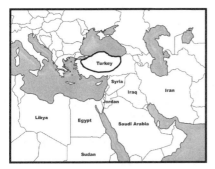
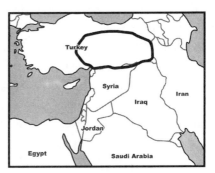

Togormah: Eastern Turkey   *Gomer: North-Central Turkey*

THE LITERAL EVIDENCE

But beyond so much of the geographic weight of this prophecy falling on Turkey, the Bible also ties this coalition to modern day Turkey in a very direct way. Zechariah 9:13 confirms that the final end time battle will be between Israel and Yavan /Ionia (often translated as Greece) which is in Turkey today: "I will bend Judah as I bend my bow and fill it with Ephraim. I will rouse your sons, O Zion, against your sons, O Greece [Yavan, Ionia], and make you like a warrior's sword." (Zechariah 9:13) According to Jamieson-Fausset-Brown Bible Commentary: *Javan*—the Ionians or Greeks: for the Ionians of Asia Minor were the first Greeks with whom the Asiatic peoples came in contact with.

The key element of this passage is the reference to the sons of Zion (that is the Jews) fighting against the sons of Greece (Yavan, Ionia)—which is in Asia Minor or modern Turkey.

The other important argument that I need to make here is that if the Bible indeed intended a *lineage* of Javan; "sons of Javan", then we must apply the same for "sons of Zion". Yet there is no such person named *Zion*. The Bible is pointing to geographic locations and not lineage. This is a common problem with many of the modern Western analysts of prophecy.

What is translated as *Greece* is the Hebrew word *Yavan*.

First, let me clarify, when the Bible translation says "Greece," this should not be confused by popular Western thinking as Athens or Cyprus. Yavan was a descendant of Noah who came to live on the Western coast of Asia Minor, or modern day Turkey in the area that came to be known as *Ionia*.

While Yavan is a term that can, in a broader sense, imply all of the ancient Greek Empire, it is most specifically a reference to Ionia in Asia Minor, or Turkey. Again, the verse that we are discussing is ultimately for the Last-Days. As such, it is most clearly speaking about the citizens of Israel fighting against the Turks who are attempting to occupy their land. And so once again, we have a very clear and direct passage that points very specifically to Turkey as the lead player in this Last-Days invasion.

One cannot separate Zechariah 9 from Ezekiel 38. In both passages, the Messiah is present. We will discuss this in more detail as we move on.

The casting of the Ezekiel 38 alliance into hell is mentioned in Ezekiel 30 where the literal name *Lydia is associated with several of the nations in the Ezekiel 38 coalition*: "Cush and Put, Lydia and all Arabia, Libya and the people of the covenant [league] land will fall by the sword along with Egypt." (Ezekiel 30:5) Lydia undisputedly refers to the western region of Turkey. The same event is seen in Jeremiah: "Come up, ye horses; and rage, ye chariots;

and let the mighty men come forth; the Ethiopians and the Libyans, that handle the shield; and the Lydians, that handle and bend the bow." (Jeremiah 46:9)

Here, the Bible clearly connects the Gog coalition with Lydia (Turkey). "There is *Meshech, Tubal*, and all her multitude: her graves are round about him: all of them uncircumcised, slain by the sword, though they caused their terror in the land of the living." (Ezekiel 32:26) Why do we have Meshech, *Tubal, Beth-Togarmah* and *Gomer* included, yet *Russia*, the supposed leader of this coalition missing? These nations are "in league" (KJV, NASB, ASV, DBY, JPS, WBS, WEB) or "covenant" and allied with Egypt.[37] In fact, the prior chapter (Ezekiel 29) also identifies Turkey with Mesheck: "Javan (Ionia, Turkey), Tubal, and Meshech, they were thy merchants: they traded the persons of men and vessels of brass in thy market." (Ezekiel 29:13)

Why does the Bible so consistently group these nations and regions together? The answer is that they were closely related in Ezekiel's day and were understood by any who read the book in its original context.

I have much doubt that Russia would lead any Islamic invasion of Israel and threaten its own existence. When the Gog and Magog invasion occurs, the primary player will be Turkey which I have argued for years. I first predicted that it would turn toward fundamental Islam which it increasingly has, particularly over the past few years. I had concluded these things during the days when the world viewed Turkey only as a secular and moderate Muslim nation. Sadly, many still do.

The emphasis on a Turkish ruler being called "The Assyrian" would validate our Turkey argument because the Assyrian Empire and Turkey significantly overlap, but Russia and Assyria are two entirely different geographic locations that never overlap.

Obviously, the Lord directed Ezekiel to significantly highlight Turkey with the combination, "of the land of Magog, the chief prince of Meshech and Tubal." The other three nations mentioned: Libya, Sudan and Iran, together with Turkey form a perfect circle around Israel. Turkey covers Israel's entire northern horizon, while Iran is east of Israel, Sudan is south, and Libya is to the west. Israel finds herself surrounded on all four corners by the Islamic coalition. While many Bible teachers have for years prophesied a coming invasion of Israel headed by Russia, we see that the Bible simply does not substantiate this position. Instead, we see an Islamic Invasion of Israel, most likely led by Turkey and involving Iran, Libya, Sudan, Syria and several other Islamic nations.

GOG

Gog or "Gygez" was a real historic person from Turkey. This is perhaps the name preserved in Scripture as "Gog" (Ezekiel 38:2). "Gog" is the reference used in the past to refer to "Gugu" of Lydia in Turkey.[38] Esarhaddon (681-668 BC) records his defeat of the Gimirrai, while King Ashurbanipal tells us in his records of the Cimmerian invasion of Lydia in the days of the Lydian king Gugu (Gygez, Gogaz) around the year 660 BC. This is the same general period that Ezekiel was writing his prophecy.

Like other places in the Bible in which God refers to the Antichrist as the Prince of Tyre, or the King of Babylon, or the Assyrian, here He is calling the Antichrist "Gog" as a throwback to Gygez, a real historic figure from Lydia (Turkey). In fact, the Gomer were Turkic peoples who were descendants of tribes people recorded in history as the Oguz.[39]

They founded the *Gokturk Empire* in the 6th century, 522 CE, and were defeated in 745 CE by the Uygurs, an ethnically related Turkic tribe. "Gokturk," with the "Gok" part being the distinguishing name of this particular Turkic tribe, is remarkably similar to "Gog" and again reinforces the point that the Biblical Gog is a ruler from the Turkic region of Asia Minor.

After several conquests among the diverse Turkic tribes, the Ghaznavids, under the leadership of Sevuktekin in 963 AD, established the first Muslim Turkish state. The Oguz Empire emerged once more upon the defeat of the Ghaznavid dynasty in 1040 CE and was assimilated by the Oguz.[40] After the expansion of Islam, the empire came under the leadership of Tugrul Bey and Cagry Bey, grandsons of Seljuk, whose name was adopted for the Seljuk Dynasty. The Empire covered the region of Anatolia, Northern Iran, Syria, Iraq, Southern Caucasus, and Azerbaijan under Turkish rule under the leadership of Alp Arslan and Malik Shah in the 11 century.

The Seljuk Dynasty declined steadily during the 13th century and the land of Seljuk Sultanate was divided among chieftains. The Mongol conquest in 1243 marked the end of the Seljuk Dynasty. Ertugrul Gazi ruled the lands around Söğüt, a division of the Seljuk Sultanate. Upon his death in 1281, his son, Osman (Uthman), expanded the territory known by his name as the Ottoman Empire. (Guide Martine, History, the Seljuks)

Archaeology can sometimes be the best forensic science when examining prophecy. In the case of Gog, the Bible uses past names, past leaders, and past locations to be introduced in the future. Gyges was first known to the Greeks as "tyrant" and the one who introduced "tyranny" to the Greeks: he was called *"tyrannous"* or the tyrant one[41] *Archagetes* means to be "further" and is applied both to divinities and to military leaders—in other words, a military leader who makes himself to be further, or greater than he is— a god.

This is exactly how the Antichrist is portrayed in the Bible (Isaiah 14). The same is said of Nimrod in Micah 5. Thus, after all that we have so far discovered, we are not surprised to learn that Gyges of Lydia (Turkey), the first to be called a tyrant, bears a striking similarity with the Biblical Antichrist.[42]

Turkey is far more qualified to lead an Islamic coalition than Russia could ever be. All of the nations allied with Magog and all the alliances throughout the Bible are all Muslim. Why would Ezekiel 38 be any different? "I will turn you around, put hooks into your jaws, and lead you out, with all your army, horses, and horsemen, all splendidly clothed, a great company with bucklers and shields, all of them handling swords. Persia, Ethiopia, and Libya are with them, all of them with shield and helmet; Gomer and all its troops; the house of Togarmah from the far north and all its troops—many people are with you." (Ezekiel 38:4) In Ezekiel 38 we have Persia, Phut and Cush. Persia is very easy to identify:

PERSIA-IRAN

Essentially, Persia is modern-day Iran. Many Iranians in America, if asked where they are from, will simply say they are Persian. In fact Iran was still called Persia until 1935. Obviously Iran is an Islamic fundamentalist nation.

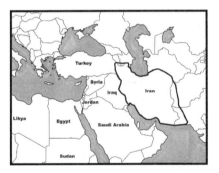

Persia: The Modern Islamic Republic of Iran

CUSH: SUDAN, SOMALIA

Not to be confused with modern Ethiopia, Cush of Ezekiel's day was simply the region immediately south of Egypt often called *Nubia*. In Scripture, Cush was often associated with Egypt and was a border nation to her: "I will make the land of Egypt a ruin and a desolate waste from Migdol," (Northern Egypt) "to Aswan," (Today in southern Egypt) "as far as the border of Cush." (Ezekiel 29:9-10)

The only legitimate identification of Cush then is modern Sudan, officially known as *The Islamic Republic of Sudan* since 1989. While Sudan does have a large Christian minority, it is ruled by the Muslim majority. Today Sudan is an absolute cesspool of Islamic oppression toward Christians and anyone who is not an Arab Muslim. The Sudanese Arab Muslim Government is even killing the native African Muslims.

The region of Cush could also extend to the south of Sudan into Somalia. Somalia is a rabidly Islamist nation that may very well be included in the invasion.

PUT OR PHUT

Biblically, Put (or Phut) is the region west of Egypt. Today this is the nation of Libya. The Septuagint translates the word Put here as *Libue*. Most modern scholars seem to agree with this interpretation. Algeria, Morocco, Tunisia and Mauritania could also be included here as well. Once again, we again have another region that is entirely Muslim.

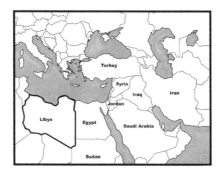

Put or Phut: General Region of Modern Day Libya

⤳61⤶
Ezekiel 38
Is Armageddon

THE SIGNIFICANCE OF SEPARATING THIS BATTLE

Many prophecy teachers in the West teach that the invading coalition of nations described in Ezekiel 38-39 is not the army of Antichrist, but of another army entirely led by some other evil world leader who is destroyed prior to Christ's coming to defeat Antichrist.

The reason for this view is simply because Ezekiel 38-39, which clearly describes a Muslim coalition of nations does not support their European Antichrist paradigm. For this reason they are forced to find a way to divorce the battle of Gog and Magog from the main event when Christ returns to the earth for the showdown with Antichrist. Most western prophecy teachers claim that Islam will be defeated and out of the scene before Antichrist emerges from Europe as a world leader.

Ezekiel 38 is indeed Armageddon for several reasons:

1. ISRAEL WILL BE PURE

"I will make known my holy name among my people Israel. I will no longer let my holy name be profaned, and the nations will know that I Jehovah am the Holy One in Israel." "It is coming! It will surely take place, declares Jehovah the Sovereign. This is the day I have spoken of," (Ezekiel 38:23-39:7-8)

2. THE GENTILES WILL KNOW GOD

God Himself says that after the defeat of Gog and his armies, all of the Gentile nations as well as Israel will be convicted of their unbelief and will know that He (Jehovah) is God: "And so I will show my greatness and my holiness, and I will make myself known in the sight of many nations. Then they will know that I am Jehovah.' I will send fire on Magog and on those who live in safety in the coastlands, and they will know that I am Jehovah..."

The text of Ezekiel 38 describes the heathen as finally knowing who the true God is "the heathen may know me" "And thou [Gog] shall come up against my people of Israel, as a cloud to cover the land; it shall be in the latter days, and I will bring thee against my land, that the heathen may know me, when I shall be sanctified in thee, O Gog, before their eyes." (Ezekiel 38:16)

How could these be "heathen?" All these nations in Ezekiel 38 are Muslim nations. Why would the Bible call people who claim to believe in Abraham and Jesus as heathen? To me this is one dilemma I had when I read the text as a Muslim, I realized that I must be on the wrong side. Worshipping Allah according to the Bible cannot be the same as worshipping Jehovah. You could imagine my dilemma when I first read this. I had to make a choice—Allah or Christ. I chose Christ. This event happens, "in the latter days," a war between Israel and these "heathens." Muslims call us *Kuffar* (heathen, infidels), for we do not believe in Allah. From their perspective, we are unbelievers—we reject Allah and Muhammad. Yet the Bible declares Muslims to be heathen. Islam turns everything upside down. Take for example, Islam claims that there is "no compulsion in religion," yet we are the ones who carry out this mandate, they don't. They should be happy with us for carrying out that commandment. Yet they are not. Islam is spread by the force, yet keeps certain abrogated peace verses for the sake of deception.

The "smarty-pants atheists" in the West condemn us (Christians) because we (according to them) are always condemning everyone who doesn't believe, to hell. In reality it is us who are damned whether we agree with Muslims or we don't. We are proud *Kuffar*. Actually I am considered a *Murtad*, one who once believed in Islam, then left. I get a much harsher punishment than you. I have 72 hours to change my mind or die. You might end up simply paying the *Jizyah* tax if they decided to spare you the sword. What you need to realize about Islam, regardless if it is the "moderate" brand (if indeed there is such a thing) or the fundamentalist brand. Islam is like the Hotel California, you can check out anytime you like, but you can never leave—unless you are carried out in a coffin, with or without your head. So when you are given a choice by a Muslim to embrace Islam—choose wisely. You are better off telling them that you would rather remain a *Dhimmi*—a subjugated person under Islamic rule. I need to fight just a little longer in the hope that this battle to come and go, (unless we have a pre-Tribulation Rapture). But after this Battle, *God's name will never again be profaned.*

After the war of Gog and Magog there will be no more blasphemy, no more, "There is no god but Allah and Muhammad is his messenger." The only creed will be "There is no God but Jehovah and Jesus is His Son."

3. CHRIST IS PRESENT

In both battles—Gog and Armageddon—Christ is present with the greatest earthquake: "And all the men that are upon the face of the earth shall shake at my presence." (Ezekiel 38:20)

Who is present? God is present—in the flesh. This is indeed the last battle, with Jesus scoring a great victory on behalf of his people against their enemies.

If one doubts that Messiah is on earth, the text in verse 7 should leave no doubt. "And the heathen shall know that I am Jehovah, the Holy One in Israel," (39:7).

Did you see that?

The Holy One is in Israel.

Other parts of Scripture use the phrase "the Holy One of Israel," but here the Messiah is actually present on the Earth in the Land of Israel.

This "in" is crucial. It's like DNA evidence in a court of law.

No serious Bible student can doubt the fact that this event is anything other than the Messiah fighting the Antichrist.

We also have verse 19, which states, "My fury shall come up in my *face*." (Ezekiel 38:18).

This is a literal face—he is furious and angry.

Not only is Christ present, but the destruction of both Gog and the

Antichrist is accompanied by an earthquake of unparalleled proportions: "For in my jealousy and in the fire of my wrath have I spoken. Surely in that day there shall be *a great shaking in the land of Israel;* So that the fishes of the sea, and the fowls of the heaven, and the beasts of the field, and all creeping things that creep upon the earth, and all the men that are upon the face of the earth, shall shake at my presence, and the mountains shall be thrown down, and the steep places shall fall, and every wall shall fall to the ground," (Ezekiel 38:19-20).

Shake at my presence? In the same verse, we read about the earthquake and his presence on earth. This is not a small event. Every creature on the earth will shake at the presence of Jesus.

The Book of Revelation also tells us that this event occurs when the Antichrist's armies are gathered together against Israel: "Then they gathered the kings together to the place that in Hebrew is called Armageddon...And there was a great earthquake, such as was not since men were upon the earth, so mighty an earthquake, and so great...and the cities of the nations fell...And every island fled away, and the mountains were not found," (Revelation 16:18:-20).

Both descriptions tell us that the mountains are "thrown down." In other words, no nations are left. Only one kingdom remains—The Kingdom of Messiah.

Zechariah describes the same event from his own prophetic perspective: "I will gather all the nations against Jerusalem to battle...Then Jehovah will go forth and fight against those nations, as when He fights on a day of battle. In that day His feet will stand on the Mount of Olives, which is in front of Jerusalem on the east; and the Mount of Olives will be split in its middle from east to west by a very large valley, so that half of the mountain will move toward the north and the other half toward the south," (Zechariah 14:1-4).

When did Jehovah have feet?

Zechariah 14 gives both accounts—the final victory of Jehovah-God and the great earthquake. Ezekiel 38:19-20 does as well.

The war of Ezekiel 38 is massive. Everything about the events, indicate that this war is no mere opening act for the Great Tribulation. It is the magnificent capstone of that period and will have a decisive effect on all nations worldwide.

If the war of Gog and Magog occurs just prior to Christ's coming and is a separate event from Armageddon, then do we have two separate battles for Christ, one to fight Gog and the other to fight Antichrist? How many comings are there?

The return of Christ for this battle is well defined in the Book of Joel: "Let the nations be roused; let them advance into the Valley of Jehoshaphat, for there I will sit to judge all the nations on every side...Jehovah will roar from Zion and thunder from Jerusalem; the earth and the sky will tremble. But Jehovah will be a refuge for his people, a stronghold for the people of Israel." (Joel 3:12, 16).

Many Western scholars agree that Zechariah 14 and Joel 3 speak of the coming of Christ. Yet, because Ezekiel 38-39 describes the names of nations coming for war, and because they do not match the European Western mold, these scholars will separate the verses from their obvious context. They attempt to create a different mold and force the Bible to fit into their mold, rather than forcing their prophetic scenarios to conform to what the Bible says. The Book of Revelation, unlike any other book in the New Testament literally oozes with references, direct citations, allusions and even many echoes of hundreds of passages from the Old Testament. In fact, nearly every verse in the Book of Revelation is founded on an Old Testament passage. Can you guess which passage Revelation 19 and the Battle or Armageddon is primarily founded on? You guessed it—Ezekiel 38 and the Battle of Gog and Magog. Nearly every Commentary on Revelation that one can find will affirm this fact—except those written by the European Antichrist theorists—they do their best to hide this fact.

Another powerful reason to recognize the fact that Gog is Antichrist is because Ezekiel makes it clear that all prophets speak of Gog: "This is what Jehovah the Sovereign says: Are you (Gog) not the one I spoke of in former days by my servants the prophets of Israel?

At that time they prophesied for years that I would bring you against them," (Ezekiel 38:17).

When this event happens, the Lord asks, are you not this one spoken of by the prophets? The word *prophets* is plural—*many prophets*, or even all of them that prophesied prior to Ezekiel.

If Israel's prophets speak of Gog and Magog, then where are all of the references? If one denies that Gog is the Antichrist, then one will be very hard pressed to find any of these references without seriously stretching the Scriptures. In fact, I have yet to see a single treatment of this subject by someone who claims that Gog is not the Antichrist. But if we take the position that Gog is the Antichrist, it is easy to find numerous passages throughout the prophetic books that mention the Antichrist and his army.

The next argument lies in the fact that the enemy armies are eaten by wildlife in both battles. The specific descriptions concerning the destruction of Gog and his armies and the defeat of the Antichrist mirror one another almost perfectly. Consider the striking similarities between the following two invitations given to the birds of the air and the animals to feast on the flesh of the fallen soldiers.

Gog: "Call out to every kind of bird and all the wild animals: 'Assemble and come together from all around to the sacrifice I am preparing for you, the great sacrifice on the mountains of Israel. There you will eat flesh and drink blood. You will eat the flesh of mighty men and drink the blood of the princes of the earth...At my table you will eat your fill of horses and riders, mighty men and soldiers of every kind,' declares Jehovah the Sovereign," (Ezekiel 39:17-20).

Antichrist: "And I saw an angel standing in the sun, who cried in a loud voice to all the birds flying in midair, 'Come, gather together for the great supper of God, so that you may eat the flesh of kings, generals, and mighty men, of horses and their riders, and the flesh of all people, free and slave, small and great,'" (Revelation 19:17).

The enemy is destroyed by the sword in the God and Magog battle and in Armageddon. You might ask, so what?

I mention this because experts who claim that the Gog and Magog battle is separate from Armageddon, base their theory on the fact that Gog and Magog are destroyed miraculously by God through hail and pestilence while the Antichrist is killed by the sword.

The fact of the matter is that both armies are destroyed by both hail, fire, and *by the sword*, yet in both the Gog and Magog battle as well as Armageddon, there is the mention of the destroying sword that God will bring against the invading armies: "I will call for a sword against him [Gog] on all My mountains, declares the Lord GOD...You will fall on the mountains of Israel, you and all your troops and the peoples who are with you," (Ezekiel 38:21-22).

Similarly, concerning the destruction of the Antichrist and his armies, we read, "His name is called The Word of God...From His mouth comes a sharp sword, so that with it He may strike down the nations." (Revelation 19: 15) This of course is the same sword that we read about in Isaiah 34—the sword of the conquering Messiah against Edom: "My sword has drunk its fill in the heavens; see, it descends in judgment on Edom, the people I have totally destroyed. The sword of the LORD is bathed in blood, it is covered with fat, the blood of lambs and goats, fat from the kidneys of rams. For the LORD has a sacrifice in Bozrah and a great slaughter in Edom." (v. 5-6)

Both the Battle of Gog and Magog and Armageddon experience great hailstones. The Antichrist's army is destroyed by a sword, hailstones, earthquakes, and disease. When teachers choose one and ignore the others, we end up with a mess. The argument that all Gog's army are destroyed miraculously and Antichrist is not has been repeated a thousand times, but it is still a clear error. It's like saying that the stone—not God, who directed the hand of David to kill Goliath.

David slung the stone. Yet, it was God who established the miracle. Israel is also another case. Did Israel use weapons in 1948 and 1967? Sure they did. But God's hand was in the battle. You might argue that Israel is secular, so God couldn't have stood with them. Well, read Ezekiel 38 again. God will change the status quo and Israel will turn back to Him.

Beyond there being a sword and great earthquake, there is also the similarity of great hailstones that will rain on the armies of both Gog and the Antichrist.

Gog: "I will rain upon him, and upon his bands, and upon the many people that are with him, an overflowing rain, and great hailstones, fire, and brimstone," (Ezekiel 38:22).

Antichrist: "Then they gathered the kings together to the place that in Hebrew is called Armageddon... Then there came... From the sky huge hailstones of about a hundred pounds each fell upon men. And they cursed God on account of the plague of hail, because the plague was so terrible," (Revelation 16:16-21).

The enemy comes from the North in both battles.

Perhaps the strongest argument that Gog is the Antichrist is that whenever the direction from which the Antichrist is coming is mentioned, it is always the north, and never the European west. Yet, there isn't a single verse in Scripture mentioning a European western invasion. You can try. It simply doesn't exist. Yet, people cling to the theory of a western invasion developed from allegories in Revelation and Daniel.

Western prophecy analysts have always argued that the Antichrist comes from Western Europe without providing a single text from the Bible as evidence.

"But I will remove far off from you the northern army," (Joel 2:20).

"And the LORD shall be seen over them, and his arrow shall go forth as the lightning: and the Lord GOD shall blow the trumpet, and shall go with whirlwinds of the south. The LORD of hosts shall defend them; and they shall devour, and subdue with sling stones; and they shall drink, [and] make a noise as through wine; and they shall be filled like bowls, [and] as the corners of the altar. And the LORD their God shall save them in that day as the flock of his people: for they [shall be as] the stones of a crown, lifted up as an ensign upon his land," (Zechariah 9:14-16).

If the Messiah is going from the south, where is He going to?

He is going NORTH.

In that day, He will save Israel. Analysts agree that this is Armageddon. Why, then, did many overlook the fact that the enemy comes from the northern regions and not Western Europe?

The weapons are destroyed in both The Gog and Magog battle and in Armageddon. After the destruction of Gog, the peoples of Israel will burn the weapons of war that have been scattered on the battlefield. "Then those who inhabit the cities of Israel will go out and make fires with the weapons and burn them, both shields and bucklers, bows and arrows, war clubs and spears, and for seven years they will make fires of them: 'They will not take wood from the field or gather firewood from the forests, for they will make fires with the weapons; and they will take the spoil of those who despoiled them and seize the plunder of those who plundered them,' declares the Lord GOD," (Ezekiel 39:8-9).

I always hear the argument that the seven years of burning weapons must take place at the beginning of the seven-year Tribulation period because it takes 7 years to burn these weapons. This argument is used to prove that this event cannot be Armageddon. But the burning weapons are not sufficient evidence that the event happens in the beginning of the seven-year false peace treaty.

First, it is wrong to call the seven-year false peace treaty offered by the Antichrist the "Seven-Year Tribulation." The Tribulation begins in the middle, when the Antichrist reneges on his deal. In reality, the tribulation is 3½ years.

Such an event, of course—the burning of weapons for 7 years—would not take place unless Israel no longer needed weapons.

Would it make sense to burn weapons at an hour of need? I could understand them burning weapons the first 3½ years, but why would they still burn the weapons after the middle of the 7 years? They will need all of the weapons they can get.

This theory makes no sense.

In fact, it further proves the case that Gog and Magog is indeed the final war. There is no longer a need for weapons. They will burn into the Millennium.

As such, this passage is also highly reminiscent of the Prophet Micah's descriptions of the Messianic period of the millennium: "And he shall judge among many people, and rebuke strong nations afar off; *and they shall beat their swords into plowshares, and their spears into pruning hooks*: nation shall not lift up a sword against nation, neither shall they learn war any more," (Micah 4:3).

Section IV

Western Misconceptions
Context and Allegorical Definitions

～62～
Western Misconceptions

MIDDLE EASTERN CONTEXT

We now need to address important misconceptions regarding the scope and geographical focus of Biblical prophecy. For many years, it has been taught that in the Last-Days literally every nation of the earth will be utterly dominated by the Antichrist; that there will be no place to escape from the dreaded Mark of the Beast; that every last nation of the world will come against Jerusalem. Zechariah 12 is used to validate the theory: "*all the nations of the earth*" (v. 1-3) will be gathered together to attack Jerusalem. Later, in Zechariah 14, we read that God, "*will gather all the nations to Jerusalem to fight against it.*" The Prophet Joel prophesies similarly, "I will gather all nations and bring them down to the Valley of Jehoshaphat," (Joel 3:2).

The Apostle John, using perhaps the strongest language of all, goes so far as to say that the Antichrist will be given "authority over every tribe, people, language, and nation," (Revelation 13:7).

This would seem as an ironclad case for the Antichrist ruling the entire world, which he uses in his march against Jerusalem.

The world used for "earth" in Zechariah is "*eretz,*" which most often is translated as "land." But there are many verses in the Bible that also use this same type of language, yet are clearly not speaking of the whole globe. These verses all use a Hebrew grammatical construct that is an exaggeration or an emphatic statement in order to convey their point. Using hyperbole is extremely common in eastern culture. Elaborating on the exceptions would entirely blunt the impact of the statement. For instance, imagine a speed limit sign that listed the exceptions painted on it, "speed limit 55—except ambulances, fire trucks, police giving chase, etc." Thus, exceptions cannot be ruled out on the basis of exclusive language. This type of language is actually found quite frequently in the Bible.

For instance, Daniel the prophet, speaking to King Nebuchadnezzar: "O king, the Most High God gave your father Nebuchadnezzar sovereignty and greatness and glory and splendor. Because of the high position he gave him, all the peoples and nations and men of every language dreaded and feared him," (Daniel 5:18, 19).

Did every single nation in the earth fear Nebuchadnezzar's father? Or did only those nations that had heard of Nebuchadnezzar's father dread him? Was Daniel speaking of every nation of the earth? Or only those nations that were in a close enough proximity to Babylon to be affected by her? Were the native peoples of Hawaii or Denmark living in dread of Nebuchadnezzar's father? "Of course not," Daniel's use of the phrase *"all the peoples, and nations and men of every language"* was more of an emphatic expression used to convey his point. Or how about this one: *"Men of all nations came to listen to Solomon's wisdom,* sent by all the kings of the world, who had heard of his wisdom," (I Kings 4:34)? Was Solomon's wisdom so impressive that not a single king in all the earth failed to hear of it? Was Solomon visited by Kings from China, Korea, and Scotland? More likely, this verse is simply attempting to convey the renowned Solomon that enjoyed throughout the ancient Biblical world. How about, "Howbeit every nation made gods of their own, and put them in the houses of the high places which the Samaritans had made, every nation in their cities wherein they dwelt," (2 Kings 17:29).

Did the inhabitants of every last nation of the earth have Samaritan gods in their homes? "Of course not," this passage concerns a local area where such practices were the norm. "All" is simply used to emphasize how widespread this practice was. In Isaiah 37:18, we read that, "the kings of Assyria have laid waste all the nations, and their countries." Did King Sennacherib of Assyria actually destroy all nations on the face of the earth? Was South Africa or Japan laid waste by Sennecherib? Again, "all" is simply used as an emphatic statement regarding Sennecherib's might and power. Did Alexander the Great ever occupy the whole world? He most certainly did not. And yet the Bible states, "As I was considering, suddenly a male goat came from the west, across the surface of the whole earth," (Daniel 8:5).

Do you see my point? There are numerous examples like this throughout the Bible.

Let's return to the passage in Zechariah 12 and read it in its full context. "I am going to make Jerusalem a cup that sends all the surrounding peoples reeling. Judah will be besieged as well as Jerusalem. On that day, when all the nations of the earth are gathered against her, I will make Jerusalem an immovable rock for all the nations. All who try to move it will injure themselves," (Zechariah 12:2-3).

Who does this passage specifically say will attack Jerusalem? The answer is, "The surrounding peoples." Today, the nations that encircle Israel on every side are Muslim. The Prophet Joel confirms this, as well. Speaking of the final attack against Jerusalem, Joel prophesied, "I will gather all the nations and bring them down to the valley of Jehoshaphat.

Then I will enter into judgment with them there on behalf of My people and My inheritance, Israel, whom they have scattered among the nations; and they have divided up My land... Hasten and come, all you surrounding nations... for there I will sit to judge all the surrounding nations," (Joel 3:2, 4, 9-12).

Once again, Joel, like Zechariah, specifies just who the nations are. Who are these "surrounding nations"? Does this include New Zealand, Canada, Greenland and Papua New Guinea? Or is this prophecy speaking about the sea of Islamic nations that surround Jerusalem on every side—exactly how it is today? The verse actually specifies at least two of the guilty parties involved. It says, "What are you to Me, O Tyre, Sidon, and all the regions of Philistia? If you do recompense Me, swiftly and speedily I will return your recompense on your head." Tyre, Sidon, and Philistia are references to the regions of Lebanon and the Gaza Territories. Certainly these qualify as the peoples that surround Israel. In fact, this pattern is found quite extensively through the prophets.

Ezekiel, for instance, also specifies who the nations are that will attack Israel and incur God's judgment at the end of the age. "O mountains of Israel, This is what Jehovah the Sovereign says to the mountains and hills, to the ravines and valleys, to the desolate ruins and the deserted towns that have been plundered and ridiculed by the rest of the nations around you—this is what Jehovah the Sovereign says: In my burning zeal I have spoken against the rest of the nations, against all Edom, for with glee and with malice in their hearts they made my land their own possession so that they might plunder its pastureland.'... Then the nations that are left round about you will know that I, Jehovah, have rebuilt the ruined places and planted that which was desolate; I, Jehovah, have spoken and will do it," (Ezekiel 36:4, 5).

Notice the pattern. First, there is specific mention of "the nations around you." Then one of them is named: Edom. While Edom is used as a general term referring to the enemies of the Jews who lived to the east of Israel, today this would most specifically be Jordan and Saudi Arabia. The Bible makes every effort to clarify the nation's roundabout: "And render unto our neighbors sevenfold into their bosom their reproach, wherewith they have reproached thee, O Lord," (Psalm 79:12). Do Israel's "neighbors" include Sweden?

"Thus Says Jehovah against all mine evil neighbors that touch the inheritance which I have caused my people Israel to inherit," (Jeremiah 12:14). The neighbors are all Muslim.

"When I gather the people of Israel from the nations where they have been scattered, I will show myself holy among them in the sight of the nations. Then they will live in their own land, which I gave to my servant Jacob. They will live there in safety and will build houses and plant vineyards; they will live in safety when I inflict punishment on all their neighbors who maligned them. Then they will know that I am Jehovah their God," (Ezekiel 28:25).

NATIONS ATTACK ANTICHRIST

A nother reason the position that every nation will fall to Antichrist is impossible, is the fact that some will resist the Antichrist and attack him. "Many countries will fall, but Edom, Moab and the leaders of Ammon will be delivered from his hand," (Daniel 11:40-45). The Bible says "many countries," not "all". Elsewhere, we read that Chittim will come against him. Daniel 11:30 says that ships of Kittim (often translated as "out of the west") will come against the King of the North (Antichrist). "For the ships of Kittim shall come against him." Chittim refers to the islands and coastline of the Mediterranean and in a wider sense, the Roman legions, or Europe. In Numbers 24:24, Balaam foretold, "that ships shall come from the coast of Kittim, and afflict Eber." Josephus identifies Kittim as Cyprus, whose ancient capital was called Kition by the Greeks. Cyprus also extended to include lands west of Syria, all of Greece, and as far as Illyricum and Italy. Note that none of these lands are Muslim. The name was first used to identify the Phoenician port of Citium in Cyprus. In fact, Kittim actually appears in the Dead Sea Scrolls and is even translated as "Romans" in the Septuagint.[1]

In general, the term Kittim was used to refer to all the islands and settlements along the seacoasts, as well as to the people who succeeded them when the Phoenician power decayed. Thus, Kittim generally refers to the islands and coasts of the Mediterranean and the races that inhabit those areas.

If the Antichrist were to come from the Western Roman Empire of Europe, the ships of Kittim would not come against him.

To answer the question, *are any European nations mentioned in the Bible*? Yes. The *ships of Chittim* in the Septuagint are literally the European nations from Cyprus to Italy to Spain. According to the prophecy of Daniel 11 they attacked Antiochus who was a foreshadow of the Antichrist, as such, this passage could very well involve a dual fulfillment, and we could have a prophecy about a European attack against the forces of the Antichrist.

Consider Turkey's army. It supersedes the combined forces of Britain, Italy and France. Yet Turkey is no match for Rome's fleet (ships). "Our fleet cannot, perhaps, compare with the fleet of Italy, but our army is mighty," explains Zia Pasha, Turkey's ambassador to the United States. Turkey's army is stronger, but Italy's fleet can defeat Turkey.[2]

No European country is featured in End-Times prophecy as receiving a judgment of wrath. Rome is mentioned several times, and Spain twice, without a single reference to judgments.

Islam wants to conquer Rome (see the photo below).

Ezekiel 28 also confirms that the most powerful nations on earth will attack Antichrist. "Behold, therefore I will bring strangers upon thee, the terrible of the nations: and they shall draw their swords against the beauty of thy wisdom, and they shall defile thy brightness," (Ezekiel 28:7). The term "terrible" implies "very powerful."[3]

God will rise up several nations to attack the Antichrist. Therefore, it cannot be true that *every* nation of the earth will fall to the Antichrist and attack Israel. There have always been attempts to establish a One-World Government, yet they have never succeeded.

Far too many in the West fail to remember the actual context of the Bible. Too many Westerners read the Bible narcissistically. Many books have been written that revolve around the West and interpret history through a Western-centric lens. When I opened the Bible for the first time, I read about the places where I grew up. I read about Bethlehem and Jericho. Far too many Westerners have missed the obvious fact that the Bible is thoroughly Middle Eastern. In the Biblical worldview, Jerusalem is the center of the earth, not Europe or America. The biblical prophecies about the End-Times are no different.

≈ 63 ≈
Western Misconceptions
And The Challenge

Speaking to a Western audience of several prominent prophecy authors in Dallas, Texas, I asked a Jesus-style question: "Besides the argument over whether Magog is Russia, can you cite any literal reference to a nation that God destroys in the End-Times that is not Muslim?"

I waited and waited. No one responded. I then asked, "Why are you not raising your hands? Is it because you cannot find any? Or is it because you have written all these books which you cannot recant?"

I have asked the same question to thousands in churches throughout the U.S., Canada, and England. Yet, to this day, no one has disagreed with me that there are no literal references to non-Muslim nations that God destroys in End-Times anywhere in the Bible.

SHIPS OF TARSHISH

Many teachers of Bible prophecy claim that the European Union is the Antichrist's dominion. They claim the Biblical Tarshish is Spain or Britain, but do not support this notion Biblically. They claim that the "merchants of Tarshish and all the young lions thereof" (Ezekiel 38:13) are other European countries. It is important to distinguish between "ships of Tarshish" and the "merchants of Tarshish" as nations that simply traded with Tyre. For example: "The burden of Tyre. Howl, ye ships of Tarshish; for it is laid waste, so that there is no house, no entering in: from the land of Chittim it is revealed to them," (Isaiah 23:1). In this verse, "Ships of Tarshish" points to Tyre (Lebanon). Here, the Bible ends speculation that "Ships of Tarshish" is any European entity.

Tarshish is cited in several passages. Many writers point to Ezekiel 27:12, noting that since only Britain or Spain manufactured tin, and because Britain still manufactures tin, then it must be Tarshish. But this theory has several serious flaws.

For this to be true, Britain and Spain must also manufacture silver, lead and iron. "Tarshish was thy merchant by reason of the multitude of all kinds of riches; with silver, iron, tin, and lead, they traded in thy fairs." (Ezekiel 27:12) Only Turkey was renowned for its production of silver, iron, tin and lead altogether.

For the next argument we turn to Jonah who in attempting to flee to Tarshish from Israel boarded a ship at the port of Joppa (Israel) on the Mediterranean coast. (Jonah 1:3). This would indicate that Tarshish lies to the west. This is true, but the ships could also sail westward to Turkey and Lebanon. Even so, many modern authors are divided between Tartessos in Iberia (Spain) and Tarsus in Cilicia (Turkey). Cilicia was the ancient name of southern Turkey. Göltepe in Turkey was associated with tin mining; Kestel, located in the central Taurus Mountains of Turkey, also produced tin. Josephus cites "Tharsus" in Turkey "Tharsus to the Tharsians, for so was Cilicia of old called; the sign of which is this, that the noblest city they have, and a metropolis also is Tarsus."[4] Josephus, citing from the Hebrew Bible, notes that Tarshish is a descendant of Japheth (Greek: Iapetos/Japetus) and Javan (Hebrew: Javan), associated with the Greek Ionia, a province in modern western Turkey.

The ancient Greek historian Athendorus, a citizen of Tarsus, traces the genealogy of Japetus, the ancestor of Javan, for Tarsus: "Athendorus, the Tarsian, said that the city was originally called Parthenia, from Parthenius, son of Cydnus, the grandson of Anchiale, daughter of Japetus..."[5]

Charles F. Pfeiffer, editor of The Biblical World, a Dictionary of Biblical Archaeology, states, "Ancient Anatolia was famous for its metals, which were carried in Phoenician ships as trade items to other parts of the ancient Near Eastern world. Phoenician inscriptions have been found at Karatepe, in Cilicia." Silver heads the list of precious metals associated with Tarshish, and ancient Assyrian sources noted that the Taurus Mountains above Tarsus were referred to as the Silver Mountains. In fact, modern metallurgy maps indicate that every single metal associated with Tarshish can be found in the Taurus Mountains. "Silver beaten into plates is brought from Tarshish," (Jeremiah 10:9).

The Bible itself indicates that Tarshish was a producer of silver. This cannot be Britain or Spain.

Harper's Bible Dictionary describes Tarsus: "Tarsus, the capital of Cilicia...The city was built on the banks of the swift Cydnus River, 10 miles from the Mediterranean and 30 miles south of the Taurus ("Silver") mountains, which were veined with lead and silver. "Archaeologists found evidence of smelters in the vicinity of Tarsus in antiquity," as noted by MacQueen. The final shaping into tools and weapons was done locally, and areas devoted to this have been found at Bogazkoy and Tarsus marked by the presence of large quantities of slag. Tarsus also produced a clay crucible with bronze adhering to it."[6]

Since Bronze is an alloy of tin and copper, the natives of ancient Tarsus had to have had access to tin in order to make the bronze. Hodges notes that the Assyrians were interested in controlling the tin resources of Eastern Anatolia (Turkey). There can be little doubt that Sargon's chief concern in this enterprise was to control the sources of supply of his raw materials. One is tempted, therefore, to suppose that much of the tin required for bronze making came from the mountains of Syria and Turkey. No later than the Early Bronze Age, Anatolian bronze objects were utilizing tin. The Larousse Encyclopedia of Prehistoric describes bronze production: "It seems certain that bronze and bronze working originated in the Middle East, where Anatolia and Armenia were mining regions...between 2300-2000 BC...the quantity of the bronze with an already remarkably high tin content is impressive."[7]

Aslihan Yener, assistant professor at the university of Chicago's Oriental Institute, discovered an Early Bronze Age tin mine, 60 miles north of Tarsus. Aslihan Yener believes that a mine and ancient mining village she has found in the central Taurus mountains of Turkey shows that tin mining was a well developed industry in the area as early as 2870 BC...the mine at a site called Kestel—some 60 miles north of Tarsus, on the Mediterranean coast— has two miles of tunnels...nearby stands the mining village of Goltepe, which was probably occupied by 500 to 1,000 persons more or less continuously between 3290 and 1840 BC...the site contains no evidence of copper metallurgy...it did not produce bronze; instead it produced tin for export...Yener and her colleagues have analyzed tin-rich slag from 50 crucibles discovered at Goltepe. Within the total one metric ton of metallurgical debris in the form of crucible and vitrified materials, she has excavated some that have 30 percent tin content (a high percentage) still intact in the crucible.[8]

If the peoples of Cilicia were capable of mining tin in the Early Bronze Age, they certainly did not need to sail to Spain to get tin to make it. Ezekiel 38:13 describes merchants of Tarshish: "Sheba and Dedan and the merchants of Tarshish with all its villages will say to you, 'Have you come to capture spoil? Have you assembled your company to seize plunder, to carry away silver and gold, to take away cattle and goods, to capture great spoil?'"

While this does not conclude which side Sheba, Dedan, and the Merchants of Tarshish are on, it is clear that grabbing booty is an Islamic trait that these nations might enjoy copying. Isaiah, however, tells us about the judgment of the ships of Tarshish, "The burden of Tyre. Howl, ye ships of Tarshish; for it is laid waste, so that there is no house, no entering in: from the land of Chittim it is revealed to them. Be still, ye inhabitants of the isle; thou whom the merchants of Zidon, that pass over the sea, have replenished," (Isaiah 23:10). So while the judgment is against "the ships of Tarashish", it is revealed from the land of Chittim (Rome, Europe).

Isaiah 23:6 says, "Pass ye over to Tarshish; howl, ye inhabitants of the isle." This place is somewhat related to Tarshish and is in close proximity to her in order to "pass over" to her. If Tarshish is Spain, how is Tyre to pass over such a far place? There are some who claim that Tarshish is Europe, noting a prophecy in Isaiah 60 that seems to hint to western ships that carried immigrant Jews to Israel.

"Surely the isles shall wait for me, and the ships of Tarshish first, to bring thy sons from far, their silver and their gold with them, unto the name of the LORD thy God, and to the Holy One of Israel, because he hath glorified thee." (Isaiah 60:9)

However, this will be fulfilled in the Messianic Kingdom, when all the nations that hated Israel will participate in bringing the exiled Jewish captives back to their land: "The multitude of camels shall cover thee, the dromedaries of Midian and Ephah; all they from Sheba shall come: they shall bring gold and incense; and they shall show forth the praises of the LORD. All the flocks of Kedar shall be gathered together unto thee, the rams of Nebaioth shall minister unto thee: they shall come up with acceptance on mine altar, and I will glorify the house of my glory," (Isaiah 60:6-7). They will even flock from Saudi Arabia to worship the real God—the Holy One of Israel!

It is obvious that the Arabs will participate in helping the surviving Jews after Christ returns and completely defeats the Muslim nations. If Europe today is the candidate for the "ships of Tarshish," which carry Jews back to the homeland, it's hard to imagine Arabs (Midian, Kedar, Sheba) ever doing such thing. If anything, the Arabs today would rather drown the Jews in the sea than extend assistance to carry them to the land of Israel. Biblical Tarshish is lumped together with Turkic regions. Isaiah clarifies the issue: "And I will set a sign among them, and I will send those that escape of them unto the nations, to Tarshish, Pul and Lud, that draw the bow, to Tubal, and Javan, to the isles afar off, that have not heard my fame, neither have seen my glory; and they shall declare my glory among the Gentiles," (Isaiah 66:19).

Here, Tarshish, Pul, Lud, Tubal and Javan are thrown together in one "that draws the bow," and all these are in Turkey. Why should only Tarshish be identified as Spain or England?

THE ETHIOPIA QUESTION

Ezekiel 38 mentions Ethiopia, which many Westerners interpret as modern day Ethiopia, a predominately Christian nation. So does that mean Christian Ethiopia will join the Islamic coalition against Israel? This interpretation poses several problems. According to the Encyclopedia of the Orient, Cush is the "Ancient kingdom of Nubia in today's northern Sudan, whose rulers conquered southern Egypt in the 8th century BC and established a capital at Napata."

The Sudan is one of the most strident, fundamentalist Islamic states. Two million Christians have been slaughtered or starved in the last twenty years there in a Christian holocaust carried out by the Arab Muslims—all in the name of Islam. Even though Sudan is prominently Catholic, Muslims see no difference between Protestants and Catholics. Yet, the Catholics are accused of being part of the Harlot of Revelation. A study of Scripture shows this to be pure conjecture based on an old interpretation that depended on the animosity between Protestants and Catholics.

One can see on any Biblical map that Cush borders Egypt. Isaiah describes the destruction of Egypt from the Aswan Dam (Syene) to the borders of Cush: "Behold, therefore I am against thee, and against thy rivers, and I will make the land of Egypt utterly waste and desolate, from the tower of Syene even unto the border of Ethiopia," (Ezekiel 29:10).

If Egypt borders Cush, and is also adjacent to Sudan, then Cush could definitely be the nation of Sudan.

THE KINGS OF THE EAST QUESTION

Some scholars think China is "the Kings of the East," with its 200 million-man army invading Israel. This conclusion is based on one verse: "And the sixth angel poured out his vial upon the great river Euphrates; and the water thereof was dried up, that the way of the kings of the east might be prepared," (Revelation 16:10).

This interpretation, of course, isolates the text without exploring the rest of Scripture regarding literal nations from the east. In all of Scripture, not a single passage connects "Kings of the East" with China. The real connection is rarely considered. "Now when Jesus was born in Bethlehem of Judea in the days of Herod the king, behold, there came wise men from the east to Jerusalem," (Matthew 2:1). We know that these wealthy kings of the east were from the regions of Babylonia and Persia. Why not consider this option? Westerners argue that the reason the Kings of the East in Revelation come from China is the staggering number of soldiers—a 200-million-man army. But Islam can easily muster this if you consider Iraq, Iran, Afghanistan and Indonesia east of the Euphrates with several kings. Why do so many apply Revelation's prophecies to a future attack upon Israel by Russia or China? The rise and conquest of Christian nations by Islamic warriors for the past 1,400 years was recognized as literal fulfillment of Bible prophecies by the great majority of Bible commentators of previous centuries, including Martin Luther and Sir Isaac Newton. Many correctly suggested that the 200-million warriors described in Revelation 9:16 were figurative and inclusive of all Islamic warriors and sympathizers throughout the centuries-long war against non-Islamic territories.

Others surmise "Sinnim" or China (note Isaiah 49: 12) by referring to those people living in eastern most part of the known world. However, Isaiah 49:12 does not refer to any wars, punishments, or tribulation against that country, but rather the return of the Jewish people from there to Israel. "Behold, these shall come from far: and, lo, these from the north and from the west; and these from the land of Sinim," (Isaiah 49:12). This is not evidence that China is destroyed. If Sinnim is indeed China, then the Chinese Jews will have a phenomenal homecoming party!

≈64≈
Western Misconceptions
The Key to Unlocking Symbolism

Surely we have considered much evidence for God's war on Islamic terror, and used literal references to prove it. Now we can apply that evidence that we have discussed to the allegorical passages in Scripture in order to form a clear and complete image from this vast prophetic puzzle. But before we do that, we need the key that unlocks the meaning behind the allegorical words and helps us understand biblical symbolism.

The Bible is the finest, richest literature imaginable. It has been shaped and enlivened by the same oral and written traditions that humankind has used since Adam and Eve. It is filled with dazzling figurative language, poetry, prophecy and historical allusions. Trained Bible scholars must possess an array of tools, including knowledge of metaphor, simile, allegory, personification, and symbolism, as well as a thorough knowledge of the times in which the Bible's authors lived. Otherwise, attempts at interpreting the Scriptures can be likened to those of the lazy student who simply says, "The poem means whatever I want it to mean." No—the poem means what its author intended it to mean. Even worse are those who approach a poem and claim it isn't actually a poem, but rather a science manual or a historical narrative.

His conclusions will be atrocious.

The purpose of studying the Bible is to properly understand the meaning of any passage as the author intended it to be understood. The Bible is God's Word and He means for us to understand what He says, not what we would like Him to say.

We do not wish to come away from the Bible with our own ideas about the future, but rather we hope to learn what God is telling us. "Knowing this first, that no prophecy of Scripture is of any private interpretation," (II Peter 1:20).

The Bible is constant and does not change meaning with every altering wind. For the last 500 years, the prevailing wind within the Protestant Church has suggested that the Antichrist will come out of the Roman Catholic Church or that we are somehow moving toward a One-World-government.

While there are indeed satanic forces that would like to unite the world for their own purposes, a close examination of the Scriptures tells us that Satan will not succeed. This theory of Antichrist controlling the whole world is completely wrong—God intervened in the Tower of Babel, during Satan's first attempt for control of the world. This story will repeat itself when Christ intervenes and comes down to stop the Antichrist from establishing a One-World Government—an Islamic Caliphate. He intervened in the Tower of Babel, and He will intervene in Armageddon.

We must allow the Bible to speak its own language, so let us look at the main symbols and decipher the keys to unlock the puzzle:

1. MOUNTAINS AS KINGDOMS

Many of the symbols used during Biblical times are still commonly understood in many cultures today, but they are not easy for many Westerners. Thus, we need a little background information. The Bible often uses mountains as a symbol representing a kingdom or an empire: "It shall come to pass in the Last-Days that the mountain of the LORD's house shall be established in the top of the mountains," (Isaiah 2:2-4). In other words, God's Kingdom will be over all other kingdoms, this is pretty simple.

In the east, this language is common. But western misconceptions and lack of understanding have caused much confusion. In the West, many are waiting for the Catholic Church to arise to power. Rome, after all, is the city of seven hills (Mountains). But listen to Ahmadinejad of Iran in one of his "I have a dream" speeches: "Do not doubt, Allah will prevail, and Islam will conquer mountain tops of the entire world."[9] The mountaintops Ahmadinejad is speaking of are the great kingdoms and governments of the West—Great Britain and America. This is the proper eastern allegoric usage for the word "Mountain". Many passages in the Bible confirms the usage of this word "mountains" as kingdoms: "My sheep wandered through all the mountains, and upon every high hill: yea, my flock was scattered upon all the face of the earth, and none did search or seek after them," (Ezekiel 34:6).

God's sheep, the Jews, were scattered in the Diaspora into many different nations. The word "mountain" is symbol for a nation, empire, or kingdom: "Behold, I am against thee, O destroying mountain, says Jehovah, which destroys all the earth: and I will stretch out mine hand upon thee, and roll thee down from the rocks, and will make thee a burnt mountain," (Jeremiah 51:25).

Here, God rails against the Babylonian Empire—the "destroying mountain," which he will make into a "burnt mountain".

And in Daniel 2: "Then was the iron, the clay, the brass, the silver, and the gold, broken to pieces together, and became like the chaff of the summer threshing floors; and the wind carried them away, that no place was found for them: and the stone that smote the image became a great mountain, and filled the whole earth," (Daniel 2:35).

From the stone (Messiah) will come the "great mountain" which is the Kingdom of God. The mountain will fill the whole earth. In other words, the Kingdom of God will rule over all the earth. "Therefore we will not fear, though the earth give way and the mountains fall into the heart of the sea, though its waters roar and foam and the mountains quake with their surging...Nations are in uproar, kingdoms fall; he lifts his voice, the earth melts," (Psalms 46:2-3, 6). If one reads these passages replacing the word mountain with kingdom and waters or seas with peoples, tribes, and different ethnic backgrounds, then it is easy to understand the picture. In verse 6 above, the Bible even gives the explanation—mountains falling (v. 2) are kingdoms falling (v. 6).

Christ spoke of having the faith of a mustard seed, that we can move mountains. Are these literal mountains? No. These are governments and kingdoms. Exactly what the disciples and the first believers did. They eventually changed the Middle East which was all converted to the faith.

2. WATERS ARE MIXED ETHNIC GROUPS.

In addition to mountains symbolizing nations, Revelation 17:5 tell us that "waters" and "rivers" represent peoples: "And he says unto me, The waters which thou saw, where the whore sits, are peoples, and multitudes, and nations, and tongues."

The primary source for understanding the meaning of a word or symbol is always the text itself. Sometimes, a passage may not be properly understood unless one understands what has been made clear in another text elsewhere in the Bible. "And there was given him dominion, and glory, and a kingdom, that all people, nations, and languages, should serve him: his dominion is an everlasting dominion, which shall not pass away, and his kingdom that which shall not be destroyed," (Daniel 7:14). "*He Shall Have Dominion Also From Sea to Sea, and From the River Unto the Ends of the earth,*" (Psalm 72:8).

These two passages actually are saying the same thing. While Daniel specifically says that Christ will rule over "people, nations and languages," the Psalm refers symbolically to "waters, seas, and rivers." But they are both, in fact, declaring the same message.

As we move on, we will see many other common Biblical symbols used. Once you begin to understand these symbols, the passages actually become fairly clear, and their message is always consistent. Now let's examine Isaiah 64:1-3: "Oh that thou would rend the heavens, that thou would come down, that the mountains might flow down at thy presence,

As when the melting fire burns, the fire causes the waters to boil, to make thy name known to thine adversaries, that the nations may tremble at thy presence! When thou didst terrible things which we looked not for, thou camest down, the mountains flowed down at thy presence." "Waters to boil" means the nations will rage.

"I will make waste mountains and hills, and dry up all their herbs; and I will make the rivers islands, and I will dry up the pools" (Isaiah 42:15).

Interpretation: He will waste "the rivers islands, and...will dry up the pools" tells us that peoples, tribes, and tongues will cease to exist. We can now apply some of these symbols to this passage from Isaiah.

"When you pass through the waters, I will be with thee; and through the rivers, they shall not overflow thee: when you walk through the fire (war), you shall not be burned neither shall the flame kindle upon you," (Isaiah 43:2).

Interpretation: When you Israelites "pass through waters" face the people against you, and you will prevail. And when you walk through fire (the agonies of war and hate) and they declare war against you, you will not be hurt; you will prevail.

3. A HEAD IS A KINGDOM

"This calls for a mind with wisdom. The seven heads are seven mountains on which the woman sits. They are also seven kings," (Revelation 17:9). We already know that a mountain is a kingdom; a head also is a Kingdom. A kingdom is obviously ruled by a king: "they are also seven kings." One cannot have a kingdom without a king. "One of the heads of the beast seemed to have had a fatal wound, but the fatal wound had been healed," (Revelation 13:3). One of the kingdoms is destroyed and comes back to life. One cannot isolate the kingdom from the king. The death of the head is the ending of the kingdom.

4. WOMAN IS A SPIRITUAL ENTITY WITH A LITERAL KINGDOM AND CAPITAL

"And the dragon was wroth with the woman, and went to make war with the remnant of her seed, which keep the commandments of God, and have the testimony of Jesus Christ." (Revelation 12:17) This is the kingdom of Israel with its capital, Jerusalem.

A woman could also be the kingdom of Christ, even prior to its establishment as the Bride of Christ with a capital in Jerusalem, which later becomes the heavenly Jerusalem.

Also, a woman, in the case of the harlot, represents followers of a false religion as John saw in the desert. "Then the angel carried me away in the Spirit into a desert. There I saw a woman sitting on a scarlet beast that was covered with blasphemous names and had seven heads and ten horns," (Revelation 17:3). "...The woman which thou saw is that great city, which reigneth over the kings of the earth," (Revelation 17:18).

This city rules this literal kingdom spiritually, much like Jerusalem, which is the center of Judaism. Jews would say, "Am Yesrael Chai." The word "Am" means nation. Islam uses the same language: "Umma-t Al-Islam," the Nation of Islam. This unites Muslims under one spiritual kingdom with the capital in Mecca.

Bear in mind that the above verse is in Greek, and a "city" in the Bible doesn't always denote a single place. For instance, today the nation of Israel is called Medinat Yesrael in Hebrew. In Aramaic or Arabic, the word Medinat is "a city." In the ancient context, for example in Jeremiah, Gilead actually speaks of all of Judah as one city. The same is true for "house", which is not a single house but all the people of Judah. "For thus Says the LORD unto the king's house of Judah; Thou art Gilead unto me, and the head of Lebanon: yet surely I will make thee a wilderness, and cities which are not inhabited." Judah itself will be a wilderness like cities devoid of their people. (Jeremiah 22:16)

5. BEASTS ARE EMPIRES LED BY KINGS

A common assumption is that "the beast" of Revelation is a man. However, it is clear from Scripture that a single entity does not necessarily represent a single being. For instance, in Revelation 19:7, we read, "Let us be glad and rejoice, and give honor to him: for the marriage of the Lamb is come and his wife hath made herself ready." Just as the wife (bride) of Revelation 19:20 represents many people from different nations, tribes and different tongues, the beast of Revelation 19:7 represents a nation or an empire—a collective group of many people. The metaphorical use of the beast and the bride is consistent with use of figures of speech throughout Scripture. Every instance of the word beast in Daniel 7: 5-7, 11, 19, and 23, is a reference to an empire—with rulers or kings represented by horns. These rulers are represented also with the word "beast" when they come out of the earth. "These great beasts (empires) are four in number are four kings (horns) who will arise from the earth."

A beast always represents a group of people from every nation, tribe, and tongue that follows a false religion and its leader (horn). So, when the beast is taken and the "false prophet" with him, we understand that the empire and its leader (the horn) are removed. We know from Scripture that Satan seeks to be like God, to rule the earth, to have his own kingdom. With this in mind, we see that an Islamic revival is quite plausible as Satan attempts to woo followers.

Jesus, our Messiah, desires His Bride (the saints) for love, forgiveness and reconciliation, and Satan desires his kingdom for destruction—parallels at opposite ends of the moral spectrum.

Just as the Bride awaits the coming Bridegroom, Islam is waiting for the leader they call the Mahdi, who will lead them in the footsteps of his predecessor Mohammed. Thus, we see the beast of Revelation 13:3 waiting and determined to follow the previous beast whose "deadly wound was healed."

6. A NAME IS A DECLARATION OF FAITH—A CREED

When Psalm 83:16 states, "That they may seek your name O Lord," the Bible is not giving us the literal name of God but the definition Him—Emanuel is a name which means "God with us." "His name shall be called wonderful, counselor, Mighty God, Everlasting Father, Prince of Peace." No one accepts the names of the true God except the ones who believe in His attributes—that Messiah is Almighty God and the God with us. We need to think more deeply when we study Scripture. Names in the east always regard the creed, attributes, descriptions and the titles of the person they signify.

In the same way is the name of the beast a blasphemous declaration that puts in God's place someone else other than His son. This is crucial for us to understand, for the harlot of Revelation has names (creeds) of blasphemy on her forehead, and so do the followers of the Antichrist. The followers of Antichrist would then have a creed of blasphemy on their hands and foreheads, which is exactly what we see many Muslims do in our day.

7. FISH ARE FOLLOWERS

Jesus wanted us to fish (gain followers). Similarly, the Antichrist will have his fish. "But I will put hooks in thy jaws, and I will cause the fish of thy rivers to stick unto thy scales, and I will bring thee up out of the midst of thy rivers, and all the fish of thy rivers shall stick unto thy scales," (Ezekiel 29:4).

With our understanding of the meaning of water, it is easy to understand the rest: I will make you to fall into a trap like a fish caught on a hook, and your followers (all the fish) of thy rivers (the different ethnic backgrounds of peoples and languages) will follow you and fall. The rest of the verses is easy: "And I will leave thee thrown into the wilderness, thee and all the fish of thy rivers: thou shall fall upon the open fields; thou shall not be brought together, nor gathered: I have given thee for meat to the beasts of the field and to the fowls of the heaven," (Ezekiel 29:5).

Interpretation: You will fall in the desert (wilderness) with all your people (fish of thy rivers), and you will not be redeemed (not be brought together, nor gathered).

Jesus uses a similar metaphor as He had His followers catch fish, saying they will be "fishers of men."

We are also fish that follow our master.

Antichrist finally loses his grip on his fish: "And I will make the rivers dry, and sell the land into the hand of the wicked: and I will make the land waste, and all that is therein, by the hand of strangers: I the LORD have spoken it." (Ezekiel 30:12).

Interpretation: I will make the land empty of people (the dry river) and wicked strangers will destroy them.

Now review the passage from Daniel: "And there was given him dominion, and glory, and a kingdom, that all people, nations, and languages, should serve him: his dominion is an everlasting dominion, which shall not pass away, and his kingdom that which shall not be destroyed," (Daniel 7:14). Compare this with the passage from Psalm 72:8: "He Shall Have Dominion Also From Sea to Sea, and From the River Unto the Ends of the earth." These two passages carry the same message. However, the passage from Psalms refers to peoples, nations, and tongues as waters, seas, and rivers.

8. A STONE OR ROCK IS MESSIAH

This needs no explanation. In Daniel 2, a stone strikes the statue structure at the feet of iron and clay. This stone is none other than King Messiah. He is also called "The Rock of All Ages" and the "Chief cornerstone that the builders rejected." The expression of Him being a rock is well known in Christian history. Much tradition recognizes this symbol. In Bethlehem, it is common when one begins building the foundation of a home to slaughter a lamb and pour its blood on the bedrock. Sometimes families even bury the lamb in the foundation. No one can build a solid home unless it's built on solid rock and the blood of an innocent lamb is shed.

9. TREES AND BIRDS ARE FALLEN ANGELS

Allegoric trees and birds in the Bible, with the exception of olive trees, often correlate to fallen angels. One example: "Behold, the Assyrian was a cedar in Lebanon with fair branches, and with a shadowing shroud, and of a high stature; and his top was among the thick boughs. The waters made him great, the deep set him up on high with her rivers running round about his plants, and sent out her little rivers unto all the trees of the field," (Ezekiel 31:3-4).

Interpretation: The Assyrian (Satan) was made the greatest among all the angels (a great cedar tree of beauty and importance), and the peoples and nations made him great, and they streamed to worship him and sent out ambassadors to serve him (waters, rivers running round about, little rivers).

10. STARS AS ANGELS

In Revelation 12:4, Satan and his fallen angels are cast out; the dragon, "drew a third of the stars of heaven and threw them to the earth." This is also clear in Daniel 8:10, where the stars are the fallen angels: "And it waxed great, even to the host of heaven; and it cast down some of the host and of the stars to the ground, and stamped upon them." These "stars" (fallen angels) are cast down to earth. So when the Bible addresses Lucifer in Isaiah 14:12 as the son of the morning [star]—he is an angel. This fallen angel is described as possessing a man (v. 16); it is clear that the Antichrist will be a man with Satan dwelling in him.

Obadiah 1:4 is a prophecy concerning Petra in the land of Edom; with a long-term fulfillment, "Though thou exalt thyself as the eagle, and though thou set thy nest among the stars, thence will I bring thee down, Says the LORD." Also "I will exalt my throne above the stars of God," (Isaiah 14:13).

Satan set his nest amongst the stars (angels). As we know from Scripture, Satan took pride in his own wisdom and exalted himself as God, rebelling against the hosts of heaven. When he was cast down from heaven (a fallen angel), he took one third of the angels with him. This passage from Obadiah refers to the height of his pride—"nest among the stars [angels]"—and to his destruction: "Thence I will bring thee down."

11. DRAGON IS SATAN

I shall start with the simple examples: "Michael and his angels fought against the dragon," (Revelation 12:7). A war between Michael and Satan in which Michael the Archangel is victorious.

"And the great dragon was cast out, that old serpent, called the Devil, and Satan, which deceives the whole world: he was cast out into the earth, and his angels were cast out with him." (Revelation 12:9). Obviously, Satan is cast out of heaven to dwell in the body of the Antichrist, who is called the dragon as well." I am against thee, Pharaoh King of Egypt, the great dragon that lays in the midst of his rivers," (Ezekiel 29:3). This is Satan dwelling in the Antichrist; he is called "the dragon." When he rules Egypt, God gives him a nickname: "Pharaoh." At this point, he is Satan in the flesh. Then he sets himself against Israel: "And there appeared another wonder in heaven; and behold a great red dragon, having seven heads and ten horns, and seven crowns upon his heads." (Revelation 12:3).

Now that we know and understand the keys to unlock the meaning of this, let's delve into and unlock some important allegoric end time prophecies.

Section V

Unlocking Allegories
Revelation and Daniel
(Rome or Islam)

≈ 65 ≈
Unlocking Allegories
The Seven Heads Are Not Rome

In the Book of Revelation, the Apostle John gives us a very vivid description of an End-Times beast: "There I saw...a scarlet beast that was covered with blasphemous names and had seven heads and ten horns," (Revelation 17:3). The seven heads are seven empires that have existed throughout history, yet re-arising all at once in the end.

As usual, whenever a Biblical prophecy contains symbolism, the Bible clarifies and explains the passage for us: "This calls for a mind with wisdom. The seven heads are seven mountains on which the woman sits. They are also seven kings. Five have fallen, one is, the other has not yet come; but when he does come, he must remain for a little while. The beast who once was, and now is not, is an eighth king. He belongs to the seven and is going to his destruction," (Revelation 17:9-11).

There are several reasons why Revelation 17 cannot be referring to Rome or Europe, but rather to the Islamic Empire.

The seven heads are not Rome or the Vatican. They are seven heads and are called seven mountains and seven kings. Mountains as we have seen are symbolic of kingdoms or empires. The correlation between Kings and Kingdoms makes seeing the hills—more literally as "mountains" or "mounts"—as kingdoms or empires as the most natural interpretation, rather than trying to find a literal reference here to hills.

Although this passage has been widely interpreted as a reference to Rome, "the city on seven hills," the actual context does not allow for such an interpretation. How could Rome be situated on seven hills that are also seven kings, each with a name of blasphemy on it? That simply doesn't make any sense. An attempt to find in this passage a reference to Rome is founded on irresponsible hermeneutics.

This passage gives us an insight into the fact that before Jesus returns, there will actually have been a total of eight "Beast" empires. The eighth empire will be ruled by the Antichrist, the beast who once was, and now is not, is an eighth king.

How can this passage help us gain insight into the identification of the final Antichrist Empire? First, we see that at the time that it was written, five of the empires had already fallen. This is seen in the phrase, "five have fallen." These empires are:

1. The Egyptian Empire
2. The Assyrian Empire
3. The Babylonian Empire
4. The Persian Empire
5. The Greek Empire

    After these five, the angel tells John that one mountain (empire) "is." At the time that John wrote the Book of Revelation, this was the Roman Empire. It ruled the Middle East, Northern Africa and much of Europe.

6. The Roman Empire

    The purpose of this prophecy is to give the composite of the last empire and the sequence of kingdoms up until the seventh, in order to pinpoint exactly this empire and it's revival as the eighth under the Antichrist. This is basically the summary of a prophetic riddle.

So the seventh empire is the one we need to identify.

According to the verse above, the eighth empire will be a resurrection or a revived version of the seventh empire. "The beast who once was, and is not, is an eighth king." Let me just paraphrase this portion for clarity:

"The seventh beast (empire) that will come into existence, and then ceases to exist, will come back as the eighth and final empire."

During John's day, the seventh empire did not yet exist. This would dismiss the empire that John was under: the Roman Empire.

The seventh Empire must sprout from the Egyptian, Assyrian, Babylonian, Persian or Grecian Empires, yet encompasses all; the seventh will include them. So will the eighth, which is a revival of the seventh.

So, if we are now waiting for the final eighth empire, then what was the seventh? What empire followed Rome?

The most common belief, held almost universally by Bible teachers, is that the Antichrist Empire will be a revived Roman Empire. There are some glaring problems with this theory:

First, Rome was the sixth empire. If Rome was the sixth, and it comes again as the seventh, then what do we do with the eighth? Do we have three revivals of the Roman Empire?

This theory has a gaping hole. Is Rome the sixth, seventh and also the eighth empires? Neither Scripture nor history nor common sense supports this notion. Yet many prophecy teachers ignore this glaring problem.

Secondly, every one of the previous six empires ruled the Middle East, including Jerusalem. This is very important. We must always remember that the Bible is thoroughly Jerusalem-centric. It is not America-centric, nor is it Euro-centric. In the Biblical view of things, Jerusalem is the center of the earth. This is in fact the overarching context of Scripture. This point cannot be underscored enough. Any theory that revolves around a revived Roman Empire based in Europe—for instance on the European Common Market—is a foreign concept to the Bible.

The third crucial point is that if we look at the first six empires, by and large, each succeeding empire either destroyed or absorbed the empire that preceded it. There is a very natural succession. If we look at each empire, we see that they all fulfill these two characteristics: they ruled over Jerusalem and they defeated or absorbed their predecessor.

The Egyptian Empire ruled all of Egypt and Israel, as well. The Assyrian Empire defeated the Egyptian Empire and likewise ruled over a vast portion of the Middle East, including Israel. After this, the Babylonian Empire defeated the Assyrian Empire and became even larger than its predecessor, again, ruling over Israel. Such is the pattern with each successive empire: The Medo-Persian Empire succeeded the Babylonian Empire only to be succeeded by the Greek Empire. The Greek Empire was in turn succeeded by the Roman Empire—which leads us to the seventh empire.

Who overcame the Roman Empire? This is what we need to find out.

≈ 66 ≈
The Fall of
The Roman Empire

In 395 A.D., The Roman Empire was divided into two portions, the eastern and the western. The Eastern portion became known as the Byzantine Empire. "From its early days as a monarchy, through the Republic and the Roman Empire, Rome lasted a millennium...or two. Those who opt for two millennia date Rome's fall to 1453 when the Ottoman Turks took Byzantium (Constantinople). Those who opt for one millennium, agree with Roman historian Edward Gibbon. Edward Gibbon dated the fall to September 4, A.D. 476 when a so-called barbarian named Odoacer (a Germanic leader in the Roman army), deposed the last western Roman emperor, Romulus Augustulus, who was probably partly of Germanic ancestry. Odoacer considered Romulus so paltry a threat he didn't even bother to assassinate him, but sent him into retirement."[1]

Some argue that Rome did not fall and that it still exists, but the majority of historians agree that Rome is long gone. The great historian Edward Gibbons, in The Fall of Rome, describes the end of the Roman Empire in the East: "I have now deduced from Trajan to Constantine, from Constantine to Heraclius, the regular series of the Roman emperors; and faithfully exposed the prosperous and adverse fortunes of their reigns. Five centuries of the decline and fall of the empire have already elapsed; but a period of more than eight hundred years still separates me from the term of my labors, the taking of Constantinople by the Turks...I have already noticed the first appearance of the Turks; and the names of the fathers, of Seljuk and Othman, discriminate the two successive dynasties of the nation, which emerged in the eleventh century from the Scythian wilderness. The former established a splendid and potent kingdom from the banks of the Oxus to Antioch and Nice; and the first crusade was provoked by the violation of Jerusalem and the danger of Constantinople. From a humble origin, the Ottomans arose, the scourge and terror of Christendom. Constantinople was besieged and taken by Mahomet II. and his triumph annihilates the remnant, the image, the title, of the Roman empire in the East... In the East, the victorious Turks had spread, from Persia to the Hellespont, the reign of the Koran and the Crescent: the West was invaded by the adventurous valor of the Normans; and, in the moments of peace, the Danube poured forth new swarms, who had gained, in the science of war, what they had lost in the ferociousness of manners."[2] According to the Bible, any fall is initiated by the loss of the horn. From that perspective, The Roman Empire didn't actually completely fall until the eastern portion of the Empire finally collapsed in 1453 A.D. to the Muslim Turks led by Mehemet II.

Likewise, it was the Islamic Caliphate of Umar Ibn al-Khattab that took Jerusalem in 637. Thus, we see that it was the Islamic Empire—culminating with the Ottoman Empire—that succeeded the Roman Empire and ruled over the entire Middle East, beginning with Jerusalem, for over thirteen hundred years and continued right up until 1924.

In 1453, the Muslim Turks introduced the use of gunpowder in warfare, brought their cannons to the gate of Constantinople and stormed the Christian capital after a siege. The Greek Emperor was killed; the great church of St. Sophia was plundered of its treasure and turned into a mosque.

Mehmet II renamed the city Istanbul. To further glorify the city, he built mosques, palaces, monuments and a system of aqueducts. The city was now officially claimed for Islam. New rules and regulations came about for the conquered. The Greeks formed communities within the empire called milets. The Christians were still allowed to practice their religion, but had to dress in distinguishing attire and could not bear arms, and so came the end to the great city of Constantinople and the Roman Empire.[3]

It is noteworthy to mention that it was the struggle with Islam that caused Europe's loss of access to the Black Sea, depriving her of a land route to India. The search for a new sea route brought about the discovery of the New World, and, as such, America was born.

Because American commerce in the Mediterranean was being destroyed by Muslim pirates, the Continental Congress agreed in 1784 to negotiate treaties with the four Barbary States. Congress appointed a special commission consisting of John Adams, Thomas Jefferson, and Benjamin Franklin, to oversee the negotiations.

Lacking the ability to protect its merchant ships in the Mediterranean, the new American government tried to appease the Muslim slavers by agreeing to pay tribute (Jizyah) and ransoms in order to retrieve seized American ships and buy the freedom of enslaved sailors.

Adams argued in favor of paying tribute as the cheapest way to get American commerce in the Mediterranean moving again. Jefferson opposed. He believed there would be no end to the demands for tribute and wanted matters settled "through the medium of war." He proposed a league of trading nations to force an end to Muslim piracy.

In 1786, Jefferson, then the American ambassador to France, and Adams, then the American ambassador to Britain, met in London with Sidi Haji Abdul Rahman Adja, the ambassador to Britain.

The Americans wanted to negotiate a peace treaty based on Congress' vote to appease. During the meeting Jefferson and Adams asked the ambassador why Muslims held so much hostility towards America, a nation with which they had no previous contacts.

In a later meeting with the American Congress, the two future presidents reported that Ambassador Sidi Haji Abdul Rahman Adja had answered that Islam "was founded on the Laws of their Prophet, that it was written in their Qur'an that all nations who should not have acknowledged their authority were sinners, that it was their right and duty to make war upon them wherever they could be found, and to make slaves of all they could take as Prisoners, and that every Musselman (Muslim) who should be slain in Battle was sure to go to Paradise."

For the following 15 years, the American government paid the Muslims millions of dollars for the safe passage of American ships or the return of American hostages. Most Americans do not know that the payments in ransom and Jizyah tribute amounted to 20 percent of United States government annual revenues in 1800.

Not long after Jefferson's inauguration as president in 1801, he dispatched a group of frigates to defend American interests in the Mediterranean, and informed Congress.

Declaring that America was going to spend "millions for defense but not one cent for tribute," Jefferson pressed the issue by deploying American Marines and many of America's best warships to the Muslim Barbary Coast.

The USS Constitution, USS Constellation, USS Philadelphia, USS Chesapeake, USS Argus, USS Syren and USS Intrepid all fought.

In 1805, American Marines marched across the dessert from Egypt into Tripolitania, forcing the surrender of Tripoli and the freeing of all American slaves.

During the Jefferson administration, the Muslim Barbary States, crumbled as a result of intense American naval bombardment and on shore raids by Marines. They finally agreed officially to abandon slavery and piracy. Jefferson's victory over the Muslims lives on today in the Marine Hymn with the line "From the halls of Montezuma to the shores of Tripoli, we will fight our country's battles on the land as on the sea." It wasn't until 1815 that the problem was fully settled by the total defeat of all the Muslim slave trading pirates.[4]

Shortly thereafter, the Christian world leveled a significant blow to Islam in 1924, after the fall of the Ottoman Empire. The Office of the Caliph was abolished. So while it was the Islamic Empire that ultimately succeeded the Roman Empire, it was the Christian West that offered Islam a series of defeats that led to the severing of its head, the office of the

Caliph in 1924. The only empire that fulfills the patterns necessary to be considered the seventh empire is the Islamic Empire that culminated with the Turkish/Ottoman Empire.

This, of course, corresponds perfectly with Ezekiel's list of nations with such a heavy emphasis on Turkey.

On the following pages are eight maps; a map of the Promised Land and the seven Biblical world empires as they relate to the Promised Land. Each map also has modern national boundary lines.

THEY FIT LIKE A GLOVE

By super-imposing every single literal reference discussed in Part III onto the allegorical picture of the seven mountains, we find that they match perfectly. Here are but a few examples:

The Egyptian Empire—today is Muslim. Christ fights against them in Isaiah 19.

The Assyrian Empire—today is Muslim. Christ fights against them in Micah 5, Isaiah 14.

The Babylonian Empire—today is Muslim. Christ fights against the King of Babylon in Jeremiah 49-51.

The Persian Empire—today is Muslim. Christ fights them in Ezekiel 38, 39.

The Greek Empire—today is Muslim. Christ fights them in Zechariah 9:13, 14 and Ezekiel 38.

The Eastern Roman Byzantine Empire—today is Muslim. Christ fights against these regions in Zechariah 9:13, 14 and Ezekiel 38.

The Muslim Empire – encompasses all the above.

Now consider the following maps:

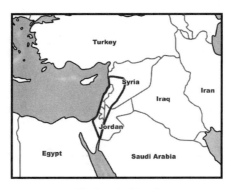

The Promised Land

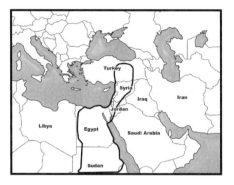

The Egyptian Empire: 3100 BC - 1070 BC

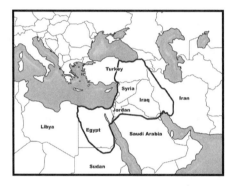

The Assyrian Empire: 1800 BC – 609 BC

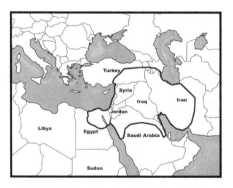

The Babylonian Empire: 1764 BC – 689 BC

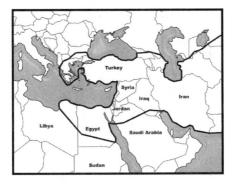

Medo-Persian Empire: 550 BC - 330 BC

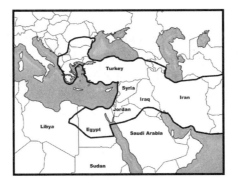

Macedonian Greek Empire: 350 BC - 64 BC

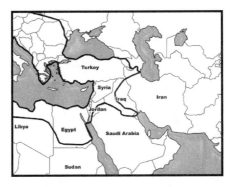

Roman Empire: 27 BC – 1453 BC

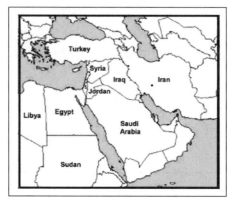

Islamic Empire: 700 AD – 1924 AD - Present Day

We see that, with each succeeding empire, the areas controlled grew larger. Eventually, the Islamic Empire came to control the entire region pictured in the map. This is a somewhat accurate portrayal of the eighth and final Antichrist Empire.

The literal and allegorical all fit together—like a hand and glove.

～67～
Unlocking Daniel 2
Nebuchadnezzar's Statue

As the famous Bible story goes, King Nebuchadnezzar of Babylon had a dream about a massive statue that was made of various metals. The king was determined to understand the meaning of this dream, but none of the Babylonian priests, astrologers or wise men could help him. Finally, Daniel, one of the Hebrew exiles, was called before the king to do what no one else could. Not only did God supernaturally reveal to Daniel the meaning of the dream, but he enabled Daniel to understand its meaning. Our examination of this passage begins with Daniel explaining to the king the meaning of his dream: "You, O king, were looking and behold, there was a single great statue; that statue, which was large and of extraordinary splendor, was standing in front of you, and its appearance was awesome. The head of that statue was made of fine gold, its breast and its arms of silver, its belly and its thighs of bronze, its legs of iron, and its feet partly of iron and partly of clay. You continued looking until a stone was cut out without hands, and it struck the statue on its feet of iron and clay and crushed them. Then the iron, the clay, the bronze, the silver, and the gold were crushed all at the same time and became like chaff from the summer threshing floors; and the wind carried them away so that not a trace of them was found. But the stone that struck the statue became a great mountain and filled the whole earth." (Daniel 2:31-35)

Daniel goes on to explain to Nebuchadnezzar that each component of the statue represents a kingdom or empire that will succeed his. "You, O king, are the king of kings. The God of heaven has given you dominion and power and might and glory...you are that head of gold." But after Babylon, other kingdoms followed. By far, the predominant position throughout history by both Jewish and Christian interpreters has been that this dream portrays the following four kingdoms: Babylon, Medo-Persia, Greece, and Rome.

While the first three in the sequence are accurate, there are some very serious problems with seeing Rome as the fourth. Below I will explain why. It is crucial to understand that the statue represents past kingdoms that are all destroyed together when Christ returns:

"You continued looking until a stone was cut out without hands, and it struck the statue on its feet of iron and clay and crushed them." The stone is Messiah.

Yet, the Bible teaches without question that Messiah destroys all parts of the structure (gold, silver, bronze, iron, and clay) together when He comes. "Then the iron, the clay, the bronze, the silver and the gold were crushed all at the same time and became like chaff from the summer threshing floors; and the wind carried them away so that not a trace of them was found But the stone that struck the statue became a great mountain and filled the whole earth." (Daniel 2:33-35)

THIS IS THE FUTURE, NOT HISTORY

The stone, at this point, establishes the Kingdom of Messiah; it becomes a great mountain (kingdom). When Jesus returns, he will destroy all these empires—at the same time, as the text literally states. (v. 34) This would be Iraq and Arabia (Babylon), Iran (Persia), Turkey and the Middle East (Greece), and, of course, the Islamic Empire, which includes all of these.

If the statue represents ancient Babylon, Persia, Greece and Rome as commonly thought, then why do we see all these empires destroyed in the end when Christ returns? If Daniel 2 speaks of history, how is the gold, strictly representing ancient Babylon, now destroyed by the Messiah when He comes? The Biblical statement is clear: "[He] crushed all at the same time," (v. 34).

Then you have the iron. The text insists that the iron crushed all the previous metals. Yet, it is understood by many westerners that the iron is Rome. Did the Roman Empire crush ancient Babylon/modern Iraq? No. Only for a few months in A.D. 116 under Emperor Trajan did the Roman Empire ever extend its territories toward Babylon. But they were almost immediately beaten back. The Roman Empire and the Babylonian Empire really do not overlap. The Roman Empire is significantly west. Did the Roman Empire ever extend it control over the regions of Persia/modern day Iran? The answer is never. Thus, if the Roman Empire were utterly destroyed, much of the other empires would be left unscathed. Yet the text is clear that when the fourth Empire is destroyed, this will include all of the others as well.

IBIN EZRA – THE FOURTH IS MUSLIM

We cannot study prophecy without understanding the dual nature of its fulfillment. Daniel 2 can, and will, parallel ancient events, but the book is ultimately concerned with the End Times. Daniel 2 is regarding a rise of 10 toes in the ends of days that will come up from the 4 ancient empires that make up the Empire of Antichrist.

The four Empires described in this passage are not what western students think, they are:

1. Babylonian Empire
2. Medo-Persian Empire
3. Greek Empire, (or possibly the Greco-Roman Empire)
4. Islamic Empire.

By the Islamic Empire, I mean the various manifestations of the Islamic Caliphate, which culminated in the Ottoman Empire. The position I hold is not unique, but was first taught by classical Jewish sages and rabbis. Among the most well-known sages and rabbis who support this view are Ibn Ezra, one of the most distinguished Jewish writers of the Middle Ages, Rabbi Yechiel Hillel ben Altshuller, author of the famous Metzudos, and, in a somewhat modified fashion, by the revered Rabbi Saadia Gaon (who sees the fourth Beast as consisting of both the Arab and the Roman Empires). According to Ibn Ezra, "Rome is included in the third kingdom as relatives of the Greeks. The Romans are considered to be the Kittim mentioned in Numbers 24:24. In Genesis 10:4, Kittim are the sons of Yavan (Greece)."[5]

Ibn Ezra, argues that while there are reasons to understand why Rome is not mentioned in the dream, the complete omission of the mighty and extensive Arab kingdom is simply too big of an oversight that needs to be explained by those who hold to the Roman interpretation. I agree.

The fourth kingdom, according to Ibn Ezra, is the Arab Muslim kingdom.

The notion that Rome is included in the third kingdom may be supportable by the view of many historians who see the Roman Empire as an extension of the Greek Empire rather than a different entity altogether. Keep in mind, the text insists that the thighs (the third entity), is bronze. This was the Grecian Empire and connects to the iron legs. The iron legs are an extension of the Grecian (bronze). In other words, the iron is of the bronze. This would eliminate Western Europe. Now, many define a particular nation by language, border, and culture. The Roman and Greek Empires in many ways shared all of these things as well as a common religion. However, it is also quite possible that the Roman Empire itself is not even considered in this passage.

BABYLON'S "FUTURE-HISTORY"

One reason to consider the idea that the Roman Empire is not emphasized in this passage is simply due to its context. While the Roman Empire followed the Greek Empire, this is only so if we view this passage from a Western perspective. We have already discussed the fact that the Bible is thoroughly Jerusalem-centric. However, we must remember the context of the Book of Daniel and, more specifically, this particular passage and this particular dream. This passage deals with a dream that was given to Nebuchadnezzar, the Babylonian King, the ruler of all of ancient Mesopotamia. Once again, our Western-centric lenses have caused us to miss the obvious: the short-term application of the first part of this dual prophecy. God was not so much explaining to Nebuchadnezzar the "future-history" of the Western world, but rather the "future-history" of the regions that he ruled over; namely Babylon and greater Mesopotamia. This dream was a description of the future of the Babylonian Empire and the primary empires that would rule over it after Nebuchadnezzar.

While Rome was most certainly an important empire in world history, its real significance to the Mesopotamian region is, in fact, fairly minimal. Even during the period of the Roman Empire's greatest eastward expansion, it was never able to fully secure control over the regions east of the Euphrates River. In the year 116 A.D. under Emperor Trajan, the Romans made some incursions into portions of Mesopotamia. But it was within months, in 117 A.D. at the death of Trajan, that the Romans lost southern Mesopotamia and completely retreated from the region. They were never able to secure control over the region east of the Euphrates in any substantial way. Because Nebuchadnezzar's dream covered a thirteen hundred year period, dealing with only the significant conquering empires, the Roman Empire is essentially a mere footnote in Babylonian/Mesopotamian history, and, thus, it was not emphasized in Nebuchadnezzar's dream. But the primary empires that would actually conquer and rule over Babylon were all laid out consecutively in the dream.

Rome never conquered the previous empires. Perhaps the most obvious flaw in this interpretation is the single description used to define this fourth kingdom: "There will be a fourth kingdom, strong as iron—for iron breaks and smashes everything—and as iron breaks things to pieces, so it will crush and break all the others," (Daniel 2:40). When one is attempting to determine which Empire is the best candidate for the fourth Empire, this passage is the clearest criterion.

Again, did Rome crush or even conquer all of the other empires? Did Rome crush the Babylonian Empire (Iraq), the Medo-Persian Empire (Iran), and the Greek Empires? The clear answer is no, it did not. It is almost surprising that such a wide range of interpreters has overlooked this fact for so long. The fourth empire would crush and break all three of the other empires.

A BRIEF HISTORY OF MESOPOTAMIA

After his rule, Nebuchadnezzar's Empire was first conquered by the Persians under Cyrus and then by Greece under Alexander the Great. After Alexander's death in 323 B.C., his empire was divided and the region of Babylon and Persia was given to one of his generals named Seleucus. Seleucus and his successors ruled the region for roughly 130 years until 190 B.C. when the Persian people (called the Parthians) arose again and took control of their former empire. Thus, after having been controlled by the Greeks for well over a hundred years, the Persians again controlled the region.[6]

Later, after the Parthian Empire, another Persian people—the Sassanid Dynasty— rose up and gained control over the region. Throughout the Partho-Sassanian period, the people maintained a strong mixture of both Hellenistic (Greek) and Persian identity and culture. For this reason, within Nebuchadnezzar's dream, there was no distinction made between the Persian or the Greek Empires and the later Parthian or Sassanid period. It was not until the mighty Islamic Caliphate came and conquered the entire region that the dream describes the next phase of the statue.

During the period of Rome's rule, the region to the east of the Euphrates River (Mesopotamia) was controlled by the Parthian Empire, not the Romans: "The wars between Rome and the Parthian Empire, which took place roughly from 53 BC to 217 AD, were a unique episode in classical history. Although Rome conquered nearly the entire civilized world around the Mediterranean, Rome could never conquer Parthia."[7]

Consider the following description of the Parthians as recounted by Justin's History of the World: "The Parthians, in whose hands the empire of the east now is, having divided the world, as it were, with the Romans, were originally exiles from Scythia... Being assailed by the Romans, also, in three wars, under the conduct of the greatest generals, and at the most flourishing period of the republic, they alone, of all nations, were not only a match for them, but came off victorious"[8]

While the Emperor Trajan did cross the Euphrates River and gain control over a small portion of Mesopotamia, within one year, Trajan had died and his victory and control dissolved.[9]

DID ROME CONQUER THE BABYLONIAN OR THE PERSIAN EMPIRES?

Again, the Roman Empire only controlled the ancient city of Babylon for a few months. While Rome did indeed conquer most of Western Europe and the region surrounding the Mediterranean it could never maintain any significant control of the regions that were the primary stronghold of the Babylonian Empire—namely the regions east of the Euphrates River, modern day Iraq and Iran. The guerilla warfare used by tribal peoples of Parthia simply proved to be too much for the Roman soldiers to withstand. Rome most certainly did not "crush" the Babylonian Empire, and really never even came within a few hundred miles of ever seeing the capitals of Persia.

DID ROME CRUSH THE GREEK EMPIRE?

While the Roman Empire did assume control of the some of the regions that were once controlled by the Alexandrian Hellenistic Greek Empire, it was, in fact, the Hellenistic/Greek culture that came to dominate the Roman Empire. The New Testament, which was written during the Roman period, was written in Greek, not Latin. In other words, the Roman Empire may have assumed control of some of the western regions once controlled by the Greek Empire, but it most certainly did not "crush" it.

Consider the following maps:

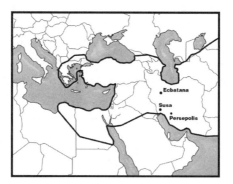

*In the Medo-Persian Empire, notice the locations of
Ecbatana, Susa, and Persepolis, the capitals of the
Median and Persian Empires. Rome never con-
quered these cities.*

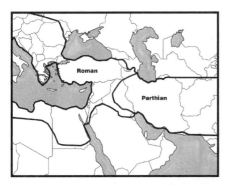

The Roman and Parthian empires at the height of their eastward expansion the small finger extending toward the Persian Gulf was held for only a few months.

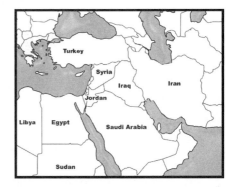

Nearly the entire region included in this map of the Middle East came to be conquered by Islam.

ISLAM CRUSHED ALL

While the Roman Empire did not fulfill the necessary requirements to be considered as the fourth empire of Daniel 2, there was an empire that did. The Islamic Empire fulfilled these requirements completely. Islam conquered all of the three previous empires—Babylonian, Medo-Persian, and the Grecian. Bear in mind, Islam also conquered the Roman Empire, which had ceased to exist in Europe. Revelation 13 insists that the fourth beast constitutes the three previous empires. This must exclude Europe. Islam conquered the entire eastern Byzantine Roman Empire and large portions of what was the Western Roman Empire. That included Iraq (Babylon), and Iran (Persia). The Roman Empire cannot make this claim and thus only Islam meets the biblical criterion of Daniel 2:40.

~68~
Arabization

✦

It is crucial for Westerners to understand that the fundamental duty of Islam is to Arabize the world—to unite humanity under one language, one government, and one religion: Islam. It is an attempt to reverse what God did at the Tower of Babel.

In the case of the Islamic Caliphate, "crush" is most certainly an appropriate description for what occurred when Islam conquered any region. Remember: language, borders, culture. Islam ran rough-trod over all of these. That is what it means to "crush." Babylon changed its language to Arabic and its religion to Islam. Persia also lost its religion, adopted the Arabic alphabet, and kept its language. Other nations, like Egypt, also completely lost their ancient religion and language, and adopted Arabic. These civilizations were all lost to Islam, and only some kept their language. In fact, it would require volumes to recount all of the history, culture, and religious influence that have nearly been erased by more than a millennium of Islamic dominance.

ARABIZM

Western students focus on Daniel 2:41 which points to the nature of the two materials (Iron and Clay) as being partly weak and partly strong, but verse 43 is rarely addressed in full: "And in that you saw the iron mixed with common clay, they will combine with one another in the seed of men; but they will not adhere to one another, even as iron does not combine with pottery."

The other meaning of this riddle in this verse needs to be noted; the underlined words "mixed" and "combine" are actually the same words translated differently from the Aramaic, the original language of much of the Book of Daniel. The word is actually "Arab." *Strong's Concordance* confirms this:

"mArab {ar-ab'}; from ʿarab' (6150) in the figurative sense of sterility; Arab (i.e. Arabia), a country East of Palestine: --Arabia." "or mereb (1 Kings 10:15), (with the article prefix), {eh'-reb}; from ʿarab' (6148); the web (or transverse threads of cloth); also a mixture, (or mongrel race): --Arabia, mingled people, mixed (multitude), woof."

And thus this passage can read: "And just as you saw the iron mixed with baked clay, so the people will be mixed (Arabized) with the seed of men (through intermarriage) and will not remain united, any more than iron does not mix with clay."

מְעָרַב

m'arav

"mingled" or "mixed"

עֲרַב

arav

"Arab"

Within Daniel 2:43, *"the people will be a mixture and will not remain united, any more than iron mixes with clay."* The Aramaic phrase *la Muta'arreb* also means, "does not Arabize." This Arab-mixed kingdom would not become totally Arabized. This duality in meaning and interpretation (mixing and Arabizing) is not mine alone—Ibin Ezra, one of the foremost respected Jewish writers, supported it: "Ibn Ezra is of the opinion that the Greek Kingdom represented by the leopard includes the Roman Empire, for ethnically the Romans were related to the Greeks. The Kittim, identified as descendants of the Romans were related to the Yavan (Greece)...The fourth animal then represents the rule of the Arabs."[10] "Rabbi Saadiah Gaon [believes that] the fourth animal in the vision includes both the Roman and the Arab empires."[11] "Ibn Ezra is troubled by the absence of the kingdom of Ishmael, viz. the Arabs and the Turks, who were very powerful in his time. He therefore concludes that the...fourth kingdom is the kingdom of Ishmael. Mezudath David follows this view."[12]

If one insists on the single usage of Muta'areb to only *mix* without *Arabize*, and the analysis of our duality of usage must be rejected, then another common example of a play on words in the Book of Daniel must also be rejected—the divine handwriting on the wall. In Daniel 5, Belteshazzr the final Babylonian king was told that his empire would be divided (*peres*) to the Medes and the Persians (Aramaic: *Paras*). Reading the word peres (meaning divided): "Peres—your kingdom has been divided and given over to the Medes and Persians," (Daniel 5:28).

So who divided the Babylonians? The Bible tells us Peres (Persia), which literally meant also to divide, *"To mix with the seed of men."* if one still rejects the meaning of the word Muta'arreb as to Arabize, but insists that it only mean "to mix", we would still conclude that mixing the seed of men would mean losing ethnicity by intermarriage. (RSV, ESV, NTL) The attempt to mingle the nations through intermarriage is an attempt to unite the world and reverse the Tower of Babel account through Islam has been fruitless. It partially worked in the Middle East where Egyptians, Syrians, Lebanese, and many others consider themselves Arabs and spoke Arabic, while Turks, Persians, Indonesians and others still hold onto their language, culture, and ethnicity. No other empire has done this.

Islam's attempt from its earliest days has been to Arabize the whole world through Islam.

However, the Persians and Turks who came from the brass (Greco-Roman) kingdoms never fully Arabized. Because the various descendants of Ishmael and Esau had intermarried among the various desert tribes, they had actually become known as "the mixed ones." Daniel 2:43 speaks of the type of mixed peoples that would make up the final Antichrist Empire. As we saw in the handwriting on the wall account, this is not without precedent in the Book of Daniel.

Elsewhere, the Bible uses word play with the words, *Eber* or *Abar*. The word used for "Hebrew" literally means, "to cross, come through, pass over." It's a fitting term in light of Moses and the Israelites' passage through the Red Sea, Joshua and the Israelites' passage over the Jordan and Abraham's departure from Ur and crossing over the Promised Land. But to be an Arab meant that one was from a mixed people who were lost scattered wanderers.

A KINGDOM DIVIDED

Beyond being an Arab Empire or an attempt to make it so, the Last-Days Empire is also said to be a divided (*peleg*) empire. The division, of course, that this passage speaks of is truly an appropriate description of the Islamic world, as it has existed from its earliest days until modern times with its various sectarian divisions. "In that you saw the feet and toes, partly of potter's clay and partly of iron it will be a divided kingdom," (Daniel 2:41).

One need only look to modern Iraq's Sunni and Shi'a sectarian battles to observe how divided the Islamic world truly is. This division of the final Antichrist Empire is also seen in the fact that even at the time they attack Israel, they will not be able to resist their own disputes. Thus, Ezekiel tells us that, *"Every man's sword will be against his brother,"* (Ezekiel 38:21). Once again, this resembles precisely what one finds today in the Palestinian Territories and Iraq and much of the Muslim world.

69

Daniel 2
Four or Five Empires: Or Both?

As we discussed Revelation 17, we saw that the Antichrist Empire was specified as being the eighth empire—or a revival of the seventh empire that would arise after being healed of a "fatal head wound." So how many empires are there, seven or eight?

Well, both are correct—the eighth is a re-creation of the seventh. This is what the text is trying to tell us.

The concept of an empire-revival is also found in Daniel 2. We have 4 sections to the statue, yet we also have 5—both are correct, since the fifth is a re-creation of the fourth.

Here, we will see that Nebuchadnezzar's Dream also lines up perfectly with Revelation 17. The last empire of Nebuchadnezzar's dream is comprised of two distinct phases of the same empire. They are related, but they are distinct. These two empires correspond to the seventh and the eight empires of Revelation 17. The first key to seeing this two-fold phase of the last empire is seen in the following portion of the above passage:

"The head of that statue was made of fine gold, its breast and its arms of silver, its belly and its thighs of bronze, its legs of iron, its feet partly of iron and partly of clay," (Daniel 2:32-33). While many modern translations might blur this point, if one were to examine the actual Aramaic text, the most literal translation possible would read as follows: Image –Head – Fine – Gold – Breast – Arms – Silver – Belly – Thighs – Brass – Legs - Iron – Feet – Part – Iron – Part Clay

Now we will arrange it a little differently, yet in the exact order that it appears in the verse. What we will see is that there are five distinct elements, and thus five distinct components to the statue:

IMAGE		
Head	Fine Gold	First
Breast Arms	Silver	Second
Belly, Thighs	Brass	Third
Legs	Iron	Fourth
Feet	Part Iron, Part Clay	Fifth (re-creation of Fourth)

With this arrangement by following the text, it is easy to see that there are not simply four, but rather five phases. Keeping in mind that the fifth is a re-creation of the fourth, we have fine gold, silver, brass, iron, and a mixture of iron and clay. The passage continues, "This was the dream; now we will tell its interpretation before the king. You, O king, are the king of kings, to whom the God of heaven has given the kingdom, the power, the strength and the glory; and wherever the sons of men dwell, or the beasts of the field, or the birds of the sky, He has given them into your hand and has caused you to rule over them all. You are the head of gold. After you there will arise another kingdom inferior to you, then another third kingdom of bronze, which will rule over all the earth. Then there will be a fourth kingdom as strong as iron; inasmuch as iron crushes and shatters all things, so, like iron that breaks in pieces, it will crush and break all these in pieces," (Daniel 2:36-40).

There are a few important observations that need to be highlighted here. First, we need to take note of the unqualified description of the fourth kingdom: "there will be a fourth kingdom, strong as iron." The fourth kingdom will not be partially strong and partially weak. It is simply described as "strong as iron." However, when we look at the descriptions of the feet and the toes, they are completely different. In these descriptions, the kingdom is only partially strong—but it is also partially brittle. Compare the descriptions below:

Legs: "there will be a fourth kingdom, strong as iron," (Daniel 2:40)

Feet: "this kingdom will be partly strong and partly brittle," (Daniel 2:43).

For those who would argue that the statue contains only four phases, the question needs to be asked: How can the very same kingdom be described in one sentence as "strong as iron," while in the very next sentence be described as only having "some of the strength of iron in it" and "partly strong and partly brittle?"

Upon examining the passage, one must conclude that there is both a fourth and a fifth division of the statue. However, because there is also continuity between the legs and the feet that are seen in the element of iron, there is also reason to believe that these last two empires are, in fact, related.

Many modern interpreters have rightly recognized the fact that the last empire in Nebuchadnezzar's dream consists of a two-fold division. Of course, most of these scholars and Bible teachers have claimed that the fourth empire is the Roman Empire and that the fifth empire is a revived Last-Days version of the Roman Empire. Again, in light of all that we have already learned, we know that this last dual-phased empire cannot be the Roman Empire, but rather represents two distinct phases of one Arab-Islamic Empire. Again, in Revelation 17 the last empire (the seventh-eight empire) follows and is distinct from Rome.

The fourth kingdom in Nebuchadnezzar's dream represents the various manifestations of the Islamic Empire that existed for over thirteen hundred years, culminating in the Ottoman Empire. This Empire was essentially fatally wounded in 1924 with the abolition of the Caliphate and the division and colonization of the Middle East by the Western powers. But the fifth empire of Nebuchadnezzar's Dream, represents the revival of the Islamic Empire that we are presently seeing arise in fractions before our very eyes.

I know that someone will object, saying that the Western powers that wounded Islam would qualify to be the next empire in the prophecy; yet the Bible gives the cut-off at the seventh in Revelation 17 and the fourth in Daniel 2. Also, it is necessary to have someone available to fatally wound that empire in order to fulfill this prophecy. So the British Empire that wounded it cannot be the one that is wounded. This would be illogical.

In summary, the empires of Nebuchadnezzar's dream are as follows:

Head	Gold Babylonian	Iraq and Arabia
Chest-arms	Silver Medo-Persian	Iran
Belly-thighs	Bronze Greco-Roman	Turkey-Mid-East
Legs -Iron	Islamic	Ottoman Empire
Feet-Toes Mixture	Islamic-Revived	Ottoman Revived

Daniel 2 confirms what we have already learned concerning the final Antichrist Empire in Revelation 17. In Revelation 17, the final Antichrist Empire is a revived version of the seventh empire, which we identified as the Islamic Empire. So also here in Daniel 2, the last empire is the two-fold fourth/fifth empire, which also is the Islamic Empire. Piece by piece, passage by passage, when the religion of Islam is plugged into the puzzle, every piece fits perfectly. There is no forcing or bending of the pieces required.

≈ 70 ≈
Am I The Only One?

‡—※—‡

To most who read this book, the Islamic End-Times thesis represents something radically new. The majority of popular modern End-Times theories teach that the Antichrist will proceed from a revived European Roman Empire. Because the Islamic end time theory is a "new" theory, many will view it with deep suspicion. If Joel and I were introducing a new theory about the nature of Christ or about the atonement, then we would both expect to be stoned to death or at the least disregarded and shunned for our heretical views. Yet we are not introducing any heresies here. We are simply adjusting common views in light of current events. But when it comes to eschatology, the Church has, in fact, never had any universal orthodox position regarding the End-Times and the identity of the Antichrist. Many theories have abounded throughout Church history and the European Theory is certainly not the only option given. Not only is it correct to assume that the Church would gain greater clarity as the day draws nearer (II Peter 1:19), but the truth is that what we are presenting here is nothing new at all. Since the earliest days of Islamic conquest, many great Christian leaders have seen Islam as the fulfillment of the Biblical Antichrist prophecies. Likewise, many commentators, both Jewish and Christian, have seen the weight of Scriptural evidence pointing to the Middle East rather than Europe as the location from which the Antichrist and his Empire would rule. What we are presenting in this book is far from a novel theory. By claiming Islam as the fulfillment of the Antichrist prophecies, we are joined by many of the greatest Jewish and Christian commentators.

IS TRADITIONAL WESTERN INTERPRETATION WRONG?

Yes and no. The traditional western interpretation correctly sees the ancient empires, yet misses their dual fulfillment. The lion, for instance, was the animal most often historically associated with Babylon. The prophet Jeremiah, for instance, refers to Babylon as a lion. The lion motif is found abundantly in ancient Babylonian art and architecture. Likewise, the description of the bear matches the unbalanced character of the Medo-Persian Empire, in which Persia exerted far greater influence over the Median portion of the empire. Here, the bear arose on one side (Persia without Media); we see one side rising and the other remains. Iran is rising, but Media (Kurdistan) is not. The leopard, known as a swift and stealthy predator, seems to be a clear reference to Alexander the Greats' agile military prowess and the incredible speed with which he conquered the ancient world. Finally, the fourth beast represented here is clearly the same empire that is seen in the fourth kingdom of Nebuchadnezzar's statue, as well as in the Book of Revelation.

As for the fourth, many prophecy aficionados have been waiting for Europe to emerge as the iron-toothed beast of Daniel 7. According to this common expectation, then, Europe which today is liberal will someday emerge as a vicious and unstoppable military machine that will kill and trample down the whole earth, leaving untold millions of victims in its wake. If this theory were accurate, then what is today arguably the most toothless group of nations in history would indeed need to grow the iron teeth of which the passage speaks. Will the toothless truly become ruthless? I doubt it. In all cases, when iron is used as symbol, it signifies ruthlessness.

Am I the only one in the world saying that Islam is the beast? "Hardly," I am not presenting a private interpretation. I am simply adding my perspective from a lifetime of experience with Islam. In fact, many great theologians agree.

JOHN WESLEY

"Indeed, the iron teeth closely match Islam." John Wesley explains, "Ever since the religion of Islam appeared in the world, the espousers of it...have been as wolves and tigers to all other nations, rending and tearing all that fell into their merciless paws, and grinding them with their iron teeth; that numberless cities are raised from the foundation, and only their name remaining; that many countries, which were once as the garden of God, are now a desolate wilderness; and that so many once numerous and powerful nations are vanished from the earth! Such was, and is at this day, the rage, the fury, the revenge, of these destroyers of human kind."[13]

HILAIRE BELLOC (1938)

"Will not perhaps the temporal power of Islam [will] return and with it the menace of an armed Mohammedan world, which will shake off the domination of Europeans—still nominally Christian—and reappear as the prime enemy of our civilization? The future always comes as a surprise, but political wisdom consists in attempting at least some partial judgment of what that surprise may be. And for my part I cannot but believe that a main unexpected thing of the future is the return of Islam."[14]

BISHOP FULTON J SHEEN
"Today (1950), the hatred of the Moslem countries against the West is becoming hatred against Christianity itself. Although the statesmen have not yet taken it into account, there is still grave danger that the temporal power of Islam may return and, with it, the menace that it may shake off a West which has ceased to be Christian, and affirm itself as a great anti-Christian world Power."[15]

GREGORY PALAMUS OF THESSALONICA (1354)
"For these impious people, hated by God and infamous, boast of having got the better of the Romans by their love of God...they live by the bow, the sword and debauchery, finding pleasure in taking slaves, devoting themselves to murder, pillage, spoil...and not only do they commit these crimes, but even — what an aberration — they believe that God approves of them."[16]

Jesus said, "The time will come, that whosoever kills you will think that he does God a service" (John 16:2).

VERNON RICHARDS
"The true Islamic concept of peace goes something like this: Peace comes through submission to Muhammad and his concept of Allah (i.e., Islam). As such the Islamic concept of peace, meaning making the whole world Muslim, is actually a mandate for war. It was inevitable and unavoidable that the conflict would eventually reach our borders, and so it has. "This is Islam's latest attempt to conquer the infidel world. Why do you suppose they waited until three centuries after the siege and battle of Vienna before they tried again? Was it because they saw an opportunity to get after us for the first time since 1683, because political correctness and the apologists it brought in train softened us up, and made us totally unaware of how evil and intolerant Islam really is, and gave them that window of opportunity to once again threaten our civilization with doom."[17]

JOSIAH LITCH (1840)
In his Fall of the Ottoman Roman Empire, Litch predicted the fall of the Ottoman Empire two years in advance to the exact day. He also interpreted the star of Revelation as the ushering in of Islam: "A star, in the figurative language of Revelation, is a minister of religion. See Revelation 1:20...A fallen star then would signify a fallen or heretical minister of religion. This was undoubtedly the Arabian imposter, Mahomet. [Mohammed] There is so general an agreement among Christians, especially protestant commentators, that the subject of this prediction is Mahommedism [Islam]"

I have included an article from Litch in Appendix C detailing his interpretation.

SIR ROBERT ANDERSON

Sir Robert Anderson, perhaps one of the leading scholars of prophecy who unlocked the seventy weeks of Daniel stated: "Verse 7 indicates that the rise of all these kingdoms was future." He continues: "In the history of Babylonia there is nothing to correspond with the predicted course of the first Beast, for it is scarcely legitimate to suppose that the vision was a prophecy of the career of Nebuchadnezzar. Neither is there in the history of Persia anything answering to the bear-like beast with that precision and fullness which prophecy demands. The language of the English version suggests a reference to Persia and Media but the true rendering appears to be; 'It made for itself one dominion,' instead 'it raised up itself on one side.'"[18]

Anderson gets it. Even today this "bear" is rising in a lop-sided fashion. We have Iran (Persia) rising without Media (Kurdistan).

Anderson continues, "While the symbolism of the sixth verse seems at first sight to point to the Grecian Empire, it will appear upon a closer examination that at its advent the leopard had four wings and four heads. This was its primary and normal condition, and it was in this condition that dominion was given to it. This surely is very different from what Daniel 8:8 describes is the history of Alexander's Empire realized, viz., the rise of a single power, which in its decadence continued to exist in a divided state."

He then comes to the following conclusion: "Each of the three first empires of the second chapter (Babylon, Persia, and Greece) was in turn destroyed by its successor; but the kingdoms of the seventh chapter all continued together upon the scene, though the dominion, was with the fourth (Daniel 7:12). The verse seems to imply that the four beasts came up together, and at all events there is nothing to suggest a series of empires, each destroying its predecessor, though the symbolism of the vision was (in contrast with that of ch.2) admirably adapted to represent this."[19]

Anderson is correct. Today, we see these three kingdoms rising to power—Iraq (Babylon), Iran (Persia without Media), and Turkey (Ionia, Greece). They are all rising together, and all are symbolically and historically connected to the empires that Daniel predicted. Expect the bear (Iran) to consume three ribs, which may be the splintering of Iraq into three sectors.

Concerning the Roman Empire, Anderson writes: "it must be owned that there was nothing in the history of ancient Rome to correspond with the main characteristic of (the fourth) beast unless the symbolism used is to be very loosely interpreted. To 'devour the earth,' 'tread it down and break it in pieces,' is fairly descriptive of other empires, but

Ancient Rome was precisely the one power that added government to conquest, and instead of treading down and breaking in pieces the nations it subdued, sought rather to mould them to its own civilization and polity. All this – and more might be added – suggests that the entire vision of the seventh chapter may have a future reference."[20]

Anderson believes that Daniel 7 is speaking only of the End-Times empires that exist simultaneously. Amazingly, he stated that the Middle East would be the primary area of conflict.

Anderson continues: "Now, Daniel 2 expressly names the Mediterranean ("the Great Sea") as the scene of the conflict between the four beasts. But there is no doubt that Egypt, Turkey, and Greece will be numbered among the ten kingdoms"[21]

In Daniel 11:40, Egypt (King of the South) and Turkey (King of the North) are expressly mentioned by their prophetic titles as separate kingdoms.

LEVANT—NOT ADRIATIC (GRECIAN-ISLAMIC, NOT EUROPEAN)

Perhaps the best case for a Seleucid-Grecian and not a European Empire comes from Scripture. Anderson agrees: "To the scheme here indicated the objection may naturally be raised: Is it possible that the most powerful nations of the world, England, Germany, and Russia, are to have no part in the great drama of the Last-Days? But it must be remembered, first, that the relative importance of the great Powers may be different at the time when these events shall be fulfilled, and secondly, that difficulties of this kind may depend entirely on the silence of Scripture, or, in other words, on our own ignorance. I feel bound to notice, however, that doubts which have been raised in my mind regarding the soundness of the received interpretation of the seventh chapter of Daniel point to a more satisfactory answer to the difficulties in question. It has been confidently urged by some that as the ten toes of Nebuchadnezzar's image symbolized the ten kingdoms – five on either foot – five of these kingdoms must be developed in the East, and five in the West. The argument is plausible, and possibly just; but its chief force depends upon forgetting that in the prophet's view the Levant and not the Adriatic, Jerusalem and not Rome, is the center of the world."[21]

Anderson finds problems with the revived "European" empire theory. He seems to advocate for a focus on the Levant (Eastern) rather than the Western Roman Empire.

CYRIL OF JERUSALEM, (315-386)

Amazingly, even before the advent of Islam, there were those who looked toward the Middle East for the fulfillment of the Antichrist prophecies. Cyril was a distinguished theologian and Father of the early Church. In his Divine Institutes, Cyril discusses the fact that the Antichrist will proceed forth from the region of ancient Syria, which extended from modern day Syria well into portions of Asia Minor (Turkey): "A king shall arise out of Syria, born from an evil spirit, the over thrower and destroyer of the human race, who shall destroy that which is left by the former evil, together with himself... But that king will not only be most disgraceful in himself, but he will also be a prophet of lies, and he will constitute and call himself God, and will order himself to be worshipped as the Son of God, and power will be given to him to do signs and wonders, by the sight of which he may entice men to adore him... Then he will attempt to destroy the temple of God and persecute the righteous people."[22]

The idea that the Antichrist will come from the Middle East is certainly not new.

SOPHRONIUS, PATRIARCH OF JERUSALEM (560-638)

Sophronius was an Arab Christian who became the Patriarch of Jerusalem in 634 and remained so until his death four years later. It was during these years that the Muslim armies under Caliph Umar invaded and conquered Jerusalem. Several historical references attest to the fact that Sophronius identified the Muslim occupation of Jerusalem and the Temple Mount as the fulfillment of the "abomination that causes desolation" that is always associated with the coming of the Antichrist. Sophronius laments the circumstances under which the Church in Jerusalem found itself and refers to the Muslim occupiers as being followers of Satan: "Why are the troops of the Saracens attacking us? Why has there been so much destruction and plunder? Why are there incessant outpourings of human blood? Why are the birds of the sky devouring human bodies? Why have churches been pulled down? Why is the cross mocked? Why is Christ, who is the dispenser of all good things and the provider of this joyousness of ours, blasphemed by pagan mouths... the vengeful and God-hating Saracens, the abomination of desolation clearly foretold to us by the prophets, overrun the places which are not allowed to them, plunder cities, devastate fields, burn down villages, set on fire the holy churches, overturn the sacred monasteries... Moreover, they are raised up more and more against us and increase their blasphemy of Christ and the Church, and utter wicked blasphemies against God. Those God-fighters boast of prevailing over all, assiduously and unrestrainedly imitating their leader, who is the devil, and emulating his vanity because of which he has been expelled from heaven and been assigned to the gloomy shades."[23]

MAXIMUS THE CONFESSOR (580-662)

Maximus was an important theologian and scholar of the early Church who helped defeat the Monothelite heresy, which claimed that Christ only possessed a divine and not a human will. Maximus witnessed the rise and spread of the Islamic Empire in his day. He described the invading Muslims as "a people who... delight in human blood... whom God hates, though they think they are worshipping God." He also referred to the Muslim invasions as "announcing the advent of the Antichrist." And so we see that even at such an early period of Islam's growth, a clear association of Islam with the Antichrist prophecies was being articulated.[24]

JOHN OF DAMASCUS (676-749)

John of Damascus is another very important figure in the early Church. He was born into a privileged Christian family in Syria, but later become a presbyter and monk. His grandfather had been the administrator of Damascus at the time the Muslims took it, and he actually grew up and served in the court of the Caliph. He was thoroughly familiar with Islam and thus, in his famous book, Against Heresies, he devotes a whole chapter to the discussion of Islam. "And there is also up until now a strong and people-deceiving superstition among Ishmaelites, that is the forerunner of Antichrist. And this [superstition – Islam] is born from Ishmael, who was born from Hagar to Abraham, from which they are called Hagarenes and Ishmaelites. And they call them Saracens, (those empty of Sarah), because of what was said by Hagar to the angel: 'Sarah has sent me away empty.' So then, these were idolaters and reverenced the morning star and Aphrodite, who they indeed named Akbar in their own language, which means great. Therefore, until the time of Heraclius, they were plainly idolaters. From that time and until now came up among them a false prophet called Muhammad, who, having encountered the Old and New Testament, as it seems, having conversed with an Arian monk, he put together his own heresy."[25]

Even as early as 50 years after Islam was birthed, learned Christian leaders who were familiar with Islam were referring to it as a forerunner of the Antichrist. The Muslim invasions heralded "the advent of the Antichrist." Interestingly we see John of Damascus pointing to Islam as a Christian heresy connected to an Arian monk, and his connection to Aphrodite, the moon-goddess. This is proven archeologically by early Islamic coins.

EULOGIUS, PAUL ALVARUS, AND THE MARTYRS OF CORDOVA (9TH CENTURY)

Many Christians from Cordova, Spain were martyred during what is ironically often taught to be a period of exemplary peaceful co-existence between Christians and Muslims under Islamic rule. In the 850's in Andalusian Spain, most Christians seemed to have assumed a position of quiet submission to Muslim rule, turning their heads to the daily inequalities suffered by Christians at the hands of their Muslim overlords. Yet there remained a remnant of faithful Christians who refused to submit to the status quo of silence. During this time, well over 50 Christians were put to death for publicly confessing that they believed Muhammad to be a false prophet and the precursor to the Antichrist. Six Christians were called before authorities and asked to recant their denial of Muhammad as a true prophet. The six replied: "We abide by the same confession, O judge that our most holy brothers Isaac and Sanctius professed. Now hand down the sentence, multiply your cruelty, be kindled with complete fury in vengeance for your prophet. We profess Christ to be truly God and your prophet to be a precursor of antichrist and an author of profane doctrine." [26] Amazing, would one find such faith and bravery among today's Christians? Indeed, false Christians existed even in these times. A controversy erupted where many who claimed to be Christians accused these martyrs of deserving their deaths for provoking the anger of Muslim authorities. Only two people defended the martyrs—monks named Eulogius and Paul Alvarus. Eulogius, later martyred, as well, praised the Christians who he said, "marched out against the angel of Satan and the forerunner of Antichrist," that is "Muhammad, the heresiarch."[27]

Paul Alvarus went even further, writing a whole book entitled Indiculus Luminosus (The Illuminated Instructions), in which he argued that Muhammad was the forerunner to the Antichrist and the eleventh horn of Daniel.

MARTIN LUTHER

Martin Luther (1483–1546) was, of course, a German monk who became the father of the Protestant reformation. While many are aware of the fact that Luther came to view the Roman Catholic Papacy as the seat of the Antichrist, few are aware that he also thought the Muslim people (which he referred to as "the Turks") comprised the eastern segment of the Antichrist Kingdom: "The Pope is the spirit of antichrist, and the Turk (Muslim) is the flesh of antichrist. They help each other in their murderous work. The latter slaughters bodily by the sword; and the former spiritually by doctrine"[28]

JOHN CALVIN (1509-1564)

John Calvin also determined the Antichrist Kingdom would consist of both the Western Roman Catholic Church and the Eastern Ottoman (Muslim) Empire. To Calvin, both the Catholic Church and Islam were equally deserving of the title of Antichrist: "As Muhammad says that his Qur'an is the sovereign wisdom, so says the Pope of his own decrees. For they be the two horns of Antichrist."[29] Elaborating on the prophecy of Daniel 7, Calvin commented that, "It does seem that the fourth iron kingdom was in fact both the pre-Papal and the pre-Islamic undivided Pagan Roman Empire, as well as the later Western-Roman Papal and the contemporaneous Eastern-Roman Islamic Empire into which it then subdivided... Thus they correspond to the two legs of the later Roman Empire – Islam and the Papacy."[30]

Referring to the great Antichrist apostasy, Calvin again pointed his finger at both the religion of Islam and the Catholic Church: "The defection (apostasy) has indeed spread more widely! For, since Mohammed was an apostate, he turned his followers, the Turks, from Christ...The sect of Mohammed was like a raging overflow, which in its violence tore away about half of the Church. It remained for the Papal Antichrist to infect with his poison the part which was left."[31]

And speaking of the Antichrist, Calvin made this connection to Muhammad: "In Daniel 11:37, that Prophet predicted the coming of a terrible tyrant. This is how he described that tyrant: 'Neither shall he pay regard to the God of his fathers, nor to the desire of women.' Applied to the Unitarian Muslims, this might well mean that they would ignore the Trinitarian God of their forefathers—and with their licentiousness and polygamy also disregard the desire of women to conclude monogamous unions. Some refer this prophecy to the Pope and to Mahomet—and the phrase 'the love of women' seems to give probability to this view. For Mahomet allowed to men the brutal liberty of chastising their wives, and thus he corrupted that conjugal love and fidelity which binds the husband to the wife.... Mahomet allowed full scope to various lusts—by permitting a man to have a number of wives. This seems like an explanation—of his being inattentive to the love of women."[32]

So while many Protestant prophecy teachers today still hold to the notion that the Roman Catholic Church is the Antichrist, nearly all are unaware that Islam held an equally prominent position in the eschatology of many of the great reformers.

JONATHAN EDWARDS (1703-1758)

Jonathan Edwards was a great American congregational preacher and revivalist. He was also president of Princeton University. Edwards, like Luther and Calvin, saw Islam as one of the premiere—though not exclusive—elements of the Antichrist Kingdom. Referring to the three unclean spirits that proceed forth from the mouth of the dragon in Revelation 16:14, Edwards commented that, "there shall be the spirit of popery, the spirit of Mahometanism (Islam), and the spirit of heathenism all united." Referring to the False Prophet of Revelation 13, Edwards says that, "here an eye seems to be had to Mahomet (Muhammad), whom his followers call the prophet of God."[33]

Like most of the reformed theologians that came before him, Edwards held to a historicist interpretation of the Book of Revelation. That is to say, he considered Revelation a treatise about the whole period from the birth of Christ to the conclusion of this age. In looking at the demonic locusts and horsemen in Revelation 9, Edwards saw a clear allusion to the Muslim armies: "Satan's Mahometan (Muslim) Kingdom shall be utterly overthrown. The locusts and the horsemen in the 9th chapter of Revelation have their appointed time set there, and the false prophet shall be taken and destroyed. And then— though Mahometanism has been so vastly propagated in the world, and is upheld by such a great empire—this smoke, which has ascended out of the bottomless pit, shall be utterly scattered before the light of that glorious day, and the Mahometan Empire shall fall at the sound of the great trumpet which shall then be blown."[34]

Edwards's comments about the Locusts are rooted in the fact that in ancient history, Arabs were associated with locusts. Even the Hebrew words for "locust" and "Arab" are almost identical. In many verses in the Bible, locusts (Arabs) come against Israel for battle. The Arab word for locust is Gindib. The Monolith of Shalmeneser III from Kurkuk, the oldest account from Babylon and the oldest document mentioning Arabs, lists Gi-in-di-bu' Ar-ba-a-a regarding Arabs and their territory called "Gindibu."[35]

While the position that Islam is the Antichrist may not be the premiere position held by today's prophecy scholars, let it not be said that what is presented in this book is a new or novel theory. Ultimately, you must decide which theory you believe is more grounded in Scripture, the European position held by many of today's prophecy teachers, or the Middle Eastern/Islamic position that has been held by many other great leaders throughout Church history.

❧ 71 ❧
Vision of The Four Beasts
(Muslim, Not European)

Daniel 7 describes a "night vision" with four bizarre beasts; each one emerges out of the sea (peoples and nations). Most scholars agree that these four kingdoms correlate precisely with the four kingdoms in Nebuchadnezzar's dream. Yet, the theme (like Daniel 2) is primarily an end-time passage.

"The first was like a lion

1. and it had the wings of an eagle. I watched until its wings were torn off and it was lifted from the ground so that it stood on two feet like a man, and the heart of a man was given to it. And there before me was a second beast, which looked like a bear

2. It was raised up on one of its sides, and it had three ribs in its mouth between its teeth. It was told, 'Get up, and eat your fill of flesh!' After that, I looked, and there before me was another beast, one that looked like a leopard

3. And on its back it had four wings like those of a bird. This beast had four heads, and it was given authority to rule. After that, in my vision at night I looked, and there before me was a fourth beast—terrifying and frightening and very powerful. It had large iron

4. teeth; it crushed and devoured its victims and trampled underfoot whatever was left. It was different from all the former beasts, and it had ten horns," (Daniel 7:4-7).

THE BRONZE

The bronze nails in Daniel 7:19 point to a Grecian, not Roman, Antichrist. "Then I wished to know the truth about the fourth beast, which was different from all the others, exceedingly dreadful, with its teeth of iron and its nails of bronze, which *devoured*, broke in pieces, and trampled the residue with its feet," (Daniel 7:19).

We have textual evidence for the Grecian nature of the Antichrist kingdom. "*Its nails of bronze*" must be alluding to the correlation of the ten toes to the Grecian Empire. This is deduced because bronze as is accepted by biblical scholars represents Greece, the third metal component of the statue in of Daniel 2. No one argues that bronze is not Greece. Yet the Grecian Empire was primarily Middle Eastern and not European. While many are convinced that the legs of iron in the statue of Daniel 2, represents the Roman Empire, few consider the fact that the legs extend from out of the bronze thighs, which again is the Grecian Empire. Comparing the Islamic Empire with the Grecian Empire, we see that they are nearly identical. Yet the Roman Empire when compared to the Grecian Empire is significantly different with only minor overlapping. While the Grecian Empire extended all the way to India, the Roman Empire's furthest Eastern expansion barely reached the Euphrates River.

Although many argue that iron is Roman, this is a false assumption. Scripture does not validate Iron as Roman. But even if we accepted that Iron did represent Rome, it would also have to be admitted that the passage at the least is alluding to a Greco-Roman Antichrist specifically from the Grecian parts of the Roman Empire. Regarding the other metals, there is no dispute.

So, when we view the iron, we cannot isolate it by itself. The bronze is in it—this would agree with Ibin-Ezra's position and others who saw a combined Greco-Roman Antichrist.

When we view Daniel 7, the fourth kingdom, we cannot separate it from verse 19 (nails of bronze). Out of these will come ten kings, represented in the vision by ten horns. "After that, in my vision at night I looked, and there before me was a fourth beast—terrifying and frightening and very powerful. It had large iron teeth; it crushed and devoured its victims and trampled underfoot whatever was left. It was different from all the former beasts, and it had ten horns," (Daniel 7:7).

These are the same ten horns that we have already seen in Revelation 17. The ten kings will be conquered by another king—an eleventh (the little horn)—who is the Antichrist, the ruler over the entire fourth kingdom. "While I was thinking about the horns, there before me was another horn, a little one, which came up among them; and three of the first horns were uprooted before it. This horn had eyes like the eyes of a man and a mouth that spoke boastfully... Then I continued to watch because of the boastful words the horn was speaking. I kept looking until the beast was slain and its body destroyed and thrown into the blazing fire," (Daniel 7:8, 11).

Having seen that the fourth kingdom of Nebuchadnezzar's dream (Daniel 2) and the fourth beast (Daniel 7) are the same, we may also confidently conclude that the fourth beast is the Islamic Empire. While the fourth beast represents the Islamic Empire initiated by Muhammad in the seventh century, the ten horns and the "little horn" or the eleventh horn, represent the future and final phase of the Islamic Empire that will fulfill the Biblical prophecies concerning the Antichrist and his empire.

≈ 72 ≈

Revelation 17 And The Beasts Of Daniel

Revelation 17 gives us an insight into the identification of the eleventh horn: the final Antichrist Empire. First, we see that at the time it was written, five of the empires had already fallen. This concluded 8 horns, and 2 more after the Grecian:

1. The Egyptian Empire   1 horn   plucked by Assyrian
2. The Assyrian Empire   1 horn   plucked Babylonian
3. The Babylonian Empire   1 horn   plucked by the Persian
4. The Persian Empire   1 horn   plucked by the Grecian
5. The Greek Empire   4 horns plucked by the Roman
6. The Roman Empire   1 horn   plucked by the Islamic
7. Islamic Empire   1 horn   plucked by the West

———
10 horns

8. Eighth (revival of the seventh) 11th horn to be plucked by Jesus
Note that Alexander's empire broke into 4 kingdoms.

DANIEL 2 AND DANIEL 7—ONE AND THE SAME

The first obvious reason to consider that the fourth kingdom of Nebuchadnezzar's Statue and the fourth beast of Daniel's night vision are one and the same is simply because all of the other kingdoms in each respective passage correlate perfectly. Thus, it also follows to reason that the fourth kingdoms, like all of the other previous kingdoms, would likewise correspond. Second, in both cases, it is the specific element of iron that is highlighted as a significant aspect of their physical makeup. And third, both kingdoms are said specifically to crush and trample all of the three empires that came before them. Consider the striking similarities between the two descriptions. In Nebuchadnezzar's Statue, we see, "a fourth kingdom, strong as iron—for iron breaks and smashes everything—and as iron breaks things to pieces, so it will crush and break all the others," (Daniel 2:40).

In Daniel's night vision, we see "a fourth beast—terrifying and frightening and very powerful. It had large iron teeth; it crushed and devoured its victims and trampled underfoot whatever was left," (Daniel 7:6).

Clearly, we are dealing with the same kingdom. But the final reason to see both fourth kingdoms as one and the same is found in the nature of the decline of both. Both kingdoms are destroyed utterly and completely upon Christ's return. In Nebuchadnezzar's Dream, we see that when the rock—representing the Kingdom of God—strikes the statue and destroys the final empire, all of the other empires are crushed and blow away like dust. "A rock [the Kingdom of God] was cut out, but not by human hands. It struck the statue on its feet of iron and clay and smashed them. Then the iron, the clay, the bronze, the silver and the gold were broken to pieces at the same time and became like chaff on a threshing floor in the summer. The wind swept them away without leaving a trace. But the rock that struck the statue became a huge mountain and filled the whole earth," (Daniel 2:34-35)

Notice that the first three empires and the fourth are broken "*at the same time.*" After the fall of the fourth empire, all of the other three cease to exist, as well. Likewise, in Daniel 7:11-12, we are told that when the destruction of the fourth beast will be complete and absolute. "Then I continued to watch because of the boastful words the horn was speaking. I kept looking until the [fourth] beast was slain and its body destroyed and thrown into the blazing fire. The other beasts had been stripped of their authority, but were allowed to live for a period of time," (Daniel 7:11-12).

Many have misinterpreted this verse to mean that *after* the fourth beast kingdom is destroyed by God, *then* the other three kingdoms will be stripped of their authority but will be allowed to continue living for a period of time. However, the verse is simply comparing the manner of decline that the first three empires undergo as opposed to the sudden, utter destruction that the fourth beast would experience. In other words, while the first three empires each lived on in the empires that followed them, the death of the fourth empire would be utterly complete when Christ returns. No lingering remnants of life would exist "But the court will sit, and his power will be taken away and completely destroyed forever," (Daniel 7:26).

The fourth empire would not gradually decay and sputter out as those that preceded it. Nor would it be absorbed into another empire that conquered it. This was precisely the case with the other three empires. For instance, when Cyrus took Babylon, he stripped the Babylonian king of his authority. But the Babylonian citizens and culture in many ways lived on under Medo-Persian rule.

The same can be said of the Medo-Persian Empire after it was defeated by Alexander, and likewise for the Greek Empire after the Romans conquered it. An important aside, it should also be pointed out that *the Roman Empire experienced a very slow death*.

As such, it most certainly may not be said—as Preterists claim—that the fourth beast, which would be utterly and decisively destroyed, could find its ultimate fulfillment in the historical Roman Empire. This passage is quite damning to Preterism. The empire that this passage is speaking about will find its complete and absolute cessation under the judgment of God *at the end of this age*. And not just the last kingdom, but all four—*they will all be destroyed at the same time*. This proves that the final empire will encompass the previous three. After this time, the Kingdom of God and all the kingdoms of the earth will be given to the saints of the most high. "Then the sovereignty, power and greatness of the kingdoms under the whole heaven will be handed over to the saints, the people of the Most High. His kingdom will be an everlasting kingdom, and all rulers will worship and obey him," (Daniel 7:26-27)

∼ 73 ∼
Unlocking Daniel
And The Little Horn

THE VISION OF THE RAM AND THE GOAT

The next snapshot of the final Antichrist Empire again comes from the Book of Daniel. This vision, in fact, was given to Daniel quite sometime after the vision of the four beasts. "In the third year of King Belshazzar's reign, I, Daniel, had a vision, after the one that had already appeared to me," (Daniel 8:1).

This time, Daniel sees two animals; the first is a ram with two horns. "I looked up, and there before me was a ram with two horns, standing beside the canal, and the horns were long. One of the horns was longer than the other but grew up later. I watched the ram as he charged toward the west and the north and the south. No animal could stand against him, and none could rescue from his power. He did as he pleased and became great," (Daniel 8:2-4).

Next, we are introduced a goat with one large horn: "As I was thinking about this, suddenly a goat with a prominent horn between his eyes came from the west, crossing the whole earth without touching the ground. He came toward the two-horned ram I had seen standing beside the canal and charged at him in great rage. I saw him attack the ram furiously, striking the ram and shattering his two horns. The ram was powerless to stand against him; the goat knocked him to the ground and trampled on him, and none could rescue the ram from his power. The goat became very great, but at the height of his power his large horn was broken off, and in its place four prominent horns grew up toward the four winds of heaven," (Daniel 8:5-8). These verses refer to the dominance of the Medo-Persian Empire, "Ram with two horns", by Alexander the Great's Macedonian Greek Empire, "Goat". After this, the goat with only one horn is broken symbolizing Alexander the Great's death. Then his generals fought until only four remained alive. These four eventually called a truce and divided the empire into four segments: the north, south, east, and west, each division named after its respective ruler as follows:

1-North	Selucus	Central Turkey, Syria, Iran and Central Asia
2-South	Ptolemy	Egypt and North Africa
3-West	Cassander	Greece and South-Eastern
4-East	Lysimachus	Western Turkey

So the four horns represent the four divisions of Greece after Alexander. This correlates with the third beast of the last vision—the *four*-headed leopard.

What is interesting about this passage is that it is so prophetically precise that many liberal or atheist scholars have fought tooth and nail to disprove its timing, insisting that the prophecy was written well after these events occurred.

After the clash between the ram and the goat, we are introduced to another horn, similar to the little horn of Daniel 7. This horn is also described as "another horn" which started small: "And out of one of them came forth a little horn, which waxed exceeding great, toward the south, and toward the east, and toward the pleasant land. And it waxed great, even to the host of heaven; and it cast down some of the host and of the stars to the ground, and stamped upon them. Yea, he magnified himself even to the prince of the host, and by him the daily sacrifice was taken away, and the place of his sanctuary was cast down. And an host was given him against the daily sacrifice by reason of transgression, and it cast down the truth to the ground; and it practiced, and prospered," (Daniel 8:9-12).

Scholars universally point to Antiochus IV Epiphanies of the Seleucid division, as the fulfillment of this passage. However, while this is true, Antiochus was also a type. His power and influence grew "to the south and to the east and toward the Beautiful Land"—Israel. This clearly refers to the End-Times Antichrist. He said: "I am going to tell you what will happen later in the time of wrath, because the vision concerns the appointed time of the end. The two-horned ram that you saw represents the kings of Media and Persia. The shaggy goat is the king of Greece, and the large horn between his eyes is the first king. The four horns that replaced the one that was broken off represent four kingdoms that will emerge from his nation but will not have the same power. In the latter part of their reign, when rebels have become completely wicked, a stern-faced king, a master of intrigue, will arise. He will become very strong, but not by his own power. He will cause astounding devastation and will succeed in whatever he does. He will destroy the mighty men and the holy people. He will cause deceit to prosper, and he will consider himself superior. When they feel secure, he will destroy many and take his stand against the Prince of princes. Yet he will be destroyed, but not by human power," (Daniel 8:19-25).

It is clear that the "little horn" is the End-Time Antichrist, who causes one-third of the angels to fall, "And it waxed great, even to the host of heaven; and some of the host and of the stars it cast down to the ground, and trampled upon them. Yea, it magnified itself, even to the prince of the host; and from him the continual burnt-offering was taken away, and the place of his sanctuary was cast down," (Daniel 8:10-11). Antiochus cannot be the one cast down with heavenly stars (fallen angels).

But here is the most important aspect of this prophecy: The little horns of Daniel 7 and Daniel 8 both point to the Antichrist. These are simply two snapshots taken from different angles. One snap-shot pictures the Antichrist emerging forth from out of the fourth Beast, while the second snap-shot portrays the Antichrist as emerging forth from the Seleucid division of the Greek Empire. But those who argue that the fourth Beast is the Roman Empire are forced to take the obviously inconsistent position that the "little horn" in Daniel 7 is the Antichrist, while the little horn in Daniel 8 is not. They are forced to do this because their mistaken assumption that the Antichrist will come from Europe is not supported by the Antichrist emerging from out of the regions of the Seleucid division of the Greek Empire. And so what do they do? As usual, they take a pick and choose approach. They accept the passages that seem to support their positions and then disregard or ignore those that do not. Many force a migration of Antichrist from Greece to western Europe.

When one sees the Antichrist emerging forth from the fourth Beast of Daniel 7 to be an Islamic Empire, as well as from the little horn of the Shaggy Goat which is The Seleucid division of the Greek Empire, then all of the pieces fit together as smoothly as and as easily as greased frog skin. And that is certainly something that the European Roman Empire theorists can never claim.

≈ 74 ≈
Unlocking Daniel 11
And The Little Horn

━┼━╼═╾·✳·╾═╼━┼━

The secret to unlocking much of the Bible is to look at the duality and type fulfillments. I cannot stress this enough. When you read Scripture, try to find repeated themes and you will discover how rich the Word of God really is. We find this in Daniel 11:21-35 which focuses on the Antichrist (King of the North). In Daniel 11, the King of the North, just like the "little horn" in Daniel 8 expresses a brutal persecution of the Jewish people and sets up the final abomination that causes desolation:

> "His armed forces will rise up to desecrate the temple fortress and *will abolish the daily sacrifice*. Then they will set up the *abomination that causes desolation*. (v. 31) With flattery he will corrupt those who have violated the covenant (v. 32), but the *people who know their God will firmly resist him. Those who are wise will instruct many*, though for a time they *will fall by the sword* or *be burned* or *captured or plundered*. (v. 33) When they fall, they will *receive a little help* (v. 34), and many who are not sincere will join them. *Some of the wise will stumble, so that they may be refined, purified, and made spotless until the time of the end*, for it will still come at the appointed time. (v. 35) Then the king shall do according to his own will: he shall exalt and magnify himself above every god, shall *speak blasphemies against the God of gods*, and shall prosper till the wrath has been accomplished; for what has been determined shall be done. (v. 36) *He shall regard neither the God of his fathers nor the desire of women*, nor regard any god; for he shall exalt himself above them all. (v. 37) But in their place *he shall honor a god of fortresses*; and a god which his fathers did not know he shall honor with *gold and silver, with precious stones* and pleasant things. (v. 38) Thus he shall act against the strongest fortresses with a *foreign god*, which *he shall acknowledge*, and advance its glory; and he shall cause them to rule over many, and *divide the land for gain*. (v. 39) "At the time of the end the king of the South shall attack him; and the king of the North shall come against him like a whirlwind,

with chariots, horsemen, and with many ships; and he shall enter the countries, overwhelm them, and pass through. (v. 40) He shall also enter the Glorious Land, and many countries shall be overthrown; but these shall escape from his hand: *Edom, Moab, and the prominent people of Ammon*. (v. 41) *He shall stretch out his hand against the countries, and the land of Egypt shall not escape*. (v. 42) He shall have power over the treasures of gold and silver, and over all the precious things of Egypt; also the [1]Libyans and Ethiopians shall follow at his heels. (v. 43) But news from the east and the north shall trouble him; therefore he shall go out with great fury to destroy and annihilate many. (v. 44) And he shall plant the tents of his palace between the seas and the glorious holy mountain; yet he shall come to his end, and no one will help him. (v. 45)" (Daniel 11:31-45)

"At that time Michael shall stand up, The great prince who stands watch over the sons of your people; And there shall be a time of trouble, Such as never was since there was a nation, Even to that time. And at that time your people shall be delivered, Every one who is found written in the book. (v. 1) And many of those who sleep in the dust of the earth shall awake, Some to everlasting life, Some to shame and everlasting contempt. (v. 2) Those who are wise shall shine Like the brightness of the firmament, And those who turn many to righteousness Like the stars forever and ever. (v. 3) 'But you, Daniel, shut up the words, and seal the book until the time of the end; many shall run to and fro, and knowledge shall increase.' (v. 4) Then I, Daniel, looked; and there stood two others, one on this riverbank and the other on that riverbank. (v. 5) And one said to the man clothed in linen, who was above the waters of the river, "How long shall the fulfillment of these wonders be?" (v. 6) Then I heard the man clothed in linen, who was above the waters of the river, when he held up his right hand and his left hand to heaven, and swore by Him who lives forever, that [4] it shall be for a time, times, and half a time; and when [5] the power of the holy people has been completely shattered, all these things shall be finished. (v. 7) Although I heard, I did not understand. Then I said, "My lord, what shall be the end of these things?" (v. 8) And he said, "Go your way, Daniel,[6] for the words are closed up and sealed till the time of the end. (v. 9) [7] Many shall be purified, made white, and refined, but the wicked shall do wickedly; and none of the wicked shall understand, but the wise shall understand. (v. 10) "And from the time that the daily sacrifice is taken away, and the [8] *abomination of des-*

olation is set up, there shall be one thousand two hundred and ninety days. (v. 11) Blessed is he who waits, and comes to the one thousand three hundred and thirty-five days. (v. 12) "But you, go your way till the end; for you shall rest, and will arise to your inheritance at the end of the days. (v. 2)" (Daniel 12:1-12)

The italicized verses have already been shown to parallel Islam. Western Bible scholars who support the re-establishment of Israel and believe that God appointed the Arch-Angel Michael to watch over Israel agree that these scriptures pertain to the Antichrist persecuting Israel and the saints. It is mostly the Anti-Israel groups that still see these as history. As such, a deliberate measure of violence must be inflicted either upon the passage or history for one to interpret this portion of the passage through a Preterist lens. Clearly, this corrupt view cannot escape the clear text: "He will be successful until the time of wrath is completed, for what has been determined must take place," (Daniel 11:36). This is referring to the End-Times (time of wrath) just before the return of Christ and events prior to the resurrection of the dead. "At that time, Multitudes who sleep in the dust of the earth will awake: some to everlasting life, others to shame and everlasting contempt," (Daniel 12:1-2).

Preterists (those who believe that the majority of Biblical prophecies was fulfilled in the first century) seem to ignore this portion: "Then the king shall do according to his own will: he shall exalt and magnify himself above every god, *shall speak blasphemies against the God of gods,* and shall prosper till the wrath has been accomplished; for what has been determined shall be done. *He shall regard neither the God of his fathers nor the desire of women,* nor regard any god; for he shall exalt himself above them all. But in their place *he shall honor a god of fortresses*; and a god which his fathers did not know he shall honor with *gold and silver, with precious stones and pleasant things.* Thus he shall act against the strongest fortresses with a *foreign god,* which *he shall acknowledge,* and *advance its glory*; and he shall *cause them to rule over many,* and *divide the land for gain,*" (Daniel 11:36-39). There were no events in his life and career that can be found that historically correlate with Antiochus exalting "himself above every god." Nor did he reject the gods of his fathers. On the contrary, Antiochus worshipped the same pantheon of Greek gods as any other Greek. In fact, Antiochus even set up an altar to Zeus in the sanctuary of the Jewish Temple. Beyond this, Daniel says that Antiochus would meet his death in Israel. However, history records that Antiochus in fact died in Persia. The question that begs an answer to the false accusation of the Antichrist being a Jew is, "Why would God choose Antiochus (a gentile) for a type of Antichrist, then choose a Jew?"

The Antichrist's god is different than Antiochus. At a glance, this passage appears to say that this evil one will not honor any god, but will exalt himself above all gods. Yet on the other hand, he is also said to honor a "god of fortresses" and to employ the help of "a foreign god." He is not an atheist, as some claim. He simply rejects all gods, except his foreign god of war (god of fortresses). This would match perfectly the ideology of Muhammad and the Mahdi, who are commanded to advance the cause of Allah with the banner "There is no god but Allah."

The part of the vision that has to do with the End times begins in Daniel 11:21: "There shall arise a vile person, to whom they will not give the honor of royalty; but he shall come in peaceably, and seize the kingdom by intrigue."

God sees the Antichrist as a "vile person." He rises to power peaceably by means of intrigue—clever plotting and politics. Today in Turkey, the Islamist party is not accepted by their predecessors and their attempt to reinstitute the Caliphate is rejected. This soon will change this since the Antichrist gains support peaceably and through trickery (v. 22), but then use force to crush his opposition and strengthen his position. We know from Daniel 9:26-27 that the Antichrist makes a peace covenant; therefore, the "prince of the covenant" is clearly the Antichrist.

This league or covenant appears to be a peace accord, as well as some sort of religious pact—possibly one that tackles the thorny issue of coexistence between Jews, Muslims, and Christians in the Middle East, and by which Jerusalem could be declared an international city with free and equal access guaranteed to people of all faiths. This covenant could also clear the way for the Jews to finally be able to rebuild their Temple on Jerusalem's Mount Moriah and resume animal sacrifices on its altar—something that hasn't happened since the last Temple was destroyed in 70 A.D In Daniel 11:31, the Antichrist puts a stop to the daily sacrifices, so obviously they must be resumed between now and then, and the signing of the covenant seems a likely time for that.

"For he shall come up and become strong with a small number of people"—or "a small people." The Antichrist rises to power through his popularity with the "small" or poor people of the world, the masses, who respond to his political and economic policies. Or he does it with the help of a "small" elite group of insiders.

"He shall disperse among them the plunder, spoil, and riches," (v. 24). This would fit Islam perfectly. If one searches Islam for "Ghana'em", it sounds as if he will distribute the wealth to win the support of the poor in the countries he conquers. So does the phrase found in verse 39, where it says he will "divide the land for gain"—his main crime of dividing Israel. "He shall do what his fathers have not done, nor his forefathers." Like Muhammad's expansions and exploits, after him Umar, then Saladin, the Mahdi will do the same. He will expand the Islamic kingdom by advancing to Egypt, Libya, and Sudan. This is evident from verse 25: "He (the Antichrist) shall stir up his power and his courage against the king of the South with a great army. And the king of the South shall be stirred up to battle with a very great and mighty army, but he shall not stand, for they (the Antichrist and his forces) shall devise plans against him."

It sounds like the king of the South has an even greater force than the Antichrist at this point. The tide of battle turns when the king of the South (Egypt) is betrayed by some of his own people. "Yes, those who eat of the portion of his delicacies shall destroy him; his army shall be swept away, and many shall fall down slain," (v. 26). We have seen Anwar Sadat, the late Egyptian President, betrayed and killed by Islamists, and this is similar since the majority of Egyptians are Muslim fundamentalists.

The Little Horn And The Rest Of Scripture Fits Like A Glove

The Little Horn must come from the Seleucid Division of the Grecian Empire. This would definitely discount any European Roman entity.

THE LITTLE HORN CONNECTS TO THE ANTICHRIST IN DANIEL

The Bible states in Daniel 8:9, "out of one of them (the 4 Grecian horns) came forth a little horn, which waxed exceeding great, toward the south, and toward the east, and toward the pleasant land," he must come from the Grecian Empire—the Eastern part of the Roman Empire and north of Israel. Since he is going south he must be coming from the north parts in relation to Israel, exactly as specified in Ezekiel 38, and Joel 3.

LITTLE HORN CONNECTS TO GOG

It all connects. Even my argument that Gog is the Antichrist cannot be escaped. He comes from the eastern part of the Roman Empire, the Grecian side; so does the little horn out of the 4 Grecian horns. Like Antiochus the Syrian, Gog also connects to the Seleucid Dynasty. Seleucus became king of the eastern provinces—more or less modern Afghanistan, Iran, Iraq, Syria, and Lebanon, together with parts of Turkey, Armenia, Turkmenistan, Uzbekistan, and Tajikistan.[36]

LITTLE HORN CONNECTS TO BEAST OF REVELATION 13

Revelation 13 describes the End-Times beast in terms of regions:

Leopard (Grecian), Lion (Babylonian), and Bear (Medo-Persian).

All three Empires ruled the region of Asia Minor, i.e. the Seleucid portion of the Grecian Empire. Scripture places the land of Gog north of Israel, and Asia Minor is north of Israel. All prophetic writings must pinpoint the region, and indeed they do.

LITTLE HORN CONNECTS TO MATTHEW 24:15

Jesus' own words are clear in Daniel. The abomination of desolation is the one described by Daniel (11:31) with a further reference to its appearance in the holy place in Daniel 12:11. Daniel 9:27 contains a third reference, as does Daniel 8:13.

The Bible does not once mention any future leader coming from the West. Daniel 11:31 describes a final evil ruler, the "King of the North," who sets up "the abomination of desolation" and puts an end to temple sacrifices.

Therefore, in accordance with Matthew 24:15 and Daniel 8:9, we must conclude that Antichrist is "From one of the prominent horns came a small horn whose power grew very great. It extended toward the south and the east and toward the glorious land of Israel."

Even the ancient commentators agree. Early Church Father Jerome, in his Commentary on Daniel, writes: "Most of our commentators refer this passage to the Antichrist, and hold that that which occurred under Antiochus was only by way of a type which shall be fulfilled under Antichrist."[37]

≈ 76 ≈
Unlocking Daniel 9 And The Evil Prince To Come (Muslim, Not European)

+═══╬═══+

The next significant prophetic passage to unlock the origin of Antichrist is the last portion of Daniel 9:26. The particular verse that we will examine is sandwiched in the middle of a very significant prophetic passage. This passage deals with a specific period of time referred to as "seventy sevens." Here, we will focus exclusively on verse 26. Let's begin by looking at it in its immediate context: "Know and understand this: From the issuing of the decree to restore and rebuild Jerusalem until the Anointed One, the ruler, comes, there will be seven 'sevens' and sixty-two 'sevens.' It will be rebuilt with streets and a trench, but in times of trouble. After the sixty-two 'sevens,' the Anointed One will be cut off and will have nothing," (Daniel 9:25-26).

This portion of the prophecy is speaking of Jesus—the Anointed One, the ruler—who was "cut off" at the crucifixion. From here, the prophecy jumps forward to the destruction of the Temple—"the sanctuary"—in Jerusalem in AD 70. "The people of the prince who is to come shall destroy the city and the sanctuary," (Daniel 9:26).

To solve this riddle and find the right piece of the puzzle regarding the Antichrist's origin, pay attention to the following underlined and numbered words in italics: "Know therefore and understand, that from the going forth of the command to restore and build Jerusalem Until Messiah the Prince, there shall be seven weeks and sixty-two weeks; the street shall be built again, and the wall, even in troublesome times. And after the sixty-two weeks Messiah shall be cut off, but not for Himself; And the *people* [1] of the *prince* [2] *who is to come* shall destroy the city and the sanctuary. The end of it shall be with a flood, And till the end of the war, desolations are determined. Then *he* [3] shall confirm a covenant with many for one week; But in the middle of the week He shall bring an end to sacrifice and offering. And on the wing of abominations shall be one who makes desolate, Even until the consummation, which is determined, Is poured out on the desolate." (Daniel 9:25-27)

The argument for the Roman Antichrist stems from an incomplete analysis of verse 26, which assumes that "the people of the prince" must be Romans. After all, the Romans were the ones who destroyed the Temple, were they not? While it is certainly understandable how a quick reading of this verse could lead one to conclude this, when one scratches below the surface, this verse actually drives a nail in the coffin of this theory. The first things we need to analyze are the identities of [1] The People of the Prince [2] The prince [3] He, the one that confirms the covenant for seven years.

1. Who is this "prince"? When did he come? Has he come yet? If so, when?
2. Who are "the people of the prince"?
Once you answer these questions and read the text again, you will get it.

1. WHO IS THIS PRINCE? WHEN DID HE COME?
Let us assume that "the prince" has come and respond to some wrong assumptions. Many Western students of prophecy assume that the prince has already come, because Titus the Roman general was the one who destroyed the Temple. Thus Titus is often identified as "the prince" who is to come.

But, this can never be so because the "he" in verse 27 ("*And he shall confirm the covenant with many for one week*") cannot refer to Titus who never engaged in a seven-year peace treaty.

Neither did Titus commit an abomination of desolation. "And on a wing of the temple he will set up an abomination that causes desolation."

Some even go so far as to place an unjustified break, concluding that the "he" is indeed the Antichrist and destroyer of the Temple, but the prince must be Titus.

Titus can never be this "he".

The only way for this interpretation to be accurate would be for Titus to come back from the dead. Is that what these interpreters wait for?

This would be utter nonsense. The "he" pertains to the prince. Period. We cannot ignore the grammar. The prince must be the one who established this seven-year peace treaty. There is no way to escape this.

So the correct and only answer to the question is that the *prince* is the Antichrist.

He has not yet come.

Western prophecy teachers generally agree that the prince must be the Antichrist. Thomas Ice agrees: "This prince has to be someone who comes after Christ. The only two viable possibilities is that it could either refer to a Roman prince who destroyed Jerusalem in AD 70 or a future Antichrist."[38] John Walvoord, Dwight Pentecost, and the majority of prophecy scholars agree that the prince must be the Antichrist.

There are some strange interpretations, however. Doug Bachelor, a Seventh Day Adventist pastor states: "He (The Messiah) will confirm the covenant with many for one week.

But in the middle of the week, he'll bring an end to sacrifice. When he died on the cross what happened? The veil was ripped and he brought an end to the sacrificial system. This isn't the anti-Christ this is Jesus. It blows my mind when I hear Evangelicals say this is the Antichrist. That is a Jesuit teaching. That this has found its way into the Protestants churches, its just an abomination of desolation!"

Bachelor blames Evangelicals and Catholics for what he perceives as a misinterpretation. Yet this interpretation that this "prince" is Antichrist preceded both Evangelicals and Catholics. Paul stated, "that he sits as God in the temple of God, showing himself that he is God," (2 Thess. 2:4). This is confirmed by Irenaeus[39], Clement[40], Origen 41 and Hippolytus.[42]

Yet this interpretation doesn't stand merely because the Church fathers said it. An inductive analysis will show that it is mentioned in other parts of the Bible. Logically, how could the Messiah commit an abomination?

2. WHO ARE THE PEOPLE OF THE PRINCE?

Now we come to the second part of this riddle. Because the prince must be the Antichrist, then who are his people? When did they destroy the Temple? Once you begin to put this puzzle together, the picture is quite amazing.

The temple was destroyed in 70 A.D. Who were the "people" that destroyed it?

Remember, there is a reason why the text says "the people of the prince." God wants you to find out who these people are, for they will be "the people" of the Antichrist. Also, there is a reason why the text says, "who is to come"—it speaks of the future. These people will destroy the temple, shortly. They are of the same lineage of the Antichrist, the *prince*—*they are the "people of the prince."* His lineage, and his predecessors. So who were these people that destroyed the Temple in 70 AD?

Yes, they were Roman legions and Roman citizens. Therefore, many scholars erroneously conclude they are of European descent and heritage, as well.

But there is more to this picture than is immediately apparent. If we look deeper, we quickly find that while the people who made up the Roman legions that destroyed Jerusalem were mostly Eastern Roman Citizens, they were not Europeans. In fact, they were primarily from the Middle East—Arabs, Syrians, and Turks.

It is crucial to note that Titus led *the Eastern Legions of the Roman Empire*, not the Western. After Vespasian emerged as the head of the Eastern Legions to challenge Vitellius, Julius Alexander, the Prefect of Egypt, then proclaimed Vespasian to be Emperor. He and Titus became consuls in 70 A.D.

So, lets read the passage in context, *"the people (ancestors) of the Prince (Antichrist) who is to come (during the Tribulation),* will sack Jerusalem and the Temple." In other words, the people are the ancestors of the prince who will bring a seven-year peace treaty.

In 70 AD, Titus, the Roman General who led the armies that attacked Jerusalem and destroyed the temple, surrounded the city with three legions on the western side and a fourth on the Mount of Olives to the east.[43] Titus put pressure on the food and water supplies by allowing thousands of pilgrims to enter the city to celebrate Passover, and then refusing to allow them to leave. Many of the citizens fought hard, and at one point, Titus was nearly captured. But in the end, much of the population was killed, dispersed or enslaved. The city was significantly broken down and the Temple was destroyed. The four specific legions under Titus were: Legion XV Apollinaris, Legion V Macedonica, Legion XII Fulminata, and Legion X Fretensis.

For some reason, possibly due to the fact that the capital of the Roman Empire was in Rome—and thus in Europe—many seem to forget that the Roman Empire also included a vast portion of the Middle East. Because most of the Roman soldiers were recruited from the provinces where their garrisons were located, the legions that were stationed in the Middle East were also primarily Arab and, most specifically, Syrian and Turkic.

Commenting on the predominant Syrian makeup of the Roman garrisons in the region, the Jewish historian Josephus stated, "The greatest part of the Roman garrison was raised out of Syria; and being thus related to the Syrian part, they were ready to assist it."[44] "So Vespasian sent his son Titus from Achaia, where he had been with Nero, to Alexandria, to bring back with him from thence the fifth and. the tenth legions, while he himself, when he had passed over the Hellespont, came by land into Syria, where he gathered together the Roman forces, with a considerable number of auxiliaries from the kings in that neighborhood."[45]

The historian Tacitus recounts the destruction of the Temple: "early in this year Titus Caesar, who had been selected by his father to complete the subjugation of Judaea...He found in Judaea three legions, the 5th, the 10th, and the 15th, all old troops of Vespasian's. To these he added the 12th from Syria, and some men belonging to the 18th and 3rd, whom he had withdrawn from Alexandria (Egypt). This force was accompanied by twenty cohorts of allied troops and eight squadrons of cavalry, by the two kings Agrippa and Sohemus, by the auxiliary forces of king Antiochus, by a strong contingent of Arabs, who hated the Jews with the usual hatred of neighbors, and, lastly, by many persons brought from the capital and from Italy by private hopes of securing the yet unengaged affections of the Prince. With this force Titus entered the enemy's territory, preserving strict order on his march, reconnoitering every spot, and always ready to give battle. At last he encamped near Jerusalem."[46]

Josephus recounts how the armies were collected: "But as to Titus, he sailed over from Achaia to Alexandria, and that sooner than the winter season did usually permit; so he took with him those forces he was sent for, and marching with great expedition, he came suddenly to Ptolemais, and there finding his father, together with the two legions, the fifth and the tenth, which were the most eminent legions of all, he joined them to that fifteenth legion which was with his father; eighteen cohorts followed these legions; there came also five cohorts from Cesarea (Cappadocia Turkey), with one troop of horsemen, and five other troops of horsemen from Syria. Now these ten cohorts had severally a thousand footmen, but the other thirteen cohorts had no more than six hundred footmen apiece, with a hundred and twenty horsemen. There were also a considerable number of auxiliaries got together, which came from the kings Antiochus, and Agrippa, and Sohemus, each of them contributing one thousand footmen that were archers, and a thousand horsemen. Malchus also, the king of Arabia, sent a thousand horsemen, besides five thousand footmen, the greatest part of which were archers; so that the whole army, including the auxiliaries sent by the kings, as well horsemen as footmen, when all were united together, amounted to sixty thousand, besides the servants, who, as they followed in vast numbers, so because they had been trained up in war with the rest, ought not to be distinguished from the fighting men; for as they were in their masters' service in times of peace, so did they undergo the like dangers with them in times of war, insomuch that they were inferior to none, either in skill or in strength, only they were subject to their masters."[47]

Again, speaking of the great enmity the Syrians had for the Jews of Jerusalem, Josephus recounts that the Syrians and the Arabs who were camped outside of the city of Jerusalem actually disemboweled more than two thousand Jews who had escaped, in order to search for gold that they might have swallowed. "The multitude of the Arabians, with the Syrians, cut up those that came as supplicants, and searched their bellies. Nor does it seem to me that any misery befell the Jews that was more terrible than this, since in one night's time about two thousand of these deserters were thus dissected."[48]

Indeed, the majority of the "Roman" soldiers that destroyed Jerusalem were Arabs, Syrians, and Turks. When we look at the four Roman legions that were under Titus during the siege against Jerusalem, we see that they were from the Eastern portion of the Empire and were primarily from Syria or eastern Turkey. Below are the four legions that were under Titus during the Jewish Roman war and the locations that history records for their garrisons:

Legion 10 Fretensis :	Turkey, Syria
Legion 15 Apollinaris:	Syria
Legion 12 Fulminata:	Melitene: Eastern Turkey, Syria
Legion 5 Macedonica :	Moesia: Serbia, Bulgaria

These four legions were all involved in the destruction of Jerusalem and the Temple. The legion, in particular, that went through the wall breach and set fire to the Temple was known as X Fretensis or the Tenth Legion. It was this particular legion that actually pulled down the entire Temple and made the Temple Mount its new base. The map below reveals where the tenth legion was garrisoned and where the soldiers were from.[4]

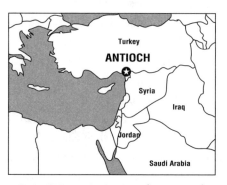

Legion X Fretensis: Garrisoned near Antioch

It should also be pointed out that each Legion was composed of several smaller "cohorts." Below is a list of the actual cohorts that comprised the tenth legion and where they originally came from:

A. Thracum: Syria (Syrians)
B. IV Cohort Thracia: Bulgaria and Turkey (Turks)
C. Syria Ulpia Petraeorum: Petra in Edom (Nabatean Arabs)
D. IV Cohort Arabia (Arabs)

Again, these were a mixture of Syrians, Turks and Arabs. While the people who destroyed the temple were indeed Roman citizens, they were not primarily Europeans or Italians, but rather the peoples that lived in Syria and Eastern Turkey during the first century. This verse is concerned with the *heritage* and *lineage* of the people as restricted by the text "*people of the Prince*" and not their allegiance to Rome. This is why the text is written in this way. It insists on this connection. Once again, the Bible has led us to the same region. In context, the "people of the prince" are simply the people of the Antichrist; the Hebrew

"Am" for people is persons, members of one's people, compatriots, countrymen, kinsman and kindred. (Strong's 5971)

Even if we take the meaning of "Am" as "nation", how will the construct of this verse with such meaning be logical? "The nation of the Antichrist" That is entirely futuristic. How can someone conclude that the Antichrist is Roman with this interpretation? It proves nothing, since the nation of the Antichrist would not be known from such a construct. The only logical construction for the context of "Am" is "the kindred" of Antichrist—his ancestors, his kinsman.

The Antichrist will be from among the people who still live in the Middle East—those who destroyed the city and sanctuary in Titus' time. This is the natural way to read the text, especially since connecting the people with the prince is widely accepted.

DANIEL WAS SPEAKING OF THE END

The reason that I am able to take such a non-traditional position with confidence is most certainly not because of any particular superior intelligence or mystical gifted-ness at interpreting the Bible, *of course not*. Nor do I think lightly of the cumulative wisdom of western Christians currently or the interpreters of old. Neither am I correcting a huge volume on Bible Prophecy, for I too believe in the Rapture, Tribulation, Millennium, recreation of Israel, 144,000 witnessing Jews in Israel, the Falling Away, the coming of the Antichrist, the coming two witnesses, their death on the streets of Jerusalem, and so much more.

In fact, western interpreters agree that Islam is involved. The question I am presenting, though, is: "Does Islam play the *main* roll?" Or a major roll. At least we all agree on the latter.

The reason that such confidence can be expressed regarding the interpretations offered here is quite simple: today we have a greater advantage than those in the past because God has specifically promised, "But you, Daniel, shut up the words, and *seal the book* until the ti*me of the end*; many shall run to and fro, and knowledge shall increase," (Daniel 12:4).

The prophecy of Daniel is *sealed* and is regarding the "time of the end." He will unlock the Book of Daniel to the Church. Isaac Newton, Matthew Henry and many of those before us understood that the book of Daniel, and by extension Revelation, would not be fully understood until the "time of the end."

Do I claim to unlock it? No. Sealed means sealed. The closer we get, the more we will all understand Daniel, whose focus is on the end: "At that time Michael, the great prince who protects your people, will arise. There will be a time of distress such as has not happened from the beginning of nations until then. But at that time your people—everyone whose name is found written in the book—will be delivered. Multitudes who sleep in the dust of the earth will awake: some to everlasting life, others to shame and everlasting contempt. Those who are wise will shine like the brightness of the heavens, and those who lead many to righteousness, like the stars for ever and ever," (Daniel 12:1-3).

Some claim that the angel here is merely speaking of the period surrounding and following Jesus' ministry at the inauguration of the Kingdom of God. But that is not specifically what this passage is speaking about. The passage says that, "*Multitudes who sleep in the dust of the earth will awake: some to everlasting life, others to shame and everlasting contempt.*" This is not speaking of the "End-Times" in a broader, general sense, but rather in the ultimate "Last-Days" when the resurrection of the dead takes place. The angel continues, "But you, Daniel, close up and seal the words of the scroll until the time of the end. Many will go here and there to increase knowledge...I (Daniel) heard, but I did not understand. So I asked, 'My lord, what will the outcome of all this be?' He replied, 'Go your way, Daniel, because the words are closed up and sealed until the time of the end. Many will be purified, made spotless and refined, but the wicked will continue to be wicked. None of the wicked will understand, but those who are wise will understand... As for you, go your way till the end. You will rest, and then at the end of the days you will rise to receive your allotted inheritance,'" (Daniel 12:5-13).

And so the question needs to be asked: *God has made it clear that this book would be locked up and sealed until the time of the end. Why, then, do so many cling to the most commonly accepted, most popular interpretations of this book?* If the book has truly been sealed until the time of the end, then it also stands to reason that the most popular, the most common interpretation, (The Roman Empire Theory) is also the most unlikely meaning of the prophecy.

It is actually the most traditional historical interpretations of the various prophecies that are the least likely to offer a complete and accurate interpretation. Just as the Messianic fulfillments were understood by only a few, so it is with the prophecies of his return. But if the interpretation offered in this book, namely that the Islamic and not the Roman Empire is the fulfillment of Daniel's prophecies, then it also stands to reason that the book is now beginning to be unsealed and the "Last-Days" that have forever been on the horizon are in fact now upon us.

~77~
Unlocking
Revelation 12 And 13

ISLAMIC SEVEN HEADED BEAST

The next significant snapshot of the final beast empire is found in the Book of Revelation, chapters 12 and 13. This passage ties into several of the previous prophetic snapshots using familiar symbolism. In Revelation 12, we are first introduced to a woman who is about to give birth. This woman is understood to represent the Jewish people, who corporately brought the Messiah into the world. But immediately after being introduced to the woman, we see that even as she is about to give birth, a dreadful and murderous red dragon stalks her. The dragon, of course, represents Satan. "Then another sign appeared in heaven: an enormous red dragon with seven heads and ten horns and seven crowns on his heads. His tail swept a third of the stars out of the sky and flung them to the earth. The dragon stood in front of the woman who was about to give birth, so that he might devour her child the moment it was born. She gave birth to a son, a male child, who will rule all the nations with an iron scepter. And her child was snatched up to God and to his throne," (Revelation 12:3-5).

The child being snatched up to God and to His throne is obviously a reference to the ascension of Jesus after the cross.

After this, we are told that there was a war in heaven, whereby

"the great dragon was hurled down—that ancient serpent called the devil, or Satan, who leads the whole world astray. He was hurled to the earth, and his angels with him," (Revelation 12:9). This fits the Grecian Antichrist: "Out of one of them came another horn, which started out small but grew in power to the south and to the east, and toward the beautiful land. It grew until it reached the hosts of the heavens, and it threw the starry hosts down to the earth and trampled it." (Daniel 8:10)

After this, Satan the dragon pursued the Jewish people as well as "her offspring"—the gentile followers of the Messiah, who came to be known as Christians. "Then the dragon was enraged at the woman and went off to make war against the rest of her offspring—

those who obey God's commandments and hold to the testimony of Jesus," (Revelation 12:17).

As we turn to chapter 13, we see that the dragon is shown standing on the shore of the sea. Then, as if he were some dark sorcerer, he summons a gruesome beast from the depths of the ocean. "And I saw a beast coming out of the sea. He had ten horns and seven heads, with ten crowns on his horns, and on each head a blasphemous name. The beast I saw resembled a leopard, but had feet like those of a bear and a mouth like that of a lion. The dragon gave the beast his power and his throne and great authority," (Revelation 13:2-3).

The first interesting observation that may be made about this beast is that it has body parts from each of the previous four beasts we examined in Daniel 7. The beast has the body of a leopard, the feet of a bear, and the mouth of a lion. As such, we may assume that the final beast empire will to some degree be a conglomerate of the Lion, Babylonian Empire (Iraq), the Bear, Medo-Persia Empire (Iran), and the Leopard, Macedonian Greek Empire (Turkey).

This is significant. Does this sound like a European Beast? Or is it a Middle Eastern/Islamic Beast? Again, we see a perfect fit with the rest of our analysis of Scripture.

We also see that the beast shares some very similar features with the dragon. Like the dragon, the beast also has seven heads and ten horns. Here, we have a perfect example of how understanding a previous passage helps us to understand a later passage. The ten horns represent ten rulers that will arise from the final beast empire; the number of horns from each empire. We know this because the angel made it very clear in Daniel 7, and just as Daniel was a roadmap for the ancients to recognize Antiochus, Revelation is a roadmap for us to recognize the Antichrist. Everything will be fulfilled to the jot and tittle. The seven heads, on the other hand, represent authority or government, (as in: head of state). The seven heads represent the seven beast empires that persecuted the nation of Israel, and in its re-created state will persecute her offspring—the Christians. So just to recap, the seven heads are the following:

The Egyptian Empire
The Assyrian Empire
The Babylonian Empire
The Medo-Persian Empire
The Macedonian Greek Empire
The Roman Empire
The Islamic Empire

THE WOUNDED EMPIRE

But then we are given some key information concerning one of these empires: "One of the heads of the beast seemed to have had a fatal wound, but the fatal wound had been healed." (Revelation 13:3)

One of the heads, that is one of the seven beast empires, has a head wound. Again, we have already learned from our study of the previous snapshots of the beast empire that the empire specifically that suffers the head-wound—an apparent death—is the Islamic Empire. This head-wound may be understood as the abolition of the Caliphate that occurred in 1924. Yet, presently, the Islamic Empire is arising anew. It is reconsolidating its power and developing new bonds of unity. Soon the head—the Caliphate—will be revived, healed and restored.

Thus, based on this passage, what we may expect to see emerge in the possible near future is ten rulers or leaders from the Islamic world that will form some sort of partnership, league, union or coalition. When this partnership emerges, these then would be the ten kings mentioned both in Daniel and here in Revelation 13. Then we are told that another king will arise, and will displace three of these kings, ultimately taking a leadership position over the fragmented empire. This individual will be recognized by at least a portion of the Muslim world as either the Caliph or the Imam Mahdi or both. This will be the Antichrist. While there are yet many specific circumstances that need to fall into place in order for this whole scenario to fully become a reality, the truth is that it is not an unimaginable scenario. Dozens of world circumstances are all seemingly now merging toward making this scenario a reality.

When this scenario does become a reality, the Bible says that the reaction of the rest of the world will be astonishment and a deep sense of fear. "The whole world was astonished and followed the beast. Men worshiped the dragon because he had given authority to the beast, and they also worshiped the beast and asked, 'Who is like the beast? Who can make war against him?'" (Revelation 13:3-4)

Later, a similar description is given concerning the emerging revived Islamic Empire: "The inhabitants of the earth whose names have not been written in the book of life from the creation of the world will be astonished when they see the beast, because he once was, then he was not, and yet came again," (Revelation 17:8).

Chapter 13 concludes with some strong descriptions of what the Antichrist and his empire will do and how they will act when they are revived and brought together. The descriptions are again very similar to what we have already found in the Book of Daniel. "The beast was given a mouth to utter proud words and blasphemies and to exercise his authority for forty-two months. He opened his mouth to blaspheme God, and to slander his name and his dwelling place and those who live in heaven. He was given power to make war against the saints and to conquer them. And he was given authority over every tribe, people, language, and nation. All inhabitants of the earth will worship the beast—all whose names have not been written in the book of life belonging to the Lamb that was slain from the creation of the world," (Revelation 13:1-8).

Section VI

Solving Mysteries
Unlocking
The Mark of the Beast

≈78≈
The Dilemma

Of all of the mysteries Bible students have wrestled with throughout the millennia, the infamous *Mark of the Beast* is perhaps the most dogged and stubborn of all. From the earliest days of the Christian Church, believers have struggled to understand the nature of the Mark of the Beast. What exactly is this *mark*? And what is its relationship to the infamous number 666? The verses that speak of these things are few and cryptic. They are only found within the pages of the Book of Revelation—"a mystery within an enigma," as they say.

In the earliest days of the Church, some sought to use the *Gematria*—a mystical form of numerology—to unlock this mystery. They hoped to find the number 666 encoded within the names of archenemies of the Church, such as the assorted heresiarchs or the persecuting Roman Caesars.

MODERN BIZARRE CONCLUSIONS

In the last century, many bizarre and even humorous speculations on this subject have surfaced. In the early 1970's, various Protestant End-Time thrillers popularized the idea that in the Last-Days, the actual number 666 would be visibly tattooed on people's foreheads or wrists as an indicator that they had submitted to the Antichrist. In these days of unprecedented technological advancement, in which microchip implants and invisible barcode tattooing exist, some Christians anxiously await the day when all people will be required to receive a microchip implant or an invisible *Universal Product Code* tattooed on their wrists or foreheads.

And if those who hold to this notion were not anxious enough, in recent years, the microchip implant has achieved a wide spread usage for pets. Perhaps there is something to the notion that the prophesied "mark" will be some form of technological personal identification system; but to be honest with you, I don't think so. I'm not implying that this technology will not eventually be used in abundance throughout the world—in the same way that ATM bankcards are commonly used throughout the world. But I seriously doubt there will ever be a global enforcement of this technology for religious purposes. Perhaps this scenario makes some sense to those who know nothing of life outside of the highly technological West, but in many parts of the world—*particularly the portion that Biblical prophecy focuses on*—there are still far too many people who live in pre-industrialized societies. Shifting their cultural paradigm to accommodate sophisticated technology would be nearly impossible. Can we really expect modern technologies, such as invisible bar-code tattoos, to penetrate every last corner of the world? I see no reason to believe that the UPC code or microchip implant is what the Bible calls the Mark of the Beast.

THE SIMPLE APPROACH

As I said at the beginning of this book, my goal is to help the reader see things in a different light, through Eastern eyes—through the eyes of a native Arab speaker and a former Muslim.

I've always been of the opinion that our interpretations and ideas about the future as seen through Biblical prophecy should be fairly real world. I am uneasy about many of the various prophetic scenarios that read like sub-standard science fiction fantasies or offbeat comic books. I think that after you have completed this portion of the study, you will agree that what I suggest makes sense and demystifies the subject. It is certainly a more plausible alternative than many of the sensational ideas about the Mark of the Beast being offered today.

∽79∾

Unlocking The Name Of The Beast

THE MARK IS THE NAME OF THE BEAST

The mark of the beast is defined in Revelation 13 as "the mark, which is the name of the beast." First we need to understand that in the Bible, a "name" does not always indicate a literal name, as the modern Western mind understands the term. In the Bible, someone's "name" is essentially a reference to the nature, character, and mission of the one who possesses it. It need not indicate a literal name per se, as it commonly does in the West.

Consider, for example, the following references to Jesus: "He is dressed in a robe dipped in blood, and his name is the Word of God," (Revelation 19:13). Or, "On his robe and on his thigh he has this name written: King of Kings and Lord of Lords," (Revelation 19:16). There is also the well-known passage in Matthew from the prophecy of Isaiah: "His name shall be called Immanuel which means God with us," (Matthew 1:23). In all of these passages, the "names" of Jesus are never literal names.

If Isaiah prophesied that His Name shall be called Immanuel, and we insist on the literal name Immanuel, then Jesus would not be Messiah because his literal name is Yeshua and not Immanuel. We must think beyond the surface.

The mistake of not applying the same concept to the Beast is not as drastic. Yet, can you see the problem with identifying political figures to the Name of the Beast?

This method of applying literal names would be fatal for the case of the Messiah. This is why we need to hermeneutically apply the interpretation of the word "Name" in allegoric sense from previously fulfilled prophecies, and not a literal one.

THE NAME IS A CREED

So, in the case of the Messiah, Mary and Joseph did not call him Immanuel, nor did Jesus' friends call him "the Word of God." Instead, these are all titles and/or descriptions that refer specifically to the nature and the character of Jesus.

Also, the creed, or declaration of faith, in this Messiah matches His name: for we believe in God with us, and the Word was God, and He is also called Mighty God. (Isaiah 9:6) Those who call Jesus by these names affirm that they worship "the man-befriending God", who "for our salvation, came down from heaven and was incarnate of the Holy Spirit and the Virgin Mary," (Nicene Creed). He is "the word which became flesh and dwelt amongst us," (John 1). In conclusion, the name is a creed, dogma, article of faith, or statement of faith.

THE NAME OF BLASPHEMY

The significance of the Name of the Beast is that it is The Name of Blasphemy. (Revelation 13:1) Biblically speaking, blasphemy is an anti-Yahweh or anti-Christ word or deed—to claim the attributes of God, claim to be Messiah, deny the Holy Spirit, deny the trinity, the cross, or even denying God's edicts and declarations—are all blasphemy. Satan blasphemed when he said, "I will be like the Most High," (Is. 14:14). Satan has always desired to be like God. He wishes to be considered equal to or greater than Yahweh. The name Allah in Islam is always used in conjunction with the word Ta'ala, The Most High. If we look again at the verse, we see that the Name of the Beast is not simply a name of blasphemy, but rather it is the name of blasphemy. It is the highest quintessential blasphemy— it claims to possess the attributes or nature of Yahweh, the God of the Bible. As such, the Name of the Beast is a claim to be equal to or greater than God and the Messiah. The Name of the Beast will contain or imply some form of anti-Yahweh and anti-Christ doctrinal or creedal language that will exalt another above Yahweh.

We know that the Antichrist will be the premiere representative of a faith that worships not the God of the Bible, but rather the adversary, Satan disguised as God. The god of the Antichrist will not only be God's premiere enemy, but he will masquerade as the Most High God.

This masquerading serves a two-fold purpose. First, of course, it fulfills Satan's desire to be like God. Secondly, it confuses and deceives mankind into offering their worship to him instead of God.

THE SHAHADATAN: ISLAM'S BLASPHEMOUS CREED

As we have already seen, the theology of Islam thoroughly—even systematically—fulfills all of the definitive elements of anti-Yahweh, anti-Christ theology as specified by John the Apostle in his first epistle. Beyond denying the Trinity, Islam also denies the Divine Incarnation of Jesus Christ as the Son of God, as well as his death, burial and resurrection. But beyond all of this, Islam has memorialized its anti-Yahweh, anti-Christ theology specifically in a creedal formula.

The Shahadatan is the Islamic creed or declaration of faith. In Arabic it reads as follows: La ilaha il Allah, Muhammadan Rasul-Allah.

This means: "There is no God but Allah and Muhammad is The One sent by Allah [The Messenger of Allah]"

The two elements of this creed are the following:

Allah is the only One True Supreme God and Muhammad (The Praised One) is the seal and final messenger of Allah.

These two components of the Shahadatan, in a very succinct manner, perhaps better than any creedal statement could, perfectly fulfill both dimensions of the definition of blasphemy that we just discussed. First, it attempts to claim that another god other than Yahweh is the Only True God.

And secondly, the Shahadatan is blasphemous toward the God of the Bible because it attempts to place Muhammad in the position that only Jesus the Messiah can fill. Muslims identify Muhammad as Al-Insan Al-Kamel, the perfect man; Rahmatan-lil-A'alameen, a mercy to all mankind; Al-rasul Al-A'tham, greatest of all sent by God; Shafi, Healer; Munji, saviour; Mahdi guided one/deliverer; Mustafa, chosen; Amir, the prince; Awal, first; Akher, last; Rasul Al-Malahim, messenger of the Last-Days battles, and finally Muhammad, the praised one.

Such are the blasphemous names of Muhammad.

Yet despite the quintessentially blasphemous nature of the Shahadatan, it is recited into the ear of every Muslim child the moment after they are born. It is the verbally expressed, outward sign of conversion to Islam. According to Biblical theology, the Shahadatan could not be more perfectly blasphemous.

AN INDICATOR OF ALLEGIANCE

The next obvious and essential observation that needs to be made is that all four of these elements—the Mark, the Name, the Number, and the Image of the Beast—are indicators of allegiance and submission to Beast. "If anyone worships the beast and his image and receives his mark on the forehead or on the hand, he, too, will drink of the wine of God's fury, which has been poured full strength into the cup of his wrath. He will be tormented with burning sulfur in the presence of the holy angels and of the Lamb. And the smoke of their torment rises forever and ever. There is no rest day or night for those who worship the beast and his image, or for anyone who receives the mark of his name." This calls for patient endurance on the part of the saints who obey God's commandments and remain faithful to Jesus (Revelation 14:9-12).

In the simplest of terms, the Mark of the Beast is essentially the emblem, the symbol, or the identifying mark of the coming Beast kingdom. By donning this mark, people will identify with the Kingdom of the Beast and the values and beliefs that this kingdom represents.

The next point is essential: The Mark of the Beast (the identifying symbol of the Antichrist kingdom) is not something that someone might accidentally embrace or receive. It is rather, an outward indicator of an inward allegiance or submission to the Beast. It is something that one must choose to accept.

The Scriptures make it clear that anyone who receives the Mark of the Beast will spend eternity in hell. One cannot accept the Mark of the Beast without also implicitly denying Christ. Biblically speaking, it is only a denial or rejection of Christ and his Gospel that can cause any individual to end up in hell. Sadly, I've actually spoken with a few individuals who, although they reserve absolutely no room in their lives for Christ, adamantly swear that they will never accept the Mark of the Beast! The Mark of the Beast is not some loophole or back door clause that Satan will use to bypass God's normal Biblical standards of justice in order to slip as many people into hell as he can. Yet, as foolish as this may sound, there are many who perceive the Mark of the Beast in precisely this way. In receiving the Mark of the Beast, there is an implicit acceptance and identification with a very specific anti-Yahweh and anti-Christ theology.

≈80≈
Unlocking The
Number Of The Beast

✦━━✦━━✦

In all of the various attempts to explain the meaning of the number 666 throughout the history of the Church, none make enough sense to gain any measure of universal recognition. Some scholars claim that the number 666 represents the fullness of fallen and rebellious mankind. But this theory fails to explain why there is a Name, a Mark, a Number and an Image of the Beast. Why does God give us different flavors? This symbol represents something utterly blasphemous and this vague explanation does virtually nothing to help us identify any specific Antichrist system or its leader. Perhaps the most commonly accepted interpretation is that the number 666 is to be solved by a mystical form of Hebrew numerology called the Gematria. But the Bible gives us a strong exhortation to use wisdom to discern this issue "This calls for wisdom" (Revelation 13:18) How would such puzzling numerological symbolism convey any such wisdom?

In short, the Gematria is a mystical form of numerology that assigns a numerical value to each letter from any given name. After the sum total of all of the letters are added up, the final result is the number of that individual's name. If this sounds strange, that's because it is. In fact, the use of the Gematria is closely rooted to a form of Jewish Kabalistic mysticism—a practice that many have labeled as occultist. American pop-star Madonna—not exactly anyone's role model of Biblical virtue—is a strong devotee of a pop-form of Kabala. In any case, because of the possible occultist dimensions of this practice, some interpreters have suggested that this passage in Revelation has nothing to do with the Gematria. The use of the Gematria has been used by some to create a myriad of Antichrists: American President William Jefferson Clinton, Ronald Wilson Reagan, George W. Bush, Bill Gates, Mikhail Gorbachev and nearly every other world leader or high-profile power broker you can imagine all have had their names manipulated in various ways to equal 666. Yet no one knows if this Gematria should be applied in English, Hebrew, Latin or Greek; neither does the Bible give us any indicator as to what we should use. Do we use Greek because the Book of Revelation was written in Greek?

Some researchers, including the Roman Catholic priest Louis Maracci and English Scholar Humphrey Prideaux, have reportedly found in the Byzantine name Maometis the number of the Beast:

M(40)A(1)O(70)M(40)E(5)T(300)I(10)S(200) in Greek Gematria totals 666.

Or do we use Hebrew because it is the original Biblical language? Since Hebrew doesn't really use vowels, this could be difficult. For example, in Hebrew, George is spelled "Jorj" or even "Jrj". Do we use the middle name, or simply the first and last name? In President Clinton's case, there is the question of whether to use Bill or William? Should the title of "President," be retained or not? Should the whole name add up to 666 or should each name—the first, middle and the last name—simply add up to 6, thus leading to three sixes? Are you beginning to see the many problems with this approach?

Others have suggested that the number 666 will only serve as a confirming equation after the Church has already solved the mystery. But this certainly seems rather anti-climatic. For if this is the case, what is the real purpose of this passage? Why is there such a strong command to discern this number?

There are other problems with this method as well. The oldest Biblical fragment that contains this passage, the Oxyrhynchus Papyri LVI 4499 does not have the number 666. Instead it has the number 616.

Figure 1 The newest volume of Oxyrhynchus (P.Oxy. LVI 4499). The earliest known witness to this particular section of the Book of Revelation (late third / early fourth century). The number—chi (hexakosiai - 600), iota (deka - 10), stigma (hex - 6)—is in the third line of the fragment.

In his Against Heresies, Ireneaus mentions that he was aware of several texts of the Book of Revelation that contained the number 616 rather than 666. Irenaeus claimed that the presence of 616 was due to a scribal error. 1 Nevertheless, from this record, we know that the Oxyrhynchus fragment is more than a mere anomaly. Apparently the number 616 was commonly accepted in certain quarters of the early Church. Also, Irenaeus does not mention this one variant reading, but rather "various readings"—plural. Even in the early Church, there was more than one variant. Manuscript evidence also provides us with at least one early text where the number 665 is found instead of either 666 or 616. 2

Could it be possible that certain scribes viewed what were thought to be three Greek letters (Chi Xi Stigma), when in reality these were three squiggles or foreign symbols. Perhaps that is the reason they could not make up their minds as to which of the Greek letters these resemble?

One thing we know for certain, whatever this Gematriatic "number" is, it must also correlate with what we know about the Name of the Beast—its blasphemous anti-Yahweh and anti-Christ creed. If you accept all the evidence I presented regarding Islam being the Antichrist, then this symbol must be understood by the language of Islam—Arabic.

THROUGH EASTERN EYES—IT'S AN ISLAMIC CREED

As a former Muslim, I first noticed when reading these passages that they closely mirror certain customs of my people, who put badges on their foreheads and arms with blasphemous declarations scrawled on them with these very symbols. In fact they wear these badges with identical symbols in every Muslim demonstration or gathering. They do this in obedience to the Qur'an which spoke of the end days regarding the "beast of the earth" and how this beast will mark all Muslims on the forehead in order to distinguish them from non-Muslims. (Qur'an 27:82) This piece of information led me to believe that Islam is the missing link to this prophetic puzzle. Yet I needed to examine the text as far back as I could go. I expected to find an Islamic declaration of some sort. As soon as I began to examine the Codex Vaticanus (AD 350) Greek text of the Book of Revelation, I immediately noticed that the supposed Greek letters (Chi Xi Stigma) that are used to translate to the number 666 very much resemble the most common creed of Islam Bismillah (or Basmalah), written in Arabic. Bismillah literally means "In the Name of Allah," and is followed by the symbol of crossed swords, which is used universally throughout the Muslim world to signify Islam.

The Basmalah is as follows:

مسب هللا ميحرلا نمحرلا

bismi-llāhi ar-raḥmāni ar-raḥīmi

Keep in mind that Arabic is from right to left, let's look at each word:

 Bismi (Name of)

llah (Allah)

Only the first two words (Bism, Allah) are necessary to constitute the Basmalah. Al-Rahman and Al-Raheem are generally added.

Image 2   Image 3   Image 4

Image 2 is from the Codex Vaticanus, A.D. 350 Bismillah (In the name of Allah) is clearly visible. The word "Allah" is at an upward angle and the two swords are clear. Allah written in an upward fashion should not be an issue. It is common since in many Islamic badges, banners, or coins such words are written sideways or would follow a circle of the crescent and such.

Image 3 is a coin from the Umayyad Muslim era with the word 'Allah' vertically as seen on the right, vertical 'Allah' can be seen on the left side of the coin, and is identical to what was written in Codex Vaticanus seen above the middle word in image 2, or the word seen in image 4.

Image 5   Image 6

Image 7
Arabic in Persian Script
In the name of Allah
(Bismillah) Most Gracious Most Merciful

Image 4, Bismillah with the word Allah is adjusted horizontally as Arabic would read.

Image 5 on the top line, we have arranged the actual words (from right to left) Bism (In the name of), then Allah followed by the crossed swords of Islam, taken from an Islamic emblem. Below them are the Greek letters Chi Xi Stigma. Notice the striking similarities between the letters, words, and symbols. Of course, the clearest resemblances are the name Allah and the Jihad symbol.

Image 6 Here we have placed the Greek Xi exactly as it appears in the Codex Vatanicus Manuscript next to a flipped Allah.

Image 5 to be compared with image 4, from right to left, the first word "Bism."

Bismillah (In the name of Allah,) is the most commonly used phrase throughout all of Islamadom, even more than the declaration of faith itself—the Shahadatan. It is written or recited at the beginning of every letter, every ceremony, every speech, every sacred recitation, every Qur'anic chapter, and before the slaughter of any animal.

In light of this, is it possible that the Apostle John, while receiving his divine revelation, did not see Greek letters, but instead was supernaturally shown Arabic words and an Islamic symbol, which he then faithfully recorded?

Could it be that years after John recorded these images; scribes commissioned to copy the text were unable to recognize the foreign words and symbols and thus thought them to be Greek letters? Might this be why some texts record them differently?

Remember, the Biblical requirement that the Name and the symbol (mark) both fulfill the same meaning—the Name of Blasphemy, or the name of Allah. While the Name of the Beast is also the Name of Blasphemy, so this mark is a similarly blasphemous name and slogan—that of the god that will be worshipped by the final Antichrist Empire. If this is so, how would the English translation of Revelation 13:18 read?

First let's look at how the translators have dealt with the verse. More than likely, it was transliterated word for word, and then ascribed the interpretation most logical for its context:

Hode	here
Esti	is
Sophia	wisdom
Echo	let him that
Nous	understanding
Psephizo	count/decide/reckon
Arithmos	the number/multitude
Therion	of the beast
Gar	for
Esti	it is
Arithmos	the number/multitude
Anthropos	of a man
Kai	and
Autos	his
Arithmos	number/multitude
Chi xi stigma	666

(Revelation 13:18)

Now consider the alternate translation that the Allah Theory could produce. The Greek word Psephizo, translated above as "count," can also quite naturally mean "reckon" or "to decide." Likewise, the Greek word Arithmos, translated above as "number" can also mean "an indefinite number or multitude," "multitude" in the case of more than one, such as a multitude of people. With this in mind, consider the following translation, as it makes very good sense:

"Here is wisdom. Let him that hath understanding reckon (or decide, discern) the multitude of the beast, for it is the multitude of a man [that is, Muhammad and or the Mahdi-Antichrist] and his multitude [are identified through the following] 'In the Name of Allah and the two swords (or Jihad).'"

In fact, at least one translation has used a similar construct. The Restoration Scriptures True Name Edition, a commonly used Messianic Bible Version has translated this verse as: "And that no man might buy, or sell, except he had the mark, or the name of the beast, in their right hand, even the multitude who have his name." (Revelation 13:17) These are a multitude of (Muslim) followers of a man (the Mahdi/Antichrist).

Reading the Messianic Restoration Bible makes very good sense. It seems to employ inductive application more accurately. The usage of "multitude" for people is in fact supported throughout Scripture. Compare this possible translation with the following passage concerning the multitude of the Beast: "And he Says unto me, the waters which thou saw, where the whore sits, are peoples, and multitudes, and nations, and tongues." (Revelation 17:15)

The whore sitting on the beast controls the "multitudes," which are peoples and nations who are part of the Beast Empire. Beyond this, according to the Book of Daniel, these "multitudes" will worship "a god of fortresses"—or more clearly, a god of war. Surely this is the best description that could be used to describe Allah, the god of Islam. Regarding Antichrist and his multitude (followers) Ezekiel also confirms, "This is Pharaoh and all his multitude, Says the Lord GOD." (Ezekiel 31:18)

Likewise, I am not surprised then to see many similarities between the symbols of the various Islamic Jihad groups and the symbols I have just highlighted as the identifying names and symbols of the Beast. The following banner of Islam is nothing new. It even includes the Shahadatan, which meets both requirements from the Bible for a mark and a name. The two swords with the Shahadatan have also been the mark of Islamic Jihad throughout the ages including Arabia where it originated from.

Hamas Emblem

As an interesting piece of trivia, even in lyrics of the rock-and-roll song Bohemian Rhapsody, "Bismillah" is used in connection with Beelzebub (Ba'al of the flies, or Lord of the flies). Beelzebub, according to Scripture, is another name for Satan. The lyrics of this song are:

> But I'm just a poor boy and nobody loves me
> He's just a poor boy from a poor family
> Spare him his life from this monstrosity
> Easy come easy go – will you let me go
> Bismillah! No – we will not let you go – let him go
> Bismillah! We will not let you go – let him go
> Bismillah! We will not let you go – let me go
> Will not let you go – let me go (never)
> Never let you go – let me go
> Never let me go
> No, no, no, no, no, no, no –
> Oh mama mia, mama mia, mama mia let me go
> Beelzebub has a devil put aside for me, for me, for me...

Freddy Mercury, the author of this song, a homosexual and a Zoroastrian, adopted Bismillah from his Iranian heritage. But it is certainly interesting that he tied it to Satan and not Allah. In the song, Satan (Beelzebub) has assigned to him a devil that will not let him go.

Muslims do believe, in accordance with their prophet Muhammad that a devil is assigned to them and even has dwelt in every Muslim. Abu Tha'labah al-Khushani said: "The Messenger of Allah said: 'The Jinn [devils] are of three types: a types that has wings, and they fly through the air; a type that looks like snakes and dogs; and a type that stops for a rest then resumes its journey.'"[3] Allah's Apostle said: "There is none amongst you with whom is not a legion from amongst the Jinn (devil). They (the Companions) said: Allah's Apostle with you too? Thereupon he said: Yes, but Allah helps me against him and so I am safe from his hand and he does not command me but for good."[4]

In the film Kingdom of Heaven, Saladin (Salahuddin) wears on his arms the badge of Islam "Bismillah," with the words Al-Rahman Al-Rahim (most compassionate most merciful). The director of the movie was a stickler for historical accuracy. Muslims used to wear this symbol as a badge of identification. If one is looking for a literal name, "Bism" actually means "name." If we are looking for the name for this Satan, "Allah" is definitely one—it fits both a creed and a literal name. Why must we spend endless hours trying to use some strange Hebrew numerology to try to figure out if someone's name equals 666 when we already have a perfect fulfillment of the Mark of the Beast right before us?

≈81≈

Unlocking The Mark Of The Beast

FIRST TEST THE SPIRITS

So what's the danger in taking the mark? What is the problem of accepting Allah and Muhammad into your heart? Well, it's eternal damnation. The choice is yours. If you are Muslim, this is your chance to come to Christ and be saved before this marking takes place.

Am I spreading fear? Sure I am. The same way that I scare my teenage children when I tell them that promiscuous sex can cause them to get AIDS. A monogamous marriage can save them from a lot of hell. Islam offers a deadly chalice filled with blasphemy. Muslims claim that faith in God requires us to utter the formula, "There is no God but Allah and Muhammad is His messenger." First of all, the phrase has a major problem—the word "Allah." The notion that Allah simply means "god" is an utter lie that is easy to refute. Allah can never simply mean "god", even if it evolved from common usage in Arabic. Allah is the name of a deity just as Jehovah is a name of a different deity. The Arabic word for God is "*Al-Ilah*" (The God) or "*Al-Rab*" (The Lord). The fact that Allah is a name can be seen in viewing the most common phrase that is used by Muslims: "Bismillah" or "BismAllah", which means "In the Name of Allah." In many English Qur'ans, it is at the beginning of every chapter translated falsely as, "In the Name of God." To test my claim here, that Allah can never mean God; the next time you run into a Muslim, ask him what must you do to convert to Islam. He will be elated of course, then will quickly respond: "Just utter the creed, there is no God but Allah and Muhammad is His messenger." Then ask him what "Allah" means. He will gladly say "God." Then ask him, "If Allah simply means God, why then insist that I declare that 'There is no God but Allah?' Why cannot I simply say, 'There is no God but God?' Why must I utter this creed in Arabic?" Tell him that you insist in only uttering the phrase, "There is no God but God" He will insist that this is not acceptable for an Islamic conversion. Ask him, "Why? Doesn't Allah after all simply mean God? Isn't that what you just said? Checkmate—Jesus style.

Christians have no problem when one says of an evil person, "his God is the devil," or, "David Koresh's God must have been the devil." Dare a Westerner to tell a "moderate" Muslim "Osama Bin Laden's Allah is the devil." Try it, but before you do, make sure you have your foot on the accelerator.

If the God *Allah* and the God *Jehovah* were the same, why all the Jihad expansion and wars against Christian nations, forcing people to choose the creed or the blade? Allah is the name of an imposter. Do not drink from his chalice, but partake from the cup of Christ. Make sure that your name is registered in the Book of Life.

THE MARK

The Greek word *charagma*, used for "mark" means "a stamp, an imprinted mark" (Strong's 5480). So a follower of the Antichrist will have a stamp on some sort of material as a badge to be placed on the forehead or arm. In John's time, the use for "charagma" was reserved for slaves in what was called a *badge of servitude*" (*Strong's 5482*). So it's a badge that declares slavery and ownership by the master and followers use it to demonstrate allegiance to this master. This would fit with Islam since according to Islamic theology, Muslims are "slaves of Allah." Islam is the religion of submission.

These followers have an option to either place this *badge of servitude* on the *foreheads* or the *arms*. Western analysts think that the mark is placed on the hand. This is not necessarily the only spot. We know from the Greek word *dexios*, which could also be translated "right side", "right arm" or "right shoulder".

To become a Muslim (literally means submitter), one must confess the *Shahadatan* declaration to demonstrate allegiance and servitude to Allah and Muhammad. This submission is always combined with commitment to fight the world: "Men, do you know what you are pledging yourselves to in swearing allegiance to this man? 'Yes. In swearing allegiance to him we are pledging to wage war against all mankind'" (Ishaq: 204). "We are steadfast trusting Him. We have a Prophet by whom we will conquer all men" (Ishaq: 471). "In faith I do not fear the army of fate. He gave us the blood of their best men to drink when we led our army against them. We are a great army with a pungent smell. And we attack continuously, wherever our enemy is found" (Ishaq: 574).

This mentality can be observed in many of the arm badges and headbands they wear. These items contain Islamic mottos, creeds, words, and symbols which fulfill Scripture's mandate. Often on the forehead the bands worn read: "No god but Allah, Muhammad is his messenger." Another favorite is the crescent of Islam included with "The Islamic Organization." These all fulfill the blasphemous nature of the Mark of the Beast.

ISLAM FORCES THE BADGE ON FOREHEADS

Amazingly, and in keeping perfectly with what the Bible predicted so long ago regarding the beast and his mark, the badge is in fact an Islamic commandment from the prophet himself: "Allah will save a man from my nation above all creation on Judgment Day. In front of him will be laid 99 registers for his sins. Every register is as long as the eye can see. Then he is asked, 'Do you deny any of these?' Then he says, 'No O Lord.' Then he is asked, 'Do you have any excuse?' He responds, 'No Lord,' Then he is told, 'You have but one good deed and there will be no condemnation for you today'. A badge is brought forth. Scrolled across it are the words: 'No God but Allah, and Muhammad is His messenger.' Then he is asked to bring forth his deeds. He asks, O Lord, what is this badge that is with these registers?' He is told, 'You will receive no condemnation.' The deeds are put on one hand, and the badge in the other. Then the registers will float and the badge will outweigh the registers" (Tirmuthi 2639).

To sum it up, the "Name of the Beast" along with variations of the name of Allah, is worn as a *sign of submission* on the right arm or foreheads. Islam is submission and allegiance to a foreign god, the Shahadatan is blasphemous, the badge worn by Muslims on the foreheads—all of these things meet the Biblical requirements of the Mark of the Beast.

And just in case you are still in doubt, even the part of the Bible that predicted the beast will mark the foreheads is in the Qur'an and the Hadith: *Dabat Al-Ard* (literally the Beast out of the Earth) is an Islamic version of the account of the "Beast of the Earth" in Revelation 13:11. But unlike the Bible, in which this beast is evil, the Qur'an gives him a holy mission to revive Islam and mark the foreheads of all true Muslim believers. According to Islamic tradition, the Beast emerges in the Last-Days: "And when the word is fulfilled concerning them, We shall bring forth a Beast of the Earth to speak unto them because mankind had not faith in Our revelations" (Qur'an. 27:82). "The prophet of Islam declared, 'The first of the signs that will come is the rising of the sun from the place of its setting and the emergence of the Beast upon the people. Whichever of these two occurs before the other then the other is right behind it.'"[5]

Why do Muslims mark their foreheads with badges of submission to Allah? It comes from their belief that the hour is near: "The task of the Beast will be to distinguish the believers from the non-believers, with Prophet Moses's staff it [the beast] will draw a line on the forehead of every [Muslim] believer whereby his face will become bright and luminous and with the ring of Solomon it will seal the nose of every non-believer where by his whole face will become black. Thus there will be complete distinction between the Muslim and non-Muslim, so that if many parties sit at a dinner table, the Muslim and non-Muslim will be distinguished."[6]

Can you imagine my shock when I studied the Bible? I was taught that a Beast would come "out of the earth" and he would mark the foreheads of all true Muslims. Do you see how Satan has turned everything upside down for Muslims? As a Muslim, I wanted the Mark of the Beast! Not surprisingly, according to Islamic tradition, this Beast comes out of Mecca. "The Beast will come out from Al-Masjid Al-Haraam in Makkah." "The Prophet took me to a place in the desert, near Makkah. It was a dry piece of land surrounded by sand. The prophet said, 'The Beast will emerge from this place.' It was a very small area."[7] Even as the Last-Days Beast religion has emerged out of Mecca so also Islam has the Beast emerging out of Mecca.

Amazingly, in the Bible, the angel took John to the desert to see the "woman," or the "prostitute" riding a beast that most likely comes out of the desert of Arabia. Mecca is the "holiest" and most central location in all of Islamadom. What is evil to us is holy to them. According to Islamic tradition, "[The] Beast is some form of ultra-conglomerate of many different animals."[8]

PLEDGING ALLEGIANCE TO THE BEAST

In the early days of Muhammad's career, he often asked those who had expressed a desire to follow him to make a pledge of allegiance or submission to him. This pledge is known as bay'ah. It is an outward oath or pledge promising allegiance—complete submission even—to the ruler.[9]

After Muhammad died, this practice of making a pledge was carried on under the Caliphs. The Muslims would make a pledge of allegiance to the Caliph, and likewise the Caliph would make a pledge of allegiance to Allah to rule strictly according to Islamic law. Many modern Islamist books and articles that speak about the restoration of the Caliphate present the giving of the *bay'ah* (allegiance) as a very common theme.

Like anxious children waiting and planning for Christmas morning, many very eager Islamists look forward to the day when all citizens of Dar-al-Islam (the regions and lands under the authority of the Caliphate) will be required to make the bay'ah pledge to the Caliph. According to Islamic tradition, those who do not make this pledge will die the death of an idolater: "One who withdraws his hand from obedience to the Ruler (Emir) will find no argument in his defense when he stands before Allah on the Day of Judgment, and one who dies without having bound himself by an oath of allegiance (bay'ah) to an

Emir will die the death of one belonging to the days of Jahillyya (Pre-Islamic ignorance and idolatry)."[10]

Similar to the Antichrist, anyone who refuses to give allegiance will be killed. The evidence of the mistreatment of Christians and Jews in the Islamic system is immense, but it will of course only increase in the days to come. This is what the Bible warned when it stated that whoever did not accept the Mark of the Beast will be killed.

≈ 82 ≈
Unlocking The
Image Of The Beast

✦━━✦·✳·✦━━✦

Possibly influenced by Laserium shows and Star Trek, many prophecy analysts attempt to take the passage of Revelation 13:15 literally. Thus many are expecting the Antichrist to produce a literal animated statue that will speak, which everyone will be commanded to bow to: "He was given power to give breath to the image of the first beast, so that it could speak and cause all who refused to worship the image to be killed." But whenever one interprets a passage that was intended to be allegorical or an allegorical passage that is intended to be interpreted literally, they have fallen prey to a common pitfall. The prophecies concerning Israel's return to the land were always intended to be taken literally, yet for decades the Church allegorized these passages and interpreted them as referring to itself. The Seven Mountains of Revelation 17 are another prime example of symbolism that has been improperly interpreted literally. Imagine what kind of interpretation we get if we literalize, "the dragon was enraged at the woman." The Bible would become a child's fairy-tale. How can anyone literalize, "and I saw a beast coming out of the sea?" What about: "one of the heads of the beast seemed to have had a fatal wound, but the fatal wound had been healed?" Many interpret this passage to man that the Antichrist will die from a fatal head wound and then come back to life. But if this scenario were true, then this would mean that Satan would be a giver of life. But this is absurd.

In seeing these absurdities, we can see the need to dig deeper into the allegoric meaning of certain passages. So how are we to understand this passage then: "He was given power to give breath to the image of the first beast, so that it could speak and cause all who refused to worship the image to be killed?" The obvious interpretation is that the prior beast *kingdom* that was wounded shall come back to life again. This is simply a revival of a wounded kingdom—not an individual. When we examine Scripture, first we must commit ourselves to some deeper investigation and then we must allow the Bible to interpret itself. The concept of reviving and creating an image of the Beast is something that the Scriptures give us ample information to understand properly. If we search through the Bible for various usages of the word "image," we will gain significant insight into the nature of what this passage is actually talking about. There are several aspects to the meaning of this "image":

1. AN IMAGE AS IN A TEMPLE OBJECT

The Bible describes "an image" as a religious or national symbol set up in the Temple, "For the Israelites will live many days without king or prince, without sacrifice or sacred stones, without ephod or an *image*" (Hosea 3:4). When Israel was destroyed as a kingdom, it lost everything. It lost it's centralized national religious institution with the destruction of the Temple (sacrifice, ephod), and also lost its national symbols—the Ark of the Covenant, Menorah, and the rest of the Temple articles. Islam also has a Temple for Allah (the Ka'ba) along with Temple articles (the Black Stone) as we will discuss in more detail later. Jehovah's Temple articles in Jerusalem were a shadow of greater things to come—the Messiah, while Allah's Temple articles (the Black Stone) resemble a shadow of Satan's coming—the Antichrist.

2. AN IMAGE AS IN A NATIONAL EMBLEM

An example of this would be the image of Caesar imprinted on coins that represented the Roman Empire. The Mark of the Beast might be an emblem or symbol of the Beast Empire that carries with it a blasphemous creedal element. An official image or emblem of a kingdom gives it a sense of national identity: "He ordered them to set up an image in honor of the beast who was wounded by the sword and yet lived" (Revelation 13:14). This "image" of the Beast (empire) would constitute the replicating of the old monster—the ruthless Islamic Empire that fell. This is the primary meaning of the verse. However, it is not the only explanation of every verse containing the word "image". To make or carry an image, a flag or an emblem of something, is akin to showing support and allegiance to whatever the image or emblem represents. That is, the followers of the Beast will declare their support and submission to the Beast Empire and all that it stands for. The followers will espouse its purpose, its ideology or doctrines and its goals. These emblems that once died with the old kingdom are revived again, as we see in Islam. An image could be a mark of Satan that identifies his followers. The Antichrist will, in this way, mark his followers with a blasphemous creed.

3. AN IMAGE AS IN AN IDOL

An Image also could represent an idol—a medium that represents a living being. One could erect an idol to a god. King Nebuchadnezzar erected a massive image (a dead idol) of himself and demanded all of his subjects to bow and worship it. This is an example of idolatry. This could easily apply to Satan, who is called Ba'al, Bel, and Beelzebub. One could erect an image of Ba'al (Satan) that would serve as a medium and a representation of Satan worship. This type of image is not restricted to a statue however; it can even be a stone such as the black stone meteorite in the Kaba in Mecca, "At last the mayor was able to quiet them down enough to speak. 'Citizens of Ephesus,' he said. 'Everyone knows that Ephesus is the official guardian of the temple of the great Artemis, whose image fell down to us from heaven'" (Acts 19:35). The image of Diana was not represented by a statue, but a Black Stone which was worshiped in Ephesus identified as The Image of Diana. Yet, these images are all symbolic of Satan worship, "What say I then? That the idol is any thing, or that which is offered in sacrifice to idols is any thing? But I say, that the things which the Gentiles sacrifice, they sacrifice to devils, and not to God: and I would not that ye should have fellowship with devils" (I Corinthians 10:19-20). Satan sets up idols as representations of himself until he comes down to earth and establishes himself as the Antichrist in human form.

4. IMAGE AS IN LIKENESS

"For whom he did foreknow, he also did predestinate to be conformed to the image of his Son, that he might be the firstborn among many brethren" (Roman 8:29). In this case, "image" is in matter of likeness.

5. THE ULTIMATE IMAGE

The ultimate image would be the Antichrist himself, which will be the manifestation of Lucifer in a human image. In the end, the living image of Satan will attempt to replace Christ—this is the Antichrist.

DESTROYING CHRISTIAN IMAGES

Islam wants to destroy every image that represents Jehovah. This is why Muslims want to destroy Jewish and Christian symbols. But the reason that Muslims desire to destroy Christian and Jewish "images" is because Islam desires to destroy Christianity and Judaism altogether. According to Islamic tradition, when Jesus returns, he does not merely come to convert most Christians to Islam but to literally abolish Christianity. This fact is understood when we analyze a very well-known tradition which states that when Jesus returns he will "break the cross, kill swine, and abolish Jizyah. Allah will perish all religions except Islam." The three actions are based on the notion that Jesus will assault all of the symbols of Christianity in order to abolish it as a religion. Shafi and Usmani explain that to "break the cross" means to "abolish worship of the cross."[11] Muslims believe that Jesus will break or remove all crosses from the rooftops and steeples of churches throughout the earth. This action is understood as a clear statement regarding Jesus' disapproval of the notion that he was ever crucified on a cross. The killing of the swine is so that the "Christian belief of its lawfulness is belied." The reason for abolishing the Jizyah tax (the compulsory poll-tax that non-Muslims must pay in order to live in a Muslim land) is based on the idea that when Jesus returns, the Jizyah tax will no longer be accepted. The only choice that Christians will have is to accept Islam or die. As Sideeque M.A. Veliankode states in Doomsday Portents and Prophecies, "Jesus, the son of Mary will soon descend among the Muslims as a just judge. Jesus will, therefore, judge according to the law of Islam...all people will be required to embrace Islam and there will be no other alternative."[12]

Harun Yahya, in his book Jesus Will Return, affirms that, "Jesus will remove all systems of disbelief in that period." Classic Muslim jurists also confirm these interpretations. Consider, for example, the ruling of Ahmad ibn Naqib al-Misri (d. 1368) from The Reliance of the Traveller, the classic Shafi manual of Islamic jurisprudence: "...the time and the place for the poll tax is before the final descent of Jesus (upon whom be peace). After his final coming, nothing but Islam will be accepted from them, for taking the poll tax is only effective until Jesus' descent (upon him and our Prophet be peace)."[13]

DESTROYING ISLAMIC IMAGES
CRESCENT MOON—THE IMAGE OF THE BEAST

So while Islamic tradition claims that Jesus will return and destroy all symbols of Christianity, there are also significant parallels in Psalm 83 and Judges 8:21 that say He will, in fact, destroy the symbols of Islam. Psalm 82-83 claims there will be a war between Messiah and the Antichrist. The Gideon-Messiah or War-Messiah who comes to rescue Israel will carry out an important task: "Do to them as you did to Midian, as you did to Sisera and Jabin at the river Kishon, who perished at Endor and became like refuse on the ground. Make their nobles like Oreb and Zeeb, all their princes like Zebah and Zalmunna, who said, 'Let us take possession of the pasturelands of God'" (Psalm 83:9-12).

After listing several Muslim nations that form an End-Time alliance to destroy Israel, the Psalmist prays: "Make their nobles like Oreb, and like Zeeb: yea, all their princes as Zebah, and as Zalmunna." But what happened in the story of Zebah and Zalmunna? The answer is found in Judges 8:21: "Then Zebah and Zalmunna said, 'Rise yourself, and fall upon us; for as the man is, so is his strength.' And Gideon arose and slew Zebah and Zalmunna; and he took the crescent ornaments that were on the necks of their camels" (Psalm 83:11).

Later in verse 26, the Bible says that the Midianite kings were wearing the same crescent ornaments around their necks. After Gideon stripped all of the crescent ornaments off of the slain kings, the people and the camels, he melted the gold. The story of Gideon is the story of Messiah. It is also the story of David and Goliath—a parallel to the showdown between Christ and the Antichrist, who blasphemes the God of Israel and proclaims, "I am against you O Most Haughty One" (Jeremiah 50:31). David, with precision bombing, lodges a stone into Goliath's forehead. This is what happens to Babylon and the Antichrist. "Their arrows shall be like those of an expert warrior; furthermore, none shall return in vain" (Jeremiah 50:9). This is modern precision bombing. Not a single missile will miss it' target. Bel, the moon-god, will also be destroyed and all the idols of the crescent moon taken away, "Bel is shamed. Merodach is broken in pieces; Her idols are humiliated, Her images are broken in pieces" (Jeremiah 50:2). Bel, or Ba'al, the cult of the crescent-moon is finally destroyed. Bel has always been symbolized by the crescent-moon.

Psalm 83 gives us the summary of the confrontation with Islam, in which God will do to the enemies of Israel what Gideon did to Midian. It is crucial to understand that Gideon as a judge of Israel is a prophetic type of Jesus. He is symbolic of the fighting Messiah. Joseph is symbolic of the suffering Messiah, and David of the King Messiah. So if we want to find out more about what Christ does when He comes to judge, we need to study Gideon. Instead of the Muslim Jesus returning to destroy crosses, we see that a far more ancient Biblical prophecy reveals that when Jesus returns, He will destroy all of the pagan crescent-moon images of Islam. In the same way that Israel, at various times, had to remove the Ashera poles from the high places, so will the crescents also be removed from the highest places (the minarets) during the rule of the Messiah.

THE CRESCENT IS SATAN'S SYMBOL

In Judges 8:21, the word used for crescent is saharon, which literally means crescent moon. It comes from the root of sahar, which is literally used for the name of Satan in Isaiah 14 as Hilal ben Sahar. Hilal, or heylal, is the word that the King James Bible translates as Lucifer. The full phrase actually means "morning star/crescent moon," which is the very symbol of Islam. In other words, the symbol of Islam and the name of Satan are one and the same. This is significant and is a very clear hint into the spiritual origins of Islam and the Antichrist.

So we see that the ancient enemies of Israel worshipped a god that was symbolized by the image of the crescent moon. To this day, this has not changed. In fact, all evidence points to the fact that Allah is simply another name for Bel or Baal, which simply means "lord" and is also a title of reverence to the Babylonian moon-god. The Romans had the same god, and so did the Greeks, who worshipped Gog (Gygez), a war deity called Men. This is also the god that Abraham left behind for Jehovah, the One True God. It comes as no surprise then that Jesus referred to Satan as Beelzebub (Baal Thubab, Arabic) (Matthew 12:24-27). The Hastings Encyclopedia of Religion and Ethics confirms the fact that the Arab name Allah correlates to Bel: "Allah is a pre-Islamic name... corresponding to the Babylonian god known as Bel."[14]

Gideon was named as "Jerub-Ba'al", the one who contends with Ba'al the moon god. Gideon was a type of the warring Messiah because he fought Ba'al. Likewise Christ, the ultimate Jerub-Ba'al will fight Ba'al in the flesh, and bruise his head, completing what was promised in Genesis 3:15.

Dr. Arthur Jeffrey, professor of Islamic and Middle East Studies at Columbia University and one of the world's foremost scholars on Islam, wrote that the name, "Allah" and its feminine form "Allat," were well known in pre-Islamic Arabia and were found in inscriptions uncovered in North Africa. According to Jeffrey's, Allah, "is a proper name applicable only to their peculiar god." He adds, "Allah is a pre-Islamic name corresponding to the Babylonian god known as Bel."[15] "Bel simply means 'lord' and this is a title of reverence to the moon-god Sin."[16]

But maybe you have not seen the significance of all of this. Perhaps Isaiah can add the convincing final piece to complete this puzzle on why this is the moon-god of Islam. Isaiah gives us a powerful picture of what Bel (a.k.a. Allah) will do at the end of the age. Most Westerners miss the hint in the famous passage: "I have sworn by myself, the word is gone out of my mouth in righteousness, and shall not return, That unto me every knee shall bow, every tongue shall swear" (Isaiah 45:23-46:1). This verse is later echoed in the New Testament: "every knee shall bow, every tongue shall confess... that Jesus Christ is Lord" (Philemon 2:8-10). A few verses later, Isaiah also tells of one being in particular who is among them: "Bel bows down, Nebo stoops; Their idols were on the beasts and on the cattle" (Isaiah 46:1). Bel will bow down before God. This is none other than the image of Allah-Satan, the crescent-moon. In the purest form of poetic justice, the demonic god of Islam will bow low before Jesus, the Mighty One of Israel which the beasts wore on their necks: "Their idols were on the beasts and on the cattle" the very symbol that Gideon removed—the crescent moon in Judges 8:21.

THE DESTRUCTION OF BABYLON THROUGH MESSIAH

The connection of this to the Harlot of Babylon can be found in the context of Isaiah 45-47: "The Lady of Kingdoms" (Isaiah 47:5); a place that lives in pleasures (Isaiah 47:8); which no one sees and sins in secret (Isaiah 47:10). Such references must be linked to the Harlot of Babylon in Revelation 17. Unlike the West, which sins in the open, Arabia practices its sins in secret. Yet the God of Prophecy challenges Islam, "Remember the former things of old, For I am God and there is no other, I am God and there is none like Me. Declaring the end from the beginning, And from ancient times things that are not yet done, Saying My council shall stand, And I will do all my pleasure" (Isaiah 46:9-10). If Islam is true, then why has Israel returned as God declared, "For Israel My glory" (Isaiah 46:13). God declares to the heathen Muslims that Messiah will come down to destroy their Babylon through His Son: "He shall do His pleasure on Babylon; And His arm shall be against the Chaldeans" (Isaiah 48:14). God's "arm" is Messiah.

CHRIST CONFRONTS ISLAM WITH THE TRINITY

Speaking to this Harlot "Lady of Kingdoms" and in a challenge to Islam, the Lord Jesus Christ declares what Islam denies; His part in the Trinity: "Come near to Me, hear this; I have not spoken in secret, from the beginning; From the time that it was, I was there, And now the Lord God and His Spirit Have sent Me" (Isaiah 48:16). Jesus is telling them (Mystery Babylon) of His nature and attributes that they have denied. In one solid verse, we see that, "From the time that it was (from the beginning was The Word), I was there; and now the Lord God (The Father) and His Spirit (The Holy Spirit) Have sent Me (The Son)."

It is amazing that few Westerners see the context of this—how the Messiah is denouncing Mystery Babylon and her denial of the Trinity. He confronts the Babylonian Antichrist spirit of I John 2:22.

CRESCENT MOON—SATAN'S IMAGE AND TITLE

In Isaiah 14, we find the story of the sin and the fall of Satan. What we will discover when we analyze the passage a bit closer are some very telling points. The passage reads as follows: "How art thou fallen from heaven, O Lucifer, Son of the Morning! How art thou cut down to the ground, which didst weaken the nations! For thou hast said in thine heart, I will ascend into heaven, I will exalt my throne above the stars of God: I will sit also upon the mount of the congregation, in the sides of the North: I will ascend above the heights of the clouds; I will be like the most High" (Isaiah 14:12-14).

In this passage we are given the name Lucifer, which has through the ages come to sig-nify Satan. In truth, the passage doesn't so much give us a proper name as it provides us with a description of who Satan really is. In Hebrew, the name for this Lucifer is three words: *Heylal Ben Shahar*. Translated fully, this means "Shining One Son of the Morning Star", or "the Shining Brilliant One." "Etymologically, Hebrew *Helel* corresponds to the *Ugaritic hll* which occurs in the following expressions: *bnt hll snnt*, Daughters of Bright-ness, swallows, or perhaps 'Shining Ones' and *bnt hll b'l gml*, 'Daughters of Brightness, Lord of The Crescent Moon."[17] Hilal is an Arabic word that means "Crescent Moon".[18] When we put the whole phrase together, *Heylal Ben Shachar* simply means "Crescent Moon, Son of the Morning Star" (or the Dawn)—or in simpler terms, a crescent moon with a star lingering over it. Of course, this is the very symbol and image of Islam. Remember, we are discussing the "image" of the Beast. Nearly every Islamic flag carries this symbol. Nearly every mosque displays this symbol on the pinnacle of its dome and/or its minarets. Consider the implications of this. Islam applies to itself the very description that the Bible uses to describe Satan. When it comes to Islam, everything is upside down. But what makes this so damning to Islam is that Hilal was the very name of the Lord of the Ka'ba, according to Muhammad's biographer, Ibn Hisham. He admits that the pagan Kinanah tribe and Quraysh (Muhammad's tribe) called the supervising god of the *Kaaba IHLAL*. They called the Kaaba "*Beit-Allah*", the house of Allah![19]

～83～

Both Bow
To An Image

THE "BLACK STONE" AND APHRODITE

Both Antichrist's followers and Muslims bow to an image. The great idol of Islam, the Black-Stone and its veneration has been around from time immemorial. Yet despite the very clear correlations, few prophecy Analysts have ever linked this to what has already been spoken of in the Book of Acts: "Everyone knows that Ephesus is the official guardian of the temple of the great Artemis, whose image fell down to us from heaven" (Acts 19:35), The image of Artemis is strikingly similar to the meteorite stone image in Mecca which Allah commands 1.3 billion Muslims to literally bow down and prostrate themselves toward at least seventeen times during their five daily prayers.

John of Damascus (676-749) who lived at the advent of Islam and served in the court of the Caliph, and was thoroughly familiar with Islam from it's inception, writes in his work, Concerning Heresy, "So then, these were idolaters and reverenced the morning star and Aphrodite, who they indeed named Akbar in their own language, which means 'great'" [20] The Islamic connection to Aphrodite is evident in the Muslim cry "Allah Akbar" (Allah is Great). Aphrodite is actually Allat, the feminine root of the name Allah. Even the Greek historian Herodotus, writing in the 5th century B.C., considers Allat the equivalent of Aphrodite: "The Assyrians call Aphrodite Mylitta, the Arabians Alilat." [21] According to the Book of Idols (Kitab al-Asnām) by Hishām b. al-Kalbi, the pre-Islamic Arabs believed Allāt resided in the Kaaba and also had an idol for her inside the sanctuary: "The Quraysh, as well as all the Arabs, were wont to venerate Allāt. They also used to name their children after her, calling them Zayd-Allāt and Taym-Allāt." [22]

Even the Bible confirms this style of naming. The name Sanballat (Nehemiah 2:19) is a derivative of two words; Sin (the Moon-god), and Allat (Aphrodite), the feminine of Allah and one of his three daughters. Such names existed long before Muhammad, whose father's name, Abd-Allah, means "slave of Allah", the Moon-god. Sanballat was known to have harassed Israel as they were attempting to build the Temple, alongside with Tobiah the Amonite and Geshem the Arab. Nothing has changed. Today these same people with an evolved form of the same religion still harass Israel and are the main obstacle to the rebuilding of the Temple.

THE BLACK STONE AS SATAN'S STAR AND IMAGE

But what is this whole thing about venerating an asteroid? What is this whole image about? Does the Bible warn us of this? The Bible is so clear in exposing this issue. Jehovah simply wants us to dig deeper. Lucifer's image is depicted in Revelation 8 and 9 showing Satan wanting to be worshipped. He is a star that fell from heaven: "And the fifth angel sounded, and I saw a star fall from heaven unto the earth: and to him was given the key of the bottomless pit" (Revelation 9:1). This "him" cannot be an object, but rather Satan himself, a living being (him) cast out of heaven as described in Isaiah 14 and Revelation 8:10.

The most important verse in the Qur'an that describes Allah is perfectly mirrored in Isaiah 14. In Isaiah 14, it is Satan or Lucifer that is described as the Bearer of Light, and in the Qur'an it is Allah that is depicted as a lamp (light, torch). In the chapter of the Star, we read: "Allah is the light of the heavens and the earth; a likeness of His light is as a niche in which is a lamp, the lamp is in a glass, (and) the glass is as it were a brightly shining star" (Qur'an 24:35-36). Compare this with Revelation 8:10: "And the third angel sounded, and there fell a great star from heaven, burning as it were a lamp and it fell upon the third part of the rivers and upon the fountains of waters."

Take note of the fact that the death of one-third of the earth's population occurs during the rise of the eighth empire, which will be an Islamic empire. Satan, who is the fallen star, and the destroyer who is unleashed, will precede the "mountain" (empire) that will cause one-third of mankind to die. The Black Stone of Mecca owes its reputation to the tradition that it fell from the "heavens." Like the Black Stone of Aphrodite, the Black Stone of Mecca is also clearly an "image" of Satan. Yet this Satanic image that is created by the Beast in Revelation 13:15 which can speak and cause all who do not worship it to be killed, is mentioned as a holy thing by Muhammad. In an Islamic tradition authenticated by At-Tirmidhi, Al-Abani notes, "Allah will raise up the stone [the Black Stone] on the Day of Judgment, and it will have two-eyes with which it will see and a tongue which it talks with, and it will give witness in favor of everyone who touched it in truth." According to Muslim traditions, the Black Stone is even the redeemer of Muslims. Al-Tirmidhi notes that many years ago, the Black Stone was, "whiter than milk; it was only later that it became black as it absorbed the sins of those who touched it."

Note: Also, Jesus is referred to as the Cornerstone ... the Rock upon which to build a house (wise man builds on Rock vs. sand. Is Satan mocking him again w/ Black Stone?

389

The blasphemy doesn't stop here. The Black Rock, the image of Satan, the Fallen Star, which attempts to take the place of Christ the Great Redeemer is called by Mohammed, the son of perdition Yameen Allah. This means that it is "the right hand of Allah" with which "he touches his servants."[23] It is the visible right hand of the invisible Allah.[24] It is even the Shekina Glory, which dwells in all believers. Venerating it and rotating seven times around it will cleanse the Muslim of all prior sins.

The veneration of Satan through this act of rotating around an idol image is even alluded to in the Bible and rarely understood by Western Analysts. Ezekiel 31:3 declares: "Behold, the Assyrian (the Antichrist, Satan in the Flesh) was a cedar in Lebanon with fair branches, and with a shadowing shroud, and of a high stature; and his top was among the thick boughs. The waters made him great, the deep set him up on high with her rivers running round about his plants, and sent out her little rivers unto all the trees of the field." If we exercise what we learned from Part IV (how to interpret allegoric symbols), we can apply what we learned in the following interpretative paraphrase: "Behold, Satan, a beautiful angel clothed in beautiful covering, an angel with high status. Peoples and multitudes from every nation made him great, and the underworld set him up high with the multitudes running round about his idol and sent out all the people to all the idols that were set for him." This is exactly what we see in the Muslim Hajj, which Muslims do yearly to have their sins forgiven by the right hand of Allah. They come from all over the world to the Ka'ba and roam round about it. In addition, Jeremiah 51:44 tells us, "I will punish Bel in Babylon, And I will bring out of his mouth what he has swallowed; And the nations shall not stream to him anymore." The nations will not flock to Babylon and Bel, the Moon-god, will be ashamed in her. No longer will the nations flock to Mecca to worship Satan. This punishment is not a historic one; it refers to Jerusalem and the invasion of the Temple Mount: "strangers have come into the sanctuaries of the Lord's house" (Jeremiah 51:51). In the Last-Days, there will be two opposing houses, one dedicated to Jehovah and the other to Satan. The "shadowing shroud" in Ezekiel 31:3 could be the black cloth that covers the prostitute Ka'ba in Mecca and the streams perhaps refers to the hordes of people from all over the globe who come to worship Satan by running around his idol and bowing to it by the millions.

The Hajj (pilgrimage). In the center is the Ka'ba. One can see the multitudes spinning round about it. As they complete their spin (7 times around) others come in from the outer multitudes and continue the spin.

The reference to a prostitute in Revelation 17 regarding the "Whore of Babylon" is no coincidence, "And the woman (whore) was arrayed in purple and scarlet color" (v. 17) resembles the near copulating with the Ka'ba's Black Stone, which historically was dedicated to Aphrodite the prostitute goddess that was called "Aphrodite Porne" (Aphrodite the Prostitute), "the goddess adorned in purple", similar to the depictions given in Revelation 17:4.

John of Damascus notes, "After the Haj was reformed by Muhammad, the "rubbing and kissing the [of the Black Stone]...was extremely passionate." Muslim tradition even perpetuates the blasphemy that, "Abraham had sexual intercourse with Hagar on it" (Sahas. Heresy, Pages 88-89). Francis Burton (Vol 3, page 295) writes regarding the Ka'ba, "the part of the cover (Kiswa), covering the door, is called [a Burka] just like the veil the Arabic women are wearing in front of their face...in fact, Arab mystics even compare the Ka'ba to a virgin, adorned with her finest wedding dress."

During their Hajj pilgrimage, Muslims kiss, rub and caress the Black Rock.

Before Muhammad encountered the angel of light in the cave of Hira, he was engaged in what was known in Arabia as Tahannuth (religious devotion to pagan idols). "The Apostle would pray in seclusion on Hira every year for a month to practice Tahannuth as was the custom of the Quraysh in the heathen days. After praying in seclusion, he would walk around the Ka'ba seven times."[25] In other words, Muhammad was a heathen and the Islamic Pillar that requires fasting during the month of Ramadan was a purely pagan tradition, as was going around the Black Stone. Today Islam still practices Tahannuth with it self-justification and meditation during the pagan holy month of Ramadan.[26] There is nothing new; but instead of calling it Tahannuth, now they just call it Hajj. There is an array of evidence that black stones were commonly worshipped in the Arab world. In 190 A.D., Clement of Alexandria mentioned, "The Arabs worship stone." He was alluding to the black stone of Dusares at Petra. In the 2nd century, Maximus Tyrius wrote, "The Arabians pay homage to what god I know not, which they represent by a quadrangular stone." Maximus was speaking of the Ka'ba (the Cube) that contains the Black Stone.[27] Even the ancient worship of Cybele pronounced Kybele is interestingly the same word Muslims use for the direction of prayer towards the Black Stone called the Qibleh. The stone associated with Cybele's worship likely originated at Pessinus, Pergamum, or on Mount Ida, "a small dark sacred stone not formed into any iconographic image that had fallen to the shrine of Pessinous from the sky."[28]

Alongside Isis, Cybele retained prominence in the heart of the Roman Empire until the fifth century when the stone was lost. Her cult prospered throughout the empire and it is said that every town or village remained true to the worship of Cybele.[29]

Islam began as a heretical Arab Christian cult focused on Aphrodite and the Morning star. This was confirmed during that era by John of Damascus (676-749), who called Islam a "superstition among the Ishmaelites that is the forerunner of Antichrist." According to John, Muslims were, "idolaters [who] reverenced the morning star and Aphrodite, who they indeed named Akbar."[30] Today they call this idol Allah, but the same satanic spirit that was worshipped then is still worshipped today. Satan manifests himself in many ways, but today Satan's greatest manifestation in the earth is through the "god" that is worshipped as Allah by over 1.3 billion people.

Section VII

Unlocking
Mystery Babylon
The Mother Of Harlots

≈84≈
The Harlot's Connection
To Arabia

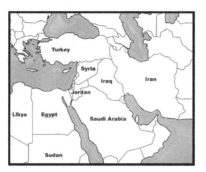

For many years, the teaching that the Harlot of Revelation is Rome or the Catholic Church has reigned within many Protestant circles. Today, most Western Analysts have diverged from this theory, and rightly so. Yet the problem of searching for alternatives leaves many in the dark—most Western Analysts are looking for a global Harlot that combines all religious systems and is political in nature, like Rome was. Yet neither Rome nor this "combination universal religion" Harlot conforms to many of the basic Scriptural descriptions of the Harlot. I have compiled seven reasons to prove this point. The Harlot described in the Bible must be in Arabia.

ISAIAH'S ORACLE AGAINST BABYLON

The Harlot *must* be connected to Arabia, not Rome or New York or any other nation or city. In Isaiah 21:9, Isaiah levels a prophetic oracle against Babylon: "Babylon is fallen, is fallen," is the same announcement used in Revelation 18:1-2. Yet this prophecy is not ultimately about ancient Babylon (Iraq), but the Mystery Babylon of Revelation. Ancient Babylon was simply a type of the Last-Days Babylon. The names in this prophecy are all areas in Arabia:

"The burden against Dumah" (v. 11)

"The burden against Arabia" (v. 13)

"All the glory of Kedar will fail" (v. 16)

Dumah and Kedar are in Arabia as the text shows: "All the glory of Kedar will fail" (v. 16). All of the locations mentioned in Isaiah 21 are in the desert of Arabia, the region of Revelation 17 which is surrounded by many waters (seas). Arabia in fact, is referred to by all Muslims as *Al-Jazeera Al-Arabia*, literally the *Arab Island* or the *Arab Peninsula* or the "Desert of the Sea" (v. 1). Even National Geographic[1] and Bernard Lewis [2] recognize it as such.

Isaiah 21 also agrees with several passages in Jeremiah and Revelation that refer to Babylon. Contenders to this interpretation would have a difficult time refuting the very direct Biblical references. The names used in these passages make it clear that the reference is not to Rome or literal Babylon on the Euphrates river. Not once do they speak of Rome, Nineveh, Ur, Babel, Erech, Accad, Sumer, Assur, Calneh, Mari, Karana, Ellpi, Eridu, Kish, or Tikrit. All of these literal locations are in Arabia, which was part of the ancient Babylonian Empire.

There are many conjectures concerning Mystery Babylon. Some say that Babylon is the United States of America or the Vatican. However, none of these theories are supported by the text. Either students of the Bible build a mold from Scripture or they make the Scriptures fit their theories. There are really only these two choices. Once we read the text of Isaiah 21, it becomes quite clear: "*An oracle concerning the Desert by the Sea*" (Isaiah 21:1). This is not the Tigris and Euphrates rivers in Iraq, but on a literal sea surrounded by the mass of waters in the Persian-Arab sea, Indian Ocean, and Red Sea. It is also thought that "the sea" may be a reference to the Nufud desert, a virtual ocean of enormous sand dunes.[3] The camel was called the ship of the desert, the only formidable vehicle to transport through the sea of sand.

ISAIAH 21

[1)]The burden of the desert of the sea. As whirlwinds in the South pass through; so it cometh from the desert, from a terrible land. [2)]A grievous vision is declared unto me; the treacherous dealer deals treacherously, and the spoiler spoils. Go up, O Elam: besiege, O Media; all the sighing thereof have I made to cease. [3)]Therefore are my loins filled with pain: pangs have taken hold upon me, as the pangs of a woman that travails: I was bowed down at the hearing of it; I was dismayed at the seeing of it. 4)My heart panted, fearfulness affrighted me: the night of my pleasure hath he turned into fear unto me. 5)Prepare the table, watch in the watchtower, eat, drink: arise, ye princes, and anoint the shield. 6)For thus hath the LORD said unto me, Go, set a watchman, let him declare what he sees. 7)And he saw a chariot with a couple of horsemen, a chariot of asses, and a chariot of camels; and he hearkened diligently with much heed: 8)And he cried, A lion: My lord, I stand continually upon the watchtower in the daytime, and I am set in my ward whole nights: 9)And, behold, here cometh a chariot of men, with a couple of horsemen. And he answered and said, Babylon is fallen, is fallen; and all the graven images of her gods he hath broken unto the ground. 10)O my threshing, and the corn of my floor: that which I have heard of the LORD of Hosts, the God of Israel, have I declared unto you. 11)The burden of Dumah. He calls to me out of Seir, watchman, what of the night? Watchman, what of the night? 12)The watchman said, The morning cometh, and also the night: if ye will enquire, enquire ye: return, come. 13)The burden upon Arabia. In the forest in Arabia shall ye lodge, O ye traveling companies of Dedanim. 14)The inhabitants of the land of Tema brought water to him that was thirsty; they prevented with their bread him that fled. 15)For they fled from the swords, from the drawn sword, and from the bent bow, and from the grievousness of war. 16)For thus hath the LORD said unto me, Within a year, according to the years of an hireling, and all the glory of Kedar shall fail: 17)And the residue of the number of archers, the mighty men of the children of Kedar, shall be diminished: for the LORD God of Israel hath spoken it.

Some might argue that the context of Isaiah 21 is only historical. But it is difficult to ignore the multiple references throughout the Book of Isaiah to Kedar, Tema, Dedan and Dumah. Dumah is in Saudi Arabia near Yathrib (Medina), and today is known as "Dumat el-Jandal." Dumah, one of the sons of Ishmael, is also associated with Edom and Seir in Isaiah 21:11. It is believed by many that Kedar, another of Ishmael's sons, is the line from which Muhammad descended. It is likely that Mecca is the "glory of Kedar" mentioned in verse 16. Historians generally identify Dumah with the Addyrian Adummatu people.[4] By these and other references, we can conclude that Dumah stands for Arabia.

We will also examine the crucial text of Isaiah 34 with the destruction of Edom, including its oil. It would be impossible to allude to Isaiah 34 as a historic reference because the purpose of the destruction against Edom there is over the final Battle of Jerusalem, in which the Lord Himself will be present and fighting. In Habakkuk 3 this takes place in "Median" which is in Arabia. The Psalms even give us a literal reference to *Edom* being the daughter of *Babylon* (born of Babylon): "Remember, O Lord, against the sons of Edom the day of Jerusalem, who said, 'Raze it, raze it, to its very foundation! O daughter of Babylon, who are to be destroyed'" (Psalm 137: 7-8).

Arabia is definitely the daughter of Babylon since it was made so by Nabonidus, who extended Babylon to Yathrib (Medina). This is a well-documented historic fact in which the Babylonian worship of the Moon-god was introduced to Arabia by Nabonidus.

In all of these Old Testament prophecies concerning the utter destruction of Babylon, they cannot be speaking of the ancient city of Babylon because it was inhabited for roughly five hundred years after these prophecies were given until around 141 B.C. when the Parthian Empire took over the region and the city was emptied of inhabitants. After this, the city slowly decayed. But it never suffered a fate anywhere near the utter destruction that was suffered by Sodom and Gomorrah—with fire raining down from heaven as many of these prophecies describe.

THE GEOGRAPHIC LOCATOR

Speaking of the destruction of Mystery Babylon, we read: "No Arab will pitch his tent there, no shepherd will rest his flocks there" (Isaiah 13:20). This cannot be attributed to Rome as some teach. Arabs never pitch their tents there. The ultimate fulfillment of this verse is the destruction of the Last-Days Babylon. We know this because the passage speaks about: "the day of the Lord" (v. 9) with the "heavens not giving light" (v. 10). This is not historical, but End-Times related.

When the Harlot is destroyed, the smoke from her judgment will be seen from afar. One is immediately reminded of the scene from Manhattan on 9/11 when news cameras relayed images of the World Trade Center from across the harbor. One could see smoke and debris from the decimation of the Towers trailing off into the sky and over the ocean. Likewise, based on all that we read about the Harlot, she will also possess a long and visible shoreline that may be observed from opposing lands and by ships at sea. Where are these sea captains when they hear and view this destruction? Jeremiah tells us they will be in the Red Sea: "The earth is moved at the noise of their fall, at the cry the noise thereof was heard in the Red sea" (Jeremiah 49:21).

Is Rome, literal Babylon, or America situated on the Red Sea? The Red Sea is a geographic indicator as to where the Last-Days Babylon will be located. Look at Mecca on any map and you will see that it sits near the Red Sea. Some may object that Jeremiah 49 is speaking about Edom, which was primarily located in modern day Jordan. Yet in Ezekiel 25 "Edom" stretches from Teman (Yemen) to Dedan (Saudi Arabia)" (v. 13). Greater Edom included all of the west coast of the Arabian Peninsula.

Notice the description of her destruction: "'As Sodom and Gomorrah were overthrown, along with their neighboring towns,' says the LORD, 'so no one will live there; no man will dwell in it,'" (Jeremiah 49:18). How was Sodom and Gomorrah destroyed? Was it not fire that rained down from heaven? Was ancient Edom ever completely destroyed like this in history? Jeremiah 49 is ultimately speaking of the Last-Day's judgment of Mystery Babylon that is associated with Edom. Throughout the Bible, only Mystery Babylon is also described as being completely and utterly destroyed in this same way. Beyond this, the passage specifies that the region we are dealing with contains the cities of Teman and Dedan which are nowhere near Iraq, or ancient Babylon.

The Bible also tells us that the Kurds (Medes) will be against Babylon. This is likely a dual fulfillment since today, the Kurds are hated by all of their neighbors: "Behold, I will stir up the Medes against them, who will not regard silver; and as for gold, they will not delight in it; Also their bows will dash the young men to pieces, and they will have no pity on the fruit of the womb; their eye will not spare children" (Isaiah 13:17:18).

∼ 85 ∼
The Harlot's Connection To A Desert

───✳───

The Harlot of Babylon is described as being in a literal desert location: "Then the angel carried me away in the Spirit into a desert. There I saw a woman (a prostitute) sitting on a scarlet beast" (Revelation 17:3). It then should be of no surprise that Jesus warned us that before He comes, religious imposters will come out of the desert: "So if anyone tells you, 'There he is, out in the desert,' do not go out" (Matthew 24:26). Many commentators overlook this literal description of the Harlot.

It is largely agreed to by most that the Beast is the governmental aspect of the Antichrist empire, and that the Harlot woman city is the spiritual driver of this Beast mechanism. So the angel takes John into a desert to observe the Harlot. There, in the desert, she is also seen "sitting on many waters (peoples)." She is the spiritual source that influences these different ethnic peoples. However, later in verse 17, the angel explains to John that "the waters" which the Harlot sits upon should be understood allegorically as representing "peoples, multitudes, nations and languages." The woman exerts a strong measure of spiritual influence over a great mixture of multitudes of different ethnicities and languages.

The combination of these three descriptions (city, desert, sitting on many waters) also matches Isaiah 21, where Babylon is described as "the Desert by the Sea."

While some insist that some of the Biblical descriptions of the Last-Days Harlot may bear some similarities to Rome, New York, or America when read by Western minds, the point is that all of the Biblical descriptions must be met, not just a few. Whatever solution to this puzzle one ultimately accepts, it must be both reasonable, and it must conform to all the relevant Scriptures. Does Rome, The United States, or New York City sit in a literal desert? If not, then these entities cannot be the fulfillment of these Biblical prophecies. Yet Saudi Arabia fulfills this description exactly.

≈ 86 ≈
The Harlot's Connection To Oil

+≡·✳·≡+

O nce we have established the connection of Mystery Babylon to Arabia and the desert, we can apply our literal findings to the allegoric references. The Bible gives us some allegoric clues about this Harlot as a provider of wine that intoxicates the nations (Revelation 17:2). Many Western Bible teachers associated the wine held in a chalice by the prostitute with the Catholic Church and the golden chalice used during communion. This conclusion is hardly hermeneutically responsible or Berean. While many of the Old Testament prophets spoke regarding Mystery Babylon, no passage in the Bible directly addresses the Harlot as does Revelation 17 and 18. As Revelation 17 begins, the Apostle John is introduced to the Harlot.

> "One of the seven angels who had the seven bowls came and said to me, 'Come, I will show you the punishment of the great prostitute, who sits on many waters. With her the *kings of the earth committed adultery* and the inhabitants of the earth were *intoxicated with the wine of her adulteries*.' Then the angel carried me away in the Spirit into a desert. There I saw a woman sitting on a scarlet beast that was covered with *blasphemous names* and had seven heads and ten horns. The woman was dressed in purple and scarlet, and was glittering with *gold, precious stones, and pearls*. She held a golden cup in her hand, filled with abominable things and the filth of her adulteries. This title was written on her forehead: 'Mystery Babylon The Great— The Mother of Prostitutes and of the Abominations of the earth.' *I saw that the woman was drunk with the blood of the saints*, the blood of those who bore testimony to Jesus... The woman you saw is the *great city* that *rules over the kings of the earth*" (Revelation 17:1-6, 18).

There are two very important descriptions of the Harlot that stand out: First, she exists geographically in a desert region. And secondly, we see that the "kings of the earth" figuratively commit adultery with her in order to obtain her "wine" in exchange for betraying God's people. What desert "wine" intoxicates the earth, and causes this desert region to grow rich? What false religion teaches that the blood of Christians and Jews should be shed? What desert nation today is the geographical womb from which this false harlot religion was birthed?

THE WINE IN JOEL 3

Amazingly, in Joel 3, the Bible talks about both this wine as well as the harlot, including the reason for God's judgment against the nations:

"For behold, in those days and at that time, when I restore the fortunes of Judah and Jerusalem, I will gather all the nations and bring them down to the valley of Jehoshaphat. Then I will enter into judgment with them there on behalf of My people and My inheritance, Israel, Whom they have scattered among the nations; And they have divided up My land. They have also cast lots for My people, traded a boy for a harlot, and sold a girl for wine that they may drink" (Joel 3:1-3).

It is sad that most claiming Christians do not know that the *division of Israel* and the *treatment of the Jews* is the main basis by which Jesus will judge the nations. Yet, many will bare the shame of ignoring one of the most important texts in Scripture. It is both fascinating and frightening to see such familiar elements of modern-day Middle Eastern politics portrayed in this ancient End-Time prophecy. Among the various crimes that the nations commit against God and His people, they are guilty of "dividing up My (God's) land." This is exactly what we see today as Israel is continually pressured to carve out Judea, the very heart of Israel, in order to create a Palestinian state and ultimately attempt to destroy Israel.

In typical Hebrew prose, we see the price paid for this sale of Israel whom God calls "My people": "They have also cast lots for My people, traded a boy for a harlot and sold a girl for wine that they may drink" (Joel 3:3). We see that the nations will sell out Israel in order to coddle the Harlot and obtain her wine. The timing context of this passage is the End-Times: "at that time, when I restore the fortunes of Judah and Jerusalem" (Joel 3:1).

I propose to you that the Harlot uses both Islam and oil as her "wine," through which she seduces the nations of the world into committing spiritual adultery with her and compromising Israel. Of course, this is probably quite a new paradigm for many Western students of the Bible, but in the East, the new converts from Islam get it—quickly. This wine cannot be a simple issue, "For all the nations have drunk the maddening wines of her adulteries" (Revelation 18:3).

Babylon is judged because of her "maddening" influence that has used oil to turn many nations against Israel. By "maddening," the text means an irrational hatred that fills the hearts of those who partake of her idolatrous doctrines. Even as the spirit of Islam today causes men to become mad with hate and rage, so also we see that the religion of the Harlot has the same effect. In the New Testament, when one becomes a follower of Jesus, they are filled with the Holy Spirit and bear the corresponding fruit in their lives: love, joy, patience, kindness and peace, etc. Islam produces the opposite.

Besides the spiritual aspect of the Harlot's influence (Islam), we also see a financial dimension: The oil is used as a means to pressure and even blackmail nations. Today we live in a world that is addicted to oil. In the days to come, we will see the truly maddening effects of the Harlot's influence when her "wine" is held as a carrot at the end of a stick from her oil-addicted clients. OPEC very recently announced that it has decided not to increase oil production in Saudi Arabia. The purpose of this is clearly to hurt the United States. In the 1970s, we saw the effects of the OPEC embargo when Saudi Arabia first woke up to her power. Should we be surprised that immediately after the formation of OPEC, the next organization to be formed was OAPEC (the Organization of Arab Petroleum Exporting Countries), whose purpose was to exert pressure on the West specifically over its support of Israel?

In the years to come, we will see how desperate the addicts can become when Saudi once again uses her "wine" to affect the policies of foreign nations. In summary, one needs to ask, what Arab, Islamic, desert nation today both ideologically and financially supports the export of Fundamental Islam (the Antichrist religion) to the world? What Arab nation is the most likely to use oil-influence to affect the policies of foreign nations? What Arab nation's oil net exports and production are more than three times higher then any other Arab member of OPEC?

Remember, the Bible says that, "...the merchants of the earth are waxed rich through the abundance of her delicacies" (Revelation 18:3). The merchants of the earth have grown rich due to the abundance of this delicacy she offers: "O you who dwell by many waters, abundant in treasures, your end has come" (Jeremiah 51:13).

LITERAL OIL—ISAIAH 34

Many may still argue that the oil in Revelation 17 is an allegory of something spiritual. Once we study Isaiah 34, however, you will no longer have any doubts. In nearly identical language to what we have already read concerning Mystery Babylon in Revelation 17,18, we read:

"For it is the day of Jehovah's vengeance, and the year of recompenses for the controversy of Zion. Its streams shall be turned into pitch and its dust into brimstone; its land shall become burning pitch. It shall not be quenched night or day; its smoke shall ascend forever" (Isaiah 34:8-10).

Incredibly, almost three millennia before the discovery of fuel oil, Isaiah predicted the burning of the very thing that was used in Babel to build a name for the rebellious ones— the pitch. Pitch is bitumen and tar, which technically is simply crude oil. Have you ever wondered why God calls the Antichrist "Nimrod" in Micah 5? His roots go back to Babel.

Notice that the land shall not be "like" burning pitch but shall actually become burning pitch—there is no simile here. This prophecy could only be fulfilled in an oil rich land. The word for "streams" (nachal) is not water streams but "torrent," "torrent-valley," "wadi /valley," "mine," or "tunnels," and thus need not be understood strictly as streams of water. Obviously water would never burn like pitch as the verse mandates. The picture painted is literally of a land that turns into a river of burning wells (tunnels) of petroleum. This is also confirmed in Revelation 18 regarding the harlot city:

"And the kings of the earth, who have committed fornication and lived deliciously with her, shall bewail her, and lament for her, when they shall see the smoke of her burning" (Revelation 18:9). "And cried when they saw the smoke of her burning, saying, 'What [city is] like unto this great city!'" (Revelation 18:18)

Remember the oil fields during Gulf War I, when Saddam Hussein set the oil wells on fire? Even during the day, the skies were black with smoke. This is precisely how Isaiah the prophet portrays Babylon's End-Time judgment. In Revelation, we read that God will, "Mix her a double portion from her own cup. Give her as much torture and grief as the glory and luxury she gave herself" (Revelation 18:4-7). This chalice of Mystery Babylon is the same as in Jeremiah 51: "He shall recompense her. Babylon was a golden cup in the Lord's hand that made all the earth drunk. The nations drunk her wine; Therefore the nations are deranged" (Jeremiah 51:7). When God issues a judgment, he hands over this cup to the Harlot and makes her drink. From the very cup that she used to establish her influence, from the abundance of her oil wealth, she will be fed a double portion of punishment by the very product that she used to establish herself and her power by her own burning with it. Though she has funded the export of this Abaddon destroyer called by the West "radical Islam" and the terrorists who have turned the world upside down, so also will the radical Islamists eventually turn on Saudi Arabia and give her something twice as bad as anything that any other nation has seen. She will be burned—in one hour, she will fall. Therefore the kings of the earth shall weep and mourn for their oil, but their oil will go up in flames. All this is what the Bible declares to be, "Jehovah's vengeance, and the year of rec-ompenses for the [legal] controversy of Zion." This cannot be ancient Babylon. God Him-self finally executes judgment on Israel's behalf with a great destruction. The same rendering is in Jeremiah 51:11: "the vengeance for His Temple." Again, this judgment against "Edom" extends from Teman to Dedan:

"Thus Says the Lord GOD; 'Because that Edom hath dealt against the house of Judah by taking vengeance, and hath greatly offended, and revenged him-self upon them.' Therefore thus Says the Lord GOD; 'I will also stretch out mine hand upon Edom, and will cut off man and beast from it; and I will make it desolate from Teman; and they of Dedan shall fall by the sword'" (Ezekiel 25:12-13).

Teman is a place name meaning "right side" that is "southern." The Edomites were a clan descended from Esau (Genesis 36:11, Genesis 36:15; 1 Chronicles 1:36). Teman was a city that was associated with the Edomites (Jeremiah 49:7, Jeremiah 49:20; Ezekiel 25:13; Amos 1:12; Obadiah 1:9; Habakkuk 3:3). Teman has often been identified with Tawilan, fifty miles south of the Dead Sea, just east of Petra, though archaeological evidence does not confirm the site as the principal city of southern Edom. Others understand Teman to designate southern Edom in general. To others still, the link with Dedan (Jeremiah 49:7; Ezekiel 25:13) suggests Tema on the Arabian Peninsula.5 Because the Bible chose to iden-tify Teman with Dedan, we need to accept that Teman is in South Central Arabia in Yemen. Dedan is well defined and was an ancient city in central Saudi Arabia that is now known as Al-Ula. 6 The Lord made the geographical location of Mystery Babylon quite clear for anyone who would seek it out.

THE EXTENT OF ARABIA'S DESTRUCTION

This destruction of Arabia is complete and fits the description made by several prophets whose prophecies correlate with Isaiah 34:

"Therefore in one day her plagues will overtake her: death, mourning, and famine. She will be consumed by fire, for mighty is the Lord God who judges her. When the kings of the earth who committed adultery with her and shared her luxury see the smoke of her burning, they will weep and mourn over her. Terrified at her torment, they will stand far off and cry: 'Woe! Woe, O great city, O Babylon, city of power! In one hour your doom has come!... Every sea captain, and all who travel by ship, the sailors, and all who earn their living from the sea, will stand far off. When they see the smoke of her

burning, they will exclaim, 'Was there ever a city like this great city?'"
(Revelation 18:8-10, 17-18)

Ships on the Red Sea can easily see Arabia's destruction. The Harlot will be destroyed violently and swiftly "and in one day," "with such violence," she will be "consumed with fire." The judgment on the Harlot is permanent. There will never be heard in this city the sound of music or musicians. Workers will never rebuild the city. The sound of tradesman will never be heard or seen in her again. All agriculture will cease. There will be no weddings. All signs of human habitation will be permanently eliminated. Apart from Sodom and Gomorrah, this type of utter destruction has never been seen in any other city, including Hiroshima and Nagasaki. "After her destruction, Babylon will merely be a home for demons, evil spirits, and scavenging desert creatures" (Revelation 18:1-2).

This is in line with the ancient Eastern perception that desolate desert wastelands were the dwelling place of demons and unclean spirits. The point being emphasized is that after Babylon is destroyed, there will be absolutely no human life ever found there again. Jeremiah agrees; he describes this: "So desert creatures and hyenas will live there, and there the owl will dwell. It will never again be inhabited or lived in from generation to generation" (Jeremiah 50:39). Isaiah confirms a similar fate: "It shall be a habitation of jackals" (Isaiah 34:14). And again later, the destruction of Babylon is described as being absolute. Isaiah speaks of this event: "For I will rise up against them, says the Lord of hosts, and cut off from Babylon its name and remnant, and offspring and posterity, says the Lord...I will sweep it with the broom of destruction" (Isaiah 12:15). The broom of destruction? Anyone who has seen footage of a nuclear explosion has seen the fury and the power of the ominous cloud that sweeps up everything in its path. Could this verse be describing a nuclear explosion? "And I will show wonders in the heavens and in the earth; Blood and fire and pillars of smoke" (Joel 2:30). Could the pillars of smoke be the scene of mushroom clouds from a nuclear explosion?

HOW COULD THE BEAST DESTROY THE HARLOT?

Revelation 17 tells us that the Beast hates the Harlot. He will ultimately turn on her, killing her, devouring her, and burning her body with fire:

> *"The beast and the ten horns you saw will hate the prostitute. They will bring her to ruin and leave her naked; they will eat her flesh and burn her with fire.* For God has put it into their hearts to accomplish his purpose by agreeing to give the beast their power to rule, until God's words are fulfilled. The woman you saw is the great city that rules over the kings of the earth" (Revelation 17:16-18).

How can this be? Some may argue that Muslims would never attack such Islamic "holy" sites as Mecca and Medina. If we take the Western view of Rome being the Harlot, one could argue the same, how could Europe burn and destroy Rome?

Yet when it comes to Mecca, plenty of Muslims have attacked the city before. In the late 7th Century, Al-Hajjaj bin Yousef Al-Thaqafi (a Muslim) laid siege to Mecca and destroyed much of the Ka'ba with stones launched from catapults. During the First World War, Saudi Arabia was actually occupied by the Turkish Ottomans. The Turks deeply resented Arab imperialism that had spread through the vast Islamic empire and made strong attempts to restrict Arab culture and language throughout their empire. This enmity and resistance was so severe that the Arabs were persuaded by the British through their envoy, T. E. Lawrence (also known as "Lawrence of Arabia"), to revolt against the Ottoman occupation and help the allies. The Turks bombarded the mosque of the Ka'ba, the most sacred shrine of all Islam. One shell actually hit the Ka'ba, burning a hole in the "holy carpet" and killing nine Arabs who were kneeling in prayer. In modern times, the same disregard for Mecca by Muslims has been seen. On November 20, 1979, over 500 militants and their leader attacked the false Islamic Mahdi, Juhaiman ibn Muhammad ibn Saif al Utaiba.[7] In the 1980s, on several occasions, followers of Ayatollah Khomeini disrupted the annual hajj, or pilgrimage to Mecca. Most of this was quelled by heavy security controls, but in July 1987, over 400 people died as a result of a serious riot instigated by thousands of Iranian pilgrims.[8] Three years later, during Gulf War I, Saddam Hussein sent numerous scuds flying over Saudi Arabia, disregarding the high risk they would pose to the Islamic "holy land." There were no protests from Muslim nations. And as recent as 2003, three al-Qaeda militants blew themselves up during an attack in Mecca.[39] The idea of Muslims attacking Mecca or Saudi Arabia is far from impossible. The day is drawing near when the emerging Beast Empire led by Turkey and Iran will attack Mecca and destroy the Arabian Harlot.

THE DESTRUCTION OF MECCA AND MEDINA IN ISLAMIC PROPHECY

Confirming what the Bible which predicts as the destruction of this Harlot by the Beast that she rides is an Islamic prophecy that predicts the destruction of it's bride Mecca by Muslim nations: "The final battle will be waged by Muslim faithful coming on the backs of horses...carrying black banners. They will stand on the east side of the Jordan River and will wage war that the earth has never seen before. The true Messiah who is the Islamic Mehdi...will defeat Europe...will lead this army of Seljuks, He will preside over the world from Jerusalem because Mecca would have been destroyed..." (Yawm Al-Ghadab, Safar Alhwaly).

Medina is not immune of this destruction: "The flourishing state of Jerusalem will be when Yathrib (Medina) is in ruins, the ruined state of Yathrib will be when the Great War comes, and the outbreak of the Great War will be at the conquest of Constantinople and the conquest of Constantinople when the *Dajjal* (the Antichrist) comes forth. He (the Prophet) struck his thigh or his shoulder with his hand and said: This is as true as you are here or as you are sitting."[10] *Yathrib* is another name for Medina, the city of the Prophet Muhammad, the second holiest city to Islam. Constantinople is Istanbul in Turkey. Many radical Muslims perceive that Istanbul has been under the control of secular hypocritical Muslims until its recent restoration to the Islamists. So according to this prophesy, after the fall of Istanbul to the true Muslims, (which, through recent elections in 2007, has just occurred) Medina will be destroyed.[11]

In the Last-Days, a coalition of radical Islamic nations will turn on and destroy Saudi Arabia. The prophecies by which radical Muslims live dictate just such an event. Thus, if the day comes that radical Muslims actually destroy Saudi Arabia, it is also very likely that this prophecy will embolden and empower them to imagine that they are acting according to Allah's plan.

≈ 87 ≈
The Harlot's Connection To A False Religion

✦═══✳═══✦

The Harlot, in many ways, might be likened to Dr. Frankenstein. The Beast is the monster that the Harlot has created.

The Beast is a coalition of ten kings representing the seven kingdoms in the past, under the authority of the Antichrist. The Harlot is a distinct and separate *geographically definable entity* that represents the primary *religious source* of the Antichrist's religion. The Harlot is sitting atop a scarlet Beast. This beast is the final Islamic Empire of the Antichrist that we have already discussed in detail. This close, seemingly symbiotic relationship of rider and steed should not be dismissed as an irrelevant component of this picture. The Lone Ranger had Silver and the Harlot has the Beast. There is a very close relationship that is evident between the two. Beyond the fact that the Harlot is riding the Beast, there are other noteworthy similarities that the two share. First, the woman is dressed in scarlet; the Beast likewise is portrayed as a scarlet Beast—the two match. Secondly, even as the Beast Empire will behead God's people, so the Harlot is drunk on the blood of the saints. They both share in the bloodguilt of God's people.

We have examined what "Mystery Babylon" means, but we also need to understand the meaning of the rest of her title: "The Mother of all Prostitutes and Abominations of the earth" (Revelation 17:5). The first thing that we need to understand is that this title is a typical Eastern sort of phrase—the kind of phrase Ahmadenijad uses when he says that Islam will be on top of all the mountains. Remember Saddam Hussein's comments in the days leading up to first Gulf War? He declared that the U.S. and Iraq were about to engage in "the mother of all battles." Of course, in typical megalomaniacal game-talk, he also declared that America was about to experience "the mother of all defeats." The term "Mother of" is simply an Eastern way of expressing a superlative; it is the biggest, the worst, the unmatched, and most significant of all.

I point this out because many mistakenly interpret "Mother of" here to mean *the source* of all other forms of idolatry. The Eastern-minded reader; however, immediately recognizes that the purpose of this phrase is to portray the Great Harlot as the greatest manifestation of spiritual infidelity against the God of the Bible that has ever existed throughout the history of the world. So the Harlot is the greatest of all spiritual prostitutes, but she is not necessarily the source of all other false religions. Throughout history, many "prostitutes" or false religions exist and have existed, but the Great Harlot is portrayed here as being by far the most significant of them all. The Harlot's false religion is also a mystery in that like no other pagan religion, it sprouts from a mixture of a heretical Christian cult and a pagan Moon-god religion that has attempted to cloak itself with certain Jewish and Christian elements in order to appear as a Biblical faith and the rightful successor of the Judeo-Christian tradition.

When the veil is pulled back, Islam's true nature and pagan source becomes apparent: It is a religion that denies the essence of God, contradicts His character and blasphemes His attributes.

GALATIANS 4—THE TWO COVENANTS

Galatians 4 speaks of two covenants: one is true and the other is false: "for these are two covenants." The first is crucial for our study; "the one from mount Sinai, which gives birth to bondage, which is Hagar. For this Hagar is mount Sinai in Arabia" (Galatians 4:24-25).

The covenant of bondage is allegorized by Mount Sinai, yet the literal definition for this reference is *Arabia*. The spiritual battle, according to Galatians 4, is between Arabia (Hagar) and Jerusalem (Sarah):

> "For it is written, that Abraham had two sons, the one by a bondmaid, the other by a freewoman. But he [who was] of the bondwoman was born after the flesh; but he of the freewoman [was] by promise. Which things are an allegory: for these are the two covenants; the one from the *Mount Sinai*, which genders to bondage, which is Agar. For this *Agar is Mount Sinai* in Arabia, and answers to Jerusalem which now is, and is in bondage with her children. But Jerusalem which is above is free, which is the mother of us all. For it is written, Rejoice, [thou] barren that bears not; break forth and cry, thou that travail not: for the desolate hath many more children than she which hath an husband. Now we, brethren, as Isaac was, are the children of promise. But as then he that was born after the flesh persecuted him [that was born] after the Spirit, even so [it is] now. Nevertheless what Says the scripture? Cast out the bondwoman and her son: for the son of the bond-

woman shall not be heir with the son of the freewoman. So then, brethren, we are not children of the bondwoman, but of the free" (Galatians 4:21-31).

Most historians agree that Sinai is in Egypt, so why is this text insisting on an Arabian location? The Bible states that a religion of bondage—Islam literally means submission—came out of the desert of Arabia through Hagar (Ishmael's lineage). Even the name Sinai comes from the Moon-god's name "Sin." The desert is the "Wilderness of Sin" or the "Desert of the Moon-god." In Old Testament times, Nabonidus (555-539 B.C.), the last king of Babylon, built Tayma, Arabia as center of Moon-god worship. As Segel, a historian of the ancient Middle East has stated, "South Arabia's *stellar religion* has always been dominated by the Moon-god in various variations."[12]

THE RICH ROYAL PROSTITUTE

The Prostitute is dressed in scarlet and crimson garments that glitter with jewels, pearls, and gold. Scarlet is the color of royalty. When Jesus was taken prisoner, the Roman centurions dressed Him in a scarlet robe (Matthew 27:28) to mock His "royalty." The scarlet and crimson clothes of the Harlot also connote royalty. Because they literally glitter with gold, jewels, and pearls, she is also considered rich beyond measure.

But there is also another meaning to the color crimson. Crimson represents sinfulness. "Though your sins be as scarlet, they shall be as white as snow. Though they be red like crimson, they shall be as wool" (Isaiah 1:18). Of course, this also perfectly matches the nature of this corrupt and murderous prostitute.

What Islamic desert nation is governed by a Royal Monarchy that is known throughout the earth as being fabulously wealthy and utterly corrupt? What place is decked with gold, silver, and precious stones?

WHAT IS INTENDED BY "THE GREAT CITY"

The Harlot is described as a great city that rules over the kings of the earth. From this, we know that she is a politically and geographically definable entity that exerts a significant measure of influence throughout the world. The primary purpose however is not so much to restrict the Harlot as being a mere literal city, but rather to contrast her to the other prominent city of Revelation—the "Holy City" of New Jerusalem. One city is described as "Great" and is pictured as a foul prostitute, while the other city is "Holy" and is pictured as a pure bride, adorned for her wedding day. The intended contrast is clear: "And he carried me away in the Spirit to a mountain great and high, and showed me the Holy City, Jerusalem, coming down out of heaven from God, prepared as a bride beauti-

fully dressed for her husband" (Revelation 21:10). "Come I will show you...the Great Prostitute...Then the angel carried me away in the Spirit into a desert. There I saw a woman sitting on a scarlet beast...The woman you saw is the *Great City* that rules over the kings of
the earth" (Revelation 17:1, 3, 18).

As discussed, Galatians 4 addresses both cities—Jerusalem from above (Revelation
21:10), and the bondage from a literal Arabia, which we see symbolically in Revelation
17:1, 3, 18. Mystery Babylon is both the antithesis and the premiere antagonist of all that
Jerusalem is called to be—and will become.

What city in the earth could be viewed as the most significant religious and ideological
antagonist to an idealized Jerusalem? What desert city has attempted to usurp the position
of Jerusalem as the spiritual capitol of the world? While exiled in Babylon, the prophet
Daniel bowed in prayer several times a day toward Jerusalem. Toward what other city do a
large proportion of the people of the earth bow each day? The Qur'an literally switched the
direction from Jerusalem to Mecca, and abrogated Jerusalem as a direction of worship.

"COME OUT OF HER MY PEOPLE!"

"Then I heard another voice from heaven say: 'Come out of her, my people, so that you
will not share in her sins, so that you will not receive any of her plagues for her sins
are piled up to heaven, and God has remembered her crimes. Give back to her as she has
given; pay her back double for what she has done. Mix her a double portion from her own
cup. Give her as much torture and grief as the glory and luxury she gave her'" (Revelation
18:4-7).

God warns his people who are living in Babylon to "come out of her"—to *flee*, for she
is about to be judged severely. Here, we find a direct allusion to another Old Testament
prophecy concerning Babylon. Jeremiah 50 and 51 repeatedly reference the need to flee
Babylon with the same rendering as in Revelation. "My people, go out of the midst of her"
(Jeremiah 51:45). "Flee out of Babylon and leave the land of the Babylonians. Be like the
goats that lead the flock" (Jeremiah 50:8). "Flee from Babylon! Run for your lives! Do not
be destroyed because of her sins. It is time for Jehovah's vengeance; he will pay her what
she deserves" (Jeremiah 51:6). "We would have healed Babylon, but she is not healed: forsake her, and let us go every one into his own country: for her judgment reached unto
heaven, and is lifted up even to the skies" (Jeremiah 51:9).

Notice that those who are warned are told to flee, "every one into his own country."
This is important. Like the ancient Babylon, so also is the Last-Days Babylon filled with foreigners and expatriates. What Arab, Islamic, desert nation is filled with a massive foreign
labor-force that is only used for labor and never offered citizenship?

≈ 88 ≈
The Harlot's Connection to Slavery, Lavish Imports And Secret Sin

+‡=━‡━✳━‡=‡+

"Woe! Woe, O great city, dressed in fine linen, purple and scarlet, and glittering with gold, precious stones, and pearls! In one hour such great wealth has been brought to ruin!" (Revelation 18:16) God speaks to the heathen: "To whom will you liken Me, that we should be alike? They lavish gold out of the bag, and weigh silver on the scales; they hire a goldsmith, and he makes it a god; they prostrate themselves, yes, they worship" (Isaiah 46:5-6).

Muslims decked the black stone idol that they likened to God with gold and silver and prostrated themselves to it as Isaiah predicted. Mecca and Medina are decked with much gold, gems and pearls. Arabia is also famous for its gold markets or *souqs*. The Mall of Arabia is the home of the *Gold Souq*, which has over 450 jewelry & gold shops in one location. Mystery Babylon prides itself on such imports: "The merchants of the earth will weep and mourn over her because no one buys their cargoes any more—cargoes of gold, silver, precious stones and pearls; fine linen, purple, silk and scarlet cloth; every sort of citron wood, and articles of every kind made of ivory, costly wood, bronze, iron and marble; cargoes of cinnamon and spice, of incense, myrrh and frankincense, of wine and olive oil, of fine flour and wheat; cattle and sheep; horses and carriages; and bodies and souls of men" (Revelation 18:11-13).

Remarkably, these are the very imports of Saudi Arabia today. The items may be divided into three categories—but they all things that she cannot produce herself. The three categories are luxury items, food items—both livestock and produce—and human slaves. Saudi Arabia imports humans for various reasons; some may be legitimate, but others clearly are not. Above, we saw that there will be many foreign workers living in Mystery Babylon who will have the freedom to flee. However, we are also told that there are many slaves in Mystery Babylon. Obviously, they will not have the freedom to flee. While most would like to imagine that slavery is a thing of the past, slavery thrives in various forms in many parts of the world today. Mystery Babylon imports men, women, and children, no doubt to maintain and bolster her excessively luxurious and sinful lifestyle. Saudi

Arabia has been repeatedly condemned by numerous human-rights watch groups for its horrific treatment of its vast foreign labor-force. They have been repeatedly reported to have a serious problem with importing young women and children as sex-slaves. How in the world could this description be made to conform to the city of Rome?

SECRET SIN AND THE ARROGANT QUEEN

In Isaiah's prophecy, and confirming Revelation 18 regarding the Harlot of Babylon, we see that in the midst of all of the Harlot's sin and wickedness, she believes that no one sees her: "You have trusted in your wickedness and have said, 'No one sees me'" (Isaiah 47:10). Revelation 18 also describes the Harlot as being utterly arrogant. In her heart she boasts, "I sit as queen; I am not a widow, and I will never mourn" (Revelation 18:7). This is also confirmed in Isaiah 47: "I will continue forever— the eternal queen!...I am, and there is none besides me. I will never be a widow or suffer the loss of children." Its destruction, "will overtake you in a moment, on a single day." This never happened to the ancient Babylon. Its decay and eventual destruction was very slow and gradual over hundreds of years.

The Last-Day Babylon's excessive luxury and debauchery which the Harlot expresses that no one is aware of, is typical of the Saudi Monarchy that is known for its hypocritical outward life of public piousness and secret debauchery.

∾89∾
Objection, Your Honor

I always get an array of objections from authors who don't want to recant their previous teachings. Some of them have written several books claiming that Rome or Europe is the focus of End-Time Bible prophecy. In their view, Rome is most fitting fulfillment of the Mystery Babylon prophecies because it sits on seven hills. But the truth is, even if we take the seven hills in Revelation 17 to be literal hills, modern Rome actually encompasses more than seven hills. And Vatican Hill was not counted as one of the original seven. But why restrict this definition to Rome? Ancient Babylon did have seven *artificial* hills within its walls? Constantinople is often called the "Second Rome," and also has seven hills within its boundaries.

But these hills are not to be taken literally. The context of the passage clearly shows that these "hills" (a better translation is "mounts" or "mountains) are kingdoms. "The seven heads are seven mountains on which the woman sits. They are also seven kings" (Revelation 17:9). Kings rule kingdoms and not mountains. A mountain is a kingdom and not a hill.

Another objection I often hear is that the Greek word used for the place that John was taken is *Eremon*, and does not mean a literal desert. John was taken in the spirit to this place simply to see a vision; it was simply the theatre for this vision. But "Eremon", according to Strong's, does mean: "desert, wilderness, deserted places, lonely regions, an uncultivated region fit for pasturage." Those who try to claim that the desert was simply the theatre for John to see the vision have rendered this portion of God's Word completely irrelevant. According to this interpretation, John could have been taken to Mars or the Moon to see the vision and it wouldn't have made any difference in terms of the meaning of the passage. This is just plain silly. The desert location that John was taken is not irrelevant. In fact, it is a crucial aspect of the vision. The desert is an important description of where the Women—Mystery Babylon can be found.

Mecca sits on a barren valley surrounded by mountains.[13] *Eremon* is the best fitting term to describe Mecca and is used throughout Scripture to describe deserts: "Wherefore if they shall say unto you, Behold, he is in the desert; (eremon) go not forth behold, he is in the secret chambers; believe it not" (Matthew 24:26). This, by itself, hints that trouble and false messiahs will come from a desert. Also, John wasn't taken to the desert to see a movie (vision), but to see a woman/city. He would not have been taken to a place unassociated with the event.

This is true in other similar usages in Scripture: "The hand of the LORD was upon me, and carried me out in the Spirit of the LORD, and set me down in the midst of the valley which was full of bones" (Ezekiel 37:1). The valley was not the theatre, but where the actual event took place—in a large pit valley filled with dead dry bones of Jews. The vision of the future Temple also has the scene associated with the event: "And he carried me away in the spirit to a great and high mountain, and showed me that great city, the holy Jerusalem, descending out of heaven from God" (Revelation 21:10). The mountain was not the theatre, but where the new city was located, on a mountain. The same is true in Ezekiel 40: "In the visions of God, He brought me into the land of Israel, and set me upon a very high mountain, by which was as the frame of a city on the south" (Ezekiel 40:2). The Lord took Ezekiel to Israel's most important mountain, the Temple Mount. He didn't take him to a place unassociated with the event.

Finally, perhaps the best argument against Rome being this harlot city, is the fact that certain European countries (Rome, Spain) are specifically mentioned in the Bible, yet none with a single reference to destruction. Why?

Spain is mentioned in Romans 15:24,28 and Rome in Acts 2:10, 18:2, 19:21, 23:11, 28:14, 28:16; Romans 1:7, 1:15; Galatians 6:18; Ephesians 6:24; Philippians 4:23; Colossians 4:18; 2 Timothy 1:17, 4:22; and Philippians 1:25. The prophets never mentioned the destruction of Rome by name. Has the Almighty forgotten to literally mention it? Yet, He never forgot Arabia by name, she is mentioned in numerous passages. Are we to simply forget all of these because we don't want to contradict the teachings in so many prophecy books?

Arabia does have great influence over the kings of the earth, and offers an addictive intoxicating commodity—oil. Rome has no such addictive substance, which the Harlot city needs in order to burn forever.

The other argument that some make for Rome is that the products mentioned in Revelation are what Rome exports. Rome produces marble, gold, silver, precious stones, pearls, fine linen etc. Many think that the list of goods is what the harlot city produces: marble gemstones, fine clothes. Yet a closer look at the text reveals that the Harlot city does not produce any of these items. In fact, she is an *importer* of these goods and not a producer: "And the merchants of the earth will weep and mourn over her, for no one buys their merchandise anymore..." (Revelation 18:11). These are the products that the *Harlot city buys* from the merchants of the sea who watch her destruction from the Red Sea.

This is crucial for it nullifies the Rome argument. Why would Rome import the very items that she already manufactures? In fact, all Saudi goods are imported via the Red Sea, and the list of goods match Saudi imports perfectly—gold, silver, precious stones, pearls, fine linen, vessels of ivory, fine wood and copper ware, iron, marble, spices, perfumes, liquor, sheep, horses, slaves and the souls of men. The Harlot city also imports slaves, horses and even ivory. Arabia imports all of these, yet Rome doesn't. By the way, if you think that Saudi Arabia does not import wine because of the Islamic prohibition, guess again. Just because its done in secret doesn't mean that it doesn't take place.

So what will the supporters of the Rome theory do once they examine Revelation 18:11? Will they recant their theory? I sure hope so.

ARABIA DOES WHILE ROME DOESN'T

Arabia has a tremendous foreign work force Rome doesn't.

Arabia does not allow citizenship for immigrants, Rome does. Arabia persecutes the saints, Rome doesn't. Arabia promotes beheading, Rome doesn't: "and I saw the souls of the martyrs who were beheaded." Historically, Rome mainly practiced burning, drowning, or crucifixion while Arabia has always beheaded believers. There are many parallels in Scripture: John the Baptist, crying out in the wilderness was beheaded for exposing the truth. So it will be before Christ comes again. The John the Baptists of this world (Christians) will be sacrificed, and very few will mourn them. Who desires to behead us today? Who are these Last-Days Edomite Herods? Where are they doing their killings? Who represents Salome that Harlot, the daughter of the Edomite? Where is biblical Edom? Mecca exerts more spiritual influence of false theology on more people than any other city on earth. Today major Universities such as Harvard, Cambridge, Georgetown and many others have been bought by the Saudis to create Islamist friendly indoctrination programs. Saudi Arabia exports radical Islam to every nation in the world. Why are we having so much trouble today with radical Islam? It's because Saudi Arabia has exported Wahabbism throughout the world. Today, we have over a billion people who bow down daily towards an image in Arabia while no one bows down towards Rome or even Jerusalem. Arabia is on a desert, Rome isn't. Arabia has oil, Rome doesn't. Arabia imports slaves, Rome doesn't. Arabia imports all of the specific merchandise in Revelation 18, Rome doesn't.

And so we have come full circle. On all counts, our search until this point has led us in one direction. The only nation on earth that precisely matches all of the descriptions necessary to qualify as Mystery Babylon is most clearly the Kingdom of Saudi Arabia.

The Reality
Turkey
Summary and Current Evidence

⨂90⨂
Turkey As The Antichrist Nation
Seven Scriptural Proofs

1. EZEKIEL 38 CONFIRMS
TURKEY'S LEADERSHIP ROLE

From the prophecies examined in the Book of Ezekiel, we saw that Turkey was significantly emphasized. Of the eight locations that were specified in the Gog Prophecy of Ezekiel 38, five were located firmly within Turkey. Magog, Meshech, Tubal, Togormah, and Gomer are all areas that were within the boundaries of modern Turkey. The fact that Turkey was so heavily emphasized is not something to be ignored. God highlighted Turkey for a reason. However, it is important that this theory be confirmed by other passages, as well.

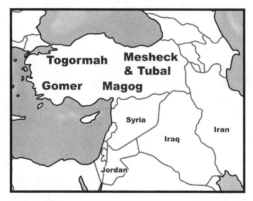

Map 1: Magog, Meshech, Tubal, Gomer and Togormah
all within the boundaries of modern Turkey

2. REVELATION 17 CONFIRMS
TURKEY'S LEADERSHIP ROLE

From Revelation 17, we concluded that the Islamic Empire, culminating in the Turkish Ottoman Empire, was the seventh Biblical Beast Empire. The capital of the Ottoman Empire was Istanbul, formerly Constantinople, the capital of the Eastern Roman Byzantine Empire. Today, Istanbul sits on the northwestern corner of Turkey. The reason that the location of the capitals of the last beast empire may be important is because as the head of the last beast empire, it is possible that it will receive the "fatal head wound" that will come back and awe the world: "One of the heads of the beast seemed to have had a fatal wound, but the fatal wound had been healed. The whole world was astonished and followed the beast" (Revelation 13:3).

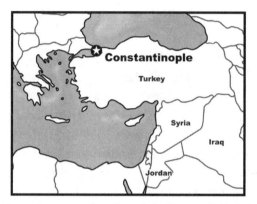

Map 2: Constantinople and Istanbul: The Capital of both the Byzantine and the Ottoman Empires

3. DANIEL 9 CONFIRMS TURKEY'S LEADERSHIP ROLE

We also examined Daniel 9, where the Bible says that it would be the "people of the prince to come" that would destroy the Jewish Temple. In other words, the ethnic peoples of whom the future Antichrist would be the leader would destroy the Jewish Temple. We saw that the primary group that carried out this destruction was the tenth legion of the Roman army (Legion X Fretensis), which was stationed in Antioch. Antioch was also the area from which the tenth legion drew most of its recruits. These soldiers were primarily Syrians and Arabs. Today, Antioch is located within the borders of Turkey, on the southeastern corner of Turkey near Syria. As such, this is yet another witness to the notion that the Antichrist would come from the region of modern Turkey.

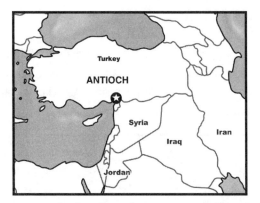

Map 3: Antioch, where the Tenth Roman Legion was garrisoned for much of the first century.

4. DANIEL 11 CONFIRMS TURKEY'S LEADERSHIP ROLE

Our fourth confirmation was found in Daniel 11, where we saw that the Antichrist was prefigured by Antiochus IV Epiphanies, the "King of the North" or the ruler of the Seleucid Division of the Greek Empire. We may expect to see the Antichrist emerge somewhere from within the region of the former Seleucid Empire. The Seleucid Empire covered a large portion of modern Turkey.

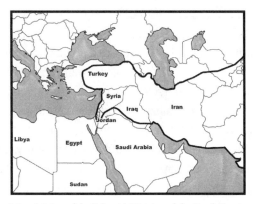

Map 4: Map of the Seluecid Division of the Greek Empire

5. ISAIAH AND MICAH
CONFIRM AN ASSYRIAN ROLL

We also studied the great emphasis that the prophets Isaiah and Micah placed on the future conflict between the Messiah and the Assyrian, who was a type of Antichrist. These prophecies also point us to the regions of the former Assyrian Empire, which engulfed a large portion of modern Turkey.

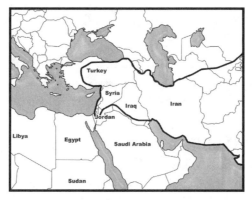

Map 5: The Assyrian Empire

6. ZECHARIAH CONFIRMS
TURKEY'S LEADERSHIP ROLE

Zechariah 9 clearly lists Yavan/Ionia (Turkey) as the primary player in the Last-Days attack against Israel. Many will have missed this prophecy due to a commonly used yet misleading translation: "I will rouse your sons, O Zion, against your sons, O Greece (Yavan, Ionia)." The key aspect of this passage is the reference to the sons of a place called Zion (Jews) fighting against the sons of a place called Yavan (Turks). Yavan was a descendant of Noah who came to live on the western coast of Asia Minor, or modern day Turkey, in the area that came to be known as Ionia. See also Joel 3:6. Zechariah 9 is clearly speaking in terms that only can be applicable to the Last-Days, and the return of Jesus the Messiah "Jehovah will appear over them." After this time, the Messiah will rule Israel and her land will be far greater than it is today:

> "He (the Messiah) will proclaim peace to the nations. His rule will extend
> from sea to sea and from the River to the ends of the earth. As for you,
> because of the blood of my covenant with you, I will free your prisoners
> from the waterless pit. Return to your fortress, O prisoners of hope; even

now I announce that I will restore twice as much to you. I will bend Judah as I bend my bow and fill it with Ephraim. I will rouse your sons, O Zion, against your sons, O Greece [Yavan, Ionia], and make you like a warrior's sword. Then Jehovah will appear over them; His arrow will flash like lightning. The Sovereign Jehovah will sound the trumpet; He will march in the storms of the South, and Jehovah Almighty will shield them. They will destroy and overcome with clingstones... Jehovah their God will save them on that day as the flock of His people. They will sparkle in His land like jewels in a crown. How attractive and beautiful they will be!" (Zechariah 9)

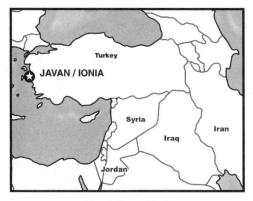

Map 6: Javan / Ionia

7. THE THRONE OF SATAN IS IN TURKEY

In Revelation chapter 2, Jesus is speaking to seven historical churches that were all situated along the west coast of Asia Minor, or modern day Turkey: "To the angel of the church in Pergamum write: These are the words of him who has the sharp, double-edged sword. I know where you live—where Satan has his throne" (Revelation 2:12-13).

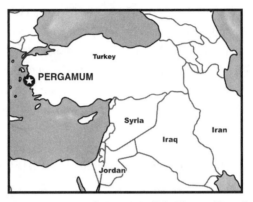

Map 7: Pergamum, the Location of "the Throne of Satan"

To many, this may be a strange question: Was there an actual literal geographic location where Satan had "a throne"? In a certain sense, yes. The verse is referring to a massive structure that sat atop a high hilltop in Pergamum. The Greeks originally built this gigantic structure in the 2nd century B.C. as a temple dedicated to Zeus. This in itself is interesting. Certain continuity exists between the various gods of beast empires. For instance, in ancient Egypt they worshipped Ra, the Sun god. In Babylon, there was Murdock, the Sun god and Sin, the Moon god (or goddess). The Greeks worshipped many gods, but viewed Zeus—the god of the sky and thunder—as the king over all of the other astral deities. Later, the Romans also worshipped Zeus under the name Jupiter. There is significant evidence to view the Allah of the Muslims as the Arab counterpart to Baal, Sin, Zeus, or Jupiter. In pre-Islamic times, Allah-worship, as well as the worship of Baal, were both astral religions in the sense that they involved the worship of the sun, the moon, and the stars.[1]

But notice that Jesus did not refer to the Pergamum Altar as the throne of Zeus, but rather as the throne of Satan. We can assume that Jesus made this point for a reason. While the various Beast Empires worshipped an assortment of gods under different names, Jesus actually referred to Zeus—the chief god of the ruling beast empire—as Satan. Zeus was Satan dressed in a Greek toga. This point is crucial as we attempt to understand the nature of the work of Satan in the earth in the Last-Days. We have already identified the re-emerging Islamic Empire as the final Beast Empire. We may also now identify Allah as Satan. This time, however, Satan is masquerading as the God of the Bible.

Not only does Jesus equate Zeus (or Jupiter) with Satan, but he also states that Satan's "throne", or spiritual base, was geographically located in Turkey. As unusual as this may sound, Satan may actually establish a geographical stronghold or a spiritual capital of sorts. This is not surprising. As late as the 19th century, this throne remained in Turkey, also the location of the capital of the Ottoman Empire. Beyond this, Pergamum was relatively close to Ionia (roughly one hundred miles north). All factors considered, this passage, by naming Turkey as the location of Satan's throne, also confirms Turkey's significant role in the Last-Days Antichrist Empire.

SATAN'S NEW HOME?

In two campaigns, starting in 1879, Satan's throne, or the Pergamum Altar, as it is now called, was excavated by a German archeological team. The altar was shipped out of the Ottoman Empire from the original location and was reconstructed in the Pergamon Museum in Berlin in the 19th century. Today, the altar still sits in Berlin where it can be seen alongside other monumental structures such as the Ishtar Gate from Babylon.

In 1934, Adolph Hitler became the dictator of Germany. Hitler ordered construction of the Tribune at Zeppelin Field in Nuremberg specifically for the purpose of his Nazi rallies. Several volumes have been written detailing the deeply occultist nature of the Nazi regime. Not surprisingly, then the Nazi architect of the *Zeppelintribune*, Albert Speer, actually used the Pergamum Altar as the model for what essentially became the premier Nazi pulpit. The Fuhrer's podium was located in the middle of the replica of the Pergamum Altar. In light of Hitler's brazen anti-Semitic spirit, and the horrors of the holocaust that accompanied his career, one can only conclude that Hitler did indeed conjure up a measure of that Satanic spirit that was present in Pergamum.

SATAN IS COMING HOME TO TURKEY

What is also interesting about all of this is that in March of 2006, the nation of Turkey, after failing to convince Germany to return the Altar decided to rebuild a perfect replica of the ancient Altar on the same ancient hill in Bergama, the location of ancient Pergamum. In March 2006, Turkish Culture and Tourism Minister Atilla Koc stated that, "There is no chance of having the altar returned from Germany, because we have no legal right. But now we have a new project. The exact copies (replicas) of those historical artifacts will be built on the original sites."[2]

This certainly makes one wonder if the same dark anti-Semitic spirit that seems to have followed this ancient Satanic altar to Germany, will now also find a welcome home in Turkey. In fact, there are many reasons to believe that this is already the case.

Let's examine the modern Nation of Turkey to see if she matches several other important political and military requirements to qualify as the leader of the Antichrist coalition.

QUALIFICATIONS TO BE ANTICHRIST

The first requirement the head nation of the Antichrist Empire must fulfill is the political capital to fill the role of mediator and guarantor of a comprehensive peace treaty between Israel and the surrounding nations that represent a threat to her: "He will confirm a covenant with many for one 'seven'" (Daniel 9:26).

In order to mediate such a covenant or treaty, this nation needs to have the reputation for being moderate and must possess the trust of the Israelis and the world. The Bible says that Israel will rely on this nation and will feel secure through the promises and terms established in the peace treaty. The Bible says that after Christ returns, "In that day the remnant of Israel, the survivors of the house of Jacob, will no longer rely on him who struck them down but will truly rely on Jehovah, the Holy One of Israel" (Isaiah 10:20). We know that Israel will trust the Antichrist because the Bible says the following about him: "On that day thoughts will come into your mind and you will devise an evil scheme. You will say, "I will invade a land of unwalled villages; I will attack a peaceful and unsuspecting people—all of them living without walls and without gates and bars. I will plunder and loot and turn my hand against the resettled ruins and the people gathered from the nations, rich in livestock and goods, living at the center of the land" (Ezekiel 38:10-13).

Another sign we should look for is latent or overt trends toward radical Islamism. Although we know that the Antichrist will initially appear to be moderate and trustworthy, he will also eventually show his true colors. And his success will come through deceit and shrewdness: "A stern-faced king, a master of intrigue, will arise. He will become very strong, but not by his own power. He will cause astounding devastation and will succeed in whatever he does. He will destroy the mighty men and the holy people. He will cause deceit to prosper, and he will consider himself superior. When they feel secure, he will destroy many and take his stand against the Prince of princes. Yet he will be destroyed, but not by human power" (Daniel 8:23-25).

Now let's compare all of the Scriptural requirements listed above to the modern nation of Turkey.

≈ 91 ≈
Turkey
The Mediator

✦

Modern Turkey fulfills the requirements of mediator nation far better than any other country in the world, hands-down. Turkey is the world's premiere mediator and bridge nation in the following ways:

Culturally and geographically situated between the East and West.

Culturally and geographically situated between the Middle East and Europe.

Politically situated between Israel and the Muslim World.

Politically and religiously situated between deceptive (moderate Islam) and more radical Muslim nations.

TURKEY AS A GEOGRAPHICAL AND CULTURAL BRIDGE

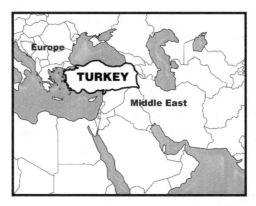

 Turkey has always enjoyed a measure of global significance because of its geographic location as the bridge or the gateway between Europe, the Middle East, and Asia. But throughout the past century, this bridge has been more than just geographic. After World War II, Mustafa Kemal Ataturk, the founder of the modern political state of Turkey, created and instituted sweeping secularist reforms to a nation that for hundreds of years had been the head of the (Islamic) Ottoman Empire. Ataturk's reforms have gone down in history as the work of a political genius. Through a seemingly foolproof system of numerous checks and balances, Ataturk ensured that only a democratic, secular government would rule Turkey for many years to come despite its Muslim dominated public. As such, throughout most of this century, Turkey has stood alone as a Muslim nation with significant secular and even Western values. But perhaps even more unique, in a sea of oftentimes-hostile Muslim nations, Turkey has also stood as a solid friend and ally to Israel and the United States. And though these friendships have experienced a cooling over the past few years, for now, the governments of Israel and the United States seem to be resting securely in the fact that Turkey is still a fully reliable ally.

However, Turkey's friendships have broadened over the past few years. Not only is Turkey an ally with Israel and the United States, but also with Iran, Syria, Pakistan, Afghanistan and nearly every other nation of significance. In the vast expanse that exists between such religiously and culturally diverse nations as the U.S. and Iran, Turkey has emerged as a nation that can relate to and bridge both worlds. In this regard, Turkey is unique in the world. Sensing the winds of change blowing throughout the globe and the opportunities that this represents, the government of Prime-Minister Recep Tayyip Erdogan and President Abdullah Gul has made sweeping efforts to position and portray Turkey as a peacemaker and mediator in nearly every single conflict that has occurred in the Middle East over the past several years. This is no exaggeration.

The most glaring example of Turkey's recent attempts at appearing to be global peacemakers, bridge-builders and general all around do-gooders is found in what is known as the United Nations Alliance of Civilizations Initiative. According to their official web-site, the Initiative, co-sponsored by the Spanish President Jose Luis Rodriguez Zapatero and Turkish Prime Minister Recep Tayyip Erdoan are summarized in the following terms: "The initiative responds to a broad consensus across nations, cultures, and religions that all societies are interdependent, bound together in their development and security, and in their environmental, economic, and financial well-being. The Alliance seeks to forge collective political will and to mobilize concerted action at the institutional and civil society levels to overcome the prejudice, misperceptions, and polarization that militate against such a consensus. The Alliance seeks to...establish a paradigm of mutual respect between civilizations and cultures."[3]

TURKEY—ISLAMIST AND MEDIATOR

In Daniel 9:27, the Antichrist will confirm a covenant with many—this deal is not only with Israel, but a peace treaty with many nations in the region. While stopping far short of promising to produce any Messianic utopia, the Alliance of Civilizations is certainly one of the most ambitious, high-level and international attempts in history to build bridges of unity between Western and Muslim nations. In light of all that we have examined and are expecting regarding the nation of Turkey, we should not be surprised to find out that they are spearheading such an initiative. By poising itself as a key mediator nation, Turkey is both positioning itself as a good candidate for admittance into the European Union, as well as increasing its regional significance and power. Professor Ruben Safrastyan, Ph.D. is the Professor of International Relations at Acharyan University in Yerevan, Armenia. He's also the Director of the Department of Turkish Studies at the Institute of Oriental Studies, Armenian National Academy of Sciences. In an article entitled, *Turkey as Mediator and Peacekeeper during Middle East Conflict*, Professor Ruben summarizes the reasons behind the recent exerted push for a mediator role in the Middle East: "The Government of the pro-Islamist Justice and Development Party (JDP) that came to power in 2002 restructured... the basic directions of the Turkish foreign policy...The Foreign Ministry of the country was instructed to improve relations with the Arab states and Iran, at the same time conserving allied relations with Israel on quite a cool level. *As a result Turkey will have the opportunity to get a mediating role both in the Middle East conflict and in the controversial relations between some Middle-Eastern countries and the West. Therefore, Turkey will become a key state in the region,* which will enhance its significance for the European Union and accelerate the process of Turkey's accession to that organization."[4]

This shift in Turkish policy was publicly displayed in Khartoum, Sudan at the Arab League Summit in 2006. In an article titled "Can Turkey Bridge the gap between Islam and the West?" Yigal Schleifer of the *Christian Science Monitor* reports that: "Prime Minister Recep Tayyip Erdogan delivered a speech at the opening of the Arab League summit in Khartoum, Sudan, where Turkey for the first time was given the status of 'permanent guest' by the organization. The prime minister's appearance at the summit—the first time a Turkish leader has done so—is the latest in a string of eyebrow-raising foreign policy moves...While the moves have ruffled feathers from Israel and Iraq to the US and European Union—which Turkey hopes to join—analysts say these aren't so much blunders as a reflection of a significant change in Turkey's Middle East foreign policy. 'Turkey wants to be a message-bringer from the Islamic world to the West,' says Huseyin Bagci, a professor of international relations at Ankara's Middle East Technical University (METU).

'The government really believes that it can be a bridge between East and West, and this is the foreign policy'...'Turkey also has another important quality in this regard, which is that it has relations with everybody [in the region]. We can effectively pass on messages. We have trust on both sides of various conflicts.' After decades of keeping the Arab and Muslim countries of the Middle East at arm's length, Turkey is trying to strengthen relations with its neighbors while at the same time recasting itself as a mediator in the region."[5]

During the past few years, Turkey has been seen mediating or offering mediation in nearly every significant Middle Eastern or Central Asian conflict. The Turkish government offered to act as a kind of mediator between the EU and the Islamic world when the controversial cartoons of the prophet Muhammad were published. Turkey has also suggested its ties to the West and its improving relations with Iran could help it act as a go-between in the diplomatic crisis over Tehran's disputed nuclear program.[6] During the conflict between Israel and Hamas in the Gaza strip in the summer of 2006, Turkey immediately volunteered to mediate a peace treaty between the two conflicting parties. The same volunteerism was offered during Israel's conflict with Hezbollah in Lebanon that summer, eventually resulting in Turkish peacekeeping troops stationed in Lebanon. After the very dramatic fall of Gaza to Hamas in the summer of 2007, Walid Salem, director of *Panorama, the Palestinian Center for the Dissemination of Democracy & Community Development in Jerusalem,* offered a comprehensive plan to correct the dire situation in Gaza. Not surprisingly, the solutions offered included a boycott of Hamas, with the only exception being the "attempt to influence their positions if still possible through relevant countries, such as Turkey."[7] And when Pakistan and Afghanistan had a dispute over illegal border crossings, where did the leaders of these countries travel to have their dispute settled? You guessed it—Turkey.

Pakistani President Gen. Pervez Musharraf and Afghan President Hamid Karzai met in Turkey with Turkish Prime Minister Recep Tayyip Erdogan mediating. Musharraf said that the meeting with Karzai had been brokered by Erdogan, who was "trying to mediate" between Pakistan and Afghanistan in the row over cross-border militant movements.

And when 15 British sailors were taken captive and held hostage by Iran in March of 2007, who was there offering mediation? You guessed it again. It was Turkey. "Turkey's bid to mediate in the escalating crisis between its eastern neighbor Iran and NATO ally Britain reflects [Turkey's] ambitions to act as a bridge between East and West, analysts said on Friday. 'As a country that has the confidence of both (Britain and Iran), Turkey is trying to ease the crisis,' said Arzu Celalifer, a researcher at the Ankara-based think-tank USAK."[8]

But for the purpose of our study, this next story is simply amazing. In February of 2007, Muslims all over the world openly expressed their outrage, claiming that Israel was violating or sabotaging the Temple Mount through its excavation work at the Mughrabi Gate. Who was called in to mediate the crisis and inspect the site? After a series of meetings in Turkey that month, Israeli Prime Minister Ehud Olmert agreed to let a Turkish delegation inspect the excavation site.

"Olmert had shown [Turkish Prime Minister Erdogan] photographs of the construction work near the Temple Mount during the Prime Minister's two-day trip to Turkey. However, the Turkish Prime Minister said Olmert had failed to convince him that the work would not harm the holy sites there... Olmert said that anyone who wanted to come look at the work taking place at the site was invited to do so, and that Israel had "nothing to hide." The issue has attracted a great deal of attention in Moslem Turkey, and before Olmert's visit Erdogan warned Israel not to increase tension over excavations at the site, saying it would lead to an uproar in the Islamic world."[9]

Think about this: in order for Israelis to do any archeological work around the Temple Mount, the ancient home of its own holy Temple, in its own country, they had to go through Turkey for permission. Truly, Turkey's political efforts to establish itself in the region as the premiere mediator nation have worked very well.

On a more global scale, when the situation in Iraq began to look as if it might not be stabilized by the United States, where did the experts turn? According to Dr. Muhammad Shamsaddin Megalommatis, an expert on the Middle East, writing for the *American Chronicle*, Turkey is "America's only honorable exit from Iraq." According to Megalommatis, "Only Turkey can avert an Islamic Terror Volcano Explosion in Iraq... Turkey can prevent the Iranian rise in power, and... impose Order and Democracy in Iraq... Turkey can help establish Order, Freedom, Democracy, and Justice in Iraq... [with] its centuries old know how, with its Ottoman experience, self-criticism and correct perception of the Wahhabi danger for the entire Mankind, with its Kemalist version of Secular Democracy for Muslims, with millions of Circassians, Turkmens, Turks and Azeris in Iraq and Iran as its natural allies."[10]

Perhaps Megalommatis is correct; perhaps in the end, it will be Turkey that will help the United States exit Iraq and restore order in the region. But the price will be heavy. Turkey will gain a foothold as a regional superpower and will increase its demand to acquire nuclear weapons. Every time the West depended on a Muslim country to neutralize another, the neutralizing country ended up becoming a ravishing beast. Afghanistan and Iraq are excellent examples. Ridding the world of Communist Russia by aiding Afghanistan ended up creating the Taliban. Aiding Iraq to neutralize Iran ended up with a war in Iraq the West still has to deal with.

Recep Tayyip Erdogan
Nov. 12, 2007

Looking to Mideast, not West, Turkey plays role of mediator
Israeli President Shimon Peres meets with Turkish Prime Minister
By Yigal Schleifer

Ankara, Turkey (JTA)—Lately, the diplomatic traffic in the Middle East seems to have found a new avenue: the Turkish capital. On Monday, both the Israeli and Palestinian Authority presidents addressed the Turkish parliament, marking the first time an Israeli head of state has spoken in the legislature of a Muslim country.

Days before that, Saudi Arabia's King Abdullah was in town for the second visit to Turkey by a Saudi monarch in the past 40 years. That trip came just a few weeks after an official visit to Ankara by Bashar Assad – the first Syrian president to have come to Turkey.

This all would have seemed nearly inconceivable only a few years ago.

For decades, Turkey kept the Arab and Muslim countries of the Middle East at arm's length as it focused on cementing its alliance with the West and distancing itself from the Ottoman Empire's Islamic past.

But now Turkey, led by the liberal Islamic Justice and Development Party, known by the acronym AKP, is trying to strengthen ties with its neighbors while at the same time recasting itself as a mediator in the region.

"This has always been part of their game plan," said Professor Henri Barkey, an expert on Turkey from Lehigh University in Easton, Pa. "The AKP has always felt that Turkey has punched below its weight internationally, that it had been too timid and sat in the corner."

Now the AKP is promoting Turkey in the role as peace broker.

In his speech to the 550-member parliament in Ankara, Israeli President Shimon Peres suggested Turkey's growing regional involvement gives it a role to play in helping solve the Middle East conflict.

"Turkey can make a unique contribution as both a global architect and a local actor," Peres said.

"We may be saying different prayers, but our eyes are turned toward the same sky and toward the same vision for the Middle East," he said in Hebrew, with translation into Turkish.

Peres and P.A. President Mahmoud Abbas came to Ankara to sign an agreement creating a joint industrial park on the West Bank-Israel boundary that is to be operated with Turkish help.

Cengiz Candar, a leading Turkish political analyst, says the industrial park project is indicative of the niche role Ankara – which has strong ties with Israel as well as Syria and Iran – would like to carve out for itself in the region.

"This whole exercise is a display of Turkey projecting 'soft power' in the Middle East," Candar said. "Turkey can play the role of a facilitator."

Turkey's newly vigorous Middle East foreign policy is not without risks, analysts warn.

Its reputation on Capitol Hill suffered damage in February 2006 when the country hosted a visit to Ankara by Hamas' leader in exile, Khaled Meshaal. Israel and members of the U.S. Congress immediately denounced the visit.

On the domestic front, Ankara's growing relations with its Muslim neighbors has led some critics from the secular establishment in Turkey to accuse the government of pursuing an "Islamic" foreign policy in the Middle East that would reorient Turkey eastward.

"Domestically there is both excitement and concern about this new foreign policy in the Middle East," said Murat Yetkin, an Ankara-based columnist for Radikal, a leading daily newspaper. "The excitement comes from rediscovering a geographical area you were once familiar with. On the other hand, there is concern about getting engaged too much."

For Israel, despite the remarkable visit to parliament by Peres, Turkey's new Middle East approach presents a mixed bag.

While it offers opportunities, such as Ankara playing the role of intermediary between Jerusalem and Damascus, the approach also diminishes some of the closeness Turkey and Israel have enjoyed in the past as isolated allies in a generally unfriendly region.

Over the last few years, the AKP government often has been more critical of Israeli actions than previous Turkish governments.

"The Turkey-Israel relationship is a lot less comfortable for Israel than it was six or seven years ago," said Alon Liel, a former Israeli diplomat in Turkey who later became chairman of the Turkey-Israel Chamber of Commerce.

Liel attributed the change to the rise of figures such as Turkish Prime Minister Recep Tayyip Erdogan and President Abdullah Gul, whom Liel said "are much more balanced in their relations with the Arab world than their predecessors."

Nevertheless, any expanded role Ankara wants to play in the Middle East, particularly that of a mediator in the Arab-Israeli conflict, will force Turkey to maintain its strong relations with Israel, Lehigh's Barkey said.

"The Turks have a potential role to play," he said. "The one very smart thing that the AKP has understood is that if you are going to have influence among the Arab countries, you have to have good relations with Israel."

~92~
Turkey
The Military Might

***

One of the main reasons Westerners believe that the Antichrist is western, is that he must have a powerful military force, and only Western nations meet this requirement. Yet, few in the West are aware of the fact that Turkey has one of the largest and most powerful militaries in the world. Among the 26 NATO member nations, Turkey has the second largest army, second only to the United States. 11 Turkey's army far supersedes the militaries of Germany, Spain, Italy, and England combined.

While the United States has roughly 2 million soldiers in its combined forces of Active Service Personnel and Reserve Troops, the Turkish army has over 4 million troops.

Because Turkey sits in such a vitally important and challenging geographic region, a powerful and agile military has also always been equally vital. Turkey is located in the Center of the Caucasus, Middle East and the Balkans; the most unstable region in the World. It is also a focal point where international geo-strategic lines and routes intersect. Turkey controls the strategic Turkish Straits; furthermore, it is positioned well to control the Suez Canal and consequently the maritime traffic in the region. Beyond all of this, in this age of uncertainty, the threat to the security of Turkey is not merely comprised of the various regimes and military powers in the region, but also of political, economic and social instabilities, border disputes, and terrorism. In light of all of this, the Turkish military has always remained strong and highly capable.

Regarding the second requirement the nation that will lead the Antichrist Kingdom must fulfill, Turkey once again meets it perfectly. Turkey most certainly has the military capital necessary to back up any comprehensive Middle East Peace plan. Turkey also has the military capabilities to attack and defeat any number of other nations in the region. Of course, Turkey's ability to attack Israel would be significantly amplified once she is joined by several other nations.

～93～
Turkey
The Hater

＋≈─⁎─≈＋

ANTI-SEMITIC AND ANTI-CHRISTIAN

Historically, until very recently, it is estimated that Muslim Turks have slaughtered an estimated 2.8 million Christians. Stanley Cohen, Professor of Criminology at the Hebrew University in Jerusalem, writes:

> "The nearest successful example [of collective denial] in the modern era is the 80 years of official denial by successive Turkish governments of the 1915-17 genocide against the Armenians in which 1.5 million people lost their lives. This denial has been sustained by deliberate propaganda, lying and cover-ups, forging documents, suppression of archives, and bribing scholars. Just as recent as 1974, secular and supposedly moderate Turkey invaded Cyprus, moved in Muslims, and ordered the Greeks to move out within 24 hours. Churches went up in flames or were converted into mosques. Seventy percent of its industry is now under Turkish control."[12]

Despite Turkey's western ties, her history is deeply underscored by an anti-Christian and Anti-Semitic spirit. Western appeasement of Islam in Turkey is based on the false assumption that Turkey, with its Kemalist views, is moderate. This view provoked fighting against Christian Serbs and Macedonians in order to support Bosnian and Albanian Muslims in Bosnia and Kosovo. Iranian Islamists and Chechens aided these groups in an attempt to re-Islamize the Balkans. And despite the supposed friendship that has existed between America and Turkey throughout much of the last few decades, this relationship taken a drastic turn in the other direction. Just before the Iraq War, the Turkish Grand National Assembly vetoed a bill to allow passage to some 60,000 American troops through Turkish territory into northern Iraq. Americans were bewildered because the Turks had always been seen as a reliable friend and partner. The Turks, however, felt America had ignored sensitivities regarding the status of northern Iraq, which borders Turkey and is often used as a launching ground by Kurdish separatists who infiltrate Turkey and carry out terrorist attacks.

Adding to this wedge, a few months later, and Turkish-American relations again took a serious blow when eleven Turkish Special Forces officers on a surveillance mission in the northern Iraqi town of Sulaymaniyah were arrested by American forces and taken to Baghdad. This became known as the "Hood Incident" because the Turks were all seen being transported with black hood-like bags over their heads. Most Americans thought very little of it. The Turks, however, who are very proud of their military and their country, were humiliated and felt enraged at the United States' disgrace of their soldiers. This was an unforgivable act in the eyes of many Turkish citizens and is remembered by them with great contempt. No official apology was ever extended apart from a note signed by Defense Secretary Donald Rumsfeld saying that America regretted the incident. This infuriated the people of Turkey, and relations between the U.S. and Turkey have suffered as a result.

GROWING HATRED

A Turkish movie entitled "Valley of the Wolves Iraq" debuted in 2006, revealing Turkish sentiments toward America. The story opens with a reference to the "Hood Incident." According to the plot, one of the arrested Turkish officers commits suicide out of shame and leaves a note for his friend Polat Alemdar, the protagonist, asking him to avenge his dishonor. Complying with the wishes of his friend, Alemdar follows the Christian fundamentalist American commander who is responsible for both the "hood incident" and the mass slaughter of thousands of innocent of Iraqi civilians. The movie stars Gary Busey, who plays a Jewish-American doctor who harvests the organs of Iraqis to be sold in New York, London, and Tel Aviv. This movie became one of Turkey's greatest theatrical hits of all time. People lined up outside of theaters to view it again and again. Turkish hatred for America and Israel is growing more each day. Many Turks believe that this movie depicts the truth about America and Israel.

Other examples of growing anti-Semitic and anti-Christian attitudes are evident in two of Turkey's best-selling books. Adolph Hitler's Mein Kampf (My Struggle) which has been subsidized and sold very cheaply by multiple publishing houses in various translations has recently become a bestseller. Another bestseller is entitled *Attack on the Pope: Who will Kill the Pope in Istanbul?* The cover of the book features a man firing a rocket propelled grenade at Pope Bendict. A study examining the rise in anti-Semitism in Turkey conducted by *The Stephen Roth Institute for Contemporary Study of Anti-Semitism and Racism* points out that in various mainstream newspapers, it is common to read anti-Semitic slurs and conspiracy theories that demonize Jews. Holocaust denial is also common. According to the study: "Translations of classic anti-Semitic tracts such as The

Protocols of the Elders of Zion and *Henry Ford's International Jew,* are sold at well-known bookstores.13

Clearly, both anti-Semitism and Anti-Christian sentiments are on the rise in Turkey.

~94~
Turkey
Fallen To The Islamists

✦

In my book *Why I Left Jihad,* I quoted Serge Trifkovic, the director of the *Center for International Affairs*, who commented on Turkey:

"The simmering Islamic volcano in the villages of Anatolia and in the poor neighborhoods of the sprawling cities makes us wonder not 'if' but 'when.' If and when Turkey becomes a fully fledged democracy, that instant it will become Islamic."[14]

I also quoted Stanley Cohen, a professor at *Hebrew University in Jerusalem*, who said: "It's still considered part of NATO and a 'friend' of the U.S. regardless that Turkey's past is rising up, as from a wounded beast, and turning into a ravishing monster. It is no wonder that The CIA's *1997 State Failure Task Force Report* identified Turkey as a nation in danger of collapse. The West needs to come to grips with the realization that Turkey is not a democracy, and any efforts to establish a democracy in it will prove fatal since democracy, like the attempts in Iraq, will only be used for electing an Islamic Sharia-driven system."

Both Trifkovic and Stanley's words predicted the situation perfectly—Turkey has now fallen to the Islamists and is it not amazing to see Stanley, a secularist, use the phrase, *"wounded beast"* to describe Turkey? This is precisely how the Bible describes the wounded defunct Ottoman Beast Empire that will revive at the end of the age. It will be near impossible for the United States to deal with Iran's nuclear weapons, the Iraq War, and Turkey's decline into Islamism simultaneously. Yet that is exactly what America is now facing. At the time of this writing, in August of 2007, the AKP Islamist party of Turkey, through completely democratic means, won the final election necessary to seize control of the entire Turkish government. This is monumental. The longest standing secular democracy in the Muslim world fell to the Islamist Party. Prime Minister Recep Tayyip Erdogan and the newly elected President Abdullah Gul now lead the AKP. The AKP also now holds a majority of Parliamentary seats. Consequently, an openly Islamist party now dominates the Turkish government and leverages Turkey's system of checks and balances completely in their own favor. Now, all they need to do is take control of the military. In order to understand the significance of this, one needs to understand who these leaders are and what they represent within the historically secular Muslim nation of Turkey.

Elisabeth Eaves of *Forbes Magazine* explains: "It all started on April 27th [2007] when Turkey's parliament, dominated by the governing Justice and Development Party, or AKP, nominated Foreign Minister Abdullah Gul for the presidency. Gul, like AKP leader Recep Tayyip Erdogan, has his roots in Turkey's Islamist movement. In recent years, AKP has taken actions seen as religiously motivated, like trying to ban adultery and encourage religious schools. Though Gul has pushed forward talks with the European Union and is widely seen as pro-Western and diplomatic, his opponents within Turkey regard him as an Islamist and thus a menace to secular government."[15]

To understand how serious the takeover of the Turkish Government by an Islamist party is, consider some of the comments made by outgoing Turkish President, Ahmet Necdet Sezer in his farewell speech. Aside from Sezer's very sober warnings, he stated the following:

"Turkey's political regime is under unprecedented threat...Political Islam is being imposed on Turkey as a model...A plot is being carried out, according to a well-defined timeline, against the Turkish Armed Forces. Foreign forces—and domestic ones, to serve their own interests—are, under the pretext of 'democracy,' trying to transform Turkey's secular republic and to create a model of a 'moderate Islamic republic' to serve as an example for Islamic countries to follow. 'Moderate Islam' would mean that the state's social, economic, political, and legal system would reflect, to some extent, the laws of the religion. By this definition, the 'moderate Islam model' might represent 'progress' for the Islamic countries—but for Turkey, it means 'regression.' This is a model of 'fundamentalism' [that Turkey rejects]."[16]

Sezer also claimed that it was only matter of time before a "moderate" Islamic government would become radical. Likewise, Dr. Megalommatis, also a supporter of the secular government in Turkey, used even stronger language to describe the seriousness of the Islamist takeover: "In Turkey, the real enemy is the Islamist movement with the lewd and gawky prime minister and foreign minister, who attempt to devise their simulative scheme of Turkey's Islamization, vulgarization, and barbarization. Playing with the divisions of Turkey's civilized political establishment, utilizing the inconsistencies of the electoral law, and relying on the perfidious support of Turkey's worst external enemies, Erdogan and Gul consist in national threat No. 1 for the entire country."[17]

If you are doubtful regarding Sezer's and Megalommatis's claims, then consider some of the comments that have been made by the architect of the recent takeover, Prime Minister Erdogan himself. Despite Erdogan's endless public expressions of being pro-democracy, pro-European Union, pro-America, pro-Israel, pro-peace, and pro-Global-unity, Erdogan was caught making the infamous quote that, "Democracy is like a streetcar. You ride it until you arrive at your destination and then you get off."[18]

It was also reported that Erdogan's undersecretary stated that it was necessary to replace secularism and republicanism with a more participatory, Islamic system.[19] On another occasion, in a rare moment of transparency, Erdogan recited the following portion of a radical Islamic poem that he wrote: "[The] Mosques are our barracks, [the] domes our helmets, [the] minarets our bayonets, [the] believers our soldiers. This holy army guards my religion. Almighty, our journey is our destiny, the end is martyrdom." If these comments had come from Osama Bin Laden or Mahmoud Ahmadinejad, they would seem in place; however, they come from one of the most powerful Muslim leaders in the Middle East. Therefore, they should be deeply disturbing to world leaders everywhere. These comments are also contradictory. They sound as if they have come from the lips of a radical suicide bomber, yet they come from the man who America and Israel trust implicitly. These comments come from the man who has helped forge the UN "Alliance of Civilizations" and who is frequently heard quoting Mevlana Jalaluddin Rumi, the famous peace-loving Sufi Muslim mystic. So who is the real Erdogan, the Muslim Ghandi or the reincarnation of Gygez? In light of the evidence that there may be more to Erdogan than we see on television, we should not be surprised to hear Professor Ruben Safrastyan refer to him as someone who is, "very skillful in political manipulations."[20]

Scripture warns, "A vile person...shall come in peaceably, and seize the kingdom by intrigue" (Daniel 11:21).

Yet another necessary requirement of the leader of the Antichrist Kingdom has found its fulfillment in Turkey. Latent or even more overt trends toward anti-Semitism and anti-Christian attitudes are clearly found in growing measure within modern Turkey. Far more significant, a potential sleeper cell, and a radical Islamist government in disguise has seized control of what has historically been the most moderate and secular Muslim nation in the world. If the nation of Turkey continues along the road that it is on, the implications for the West will be devastating. As British journalist John Hooper stated as far back as 1996, "the scope for conflict, were Turkey, like Iran, to 'go Islamic' would be immense." Nevertheless, if Turkey actually joins forces with Iran and several other Islamist nations, as the Bible says, then "immense" will not even begin to describe the devastating impact for Israel and the United Sates.

≈ 95 ≈
Turkey In Islamic Prophecy

✦

MUSLIM PROPHECY PREDICTED
THE FALL OF TURKEY TO THE ISLAMISTS

I once partook in an Irish National Television debate with Anjum Choudry, a leader of the defunct *Al-Muhajirun* terror organization in England. Choudry began spouting hatred for Kamal Attaturk, calling him a stooge who abolished the Caliphate. He claimed Islam must be re-established where it was wounded. Today, Choudry's dream is coming true—the fall of the Turkish government to an Islamist political party bears heavy prophetic significance among apocalyptically minded Muslims.

Satan, who understands the Bible, had set up his own prophecies about the first and second rise of the Turkish Empire. Among the numerous Islamic traditions, there exists a series of prophecies that speak of the fall of Constantinople to Islam. When Mehmet II, leader of the Muslim armies conquered Constantinople in 1453, he played up these prophecies to his troops, empowering them with a euphoric sense of divine purpose. "Allah will conquer Constantinople (Istanbul) for the people of His most loved friends," he said. "Verily you shall conquer Constantinople. What a wonderful leader will her leader be, and what a wonderful army will that army be!"[21]

Yet the *second* conquering of Constantinople by Islam is looming on the horizon. This one is said to be accomplished through peaceful means just prior the ends of days. *The Great War*, as it is called in Islam, will occur just after the conquest of Constantinople. "The flourishing state of Jerusalem will be when Yathrib (Medina) is in ruins, the ruined state of Yathrib will be when the Great War comes, and the outbreak of the Great War will be at the conquest of Constantinople and the conquest of Constantinople when the Dajjal (Antichrist) comes forth. He (the Prophet) struck his thigh or his shoulder with his hand and said: This is as true as you are here or as you are sitting."[22]

Just as Israel's re-taking of Jerusalem in 1967 boosted Christian moral worldwide, the re-conquering of Constantinople for Islam will empower Muslims. Several years before the fall of Turkey to the Islamist party, Muslim apocalyptic writer Sidheeque Veliankode commented that, "the first conquering of Constantinople by Mehmet II was merely a preparatory war before the actual conquest of it at the last hour. However, the Hadith commentators suggest that the overthrow of Constantinople State Government after the downfall of the Islamic Caliphate era confirms the return of the same state—God willing—to the hands of the Muslims."[23]

When searching for the Antichrist, one must never look to the Ahmadinejads or Usamas of the world, but instead to someone with a moderate mask—at least in the beginning. His sinister, rabid hatred for Jews and Christians will not be revealed until he lures the sheep into his den. Everyone in the Middle East knows Abduallah Gul, whose name literally means "the Servant of Allah the Demon."

The Islamic paradigm, as it seems from our study, is one of the most significant keys to unlock the Bible's ancient prophecies. Satan knows the Bible inside out, and thus attempts to sway the gullible by taking true prophecies and shifting the outcome. Israel won against all odds never to be pulled up again (Amos 9:15)—all I needed to do when I was Muslim was tune out the wrong channel. *This is why Christ Himself warned, Be wise as a serpent, and innocent as doves.*

≈96≈
The Reality

+≡⊱ ✳ ⊰≡+

THE RISE OF MAHDISM
AND THE CALIPHATE MOVEMENT

THE CRY FOR MAHDI—ITS NOW A REALITY

Even if you don't believe the Bible, world circumstances are now bearing out exactly what it predicts will happen. Either the prophets are prophets, or they are perfect guessers. The call for a unified Islamic coalition ruled by an Islamic dictator is now quickly becoming a reality. On September 17, 2005, the Iranian President Mahmoud Ahmadinejad addressed the United Nations National Assembly in New York City. He concluded his speech with the following declaration and prayer: "From the beginning of time, humanity has longed for the day when justice, peace, equality, and compassion envelop the world. All of us can contribute to the establishment of such a world. When that day comes, the ultimate promise of all Divine religions will be fulfilled with the emergence of a perfect human being who is heir to all prophets and pious men. He will lead the world to justice and absolute peace. O mighty Lord, I pray to you to hasten the emergence of your last repository, the promised one, that perfect and pure human being, the one that will fill this world with justice and peace."

Think about this: Before the United Nations National Assembly, in the heart of New York City, The President of Iran called out to his god to hasten the emergence of the Mahdi—the one who would ultimately cause the religion of Islam to rule over the earth and destroy all those who refuse to submit. When has this ever happened?

Western reporters scrambled to identify this mysterious *Al-Mahdi* and found him in the ancient sources of both Shi'a and Sunni holy writ. The West finally had their first introduction to Islam's awaited Messiah. On November 16, 2005, Ahmadinejad, like a Muslim John the Baptist, exhorted crowds in Tehran to pave the way, proclaiming that his main mission as the President of Iran is to "pave the path for the glorious reappearance of Imam Mahdi—may Allah hasten his reappearance."[24] As if that is not astonishing enough, according to Ahmadinejad, this Mahdi will arrive in the next two years (Jackson Diehl, Washington Post).[25] The personal relationship with this Muslim-Messiah goes beyond announcing his soon coming—Ahmadinejad even claims to converse with this Mahdi-Messiah.[26]

If one thinks this is an anomaly, think again. Iranian leaders set up an institute in 2004 for the study and dissemination of information about the Mahdi. It is fully staffed, and even produces children's magazines to influence the younger generation—a Hitler style youth brainwashing of masses who await the Grand Imam and Islam's supreme ruler and Messiah.[27]

With weapons of mass destruction and a few nuclear bombs, he might even cause lightening to come down from heaven as the predicted Mahdi will do—with one slight adjustment; however, the carrier of his nuclear-tipped Shahab will be a transit flight lobbed from an ocean-liner right over New York city. The Shahab, the choice name picked for Iran's missile, literally means lightening. Everything except the completion of his nuclear program is in place, including the reception site of Mahdi—over $20 million dollars was spent refurbishing the Mosque in Jamkaran just outside the "holy city" of Qom. It is ready for the grand finale; the countdown has begun.

HOJJATIEH—THE LUNATICS ARE RUNNING THE ASYLUM

From the birth pangs of the Holocaust, Israel was born. Why is it every time I speak to a secular audience about Israel, Muslims tell me the birth of Israel was a self-fulfilled prophecy? Did the Jews drag six million to their death in order to accomplish such a thing? What does one think about Iran's Hojjatieh Society, considered by mainstream Shi'a Muslims to be the lunatic fringe? The Hojjatieh Society is governed by the conviction that the 12th Imam's return can be hastened by the creation of a period of chaos on earth which they must fulfill. The group is so extreme that even the late hardliner Ayatollah Khomeini banned them in 1983. This is the same Khomeini who, when asked by a companion how he wanted the Ministry of Justice restructured, replied, "Anyone who is against me is against Allah and must be killed where they stand. No other justice system is required." It is easy to understand why so many claim that Ahmadinejad is a member of Hojjitieh. Ahmadinejad's mentor and spiritual advisor, Ayatollah Mesbah Yazdi, is considered by many to presently be the highest-ranking member of the Hojjatieh Society. But it is the defining element of the Hojjatieh Society that has so many concerned—as stated, Hojjatieh believes that the Mahdi's return will be preceded by world chaos, war, and bloodshed throughout the earth. After this cataclysmic confrontation between the forces of good and evil, the Mahdi will lead the world to an era of universal peace. The danger present with this volatile combination of beliefs has not been articulated any better than by former Israeli prime minister Netanyahu, who described Hojjatieh this way: "I was looking for an analogy to try to explain to Americans what it is that is so dangerous about Iran acquiring nuclear weapons. You remember those crazy people in Waco, Texas? Imagine David Koresh with nuclear weapons. Imagine David Koresh, not with hundreds of followers, but millions of followers, with nuclear weapons, wanting to obliterate America, wanting to obliterate America's allies, wanting to take over the world's oil supply. If the lunatics escape from the asylum, that is one thing; however, if they can can get their hands on a nuclear weapon, that is another. This is that kind of cult. It's the cult of the Mahdi."[29]

In truth, no one should view Ahmadinejad as a John the Baptist paving the way for Messiah. A more fitting parallel is Judas Iscariot; the zealot who many speculate attempted to force Jesus to take his throne as King of Israel by betraying him. The Hojjatieh are to the Muslim world what some Jewish Zealots were to first century Jews. They believe they can manipulate Allah and force the Mahdi to appear. Or perhaps Allah will find a better candidate with more manipulating charisma to be his right arm.

MAHDIST RUMBLINGS IN IRAQ

But among those monitoring Iran's Mahdi obsession, few point out the spread of this infestation in neighboring Iraq, in not only the Shi'a strain, but also the Sunni. In January of 2007, American troops in Iraq, like pest control, fighting from one area to another, killed Ahmed Hasani al-Yemeni, a man who had claimed to be the Mahdi. Hasani was the leader of a group known as the *Jaish al-Janna* (Army of Heaven), and had gathered between six and seven hundred followers, including many Sunni Muslims recruited from the ranks of al-Qaeda.[30]

But Jaish al-Janna is not the only Mahdist group that has recently emerged in Iraq. In fact, according to Zeyad Kesim, a monitor of key Arabic websites in Iraq, Jaish al-Janna is only the tip of the iceberg. According to Zeyad, there are now at least seven different Mahdist sects in Iraq, each one believing that the return of the Mahdi is imminent.

FALSE MAHDIS AND FALSE MESSIAHS

In the 19th century in Algeria, several individuals claimed to be the forerunner to the Mahdi. We should not be at all surprised if the Middle East soon provides us with another popular claimant to this office. This time, however, his gathering of followers will not be so localized or limited. As we witness, heads of state and numerous Muslim groups gather to proclaim his coming like a perfect storm. Timothy Furnish, American scholar of Mahdist movements, recently commented: "The historical situation in Iraq right now, with all these Mahdist and near-Mahdist claimants, reminds me very much of that in Algeria under French occupation in the mid-19th century. There, too, a myriad of Mahdist 'forerunners' emerged to challenge the French in the name of the coming Mahdi before, finally, in 1879 one Muhammad Amzian actually, publicly proclaimed himself the Mahdi... No military or political solution is going to work in Iraq until this enormously powerful eschatological element in the region (both Sunni and Shi`i) is addressed."[31]

I might add it is also very similar to two other key time periods. The first being first century Israel, where, just prior to the ministry of Jesus, many false claimants to the office of Messiah had emerged. The Bible says: "*But when the fullness of the time came, God sent forth His Son, born of a woman*" (Galatians 4:4). When Christ was born in Israel in the first century, the time was ripe socially, politically, religiously and prophetically for a messiah to emerge. Indeed, the Messiah arrived. However, many other *false* messiahs also emerged during this period. Like then, we are presently seeing yet another set of circumstances that will most assuredly lead to the emergence of a false messiah figure somewhere in the Muslim world.

This leads to the other key time period that will provide us with numerous false messiahs. This, of course, is the End-Times. What will be the sign of Messiah's coming and of the end of the age? Jesus answered: "Watch out that no one deceives you. For many will come in my name, claiming, 'I am the Christ, and will deceive many...At that time if anyone says to you, 'Look, here is the Christ!' or, 'There He is!' do not believe it. For false christs and false prophets will appear and perform great signs and miracles to deceive even the elect—if that were possible. See, I have told you ahead of time. "So if anyone tells you, 'There He is, out in the desert,' do not go out; or, 'Here He is, in the inner rooms,' do not believe it" (Matthew 24:3-5, 23-26).

Jesus made it clear that in the Last-Days, many deceivers would emerge claiming to be the Messiah or a prophet, and leading many people astray. As we look at the present explosion throughout the Muslim world of Islamic Messianism, all believers should realize that this is a clear sign that we are now approaching the End-Times.

THE TIME IS RIPE FOR A REVIVED MUSLIM CALIPHATE

It's not only a call for Mahdi, but a revival of the Caliphate as well. Muslims regard themselves as members of one *Ummah*, or community of Muslim believers. This concept dominates the Muslim world. This sense of community and loyalty to Muhammad and Allah even trumps family and other societal ties giving reason as to why many Muslims do not hesitate to kill even family members who give up the Islamic faith. Add to this the simple fact that the Islamic sacred traditions are filled with prophecies foretelling the triumph of Islam over the whole world. The eventual conquest and complete Islamization of the earth is as natural an expectation for most Muslims as the rising of the sun.

Muslims have a sense of entitlement, feeling as if world domination is simply their destiny. Therefore, for the past 80 plus years, since the actual abolition of the Caliphate, the Muslim believer has felt a deep disorder in the power balance of the world. Rather than a united Islamic Empire under a Caliph, the Islamic World has existed as a network of underachieving and defeated nation states. They see the modern Muslims states in the Middle East as a product of the evil of the Western powers (despite being secular states, Muslims often see them as Christian nations) who divide the Islamic Caliphate. At the same time, too often they are ruled by corrupt third-rate dictators who live in luxury while their people live in poverty.

Again, they often see these tyrants as being installed or supported by the evil Western powers. A people who viewed themselves as the world's foremost superpower for over thirteen hundred years has been a divided network of backwater nation states for nearly a century now. And to compound this emotional blow, this humbling has taken place during the 20th century, a time when numerous other nations—particularly those founded on Judeo-Christian principles—have excelled in everything from government to human rights, scientific breakthroughs, fiscal prosperity, education, military strength and more.

So it has been the combination of prosperity and advancement in so many parts of the non-Muslim world contrasted with the complete deterioration of the once thriving Islamic Empire that has been on display as the shame of the whole Muslim World. Add again to all this the fact that the Muslim world is an Eastern culture, where honor and shame mean everything. Overall, the psychological impact and the resentment of the Muslim world is nearly all consuming. In addition, where does this resentment and pent-up anger fall? In such a drastically disordered world, conspiracy theories and blame shifting are common outlets for anger. Muslims blame all of their ills on Israel (or, as it is so often called, "The World-Zionist Conspiracy") as well as the various Western colonizing "crusader forces" of previous centuries. Looking back at the pre-colonial days of Islamic

Empire, two thoughts often emerge in the modern Muslim mind: The first is to recapture their former glory, and the second is to punish those who have withheld it for so long. All of these aspirations are most often summarized negatively in the overthrow and destruction of Israel and the West, while they are expressed positively in the messianic expectations concerning the re-establishment of the Caliphate.

Today, the Muslim world is ripe for the re-emergence of the Caliphate. And dozens of pro-Caliphate movements are experiencing explosive growth throughout the earth. In 2007, well over 100,000 Muslims gathered in Indonesia for the Hizb-ut-Tahrir's pro-Caliphate conference. Just outside Haifa in Israel over 50,000 Muslims gathered. And in London, tens of thousands gathered. The movement has large and very active groups functioning across the globe; from Russia to England, from Indonesia to Egypt. But what very few are aware of is that despite the different names and methods of terrorist groups that appear on the news, nearly all share a similar goal: the restoration of a pan-Islamic Caliphate and the establishment of Islamic Shariah law—first among the Muslim states and then eventually in the whole earth. This holds true for both Sunni and Shi'a Islamist groups, for Al-Qaeda, Hizb-ut-Tahrir, The Muslim Brotherhood, The Iranian Revolution, and dozens of other groups as well.

PRO-CALIPHATE GROUPS OPERATING IN ISRAEL

In February of 2006, Sheikh Ismail Nawahda of Guiding Helper Foundation, preached to a gathering of Muslims on the Temple Mount in Jerusalem. He called upon them to restore the Caliphate, or, as he explained, "Genuine Islamic Rule", which would "unite all the Muslims in the world against the infidels." And only a few months later, Sheikh Raed Salah of the Islamic Movement in Israel, addressing over 50,000 Muslims just outside the Israeli city of Haifa, declared: "Jerusalem will soon be the capital of a Moslem Arab Caliphate, and all efforts by the Israeli establishment to Judaize the city will amount to nothing... soon Jerusalem will be the capital of the new Muslim caliphate, and the caliph's seat will be there."[32]

Yet despite the very real threat an Islamic Caliphate represents, liberals and the everything-is-fine-Bush-is-just-a-cowboy-reactionary-fear-monger crowd that sadly dominates much of the left-wing Western media regularly mock the idea.

PRESENT DAY REVIVAL: KHILAFAT MOVEMENT TODAY

The fact is the fervor for a renewed Caliphate is at the highest level it has reached since its abolishment. In December of 2006, the Jamestown Foundation, an international intelligence think-tank, wrote about the rising growth and appeal of pro-Caliphate groups such as Hizb-ut-Tahrir (HT). The report was based on both an in-depth analysis of statistics and trends throughout the Muslim world and direct interviews with several high-ranking HT operatives in JorDaniel Jamestown concluded that HT's influence is drastically spreading throughout the Muslim world. HT is often a gateway or a "conveyor belt" into other pro-Caliphate groups with a more violent tendency, like al-Qaeda or the Muslim Brotherhood (*Al-Ikhwan*), with which I was formerly involved.

Many surveys show that since the U.S led invasions of Afghanistan and Iraq, Muslims almost universally have seen the war against terrorism as a war on Islam. Muslims regard themselves as members of the ummah, or community of believers, that forms the heart of Islam. As the earthly head of that community, the Caliph is cherished both as memory and ideal. The caliphate is still esteemed by many ordinary Muslims. 33

The University of Maryland conducted a face-to-face survey of 4,384 Muslims between December 9, 2006 and February 15 2007 (1000 Moroccans, 1000 Egyptians, 1243 Pakistanis, and 1141 Indonesians). Andrew Bostom, author of *The Legacy of Jihad* and an expert on Islamic Jihad commented on the results: "65.2% of those interviewed—almost two-thirds, hardly a 'fringe minority'—desired this outcome: 'To unify all Islamic countries into a single Islamic state or Caliphate', including 49% of 'moderate' Indonesian Muslims. 65.5% of this Muslim sample approved the proposition 'To require a *strict* application of Shari'a law in every Islamic country.'34

How many times have you heard that "most" of the Muslims of the world are moderate and are not a threat to the West? How many times have you heard that we only need to worry about a "small minority"? Does a two-thirds sound like a small minority to you? It is time to get real.

AMERICAN INTELLIGENCE CONFIRM RISE OF CALIPHATE

Even if the University of Maryland/ WorldPublicOpinion.org poll is not enough to convince you of the real threat of an established Caliphate, consider a report released through the National Intelligence Council (NIC) in 2004. The NIC is the American Intelligence Community's foremost "center for mid-term and long-term strategic thinking". The Council is the premier think-thank consulting the United States' National Director of Intelligence. In other words, this is not a low-level partisan think-tank dispensing opinions that merely support their political agendas. The NIC's resources consist of a broad range of academics and experts from around the globe. In late 2004, the Council released a study titled *Project 2020, Mapping the Global Future*. The study explores what it deems to be the four most-likely geo-political scenarios that we should expect to see by the year 2020. One of the scenarios describes the emergence of a pan-Islamic Caliphate. The conclusions of the study are below:

"A Caliphate would not have to be entirely successful for it to present a serious challenge to the international order. This scenario underlines the saliency of the cross-cultural ideological debate that would intensify with growing religious identities...The IT revolution is likely to amplify the clash between Western and Muslim worlds... The appeal of a Caliphate among Muslims would vary from region to region, which argues for Western countries adopting a differentiated approach to counter it. Muslims in regions benefiting from globalization, such as parts of Asia and Europe may be torn between the idea of a spiritual Caliphate and the material advantages of a globalized world. The proclamation of a Caliphate would not lessen the likelihood of terrorism and in fomenting more conflict, could fuel a new generation of terrorists intent on attacking those opposed to the Caliphate, whether inside or outside the Muslim world. The nation-state will continue to be the dominant unit of the global order, but economic globalization and the dispersion of technologies, especially information technologies, will place enormous new strains on governments. Growing connectivity will accompany the proliferation of virtual communities of interest, complicating the ability of states to govern. The Internet in particular will spur the creation of even more global movements, which may emerge as a robust force in international affairs. Part of the pressure on governance will come from new forms of identity politics centered on religious convictions. In a rapidly globalizing world experiencing population shifts, religious identities provide followers with a ready-made community that serves as a 'social safety net' in times of need—particularly important to migrants. In particular, political Islam will have a significant global impact leading to 2020, rallying disparate ethnic and national groups and perhaps even creating an authority [the Caliphate] that transcends national boundaries. A combination of factors—youth bulges in many Arab states, poor economic prospects, the influence of religious education, and the Islamization of such institutions as trade unions, nongovernmental organizations, and political parties—will ensure that political Islam remains a major force."[35]

We think that the War on Terror is tough now. But this report only speculates on a very limited and struggling Caliphate. What would the ramifications of a successful Caliphate be? Far beyond drastic, the results of such a Caliphate would be *catastrophic* for the West. Nor does the report discuss what might happen if such a Caliphate were to be established far sooner than 2020. There are certainly reasons to suggest that this very well may be the case. Again, this report was released in 2004. This was before the advent of the maniacal and obviously apocalyptic Iranian President Mahmoud Ahmadinejad and his drive for nuclear capability. It preceded the clash between Israel and Hezbollah and the changes that that brought. It came before the fall of Turkey to the Islamist party. Since 2005, the difficulties in the Middle East have compounded as geo-political realities shifted more than they have in the previous twenty years. Could the emergence of a pan-Islamic Caliphate be a reality much sooner than the Project 2020 report suggests? Only God knows.

WHY THE CALIPHATE IS A THREAT TO THE WEST

The Caliphate confers legitimacy to jihad. According to Islamic law, without a Caliphate, it is not possible to declare a genuinely sanctioned pan-Islamic Jihad. Similar to the need for the President of the United States to declare a state of war, it is also necessary for a Caliph to be in office for any official pan-Islamic Jihad to be declared. But once a Caliph is in office, it is actually law for him to engage the non-Muslim world in war in order to spread Islam. This is not to say that Muslims have not conducted jihad against non-Muslims, but these have largely been the acts of small groups or individuals. In other words, jihad under a Caliph would be genuine "old school" jihad—not a bombing here or an attack there. It would become the modern world's first true full-scale global religious war. It would involve everything that the Islamic world could throw out, from economic jihad to withholding oil to cyber jihad to multi-front military conflicts.

Traditionally, the land with whom the Caliphate was at war was referred to as *Dar al-Harb*—"land of war"—in contrast to *Dar al-Salam*—the "land of peace". In particular, jihad will be declared to free the Muslim lands from any perceived control of Western powers and influence, and jihad will also be declared against any non-Muslim nations that hinder the spread of Islam.

And so we have the convergence of numerous geopolitical realities, Bible prophecy, Muslim End-Time beliefs, and even American Intelligence all pointing to the same conclusions—all confirming the many prophecies that were made in the Bible thousands of years ago. Now is the time for *believers everywhere to prepare both their hearts and their affairs*. It is time to get your house in order. And *if you are a non-believer, now is the time to reconsider your position!*

97

Gog And Magog Coalition Is Now Forming

Now we will see that coalition of Ezekiel 38 is forming right before our eyes. New developments seem to fall into place daily. This chapter will fill the reader in on just some of the latest events that significantly support the prophecy of Ezekiel 38. From this prophecy, we know that among the specific nations that will be part of the Antichrist's ten-nation coalition are: Turkey, Iran, Sudan, Syria and Libya. Many other nations will also submit or fall to the Antichrist, but the exact order of these events, we cannot be sure. Through several of the other prophecies, we know that Lebanon and the Palestinian territories will be involved as well. With Sudan, we could also see Somalia as part of the coalition. Several Central Asian states are likely, such as Afghanistan or Pakistan. With Libya, we could also see other North African nations involved—Morocco, Algeria and Tunisia, etc. Along with Turkey, we could also see the Turkic nations south of Russia: Turkmenistan, Krygistan, Uzbekistan, etc. But for now, we will stick only with the nations that we are clearly presented with in the Gog/Magog prophecy: Iran, Syria, Libya, Sudan, and Turkey.

THE EMERGENCE OF THE SHI'A CRESCENT

Analysts now nearly all agree that perhaps the most significant unintended consequence of America's war in Iraq and the toppling of Saddam Hussein is that the majority Shi'a Muslims of Iraq—those who were significantly suppressed under Saddam's regime—have arisen with great political power in Iraq. And the ripple effect this has caused is significantly changing the balance of power in the Middle East. One of the most basic elements of Middle East politics that one needs to understand is the power balance between the Sunni and the Shi'a nations. For the past 50 years, the Kingdom of Saudi Arabia (KSA) has been the top-dog oil-producing nation in the Middle East. Not only is KSA clearly the top oil producer, but she also has the greatest global percentage of readily available oil reserves. Simply put, whoever has the oil has the money and the power. KSA is also a Sunni Muslim nation. Now, standing on the other side of the ring—just across the Persian Gulf—is Iran. Iran is the second greatest oil producer in the region and is far and away the Shi'a stronghold of the earth. Since the late 1970's, when the Iranian Revolution began, Iran has been struggling to cast itself as the greatest and most powerful Muslim nation in the World. So remember this: in the power struggle between the Shi'a and the Sunni worlds, it is Saudi and Iran who stand at odds. KSA and Iran represent the leaders of the two power blocks—the Sunni and the Shi'a blocks. While not all Muslim nations are so deeply concerned about these sectarian divisions, within the Middle East proper, this power struggle is everything, seconded only by the greater Muslim world's hatred for Israel and the West. It is for this reason that the nations of Saudi Arabia, Egypt and Jordan have emerged as partners in their resistance to the growing power of what is now being called "the Shi'a crescent".

With this background set, we can now move on to see which nations are taking which side and why. While many would assume that those nations that are Sunni would join the Sunni alliance and the Shi'a would join Iran, it is not that simple. Instead, many Muslim nations are siding up according to which nations are perceived as friendly to the West and Israel versus those nations that have assumed a more Islamist and radical disposition. So on one side we have a primarily Sunni and so-called moderate Western friendly coalition, and on the other side is a divided Shi'a/Sunni coalition that is staunchly anti-West and far from moderate. This divided Sunni/Shi'a dimension to the emerging Islamist coalition fits perfectly in line with what we are expecting to see with regard to the final Antichrist coalition/kingdom in that "The kingdom will be divided" (Daniel 2:41).

THE ARAB SUMMIT

In early 2007, the Saudi Arabian government gathered together 22 Muslim heads of state, as well representatives from the United Nations (UN), the European Union (EU), Non-aligned Movement (NAM) and Organization of the Islamic Conference (OIC). The end result was the declaration of a soon-to-be Muslim/Israeli Peace Deal. News outlets across the world buzzed with anticipation. The problem; however, was that no sooner had the so-called good news been announced then certain Muslims leaders within Saudi began to betray their true colors. *The Jerusalem Newswire* reported the following barely veiled threat: "Saudi Arabia's foreign minister on Tuesday warned Israel to accept the pan-Arab peace proposal as is or face war. The Arab League convened in Riyadh on Wednesday to discuss the plan, which was first presented by Saudi King Abdullah at a Beirut meeting of the organization in 2002. It offers Israel the promise of peace with its neighbors in return for surrendering every inch of land liberated in 1967 and opening its borders to millions of foreign-born Arabs who called themselves 'Palestinian refugees.' Israel's failure to accept these 'generous' terms means it must want war, Saudi Foreign Minister Saud al-Faisal told Britain's Daily Telegraph. If Israel refuses, that means it doesn't want peace and it places everything back into the hands of fate. They will be putting their future not in the hands of the peacemakers but in the hands of the lords of war."[36] Shortly thereafter, Prime Minister Ehud Olmert expressed his positive outlook regarding the potential for peace with the surrounding Muslim nations.[37] *The Middle East Online* reported Olmert's glowing outlook: "Israeli Prime Minister Ehud Olmert said in interviews published on Friday that the Jewish state could clinch global peace with its enemies within five years, after Arab leaders revived a peace plan. Asked whether he meant 'all of the Arab world', Olmert said 'yes'. 'A bloc of states is emerging that understands they may have been wrong to think that Israel is the world's greatest problem,' he said in an interview with the liberal Haaretz. 'That is a revolutionary change in outlook.'"[38]

In light of the various blatantly anti-Semitic statements and threats that are made regularly by leaders throughout the Middle East, one cannot help but view such an optimistic outlook as being ridiculously naïve. As Palestinian leaders regularly claim that Islam commands destroy Israel and that they will never accept a peace with the Jews, Olmert and others like him still believe that peace with the Palestinian people is possible. This is 1938 all over again. I remind you of Neville Chamberlain's now infamous declarations of optimism regarding the peace agreement that he had established with Adolph Hitler. On September 30, 1938 the newspaper read as follows: "PM Neville Chamberlain arrived back in the UK today, holding an agreement signed by Adolph Hitler which stated the German leader's desire never to go to war with Britain again. Mr. Chamberlain declared the accord with the Germans signaled 'peace for our time,' after he had read it to a jubilant crowd gathered at Heston airport in west London. The German leader stated in the agreement: 'We are determined to continue our efforts to remove possible sources of difference and thus to contribute to assure the peace of Europe.'"[39]

Likewise, and even more frightening, is the Apostle Paul's warning to the Church regarding Christ's return: "Now, brothers, about times and dates we do not need to write to you, for you know very well that the day of the Lord will come like a thief in the night. While people are saying, 'Peace and safety,' destruction will come on them suddenly, as labor pains on a pregnant woman, and they will not escape" (1 Thessalonians 5:1-3). But beyond the fact that the Saudi Initiative peace deal is truly a joke, it is also not really even an *Arab* peace deal at all, rather a plan set-forth by the leaders of the Sunni nations, who are trying to protect their own power while isolating Iran, Syria and any other nations that do not wish to bow to the Saudi power block. As a result, this "peace plan" has actually caused Ezekiel's coalition of radical nations to continue strengthening their ties. It has been almost eerie to watch as it unfolds.

TAKING SIDES

One of the most obvious developments is that Libya's President Qaddafi boycotted the Saudi gathering. According to Qaddafi the event was sowing division amongst the Muslim community because Iran and Syrian leaders weren't invited: "I will not take part in a summit that splits Islam in two and pits Sunni and Shi'a against each other," he said in an interview on Al-Jazeera television..."I will not take part in a summit that pits Arabs against the Fars (Iranians)...to benefit the colonial (Western) powers," Qaddafi said.[40]

Qaddafi made his feelings clear when he stated directly that "Libya has turned its back on the Arabs (read: Saudi Arabia and its allies), and has despaired of them. The Arab nation's time is up, and it is on its way to disintegration...I will not be a party to a conspiracy to mobilize the Arabs against the Persians. Only the forces of colonialism benefit from such a conspiracy. I will not be a party to a conspiracy that splits Islam into two - Shiite Islam and Sunni Islam—mobilizing Sunni Islam against Shiite Islam."[41]

Moreover, of course by referring to the "Arab's" time being up, Qaddafi is referring to Saudi Arabia and its allies. Observers of the Middle East have not missed this dynamic of siding with Iran as well as Hezbollah. Because of Iran's firm stand against America and Israel, as well as Hezbollah's alleged successes against Israel in 2006, many more radically minded Muslims have begun to side with Iran and turn against the Saudi power block. On one side, they see Iran and Hezbollah acting valiantly against the infidels and on the other hand, they see the Saudi block as being compromised and in bed with the West. This move of support for Iran is seen not only by Libya's Qaddafi, but also in many Sunni Muslims who, over the past few years, have converted to Shi'a Islam. "Mustafah al-Sada, a religious Shiite Muslim, told al-Arabia that many Sunnis are now asking him, 'What must I do to become a Shiite?' Al-Sada said that he knows of 75 Sunnis from Damascus who have converted to the Shiite sect since the beginning of the [Israeli/Hezbollah] war...Munir A-Sayed, a 43-year-old lawyer says: 'I'm Sunni, but I belong to Hassan Nasrallah...I've converted politically,' he explained."[42]

A spokesman for the Reform Party of Syria went even further elaborating that "whole villages and urban areas are adopting the Hezbollah model whereby clinics, schools, and social services are provided by Iran in return for Syrians to convert to Shi'ism."[43]

According to some reports, officials in Damascus were not happy with this trend. However, other Syrian political commentators have claimed that the Syrian regime is actually encouraging an increase in Iran and Hezbollah's popularity in order to hold up President Bashar Assad's own popularity. As evidence for this claim, they point to the surfacing of stickers and posters that have typical Middle Eastern iconic images of Hezbollah's Nasrallah, Syrian President Bashir Assad and Iranian President Mahmoud Ahmadinejad all together like the three Musketeers.

QADAFI CALLS FOR A FATAMID CALIPHATE

Beyond Iran and Hezbollah's growing Shi'a influence, even more significant—and actually quite shocking—was Libya's blatant appeal to Iran for a Libyan/Iranian unity when Qaddafi made a public call for the establishment of a Fatimid Caliphate on Easter Weekend, 2007. Let me explain what this meant. The Fatimids were a Shi`a group that controlled much of North Africa during the 10th century. After conquering Egypt, they transferred their headquarters there from 969-1171. The Fatamids were an imperial militantly-expansionist state. They desired to overthrow their main opponents, the Sunni empire of the Abbasids, who were centered in Baghdad and the Ummayids, who controlled Spain. At their height, The Fatamids ruled Egypt, much of what are now Israel, Palestine and Syria, as well as Saudi Arabia's western region encompassing Mecca and Medina; their desire was ultimately to conquer the entire Muslim world. According to Middle East scholar Timothy Furnish, the fact that Libya, which is a Sunni majority nation, would call for a return to a Shi'a Caliphate is not something to be brushed aside lightly.[44]

Furnish is correct. This call from Qaddafi was a direct appeal for an Iranian/Libyan axis to stand against the Saudi/Sunni power block. In other words, as if foreseeing the strong horse of the future, Libya is trying to get on board with Iran. Further supporting this idea of a blossoming Iranian/Libyan alliance is the fact that the Iranian revolution both historically and in very recent days has also, like Qaddafi, made some strong appeals for Sunni/Shi'a unity, all the while papering over fourteen hundred years of division. The mixed Sunni/Shi'a makeup of the forming coalition is significant in that it fulfills the "kingdom will be divided" prophecy in Daniel 2. As an Arab/Persian coalition, it would also fulfill the prophecy, which says the people of the Antichrist Kingdom would be "a mixture" (Daniel 2:43).

IRAN AND SYRIA ARE UNIFYING

Of course, for those that follow Middle East news, little needs to be said regarding the growing alliance between Syria and Iran. This alliance has been seen in numerous meetings between Syrian President Bashir Assad and Iranian President Mahmoud

Ahmadinejad. Syria and Iran also entered into a mutual war agreement. In the case of war (whether offensive or defensive, it was never declared), either nation will fight on the behalf of the other. And on June 9, 2007, it was reported that Syria and Iran were in intense war consultations planning on a collaborated attack against Israel. One Israeli intelligence news outlet reported on some of the happenings, "...two high-ranking Iranian delegations spent time in Damascus. One was composed of generals who held talks with Syrian leaders on coordinated preparations for a Middle East war in the coming months. At the Iranian end, a similar high-ranking Syrian military delegation called in at Iranian army and Revolutionary Guards headquarters to tighten operational coordination between them at the command level, as well as inspecting the Iranian arsenal. The Syrian general staff will draw up a list of items it is short of for a possible military confrontation with Israel..."[45]

And of course, Iran and Syria are largely seen by Western and Israeli intelligence as the primary influence in the fall of the Gaza strip to Hamas. So once again, Iran, a Shi'a nation is deeply invested in supporting Hamas, a Sunni group. Again, the purpose of Iran is to establish influence and power using any means or any alliances necessary.

SUDAN AND IRAN ARE UNIFYING

The budding alliances between Iran, Syria, Libya, Hezbollah and the Palestinian Hamas are certainly not where the story ends. For among the nations that are also specifically mentioned by Ezekiel, is SuDaniel Not surprisingly then, Sudan—a renegade regime that is brazenly supporting a racially motivated genocide in its midst—are quickly becoming bosom buddies. In January of 2007, Iranian President Ahmadinejad visited Sudan to express his support for the Sudanese government and to stand united with them against the United States and the West. Al-Jazeera reported: "On his first visit to Sudan, Ahmadinejad extended full support to (Sudanese President) Bashir, blaming the United States and its Western allies for the region's troubles. Ahmadinejad stressed that Iran considers progress, dignity and power of Sudan as important as its own, and extends ideological support to the country. 'There is no limit to the expansion of relations with Sudan,' he said. For his part, Sudan's President al-Bashir said Tehran was within its absolute right to pursue a nuclear program."[46]

And in March of 2007, despite Western pressure aimed at convincing Iran and Sudan to accept terms imposed by the U.N. Security Council, the two nations, at least rhetorically, continued to harden their defiance against the rest of the world. While Iran refused to discontinue its uranium enrichment, Sudan refused to allow any international forces into Darfur to protect villagers who have been systematically massacred by the Government supported Arab Muslim *Janjaweed*.[47]

Then, as the UN deadline for Iran to suspend its nuclear activities loomed in April, Iran, rather than taking even a slightly humble posture, not only announced that it had achieved nuclear capability, but that it would also give this technology to other countries.

Although Ayatollah Ali Khamenei, Iran's supreme leader, was not quoted as saying who might be a recipient of the nuclear know-how, he made the comment during a meeting with Sudanese president Omar al-Bashir, who last month said his country would look into the possibility of nuclear power.[48]

This report becomes even more frightening in light of the CIA warning to the US Congress in January of 2007 to the effect that Libya, Syria and Sudan were all mutually pursuing weapons of mass destruction. "As the United States is consumed with proliferation crises in Iraq and North Korea, other counties such as Libya, Syria and possibly Sudan are quietly trying to acquire or expand secret arsenals of weapons of mass destruction, the CIA has warned."

The US Central Intelligence Agency has also concluded that suspected terror mastermind Osama bin Laden, blamed for the September 11 attacks on the United States, "has a more sophisticated biological weapons research program than previously discovered. Nuclear, chemical, biological, and ballistic missile-applicable technology and expertise continues to gradually disperse worldwide."[49]

So to recap: We have the blossoming alliance between Iran, Sudan, Libya, Hamas and Syria, the specific nations that the Bible said would unite in a bid to destroy Israel and dominate the region. Meanwhile, Turkey, the nation that will lead these nations has fallen to the Islamist party and is establishing itself as a leader in the region. Three thousand years ago the Hebrew prophets made these prophecies. Today they are all coming together with staggering accuracy. We have reached a time in history when we can actually watch as these things come together. The end of this age and the beginning of next is no longer on the horizon—it is now literally looming right before us.

The Reality
Islam's Explosive Growth

Muslims are increasing more then any other religious group in the world. Their growth rate is four times faster than Christians. 50 Presently, those who practice Islam make up approximately one-fifth of the world's population. One seasoned Bible teacher from England, after reviewing the statistics, recently commented that, "if present trends continue, half of all global births will be in Muslim families by the year 2055".51 Something dramatic and revolutionary is happening before our eyes, and most Western Christians are oblivious to it.

Not only are Muslims the fasting growing religious group in the world, but also in the United States, Canada and Europe.52 The annual growth rate of Muslims in the US is approximately 4%, but there are also strong reasons to believe that it may have risen to as high as 8% over the past several years. There are two primary reasons for the growth of Islam. They are birthrates and conversions. In this chapter we will briefly walk through each of these two factors in order to paint a realistic picture of what the immediate global future will look like.

THE DEMOGRAPHICS DON'T LIE

An article featured in the Brussels Journal, entitled "The Rape of Europe", reported the German author Henryk M. Broder telling the Dutch newspaper De Volkskrant (12 October) that young Europeans who love freedom, better emigrate. Europe as we know it will no longer exist 20 years from now. Whilst sitting on a terrace in Berlin, Broder pointed to the other customers and the passers-by and said melancholically, "We are watching the world of yesterday."53

Broder is correct. Any simple examination of the present birth rates of the native Europeans versus Europe's Muslim immigrant population leads us to one very clear and ominous conclusion: Europe will soon pass away and will become what many observers have dubbed Eurabia. Author Mark Steyn, in his New York Times bestseller America Alone, drives this point home in a way that leaves little room for challenge. Steyn notes that "In

1970, the developed nations (the non-Muslim majority nations of the world) had twice as big a share of the global population as the Muslim world: 30 percent to 15 percent. By 2000, they were at parity: each had 20 percent... The salient feature of Europe, Canada, Japan, and Russia is that they are running out of babies. What's happening in the developed world is one of the fastest demographic evolutions in history."[54]

In other words, most of the developed non-Muslim nations are simply not having enough children to maintain their populations. Meanwhile, Muslims are having far more children than any other group on the earth. It is only a matter of time then before many European nations are overrun by Middle-Eastern and Northern African immigrants—and thus Islam. Consider the following figures: "The number of Muslims in contemporary Europe is estimated to be 50 million. It is expected to double in twenty years. By 2025, one third of all European children will be born to Muslim families."[55]

Did you catch that? At present birth rates—in less than twenty years—one third of all Europeans will be Muslim. Once thriving Christian nations are literally breeding (or failing to breed) themselves into absolute extinction.

"In 2050, 60% of Italians will have no brothers, no sisters, no cousins, no aunts; no uncles. [56] The other 40% will be Muslim. By mid-century, the tiny Muslim nation of Yemen will have a greater population than Russia, one of the largest countries in the world. Seventeen European nations are now at what demographers call 'lowest-low' fertility: 1.3 births per woman. In theory, those countries will find their population halving every thirty-five years or so. In practice, it will be much quicker than that, as the savvier youngsters figure that there's no point in sticking around a country that's turned into an undertakers waiting room."[57]

Facts and figures like this can roll on and on. In the United Kingdom, Muhammad is already the most popular name for boys. In Spain, as the native Spanish population is literally knocked in half every generation. The Muslim immigrant population is doubling in far less time. The result is that Spain will be majority Muslim before we know it. The same can be said for France—and soon enough, for most of Europe. Consider the following statistics regarding the percentage of the population that is under the age of fifteen: "Spain and Germany have 14%, the United Kingdom 18%, the United States 21%—and Saudi Arabia has 39%, Pakistan% percent, and Yemen 47%."[58]

Is it hard to extrapolate the meaning of these figures? Whoever has the youth has the future. The simple fact of the matter is that within only a couple of generations—well within this century—the Western world as we know it will completely cease to exist. For this reason and more, I say that Islam is the future, albeit only temporarily so.

CONVERSION TO ISLAM

Beyond the most obvious and ominous factor of demographics, there is also the potential for a genuine global Islamic revival. The Bible makes it very clear that just prior to the return of Jesus, there would be what is called the "great apostasy". Islam is fully capable of fulfilling this prophecy. Whether you believe it or not, every year, tens of thousands of Americans convert to Islam. Prior to 2001, most reports seem to have the number roughly around 25,000 American converts per year. [59] This may not sound like that much, but this yearly figure, according to some Muslim American clerics, has quadrupled since 9-11.[60]

Since 9-11, the number of American converts to Islam has skyrocketed. As early as one month after the World Trade Center attacks, reports were flowing in from Mosques all over America. Ala Bayumi, the Director of Arab affairs at the Council for American Islamic Relations (CAIR) on November 11, 2001, in the London daily newspaper, Al-Hayat said this: "Non-Muslim Americans are now interested in getting to know Islam. There are a number of signs... Libraries have run out of books on Islam and the Middle East... English translations of the Koran head the American best-seller list... The Americans are showing increasing willingness to convert to Islam since September 11... Thousands of non-Muslim Americans have responded to invitations to visit mosques, resembling the waves of the sea crashing on the shore one after another..."[61]

After testifying to the dramatic strides that Islam had taken as a result of the 9-11 attacks, Bayumi goes on to say:" Proselytizing in the name of Allah has not been undermined, and has not been set back 50 years, as we thought in the first days after September 11. On the contrary, the 11 days that have passed are like 11 years in the history of proselytizing in the name of Allah."[62]

In an article from the British newspaper, The Times of London, January 7, 2002, just four months after 9-11 we read:

> "There is compelling anecdotal evidence of a surge in conversions to Islam since September 11, not just in Britain, but across Europe and America. One Dutch Islamic center claims a tenfold increase, while the New Muslims Project, based in Leicester, [England] and run by a former Irish Roman Catholic housewife, reports a 'steady stream' of new converts."[63]

But here's another sad aspect of these figures: Over 80% of American converts to Islam were raised in a Christian Church.[64]

If the higher figures of conversion are accurate, that would mean that as many as 60,000 Americans, who were raised in a Christian home, are converting to Islam annually. I have one acquaintance who, although he was a pastor's son raised in a deeply religious and traditional Christian family, nevertheless converted to Islam in college. I have read numerous testimonies of bishops and priests, missionaries, divinity students, and normal everyday Christians who have converted to Islam. Some are even self-described former "spirit filled Christians."

If this is the case, some might object, then why aren't these statistics more widely known? You may be wondering why you do not personally know anyone who has converted. There are easy answers to these questions. One of the primary reasons that these trends have gone largely unnoticed is because most American Muslims are concentrated in the larger metropolitan centers. The greater Chicago metropolitan area, for instance, is home to well over 350,000 Muslims. Greater New York City has twice that with over 700,000 Muslims. [65]

The other important statistic that sheds light on why this issue isn't more commonly discussed specifically in white American churches is sadly because 85% of American converts to Islam are African-American. White Christian America has not nearly been as impacted by this phenomenon as African-Americans have. It is a very sad commentary on the discontinuity and disunity of the American Church. Islam is absolutely sweeping through the inner cities of America. One Muslim authority estimates that by the year 2020, most American urban centers will be predominantly Muslim.[66]

But as the number of conversions increase, the face of the Muslim convert is changing as well. Shortly after 9-11, National Public Radio did a special on Islam and those who had converted after 9-11. "One of the most important topics [in an NPR broadcast] was an interview with several young women at American universities who recently converted to Islam through the Islamic Society of Boston. They hold advanced degrees from universities in Boston, such as Harvard, and they spoke of the power and the greatness of Islam, of the elevated status of women in Islam, and of why they converted to Islam. The program was broadcast several times across the entire U.S."[67]

From an article in The New York Times, October 22, 2001, we read a portion of Jim Hackings story, "Nine years ago, Jim Hacking was in training to be a Jesuit priest. Now, he is an admiralty lawyer in St. Louis who has spent much of the last month explaining Islam at interfaith gatherings... He made the Shahadah [Muslim Conversion ceremony] on June 6, 1998. 'The thing I've always latched to is that there's one God, he doesn't have equals, he doesn't need a son to come do his work'" (emphasis mine).[68]

A typical testimony of a former Christian convert reads:

"As a child, Jennifer Harrell attended church and Sunday school. In high school, she was on the drill team and dated a football player. After college, she became a Methodist youth minister. At age 23, she became a single parent. At age 26, she became a Muslim. "I grew up in Plano doing all the things I thought I was supposed to do,' said Ms. Harrell, 29, of Dallas. 'I went to church. I went to parties. Nevertheless, I wasn't concerned about heaven or hell. I took it all for granted.' Eventually, she took a job in sales, where she was introduced to Islam by Muslim co-workers. One of them loved to debate religion, which stirred Ms. Harrell to rethink her Christian faith. She studied the Bible, but also Islam in order to do a better job of defending her faith. Instead, she became intrigued that Muslims prayed five times a day, fasted and gave alms as a way of life. 'I wasn't the type of Christian who prayed every morning,' she said. She said Muslim beliefs about Jesus made more sense to her because they revere him as a prophet and not God's son. 'When I was a Christian, I never understood why Jesus had to die for my sins,' Ms. Harrell said. 'I mean, they're my sins.' Before becoming a Muslim, she visited a Christian minister. She said she asked why Christians ate pork, why women didn't cover their heads in church, and why Christians dated. 'I wanted him to defend the Bible,' she said. 'I gave him everything that I had found wrong with Christian interpretation.' His answers didn't satisfy her." [69]

Stories like Jim Hackings and Jennifer Harrell are legion. I have probably read a hundred of them. I have witnessed several instances of people who joined Internet discussion groups out of curiosity, simply wanting to learn more about Islam. Sometimes only weeks or months later, I would find that these individuals either had converted to Islam or were strongly considering conversion. Many referred to themselves as Christians when they began with these groups. These were all Westerners, generally American, Canadian or British.

A NEW MONOTHEISTIC OPTION

In the past, whenever most Westerners have decided that they believe in a personal God and have made a decision to make this new faith a primary aspect of their life, they usually have found the expression for their faith in a Christian church. As Islam spreads in the West, many are realizing that Christianity is not the only monotheistic option available to them. Sadly, many are choosing Islam instead of Christianity. David Pawson, a prominent Bible teacher from England, recalls the experience of one of his friends, "A Christian friend of mine is a counselor in a state school. He was delighted when a boy he was trying to help find a purpose in life told him he had become convinced that there was a personal God in whom he could believe. To his surprise and disappointment, this English boy told him some weeks later that he had become a Muslim. He was one of many thousands who had made the same choice."[70]

As Islam grows in the West, this story is sure to be repeated many times.

A WARNING FOR ENGLAND

In his book, Islam's Challenge to Christians, David Pawson sounds what may very well be a genuine prophetic warning not only to England but also to the entire Western Church. A well-seasoned and respected leader in the Church, he recounts a recent experience he had while listening to well-known authority on Islam, Patrick Sookhedo, give a lecture. If a leader of less qualification than David Pawson made the following statement, then it is possible that it would go entirely unnoticed, but instead, we should all be very sobered by what David experienced, "In the middle of his talk, both unexpected and unrelated to its contents, I was suddenly overwhelmed with what could be described as a premonition that Islam will take over this country. (England) I recall sitting there stunned and even shaking. We were not just listening to an interesting lecture about a religion and culture, which others believed and practiced. We were hearing about our future!"[71]

In the rest of the book, Pawson walks through what he feels are some proper Christian responses to his prediction. Pawson's recommended course of action includes three primary components: reality, relationship and righteousness. I will not endeavor to expound on these three issues, as he has already done so with conviction. Of course, his warning has proven to be highly controversial throughout the Church in England. The real question, however, in the opinion of this author, is not really, whether Pawson's warning will happen or not, but rather: Will the Church in England choose to implement his recommended plan of response?

BALANCING THE FACTS

The point here is not to paint an overly dismal picture. Muslims are also converting to Christianity all over the world. Many Muslims will make the claim repeatedly that no Muslim ever leaves Islam. This claim is refuted without much effort. I recently received a letter from a well-known terrorist who is in prison in the United Sates for attempting to carry out a large-scale terrorist plot. He has now come to Christ in prison. Ramzi Yusuf, the mastermind behind the first World Trade Center Bombing, has also come to Christ while in prison. One Muslim Sheikh recently claimed that in Africa alone, there are over six million Muslim converts to Christianity annually. That would break down to about 667 an hour, or 16,000 a day. From January of 2003 to the middle of 2004, the ministry of German Evangelist Reinhardt Bonke saw, over ten million Africans make decisions to follow Jesus. A large percentage of those who made these decisions were Muslims. In fact, Muslims from all over the world are making decisions to become followers of Jesus.[72] Many of these decisions are made following a spiritual dream or a vision.[73]

There are many wonderful and powerful testimonies of the goodness of God in the lives of Muslims coming to know Jesus. In fact, the number of Muslims converting to Christianity is unprecedented. Many Christians who live in Muslim countries claim that what is taking place is nothing short of a Christian revival. Reports of high-level Imams converting to Christianity are becoming commonplace. I believe with all my heart that the Middle East will see a genuine revival of Muslims coming to a Biblical faith in Jesus. Meanwhile, Christianity in Latin America, Asia and Africa is also now experiencing explosive growth. But this does not negate the fact that the growth of Islam—primarily due to birthrate—is still much faster than that of Christianity, not only in America, Canada, England and Europe, but worldwide. Despite the reasons for its growth, it is nevertheless growing and spreading faster than Christianity. The simple fact of the matter is that much of the Western Christian Church has completely missed the undeniable worldwide relevance of Islam, both now and even more so in the immediate future.

A fair prediction is that if the time comes when Islam indeed does bypass Christianity as the world's largest religion, or even as it merely begins to draw closer to that point, there will be a tipping point whereby the rate of growth will increase exponentially. The simple fact of the matter is that everyone wants to be on the winning team. Bandwagon conversions of Westerners and the resulting confusion among faithful Christians will eventually become the rule of the day.

We cannot underestimate the power of a worldwide trend. Indeed one of the primary aspects of the Last-Days is what the Bible calls the "great apostasy," which will be a significant global falling away from the Christian faith. While Islam still exists as an insecure religion wrestling with why Allah has allowed Islam to remain an inferior presence in the earth compared to Christianity, the day will likewise come for Christians, when they have to wrestle with why God has allowed Islam to bypass Christianity in growth and influence.

The only hope for a turnaround in this trend would be a significant full-scale worldwide revival; the kind of revival that until now has never been seen. It is time for the Church to face reality. As Brother Andrew, the man who became so well known for smuggling Bibles past the iron curtain wrote in the modern Christian classic, God's Smuggler, as early as 1994, "What Communism was to the twentieth century, Islam will be for the next one hundred years."[74] After examining all of the various reasons Biblically for seeing the soon-coming emergence of a radical Islamic Empire, in fact, nearly every statistic is pointing it this very thing. And thus the world that we live in is daily creeping closer and closer to perfectly reflecting that world of which the Bible prophesied thousands of years ago when it spoke of the "End-Times."

The time is shorter than most think. Let us all hasten; therefore, to do the work of God.

⧼ APPENDIX A ⧽
My Testimony

THE CONFESSIONS OF A PALESTINIAN TERRORIST

"*Behold, I am going to make Jerusalem a cup that brings utter drunkenness to all the surrounding peoples; and when the siege is against Jerusalem, it will also be against Judah. It will come about in that day that I will make Jerusalem such a heavy stone for all the peoples; that all who attempt to lift it will rupture themselves—and be severely injured*" (Zechariah 12:2, 3).

In the ancient book of the Jewish prophet Zechariah, the God of Israel announces an amazing and fearful prediction. Looking into the distant future, He speaks of a time when all of the nations that surround Israel will gather against her for war. All who attempt to attack—or "lift" Jerusalem, God says, will find themselves "severely injured." The picture is one of a man so determined—so possessed to lift something that cannot be lifted, that he causes his own body "severe" pain and damage, even to the point that it ruptures. What is it that drives someone to attempt the impossible despite the fact that it is destroying him? Remember a trembling drug-addict or alcoholic who, somewhere along the line, becomes a slave to his addiction. The prophet declares that at the end of the age—in the Last-Days—desire for the city of Jerusalem would become like a cup of *very strong drink*. In addition, whoever drinks from this cup would become staggeringly drunk, not as if drunk from alcohol—but as *if drunk with hatred and rage*.

I know. I drank deeply from that cup for too much of my life.

I was a Palestinian terrorist, and this is my story.

My name is Walid Shoebat. I was born and raised in Beit Sahour, Bethlehem in the West Bank to a prominent family. My paternal Grandfather was the Muhktar or chieftain of the village. He was a friend of Haj-Ameen Al-Husseni, the Grand Mufti of Jerusalem, and the notorious friend of Adolph Hitler. My Maternal Great Grandfather F.W. Georgeson, on the other hand, was a great friend of Winston Churchill, who wanted nothing more then the destruction of Hitler and Nazism. I was born from parents who came from the opposite sides of the spectrum— both geographically and ideologically.

From the time and place of my birth, I lived between two opposing forces—on one side is the evil Allah, and on the other is Jesus. I was born on the first day my parents arrived in *Bethlehem*. To my father's honor, it was one of Islam's holiest days—the birthday of the Muslim prophet Muhammad. Yet the place, in which I was born, Bethlehem, to my mother's honor, was the place where Jesus was born. Muhammad denied Jesus was the one died on the cross, or that He claimed to be—The Son of the Living God.

To commemorate this great day, my father named me Walid (the child), which relates to the Arabic word *Mauled*, from Al-Maulid Al-Nabawi (the birthday of Prophet Muhammad). Walid means "the birth boy". My mother approved—to her, the name was a reference to the birth of Christ. "For unto us a child (*Yeleed*) is born" (Isaiah 9:6). *Yeleed* is the Hebrew word for Waleed (Walid).

When I became a believer and wanted to change my name to a more Christian name like Paul or John. I started to analyze my full name and it's meaning—The Child son of David, son of Peace, son of the Branch. Every one of the names where titles of Christ in the Bible—I decided to keep my name, in its original state.

My father was a Palestinian Muslim who taught English and Islamic studies in the Holy Land. My mother was an American Christian who was un-equally yoked in marriage to my father during his studies in the United States. Fearing the impact of the American way of life for their two children, my parents moved to Bethlehem, which at that time was part of Jordan Shortly after my parents arrived in Bethlehem, I was born. My father changed jobs, and we moved to Saudi Arabia and then back to the Holy Land—this time to the lowest place on earth, Jericho.

I cannot forget the first song I learned in school. It was titled "Arabs Our Beloved and Jews Our Dogs." I was only six years old. I remember wondering at that time who the Jews were, but along with the rest of my classmates, I repeated the words without any real understanding of their meaning.

As I grew up in the Holy Land, I lived through several battles between the Arabs and the Jews. The first battle, while we were still living in Jericho, was the Six Day War. This was when the Jews captured old Jerusalem and the rest of "Palestine". It is hard to describe what an immense disappointment and great shame this was to the Arabs and Muslims worldwide.

The American Council in Jerusalem came to our village just before the war to evacuate all the Americans in the area. Because my mother was an American, they offered us assistance, but my father refused any help from them because he loved his country.

I still remember many things during the war—the noise of the bombing and shelling that went on day and night for six days, the looting of stores and houses by the Arabs in Jericho, people fleeing to cross the Jordan River for fear of the Israelis.

The war was named the Six Day War because in a mere six days, the Israelis gained victory over a multi-national Arab force which mounted attacks from multiple fronts. On the seventh day of this battle, Rabbi Shlomo Goren, the chief chaplain of the Israeli Defense Forces, let loose a resounding note on the *shofar* (a rams horn), announcing the Jewish control of the Western Wall and the old city of Jerusalem. Many Jews pointed out the obvious parallels of this event to the Biblical account of Joshua and the Israelites when they took Jericho. As I found in the Biblical account of the story of Joshua, the Israelites circled the walls of Jericho for six days, and then on the seventh day, at dawn (Joshua 6:15) they circled the wall seven times. The priests blew the shofars as all the Israelites shouted with one voice. The walls fell and the Israelites took the city—Joshua had a Six Day War.

During the war, my father would sit glued to the radio listening to the Jordanian news station. He used to say that the Arabs were winning—but he was listening to the wrong station. The Israeli station was announcing the truth of their imminent victory. Instead, my father chose to believe the Arabs who claimed that the Israelis were—as always—lying and promoting false propaganda. How many of us today remember Saddam's Information Minister and all of the wild claims and false reports that he spouted in the few days leading up to the fall of Baghdad? In the Islamic world, it seems as though some things never change. After the war, to my father in Jericho, it seemed as if the walls had crumbled in on him directly.

Later, we moved back to Bethlehem where my father enrolled us in an Anglican-Lutheran school to take advantage of the superior English courses. My brother, sister, and I were the only Muslims in the school. The three of us were hated, but not because we were Muslims, but because we were half-Americans. Although it was a Christian school, it still bore the traits of the Islamization form of Christianity that infects so many of the Palestinian Christians to this day. In order to get along—and sometimes simply to survive—many Christians in Islamic dominated countries adopt the hateful attitudes of the Muslims around them towards Israel, America, and the West. Because we were half-Americans, the teachers would often beat us while the other Christian students laughed.

Eventually, my father transferred me to the Government school where I began to grow strong in the faith of Islam. I was taught that one day, the fulfillment of an ancient prophecy by the Muslim prophet Mohammed would come to pass. This prophecy foretold a battle in which the Holy Land would be recaptured for Islam and the elimination of the Jews would take place in a massive final slaughter. This prophecy is found in some of the most sacred books of Islamic traditions known as the *Sahih Hadith* (reliable traditions of Muhammad). This particular tradition reads as follows:

> "[Muhammad said:] The last hour would not come unless the Muslims will fight against the Jews and the Muslims would kill them, until the Jews would hide themselves behind a stone or a tree and a stone or a tree would say:

Muslim, or the servant of Allah, there is a Jew behind me; come and kill him; but the tree Gharqad would not say, for it is the tree of the Jews" (*Sahih Muslim Book 041, Number 6985*).

When asked where this slaughter would take place, tradition states that it would be "in Jerusalem and the surrounding area." I followed my father's example when I was a youth and always paid attention to Islam and what our Muslim teachers taught us. Like so many of my classmates, I was deeply inspired by Muhammad's dark and bloody vision. I offered my life to *Jihad*, or Holy War, eventually in order to help fulfill this prophecy. I wanted to be part of the unfolding of Muhammad's grand plan, when Islam would gain the final victory over the Jews and finally—without any further obstacles—it would rule the world.

During my early teenage years, there were often riots at school against what we called the Israeli occupation. Whenever I could, I assumed the role of agitator and instigator. I vowed to fight my Jewish enemy, believing that in doing so, I was doing God's will on the earth. I remained true to those vows as I raged against the Israeli army in every riot I could. I used any means available to inflict maximum damage and harm. I rioted in school, on the streets, and even on the temple mount in Jerusalem. All throughout high school, I was always one of the leading activists for the cause of Islam. I would prepare speeches, slogans, and write anti-Israeli graffiti in an effort to provoke other students to throw rocks at the armed Israeli soldiers. The thundering echoes of our dark chants still reverberate in my memory:

"No peace or negotiations with the enemy!"
"Our blood and our souls we sacrifice to Arafat!"
"Our blood and our souls we sacrifice to Palestine!"
"Death to the Zionists!"

My dream was to die as a *Shaheed* (a martyr for Islam). At demonstrations, I would open my shirt hoping to be shot—but because the Israelis would never shoot at the body—I never succeeded. When school pictures were taken, I would purposefully pose with a grim face anticipating that it was my turn to be in the paper as the next martyr. Many times, I came close to being killed during youth protests and clashes with the Israeli Army. My heart was resolute; nothing could take away my drive—my hatred and anger—other than a miracle. I was one of those young men that you might have seen on CNN hurling rocks and Molotov cocktails during the days of the *Intifada* or "the uprising". At the time, I would have resented the label; but the truth is that I was a young budding terrorist.

The *Islamo-Nazi* brainwashing of my teachers and Imams—of my entire culture—was having its desired effect. The interesting thing is that I was not only terrorizing others, in many ways, I also terrorized myself. My ultimate fight was to gain enough merit—to build up a solid track record of terror—in order to earn Allah's favor. I lived in fear of judgment and hell and thought that only by behaving as I did would I ever have a chance at making it into *Janna* (paradise or heaven). I was never confident that my "good deeds" would outweigh my bad deeds in the scale on the Day of Judgment I was driven by not only anger and hatred, but also spiritual insecurity and fear. I believed what I was taught; the surest way to ease Allah's anger towards my sins was to die fighting the Jews. Perhaps, if I were successful, I would even be rewarded with a special place in heaven where beautiful wide-eyed women would fulfill my most intimate desires.

It is hard to convey the degree to which someone like myself, growing up under the Palestinian education system is brainwashed. Every voice in authority speaks the same message; the message of Islam—jihad—hatred of the Jews—and things that no young mind should ever be subjected to.

I remember an occasion at Dar-Jaser High School in Bethlehem during Islamic studies when some of my classmates asked the teacher if it was permitted for Muslims to rape the Jewish women after we defeated them. His response was, "The women captured in battle have no choice in this matter, they are concubines and they need to obey their masters. Having sex with slave captives is not a 'matter of choice for slaves.'" This was not merely the opinion of the teacher, but is clearly taught in the Qur'an: "Forbidden to you also are married women, except those who are in your hand as slaves, this is the law of Allah for you" (Sura 4:24).

Elsewhere it says:

> "O prophet; we allowed thee thy wives to whom thou hast paid their dowries, and the slaves whom thy right hand possesseth out of the booty which Allah hath granted thee, and the daughters of thy uncle, and of thy maternal aunt, who fled with thee to Medina, and any believing woman who hath given herself up to the prophet, if the prophet desired to wed her, a privilege to thee above the rest of the faithful." (Sura 33:50)

We had no problem with Mohammed taking advantage of this privilege as he married around 14 wives for himself and several slave girls from the booty that he collected as a result of his victorious battles. We really never knew how many wives he had and that question was always a debatable issue to us. One of these wives was even taken from his own adopted son Zaid. After Zaid, married her, Muhammad took interest. Zaid offered her to Muhammad, but it was not until a "revelation" came down from Allah that Muhammad generously accepted Zaid's offer. Others of Muhammad's wives were Jewish captives forced into slavery after Mohammed beheaded their husbands and families. We learned these things in our Islamic studies course in High School. This was the man we were supposed to emulate in every way. This was our prophet, and from him we learned to hate Jews.

I remember one occasion in Bethlehem when all the viewers in a jam-packed theater clapped their hands with joy as we watched the movie, "21 Days in Munich." The moment we saw the Palestinians throwing grenades into the helicopter and killing the Israeli athletes, everyone in the theatre—hundreds of viewers—yelled, "*Allahu akbar!*" (Allah is the greatest!). This is the slogan of joy used by Muslims for victorious events.

In an attempt to change the hearts of Palestinians, the Israeli TV station would show Holocaust documentaries. I would sit and watch cheering the Germans while I ate popcorn. My heart was so hardened, it was impossible for me to change my attitudes toward the Jews and only a "heart transplant" would do that job.

By the grace of God, I had something that very few of my classmates had—a mother who was a compassionate and contrarian voice, patiently trying to reach me in the midst of the deafening cacophony of hatred that surrounded me. She would try to teach me at home about what she called "God's plan." She spoke to me about Bible prophecy; she said that the return of the Jews was part of this plan. God foreordained it—thousands of years before—and it was being fulfilled right before our eyes, in our day. This to her, was God's miracle in our generation for the world to see that "His will shall be done."

She also told me about many future events that were yet to be fulfilled—some of which are being fulfilled today—many of which we discussed in this book. She told me about Jesus' warnings of false messiahs and counterfeit spiritual movements, of His prophesied return to Israel and an age of peace. However, all of this had little effect on me at the time, for my resolve was solid—I would live or die fighting against the Jews. Nevertheless, a mother never gives up.

I didn't know it at the time, but an American missionary couple had influenced my mother. She had even asked them to baptize her secretly. But when she refused to be baptized in a pond full of green algae, the missionary priest had to plead to the YMCA in Jerusalem to clear the pool of men, and my mother was then baptized. No one from our family knew.

Many times my mother would take me on trips to various museums in Israel. This had a very positive effect on me and I fell in love with archeology. I was fascinated with it. In my many arguments with her, I would directly tell her that the Jews and Christians had changed and corrupted the Bible. Her response was to take me to the Scroll Museum in Jerusalem where she showed me the very ancient scroll of Isaiah—still intact. My mother made some of her most effective points using no words at all.

Despite my mother's patient and gentle attempts to reach me, I was unreachable. I would torment her with insults. I would call her an "infidel" who claimed that Jesus was the Son of God and a "damned American Imperialist." I would show her pictures in the newspaper of all the Palestinian teenagers who had been "martyred" because of clashing with the Israeli soldiers and I would demand that she give an answer. I hated her and many times, I asked my father to divorce her and remarry a good Muslim woman.

Despite all of this, it was my mother—when I was thrown in the Muscovite Prison in Jerusalem—who went to the American Council in Jerusalem to try to get me out. The Muscovite prison was a Russian Compound that served as Jerusalem's central prison for those who were caught inciting violence against Israel. My dear mother was so worried over the direction that my life was taking that her hair started to fall out. Her worries were not unfounded. During my time in jail, I was initiated into Yasser Arafat's Fatah terror group. Soon after, a well-known bomb maker from Jerusalem named Mahmoud Al-Mughrabi recruited me. The time had come for more than mere protests and riots. Al-Mughrabi and I arranged to meet on Bab-El-Wad Street at the Judo-Star Martial Arts Club run by his father near the Temple Mount in Jerusalem. He gave me a very sophisticated explosive device that he had personally assembled. I was supposed to use the bomb—an explosive charge hidden in a loaf of bread—to blow up the Bank Leumi branch in Bethlehem. Mahmoud helped me smuggle the bomb, as did the Muslim Wakf; the religious police on the Temple Mount. From the Temple Mount, I walked out onto the platform with explosives and a timer in my hand. We walked along the walls and avoided all of the checkpoints. From there, I walked to the bus station and took a bus to Bethlehem. I was fully ready to give my life if I had to. I stood before the bank and my hand was literally ready to pitch the bomb at the front doors, when I saw some Palestinian children walking near the bank. At the last moment, I threw the bomb instead on the bank's rooftop. And I ran.

As I reached the Church of the Nativity, I heard the explosion. I was so scared and so depressed that I couldn't sleep for days. I was only 16 years old. I wondered if I had killed anyone. That was the first time I came to grips with what it would be like to have blood on my hands. I didn't enjoy what I had done, but I felt compelled to do it because it was my duty.

It is also with difficulty that I recall to you this next story. It was my first attempt to lynch a Jew. Like swarms of locust, stones were flying everywhere as we clashed with the Israeli soldiers. A group of us had set fire to a row of tires to use as a blockade. One soldier was hit with a rock. He chased after the kid who had hit him. But instead, we caught the soldier. Like a pack of wild animals, we attacked him with everything we had. I had a club and I used it to pound him in the head until the club broke. Another teenager had a stick with a nail sticking out. He kept whacking the poor young man's skull until he was covered with blood. We nearly killed him. Incredibly, as if with a final burst of adrenaline, he lunged across the blockade of burning tires and escaped to the other side where the other Israeli soldiers carried him to safety.

Now, these many years later, it is hard for me to express how deeply it grieves me that I ever committed such acts. I am not the same person that I was in those days. By the grace of God, I am a changed man—a new person.

Eventually I graduated high school. My parents sent me to the United States to seek a higher education. I enrolled at what was then called The Loop College, located in the heart of downtown Chicago. When I arrived, I immediately became involved with many anti-Israeli social and political events. I still sincerely believed that the day was coming when the whole world would submit to Islam and then the whole world would realize just how much she owed the Palestinian people for all of their losses as the vanguard in the Islamic war against Israel. The Loop College was full of various Islamist organizations. When I walked into the cafeteria, it was almost like walking into an Arab café in the Middle East. Various Islamist groups operated out of the school in those days, each competing for the recruitment of the other students. I immediately began devoting my energies to serving as an activist for the PLO—The Palestinian Liberation Organization. I was supposed to be officially working as an interpreter and counselor for Arab students through an American program called CETA (Comprehensive Employment and Training Act) in which I was paid by grants from the United States Government. The truth; however, is that much of what I did involved interpreting advertisements for events whose goal it was to win American sympathy for the Palestinian cause. Actually, "win sympathy" may be a rather misleading expression. We were attempting to brainwash the Americans—all of whom we viewed as being incredibly gullible. In Arabic, the advertisements for these events would openly use Jihadist, anti-Semitic descriptions such as: "There will be rivers of blood/ Come and support us to send out students to Southern Lebanon to fight the Israelis." The English versions of the signs, on the other hand, would utilize fluffy and innocuous descriptions such as: "Middle Eastern cultural party, come and join us, we will be serving free lamb and baklava." That was 1970.

Then came Black September. Black September is the month known throughout the Middle East as the time when King Hussein of Jordan moved to quash an attempt by the PLO in Jordan to overthrow his monarchy. Many Palestinians were killed during the conflict, which lasted for almost a year until July of 71. The end result of all this was the expulsion of the PLO and thousands of Palestinians from Jordan into Lebanon.

Of course, the conflict spilled over and affected the various Arab student organizations at the Loop College. It was very disheartening and frustrating for me to watch, as I knew that without unity, the cause of Islam—the cause of the Jihad in America—would get nowhere. It was at this time that I joined *Al-Ikhwan*—the Muslim Brotherhood. The Muslim Brotherhood is a father organization to dozens of other terrorist organizations throughout the world. I was not alone in joining The Brotherhood either. There were hundreds of other Muslim students from all over the United States that joined in those days. I believed that working as an activist for the Muslim Brotherhood was the best way to help bring about a much-needed unity among Muslims; not Palestinian Muslims or Jordanian Muslims, but rather one Muslim Ummah—one universal Islamic community, under the one umbrella of Islam. To this end, a Jordanian Sheikh named Jamal Said came to the United States to recruit students. The recruitment meetings were held in basements or rented hotel rooms. Muslim students flocked from all over the U.S. to attend the meetings and listen to Sheikh Jamal Said. Jamal had an almost legendary status and reputation. He was an associate of Abdullah Azzam, who is famous throughout the Middle East for being the mentor of none other than Osama Bin Laden. People often ask me if I think that there are terrorist cells operating within the United States. There can be no question that there are. While so many of America's college students in the seventies were experimenting with drugs, protesting their government, and participating in the birthing of the "flower child" movement, they were oblivious to the other underground revolution that was being birthed by radical Muslim students across the country. Within Islam, it is taught that when the Muslims enter a country to conquer it for Allah, there are various stages to that "invasion". Those were the early stages of the most subversive movement that this country will ever know. It was the birthing of the Jihadist movement in America.

I want jump ahead and tell you about the man that I am today. In the early nineties, my very wise wife issued a challenge. Tired of listening to me argue and trying to convert her to Islam, she challenged me to study the Bible for myself to see if indeed all of the things that I had been taught about the Bible and the Jews were true or not. Thus began a radical life-changing journey. It was a journey that turned into an obsession until all my questions were answered. I would stay up late at night and read, pouring through the Jewish and Christian Scriptures. I read the Old Testament and the New. I studied Jewish history. I prayed and I wrestled with all of the things that I was discovering. Many of my beliefs that formed the very foundations of my Islamic worldview were beginning to crumble. Confronted with the obvious conflict between the worldview and the religion of my youth and the piercing quality of the Bible, I prayed to God for guidance. With all of my soul, I prayed,

"God, you are the Creator of Heaven and Earth, the God of Abraham, Moses, and Jacob, You are the beginning and the end, You are The Truth—the only truth, the Author of the true Scriptures, the one and only Word of God. I suffer to find Your truth, I want to do Your will in my life, I long for Your love and in the name of The Truth I ask You to enlighten my mind and open my eyes. Amen!"

The wonderful thing about God is that when someone sincerely and humbly cries out to Him to help him or her find truth, He always answers that prayer. Today I am a Christian. I am the founder of the Walid Shoebat Foundation. My life mission and driving passion is to bring the truth about the Jews and Israel to the world, all the while allowing Christ to bring healing to my own soul through repentance and the pursuit of reconciliation. I have set out to untiringly bring the cause of Israel to hundreds of thousands of people throughout the world. I never would have thought that God would open to me so many doors. Among the many major Universities that I have had the opportunity to speak at; Harvard, Columbia, Brandeis, USC, UCLA, Concordia and Penn State are only a few. I've shared my story on FOX, CNN, CN8, CBS, NBC, Israel National News and a host of other national and international television stations. I've addressed Archbishops, leading politicians, Congressmen, Senators and in Chile, Ireland, and the U.S. But perhaps far more important, I've had the privilege of speaking at dozens of synagogues and Jewish Conferences. I was a keynote speaker at the Aish Hatorah Partners Conference in Nov 2004 - the largest gathering of Orthodox Rabbis in the USA. I was greatly blessed to speak at the Encounter Conference London to over 2000 Orthodox Jews, the largest conference of its kind in Europe. I was the only non-Jew ever to be invited to speak in the nine years of the conference history. I thank God for giving me the opportunity to seek forgiveness and reconciliation from the Jewish people everywhere throughout the world. To anyone who will listen, I tell my story. Despite numerous threats to my life, I continue to speak out against the hatred and the Islamo-Nazi lies that I was indoctrinated under.

Until they come for me, I will continue to speak out. Yes, today I say to the whole world, *I love Jews!* I love them because of the light that has come to me through the Jewish people, the Jewish Scriptures and ultimately through the Jewish Messiah. I love the Jewish people because it was they who literally birthed Light into the world—for through them came Jesus who is the Living Light and the Truth. I no longer despise Jews because I know from the Bible that the Jews are God's chosen people whose purpose it is to give light to Arabs and to the whole world—if only we would allow them. The Bible has opened my eyes to the fact that God made the Jews a blessing to the world. In return for this blessing, God has asked all men to honor the Jews by blessing them in return. For as God said to Abraham:

"I will bless those who bless you and I will curse him who curses you, and in you all the families of the earth shall be blessed" (Genesis 12:2).

Knowing this truth has transferred my way of thinking from being a follower of Muhammad and idolizing Adolph Hitler to believing in Jesus Christ, from believing lies to knowing the truth, from being spiritually sick to being healed, from living in darkness to seeing the light, from being damned to being saved, from doubt to faith, from hate to love, and from evil works to God's grace through Christ. This is who I am today.

Praise be to Yahweh the God of Israel!

⁓ APPENDIX B ⁓
The Muslim Rape Epidemic In The West

Today's news from Germany buries the fact that the gang rapists of a 13 year-old were likely Arab Muslim immigrants:

Shock in Berlin as suspected rapists freed here is the news reported that this is part of a gang rape epidemic sweeping areas with high Arab Muslim immigration.

As is the case with young Arab Muslims throughout the west, teenage girls are generally forbidden to go out, leaving separatist gangs of predatory Arab Muslim males with highly misogynist attitudes. Harassment of females has; therefore, exploded throughout the west, most shockingly demonstrated in the recent phenomenon of gang rape for sport. Listed below is the evidence.

While these cases are primarily not related to the core group of committed Islamists within Arab Muslim immigrant populations, there is some "trickle-down" of attitudes so it is also worth noting the rape aspects of Jihad ideology as well: The Rape Jihad.

Germany

Shock in Berlin as Suspected Rapists Freed The youths, aged 13 to 15, allegedly attacked their victim as she walked home from school in the Charlottenburg district which is generally seen as safe area with low crime rates. While allegedly gang-raping the girl, the youths are reported to have filmed the sexual attack with a mobile phone camera. Media reports say the four later boasted about the rape to other school children and sent copies of the video to friends.

Police who detained the four earlier this week have so far not found any film footage of the alleged rape. There is suspicion the video pictures may have been erased and mobile phones of the suspects are being analyzed by experts in a bid to retrieve any pictures.

Adding to the potential explosiveness of the alleged rape is the fact that the four suspects are all the children of immigrant families, while the victim is German. The normally well-informed Bild tabloid said the suspects were two German-Turks, a German Russian and a German-Angolan.

Federal police statistics released on Monday show non-German youths under the age of 21 were twice as likely to be crime suspects as German nationals of the same age last year.

Officers in charge of the case are convinced the four youths carried out the gang rape and DNA tests are being carried out on sperm traces found on the victim.

Given the brutality of the attack, there has been anger over a decision by Berlin justice officials to order the youths be set free. The 13-year-old suspect is too young to be kept in detention under German law, but the other three could be held.

Berlin justice Senator Karin Schubert insists; however, that even youths suspected of violent crimes can only be kept locked up if there is a danger they will flee justice.

France

In more cosmopolitan centers like Paris and Australia, the game is blossoming. It consists in the ritual gang rape of white females, preferably , by non-white immigrants.. Once the attacker and victim have become chums, the male lures the girl to a location where his fellow gang members take their turns with her. In the case on trial in Paris, it was no fewer than 14 gang members. Unlike many victims of such fun, this young lady lodged a complaint with the police. As a result, she was gang raped a second time. This time, allegedly, by the 11 who went on trial in April.

The incident is not isolated. Police investigations of similar rapes were underway in three other French cities, and one French magistrate says the game has been going on since at least the 1980s. Their technique was to pick up a young white girl and once she had become the girlfriend of one of the members, he would allow his mates to make use of her. Furthermore, in Nice, a gang rape video of a female student is circulating freely amond Muslim immigrants. These gangs go as far as raping female accomplices. Kidnap Accomplice of Ilan Halimi Was Herself a Victim of "Tournante."

Australia

The Australian Sun-Herald reports that police data show that some 70 racially motivated rapes of young white girls, one as young as 13, by Middle Eastern immigrants have taken place in the last two years. Fifteen youths and men have been charged with more than 300 offenses relating to matters since mid-2000 alone. They are all of Middle Eastern extraction. None of those involved is presently before the courts. Those in Australia don't seem to be part of a gang initiation, but they are nonetheless, clearly racially driven. Before being brutalized, the Australian paper reports, other victims have reportedly been questioned about their Australian heritage or forced to endure taunts about their attackers. Like the rapes in France, those in Australia follow a similar pattern in which one non-white male becomes intimate with a white girl, whom he then delivers to his friends for sexual violation, beating, and humiliation.

Sweden

Swedish girls Jenny and Linda were on their way to a party on New Year's Eve when they were assaulted, raped, and beaten half to death by four Somali immigrants. Sweden's largest newspaper has presented the perpetrators as "two men from Sweden, one from Finland and one from Somalia." This is a testimony as to how bad the informal censorship of news articles is in relationship to immigration in Sweden. Similar incidents are reported with shocking frequency, to the point where some observers fear that law and order is completely breaking down in the country. The number of rape charges in Sweden has tripled in just above twenty years. Rape cases involving children under the age of 15 are six times as common today as they were a generation ago. In an online readers' poll from the newspaper Aftonbladet, 82% of the women expressed fear to go outside after dark, even though there are reports of rapes happening in broad daylight.

According to a new study from the Crime Prevention Council, it is four times more likely that a known rapist is born abroad, compared to persons born in Sweden. Resident aliens from Algeria, Libya, Morocco and Tunisia dominate the group of rape suspects. According to these statistics, almost half of all perpetrators are immigrants.

To help in the prevention efforts, a group of Swedish teenage girls has designed a belt that requires two hands to remove and which they hope will deter would-be rapists. "It's like a reverse chastity belt," one of the creators, 19-year-old Nadja Bj'rk, told AFP, meaning that the wearer is in control, instead of being controlled. Bj'rk and one of her partners now plan to start a business to mass-produce the belts.

"It is not as wrong raping a Swedish girl as raping an Arab girl," says Hamid. "The Swedish girl gets a lot of help afterwards, and she has probably been ****** before anyway, but the Arab girl will get problems with her family. For her, being raped is a source of shame. It is important that she retains her virginity until she marries." It was no coincidence it was a Swedish girl that was gang raped in Rissne. This becomes obvious from the discussion with Ali, Hamid, Abdallah, and Richard. All four have disparaging views on Swedish girls, and think this attitude is common among young men with immigrant background. "It is far too easy to get a Swedish whore girl, I mean..." says Hamid, and laughs over his own choice of words, "many immigrant boys have Swedish girlfriends when they are teenagers. When they get married, they get a proper woman from their own culture who has never been with a boy. That is what I am going to do. I don't have too much respect for Swedish girls. I guess you can say they get ****** to pieces."

Muslim Rape Epidemic in Sweden and Norway is on the rise. The number of reported rapes by ambush in 2004 continues to double, following what was already a decade of steadily increasing numbers of sexual crimes.

The number of reported rapes against children is also escalating. The figures have nearly doubled in the last ten years: 467 rapes against children under the age of 15 were reported in 2004 compared with 258 in 1995. Legal proceedings continue this week in a case involving a 13 year old girl from Motala who was said to have been subjected to a group rape by four men. (Note: These four men were Kurdish Muslims, who raped the girl for hours and even took photos of doing so.)

Norway

Rape charges in the capital are spiraling upwards, 40 percent higher from 1999 to 2000 and up 13 percent so far this year. Police Inspector Gunnar Larsen of OslOs Vice, Robbery and Violent crime division says the statistics are surprising. The rising number of rape cases and the link to ethnic background are both clear trends. While 65 percent of those charged with rape are classed as coming from a non-Western background, this segment makes up only 14.3 percent of OslOs population. Norwegian women were the victims in 80 percent of the cases, with 20 percent being women of foreign background.

Denmark

Alarmed at last week's police statistics, which revealed that in 68% of all rapes committed this year the perpetrator was from an ethnic minority, leading Muslim organizations have now formed an alliance to fight the ever-growing problem of young second and third-generation immigrants involved in rape cases against young Danish girls.

Caveats

There are two technical imprecisions in this post that were blurred for readability. Australia is not European. Also, among Western immigrants, Arabs and Muslims are different, but highly overlapping, groups. The phenomenon is highest among those who are Arab and Muslim, and largely unknown among non-Muslim Arabs.

⟨≈ APPENDIX C ≈⟩
The Three Woe Trumpets
Woe! Woe! Woe!

Fall of the Ottoman Empire,
or Ottoman Supremacy Departed, August 11, 1840
by Josiah Litch

The book of Revelation has long been looked upon as a book of inexplicable mysteries, altogether beyond the reach of the comprehension of mortals. This opinion has received too much encouragement from professed teachers and expounders of the Word of God, many of them of eminent talents and various learning. Their unguarded remarks respecting the obscurity of unfulfilled prophecy in general and the book of Revelation have done much evil in particular. The Holy Spirit is grieved, and the God of Revelation slighted and insulted, by such insinuations and remarks. How differently has the author of the book expressed himself in reference to it! He calls it, "The Book of the Revelation of Jesus Christ, which God gave unto him to show unto his servants things which must shortly come to pass."

If it is a revelation, then it is not an inexplicable mystery, but the mind of God made known to man. "Blessed," then "is he that readeth, and they which hear the words of the prophecy of this book." If God has pronounced a blessing on the reader of this book, who shall annul it?

"Woe [sic], woe, woe to the inhabiters of the earth, by reason of the other voices of the trumpet of the three angels which are yet to sound" (Revelation 8:13).

"And the fifth angel sounded, and I saw a star fall from Heaven unto the Earth; and to him was given the key of the bottomless pit" (Revelation 9:1).

A star, in the figurative language of Revelation, is a minister of religion (See Revelation 1:20). A fallen star then would signify a fallen or heretical minister of religion. This was undoubtedly the Arabian imposter, Mahomet. [Mohammed] There is so general an agreement among Christians, especially protestant commentators, that the subject of this prediction is Mahommedism [Islam] that I shall not enter into the argument at large to prove it; but in passing, shall merely give a brief exposition of the emblems used, and their application in the text.

"And he opened the bottomless pit; and there arose a smoke out of the pit, as the smoke of a great furnace; and the sun and the air were darkened by reason of the smoke of the pit" (Revelation 9:2).

The smoke was the cloud of errors that arose through his instrumentality, darkening the sun, (gospel light,) and the air, (the influence of Christianity on the minds of men). In this enterprise, he and his followers were so successful that the light of Christianity almost disappeared wherever he gained an influence; and the smoke of the pit produced nearly total darkness throughout the Eastern Church.

"And there came out of the smoke locusts upon the earth; and unto them was given power as scorpions of the earth have power." (Revelation 9:3).

That these locusts were emblems of an army is clear. "And the shapes of the locusts were like unto horses prepared unto battle; and on their heads were crowns like gold, and their faces were the faces of men. And they had hair like the hair of women, and their teeth were as the teeth of lions" (Revelation 9:8). Such is the description of a Mahommedan [Muslim] horseman prepared for battle. A horse, a rider with a man's face, long flowing beard, woman's hair, flowing or plaited, and the head encircled with a yellow turban, like gold.

"Was given power, as the scorpions of the earth have power" (Revelations 9:10). Martinicus says, "Scorpions have nippers, or pincers, with which they keep hold of what they seize, after they have wounded it with their sting"

Like the scorpion, Mahomet stung the subjects of his proselytism, infused the poison of his doctrines, and continued to hold them by the force of arms, until it had affected the whole man, and the subject settled down in the belief of his delusive errors. Wherever his arms triumphed, there his religion was imposed on men, whether they believed it or not.

"The successors of the prophet propagated his faith and imitated his example; and such was the rapidity of their progress, that in the space of a century, Persia, Syria, Egypt, Africa, and Spain had submitted to the victorious arms of the Arabian and Saracen conquerors." Ruter

Verse 4: "And it was commanded them that they should not hurt the grass of the earth neither any green thing, neither any tree [a direct command found in the Koran]; but only those men which have not the seal of God in their foreheads."

"Grass, green thing, and tree" are here put in opposition to those men who have not the seal of God. If so, they must mean those who have the seal of God—his worshipers.

"Infidels, who rejected the Christian religion, and also all idolaters, they forced to receive the Mahommedan religion [Islam], upon pain of death. However, Jews and Christians, who had their Bibles and their religion, were left to the enjoyment of them, upon their paying large sums, which they exacted. But where the payment of such sums was refused, they must either embrace the new religion or die." Smiths Key to Revelation.

Verse 5: "And to them it was given that they should not kill them, but that they should be tormented five months."

As the language thus far has been figurative, so it must be here also. To kill, signifies, a political death, or subjection. The nation of Christians who were the subjects of this plague were to be tormented five months, but not politically slain. Five months is one hundred and fifty days; each day a full solar year; the whole time, one hundred and fifty years.

Verse 6: "And in those days men shall seek death, and shall not find it; and shall desire to die, and death shall flee from them."

This, of course, is the same death as that in verse 5. Such was the misery of the Greeks, occasioned by the wars in which they were almost continually embroiled with the Mahommedan powers, that very many would have preferred an entire subjection of the empire to them, to the protracted miseries the war occasioned. Nevertheless, this was not permitted; political death fled from them.

THE EXTERMINATOR TORMENTS THE GREEKS ONE HUNDRED AND FIFTY YEARS

Verse 10: "Their power was to hurt men for five months."

1. The question arises. What men were they to hurt for five months? Undoubtedly, the same they were afterwards to slay (See verse 15). "The third part of the men," or third of the Roman empire the Greek division of it.

2. When were they to begin their work of torment? The 11th verse answers the question: "They had a king over them, which is the angel of the bottomless pit, whose name in the Hebrew tongue is Abaddon, but in the Greek hath his name Apollyon [meaning destroyer]."

   a. "They had a king over them." From the death of Muhammad the Mahommedans were divided into various factions, under several leaders, with no general civil government extending over them all. Near the close of the 13th century, Othman founded a government, which has since been known as the Ottoman government, or empire, extending over all the principal Mahommedan tribes, consolidating them into one grand monarchy.

   b. The character of the king. "Which is the angel of the bottomless pit." An angel signifies a messenger, or minister, either good or bad. The messenger was not always a spiritual being. "The angel of the bottomless pit," or chief minister of the religion which came from hence when it was opened. That religion is Mahommedism [Islam], and the Sultan is its chief minister.

"The Sultan, or Grand Signior, as he is indifferently called, is also Supreme Caliph, or high priest, uniting in his person the highest spiritual dignity with the supreme secular authority." Perkins, "World as it is," p. 36...

3. His name. In Hebrew, "Abaddon," the destroyer; in Greek, "Apollyon," one that exterminates or destroys. Having two different names in the two languages, it is evident that the character rather than the name of the power is intended to be represented...Such has always been the character of the Ottoman government...

But when did Othman make his first assault on the Greek empire? According to Gibbon ("Decline & Fall,") "Othman first entered the territory of Nicomedia on the 27th day of July, 1299"

"And their power was to torment men five month" Commencing July 27th, 1299, the one hundred and fifty years reach to 1449. During that whole period the Turks were engaged in an almost perpetual war with the Greek empire, but yet without conquering it. They seized upon and held several of the Greek provinces, but still Greek independence was maintained in Constantinople. But in 1449, the termination of the one hundred and fifty years, a change came. Before presenting the history of that change, however, we will look at verses 12-15. "One woe is past; and behold, there come two woes more hereafter. And the sixth angel sounded, and I heard a voice, from the four horns of the golden alter which is before. Saying to the sixth angel that had the trumpet, 'Loose the four angels that are bound in the great river Euphrates.' And the four angels were loosed which were prepared for an hour, a day, a month, and a year, for to slay a third part of men."

The first woe was to continue from the rise of Mohammedism until the end of the five months. Then the first woe was to end, and the second begin. Moreover, when the sixth angel sounded, it was commanded to take off the restraints, which had been imposed on the nation, by which they were restricted to the work of tormenting men, and their commission extended to slay the third part of men. This command came from the four horns of the golden altar that is before God. "The four angels," are the four principal sultanies of which the Ottoman empire is composed, located in the country of the Euphrates. They had been restrained; God commanded, and they were loosed.

In the year 1449, John Paleologus, the Greek emperor, died, but left no children to inherit his throne, and Constantine Deacozes succeeded to it. But he would not venture to ascend the throne without the consent of Amurath, the Turkish Sultan. He therefore sent ambassadors to ask his consent, and obtained it, before he presumed to call himself sovereign. Let this historical fact be carefully examined in connection with the prediction above. This was not a violent assault made on the Greeks, by which their empire was over-thrown and their independence taken away, but simply a voluntary surrender of that inde-pendence into the hands of the Turks, by saying, "I cannot reign unless you permit."

The four angels were loosed for an hour, a day, a month, and a year, to slay the third part of men. This period amounts to three hundred and ninety-one years and fifteen days; during which Ottoman supremacy was to exist in Constantinople.

Commencing when the one hundred and fifty years ended, in 1449, the period would end August 11th, 1840. Judging from the manner of the commencement of the Ottoman supremacy, that it was by a voluntary acknowledgment on the part of the Greek emperor that he only reigned by permission of the Turkish Sultan, we should naturally conclude that the fall or departure of Ottoman independence would be brought about in the same way; that at the end of the specified period, the Sultan would voluntarily surrender his inde-pendence into the hands of the Christian powers, from whom he received it.

When the foregoing calculation was made, it was purely a matter of calculation on the prophetic periods of Scripture. Now, however, the time has passed by, and it is proper to inquire what the result has been—whether it has corresponded with the previous calculation.

1. Has the ottoman independence in Constantinople departed, and is it in Christian hands? Let the following testimony answer the question...

The London Morning Herald, after the capture of St. Jean dAcre, speaking of the state of things in the Ottoman Empire, says: "We have dissipated into thin air the prestige that lately invested as with a halo the name of Mehemet Ali. We have in all probability destroyed forever the power of that hitherto successful ruler. But have we done aught to restore strength to the Ottoman empire? We fear not. We fear that the sultan has been reduced to the rank of a puppet; and that the sources of the Turkish empires strength are entirely destroyed."

"If the supremacy of the Sultan is hereafter to be maintained in Egypt, it must be main-tained, we fear, by the unceasing intervention of England and Russia."

2. When did Mahommedan independence in Constantinople depart?
In order to answer this question understandingly, it will be necessary to review briefly the history of that power for a few years past.

For several years the Sultan has been embroiled in war with Mehemet [Mohammed] Ali, Pacha [sic] of Egypt. In 1838 there was a threatening of war between the Sultan and his Egyptian vassal. Mehemet Ali Pacha, in a note addressed to the foreign consuls, declared that in the future, he would pay no tribute in the Porte, and that he considered himself independent sovereign of Egypt, Arabia, and Syria. . . . In 1839, hostilities again commenced, and were prosecuted, until, in a general battle between the armies of the Sultan and Mehemet, the Sultans army was entirely cut up and destroyed, and his fleet taken by Mehemet and carried into Egypt. This fleet Mehemet positively refused to give up and return to the Sultan. In 1840, England, Russia, Austria, and Prussia, interposed, and determined on a settlement of the difficulty; for it was evident, if let alone, Mehemet would soon become master of the Sultans throne.

The Sublime Porte, with a view of putting a stop to the effusion of Mussulman blood, and to the various evils, which would arise from a renewal of hostilities, accepted the intervention of the great powers.

Here was certainly a voluntary surrender [part of the official document reads:]

"The powers have, together with the ottoman plenipotentiary, drawn up and signed a treaty, whereby the Sultan offers the Pacha, the hereditary government of Egypt, and all that part of Syria extending from the gulf of Suez to the lake of Tiberias, together with the province of Acre, for life. The Pacha, on his part, evacuated all other parts of the Sultans dominions now occupied by him and returning the Ottoman fleet. A certain space of time has been granted him to accede to these terms; and, as the proposals of the Sultan and his allies, the four powers, do not admit of any change of qualification, if the Pacha refuse to accede to them, it is evident that the evil consequences to fall upon him will be attributable solely to his own fault.

"His Excellency, Rifat Bey, Musleshar for foreign affairs, has been despatched in a government steamer to Alexandria, to communicate the ultimatum to the Pacha" [Moniteur Ottoman, Aug. 22, 1840].

The question now comes up, when was that document put officially under the control of Mehemet Ali?

"By the French steamer of the 24th, we have advices from Egypt to the 16th. The Turkish government steamer, which had reached Alexandria on the 11th, with the envoy Rifat Bey on board, had by his (the Pachas) orders been placed in quarantine, and she was not released from it until the 16th. However, on the very day [August 11, 1840] on which he had been admitted to practice, the above named functionary had an audience of the

Pacha. He had communicated to the Pacha the command of the Sultan, with respect to the evacuation of the Syrian province, and appointed another audience for the next day. When, in the presence of the consuls of the European powers, he would receive from him his definite answer, and inform him of the alternative of his refusing to obey; giving him the ten days which have been allotted him by the convention to decide on the course he should think fit to adopt." [The London Morning Chronicle, Sept. 18, 1840].

According to previous calculation; therefore, ottoman supremacy did depart on the eleventh of August [August 11, 1840] into the hands of the great Christian powers of Europe.

Then the second woe is past, and the sixth trumpet has ceased its sounding; and the conclusion is now inevitable, because the word of God affirms the fact in so many words, *"Behold, the third woe cometh quickly..."*

END

≈ FOOTNOTES ≈

PART I

1   Indiana Jones and the Last Crusade script, Wikipedia

2   Islamic Association of Palestine, Hamas Branch, from The River to The Sea, video conference in the U.S.

3   Livingstone, Robert. Christianity and Islam: The Final Clash. Enumclaw: Pleasant Word, 2004. P.12

PART II

1   Kabbani,Shaykh Muhammad Hisham, The Approach of Armageddon? An Islamic Perspective. Canada: Supreme Muslim Council of America, 2003. p. 228

2   Ibn Kathir, The Signs Before the Day of Judgment. London: Dar Al-Taqwa, 1991. p. 18

3   Furnish,Timothy. Holiest Wars, Islamic Mahdis, their Jihads and Osama Bin Laden, 2005.

4   An Interview With Harun Yahya http://www.jesuswillreturn.com/a_3.html

5   Ibn Maja, Kitab al-Fitan #4084 as quoted by Kabbani, p. 231

6   Sunan Abu Dawud, Narrated by Umm Salamah, Ummul Mu'minin

7   "What is the Sunnah, Part 2 of 2," The Religion of Islam, http://www.islamreligion.com/articles/655/

8   Muhammad, the Prophet of Islam, from Sahih Bukhari 84.59

9   Abu Muslim, Book 041, Number 6961, In Hadiths of the 'twelve successors'

10   Mufti Muhammad Shafi and Mufti Muhammad Rafi Usmani in their book, Signs of the Qiyama [the final judgment] and the Arrival of the Maseeh [the Messiah]

11   Kabbani, p. 237

12   Al-Sadr and Mutahhari, prologue p. 3

13   Schneider, Ludwig. Israel Today, Was the Dome of the Rock a Church. 11/14/2006

14   Sahih Buhkari: Volume 8, Book 74, Number 290 Shirk: The Ultimate Crime Islam: The Religion of All Prophets http://www.islaam.ca/what-is-islam-/poly-theism-association-with-allah/shirk-the-ultimate-crime-2.html

15   John Calvin Institutes of Religion (Book 2, chapter 6:4)

16   Polycarp Letter to the Philadelphians 7:1 [A.D. 135]

17   Al-Sadi from Al-Tibyan, by Al-Tousi) See also Tafseer Al-Jalalyn 3:54, Royal Aal al-Bayt Institute for Islamic Thought, Amman, Jordan (http://www.aalalbayt.org), see also Tafsir Ibin-Abbas 3:54, and Ibin-Katheer 3:54. Also see Qurtubi, IV, pp. 98-99; cf. Zamakhshari, I, p. 366 Also see Dr. Mahmoud M. Ayoub, The Qur'an and Its Interpreters, Volume II, The House of Imran, (1992 State University of New York Press (SUNY), Albany) p. 166

18   Muhammad ibn Izzat, Muhammad. 'Arif, Al Mahdi and the End of Time. London: Dar Al-Taqwa, 1997. p 40

19   Muhammad ibn Izzat, Muhammad. 'Arif, Al Mahdi and the End of Time. London: Dar Al-Taqwa, 1997. p 16

20   Muhammad ibn Izzat, Muhammad 'Arif, Al Mahdi and the End of Time. London: Dar Al-Taqwa, 1997. p 16

21   Wikipedia, The Smithsonian Institution, Archeology and the Book of Mormon.

22   See Toby Lester (January 1999). "What Is The Koran". The Atlantic Monthly. Retrieved on 2007-10-19.

23   Tafsir Ibn Kathir Surah 2:42

24   Sunan Abu Dawood Book 14, Number 2631: Narrated Ka'b ibn Malik.

25   A Shite Encyclopedia October 1995 Revised January 2001 http://www.al-islam.org/encyclopedia/chapter6b/1.html

26   Ibn Abbas, commenting on Qur'an 3:28, as narrated in Sunan al-Bayhaqi and Mustadrak al-Hakim, said: "al-Taqiyya is the uttering of the tongue, while the heart is comfortable with faith."

27   Ibn Kathir's Tafsir -Surah 3:28

28   Maimonides, Epistle Concerning Apostasy, 1160 AD, Historical Society of Jews from Egypt.

29   Abu Hamid Imam Al-Ghazali, Ulum id Din pp. 3,137

30   Al-Sirah al-Halabiyyah, v3, p61,http://www.al-islam.org/encyclopedia/chapter6b/1.html

31   Bukhari Volume 5, Book 59, Number 369 Narrated by Jabir bin 'Abdullah

32   Islam Review, Lying in Islam Abdullah Al Araby
     http://www.islamreview.com/articles/lying.shtml

33   members.fortunecity.com/mist91/hztabuubaidajarrah.html

34   Ahmad ibn Naqib al-Misri, The Reliance of the Traveller, translated by Nuh Ha
     Mim Keller, (Amana publications, 1997), section r8.2, page 745

35   Ghazali Ulum id Din pp. 3,137

36   Islam Review, Lying in Islam Abdullah Al Araby
     http://www.islamreview.com/articles/lying.shtml

37   The Kashmir Telegraph, Jagan Kaul, April 14th 2002. See also The Danger
     Within, Militant Islam in America, by Daniel Pipes, November 2001.

38   Ayatullah Baqir al-Sadr and Ayatullah Muratda Mutahhari, The Awaited Savior,
     (Karachi, Islamic Seminary Publications, prologue, p. 1

39   Abdulaziz Abdhulhussein Sachedina, Islamic Messianism, the Idea of the
     Mahdi in Twelver Shi'ism, (Albany, State University of New York, 1981) p. 2

40   Kabbani, p. 229

41   Sefer Zerubbavel, in Midreshei Ge'ullah, p. 80ff.

42   Sunan Abu Dawud, Book 36, Number 4273, Narrated by Umm Salamah,
     Ummul Mu'minin

43   Ayatullah Baqir al-Sadr and Ayatullah Muratda Mutahhari, The Awaited Savior,
     Karachi, Islamic Seminary Publications, prologue, pp. 4, 5

44   Local Push for Islamic State, Barney Zwartz, The Age, January 9, 2007

45   At-Tabarani, Related by Abu Hurayra, as quoted by 'Izzat and 'Arif, p. 9

46   Izzat and Arif, p. 15

47   Ibid.

48   "Islam 101," From Jihad Watch, also see "Religion of Peace?" by Robert Spencer,
     Washington, DC: Regnery Publishing, Inc., 2007, p. 165.)

49   Dr. Waleed A. Muhanna, a Brief Introduction to the Islamic (Hijri) Calendar,
     http://fisher.osu.edu/~muhanna_1/hijri-intro.html

50   Sahih Ashrat as-Sa'at, as quoted in Kabbani, p. 236

51   Veliankode, p. 351

52   Sahih Bukhari: 29, 304, 1052, 1462, 3241, 5197, 5198, 6449, 6546, Sahih
     Muslim: 80, 885, 907, 2737

53   Sahih Al-Bukhari, Volume 7, Book 62, Number 64; see also Numbers 65 and 88

GOD'S WAR ON TERROR

54   Musnad Ahmad, Number 25636

55   Minister named to 'Islamic Cabinet' September 4, 2007 PJSTAR

56   Sideeque M.A. Veliankode, Doomsday Portents and Prophecies (Scarborough, Canada, 1999) p. 277

57   Ayatullah Baqir al-Sadr and Ayatullah Muratda Mutahhari, The Awaited Savior, (Karachi, Islamic Seminary Publications), prologue, pp. 4, 5

58   Abdulrahman Kelani, The Last Apocalypse, An Islamic Perspective, (Fustat, 2003), pp. 34-35

59   Muhammad, the Prophet of Islam, from Sahih Bukhari 84.59

60   Fruchtenbaum., "Nationality," pp. 17-18. From Article by Dr. Thomas Ice, The Ethnicity of The Antichrist, May 8th, 2007, Prophetic News

61   http://iisca.org/knowledge/jihad/jihad_for_allah.htm

62   Ibn Khaldun, The Muqaddimah, trans. by Franz Rosenthal (New York: Pantheon Books Inc., 1958) Vol. 1:473

63   Jurisprudence in Muhammad's Biography, Dr. Muhammad Sa'id Ramadan al-Buti (page 134, 7th edition)". http://www.secularislam.org/jihad/exegesis.htm

64   E. Tyan, "jihad," Encyclopedia of Islam, 2nd ed. (Leiden: Brill, 1965)

65   Tafsir Ibn Kathir Surah 9:123 Tafsir.com

66   Muhammad, the prophet of Islam, narrated by Al-Miqdaam Ibn Ma'di Karib, Tirmidhi & Ibn Maajah.

67   Tirmidhi, Nasaa'i and others

68   Bukhaari & Muslim

69   Al-Quds Al-Arabi London, May 11, 2001

70   USA Today, June 26, 2001).

71   The Jerusalem Post Internet Edition, 9, 6, 2001

72   Malik 362:1221

73   The Evident Smoke, 44:54 Shakir, Shakir, M. H., "The Qur'an", Tahrike Tarsile Qur'an, Inc, Elmhurst, NY, 1993

74   The Beneficent, 55:54-58 Dawood, Dawood, N. J., "The Koran", Penguin, London, England, 1995

75   p. 367_Digest of Islamic Law_ N. Bailli e, Premier Book House, Pakistan

76   Sahih Bukhari Volume 9, Book 84, Number 59, Narrated Abu Huraira

77   Joseph Farah, IslamicTerror.com? Muslim websites in West defend bin Laden, call for '5th column' World Net Daily, November 13, 2001

78   Narrated Abu Burda. Volume 9, Book 84, Number 58.

79   Narrated Anas Bin Malik, Hadith Sahih Bukhari Vol. 1 # 387

80   Christian Leaders Association 21 June, 1998. Jakarta, Indonesia

81   London Telegraph, 2004

82   Fiqh az-Zakat: A Comparative Study, Shaykh Yusuf al-Qaradawi, International Institute of Islamic Thought, 1999

83   Tabarani, as related by Hadrat Abu Umamah, as quoted by Zubair Ali, p. 43 and Abduallah, p. 55

84   Sunan Abu Dawud, Book 36, Number 4273, narrated by Umm Salamah, Ummul Mu'minin

85   Sunan Abu Dawud, Book 36, Number 4272, Narrated by Abu Sa'id al-Khudri

86   Jihad: The Origin of Holy War in Islam by Reuven Firestone, pp. 139-140, quoted by Andrew Bostom, Front Page Magazine, April 17, 2006

87   Umdat as-Salik, o9.16)

88   Discoverthenetworks.com, a guide to the political left, Yasser Arafat

89   El-Arabi (June 24, 2001

90   Discoverthenetworks.com, a guide to the political left, Yasser Arafat

91   FrontPageMagazine.com | Friday, January 27, 2006

92   Ibid.

93   From Video, Sheikh Qaradawi, speaking at the I.A.P, Islamic Association of Palestine conference, Kansas City

94   Sahih Al-Bukhari 3.891

95   Alfred Guillame, The Life of Muhammad (SiratRasul) page 507.

96   Lessons from the Prophet Muhammad's Diplomacy by Daniel Pipes Middle East Quarterly September 1999

97   IMRA Newsletter Malaysian PM's Proposal to follow Hudaibiyah Model & "Geneva Initiative" Dr. Aaron Lerner, 19 October 2003

98   Sahih Muslim, Hadith No.1731

99   From the Wagjiz, written in 1101 A. D quoted by Andrew Bostom, Islamic Holy War, and the Fate of Non-Muslims. See also Front Page Magazine, Jamie Glazov, Friday 13, 2004

100   Bassam Tibi, "War and Peace in Islam," in Terry Nardin, ed., "The Ethics of War and Peace: Religious and Secular Perspectives", Princeton, NJ: Princeton University Press, 1996, p. 130. #

101   Ibid.

102   Tibi, Bassam. "War and Peace in Islam," in The Ethics of War and Peace: Religious and Secular Perspectives, edited by Terry Nardin, 1996, Princeton, N.J., pp. 129-131.)

103   Tabandeh, Sultanhussein. A Muslim Commentary on the Universal Declaration of Human Rights, p. 17.)

104   Tabandeh, Sultanhussein. A Muslim Commentary on the Universal Declaration of Human Rights, pp. 18-19.

105   Tabandeh, Sultanhussein. A Muslim Commentary on the Universal Declaration of Human Rights, p. 37.

106   Sunan Abu Dawood Narrated by Sahl ibn al-Hanzaliyyah

107   Al Hidayah, "Mishkat" II, page 406, explanatory note

108   Sahih Hakim Mustadrak, related by Abu Sa'id al-Khudri (4:557 and 558), as quoted by Kabbani p. 233, Paving the way for the coming Mahdi

109   At-Tabarani, Related by Abu Hurayra, as quoted by 'Izzat and 'Arif, p. 9

110   El-Kavlu'l Muhtasar Fi Alamet-il Mehdiyy-il Muntazar, as quoted by Harun Yahya, http://www.endoftimes.net/08mahdiandtheendtimes.html

111   Ancient Christian Commentary Revelation page 211

112   Sefer Zerubbavel, in Midreshei Ge'ullah, p. 80ff.

113   Jihad in Islam by Sayyeed Abdul A'la Maududi, Islamic Publications (Pvt.) Ltd, p8.

114   Open letter to the Pope, the Archbishop of Izmir (Smyrna), Turkey, the Reverend Guiseppe Germano Barnardini, speaking in a recent gathering of Christians and Muslims as documented by Abdullah Al-Araby, The Islamization of America, (The Pen vs. the Sword, Los Angeles California, 2003), p. 8

115   Report in the San Ramon Valley Herald of a speech to California Muslims in July 1998; quoted in Pipes, CAIR: Moderate Friends of Terror, New York Post, April 22, 2002

116   Ahmed Reza, CAIR' responds to Reverend Franklin Graham, Shia News.com August 5, 2002

117   Daniel Pipes the Danger Within: Militant Islam in America, Commentary Magazine November 2001

118   Phillip Jenkins, The Next Christendom, the coming of Global Christianity, (Oxford University Press, New York, 2002) pg. 180

119   "The Muslim Manifesto," published by the late Dr. Kalim Siddiqui, June 15 1990, http://answering-Islam.org.uk/Terrorism/agenda.html

120   Peaceful religion is not spelled I-s-l-a-m, by Mychal Massie, World Net Daily, May 25, 2004

121   Abdul Rahman al-Wahabi, Yawmul-Ghadhab hal-Bada'a be-Intifadat Raja. The Day of Wrath

122   Abu Nu'aym and As-Suyuti, related by Thawban, as quoted by Izzat and Arif, p. 44

123   Tafsir Ibn Kathir; Al-Baqarah

124   Al Adaab: Living Islam According to the Minhaj of the True Salaf as Salihoon

125   Ibid.

126   Sharh Jawharat al-Tawhid (1990 ed. p. 186)

127   Dr. G. F. Haddad, Living Islam, The Prophetic Title: The Best of Creation

128   Ibid.

129   "The Night Journey Of Mhammad (Peace Be Upon Him) To Heaven, Muhammad Resool Allah's Journey," Waqf-Ikhlas

130   Dua'a Nudbah

131   The Night Journey Of Muhammad, Waqf-Ikhlas, Ihlas Holding A.S, Cagaloglu, Istanbul, Turkey.

132   Ibin Al-Sabbagh in AlFusul Al-Muhimma, transmitted by Ibin Abbas.

133   Narrated by Abu-Huraira, Abi Sayeed Al-Choudury, Islambasics Library, also see rudood.com, attributing deception to Allah, Scholar Abdilrahim Sharif, August 9, 2006.

134   Islambasics Library

135   Transliteration of the Beautiful names.

136   Remembering Allah the way the Prophet did, DaralislaamLive.com, December 2, 2007.

137   "In Praise of the Prophet," Shaikh Farid Ad-Din Attar, Book of God.

138   Ibid *Also see, The Asset of Supplication #600

139   W.H.T. Gairdner, The Reproach of Islam, (Foreign Mission Committee of the Church of Scotland, 1911) p. 158.

140   Karen Armstrong, Muhammad: A Biography of the Prophet (Harper Collins Books, 1993), 46.

141   A. Guillaume, The Life of Muhammad, (Oxford University Press, 2001) p. 106.

142   A. Guillaume, The Life of Muhammad, (Oxford University Press, 2001) p. 106.

143   At-Tabari Vol. 9, page 167, note 1151.

144   Sahih Bukhari Volume 6, Book 60, Number 478.

145   John Gilchrist, Jesus to the Muslims, 1986, Benoni, Republic of South Africa.

146   Narrated By Aisha, Sahih Buhkari Volume 7, Book 71, Number 660.

147   Ali Sina, The Examples of Muhammad http://www.faithfreedom.org/Articles/sinaawa40621.htm

148   A. Guillaume The Life of Muhammad: (Oxford University Press, Oxford England), p.464.

149   At-Tabari, Vol XI, The Challenge to the Empires, In series: The History of at-Tabari, (Ta'rikh al-rasul wa'l-muluk), Translated by K.Y. Blankkinship, SUNY series in near Eastern Studies, Bibliotheca Persica, State University of New York Press, Albany New York, 1993, p.44-45

150   Abu Jafar Muhammad ibn Jarir At-Tabari, the early Islamic historian and theologian recorded this event "Khalid said, O Allah, if you deliver their shoulders to us, I will obligate myself to You not to leave any one of them whom we can overcome until I make their canal run with their blood.' Then Allah defeated them for the Muslims and gave their shoulders to them. Khalid then commanded to his herald to proclaim to his men, 'Capture! Capture! Do not kill any except he who continues to resist.' As a result the cavalry brought prisoners in droves, driving them along. Khalid had detailed certain men to cut off their heads in the canal. He did that to them for a day and a night. They pursued them the next day and the day after, until they reached the Nahrayn and the like of that distance in every direction from Ullays. And Khalid cut off their heads."

151   Ibid.

152   "Chopping Heads," by Amir Taheri New York Post May 14, 2004

153   The Baburnama -Memoirs of Babur, Prince and Emperor, translated and edited by Wheeler M. Thacktson, Oxford University Press,1996, p. 188. as quoted by Andrew Bostom, FrontPageMagazine.com, May 13, 2004, The Sacred Muslim Practice of Beheading

154   Ibid.

155   Ibid.

156   Ibid.

157   CBS News, Saudi Arabia's Beheading Culture, June 27, 2004

158   Theodore Shoebat, In Satan's Footsteps, an Introduction

159   Columbia Encyclopedia, See L. Séjourné, Burning Water (tr. 1957).

160   Sahih Bukhari Volume 1, Book 3, Number 111 Narrated by Ash-Sha'bi

161   Quote from Ayatollah Ibrahim Amini, Al-Imam Al-Mahdi: The Just Leader. Amini is a professor at the Religious Learning Center in Qom, Iran, and one of the country's most respected Shi'a scholars clearly articulates this vision. of Humanity, translated by Dr. Abdulaziz Sachedina, available online at: http://al-islam.org/mahdi/nontl/Toc.htm

162   Muhammad Ali Ibn Zubair in an article entitled, Who is the evil Dajjal? Elaborates, "The Yahudis [Jews] of Isfahaan will be his [the Dajjals] main followers. Apart from having mainly Yahudi followers, he will have a great number of women followers as well."Muhammad Ali Ibn Zubair Who is the Evil Dajjal (the "anti-Christ")? Online article from http://www.islam.tc/prophecies/masdaj.html

163   Veliankode, p. 360, Sahih Bukhari Volume 3, Book 43, Number 656

164   Muhammad Ali Ibn Zubair, The Signs of Qiyama, translated by M. Afzal Hoosein Elias at http://members.cox.net/arshad/qiyaama.html

165   Albert Speer (1905-1981), Nazi Germany's Minister for Armaments 1942-45, Inside the Third Reich, chapter 6

166   Ibid.

167   Ibid.

168   Marvin Olasky, World magazine, October 23, 2004, p. 52

169   The Waffen SS by George S. Stein, 1966, page 182

170   Sahih Muslim Book 041, Number 6985

171   Daily Star, Oct. 23, 2002

172   New Yorker, Oct. 14, 2002

173   October 22, Ahmad Shama, president of MSA.

174   Palestinian Media Watch, Studies on Palestinian Culture and Society by Itamar Marcus www.pmw.org.il

175   Middle East Media Research, Friday Sermon on Palestinian Authority TV, April 17, 2002 Palestinian Authority Imam Sheikh Ibrahim Madhi at the Sheikh 'Ijlin Mosque in Gaza City www.memri.org

176   Andrew Bostom, Front Page Magazine, 11,26,2007.

177   Tirmidhi as quoted by Mohammed Ali Ibn Zubair Ali, Signs of Qiyamah (Islamic Book Service, New Delhi, 2004), p. 42 and Prof. M. Abdullah, Islam, Jesus, Mehdi, Qadiyanis and Doomsday, (Adam, New Delhi, 2004), p. 54

178   Muhammad ibn Izzat, Muhammad 'Arif, Al Mahdi and the End of Time (London,Dar Al-Taqwa, 1997), p. 40

179   Against Heresies 5:30:4.

180   Shaykh Muhammad Hisham Kabbani, The Approach of Armageddon?An Islamic Perspective (Canada, Supreme Muslim Council of America, 2003), p. 223

181   Kabbani 223-4

182   Abu Ameenah Bilal Philips, Ph.D. Ad-Dajjal, The Antichrist, (Alexandria, Soundknowledge Audio Publishers, 2001)

183   Excerpts from a Friday sermon delivered by Palestinian Authority Imam Sheikh Ibrahim Madhi at the Sheikh 'Ijlin Mosque in Gaza City, broadcast live on April 12, 2002 by Palestinian Authority television http://memri.org

184   Samuel Shahid, The Last Trumpet: A Comparative Study of Christian-Islamic Eschatology (US, Xulon, 2005), p. 254

185   Narrated By An-Nawwas b. Sam'an Abu Muslim Book 041, Number 7015

186   Shaykh Muhammad Sâlih al-Munajjid The great trial of the Dajjal

187   Taliban execute 26 male Afghans, Brian Hutchinson, Can West News Service December 19, 2006

188   Saudis put bodies of beheaded Sri Lankans on display, ETHAN MCNERN Scotsman.com February 21, 2007

189   Calvin On Islam, Revelation Prof. Dr. Francis Nigel Lee Lamp Trimmers El Paso, 2000

PART III

1   Jerome

2   Baro Desert Locust, (Raymond Dillard, The Minor Prophets, "Joel," p. 255-56)."

3   Bat YeOr, The Dhimmi: Jews and Christians Under Islam, 376

4   Wars of The World, Arab Israeli Wars, 1967

5   Position of Arab Forces May 1967 Department for Jewish Zionist   Education.

6   26-July-2006 Ancient Book of Psalms Discovered National Museum of Ireland Press Release

7   WorldNetDaily.com 'Psalm in a bog' linked to Israel's current war July 26, 2006.

8   Charles C. Ryrie, ed., The Ryrie Study Bible (Chicago, IL: Moody Press, 1978), 1285.

9   From Grace Online Library "Some editions of the New American Standard Bible include 'Rosh' in Isaiah 66:19: 'Tarshish, Put, Lud, Meshech, Rosh, Tibal, and Javan.' No other translation includes 'Rosh' in this listing. The Hebrew text does not include 'Rosh.' The Lockman Foundation's on-line version of their updated translation of the NASB does not include 'Rosh' in Isaiah 66:19."

10   Merrill F. Unger, Beyond The Crystal Ball (Chicago: Moody Press, 1974) p. 81 11 Edwin M Yamauchi, Foes from the Northern Frontier: Invading Hordes from the Russian Steppes, (Grand Rapids, MI Baker Book House, 1982).

12   Mark Hitchcock, The Berean Watchmen Ministries, The Battle of Gog and Magog, page 2.

13   Clyde E. Billington Jr., "The Rosh People in History and Prophecy (Part Three)," Michigan Theological Journal 4 (1993), 59, 61. Quoted by Mark Hitchcock, Battle of Gog and Magog, Page 7.

14   Billington, "The Rosh People (Part Three)," p. 44.

15   Billington, "The Rosh People (Part Three)," p. 48.

16   James D. Price, "Rosh: An Ancient Land Known to Ezekiel," Grace Theological Journal, Vol. 6, No. 1, 1985, p. 69.

17   The Popular Bible Prophecy Commentary, Understanding the Meaning of Every Prophetic Passage, Tim Lahaye and Ed Hindson

18   Grant Jeffrey, Final Warning, p. 123.

19   Schaff-Herzog Encyclopedia of Religious Knowledge. Dictionary Edition Schaff, Philip (1819-1893) Grand Rapids, MI: Baker. Book House, 1953 Volume 5 Page 14.

20   F. W. Gingrich & Frederich Danker, A Greek-English Lexicon of the New Testament and other Early Christian Literature, Univ. of Chicago Press, Chicago & London, 1957.

21   F. H. Colson, G.H. Whitaker, & Ralph Marcus, Philo, Loeb. Classical Library, London, 1929-1953.

22   The Central Caucasus and Bashan, Travels into the Centr Caucasus and Bashan, Including visits to Ararat and Tabreez, and Ascents of Kazbek and Elbruz, By Doglas W. Freshfield,London, Longmans Green and Co. 1869).

23   Copyright 1987 Harper & Row Publishers, page 93.

24   Achtemeier, Paul J. ; Harper & Row, Publishers ; Society of   Biblical Literature: Harper's Bible Dictionary. 1st ed. San   Francisco : Harper & Row, 1985, S. 629.

25   Hitchcock, pp, 44,45.

26   AotJ I:6. (Ketubot 13:11 in the Mishna).

27   Fred G. Zaspel, The Nations of Ezekiel 38 – 39, Who Will, Participate in the Battle?Word of Life Baptist Church, Pottsville, PA.

28   James Lloyd, Christian Media Research, April 15, 2002.

29   Hitchcock, pp, 44,45 Also see Edwin M. Yamauchi, Foes from the Northern Frontier (Grand Rapids: Baker Books, 1982), 20.

30   Mark Hitchcock, The Berean Watchmen Ministries, The   Battle of Gog and Magog, page 10.

31   Hitchcock, pp, 44,45.

32   The Battle of Gog and Magog, Mark Hitchcock, page 4.

33   Herodotus, I.14.

34   Matthew Henry's Concise Commentary.

35   Fred Zaspel, Word of Life Baptist Church, The Nations of   Ezekiel 38,39.

36   Ibid.

37   The New John Gill Exposition of the Entire Bible, Ezekiel 30:5.

38   D. G Hogarth, Section 8,9.

39   Herodotos (I.14).

40   Encyclopedia Britannica, Islamic World, Migration and Renewal (1041-1405).

41   Herodotos, I. 14.

42   Euphorion, fr. (FHG III 72);Etymologicum Magnum 771, 56; cf. Etymologicum Gudianum, Sturz 537, 26.

43   Herodotos, 1. 14.

44   Donald F. Logan, The Vikings in History, (Totowa, NJ 1994, p. 186.)

PART IV

1   Barnes Notes On The Bible, #13.
    www.gotothebible.com/Barnes/Genesis/10.html.
    http://ccat.sas.upenn.edu/nets/edition/Danielpdf Also seeAlbert.

2   BELLPORT, L.I., Sept. 26. -- Zia Bey Pasha, the Turkish Ambassador. to the
    United States, stated to-night that he had as yet received no. instructions from
    the Porte to invoke the good offices of the American Government in the way of
    restraining Italy from hostile action in Tripoli.

3   Strong's H6184 See also Ezekiel 31:12.

4   Josephus, Antiquities of the Jews, 6.1.127.

5   James Hastings, Tarsus, Vol. 4 p.686, A Dictionary of the Bible, (Peabody, Mass.
    Hendrickson Publications, 1898, 1988 reprint.

6   The Hittites and Their Contemporaries in Asia Minor. Boulder, Colorado. West-
    view Press. 1975.

7   Henry Hodges, Technology in the Ancient World, (Baltimore, Maryland, Pen-
    guin Books, 1971), p.108.

8   William Harms, "Aslihan Yener and the Bronze Age Source of Tin Found in
    Turkey," Biblical Archaeology Review, vol. 20, no. 3, May-June, 1994, pp.16-17.

9   MEMRI, July 29th, 2005)

PART V

1   The Fall of Rome – the End of the Roman Empire, by N.S Gill

2   Gibbons, The Decline And Fall Of The Roman Empire, Chapter XLVIII

3   Harris, William H & Levey, Judith S. The New Columbia Encyclopedia. (New
    York; Columbia University Press, 1975). Also see Runciman, Steven. The Fall of
    Constantinople. (London; Cambridge University Press, 1965).

4   By Ted Sampley, U.S. Veteran Dispatch, January 2007

5   Daniel A New Translation with Commentary Anthologized from Talmudic,
    Midrashic, and Rabbinic Sources, Mesorah Publications (Brooklyn, New York
    1969), p. 104

6   Rome's Enemies: Parthian And Sassanid Persians Peter Wilcox (Osprey LTD.
    New York, 1986), p5

7   Rome and Parthia at War, March 2006. All Empires, Online History Commu-
    nity Http://www.allempires.com/

8   Justin's History of the World as cited in Trogus Pompeius, in Justin, Cornelius Nepos and Eutropius, John Selby Watson, tr. (London: George Bell and Sons, 1876), pp. 272-283

9   Parthia, George Rawlinson (Cosimo, New York, 1893, 2007), pg 304-310

10   The Book of Daniel, A New Translation with Rabbinic Commentary Anthologized from Talmudic, Midrashic and Rabbinic Sources, Rabbis Nosson Scherman and Meir Zlotowitz (Mesorah, Brooklyn, 1979) , p 199

11   Ibid. p 314

12   The Books of Daniel, Ezra, Nehemiah: A New Translation of the Text, Rashi And A Commentary Digest Rabbi A.J. Rosenberg (Judaicia New York, 2000), p22

13   From "The Doctrine of Original Sin" Works, 1841

14   Hilaire Belloc, The Great Heresies, chapter 4 March, 1936, page 127-128

15   Archbishop Sheen, 1952, reprinted in the October 2001 Mindszenty Report, published by the Cardinal Mindzenty Foundation.

16   Gregory Palamus of Thessalonica, (1296-1354) Metropolitan of Thessalonica during the 14th century, wrote this commentary while living as a captive amongst the Turks in 1354

17   Vernon Richards, Oil and Jihad, Islam Undressed, Mar 29, 2005 18 Sir Robert Anderson, The Coming Prince, Appendix II, Miscellaneous: Who and When, Tregelles, p. 274.

19   Sir Robert Anderson (1841-1918), The Coming Prince, The Ten Kingdoms

20   Sir Robert Anderson(1841-1918), The Coming Prince, Appendix II, Miscellaneous: Who and When, Tregelles, p. 276.

21   Sir Robert Anderson(1841-1918), The Coming Prince, Appendix II, Miscellaneous: Who and When, Tregelles, p. 273.

22   Saint Cyril of Jerusalem Divine Institutes 7:17 A.D. 307

23   Sophronius, Patriarch of Jerusalem 636-637AD as quoted in "Seeing Islam as Others Saw It: A Survey and Evaluation of Christian, Jewish and Zoroastrian Writings on Early Islam." (Darwin Press 1997)

24   Tolan, John-Victor. Medieval Christian Perceptions of Islam. New York and London: Garland Publishing Company, 1996

25   Saint John of Damascus Against Heresies: The Fountain of Knowledge

26   Paul Alvarus, Memoriale sanctorum 2.4 (PL 115:771-2; CSM 2:403-4). As refer-
        enced in Christian Martyrs in Muslim Spain Kenneth Baxter Wolf 1999 Cam-
        bridge University Press

27   Antichrist: Two Thousand Years of the Human Fascination With Evil Bernard
        McGinn (Columbia University Press, New York, 1994), p.86

28   Martin Luther, Tischreden, Weimer ed., 1, No. 330

29   Calvin On Islam Revelation Prof. Dr. Francis Nigel Lee (Lamp Trimmers El Paso,
        2000)

30   Calvin On Islam Revelation Prof. Dr. Francis Nigel Lee (Lamp Trimmers El Paso,
        2000)

31   J. Calvin's Commentary on Second Thessalonians in his The Epistles of Paul the
        Apostle to the Romans and to the Thessalonians, Grand Rapids: Eerdmans,
        1961 rep., pp. 398-400.

32   Calvin On Islam Revelation Prof. Dr. Francis Nigel Lee (Lamp Trimmers El Paso,
        2000

33   Jonathan Edwards, The Fall of Antichrist, Part VII, page 395, New York, Pub-
        lished by S. Converse 1829)

34   Jonathan Edwards, The Fall of Antichrist, Part VII, page 399, New York, Pub-
        lished by S. Converse 1829)

35   Israel Eph'al, The Ancient Arabs, Nomads on the Borders of the Fertile Crescent
        9th to 5th centuries B.C, Chapter III, page 75. Eph'al is Assoc propfessor Biblical
        History, Tel Aviv, Israel. This is also confirmed by early Arabic sources, Ibin
        Hisham, The Life of Muhammad, 974

36   J.G. MacQueen, The Hittites and Their Contemporaries—Asia Minor, (Boulder,
        Colorado, Westview Press, 1975), p. 78.

37   St. Jerome, Commentary on Daniel Gleason Archer Translator (1958). pp. 15-
        157

38   Thomas Ice, The Seventy Weeks of Daniel, Part VIII, The Tomas Ice Collection.

39   Irenaeus, "Against Heresies," Book V, Chapter 25, The Fraud Pride and Tyran-
        ical Kingdom Of Antichrist as Described By Daniel And Paul, Early church
        Fathers Ante-Nicene Vol. 1 page 1147 [c. 130–202]

40   Clement Of Alexandria, Book III Chapter 21. Ante-Nicene Fathers Vol. 2 page
        663 [born about the middle of the 2nd century, and died between 211 and 216]

41   Orign De Principiis, Book III Chapter 46. Ante-Nicene Fathers Vol. 4 page 1224
        (185-254 AD)

42   Hippolytus, "The Refutation Of All Heresies II" The interpretation by Hippolytus, (bishop) of Rome, of the visions of Daniel and Nebuchadnezzar, taken in conjunction. Ante-Nicene Fathers Vol. 5 Page 377 [born in the second half of the 2nd century]

43   Pace, H. Geva, "The Camp of the Tenth Legion in Jerusalem: An Archaeological Reconsideration", IEJ 34 (1984), pp. 247-249.

44   The Wars of The Jews: History of the Destruction of Jerusalem By Flavius Josephus Trans.William Whiston BOOK II: CHAPTER 13:Para7

45   Flavius Josephus The Complete Works of Josephus, The Wars Of The Jews Or The History Of The Destruction Of Jerusalem Book III, Chapter 1, Paragraph 3

46   Tacitus The History New Ed edition Book 5.1 Editor: Moses Hadas, Translators: Alfred Church, William Brodribb   (Modern Library; New York, 2003)

47   Flavius Josephus The Complete Works of Josephus, The Wars Of The Jews Or The History Of The Destruction Of Jerusalem Book III, Chapter 4, Paragraph 2

48   The Wars of The Jews: History of the Destruction of Jerusalem By Flavius Josephus Trans.William Whiston BOOK V: Chapter 13: Para4

49   Pace, H. Geva, "The Camp of the Tenth Legion in Jerusalem: An Archaeological Reconsideration", IEJ 34 (1984), pp. 247-249.

PART VI

1   Against Heresies by Irenaeus.

2   http://www.csad.ox.ac.uk/POxy/beast616.htm

3   Shaykh al-Albaani said in al-Mishkaat (2/1206, no. 4148): al-Tahhaawi and Abu'l-Shaykh reported it with a saheeh isnaad

4   Hadith – Sahih Muslim 6757, Narrated Abdullah ibn Mas'ud, similar narration 6759 by 'Aisha, r.a. WWW.MUTTAQUN.COM

5   Hadith reported by "Abdullah-b-Umar, Sahih Muslim

6   Abu Huraira-Musnad Ahmad/Tirmidhi, by Shaykh Ahmad Ali in his Major Signs Before the Day of Judgment. Similar Hadeeth narrated by Ibn Majah in Kitab al-Fitan, (Hadeeth 4061), 2 - 1351, 1352 and Ahmad, Musnad, 2 - 295

7   Ibn Majah, Kitab al-Fitan, (Hadeeth 4267), Beast coming out of Mecca [The Sacred Mosque in Mecca]. This opinion is based on the Hadith reported by Tabarani on the authority of Hudhaifa-b-Usaid and Ibn Majah: 2/1352) Also see See Tadkirah and Al-Isha'ah

8   Tadhkirah al-Huffaz by al-Dhahabi)

9   Abu Muslim   Book 020, Number 4541, Narrated by Junida b. Abu Umayya. This concept is articulated in a Hadith from the collection of Abu Muslim. "The Messenger of Allah called us and we took the oath of allegiance to him. Among the injunctions that he made binding upon us were: That we would listening to and be obedient to the Ruler (Emir) in both our pleasure and displeasure, in both our adversity and prosperity—even when somebody is given preference over us, without ever disputing the powers delegated to the man duly invested with them. Obedience shall be accorded to him in all circumstances, except when you have clear signs of his disbelief in (or disobedience to) God-signs that could be used as a conscientious justification for non-compliance with his orders."

10   Abu Muslim Book 020, Number 4562

11   Mufti Muhammad Shafi and Mufti Muhammad Rafi Usmani, Signs of the Qiyama and the Arrival of the Maseeh, (Karachi, Darul Ishat, 2000), p. 60

12   Sideeque M.A. Veliankode Doomsday Portents and Prophecies.

13   Ahmad ibn Naqib al-Misri (d. 1368) from The Reliance of the Traveller.

14   The Hastings' Encyclopedia of Religion and Ethics, volume I, p.326.

15   Arthur Jeffrey, ed., Islam: Muhammad and His Religion (1958), p. 85.

16   Ibid.

17   Dictionary of Deities and Demons in the Bible, Page 393

18   Islamic and Arabic Names Collection, Muslims Internet Directory.

19   Clair Tisdall, The Original Sources of The Qur'an, Chapter II, page 13, also see Van Netton, Allah Divine Demonic, pg. 94

20   Saint John of Damascus (676-749) Against Heresies: The Fountain of Knowledge.

21   Histories 1:131

22   B. al-Kalbi, N.A. Faris 1952, pp. 14-15.

23   Wikipedia, The Story of The Black Stone and Muhammad son of Abdullah

24   IslamOnline.net Various Aspects of Haj

25   Killer Angel, George Grant, Reformer Press: p. 104

26   Wikipedia, Johann Wolfgang Von Goese, Britannica, 2002 ed. CD-ROM.

27   Islam: A Challenge to Faith, Samuel M. Zwemer, F.R.G.S, New York, 1907, Page 112

28   In Search of God the Mother, Roller, p. 265.

29   Maarten J. Vermaseren, Cybele and Attis, trans. A.M.H. Lemmers, Thames and Hudson, 1977 cited in Baring and Cashford, op. cit.

30   Saint John of Damascus Against Heresies: The Fountain of Knowledge

PART VII

1   Forder, Archibald. "Arabia, the Desert of the Sea," National Geographic (December 1909), 1039-1062.

2   Bernard Lewis, The Arabs in History, page 15, B.L London 1947

3   Ibid.

4   The 12 Tribes of Ishmael," Nabataea.net. Esarhaddon tells us that, in his attempt to subdue the Arabs, his father, Sennacherib, struck against their capital, Adummatu, which he called the stronghold of the Arabs. Sennacherib captured their king, Kaza'il, who was called "King of the Arabs". In one inscription of Ashurbanipal, Kaza'il is referred to as "King of the Kedarites". From a geographical standpoint, Adummatu is often associated with the medieval Arabic Dumat el-Jandal, which was, in ancient times, a very important and strategic junction on the major trade route between Syria, Babylon, Najd and the Hijaz area. Dumat el Jandal is at the Southeastern end of Al Jawf, which is a desert basin, and often denotes the entire lower region of Wadi as Sirhan, the famous depression situated halfway between Syria and Mesopotamia. This area has water, and was a stop over for caravan traders traveling from Tayma, to Syria or Babylonia. This strategic location effectively made Dumah the entrance to north Arabia. This oasis was the center of rule for many north Arabian kings and queens, as related in Assyrian records.

5   Holman Bible Dictionary.

6   Encyclopedia Britanica, The Online Encyclopedia, Al-Ula.

7   Holiest Wars, Timothy Furnish Praeger Publishers (2005).

8   http://www.globalsecurity.org/military/world/gulf/mecca.htm.

9   Global Terrorism Analysis, Terror In The Holy City: Analyzing The Al-qaida Attacks In Mecca By John C.k. Daly
http://jamestown.org/terrorism/news/article.php?issue_id=2898

10   Narrated Mu'adh ibn Jabal: Translation of Sunan Abu-Dawud, Battles (Kitab Al-Malahim), Book 37, Number 4281

11   Muslim tradition also describes the destruction of Mecca as well.

12   Berta Segall, "The Iconography of Cosmic Kingship," the Art Bulletin, vol.xxxviii, 1956, p.77

13   Wikipedia, Ka'ba, Before Islam

PART VIII

1   A Comprehensive Commentary on the Qur'an, Osnabruck: Otto Zeller Verlag, 1973, p. 36).

2   Replica of Bergama Altar to be Erected Monday, March 06, 2006

3   Alliance of Civilizations www.unaoc.org/aoc.php?page=2

4   Global Politician Turkey as Mediator and Peacekeeper during Middle East Conflict: Analyzing Events of Summer 2006 Prof. Ruben Safrastyan, Ph.D. - 6/13/2007

5   Christian Science Monitor Can Turkey bridge the gap between Islam and the West? By Yigal Schleifer March 29, 2006

6   Christian Science Monitor Can Turkey bridge the gap between Islam and the West? By Yigal Schleifer March 29, 2006

7   Arabic Media Internet Network Walid Salem Gaza Coup Detat June 19, 2006

8   Turkish Daily News SİBEL UTKU BİLA Turkey seeks to boost profile in captive crisis March 31, 2007

9   Jerusalem Post, Feb 16, 2007 Turkey to inspect Mughrabi excavation HERB KEINON

10   American Chronicle Turkey: America's only Honorable Exit from Iraq Dr. Muhammad Shamsaddin Megalommatis June 10, 2007

11   Dale Foster, Business, and Economic Development in Turkey, July 15, 2007.

12   Stanley Cohen, Professor of Criminology, Hebrew University, Jerusalem, Law and Social Inquiry, vol. 20, no. 1, winter, 1995, pp. 7, 50.

13   The Stephen Roth Institue for Contemporary Study of Anti-Semitism and Racism http://www.tau.ac.il/Anti-Semitism/asw2005/turkey.htm

14   Serge Trifkovic, Islam, The Sword of The Prophet, (Regina Orthodox Press) p203

15   Forbes Magazine, Turkey's Gul: President Or Polarizer? Elisabeth Eaves, May.04.07

16   The Middle East Media Research Institute Blog Turkish President Strongly Warns: Turkish Republic In Danger From Within http://www.thememriblog.org/blog_personal/en/1214.htm

17   Turkey and Israel: Facing Common Threats and Sharing Great Perspectives Bottom of Form Dr. Muhammad Shamsaddin Megalommatis July 5, 2007

18   http://www.groundreport.com/articles.php?id=2834027

19   http://www.groundreport.com/articles.php?id=2834027

20   Turkey as Mediator and Peacekeeper during Middle East Conflict: Analyzing Events of Summer 2006 Prof. Ruben Safrastyan, Ph.D. - 6/13/2007

21   Narrated from Bishr al-Khath`ami or al-Ghanawi by: Ahmad, al-Musnad 14:331 #18859; al-Hakim, al-Mustadrak 4:421-422; Tabarani, al-Mu`jam al-Kabir 2:38; al-Bukhari, al-Tarikh al-Kabir 2:81

22   Sunan of Abu-Dawood Book 37: Number 4281   Narrated byMu'adh ibn Jabal

23   Veliankode pg. 256

24   WorldNetDaily.com Iran website heralding 'Mahdi' by springtime November 16, 2005

25   Iran, Apocalypse vs. Reform, Jackson Diehl Washington Post Thursday, May 11, 2006

26   Mesmerized Media: When will Ahmadinejad's radical religious beliefs get covered? By Joel C. Rosenberg National Review September 20, 2006

27   Iran leader's messianic End-Times mission,WorldNetDaily January 6, 2006 Iran leader's messianic End-Times mission

28   The rise of Prof 'Crocodile' - a hardliner to terrify hardliners By Colin Freeman Telegraph UK November 19, 2005

29   TownHall.com Glenn Beck Interview with Benjamin Netanyahu November 17, 2006

30   The Long War Journal Jaish al-Janna and Najaf Bill Rogio January 30, 2007

31   Timothy Furnish MahdiWatch.org February 16, 2007

32   Jihadwatch.corg April 16, 2006

33   Jamestown Foundation Hizb-ut-Tahrir's Growing Appeal in the Arab World James Brandon December 14, 2006

34   Mainstream Caliphate Confessions By Andrew G. Boston Front-PageMagazine.com April 30, 2007

35   NIC Project 2020, Mapping the Global Future

36   Jerusalem Newswire Arabs to Israel: Peace on our terms or war By Ryan Jones March 28, 2007

37   AsiaNews.it April, 19, 2007 Israeli delegation to travel to Jordan to discuss Arab League peace plan

38   Middle East online March 30, 2007 Olmert: Mideast peace possible in five years Charly Wegman

39   BBC On This Day: September 30, 1938: 'Peace for our time' – Chamberlain

40   PakTribune Qaddafi says Arab summit against Iran Wednesday March 28, 2007

41   MEMRI TV http://memritv.org/Transcript.asp?P1=1421

42   YNETNEWS.com Syria: Sunnis converting to Shiites in homage to Nasrallah Rohee Namias November 8, 2006

43   YNETNEWS.com Syria: Sunnis converting to Shiites in homage to Nasrallah Rohee Namias November 8, 2006

44   History News Network: A New Empire of the Mahdi? Libyan and Iranian Pan-Islamic Agendas, Timothy R. Furnish April, 30, 2007

45   Syrian and Iranian Generals in Intensive War Consultations DEBKAfile Exclusive Report June 9, 2007

46   Al-Jazeera, Iran, Sudan stand united against Western pressure

47   Iran, Sudan Unyielding In U.N. Rift The New York Sun BENNY AVNI, March 14, 2007

48   Under Fire From the West, Iran and Sudan Cozy Up Patrick Goodenough CNSNews.com April 26, 2006

49   US EMBASSY FACT SHEET: THE IRAN AND LIBYA SANCTIONS ACT OF 1996 August 6, 1996

50   David Pawson, The Challenge of Islam to Christians (London, Hodder and Stoughton, 2003), p. 11

51   ibid

52   Bruce Mcdowell and Anees Zaka, Muslims and Christians at The Table (Phillipsburg, P& R Publishing, 1999), p. 6

53   http://www.brusselsjournal.com/node/1609

54   Steyn pg xv, xvi

55   http://www.brusselsjournal.com/node/1609

56   Steyn xvii

57   Steyn pg.

58   Steyn pg. 7

59   Bruce Mcdowell and Anees Zaka, Muslims and Christians at The Table (Phillipsburg, P& R Publishing, 1999), p. 6

60   New York Times, October 22, 2001, Jodi Wilgoren, Islam Attracts Converts by the Thousands, Drawn Before and After Attacks,

61   Al-Hayam Newspaper (London), November 12, 2001, as quoted in Middle East Media & Research Institute, November 16, 2001, Muslim American Leaders: A Wave of Conversion to Islam in the U.S. Following September 11

62   Al-Ahram Al-Arabi (Egypt), October 20, 2001, as quoted in Middle East Media & Research Institute, November 16, 2001, Muslim American Leaders: A Wave of Conversion to Islam in the U.S. Following September 11

63   The Times, (UK) January 7 2002, Giles Whittell, Allah Came Knocking At My Heart

64   Mcdowell, Zaka, p. 6

65   ibid. p. 6

66   ibid. p. 7

67   Middle East Media & Research Institute, November 16, 2001, Muslim American Leaders: A Wave of Conversion to Islam in the U.S. Following September 11

68   New York Times, October 22, 2001, Jodi Wilgoren, Islam Attracts Converts by the Thousands, Drawn Before and After Attacks

69   The Dallas Morning News – November 3, 2001, Susan Hogan

70   Pawson, p. 36

71   Ibid, 6,7

72   Al-Jazeera, December 12, 2000, "Christianization of Africa"

73   Isaalmasih.net

74   Brother Andrew, Light Force, (Grand Rapids, Fleming H. Revell, 2004), p140